AMERICAN EXPERIENCE

Immigration

AMERICAN EXPERIENCE

Immigration

Dennis Wepman

Facts On File
An imprint of Infobase Publishing

Immigration

Copyright © 2008, 2002 by Dennis Wepman

Originally published as a volume in the Eyewitness History Series.

Maps and graphs pages 414–419 and 426–434 © 2008, 2002 by Facts On File

Facts On File, Inc.
An imprint of Infobase Publishing
132 West 31st Street
New York NY 10001

Library of Congress Cataloging-in-Publication Data

Wepman, Dennis.
Immigration/Dennis Wepman.
p. cm.—(American experience)
Originally published as volume in the Eyewitness History Series.
Includes bibliographical references and index.
ISBN 978-0-8160-6240-9. (alk. paper)
I. United States—Emigration and immigration—History. I. Title.
JV6450.W43 2007
304.8'73—dc22
2007029713

Facts On File books are available at special discounts when purchased in bulk quantities for businesses, associations, institutions or sales promotions. Please call our Special Sales Department in New York at (212) 967-8800 or (800) 322-8755.

You can find Facts On File on the World Wide Web at http://www.factsonfile.com

Text design by Joan M. McEvoy
Maps and graphs on pages 414–419 and 426–434 by Patricia Meschino

Printed and bound in the United States

VB FOF 10 9 8 7 6 5 4 3 2 1

This book is printed on acid-free paper.

Note on Photos

Many of the illustrations and photographs used in this book are old, historical images. The quality of the prints is not always up to modern standards, as in many cases the originals are damaged. The content of the illustrations, however, made their inclusion important despite problems in reproduction.

To the heroes and victims of America's endlessly changing immigration policy,
and to my grandparents,
who were lucky enough to benefit from it when the going was good.

You can not spill a drop of American blood without spilling the blood of the whole world. . . . We are not a narrow tribe of men. . . . No: our blood is as the blood of the Amazon, made up of a thousand noble currents all pouring into one. We are not a nation, so much as a world. . . .

—Herman Melville, *Redburne, His First Voyage* (1849)

Contents

Preface

The literature of immigration to the United States is enormous. It includes not only documents and memoirs of virtually every national and ethnic group that has come to America since the nation's first European settlement but a voluminous body of legislative writing and the sometimes violent response to it. As all Americans except the native population of the country are either immigrants or the descendents of immigrants, it is a subject that touches the national experience very closely. President Franklin Roosevelt once addressed a meeting of the Daughters of the American Revolution—often thought of as one of the most "purely American" of groups—as "Fellow Immigrants," and, noting their shocked expressions, explained, "Remember, remember always, that all of us, and you and I especially, are descended from immigrants and revolutionaries."

To understand the history of American immigration and the character of the country to which it has contributed for nearly four centuries, it is necessary to consider several factors. Of equal importance are the conditions in their homelands that impelled the movement of great masses of people to our shores and the attractions that drew them here. Yet no less significant is the story of the often fearful trip they made, the reception they encountered, and the impact they had on American life.

The image of the New World in foreign eyes was the product both of deliberate promotion—by colonists, travel agents, and those in need of immigrant labor—and of personal accounts of the country by those who had made the journey. These descriptions—enticing or terrifying, tragic or triumphant—are seldom objective, but they provide vivid insights into the immigrant experience and contribute far more than cold government statistics to an understanding of that experience in American history.

This book presents the story of American immigration in the words of those who experienced it and of those who reacted to it. It includes glowing pictures of the new land presented by explorers and promoters, as well as selections from letters, diaries, and memoirs by immigrants recounting the dreams, the joys, the fears, and often the misery of their journeys, along with their problems of adjustment to a new life. It also includes the formal government documents, the oratory of statesmen and demagogues, and the passionate rhetoric of the press welcoming or rejecting the newcomers. When early primary sources survive in the original language, the citations have retained their quaint spelling and grammar. Where possible the text has been illustrated with pictures of the heroes and villains of the story and contemporary cartoons dramatizing the powerful feelings that successive waves of immigration aroused.

The quotations included as "Eyewitness Testimony" are identified by exact references to their original sources given in concise form when these sources are included in the bibliography. In the cases of older references taken from more recent editions, the editions used are listed in the bibliography with notes giving their original dates of publication. Thus the listing of Gottfried Mittelberger's *Journey to*

Pennsylvania in the Year 1750 . . . is dated "1960; first published 1756." Where testimony is quoted from secondary sources, the exact locations of the material in those sources are given.

Selections from the principal documents relating to American immigration are provided in Appendix A—from the Maryland Toleration Act of 1649 and the notorious Alien and Sedition Acts of 1798 to various later state and federal laws encouraging or restricting immigration. This section presents the official wording of laws defining the changing status of immigrants through the years and statements by presidents of their positions on immigration legislation. Brief biographies of the principal figures mentioned in the text are provided in Appendix B, and Appendix C shows maps of the major routes of foreign immigration to the United States and the principal areas of settlement within the country. Tabular material, including government statistics for major waves of immigration, broken down by year and place of origin, is provided in Appendix D. A glossary of terms, abbreviations, and acronyms relating to immigration has been included.

The population of America has been enriched—some would say polluted—by additions from almost every other country in the world. This growth has encountered opposition from the beginning of the nation's history, from the conflicts between colonists and Native Americans to the most recent riots in ethnically mixed neighborhoods of America's great cities. Needed for labor, immigrants have also been seen as competing for jobs. Valued for their diverse contributions to the country's way of life, they have also been resented as a threat to its national and cultural unity—and even to its racial purity. The conflict has been waged in the press and on the floors of Congress as well as on the streets and in the barrooms of its cities. The dramatic story of changing attitudes and conditions is told chronologically in these pages, but the many national groups who figure in it are also surveyed across time, from the English, Dutch, Spanish, Scandinavian, German, and French pioneers who tamed the land (and subdued the Native Americans who already occupied it) to such recent arrivals as the Hmong refugees of Southeast Asia. It covers the very different physical and emotional challenges met by the first settlers and by those who followed them, and it explores the complex social and economic questions raised by the contacts of cultures from the old world with those of the new.

Oscar Handlin began his 1952 book *The Uprooted* with the words, "Once I thought to write a history of the immigrants in America. Then I discovered that the immigrants *were* American history." Those who have come from abroad to make their homes in the New World—from Spanish conquistadores seeking gold, Pilgrims and Quakers seeking religious freedom, and political outcasts seeking refuge, to the hungry and dispossessed seeking opportunity—compose the very fabric of the country. Their accounts of the troubles they escaped and the troubles they encountered are sometimes funny but more often profoundly moving. In reading their words and those of the society that received them, you will find the story of America's national experience rendered sometimes with pride and gratitude, sometimes with bitterness, but always with rare eloquence.

Acknowledgments

A work on so wide-ranging a subject as American immigration is naturally a collaboration, incorporating the observations of nearly four centuries of writers and the research of numberless scholars. For their help in uncovering material, thanks are due to Barry Moreno and Jeffrey S. Dosik, librarians of the Ellis Island Immigration Museum, and to the staff of the New York Public Library. Thanks for their courtesy and efficiency in locating appropriate images go to the staff of the New York Public Library Picture Collection, to Marian Smith and Crystal Williams of the Immigration and Naturalization Historical Reference Library, and to Bebe Overmiller of the Prints and Photos Collection of the Library of Congress. My special gratitude to Ivy Fischer Stone and to Facts On File editors Nicole Bowen, Terence Maikels, and Liza Trinkle for their unfailing patience.

Introduction

To Americans the word *immigrant* evokes an image of desperate refugees from poverty or oppression—the people Emma Lazarus somewhat condescendingly called "huddled masses yearning to breathe free,/The wretched refuse" of Europe's "teeming shore." Many of the people who figured in the great stream of humanity that came across the Atlantic at the end of the 19th and the beginning of the 20th century were indeed often wretched enough. Driven by both economic and political forces that had reduced them to the extreme measure of abandoning their homes, they had been stripped of money and property and faced the uncertainties of a new life with little support. From 1892, when the federal government assumed responsibility for immigration and opened a receiving station on New York's Ellis Island, to 1954, when the depot was closed, more than 16 million people passed through the Port of New York, most of them with little more than the clothes on their backs.

This tremendous shift of population, representing some two-thirds of the entire immigration to the United States during that period, is the greatest movement of people in the history of the world, and it has become the defining example of the phenomenon. But the throngs that passed through the gates of Ellis Island presented only one face of an experience far larger and far more complex than the "huddled masses" arriving from Europe during those 62 years. Millions of aliens have entered the country on the West Coast, from South and Central America, and from Canada. The history of American immigration began with the first settlers who followed the original colonists in 1607 and continues to the present day. It includes people of every class and condition from every continent except Antarctica, and it has been impelled by a wide variety of conditions.

In 1782, as an American national identity was beginning to crystallize, a French immigrant named Michel-Guillaume-Jean de Crèvecoeur noted that the conditions of American life altered the minds of Europeans and erased national distinctions that had been fixed for centuries. In his *Letters from an American Farmer,* published under the name of J. Hector St. Jean, he wrote of a family "whose grandfather was an Englishman, whose wife was Dutch, whose son married a French woman, and whose present four sons now have four wives of different nations." In this blending he saw the future strength of America. "Here," he stated of his adopted country, "individuals of all nations are melted into a new race of men."

Americans saw their country as a haven for victims of foreign oppression and tried to attract European immigrants. In fact, the Declaration of Independence specifically charges King George III with trying to keep non-English settlers out of the colonies "by obstructing the laws of Naturalization of Foreigners" and "refusing to pass others to encourage their migration hither."

A century later, American philosopher Ralph Waldo Emerson expressed the same ideas as Crèvecoeur. In his journal he compared the process of fusing nationalities into a new race with "the melting and intermixture of silver and gold" to produce "a new compound more precious than any." Emerson believed that "in this continent—asylum of all nations—the energy of Irish, Germans, Swedes, Poles, and Cossacks, . . . of the Africans and of the Polynesians—will construct a new race, a new religion, a new state, a new literature, which will be as vigorous as the new Europe which came out of the smelting-pot of the Dark Ages." The amalgamationist vision was shared by Theodore Roosevelt, who, although he came of old Dutch stock, was proud to say, "We Americans are the children of the Crucible." It reached its clearest expression in the popular play *The Melting Pot* in 1908, whose title was to enter the language as a synonym for the American ethnic experience.

America's self-image as a nation of immigrants—or, indeed, as an asylum for the dispossessed of other nations—has never been universal, however. From the earliest colonial times there have been those who viewed the country as an extension of England—"one united people," as John Jay wrote in 1787, "—a people descended from the same ancestors, speaking the same language, professing the same religion, attached to the same principles of government." As the range of peoples adding to our population increased during the 18th and 19th centuries, the resistance to foreign intrusion grew. Many Americans whose ancestors came from northern Europe felt that immigrants from Asia, Africa, or southern and eastern Europe were racially inferior and polluted the racial and cultural stock of the original settlers. Others felt that large groups of people from any one region would form separate communities that spoke their own language, thus threatening the unity of the nation. And although immigrants had always been welcomed as a source of cheap labor, some workers felt that, by working longer hours for less pay, foreigners would take away their jobs.

These conflicting views of immigration have provided a recurring theme for historians and social scientists and have resulted in drastic changes in the nation's laws. For the first century of our national life, the frontiers were open and foreigners were welcomed. By the 1840s a movement called *nativism* was seeking to protect America from foreign elements; its attack focused especially on the Roman Catholic Church. When the potato famine in Ireland sent many immigrants to American shores, the conflict reached a head, and a political party was formed to fight against the government's liberal policies. Their political ambitions were never successful, but nativists were able to assert enough pressure to bring about changes in the law. In 1882 Congress passed an act prohibiting the immigration of paupers and convicts, and rigorous literacy tests for voters were instituted to prevent foreigners from entering. The Chinese Exclusion Act of that year prohibited the entry of Asian laborers and declared the Chinese ineligible for naturalization.

Immigration and laws restricting it have fluctuated throughout the years in America. During the 1920s there was a fear that alien ideas would destroy American institutions. The American Federation of Labor opposed immigration in order to protect the jobs of its members. In 1913 California prohibited Chinese and Japanese immigrants from owning land. Writers such as Madison Grant, whose 1916 book *The Passing of the Great Race* warned against the admission of Jews and eastern and southern Europeans as a threat to the racial purity of the American people, were very influential in promoting restrictive immigration laws. The National Origin Act (known also as the Johnson-Reed Act) reduced the number of admissible aliens by establishing national quotas that favored north Europeans. In the early 1930s the Great Depression led the government to institute widespread deportation of Mexican laborers.

Although World War II changed the patterns of American immigration, opening the nation's gates to many victims of the conflict, the laws continued to favor Europeans. The Displaced Persons Act of 1948 admitted 400,000 immigrants from Europe but did not apply to Asians, Africans, or Near Easterners. Writers have continued to support both sides of the issue, some arguing for the cultural and economic enrichment of the country through the contributions of foreign talent and others warning of disaster if national borders are not enforced. Today there is little public support for the idea of superior and inferior races, and the Chinese Exclusion Act and the quota system have been abandoned, but the controversy between open- and closed-door policies still rages.

The issue is a complex one, and with ever-changing world conditions it is not likely to be soon resolved. In this book there are opinions on the subject expressed by Pilgrim fathers of the 1600s and by George Washington, William Penn, Abraham Lincoln, John F. Kennedy, and George W. Bush. There are also ideas and stories from hundreds of ordinary people who lived the experience. Immigration has been one of the most important processes in American history. In these firsthand accounts, one will find many surprises and much to make one think.

CHAPTER ONE

Colonists and Immigrants
1607–1700

The New Land

Anthropologists believe that the first immigrants to America—the various peoples Columbus misnamed "Indians"—first reached the continent from Asia during an ice age, as long as 35,000 years ago. They came, as their successors did, in flight from intolerable living conditions or in search of food, comfort, and a chance for a better life.

The Western Hemisphere held out the same promise to Europeans when they first saw it at the end of the 15th century, and it was not long before the adventurous, the fugitive, and the ambitious began making their way to the New World. Explorers came first. Five years after Christopher Columbus dropped anchor at the Caribbean island of San Salvador in 1492, Italian navigator Giovanni Caboto changed his name to John Cabot and sailed under the English flag to Canada, where he laid claim to the region and sailed home at once. Other adventurers came from Spain and France and reported what they saw, and in 1565 the Spanish founded St. Augustine, Florida, the first European city in North America. The English made their first move to colonize the New World in 1578, when Queen Elizabeth granted Sir Humphrey Gilbert the authority "to inhabit and possess at his choice all remote and heathen lands not in the possession of any Christian Prince." Gilbert led expeditions for that purpose in 1578 and again in 1583. He was daring, but he was not a skillful mariner. He ran some of his ships onto a reef, lost his cargo in a storm, unknowingly signed up pirates among his crew, and drowned when his ship sank on the way home.

Gilbert's half brother, the dashing soldier and courtier Sir Walter Raleigh, accompanied him on both expeditions and in 1584 received the same royal authorization "at all times and for ever hereafter, to discover, search, finde out, and view such remote, heathen and barbarous lands, countries, and territories . . . and the same to have, hold, occupie, and enjoy . . . for ever." The next year Raleigh succeeded in founding a settlement in a region he named Virginia, both in honor of Elizabeth, the Virgin Queen, and because it was a virgin land. His passengers—husbands, wives, and children eager to make a home in the New World—settled on Roanoke Island in present-day North Carolina. In 1587 Virginia Dare became the first

1

English child born in the New World. That same year, Raleigh returned to England confident of the future of America, of which he wrote, "I shall live to see it an Inglishe nation." He was to be disappointed in that hope; when a ship arrived from England with fresh supplies in 1590, the colony had vanished. The fate of the "Lost Colony" remains a mystery, but though Roanoke did not survive, Raleigh proved that English families could create homes in the New World, and his writings inspired others to follow his path.

It was the promise of wealth in the new land that sustained the English in their colonizing ambitions at first, and the expeditions that followed Raleigh's were private business ventures. Organized by merchants as joint-stock companies with many investors, they were chartered by the throne, as a modern company is incorporated by the government. The first successful English colony in America was one of two authorized by King James in 1606. The Virginia Company of London and the Virginia Company of Plymouth, named for the cities from which they sailed, both left the same year. The Plymouth Company landed and set up a colony in Maine in 1607, but the enterprise did not succeed, and it was abandoned the next year. It was the London Company that established the first permanent English colony in America.

For the two companies, King James licensed "certain Knights, Gentlemen, Merchants, and other Adventurers . . . which are, or from time to time shall be, joined to them, which do desire to begin their Plantation and Habitation in some fit and convenient place" to form colonies "of sundry of our people into that Part of *America*, commonly called **VIRGINIA**, and other Parts and Territories in *America*, either appertaining to us, or which are not now actually possessed by any *Christian* Prince or People." The three small vessels of the London Company, the *Susan Constant*, the *Godspeed*, and the *Discovery*, set sail in December 1606 with 104 Englishmen. They did not come to build homes and raise families, but rather to

A contemporary artist depicted the arrival of the English in the Virginia colony, around 1607.
(New York Public Library Print Collection)

seek fortunes and return to England. The group consisted of "Knights, Gentlemen, Merchants, and other Adventurers," along with twenty laborers and four carpenters. No one brought his wife.

They landed at Cape Henry in April 1607, and on the 14th of the next month made their way to the calmer waters of the James River to plant their colony. Jamestown was not a healthy site. The land was marshy, the air was damp, and the soil was ill adapted to English vegetables. Furthermore, the colonists were ill adapted to gardening. They had come not to work the soil but to find treasure. As Captain John Smith, one of their first leaders, wrote in his *Generall Historie of Virginia* in 1624, there was "no talke, no hope, nor worke, but dig gold, wash gold, refine gold, load gold." Unfortunately, there was no gold in Virginia, and the knights, gentlemen, and merchants had to turn their hands to the hard work of building a city.

The next year, 1608, Samuel de Champlain and 32 men raised the French flag on a bank of the St. Lawrence River, far to the north of Virginia, and named the spot Quebec. Like the English adventurers, the French who established the first settlement in what is now Canada came for gold. And like the English, they failed to find any. Instead they traded with the Indians for furs, which they sent back to France.

English Immigration Begins: Jamestown, Virginia

The first year of the Jamestown colony was anything but a success. The pioneers were not well prepared for the tasks that confronted them, and even less for the physical demands of the land and its climate. Nevertheless, the Virginia Company continued its promotional campaign, papering England with pamphlets describing the colony as a utopia where the poorest immigrant could achieve the status of the landed gentry in England. The ads paid off well; in 1609, while the original settlers were starving and dying of malaria, 600 newcomers arrived looking for the promised land of milk and honey. In 1610 Thomas West, Lord Delaware, brought 400 more.

Almost no one in the first wave of immigrants was a knight, a gentleman, or a merchant. Some were farmers, lured by the promise of free land, or tenant-farmers driven from their homes by increased rents. Many were simply unemployed laborers and tradesmen or vagrants and thieves, all looking for a living. Probably the majority of immigrants were indentured servants, people of lesser means who paid for their passage to the New World by selling their labor for a period of time after their arrival. This system arose as a response to widespread unemployment in England, offering a solution both to the overpopulation of the old country and the need for workers in America. As Sir George Peckham, a 16th-century English explorer, wrote, "There are at this day great numbers (God he knoweth) which live in such penury and want, as they coulde be contented to hazard their lives, and to serve one yeare for meat, drinke, and apparell only, without wages, in hope thereby to amend their estates." Farmers and businesses bought the service from ship captains or agents, often at public auctions, and could command the worker's labor for terms usually running from four to seven years.

Not all the indentured servants came willingly. Some were convicts who accepted their terms as alternatives to long prison sentences or to being hanged, and many were literally kidnapped into service. The settler who bought such a laborer ran the risk that he or she might escape. However, the Virginia Company provided some protection to the buyer by offering a grant of land—called a headright—for each immigrant purchased. In addition, the servant had an incentive to carry out the contract: at the completion of the term, an indentured servant was entitled to "freedom dues"—a payment that might include money, tools, clothes, and even a plot of land.

The sending of prisoners to serve out their sentences as indentured workers was an early cause of controversy, both in the new colonies and in England itself. On the one hand, the practice cleared the country of unwanted people and helped develop its territories overseas. On the other hand, it provided unwilling immigrants who were unlikely to make good or loyal citizens. Sir Francis Bacon, an author who had served as attorney general and lord chancellor under King James, wrote in his essay "Of Plantations" in 1625, "It is a shameful and unblessed thing to take the scum of people and wicked and condemned men to be the people with whom you plant, and not only so, but it spoileth the plantation, for they will ever live like rogues, and not fall to work, but be lazy, and do mischief, and spend victuals, and be quickly weary, and then certify over to their country to the discredit of the plantation." His argument, however, was not successful. During the first century of English settlement in America, some 50,000 felons were sent to the colonies.

Life in the Jamestown colony was hard for colonist and immigrant alike. By the end of the first year, some two-thirds of the original settlers had died. Two years later, the weather was so bad that they called the season "the starving time"; during that winter, more than 80 percent of the immigrants died within six months. Of the nearly 500 inhabitants of Jamestown in 1610, only about 60 survived the winter.

Naturally, the social organization of the group disintegrated under such pressures, and the leaders of the colony seemed unable to maintain order. Only one member of the governing council, Captain John Smith, is known to have stood out as an able and courageous leader. The 29-year-old Smith was boldly critical of the policies of the Virginia Company for its promotional campaign and for the selection of people it sent to the colony. He issued the order in 1609 that "he that will not work shall not eat," and instead of bartering with the Indians for corn, he began its cultivation for the colony. Smith was a professional soldier, and his arrogance offended the owners of the company, who replaced him as leader in 1609, but he was probably the single most responsible figure in the first years of the colony.

Smith also played an important role in the tense relations between the settlers and the Indians. According to the widely repeated story—first reported by Smith himself and now generally dismissed as his own invention—the adventurous captain was captured in 1608 by the followers of Powhatan, the head of a federation of Algonquian Indians in Virginia. As he was about to have his brains dashed out on Powhatan's orders, the chief's 12-year-old daughter Pocahontas threw herself on his body, cradling his head in her arms to save his life. Powhatan was so moved by his daughter's act that he pardoned Smith. When Pocahontas later married John Rolfe, another of the settlers, the Powhatan Confederacy made peace with the colony, and the two groups maintained friendly relations until Powhatan's death in 1618.

Rolfe's marriage, and the improvement of relations with the Indians it brought, was only one of his contributions to the survival of the colony. After arriving in Jamestown in 1610 among the first group of immigrants, Rolfe devoted himself

Captain John Smith is rescued by Pocahontas in this engraving of the famous legend first published in London after 1850. *(Library of Congress, Prints and Photographs Division [LC-USZ62-109381])*

to experimenting with tobacco, a local plant whose use had been introduced to Europe a few years before. In 1612 Rolfe developed a new, superior variety and a method of curing it so that it could be exported. As beaver pelts supported Quebec, tobacco became Virginia's most important cash crop. In 1619 England imported 20,000 pounds of tobacco from Virginia, and the enormous popularity of smoking in the home country gave the foundering colony its first ray of hope for financial survival. By that year the settlers felt confident enough to take their first steps toward independence. They established a legislative assembly, the first in America, and created their own colonial government. That year the Virginia Company in London sent its first shipload of unmarried women to the colony, "whereby," as the company explained, "the Planters' minds may be faster tyed to Virginia by the bonds of Wyves and children." The dream of gold that had brought the first colonists to the land had faded, and the settlers were coming to accept the colony as a home.

The year 1619 also saw the arrival of the first Africans in the English territory of North America. Slavery was an important part of the economy of several Spanish settlements on the continent, but it had not yet appeared among the English. In 1619 a Dutch ship dropped anchor in Jamestown with 19 Africans for sale as slaves. The colonists bought them, but as indentured servants, like those who had come voluntarily from England. Like the white indentured servants, the Africans were assigned to work under contracts ranging from five to seven years, and, like other indentured servants immigrating to the colony, they were given their freedom when their contracts expired. They were not immigrants because they had not chosen to make their homes in the New World, but they were granted the same rights as those who had, and when their time was up they took their places as farmers, craftsmen, and merchants with the rest of the community.

If there was no racial conflict between Africans and whites in the first days of the Jamestown colony, things were not so tranquil with the Indians. When Powhatan died in 1618, the new leader of the confederacy he had led took a different view of the Europeans arriving in their country. As the colony grew, the Indians were driven off their lands, and they organized a desperate attack to reclaim them. On March 22, 1622, a powerful force attacked the colony and killed 347 of the settlers. The English retaliated with massacres of the Indians, and a state of war continued between the two peoples for several years before the confederacy was destroyed. The surviving Indians were then assigned limited areas for hunting and farming, and they were subject to the English law. By 1680 there were no more than 1,000 Indians left in the Virginia colony.

In the early 1620s the colony had become a fully self-supporting community, and by 1621 it established regular trade relations with the home country, shipping its tobacco by way of the West Indies, where ships stopped to pick up sugar, rum, and molasses, and then continued their voyage to England. There the products of the New World were sold and the ships collected cargoes of textiles, tools, and other manufactured goods to sell to the colonists. This three-stage system—England to North America to the West Indies and back to England—was called the *triangular trade.*

Although the sale of tobacco and other crops increased, and immigrants continued to arrive in Jamestown, the Virginia Company was not a successful enterprise. Disease, incompetent management, business conflicts within the company, and military conflicts with the Indians combined to undermine the venture. By 1624, according to one estimate, the Virginia Company had lost some £200,000. In that year it was declared bankrupt. The English government revoked its charter and took it over as a Crown Colony, administered directly by a royal governor appointed by King James I.

The New England Colonies

The English immigrants to Jamestown had come for mercantile reasons, but another group sailed for the New World in 1620 with somewhat different goals. These Englishmen had already left their homeland because of religious differences and settled in Amsterdam, Holland, in 1608. There they followed their own version of Protestantism, forming an English Separatist Church, and attempted to accommodate themselves to their circumstances.

From the beginning they were not happy in Holland. They were allowed to worship as they chose, but they were never comfortable in their new home. As William Bradford, governor of their American colony for 31 years, reported in 1651, "They heard the strange & uncouth language, and beheld the different manners & customes of the people, with their strange fashions and attires; all so farre differing from that of their plaine countrie villages" and "though they saw faire and bewtifull cities, flowing with abundance of all sorts of wealth & riches, yet it was not long before they saw the grimme & grisly face of povertie coming upon them

All of the British colonies, from Newfoundland (inset) to "Barmudas," a part of the Virginia Plantation until 1625, were printed in Nathaniel Crouch's *The English Empire in America* (1685). *(New York Public Library Print Collection)*

like an armed man." Even after moving from Amsterdam to Leyden and although they were beginning to prosper, the immigrants felt estranged, seeing their children growing away from their English customs, losing their language, and "drawne away by evill examples into extravagante & dangerous courses." After 12 years, they felt the need not only to escape the alien ways of the Dutch but to create a colony in the New World where they might lay "some good foundation . . . for the propagating & advancing the gospell of the kingdom of Christ in those remote parts of the world." Outlaws in England and aliens in Holland, they decided to establish a colony of their own.

The decision to move to "some of those vast & unpeopled countries of America, which are all fruitfull and fitt for habitation" was not unanimous. Many felt that the trip would be too perilous and too expensive and that the New World would be even harder to adjust to than Holland. Reports of the country's perils from people such as John Smith filled them with alarm about the adventure. As Bradford reported, they feared that "they should be liable to famine, and nakedness, . . . and the chang of aire, diate, & drinking water, would infecte their bodies with sore sicknesses and greevous diseases." Worse yet, they would encounter "the salvage [sic] people, who are cruell, barbarous, & most trecherous, being most furious in their rage, and merciles wher they overcome; not being contente only to kill, & take away life, but delight to tormente men in the most bloodie maner that may be, fleaing some alive with the shells of fishes, cutting of the members & joynts of others by peesmeale, and broiling on the coles, eate the collops of their flesh in their sight whilst they live, with other cruelties horrible to be related."

Fearful as the prospect was, they finally decided that it was worth the risk, for "all great & honorable actions are accompanied with great difficulties." They applied for a charter to form another settlement in Virginia, and the English government, happy to promote its colonies in North America, granted it. Their years as foreigners in Holland, excluded from the craft guilds and barred from any but the most strenuous labor, had toughened them and prepared them for the hardships that lay ahead. The little band entered into a contract with the Virginia Company of London, forming a stock company in which every emigrant over the age of 16 held one share of stock valued at £10 and agreed to work for seven years to pay back their debt. Their religious practices may have been outlawed in England, but these sober, hard-working craftsmen and farmers made ideal colonists, and the company invested in their labor quite willingly.

The voyage did not have an encouraging beginning. Of the two ships in which they originally set sail, one proved not to be seaworthy and had to turn back. Some of the group gave up the trip, and the remaining 102 crowded into the *Mayflower* and began their pilgrimage from Plymouth in September. It was a hard crossing, with many storms, and, because of either incompetent navigation or bad weather, they came to shore far north of their intended destination, on the stern and rockbound coast of Massachusetts.

The Pilgrims, as they called themselves, drew up a formal compact, or agreement, before they left the ship. Because they had landed outside the jurisdiction of the Virginia Company, they agreed to enact and keep a body of laws for the common good until they received a formal charter. They never did receive such a charter, and the compact remained their official law for as long as Plymouth remained a separate colony. Signed on November 11, 1620, the Mayflower Compact was the first document of self-government in the British colonies.

The Plymouth colony fared no better during its first winter than its predecessor in Jamestown, and, according to Bradford, by spring "out of 100 and odd persons, scarce 50 remained." Yet the Pilgrims labored resolutely, chopping trees and building homes, and when the weather allowed they were ready to plant. Contrary to their fears about the "salvage people, who are cruell, barbarous, & most trecherous," the local Indians visited them throughout the hard winter to show them their ways of hunting and fishing and how to grow corn, squash, and beans.

The Plymouth colony was organized by religious pilgrims, but in fact fewer than half of the people on the *Mayflower* were Separatists. Many were indentured servants, like the majority of the Jamestown colony. Its appointed military captain, Miles Standish, was a nonreligious mercenary hired in Holland for the trip.

Plymouth did not grow into a large, prosperous colony like Jamestown. It had no profitable crop like tobacco, and although a small trickle of immigrants joined it from year to year, it never had the manpower or financial backing to expand. Nevertheless, this little community founded as a religious brotherhood inspired many others to make the pilgrimage. When Plymouth was absorbed into the larger colonies of the area in 1691, it had grown to only 7,000 people, but it became the nucleus of the greatest and most successful colonial venture in the New World.

During the period between the founding of Jamestown in 1607 and the landing of the *Mayflower* at Plymouth in 1620, emigration to the New World became increasingly attractive in England, where conditions were unstable. The Thirty Years' War, a series of European conflicts over religious and political issues, began in 1618. The turmoil that resulted had made normal trade impossible and created an economic depression in England. It brought about higher taxes and widespread unemployment, and the Church of England became more inflexible in its demands for religious conformity. Laborers who had lost their jobs, farmers who had lost their land, and merchants who had lost their businesses all began to look to the mainland of America and the small islands in the Caribbean for a new start.

In 1630 the newly chartered Massachusetts Bay Company sent 17 ships, carrying some 20 times as many passengers as the *Mayflower* had held, to a harbor a few miles north of Plymouth. Sponsored by Puritans, a Protestant reform movement intent on "purifying" the Church of England from elaborate ceremonies, the new colony was well subsidized and equipped. A corporate colony like Jamestown, it comprised nearly 2,000 members and held a huge land-grant and the authority to engage in any kind of local business independently. The group's leadership consisted of prominent Puritans such as John Winthrop, the colony's first governor, and it included many prosperous members of the British landed gentry among its members. Like the Plymouth colony, it was predominantly composed of laborers and servants who had come as much for economic opportunity as for religious freedom, but the Puritan gentlemen who organized and governed it established its laws and policies. As lords of great estates, they lived almost as well as they had in England.

The immigrants who came without land or a high spiritual mission, however, did not have such a comfortable time. Bound for seven years by the harsh terms of their indentures, they were sometimes victimized by those who had paid their passage. The terms of their indentures often forced them into a condition not much different from the chattel slavery that was to follow for Africans. They could be bought or sold, and families could be broken up. They were sometimes subjected to whipping for laziness and worse for attempting to escape. Daniel Defoe, in his 1683 novel *Moll Flanders,* wrote that they were "brought over by masters of ships to be sold as servants. Such we call them, . . . but they are more properly called slaves." For the felons convicted of capital crimes who came to the colonies from prisons, the servitude was preferable to being hanged, but for others the conditions of their labor were harsher than penal servitude in England. Many who came of their own will regretted their decision. Elizabeth Sprigs, a servant girl in Maryland, wrote home to her father, "What we unfortunate English people suffer here is beyond the probability of you in England to conceive. . . . I, one of their unhappy number, am toiling almost day and night, . . . then tied up and whipped to that degree that you'd not serve an animal. . . . Nay, many Negroes are better used."

Not all indentured servants, however, had such an unhappy time in their service. John Hammond, who worked out his voluntary indenture in Virginia from 1636 to about 1643, wrote a pamphlet in 1656 describing his experience and advising those who wished to follow his example. "The country [Virginia] is reported to be an unhealthy place, a nest of Rogues, whores, dissolute and rooking persons; a place of intolerable labour, bad usage, and hard Diet, &c. . . . ," he wrote in *Leah and Rachel, or Two Fruitful Sisters Virginia and Maryland.* "But when ye arrive, you will find a strange alteration. . . . The labour servants are put to, is not so hard nor of such continuance as Husbandmen, nor Handicraftmen are kept at in England. . . . [L]ittle or nothing is done in winter time, none ever work before sun rising nor after sun set, in the summer they rest, sleep or exercise themselves five hours in the heat of the day, Saturdays afternoon is always their own. . . . The Women are not (as is reported) put into the ground to work, but occupy such domestic employments and housewifery as in England. . . . Those servants that will be industrious may in time of service gain a competent estate before their Freedom." However, he warned the prospective servants that their masters might take advantage of them and cautioned all who thought of accepting their terms to be careful of whom they bound themselves to. "Be sure to have your contract in writing and under hand and seal," he wrote, "for if ye go over upon promise made to do this or that, or to be free, it signifies nothing."

The stream of Protestant dissidents and the workers they carried with them became known as the Great Migration. During the next 10 years, some 21,000 men, women, and children migrated to New England under Puritan direction. Although the majority of the immigrants were farmers, craftsmen, and servants, rather than churchmen, the principal motivations of the migration were spiritual freedom to practice their religion in their own way and the opportunity to spread their beliefs to the Indians. As Puritan pastor John White wrote in *The Planter's Plea* in 1630, "Necessitie may press some; Noveltie draw on others; hopes of Gaine in time to come may prevaile on a third Sorte; but that the most, and most sincere and godly part, have the advancement of the Gospel for their main Scope I am confident." Of the benefit they were conferring on the original inhabitants of the New World by converting them to Christianity, they had no doubt. The official seal of the Massachusetts Bay Colony pictured an Indian with his arms open in welcome and the legend, issuing from his mouth, "Come over and help us."

Whatever the missionary zeal that inspired the Puritans, the religious freedom they came to New England for did not include freedom for others to follow their own spiritual paths. Although Winthrop and his son John, who later became the governor of the Connecticut colony, were democratic leaders and established open elections for their colonies, Puritan principles were rigidly enforced. The community church was the only one permitted, and everyone in the community—from landowner to indentured servant—was required to belong to it, attend its services, and live according to its stern and rigid laws. Those who fell asleep during services in the Massachusetts colony might be publicly whipped.

The laws governing private life were as strict as those of the church. In 1684 the criminal code of Massachusetts encompassed 13 capital crimes, including witchcraft, idolatry, blasphemy, adultery, and perjury. Death by hanging was ordered for any boy of 16 or older who was stubborn or rebellious or who "smote" or "cursed" a parent.

Not everyone in the New England colony accepted the strict church law, however, and as new immigrants arrived from England, conflicts were inevitable. Religious controversy led to divisions within the community. Roger Williams, a part of the first wave of the Great Migration in 1630, served as a pastor in the Plymouth colony but became critical of Puritan practices. He condemned the church's narrowness and challenged its right to appropriate land from the Indians. His independent spirit was unacceptable to the colonial leaders, and in 1635 he was placed under arrest. As Nathaniel Morton, an eyewitness to the event, described it in 1669, "The prudent Magistrates understanding, and seeing things grow more and more towards a general division and disturbance, after all other means used in vain, they passed a sentence of banishment against him out of the Massachusetts Colony, as against a disturber of the peace, both of the Church and Commonwealth."

Helped by his Indian friends, Williams spent a desperate winter in the forest and finally made his way to the head of Narragansett Bay, southwest of the Massachusetts colony. There, as Morton continued his account, "Mr. Williams sat down in a place called Providence, out of the Massachusetts jurisdiction, and was followed by many of the members of the Church of Salem, who did zealously adhere to him, and who cried out of the persecution that was against him, keeping that one principle, that every one should have the liberty to worship God according to the light of their own consciences."

These exiles established a settlement with no charter, from either the king or the Massachusetts Bay Colony, and with no financial support, but somehow they survived. By 1643 the community had grown large enough to attract its own immigrants from England, in search of the same religious tolerance that had drawn Williams away from Massachusetts, and by 1663 the several towns established in the area had received a royal charter from Charles II as the colony of Rhode Island. Religious dissidents from the strict Puritan faith were forbidden to worship in the colonies of Massachusetts and Virginia, but Rhode Island welcomed people of any religious persuasion or of no religion at all.

Another religious dissident in the Massachusetts Bay Colony did not fare so well. Anne Hutchinson was an outspoken wife and mother who had immigrated to Massachusetts in 1634. Her belief in salvation by personal experience of God, without the need for obedience to church laws, so angered the church officials in Boston that she was arrested for "traducing the ministers and their ministry." Governor Winthrop described her as "like Roger Williams or worse" in 1637, and she was convicted of sedition and banished from the colony. After a difficult journey through the forests of New England, she and her large family found their way to southern Rhode Island. But the long arm of the Massachusetts Bay Colony reached her even in Rhode Island, and in 1642 the family moved south to Long Island, near what is now Pelham Bay, New York. There she and her household of 16, including 13 of her fourteen children, were massacred by Indians the next year.

Roger Williams (1604–83), a religious dissenter in the Massachusetts colony who withdrew from it to found the Rhode Island colony, is shown in an idealized portrait in charcoal by H. Halit. *(Library of Congress, Prints and Photographs Division [LC-USZ62-109381])*

Relations between the settlers and the native population in New England were often hostile after the first few years. Although the Pilgrims were welcomed and helped by the local Indians during their hard first winter there, the friendship between the two cultures soon broke down, and it was never restored. The Europeans had come to settle the land and were prepared to purchase it for their permanent use. The grants given by the English rulers stated that they were to pay for whatever land they took over, but the Indians did not share the European idea of land ownership, thinking of the territory as belonging to all people to use equally. When the colonists began to expand beyond their first areas of settlement, fighting broke out. As the Powhatan Confederacy in Jamestown had risen up against the English in 1622, the powerful Pequot tribe in Massachusetts began resisting English expansion into their territory around 1636. In June of the next year, some 300 armed Puritans, joined by warriors of the Mohegan tribe, surrounded and destroyed the Pequot village, burning its dwellings to the ground and killing most of its inhabitants. Only about 200 Pequot survived the massacre, and they were made slaves. There was no large-scale Indian resistance in the New England colonies for almost 40 years afterward.

New Netherland and New Amsterdam

Although it was the English colonies in North America that were to form the nucleus of the new nation, the British were not the only ones to attempt to exploit the territory. The Netherlands was a small nation, but in the 17th century it was an important and powerful one, and it had colonial ambitions no less great than those of England, Spain, and France.

The Dutch East India Company, a trading corporation operating under royal Dutch authority, was seeking a northern sea route to Asia when it sent English mariner Henry Hudson across the Atlantic to explore the New World. In 1609, when Hudson found the river that today bears his name, he realized that it would not take him to China or India, but his reports of the beautiful and fertile land of the Hudson Valley convinced his employers of the possibilities of profit. By 1614 the Dutch had established a settlement at the headwaters of the river, near present-day Albany, New York. It quickly became a prosperous commercial enterprise, trading with the Indians for fox and beaver pelts, but its residents made no effort at establishing homes and had no plans to develop the colony as a permanent settlement.

The Dutch had already begun colonizing, however, and had established a foothold in the Caribbean and in Asia. Investors in the Netherlands soon began to eye the North American mainland. In 1621 the government in Amsterdam gave the newly formed Dutch West India Company a charter to conduct business and to settle the land. This large corporation formed the colony of New Netherland around Fort Orange, at the trading post near the mouth of the Hudson, in 1624. That year 30 families settled there permanently, carving out estates for themselves and building solid Dutch-style houses. Almost immediately the colony began to spread south along the Hudson Valley, and it soon came to include all the territory between the Atlantic and Delaware Bay, comprising most of present-day New York and New Jersey. Two years after the colony began, the company's director-general, Peter Minuit, made one of the most famous real-estate transactions in American history. According to legend, he purchased the island of Manhattan from the Canarsie Indians for 60 guilders—traditionally equal to 24 American dollars—worth of trinkets. With its great natural harbor, the island, renamed New Amsterdam for the Dutch capital, became the colony's trading center.

New Netherland was commercially successful, but it never became a major colonial power and did not last long. One reason for its failure to grow and become self-sufficient was its policy of allotting land only to a few rich men, called patroons, who received enormous estates stretching 16 miles along the river and as far inland as the settler could reach. The patroon had full power over this land and paid no taxes for eight years in return for his agreement to settle 50 families from the Netherlands on it. Economic conditions in the Netherlands were not so bad in the 17th century, and not many Dutch peasants wanted to move to a new country to become serfs on a nobleman's estate. By 1640 Dutch immigration had grown so little that the Dutch

West India Company tried the more modest plan of offering 200 acres to those who could promise to bring five people over, but it did not help. Where the Virginia Company's 50-acre headright, offered either to a landowner who brought one worker to the colony or to any family who came on its own, had provided a great inducement to immigrate, the less generous Dutch policy tempted almost no one. During the scant half-century that the Dutch colony in North America lasted, fewer than 6,000 people emigrated to it from the Netherlands.

Many of the immigrants to New Netherland were English—either from England or transplanted from other colonies in North America—and a good number of its residents came from other countries. It is estimated that by 1664, as many as 30 percent of the population of New Netherland was non-Dutch. One of the most striking features of the colony's port city, New Amsterdam, was its cosmopolitan character. Then, as now, Manhattan Island was home to people from many nations. In 1643, when the entire population of the colony of New Netherland was perhaps 4,000, the French priest Isaac Jogues visited New Amsterdam and noted that he had heard no fewer than 18 languages spoken on its streets.

Among the many peoples who found their way to the Dutch colony were the first Jewish families to come to the New World as a group. There had been individual Jews in the New World since at least the 1620s, but the 23 who arrived in the harbor of New Amsterdam in 1654 were the first to settle and establish a distinct Jewish presence. They had been prosperous members of a large Jewish community in Recife, Brazil, but when Portugal took over that city they had been forced to flee. Like other religious refugees, they looked to the New World for a haven.

They were not welcomed. The leaders of the Dutch Reformed Church, the official religion of the colony, were as severe and repressive as the Puritans, and they allowed little religious freedom. The governor-general, Peter Stuyvesant, tried to expel the Jewish immigrants, but seven of them were stockholders of the Dutch West India Company, and the home office in Amsterdam ordered him to allow the entire group to stay. Nevertheless, their lives were not made easy; they could engage in trade but not open retail shops, practice any craft, vote, or hold public office, and they could not worship in a synagogue or other public place. They were prohibited from serving in the public guard but were required to pay a special tax for not doing so. Some of the Jewish settlers found life under the government of the colony intolerable and left for the Netherlands or for other Dutch possessions in the Caribbean, where they could enjoy more personal freedom and opportunity. However, enough remained to establish a permanent Jewish community.

Another foreign group that secured reluctant hospitality from the Dutch government was the Swedes. The king of Sweden, observing the success of the corporations that established Virginia, Massachusetts, and New Netherland, created a Swedish West India Company and received permission from the government in Amsterdam to found a Swedish colony within the boundaries of New Netherland in 1638. Soon a community named New Sweden grew on the banks of the Delaware River, near present-day Wilmington, Delaware, and in 1640 the first Lutheran clergyman arrived. But although the government in the home country had officially sanctioned the Swedish settlement, the Dutch colonists saw the Swedes as interlopers and competitors, and relations between the two communities were strained from the beginning. The Swedish immigrants were peaceable and hard-working, and many assimilated so completely as to accept and use the Dutch language, but there were many conflicts between the two groups. In 1655 an open war broke out, and the better-armed Dutch quickly overran and occupied New Sweden.

Despite its commercial and military success, New Netherland was never able to achieve complete colonial stability or unity. One major reason was its inflexible management. Under the harsh and dictatorial rule of a series of unpopular governors-general, the Dutch colonists were frequently dissatisfied, and when commercial rivalries led to conflicts with the English, few of the Dutch supported their government. At last in 1664—a mere half-century after the Dutch settled at the mouth of the river their explorer had discovered—the English sailed four frigates into the harbor and challenged the colony. Peter Stuyvesant tried to rouse his subjects to resist, but the harsh, autocratic governor-general inspired so little loyalty that they failed to give him any support. The colony fell without a shot being fired. The English claimed it as the property of James, duke of York, and renamed it New York.

Maryland and Pennsylvania

As the Puritan colonies offered a haven of religious tolerance only for Puritans, the colony of Maryland offered the same for Catholics, but the number of people to profit by it was small. The colony was founded by George Calvert, first baron Baltimore. Calvert had been a secretary of state to James I, but, when he converted to Roman Catholicism in 1625, his political career came to an end. His plan was to establish in the New World a refuge for wealthy Catholics. The king granted him a tract in Newfoundland, in present-day Canada, in 1621, and Lord Baltimore took his family there in 1628. One winter in that frigid territory was enough for them. He wrote to the king about "the sad face of wynter upon all this land, both sea and land so frozen for the greatest part of the tyme as they are not penetrable" and "the ayre so intolerable cold as it is hardly to be endured," and after a year he came home to ask for something a little further south.

Although the Virginia colony was eager for new investment, its residents were inflexibly Protestant and did not welcome a Catholic in their midst. The king at last granted Calvert a charter for a territory just north of Virginia, in what is now Maryland. Calvert died before the charter was issued in 1632, but his son, Cecilius, second baron Baltimore, organized the colony in 1634. It was not a success at first and was slow to attract English immigrants from either the small Catholic community or the adventurous. Begun with fewer than 150 settlers, the total population in 1640 was about 400, and it fell to some 200 within the next few decades.

The direction of the colony was in the hands of a small group of upper-class Catholics, but the working community, brought over as the leaders' servants, was made up of Protestants. One estimate places the total number of Catholics in Maryland from 1661 to 1689 at about one-twelfth of the population. The religious liberty accorded to Catholics in Maryland did little for adherents of other religions, and even such tolerance as the Catholic government of Maryland exhibited was grudging. Lord Baltimore received his charter from the Protestant King James on the condition that there be no restrictions against Protestants in the new colony. The Maryland Toleration Act of 1649 specified that no Christian was to be "in any ways troubled molested or discountenanced for . . . his or her religion, nor in the free exercise thereof . . . nor in any way compelled to the belief or exercise of any other Religion against his or her consent." But the boundaries of this religious freedom were narrowly defined within the Christian faith. Anyone who "insulted" the Blessed Virgin, the Apostles, or the Evangelist was to be fined or publicly whipped, and anyone who denied the Holy Trinity or the divinity of Jesus Christ was to be hanged.

Although founded as a haven for members of the Roman Catholic faith, the colony was far from unanimous in its support of that church. When the English throne revoked the private ownership of Maryland in 1691, taking it over as a crown colony, a Protestant revolt resulted in the Church of England being established there the next year. Finally Charles Calvert, the third baron Baltimore and George's grandson, joined the Protestant Church of England himself.

The British government remained indifferent to religious controversy in the New World. Its principal interest in the colonies was commercial, and it carefully protected its financial investments there, revoking its charters and annexing the territories as Crown Colonies when they ceased to be profitable to the home country. As early as 1621, the king ordered Virginia to ship its tobacco only to English ports. In 1645 Parliament enacted the first of several increasingly repressive laws governing colonial trade, and in 1660 it passed a comprehensive statute, known as the First Navigation Act, requiring the captains and ships and at least three quarters of the crews carrying a wide variety of cargoes to or from the colonies to be English nationals. In this way the British government prevented the Dutch from selling Virginia tobacco in Europe and the French from trading in West Indian sugar.

In a lengthy and precisely worded document, the Navigation Act of 1660 spelled out an elaborate series of restrictions, concluding, "And it is further enacted . . . that . . . no sugars, tobacco, cotton-wool, indicoes [indigo], ginger, fustick [a New World tree from whose bark a dye is extracted], or other dying wood of growth, production or manufacture of any *English* plantation in *America, Asia,* or *Africa,* shall be shipped, carried, conveyed, or transported from any of the said *English,* plantations to any land, island, territory, dominion, port, or place whatsoever, other than to such other *English* plantations as do belong to his Majesty."

These statutes inhibited trade and imposed a financial strain on the settlers, but the religious practices of most immigrants remained unhampered. If full religious freedom was seldom found in the New World, America came closer to that ideal than England, and those in search of it continued to emigrate for the purpose. The first colony after Rhode Island to truly fulfill the promise of religious freedom, and to draw a sizable immigrant populace from the Old World on that basis, was Pennsylvania, which was granted a charter in 1681. Like Maryland and New York, it was a proprietary colony, built on a parcel of land given by the British government to a proprietor, or owner. Of all of the 13 colonies, none was so clearly an expression of a spiritual mission as Pennsylvania.

William Penn, the son of Admiral Sir William Penn, a British naval hero, was an Oxford-educated aristocrat who found the moral laxity of those who surrounded Charles II so distasteful that he retired from the royal court and joined a new religious group called the Society of Friends, or Quakers. This radical Protestant society, founded in England in the 1650s, rejected all church authority and relied on personal judgment in religious matters believing that God made his will known without the need of clergy. Its members often suffered public whippings or went to jail for refusing to submit to the established church. Penn himself was imprisoned several times for writing and preaching in support of the Quaker faith and spent eight months in the Tower of London on one such occasion. While he was there he wrote *No Cross,*

No Crown, a defiant pamplet expressing his willingness to suffer for his beliefs. When he expressed a desire to establish a colony in North America where anyone might worship in his own way, the king was only too glad to oblige. Granting Penn a charter to settle his Quaker friends in the New World permitted the king both to discharge a debt of about $80,000 he owed Penn's father and to purge the country of a troublesome element.

Pennsylvania (Penn's Woods), named in honor of the Quaker's father, was a large, fertile territory whose government was based on Quaker ideas and freedom of religion. Believing that "any government is free to the People under it (whatever be the Frame) where the Laws rule, and the People are a Party to those Laws," Penn established the most generous terms and the most humanitarian policies of any of the original colonies. All religions were welcome, and none was imposed, since, as Penn observed, "It were better to be of no church, than to be bitter of any." The first thing he did on arriving in Pennsylvania was to draw up a treaty with the Indians—one of the few never broken by Europeans—and to pay them for most of the land that the king had given him.

As the Quaker faith was based on fraternity—they addressed everyone as "Friend"—the new colony naturally welcomed different ethnic groups as well as different religious persuasions. The Delaware Valley already held the largest group of non-English settlers in the colonies, including as it did New Netherland and New Sweden, and Penn noted in his 1685 essay "A Further Account of the Province of Pennsylvania" that the people of the region were "a collection of Divers Nations in Europe: as, French, Dutch, Germans, Swedes, Danes, Finns, Scotch, French and English, and of the last equal to all the rest." Penn actively recruited the Welsh, who purchased 40,000 acres west of Philadelphia where they maintained their language and customs in what became known as the Welsh Tract. Having traveled as a missionary in Germany, he also welcomed German Quakers, who settled a few miles north of Philadelphia. There Franz Daniel Pastorius, a lawyer from the lower Rhineland, founded the village of Germantown with a group of his compatriots so that, as he explained in 1683, "we High-Germans may maintain a separate little province and thus feel more secure from all oppressors." Like the Welsh, the people of the region established their own distinct cultural identity, instituted their own local laws and courts, and spoke their own language. Germantown became a prosperous community of farmers, merchants, linen-makers, and craftsmen.

Quakers governed Pennsylvania as a "Holy Experiment," believing that everyone shared equally in the blessing of God. Pioneers in many social reforms, they were the first in the new land to establish humane care of the insane and to advocate prison reform. They opposed capital punishment and slavery and championed public education for the poor and equal rights for women. A modest people, they dressed simply and never wore jewelry. In Pennsylvania, everyone was equal and everyone was welcome. The colony became a haven for the outsider, and foreign nationals prospered there. Some people, both in England and in the other English colonies in the New World, felt that they prospered too much, and that they maintained their separate national identities too distinctly, threatening the unity of the British community. The colonies had not yet begun to think of themselves as a nation, but there were already those who feared immigration. Their voices were to grow louder in the centuries to come.

Chronicle of Events

1578

- Queen Elizabeth grants Sir Humphrey Gilbert a patent to explore and colonize in North America. Gilbert dies while returning from his second expedition in 1583.

1585

- *July 27*: Sir Walter Raleigh founds a colony on Roanoke Island in what is now North Carolina. It is abandoned the next year.

1587

- A second group, comprising 100 men and 17 women, attempts to settle on Roanoke Island. It disappears by 1590.

1606

- Queen Elizabeth grants charters to the London and the Plymouth Virginia Companies to establish settlements in North America.

1607

- *May 24*: Three ships containing 104 Englishmen drop anchor in the James River, Virginia, to form the first permanent English colony in North America, the Jamestown colony, as a joint business venture. By the end of the first year, almost two-thirds of the original colonists have died of disease.

1608

- Samuel de Champlain founds Quebec, the first French settlement in North America, on the St. Lawrence River in present-day Canada.
- Captain John Smith's *True Relation of Occurrences in Virginia*, published in England, encourages colonial immigration.

1609

- Six hundred immigrants from England arrive in Jamestown. They include planters, craftsmen, and, predominantly, indentured laborers. Advertising by the London proprietors promotes the colony as a land of opportunity.
- John Smith initiates the cultivation of Indian corn in the Jamestown colony.

- English navigator Henry Hudson, sailing for the Dutch East India Company, discovers and explores the Hudson River.
- The Church of England is established by law in the Jamestown colony.

1610

- Four hundred new settlers join the Jamestown colony under the leadership of Lord Delaware.

1611

- Samuel de Champlain lays out a site for a settlement that will become Montreal, Canada, in 1641.

1612

- The English settle the island of Bermuda. By 1640 the British colonies in the West Indies will hold about 20,000 people.
- John Rolfe develops a method of curing tobacco, the first crop with trading value. Two years later a profitable export trade in tobacco is established with England.

1613

- The English destroy French settlements near the Bay of Fundy between the present-day provinces of New Brunswick and Nova Scotia, Canada.

1614

- The Dutch establish a fur-trading post near the head of the Hudson River in the area of present-day Albany, New York.

1616

- John Smith publishes *A Description of New England*, which draws many immigrants to the New World and popularizes the name of the region.

1618

- The Virginia Company, in need of labor for its colony, initiates the policy of granting a "headright" of 50 acres per worker brought to the colony or per family immigrating independently. This system attracts numerous immigrants from England.

1619

- Arrival of a shipload of women to Virginia, sent by the Virginia Company to encourage settlers to establish homes, signals the colony's transition from a trading post to a permanent settlement.

- *July*: America's first legislative body, the General Assembly of Virginia, meets for the first time and establishes British law in the New World.
- *August*: Nineteen Africans are brought to Jamestown by a Dutch man-of-war as indentured servants. They have the same rights as white indentured servants and are freed after serving the terms of their indenture, usually from five to seven years.

1620

- *September 16*: Church of England Separatists, calling themselves "Pilgrims," receive a charter to settle in Virginia. Blown off course during their journey from Plymouth, England, they land in Cape Cod, Massachusetts, November 19, and establish the Plymouth colony.

1621

- Regular trade with England through the West Indies begins. It is called the "triangular trade" because ships made a three-stage journey from the colonies to the West Indies with merchandise (mainly tobacco); picked up sugar, rum, and molasses there; and proceeded to England, where they exchanged their cargo for British manufactured goods; and returned to the colonies.
- The Dutch West India Company receives a charter to establish a colony on the North American mainland.

1622

- *March 22*: Indians massacre 347 settlers in the Jamestown colony.

1623

- Colonists settle in New Hampshire and Maine under the authority of the Council for New England.

1624

- The Dutch establish Fort Orange at their fur-trading post near the head of the Hudson River.
- *May 24*: Virginia becomes a royal colony when the British government revokes its charter. The colony has lost an estimated £200,000 since its establishment.

1625

- The population of the British colonies in North America reaches 1,980, of which 1,800 are in the Virginia colony.

- The Dutch establish a fur-trading post on Manhattan Island.

1626

- The Dutch, under Peter Minuit, purchase Manhattan Island from the Indians and rename it New Amsterdam.

1628

- The Dutch Reformed Church is established in New Amsterdam and becomes the official religion.
- *September 6*: The Council for New England grants a land patent to a group of Puritans between the Charles and the Merrimack Rivers, and 50–60 colonists establish a settlement at Salem, Massachusetts.

1629

- *March 10*: Charles I dissolves Parliament. Puritans are severely persecuted by the Church of England, leading to widespread dissatisfaction and a drive to emigrate to the New World.
- *March 14*: Charles I grants a charter to the Massachusetts Bay Company.
- *April*: War between France and England ends.
- *June 17*: The Dutch West India Company grants large holdings along the Hudson and Delaware Rivers to wealthy citizens, called patroons, who agree to bring settlers to New Netherland.
- *June 27*: Four hundred twenty new settlers arrive in the Massachusetts Bay Colony.
- *July 20*: The British conquer and occupy Quebec, although war between France and England officially ended three months earlier.

1630

- *June 12*: The Massachusetts Bay Company begins the settlement of some 2,000 English immigrants under Puritan leadership in New England, initiating the "Great Migration" to the New World. In the next 10 years, Protestant reformers seeking freedom of religion lead some 21,000 immigrants to New England.

1632

- The Treaty of St. Germain-en-Laye defines the territorial boundaries of the French and English in the New World.

1634

- *February 27*: The first settlers of the Maryland colony—founded by George Calvert, Lord Baltimore, as a refuge for English Catholics—arrive. The colony is required by charter to provide religious freedom to all Christians.

1635

- The French occupy St. Christopher, the first of 11 West Indian islands that they take over during the next 21 years.
- *October*: London-born clergyman Roger Williams is banished from Salem for protesting Puritan church authority in government.

1636

- Connecticut colonists launch an attack against the Pequot Indians and destroy their main village. A massacre of the few remaining Indians, in which the Plymouth colonists take part, follows in 1637.
- *June*: Williams founds Providence, the first settlement in Rhode Island, as a refuge for religious dissenters. The Providence settlement is the first in which the church has no control over the government.

1637

- *November 17*: Anne Hutchinson is convicted of sedition and banished for disputing the authority of the church in the Massachusetts Bay Colony.

1638

- Swedes begin settlement on the Delaware River in present-day Wilmington, in the territory of New Netherland, under the authority of the Dutch government but against the will of the Dutch colonists. The settlement is named New Sweden.
- *March 7*: Anne Hutchinson founds the town of Pocasset, later Portsmouth, Rhode Island, with her husband and 14 children. In 1642 she moves to the area of Pelham Bay, New York, where she and her family are massacred by Indians.

1640

- The first Lutheran clergyman arrives in the Swedish colony on the Delaware River. The church is not established for another century.

1641

- French settlers found Montreal, Canada.

1642

- Civil war breaks out in England under Oliver Cromwell. Immigration to America increases.

1643

- *May 19*: New England Confederation is formed, including the Plymouth, Massachusetts Bay, Connecticut, and New Haven colonies.

1644

- *March*: The British government officially charters the Providence Plantation in Rhode Island, settled since 1636.

1647

- The Rhode Island colony adopts a constitution officially establishing separation of church and state, along with other liberal provisions.

1649

- Charles I of England is executed, and Oliver Cromwell establishes the British Commonwealth.
- *April 21*: Maryland Toleration Act establishes religious toleration for all Christians regardless of sectarian affiliation.

1652

- The Massachusetts Bay Colony declares itself independent of the control of the British Parliament and begins the coinage of its own money.

1654

- The first sizable group of Jews to immigrate to the New World arrives at New Amsterdam seeking refuge from Portuguese persecution in Brazil. They are admitted and allowed to engage in trade but prohibited from voting or worshiping publicly.
- *July*: The French colony of Acadia, in present-day Nova Scotia, Canada, is seized by English troops.

1655

- The Dutch occupy New Sweden, the Swedish colony on the Delaware River.

1656

- *July–August*: Members of the Society of Friends (Quakers) arrive in Boston but are expelled. The next year the Society is formally banned in Massachusetts.

1659

- *October*: The first of four executions of Quakers is carried out in the Massachusetts Bay Colony. The sentences are for returning to the colony after the Society of Friends has been expelled.

1660

- The British monarchy is restored under Charles II. The American colonies accept royal authority.
- *October 1*: Parliament passes the Navigation Act, prohibiting the shipment of certain colonial products, including sugar, cotton, and tobacco, to any country except England or her colonies.

1663

- Charles II grants a charter to Carolina, extending from Florida to Virginia and westward to the Pacific Ocean.
- A new Navigation Act in England prohibits shipment of goods to the colonies except on English ships, inhibiting trade with Europe.

1664

- *September 8*: The English take New Amsterdam from the Dutch and establish the colony of New York.

1667

- Acadia is restored to French rule.

1668

- England and France begin a struggle for control of the Hudson Bay.

1670

- The Virginia Colony assembly declares all servants brought in by sea who are not Christian to be "slaves for life."
- English nobles found Charleston, South Carolina, to develop the Carolina territory.
- Hudson Bay Company is established by England to compete with French fur traders.

1673

- French missionary priest Jacques Marquette and explorer Louis Jolliet travel from the Great Lakes to the Mississippi by boat.

1675

- *June 20*: King Philip's War between the New England colonists and the Algonquian Indians begins. The Indians are defeated the next year. The Wampanoag chief known as King Philip is shot, and his wife and children are sold into slavery.

1681

- *March 4*: William Penn and a group of Quakers found Pennsylvania as a "Holy Experiment" in religious toleration and self-government.

1682

- René-Robert Cavalier, sieur de La Salle, claims the Mississippi Valley for King Louis XIV of France, naming it Louisiana.
- *October 27*: William Penn arrives in Pennsylvania. He makes a formal treaty with the Indians and pays them for the land.

1683

- The first group of German immigrants, Mennonites and Quakers, immigrate to Pennsylvania seeking to withdraw from the world and establish their own religious community. Franz Daniel Pastorius establishes Germantown, the first German-speaking city in America, near Philadelphia. Pennsylvania provides a home during the succeeding years for such other German Protestant groups as the Dunkards, Moravians, Amish, and Schwenckfelders.

1684

- *June 21*: The British government revokes the charter of the Massachusetts Bay Colony for various independent actions, including refusing to take an oath of allegiance or to abide by the Navigation Acts and execution of British subjects for religious dissent.

1685

- In France, Louis XIV's revocation of the Edict of Nantes, guaranteeing freedom of worship to Protestants, leads to severe persecution of Huguenots. A small refugee migration results, and Huguenots settle and establish churches in Massachusetts, New York, and South Carolina.
- *February 6*: The duke of York ascends the throne of England as James II. In one of his first actions as king, James II reorganizes the Massachusetts Bay Colony, establishing the Dominion of New England, which includes New York, New Jersey, and Pennsylvania.

1689

- James II abdicates, and William and Mary ascend the throne. The new rulers take possession of some colonies as royal provinces and establish special courts to enforce the Navigation Acts.

1693

- New York officially declares the Church of England to be the official faith of the colony. Maryland, North Carolina, South Carolina, and Georgia follow between 1702 and 1758.

The ill-fated explorer and colonist René-Robert Cavelier, sieur de La Salle, standing, left (1643–87), named viceroy of North America by the king of France, was assassinated by his men. *(Library of Congress, Prints and Photographs Division, [LC-USZ62-5546])*

1699

- The French establish colonies in present-day Mississippi and Louisiana. Other French settlements and trading posts form in the Michigan and Illinois territories.

- The British pass the Wool Act, prohibiting colonies to trade in wool among themselves or with any other country except England.

Eyewitness Testimony

. . . [Y]our Highnesses may believe that this island [Hispaniola, now Haiti and the Dominican Republic], and all the others, are as much yours as Castile. Here there is only wanting a settlement and the order to the people to do what is required. For I, with the force which I have under me, which is not large, could march all over these islands without opposition. I have seen only three sailors land, without wishing to do harm, and a multitude of Indians fled before them. They have no arms, and are without warlike instincts; they all go naked, and are so timid that a thousand would not stand before three of our men. So that they are good to be ordered about, to work and sow, and to do all that may be necessary, and to build towns, and they should be taught to go about clothed and to adopt our customs.

Christopher Columbus, October 14, 1492, journal entry, "*Journal of the First Voyage of Christopher Columbus, 1492–93,*" *in Edward Gaylord Bourne,* The Northmen, Columbus and Cabot, 985–1503 *(1906), p. 145.*

The second of July, we found shallow water, where we smelled so sweet and so strong a smell, as if we had been in the midst of some delicate garden abounding with all kinds of odoriferous flowers, by which we were assured, that the land could not be far distant. . . .

The next day there came unto us many boats, and in one of them the King's brother, accompanied with forty or fifty men, very handsome and goodly people, and in their behavior as mannerly and civil as any in Europe. His name was Granganimeo, and the King is called Wingina, the country Wingandacoa, and now by her Majesty Virginia.

Captain Arthur Barlowe, a member of Sir Walter Raleigh's expedition, on arriving at the coast of present-day North Carolina on July 2, 1584, in Richard Hakluyt, Principal Navigations, Voyages, Traffiques, and Discoveries of the English Nation, *(1589), in Colbert,* Eyewitness to America *(1997), p. 12.*

At his [John Smith's] entrance before the King, all the people gave a great shout. The Queene of *Appamattuck* was appointed to bring him water to wash his hands, and another brought him a bunch of feathers, in stead of a Towell to dry them: having feasted him after their best barbarous manner they could, a long consultation was held, but the conclusion was, two great stones were brought before *Powhatan*: then as many as could layd hands on him, dragged him to them, and thereon laid his

head, and being ready with their clubs, to beate out his braines, *Pocahontas* the King's dearest daughter, when no entreaty could prevaile, got his head in her armes, and laid her owne upon his to save him from death: whereat the Emperour was contented he should live to make them hatchets, and her bells, beads, and copper; for they thought him as well of all occupations as themselves.

John Smith, recounting the story of his salvation by Pocahontas on January 5, 1608, Travels and Works of Captain John Smith *(1624), p. 400.*

I am now grown old, and must soon die; and the succession must descend, in order, to my brothers . . . and then to my two sisters, and their two daughters. I wish their experience was equal to mine; and that your love to us might not be less than ours to you. Why should you take by force that from us which you can have by love? Why should you destroy us, who have provided you with food? What can you get by war? We can hide our provisions, and fly into the woods; and then you must consequently famish by wronging your friends. What is the cause of your jealousy? You see us unarmed and willing to supply your wants, if you will come in a friendly manner, and not with swords and guns, as to invade an enemy. I am not so simple, as not to know it is better to eat good meat, lie well, and sleep quietly with my women and children; to laugh and be merry with the English; and, being your friend, to have copper, hatchets, and whatever else I want, than to fly from all, to lie cold in the woods, feed upon acorns, roots, and such trash, and to be so hunted, that I cannot rest, eat, or sleep. In such circumstances, my men must watch, and if a twig but break, all would cry out, "*Here comes Capt. Smith*"; and so, in this miserable manner, to end my miserable life; and, Capt. Smith, this *might* be soon your fate too. . . . I, therefor, exhort you to peaceable councils; and above all, I insist that the guns and swords, the cause of all our jealousy and uneasiness, be removed and sent away.

Powhatan, speech to John Smith, ca. 1609, in Drake, Biography and History of the Indians of North America, from its First Discovery *(1851), p. 353.*

The soile is strong and lustie of its own nature . . . [I]f bare nature be so amiable in its naked bed, what may we hope when Arte and Nature both shall joyne, and strive together, to give best content to man and beast? . . . We doubt not but to make there in a few yeares store of good wines, as any from the Canaries, by replanting and making tame the Vines that naturally grow there in great abundance. . . . There grows hemp for Cordage, an excellent commoditie, and flaxe for linen cloth. . . . We intend to plant there (God willing) great plentie of Sugar Canes, for which the soyle and clymate is very apt and fit; also linseed and Rapeseed to make Oiles. . . . We must plant also Orenges, Limons, Almonds, Aniseeds, Rice, Cummin, Cottonwood, Carowey seeds, Ginger, Madder, Olives, Oris, Sumacke, and many such like, . . . all very good merchandize.

> Novo Britannia, *pamphlet published by the Virginia Company to promote immigration to the Virginia Colony, 1609, in Force,* Tracts and Other Papers, Relating Principally to the Origin, Settlement, and Progress of the Colonies in North America, *Volume 1 (1836), pp. 16–17, 22.*

Every man allmost laments himself of being here, and murmurs at his present state. [They are] sutch disordered persons, so prophane, so rioutous, so full of treasonable Intendments, besides of sutch diseased and crased bodies which render them so unable, fainte, and desperate of recoverie, as of three hundred not three score may be called forth or imploied upon any labor or service. . . .

If it will please his Majestie to banish hither all offenders condemned to die, it would be a readie way to furnish us with men, and not allwayes with the worst kinde of men either for birth, spiritts or Bodie.

> *Sir Thomas Dale, governor of the Jamestown Colony, 1611, in a letter reporting on conditions to James I, in Morison,* The Oxford History of the American People *(1965), p. 51.*

Whereas, the number of one hundred children . . . were the last spring sent and transported by the Virginia Company from the city of London unto Virginia, and toward the charge for the transportation and appareling of the same one hundred children a collection of the sum of 500 pounds was made of diverse well and godly disposed persons, charitably minded toward the plantation in Virginia, dwelling within the city of London and suburbs thereof, and thereupon the said 500 pounds was paid unto the said Company for the purpose aforesaid. And, thereupon, for the good of the same children . . . it is fully concluded, ordered and decreed by and at a general Quarter Court, . . . that every of the same children which are now living at the charges, and by the provision of the said Virginia Company, shall be educated and brought up in some good trade and profession, whereby they may be enabled to get their living and maintain themselves when they shall attain their several ages of four-and-twenty

years, or be out of their apprenticeships, which shall endure at the least seven years if they so long live.

And, further, that every of the same children—that is to say, the boys at their ages of one-and-twenty or upward, and the maids or girls at their age of one-and-twenty years, or day of marriage, which shall first happen, shall have freely given and alloted unto them fifty acres of land apiece in Virginia, aforesaid, within the limits of the English plantation. . . .

> *Petition by the leaders of the Jamestown Colony to the Virginia Company in London requesting further shipment of apprentices, 1620, in Brock,* Abstract of the Proceedings of the Virginia Company of London, 1619–1624 *Volume I, (1887), p. 39.*

Having undertaken for the glory of God, and the advancement of the Christian faith and honor of our king and country, a voyage to plant the first colony in the northern part of Virginia, do by these present, solemnly and mutually, in the presence of God and one of another, covenant and combine ourselves together into a civil body politic, for our better ordering and preservation and furtherance of the ends aforesaid; and by virtue hereof to enact, constitute and frame such just and equal laws, ordinances, acts, constitutions, offices from time to time as shall be thought most meet and convenient for the general good of the colony; unto which we promise all due submission and obedience.

> *The Mayflower Compact, signed by forty-one men on board the ship carrying the Pilgrims to the Plymouth Colony on November 11, 1620, in Cheever,* The Journals of the Pilgrims in New England, in 1620 *(1849), pp. 30–31.*

[The Virginia colony] shall redeem many a wretch from the jaws of death, from the hands of the executioner. . . . It shall sweep your streets and wash your doors from idle persons and the children of idle persons, and employ them; and truly, if the country were but such a Bridewell [a prison in London] to force idle persons to work, it had a good use.

> *John Donne, English poet and clergyman, in a sermon to the Virginia Company in London, 1622, in Evans,* America: The View from Europe *(1976), p. 94.*

And such was the conceit of firm peace and amity that there was seldom or never a sword worn and a piece seldomer, except for a deer or fowl. . . . The houses generally sat open to the savages, who were always friendly entertained at the tables of the English and commonly lodged in their bed-chambers . . . to open a fair gate for their conversion to Christianity. . . .

Yea, such was the treacherous dissimulation of that people who then had contrived our destruction, that even two days before the massacre some of our men were guided through the woods by them in safety. . . . Yea, they borrowed our own boats to convey themselves across the river . . . to consult of the devilish murder that ensued, and of our utter extirpation, which God of his mercy (by the means of some of themselves converted to Christianity) prevented. . . .

On the Friday morning (the fatal day) . . . they came unarmed into our houses, without bows or arrows, or other weapons, with deer, turkeys, fish, furs, and other provisions to sell and truck with us for glass, beads, and other trifles; yea, in some places sat down at breakfast with our people at their tables, whom immediately with their own tools and weapons either laid down, or standing in their houses, they basely and barbarously murdered, not sparing either age or sex, man, woman or child; so sudden in their cruel execution that few or none discerned the weapon or blow that brought them to destruction. . . .

And by this means that fatal Friday morning, there fell under the bloody and barbarous hands of that perfidious and inhumane people, contrary to the laws of God and man, and nature and nations, 347 men, women, and children. . . . And not being content with taking away life alone, they fell after again upon the dead, making, as well as they could, a fresh murder, defacing, dragging, and mangling the dead carcasses into many pieces, and carrying away some parts in derision. . . .

Our hands, which before were tied with gentleness and fair usage, are now set at liberty by the treacherous violence of the savages . . . so that we, who hitherto have had possession of no more ground than their waste and our purchase at a valuable consideration to their contentment gained, may now by right of war, and law of nations, invade the country, and destroy them who sought to destroy us; whereby we will enjoy their cultivated places. . . .

Edward Waterhouse, an official in the Jamestown Colony, describing the Indian massacre, 1622, and defending the settlers' revenge, in Kingsbury, The Records of the Virginia Company of London *(1906–35), pp. 550–551, 556–557.*

Well beloved good friend Henry Hovener

My commendations remembered, I heartily wish your welfare for God be thanked I am now in good health, but my brother and wife are dead about a year past. And touching the business I came hither is nothing yet performed, by reason of my sickness and weakness I was not able to travel up and down the hills and dales of these countries but do now intend every day to walk up and down the hills for good Mineralls here is both golde silver and copper to be had and therefore I will doe my endeavor by the grace of God to effect what I am able to perform. . . . It may please the aforesaid Company to send me . . . two little runtletts of wine and vinegar some spice and sugar to comfort us here in our sickness. . . . And whatsoever this all costeth I will not only wth my most humble service but also with some good Tobacco, Beaver, and Otterskins and other commodities here to be had recompence the Company for the same.

Sebastian Brandt, a settler in the Virginia Colony, letter to a friend in England, January 13, 1622, (Gilder Lehrman Collection, #708), in Davis and Mintz, The Boisterous Seas of Liberty *(1998), p. 32.*

You write me of some yll reports is given of my Wyfe for beating the maid; yf a faire waye will not do it, beatinge must, sometimes upon such Idlle girrels as she is. Yf you think it fit for my wife to do all the worke and the maide sitt still, she must forbeare her hands to strike, for then the worke wll ly undonn. She hath bin now 2 years ½ in the house, and I do not thinke she hath risen 20 times before my Wyfe hath been up to call her, and many tymes light the fire before she Comes out of her bed. . . . We Cann hardly keep her within doores after we a gonn to beed, except we Carry the key of the doore to beed. She never Could melke Cow nor goat since she came hither. . . . She cannot be trusted to serve a few pigs, but my wife most Commonly must be with her.

John Winter, settler in Richmond, Maine, 1639, in John Pinney Baxter, ed., Trelawny Papers *(1884), quoted in Davis and Mintz,* The Boisterous Sea of Liberty *(1998), pp. 66–67.*

It may be thought strang that these people [the settlers of the Plymouth Colony] should fall to these extremities in so short a time, being left competently provided when the ship left them, and had in addition by that moyetie of corn that was got by trade, besides much that they gott of the Indans where they lived, by one means & other. It must be their great disorder, for they spent excessively, whilst they had, or could get it, and it may be wasted parte away among the Indeans (for he that was their cheef was taxed by some amongst them for keeping Indean women, how truly I know not). And after they began to come into wants, many sould away their cloathes and bed coverings; others (so base were they) became servants to the Indeans, and would cutt them woode and fetch them water, for a cap full of corne; others fell to plaine stealing, both night & day, from the Indeans, of which they greevosly complained. In the end they came to that misery, that some starved and dyed with could and hunger. One in gathering shell-fish was so weake as he stuck fast in the mudd, and was found dead in the place. At last most of them left their dwellings & scatered up and downe in the woods, & by the water sids, wher they could find ground nuts and clames. . . . By which their cariages they became contemned & scorned of the Indeans, and they begane greatly to insulte over them in a most insolente maner; insomuch as they lay thus scatered abroad, and had set on a pot with ground nuts or shell-fish, when it was ready the Indeans would come and eate it up; and when night came, whereas some of them had a sorie blanket, or such

like, to lappe them selves in, the Indeans would take it and let the other lye all nighte in the could; so as their condition was very lamentable. Yea, in the end they were faine to hange one of their men, whom they could not reclaime from stealing, to give the Indeans contente.

William Bradford, governor of the Plymouth Colony, 1652, describing the difficulties of the group in 1623, Of Plymouth Plantation *(1962), pp. 86–87.*

Reasons for Puritan Migration

1. It will be a service to the Church of great consequence to carry the Gospel into those parts of the world . . . & to raise a Bulwark against the kingdom of AnteChrist wch the Jesuits labour to reare up in those parts.

IN HONOR OF THE BIRTHDAY OF GOVERNOR JOHN WINTHROP, BORN JUNE 12, 1587.

John Winthrop (1588–1649) was elected the first governor of the Massachusetts colony in 1629 before the group set sail and reelected 1631, 1632, 1633, 1637–40, 1642–44, 1646–49. *(Library of Congress, Prints and Photographs Division [LC-USZ62-120506])*

2. All other churches of Europe are brought to desolation, & o[u]r sins, for which the Lord begins already to frown upon us & to cut us short, do threaten evil times to be coming upon us, & who knows, but that God hath provided this place to be a refuge for many whom he means to save out of the general calamity, & seeing the Church hath no place left to fly into but the wilderness, what better work can there be, then to go and provide tabernacles & food for her against she comes thither.

3. This land grows weary of her Inhabitants, so as man, who is the most precious of all creatures, is here more vile & base then the earth we tread upon, & of less price among us than a horse or a sheep: masters are forced by authority to entertain servants, parents to maintain there own children, all towns complain of the burthen of their poore, though we have taken up many unnecessary yea unlawful trades to maintain them, & we use the authority of the Law to hinder the increase of o[u]r people. . . .

4. The whole earth is the Lords garden & he hath given it to the Sons of men wth a genl Commission: Gen: 1:28: increase & multiply, & replenish the earth & subdue it, . . . why then should we stand striving here for places of habitation . . . & in the meane time suffer a whole Continent as fruitful & convenient for the use of man to lie waste wthout any improvement?

5. All arts & Trades are carried in that deceitful & unrighteous course, as it is almost impossible for a good & upright man to maintain his charge & live comfortably in any of them.

6. The fountaine of learning & Religion are so corrupted as . . . most children (even the best wittes & of fairest hopes) are perverted, corrupted, & utterly overthrown by the multitude of evil examples. . . .

John Winthrop, governor of the Massachusetts Bay Colony, 1629, Life and Letters of John Winthrop, *Volume I, pp. 309–311.*

What with fine woods and green trees . . . made us all desirous to see our new paradise of New England, whence we saw such forerunning signals of fertility. . . .

The form of the earth here, in the superficies of it, is neither too flat in the plains nor too high in the hills, but partakes of both in a mediocrity, and fit for pasture, or for plow, or meadow ground, as men please to employ it. Though all the country be, as it were, a thick wood for the general, yet in diverse places there is much ground cleared by the Indians, and especially about the plantation; and I am told that about three miles from us a man may stand on a little hilly place and see diverse thousands of acres of ground as good as need to be, and not a tree in the same.

It is thought here is good clay to make bricks and tiles and earthen pots, as need to be. . . . The fertility of the soil is to be admired at, as appears in the abundance of grass that grows everywhere, both very thick and long, and very high in diverse places. . . . It is scarce to be believed how our kine and goats, horses and hogs do thrive and prosper here and like well of this country.

In our plantation we have already a quart of milk for a penny; but the abundant increase of corn proves this country to be a wonderment. Thirty, forty, fifty, sixty are ordinary here. Yea, Joseph's increase in Egypt is outstripped here with us. Our planters hope to have more than a hundredfold this year, and all this while I am within compass. And what will you say of two hundredfold and upward?

It is almost incredible what great gain some of our English planters have had by our Indian corn. . . .

Reverend Francis Higginson, Puritan settler in the Massachusetts Bay Colony, 1630, New England's Plantation, or A Short and True Description of the Commodities of that Country, *in Young,* Chronicles of the First Planters of the Colony of Massachusetts Bay, from 1623 to 1636 *(1846), pp. 233, 243–244.*

My father and mother showed themselves unwilling [that I should leave]. I sat close by a table where there lay a Bible. I hastily took up the Bible, and told my father if, where I opened the Bible, there I met with anything either to encourage or discourage, that should settle me. I, opening of it, not knowing no more than the child in the womb, the first thing I cast my eye on was: "Come out from among them, touch no unclean thing, and I will be your God and you shall be my people." My father and mother never more opposed me, but furthered me in the thing, and hastened after me as soon as they could.

John Dane, a tailor among the early immigrants to the Massachusetts Bay Colony, in the early 1630s, "A Declaration of Remarkabell Providenses in the Corse of My Lyf," in the New England Historic and Genealogical Register, *No. 8, (1845), in Fischer,* Albion's Seed: Four British Folkways in America *(1989), p. 20.*

Peter Stuyvesant (ca. 1610–72), the haughty governor-general of New Netherland, arrived in New Amsterdam in 1647 and surrendered the Dutch colony to the English in 1664. *(New York Public Library Print Collection)*

Stay not among the Wicked
Lest that with them you perish,
But let us to New-England go,
And the Pagan people cherish. . . .
"The Zealous Puritan," a popular ballad from the Great Migration, 1639, in Firth, The American Garland; Being a Collection of Ballads Relating to America, 1563–1759 *(1915), p. 25.*

Stuyvesant's first arrival . . . was like a peacock, with great state and pomp. The appellation of *Lord General,* and similar titles, were never before known here. Almost every day he caused proclamations of various import to be published, which were for the most part never observed, and have long since been a dead letter. . . . At one time . . . Arnoldus Van Herdenbergh related . . . how he had appealed . . . whereupon the Director . . . interrupted and replied, "It may during my administration be contemplated to appeal, but if anyone should do it, I will *make him a foot shorter,* and send the pieces to Holland, and let him appeal in that way." In our opinion

this country will never flourish under the government of the Honorable Company, but will pass away and come to an end of itself, unless the Honorable Company be reformed.
Adriaen Van Der Donk, 1647, a Dutch lawyer, reporting on conditions in New Amsterdam to the Dutch West India Company, in Collections of the New-York Historical Society, *2d series (1849), in Colbert,* Eyewitness to America *(1997), pp. 28–29.*

We would have liked to effectuate and fulfill your wishes and request, that the new territories should no more be allowed to be infected by the people of the Jewish nation, for we foresee therefrom the same difficulties which you fear. . . . [Such a policy] would be unreasonable and unfair, especially because of the considerable loss sustained by this nation, with others, in the taking of Brazil, and also because of the large amount of capital which they still have invested in the shares of this company. Therefore, after many deliberations we have decided and resolved to apostille [order] upon a certain petition made by said Portuguese Jews, that these people may travel and trade to and in New Netherland and live and remain here, provided the poor among them shall not become a burden to the company or the community, but be supported by their own nation.
The directors of the Dutch West India Company in Amsterdam to Peter Stuyvesant, governor of the Dutch colony of New Netherland, in reply to his petition that "none of the Jewish nation be permitted to infest New Netherland," April 26, 1655, in Schappes, A Documentary History of the Jews of the United States, 1654–1875 *(1952), pp. 4–5.*

Carolina is a fair and spacious province on the continent of America. . . . The land is of diverse sorts as in all countries of the world. That which lies near the sea is sandy and barren, but bears many tall trees, which make good timber for several uses; and this sandy ground is by experienced men thought to be one cause of the healthfulness of the place. But up the river about twenty miles, where they have made a town, called Charles Town, there is plenty of as rich ground as any in the world. . . . The woods are stored with deer and wild turkeys, of great magnitude, weighing many times above 50 lb. a piece, and of a more pleasant taste than in England, being in their proper climate; other sorts of beasts in the woods that are good for food, and also fowls, whose names are not known to them. . . .

There are as brave rivers as any in the world, stored with great abundance of sturgeon, salmon, bass, plaice, trout, and Spanish mackerel, with many other most pleasant sorts of fish, both flat and round, for which the English tongue has no name. Also in the little winter they have, abundance of wild geese, ducks, teals, widgeons, and many other pleasant fowl.

Last of all, the air comes to be considered, which is not the least considerable to the well being of a plantation, for without a wholesome air all other considerations avail nothing. And this is it which makes the place so desirable, being seated in the glorious light of heaven brings many advantages. . . . If, therefore, any industrious and ingenious persons shall be willing to partake of the felicities of this country, let them embrace the first opportunity, that they may obtain the greater advantages.

Pamphlet promoting immigration to Carolina, A Brief Description of the Province of Carolina, on the Coasts of Floreda *in Carroll*, Historical Collections of South Carolina, *Volume II (1836; first published, 1666), pp. 10–13.*

Your Endeavors [to enforce religious uniformity in England] have been many; Your Acts not a Few to Enforce it, but their Consequence, whether you intended it or not, through the Barbarous Practices of those that have had their Execution, hath been the Spoiling of several Thousands of the free inhabitants of this Kingdom of their Unforfeited Rights. Persons have been flung into Jails, Gates and Trunks broke open, Goods destroyed, till a stool hath not been left to sit down on, Flocks of Cattle driven, whole Barns full of Corn seized, Parents left without Children, Children without their Parents, both without subsistence. . . .

I shall not at this time make it my business to manifest the Inconsistency that there is between Christian Religion, and a forced uniformity; not only because it hath been so often and excellently done by Men of Wit, Learning and Conscience . . . but because Every free and impartial Temper hath of a long time observ'd, that such Barbarous Attempts were so far from being indulged, that they were most severely prohibited by Christ himself. . . .

Instead of Peace, Love and good Neighborhood, behold Animosity and contest! One neighbor watcheth another . . . ; this divides them, their Families and Acquaintance. . . .

But there are . . . objections that some make against what I have urged, not unfit to be consider'd. The first is this: If the Liberty desired be granted, what know we but Dissenters may employ their Meetings to insinuate against the Government, inflame the People into a Dislike of their Superiours, and thereby prepare them for Mischief. . . . Answer. . . . What Dissenter can be so destitute of Reason and Love to common Safety, as to expose himself and his Family by plotting against a Government that is kind to him, and gives him the Liberty he desire?

William Penn, "England's Present Interests Discovered" (Gilder Lehrman Collection #1672), 1675, in Davis and Mintz, The Boisterous Sea of Liberty *(1998), pp. 100–101.*

Certain conditions, *or* concessions, *agreed upon by* William Penn, *Proprietary and Governor of the Province of Pennsylvania, and those who are the adventurers and purchasers in the same province. . . .*

I. That so soon as it pleaseth God that the abovesaid persons arrive there, a certain quantity of land, or ground plat, shall be laid out, or a large town or city, in the most convenient place . . . and every purchaser and adventurer shall, by lot, have so much land therein as will answer to the proportion, which he hath bought.

XI. There shall be no buying or selling, be it with an *Indian,* or with one another . . . but what shall be performed in public market, . . . where they shall pass the public stamp, or mark. If bad ware, and prized as good, or deceitful in proportion or weight, to forfeit the value as if good and full weight and proportion, to the public treasury of this province, whether it be the merchandize of the *Indian,* or that of the planters.

XII. And forasmuch as it is usual with the planters to over-reach the poor natives of the country, in trade, by goods not being good of the kind, or debased with mixtures . . . it is agreed, whatever is sold to the *Indians,* in consideration of their furs, shall be sold in the market place, and there suffer the test, whether good or bad; if good, to pass; if not good, not to be sold as good, that the natives may not be abused, nor provoked.

XIII. That no man shall, by any ways or means, in word, or deed, affront, or wrong, any *Indian,* but he shall incur the same penalty of the law, as if he had committed it against his fellow planter. . . .

William Penn, "Concessions to the Province of Pennsylvania,"
July 11, 1681, in Thorpe, Federal and State
Constitutions, *Volume 5, (1993), pp. 3044–3046.*

To Ye Aged and Beloved, Mr. John Higginson

There be now at sea a ship called Welcome, which has on board one hundred or more of the heretics and malignants called Quakers, with W. Penn, who is the chief scamp, at the head of them. The general court has accordingly given secret orders to Master Malachi Huscott, of the brig Porpoise, to waylay the said Welcome slyly as near as the Cape of Cod as may be, and make captive of said Penn and his ungodly crew, so that the Lord may be glorified and not mocked on the soil of this new country with the heathen worship of these people. Much spoil can be made by selling the whole lot to Barbadoes, where slaves fetch good prices in rum and sugar, and we shall not only do the Lord great service by punishing the wicked, but we shall make great good for his Minister and people.

Yours in the bowels of Christ,

Cotton Mather, Congregational minister, in a letter allegedly
written September 25, 1682, from Boston, in Corsi, Paths to
the New World *(1953), p. 13.*

Francis Daniel Pastorius (1651–1719) was the leader of the first large group of German immigrants to America and founder of Germantown, Pennsylvania. *(Library of Congress, Prints and Photographs Division [LC-USZ62-96916])*

These are the reasons why we are against the traffic of men-body, as followeth: Is there any that would be done or handled at this manner? Viz.: to be sold or made a slave for all the time of his life? How fearful and faint-hearted are many at sea, when they see a strange vessel, being afraid it should be a Turk, and they should be taken, and sold for slaves in Turkey. Now, what is *this* better done, than Turks do? Yea, rather it is worse for them, which say they are Christians; for we hear that the most part of such negers are brought hither against their will and consent, and that many of them are stolen. Now, though they are black, we cannot conceive there is more liberty to have them slaves, as it is to have other white ones. . . . Ah! Do consider well this thing, you who do it, if you would be done at this manner—and if it is done according to Christianity!

Resolution of the Germantown, Pennsylvania, Mennonites,
February 18, 1688, Mode's Source Book and
Bibliographical Guide for American Church History
(1921), pp. 552–553.

Before my laying out of this town [Germantown, Pennsylvania], I had already erected a small house in Philadelphia, thirty feet by fifteen in size. The windows, for the want of glass, were made of oiled paper. Over the door I had placed the following inscription: *Parva Domus, sed amica bonis, procul este prophani* [A small house, but friendly to the good; let the evil take themselves hence], at which our governor, when he paid me a visit, laughed heartily, at the same time encouraging me to build more.

I have obtained 15,000 acres of land for our company, in one tract, with this condition: that within one year at least thirty families should settle on it; and thus we may, by God's blessing, have a separate German province where we can all live together in one.

Inasmuch as this region lies in the same degree of latitude as Montpelier [France] and Naples [Italy], but has a much richer soil, and that better watered by its many springs and rivulets, it is but reasonable to suppose that such a country must be well calculated to produce all kinds of fruit. The air is pure and serene, the summer is longer and warmer than it is in Germany, and we are cultivating many kinds of fruits and vegetables, and our labors meet with rich reward.

Although this far-distant land was a dense wilderness—and it is only quite recently that it has come under the cultivation of the Christians—there is much cause of wonder and admiration how rapidly it has already, under the blessing of God, advanced, and is still advancing, day by day.

Francis Daniel Pastorius, An Accurate Description of the Recently Founded Province of Pennsylvania, 1700, *in Adler, et al.,* The Annals of America, *Volume 1 (1968), p. 311.*

CHAPTER TWO

The Colonies Expand
1701–1775

Religious Freedom and National Diversity

While the main motive for immigration to America was economic, money was not the only magnet that drew people to the New World. Religious discrimination—in the form of actual persecution, as in the case of the Jews, or professional and social disadvantages, as in that of the Puritans and Roman Catholics—became an increasingly important cause. In England the political power of the Anglican Church prevented dissenters from holding important offices or advancing in commerce, and many looked to the New World for improvement in their personal lives as well as for the freedom to practice their religions unhampered.

Religious tolerance was not a consistent feature of colonial America, but as different cultures came into contact, communities became more flexible. The Puritans of Massachusetts hanged two Quakers in the 1650s for remaining in the colony after they had been banished for their religious nonconformity, but the Dutch in New Netherland refused to expel English Quakers even when Director-General Stuyvesant ordered them to, and Jews were permitted to establish homes there. Although the British took over the Dutch colony without violence, the two groups of people did not always live together in harmony thereafter. Religious differences, and differences in attitude toward other religions, as well as commercial competition, were sometimes a cause of conflict in the New York colony. Puritans were denied many civil rights in New Amsterdam, and there were several military confrontations between the English and the Dutch from the 1670s to the early 1700s, but the necessity of survival imposed some degree of cooperation on the residents of the area despite whatever differences existed among them. Assimilation was inevitable, and even in the solidly Dutch and Swedish areas the movement was toward English customs.

Peter Kalm, a Swedish visitor to the colonies in the middle of the 18th century, noted that although Dutch was generally spoken in New York, the majority of descendents of settlers from the Netherlands "were succumbing to the English language. The younger generation scarcely ever spoke anything but English, and there were many who were offended if they were taken for Dutch, because they preferred to pass for English." Many, in fact, "deserted the Reformed and

Presbyterian churches in favor of the English." The Swedish immigrants of the colony surrendered their language even more readily. "We had a Swedish guide along who was probably born of Swedish parents, was married to a Swedish woman, but who could not, himself, speak Swedish," Kalm reported. "Since English is the principal language of the land all people gradually get to speak that, and they become ashamed to talk in their own tongue because they fear they may not in such a case be real English."

Immigration from England diminished after the middle of the 17th century as conditions improved in the mother country. Religious dissenters were treated with more tolerance in England, and the wave of Puritan and Catholic immigration, in flight from discrimination, ebbed. The London fire of 1666 and the plague that followed it made England fearful of losing too many laborers and skilled craftsmen to the colonies, and immigration was officially discouraged. As the settlement of the English in the Dutch territory of New Netherland proved, it was possible for the new continent to accommodate people of diverse backgrounds and ideas. The British colonies continued to look to the home country for immigrants, but the population of America was beginning to include more and more settlers from other European sources.

England considered America an extension of its empire, the promise of a glorious fulfillment of its imperial destiny. The poet John Donne, in 1622, called America "the suburbs of the Old World." The transition to the New World, while often challenging, was not a change of nationality or a loss of national culture. It was the settlers from other European countries, according to some scholars, who were the first true immigrants to America.

Like the English colonists, people from the other British Isles or from continental Europe came for a variety of reasons. Political unrest and religious persecution increasingly drove immigrants from other countries.

The Germans

No area of continental Europe was so unsettled in the 18th century as the many warring states that made up the present nation of Germany. The so-called Thirty Years' War fought between Protestants and Catholics from 1618 to 1648 reduced the population of the German states from 21 million to 13 million between those years. The hostility between England and Spain begun in 1701 further disrupted European society, and the war between France and Germany in 1709 devastated both lands. The economy was ruined—German princes levied taxes as high as 60 percent of a worker's income to pay for troops and arms—and disease and famine were widespread.

When William Penn traveled to Germany in 1677 to preach the Quaker faith, he observed the Mennonites, Dunkards, Puritanic Lutherans, Schwenckfelders, Moravians, and other Protestant sects with faiths similar to his own. Like the Quakers, they believed in a simple life withdrawn from the world and a direct relationship with God; Penn therefore saw a fruitful field for colonial recruitment. When he returned to England and obtained a grant of land in America, he wrote of his colony there, where these oppressed minorities could make a new start, free of war, religious persecution, and the impossibly high taxes their German rulers imposed on them. Translated into German, his pamphlets were distributed widely throughout the region. It is not surprising that his promotion of virgin land and religious freedom appeared as a divine deliverance to many. In 1683 Franz Daniel Pastorius and his little group of 13 families blazed a trail when they established the first German settlement in the New World (Germantown, near Philadelphia). After he sent back to Germany glowing reports of his success in the New World, his countrymen followed him gratefully.

In 1706 the Lutheran pastor Josua von Kocherthal traveled to Carolina and wrote an enthusiastic account of it. Two years later he led a group of 41 pioneers from the Palatinate, a region on the Rhine River in southwestern Germany, to the Hudson Valley in New York. There they established Newburgh, about 60 miles north of present-day New York City. The settlement was not a success and soon foundered, but although this first attempt failed, conditions in Germany were so bad that others were ready to try again. The winter of 1708–09 was a particularly severe one, and false rumor sprang up that Queen Anne of England would transport any Christian to the New World at no cost to help develop her empire. In autumn 1709 thousands from the Palatinate flocked to England to escape the conditions in their home country. Some stayed in London, others were sent to Ireland or North England, and some went to Holland; but the great majority of the 13,000 Palatine Germans went on to seek religious and civil liberty in the New World. About 650 went to Carolina, and 2,800 followed von Kocherthal's path to the Hudson Valley in New York. They were no more successful than his little group had been, but reports of their difficulties did not discourage others from making the voyage. By 1710, 4,000 immigrants from the Palatinate were arriving in North America every month. Over the next few years, so many entered America that the term Palatine was soon applied to all German immigrants. The Elector Palatine, the prince of that state, became alarmed at the depopulation of his country and tried to stem the tide. He issued an edict making emigration a capital crime, but his subjects found their way out despite his efforts. In 1714, 12 families migrated together to Virginia, where they established the community of Germanna. When 80 families joined them from Württemberg soon after, they became self-sufficient and soon attracted other Germans. Like Germantown, the settlement remained solidly German, maintaining the customs and language of their homeland.

Although the Germans prospered once they became independent in North America, the expenses of establishing themselves were great. Some had the financial help of relatives, others sold what land they had in Germany, but most were without funds to pay their fare and had nothing to sell but their labor. Many—perhaps the majority—were forced to travel by means of the redemptioner system, in which, like English indentured servants, they sold their services for a period of time in return for the passage to America. German redemptioners (so called because they redeemed their freedom by working for Americans after arriving) were the victims of the same abuses as their English counterparts, serving from three to six years without pay. Those from 10 to 15 years of age were bound until they were 21 years old. Indeed, the system has been called "white slavery," and terrible stories were told of the exploitation of these paupers, who had to work off the debts of relatives who had died on the way over from Germany. On arrival, redemptioners were sold to the highest bidder at a public auction hardly different from a slave market. Like indentured servants, they could be punished severely for carelessness or laziness and were hunted down like slaves if they attempted to escape from their masters. Despite the often-difficult conditions of their servitude, however, they continued to come. It is estimated that as many as half of the immigrants from Germany in the 18th century came as redemptioners.

Dutch shippers, who profited from the commercial traffic in human labor, dominated transportation of German immigrants. Around 1720, the recruitment of potential redemptioners became a complex business in the Netherlands, where merchants and ship owners hired agents to promote the voyage among the poor. Called newlanders, these operatives dressed in expensive clothes and flashed rich jewelry, pretending to be wealthy immigrants returning for a visit. They painted an enticing—and often quite false—picture of the glittering opportunities awaiting their potential customers. Few were able to resist the newlanders' glamorous stories of streets paved with gold, and thousands were only too glad to trade a dismal and hopeless life in Germany for a period of servitude with a prospect of wealth afterward. Of course the newlanders said nothing of the conditions of the voyage.

Whether as redemptioners or as paid passengers, German immigrants suffered terrible hardships in the ships that brought them. Bad and inadequate food, cramped quarters, and disease cost the lives of many before the ships reached their destination in the New World. The records of a ship that made the trip in 1731 notes that the passengers were reduced to eating rats, which were sold for eighteen pence each (mice went for sixpence), and that the captain deliberately starved them to increase his profit. "He succeeded too well," the report concludes, "for out of the 156 passengers only 48 reached America." Gottlieb Mittelberger, an immigrant from Württemberg writing in 1750, described his six-month voyage in vivid detail: "No one can have an idea of the sufferings which women in confinement have to bear with innocent children on board these ships. Few of this class escape with their lives; many a mother is cast into the water with her child as soon as she is dead. . . . Children from one to seven rarely survive the voyage; and many a time parents are compelled to see their children miserably suffer and die. . . . I witnessed such misery in no less than 32 children in our ship, all of whom were thrown into the sea."

Through Penn's influence, Philadelphia became the principal port of entry for European immigrants, and Pennsylvania their largest and most cosmopolitan center. The colony was attractive to all continental Europeans, but especially so to the Germans, who by the time of the American Revolution numbered no fewer than 110,000, representing one-third of the colony's population. The New York and Virginia colonies each held some 25,000, and large concentrations of Germans formed settlements in the Carolinas. By 1766 the stream of people leaving Germany for the New World had become such a flood that the rulers of many other German states besides the Palatinate imposed bans on emigration, but they had no more effect than that ordered by the elector years before.

German immigrants spread to all the American colonies. They were not welcomed in conservative New England, and few settled there, but many found homes in New York, New Jersey, Maryland, Virginia, and Carolina. In none, however, did they prosper as well as they did in Pennsylvania, where about half settled. So populous were the German communities around Philadelphia that the people became known as the Pennsylvania Dutch—a mispronunciation of the word *Deutsch* often applied indiscriminately to Germans and Swiss as well as to the natives of the Netherlands—and their Palatinate dialect became the official language of the area. Pastorius's Germantown was an orderly and peaceful place; it was said that there was virtually no crime there except neglected fences. Its court met only once every six weeks, and often closed up because there was no one to try. An example of one of the few records of an arrest was of a man named Müller, who went to jail for trying to smoke 100 pipefuls of tobacco in a day for a bet.

Although Germantown began as an agricultural community, it soon developed its own industries and has been called "the first distinctively manufacturing town in Pennsylvania," well known for its textile and paper mills, its production of carriages and coaches, and its leather industry. Nevertheless, the Germans had been drawn to America by the promise of freedom, and freedom in their new life meant land, the symbol of independence. Most of the German settlers in Germantown and elsewhere became farmers, even if that had not been their work before. Their farms were large—those in Maryland were estimated to average 370 acres—and they quickly became noted for the proficiency with which they worked the soil. Benjamin Rush, a prominent physician and close friend of Benjamin Franklin, considered them the best farmers in America. In his "Account of the Manners of the German

Benjamin Franklin (1706–90), depicted in this bust by Jean-Antoine Houdon, 1778, favored immigration to the United States but urged the new country to be cautious about whom it accepted. *(New York Public Library Print Collection)*

Inhabitants of Pennsylvania," he noted that they were "not only industrious and frugal, but skillful cultivators of the earth." Rush was especially impressed by the careful management of their resources. "They sell their most profitable grain," he observed, "and eat that which is less profitable. . . . The profit to a farmer, from this single article of economy, is equal, in the course of a lifetime, to the price of a farm for one of his children."

Immigrating in great numbers together, the Germans tended to settle in groups large enough to maintain their own national identity and language. Such city names as Germanna and Germantown reflected their determination to remain isolated from the emerging American culture. The government meetings of their communities were conducted in German, and their laws were written in it. In 1732 a German newspaper called the *Philadelphische Zeitung*, the first foreign-language periodical in the colonies, began publication in Pennsylvania and attained a considerable circulation. Some groups, like the so-called Pennsylvania Dutch, have avoided change to the present day and still speak the language their 17th-century ancestors spoke.

This cultural separatism was to lead to friction in the predominantly English-speaking colonies. The reluctance of the Germans to assimilate caused some to doubt their loyalty to colonial interests. Philadelphia's Benjamin Franklin feared that they might endanger the unity of the region. "They may soon so outnumber us," he wrote in 1753, "that all the advantages we have will, in my opinion, be not able to preserve our language, and even our government will become precarious."

The French

The French had been a presence in the New World since a year after the Jamestown colony began, when Champlain founded Quebec in 1608, but their numbers had never been great. French settlements had been established from Canada to Louisiana, but immigration to the English colonies remained sparse. It was not until 1685 that a significant number arrived from France to seek residence among the English. In that year the Catholic king Louis XIV demanded adherence to the Church of Rome from all his subjects and revoked the Edict of Nantes, which had been issued in 1598 to grant political and religious freedom to all Christian dissenters. French Protestants, known as Huguenots, became victims of severe persecution. A national decree ordered French soldiers "to kill the greatest part of the Protestants that can be overtaken, without sparing the women, to the end that this may intimidate them and prevent others from falling into a similar fault."

Several thousand Huguenots fled across the Atlantic. Since the French colonies in North America, in accordance with the royal decree, were open only to Catholics, the Huguenots sought refuge in the British colonies. Predominantly middle-class merchants, tradesmen, and skilled artisans, they had few economic problems and settled peacefully in all the 13 colonies, where they quickly assimilated. Some translated their names—the Feuillevert family became Greenleaf—and some simply adapted them to English pronunciation and spelling, like the parents of the patriot Paul Revere, whose name in France had been DeRivoir, or the Huguenot family named Beauchamps, who became Beecham. Huguenot refugees built large plantations and prospered in the textile trade and other businesses in Carolina, New York, Massachusetts, and Pennsylvania. Many became political leaders.

If the reason for the Huguenot migration was primarily religious, the next wave of French immigration to America was based entirely on political causes. In 1603 the French had established a large settlement on the northeast coast of North America in what are now the Canadian provinces of Nova Scotia, New Brunswick, and Prince Edward Island. Named Acadia, from the Indian name for the region, it was a stable French colony when the French and English began to struggle for control of North America in the first decade of the 18th century. In 1710 troops from the Massachusetts colony unsuccessfully besieged Port Royal, the capital of Acadia. Three years later the British repeated its attack and occupied the city. When hostilities between the French and the English officially ended in 1713, the Treaty of Utrecht ceded Acadia to England, but the Acadians repeatedly supported the Indians in their attacks on English settlements, and their privateers continued to prey on Massachusetts fishing boats. A French colony under English rule, Acadia never relinquished its loyalty to what had been its parent nation. When the French and the Indians combined forces to oppose the English in North America in 1754, the colony was seen as a danger to the English colonies in America.

In 1755, Britain demanded an oath of allegiance to their king from the Acadians, and when some refused it, the British governor of the colony became determined to make an example of them. The colonial militia disarmed the French settlers, took hundreds hostage, and ordered that the colony be cleared. Six thousand of the approximately 18,000 Acadians were herded aboard small vessels and transported to British colonies along the Atlantic Coast. Most of the remaining Acadians fled into the wilderness of what is now New Brunswick, where many died of starvation and exposure.

Known in French and French-Canadian history as *Le Grand Dérangement* (the Great Displacement), this dispersal of the Acadians was the first example of forcible immigration to America except for the institution of slavery. In order to prevent any organized resistance, the hapless French were deliberately scattered throughout the 13 colonies, where they faced a welcome from the English colonists that was far different from that of the Huguenots. Acadia had been English territory since 1713, so its residents were considered disloyal English subjects and were met with hostility. Despite the successful assimilation of the Huguenots, there was still much anti-French sentiment among the English engaged in competition for control of North America, and the infusion of thousands of exiles from Canada into the colonies occasioned considerable alarm.

When the French and Indian War ended in 1763, the Treaty of Paris permitted the Acadians to relocate. Some made their way back to Acadia and began to reconstruct their society, but the great majority remained in the English colonies, wandering westward until they congregated in the formerly French colony of Louisiana. Here they settled in the bayou country, which they nostalgically renamed New Acadia. They gradually adapted themselves to the semitropical Louisiana climate and topography and applied their experiences of life in Nova Scotia to their new home. Those who had been ranchers in Canada raised cattle in the prairie country for the New Orleans market; Acadian farmers settled on the rich farmlands along the Mississippi River and developed vast tracts of land. An industrious, hardworking community, the exiles prospered in their new home. Within 10 years, most Acadians achieved a standard of living equal to what they had known before their diaspora had begun. Their descendents, still a clearly defined and cohesive group, came to be known as Cajuns, an American pronunciation of *Acadians*.

The Scots, the Irish, and the Scotch-Irish

The English continued to be the main source of American immigration during the 18th century, but increasingly residents of other parts of the British Isles found their way to the New World. The Scots yearned to escape poverty and religious friction with the English in their kingdom; when Massachusetts governor John Winthrop visited Scotland in 1635 he found there a "great giddiness" to emigrate and was stopped wherever he went by people eager to question him about the New World. The few who were able to make the trip were popular additions to the new colony. Scotland was a separate country in the 17th century, however, and was barred from colonial trade by the English. Thus, few of its inhabitants could manage the expenses of the trip. In the 1680s a few hundred were brought by the proprietors of East New Jersey to settle Perth Amboy, and in 1651 the British government disposed of a few Scots captured in an uprising by transporting them to the colonies. Other political dissidents were transported to Virginia in 1652 and in 1679. But no great wave of immigration from Scotland occurred until 1707, the year the Act of Union joined Scotland and England as a single nation.

Now free to travel as citizens of Great Britain, many Scots came to North America. Some settled as merchants in the seaports along the Atlantic coast, and others came as schoolmasters, clergymen, artisans, and laborers to New York and the tobacco colonies in the South. The poor of Glasgow sold their services as indentured servants. Groups of several hundred were organized to establish Scottish communities in America in the 1730s. Governor Cosby of New York, eager to develop his colony, made a grant of land to one such group to settle near Lake George, and other settlements were formed in the Mohawk and upper Hudson Valleys.

There was no mass movement of the Irish in the 18th century, largely because Ireland was a Catholic kingdom and its inhabitants were unwelcome in the Protestant colonies. Some few had come as indentured servants, and in 1649, when Oliver Cromwell suppressed an Irish rebellion, many refugees from that war fled to America. During the next few years, Cromwell rounded up an estimated 250,000 Irish men, women, and children and sent them to the West Indies to work on the sugar plantations. Some of them and their descendents later came over to the mainland colonies, where they found a home in the Catholic colony of Maryland, established as a haven for members of that religion. Their adjustment to the New World was not easy. Until 1649, Maryland allowed only English and Irish immigrants to own property, but even that officially Catholic colony reserved its political rights to its English settlers until 1674. It was not until the 19th century, after Ireland had joined England, Scotland, and Wales as a part of Great Britain, that a sizable migration from Ireland to the New World occurred.

The greatest influx into the English colonies of "foreigners," however, was of another group from the British Isles, the people known somewhat misleadingly as the Scotch-Irish. Neither nationally Scottish nor ethnically Irish, they came from Ulster, the northernmost province of Ireland. King James I of England had relocated some thousands of Lowland Scots to this area on the border of England and Ireland in the early 17th century to serve as a buffer between the two unfriendly nations. Many had been forced to accept this painful situation because of poverty or personal misfortune, but within the century their descendents made Ulster a wealthy region. They developed a successful dairy industry and became famous for their linen and woolen goods.

Several circumstances combined to initiate a mass migration from Ulster in the second decade of the 18th century. Fear of the competition between their linen and the newly expanded cotton industry and a series of crop failures beginning in 1717 were among the first causes. Another was the fact that their wool production was so successful that the English were unable to compete with them and restricted their exports to England, Scotland, and North America. To protect the English home industry, Parliament passed a Woolen Act in 1699, prohibiting the exportation of Irish woolens except to England. Later it passed the same law for Irish export of raw wool.

More heavily invested in linen production than in that of wool, the Scotch-Irish were not profoundly affected by these measures of the English government. A more serious grievance lay in the land system imposed upon them. Absentee landlords, prohibitively high rents, and short-term leases on British-owned property deprived these independent-minded people of any security in their homes and businesses. Further, as Presbyterians, they were excluded from public office, which was open only to Anglicans.

When many leases ran out in 1717, English landlords seized the opportunity to raise the rents, and the higher rates increased the taxes proportionately. The Catholic Irish were willing to accept these hard conditions, but the Presbyterian Ulstermen began to look to the New World for a better life. The English, no longer needing the Scotch-Irish as a barrier between them and the Catholic Irish, presented no obstacles to their departure.

In 1718 a great wave of Scotch-Irish immigration to the colonies began. A decade later a series of crop failures in North Ireland made the desire to leave even more urgent. An exodus was organized by clergymen of the Presbyterian Church, the national church of Scotland, even though religious conflict with either the Anglican Church or the Roman Catholic Church of southern Ireland was not a significant cause of it. From 1718 to 1728, many inhabitants of the area were ruined by a combination of economic pressures and agricultural misfortune; the only way to escape from their situations and try their luck in the New World was to go as redemptioners. They were often exploited by "spirits" or "crimps"— the English equivalents of the German newlanders, agents of either American merchants or Irish ship captains promoting immigration. In 1728 Hugh Boulter, the Catholic archbishop of Ireland, wrote, "We have had for several years some agents from the colonies in America, and several masters of ships, that have gone about the country and deluded the people with stories of great plenty, and estates to be had . . . in those parts of the world. And they have been the better able to seduce people by reason of the necessities of the poor of late." Despite these abuses by dishonest agents and the horrors of the voyage, nearly 5,000 Scotch-Irish made the trip to America in 1718.

The first wave of Scotch-Irish immigrants went to New England, with many of them going to Worcester, Massachusetts. But the relatively settled and populous regions of eastern Massachusetts did not welcome the Presbyterian newcomers. Their religion was viewed as heresy, and the townsfolk of Worcester burned their meetinghouse. In Boston they were feared as economic competitors. In 1718 one alarmed colonist was quoted as warning, "These confounded Irish will eat us all up." In 1728 a mob formed to prevent the landing of an immigrant ship from Belfast in Boston harbor. The cold reception the Scotch-Irish received in eastern Massachusetts led them to move on to the western frontier of that colony and to

Vermont, Maine, and New Hampshire, where they established the thriving town of Londonderry, named for one of the counties in Ulster.

By 1725 Pennsylvania's economic opportunity and religious tolerance had begun to attract many of the Scotch-Irish. But the colony's liberal land policies had started to tighten up after William Penn's death in 1718, and within a few years, although they were unmolested in their worship, life for the Scotch-Irish in Pennsylvania became almost as difficult as it was in Massachusetts. They therefore began to look to the southern colonies as a destination, and during the 1730s many sailed from Ulster directly to South Carolina and Virginia. Charleston soon became second only to Philadelphia as a landing place for ships from Ulster.

Like most immigrants, the Scotch-Irish encountered physical hardships in their new homes, especially in Virginia, the Carolinas, and New England, where they generally settled on the frontiers. Their history of providing a barrier in Ulster to insulate the English from the Irish prompted colonial officials to direct them to areas where they might serve the same purpose between colonists and Indians. A hardy, industrious people, they quickly acquired the skills necessary to survive in their primitive surroundings. They learned woodcraft and became noted as Indian fighters, establishing the image of the frontiersman dressed in fringed hunting shirts and moccasins and carrying Indian hatchets. Despite their rough ways, however, they were devoted to their church and earnestly supported education. The clergyman William Tennent, soon after immigrating to Pennsylvania, founded the first Presbyterian school in the colonies in 1728, and within a few years the Scotch-Irish established Allegheny, Dickinson, and Washington and Jefferson Colleges in Pennsylvania, Hampden-Sydney in Virginia, and, in 1746, the College of New Jersey (later named Princeton University) in New Jersey.

Despite their less-than-cordial welcome by colonists who considered them rude foreigners invading their English settlements, the stream of Scotch-Irish immigrants grew to a flood by the 1720s. When the market for linen crashed in 1771, the influx increased again, reaching an annual average of 10,000 to 12,000 people. The total arriving in the half-century before the Revolutionary War has been estimated at from 150,000 to 300,000, making them the largest group of foreign immigrants to come to America in the 18th century. The name Ulster given to counties throughout the American Northeast bears witness to the Scotch-Irish impact on the American population. Only when the colonial revolution was imminent and agitation for independence had mounted simultaneously in Ireland did the English government take measures to stem the tide of Scotch-Irish immigration to its colonies in North America.

A Dumping Ground for Undesirables

If Europe, Scotland, and Ireland sent its political and religious dissidents and its poor to people the colonies, England added a steady stream of other undesirables. This policy served both as a source of labor in its developing empire and as a means of ridding itself of a social problem. Perhaps nothing so antagonized the pioneers attempting to build a viable society in the New World as the mother country's use of it as a dumping ground. As colonies with no voice in the government of the home country, they were powerless to prevent the entry of such newcomers, but many attempted to regulate or restrict it. As early as 1676, Maryland's Assembly required shipmasters to declare if they had any convicts aboard, so that they might be refused entry to the colony. Pennsylvania passed a law in 1722 imposing a tax on every criminal landed and making shipowners responsible for their passengers' good conduct. Five years later it added to its books another act requiring the owners of ships carrying immigrants to provide lists of their passengers with accounts of their intentions in immigrating and requiring non-English passengers to swear allegiance to the king. A law was passed imposing a 40-shilling tax on every immigrant entering Pennsylvania in 1729, in order "to discourage the great importation and coming in of foreigners and of lewd, idle and ill-affected persons into this province, as well from parts beyond the seas as from the neighboring colonies." In 1740 Maryland passed an act levying a tax on felons and paupers entering the colony from abroad.

Crime was widespread in England in the 17th and 18th centuries, and the severity of the law seemed to do nothing to reduce it. All classes of felonies were punishable by death, and there were some 300 felonies on the books, from stealing anything worth more than a shilling to murder. A sympathetic judge could recommend a royal pardon, usually accompanied by an order to leave the country. Transportation might also be ordered for crimes less than felonies. In 1663 Parliament enacted a law authorizing the courts to ship "Rogues, Vagrants, and sturdy Beggars" to the colonies, defining that class of petty criminals as "all persons calling themselves Schollers going about begging, all Seafaring men pretending losses of their Schippes or goods on the sea going about the Country begging, all idle persons going about in any Country begging or using any subtile Crafts or unlawfull Games . . . or fayning themselves to have knowledge in Phisiognomy Palmistry or other like crafty Scyence, or pretending that they can tell Destenyes Fortunes or such other like fantasticall imagynacons; . . . all Juglers Tynkers Pedlers . . . wandring abroad; all wandring persons and comon Labourers . . . loytering and refusing to worcke for such reasonable wages as . . . commonly given in such Parts. . . ."

In 1717 Parliament passed an act that addressed more serious crimes, authorizing "penal transportation" as a sentence for felonies. It was a popular edict in

English convicts, shown here in an 18th-century engraving, were transported to the colonies in great numbers. *(Library of Congress, Prints and Photographs Division [LC-USZ62-116241])*

England, and receiving undesirables was seen as one of the most useful services that the colonies provided the mother country. The eminent author Dr. Samuel Johnson considered Americans "a race of convicts who ought to be content with anything we allow them short of hanging."

Until 1640, all convicts entering America were sent to Virginia to restock the labor force diminished by disease and Indian attacks. Later Maryland became the favored destination. Pennsylvania got its share, but the majority of the transported criminals were channeled to the southern colonies, where the need for plantation labor was greatest. Only New England was spared these undesirable additions to its populace, because it had little market for the labor they supplied and no tobacco with which to pay for it. It is estimated that more than 50,000 convicted criminals were transported to the New World after 1717—more than 20,000 between 1750 and 1770 to the Maryland colony alone—before the Revolutionary War brought the practice of penal transportation to an end.

These "seven-year passengers" were often as reluctant to come as the colonies were to receive them. Given the choice of hanging or servitude in America, some convicted felons chose to be hanged. The voyage across the Atlantic was bad enough for the average willing immigrant, but for the convict it was barely tolerable. A visitor to a convict-ship reported, "All the states of horror I ever had an idea of are much short of what I saw this poor man in; chained to a board in a hole not above sixteen feet long, more than fifty with him; a collar and a padlock about his neck, and chained to five of the most dreadful creatures I ever looked on." As many as a quarter of the felons thus transported died before they arrived, and those who survived the trip were often too sick to work.

Once on North American soil, their lot was seldom any better than it would have been in an English jail. A number of transported felons returned to England, preferring the risk of being hanged to life in America. Some escaped their servitude and lived (or died) as fugitives in the colonies. But others survived their seven- or fourteen-year sentences and found their way to large cities, where they put their past behind them, melted into the colonial society, and made new lives for themselves.

Georgia

A class of criminal more sympathetic than felons, or even than "Rogues, Vagrants and sturdy Beggars," was that of those whom the harsh British law doomed to remain in prison indefinitely because they could not pay their debts. In 1733 a new colony was established to provide a haven for these unfortunates.

Georgia, the last of the 13 colonies, came into being because of the need for a buffer zone to protect South Carolina from the Spanish in Florida. In 1730 James Edward Oglethorpe, a member of Parliament who had long been interested in prison reform, petitioned the king for a grant of land on which he might establish a refuge for debtors and other victims of misfortune. The government saw an advantage in both Oglethorpe's humanitarian ends and the stability of its Carolina border. It also saw the possibility of developing profitable wine and silk industries in the warm Carolina climate. In 1732 King George II granted Oglethorpe a charter for all the land lying between the Altahama and the Savannah Rivers in the southern part of South Carolina. The new colony was named Georgia after King George, and its charter was different from those of most other

James Oglethorpe (1696–1785), a British philantropist and prison reformer, opened Georgia to people of all races and religions. *(New York Public Library Print Collection)*

colonies, because the motives for founding the colony were essentially idealistic. According to its terms, the territory was entrusted to a group of trustees who were forbidden to profit from holding office or owning land, and it limited family holdings to 50 acres in hopes of reestablishing the self-sufficient farmer class of England. Slavery was also forbidden. The trustees, prominent London business-men and philanthropists, appointed Oglethorpe as governor. In 1733 he founded Savannah with a first shipload of 114 settlers. The trustees mounted what has been described by a modern historian as "the biggest publicity campaign from which any English colony ever benefited." They placed long articles in all the newspapers about the rich soil, healthy climate, and liberal government of the colony and raised money by popular subscription.

Like Penn, Oglethorpe began his term with a symbolic gesture of generos-ity, paying the Creek Indians for the land that the crown had granted him to build his settlement. The laws he established forbade the introduction of slavery and the importation of hard liquor. Not all the settlers in the new colony were debtors; Georgia established an open door to all Protestants persecuted by Catholic monarchs in Europe. During the next few years Oglethorpe made good on his promise of a benevolent and paternalistic settlement. He welcomed a group of Moravians, who built the biblically named town of Ebenezer on the Savannah River, and took in several clans of Scots seeking refuge from English persecution. Georgia became an asylum for German Lutherans, English Methodists, and colonial Jews.

Oglethorpe's fair treatment of the Indians won him their trust, and when the Spanish threatened to invade from Florida, the Creek and Cherokee supported him. They relinquished much of their coastal lands to Georgia and offered to join the colony in its counterattack on Spanish posts. Oglethorpe had served in the British army while still in his teens and was no stranger to military procedure. When the Spanish seized the colony's fort on Amelia Island at the mouth of the St. Mary's River, he mobilized the few Georgians and South Carolinians he could muster and an equal number of Indians and marched on the large Spanish settlement of St. Augustine. Outnumbered by almost five to one, Oglethorpe and his men were soundly defeated. Later battles were more successful, but the small forces of Georgia were no match for the Spanish, even with the help of Oglethorpe's Indian friends.

Despite, or perhaps because of, the idealistic spirit on which it was founded, Georgia did not succeed as a proprietary colony. Its climate proved less salutary than promised—29 of the original 114 settlers died the first year—and neither grapes for wine nor mulberry trees for silkworms would grow in its soil. Almost no imprisoned debtors took Oglethorpe up on his generous offer of asylum, and of those who did, many went into debt again almost immediately. During the first eight years of Georgia's brief history as a proprietary colony, the trustees were forced to pay the costs of settling 1,810 charity cases, nearly half of them Protestants from Germany, Switzerland, Scotland, and Italy. During that time, only about 1,000 immigrants came at their own expense.

The fortunes made by South Carolina indigo and rice planters proved impossible to duplicate in Georgia without slaves, and many of the more ambitious settlers left their 50-acre grants and headed north to the colony's more prosperous neighbor. Little by little Oglethorpe's high mission deteriorated. In an effort to make the colony pay, the trustees repealed the antislavery law and permitted the importation and sale of rum and brandy. Colonists found ways to get around the land restrictions and built large plantations, worked by indentured servants or slaves. Oglethorpe spent his own fortune and went into debt trying to save his dream, but in 1743 he was dismissed on grounds of mismanagement by the trustees who had hired him and he returned home to England to be court-martialed. The charges brought against him were proved to be groundless and were dismissed, but the damage to his reputation and fortunes had been done. The British government, as a gesture of restitution, reappointed him to his seat in Parliament and awarded him the rank of general—22 years later, when he was 70 years old. He never returned to the colony he had founded.

By 1752, the colony had a population of only 1,735 white and 349 African residents. Its immigrants had found the sanctuary it had offered, but they had not prospered, and neither had the proprietors. The trustees regretfully decided to give up their utopian dream and turn the colony over to the crown as another royal province.

The Revolutionary War Begins

In the third quarter of the 18th century, the vast majority of the American population was English and considered its home English soil. Most of the immigrants that had streamed in since the first colonists settled in Virginia came from the same source. But with each year new strains were added to the original stock. The four New England colonies—Massachusetts, New Hampshire, Rhode Island and Connecticut—remained predominantly English, though many of their inhabitants were by the end of the century fourth- or fifth-generation Americans. The five southern colonies—Virginia, Maryland, North and South Carolina, and Georgia—had a considerable number of people of Scottish, Irish, and Scotch-Irish origins. The four central colonies—New Jersey, New York, Delaware, and Pennsylvania—held many people from other countries. By this time only 30 percent of the people in New York, with its Dutch beginnings, were of English birth or ancestry, and Pennsylvania had a sizable German population.

When the Seven Years' War between England and France (and its North American phase, the French and Indian War) ended in 1763, England controlled virtually all of North America, including Florida (recently acquired from Spain) and Canada, as well as a number of highly productive islands in the Caribbean. For more than a century and a half, it had permitted its colonies to develop their own society, generally maintaining a policy known as "salutary neglect." Indeed, during much of its colonial period America was given a great deal more liberty than England permitted itself. Free to include people of different religions, political beliefs, and styles of life, the colonies had their own separate assemblies to make their own

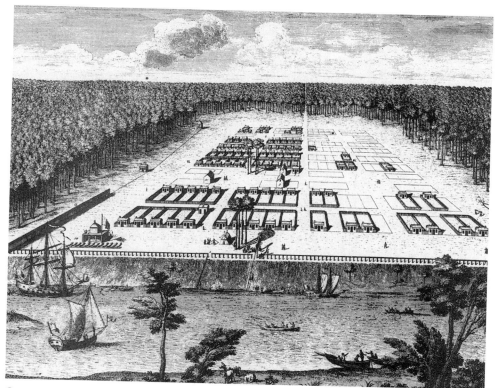

One-year-old Savannah, Georgia, had 84 identical houses, according to this illustration in a report sent to the trustees of the colony in 1734. *(New York Public Library Print Collection)*

laws and elect their own leaders. Americans had every reason to be satisfied with their relation to England, and most agreed with the loyal colonist who wrote, "Our invaluable charter secures to us all English liberties. . . . Happy, beyond Expression! in the Form of our Government—In the Liberty we enjoy."

With the end of the French and Indian War, the benefits of British protection—from Indian assaults and from French and Spanish encroachment—diminished. The dependency of the inhabitants of North America on England was weakened, and with it the emotional ties that bound them to the mother country. Most English immigrants had come to America to escape either political oppression, religious intolerance, or economic hardship to begin with, and had little love for the country from which they had either fled or been transported. England had earned no loyalty from the natives of Scotland, Ireland, and Wales, and the Dutch, Swedes, and Germans had no ties at all with that country. Thus, when the British imposed new laws on America after 1763—laws that included restrictions on American trade to protect its own industries, taxes, and import duties to reimburse it for the expenses of the French and Indian War and to support its troops in the colonies, and a ban on settlement beyond the Appalachian Mountains to keep peace with the Indians—the colonists reacted with anger. England had become an empire, and Americans were too accustomed to the independence they had enjoyed to accept imperial rule willingly. Still predominantly English in origin—some 60 percent of the white population of the colonies were of English stock—they had begun to think of themselves as Americans.

The Scotch-Irish frontiersmen resented the limits on their movement beyond the Appalachians that were enforced by British troops. The Stamp Act of 1765, imposing a tax on newspapers and official documents, outraged everyone. The Quartering Act of the same year, requiring the colonies to provide British troops with lodging, "candles, firing, bedding, cooking utensils, salt and vinegar, and five pints of small beer or cider, or a gill of rum per man, per diem," made matters even worse. Benjamin Franklin, who had protested England's transportation of felons and paupers to the colonies in the 1750s, wrote a pamphlet, *Rules by Which a Great Empire May Be Reduced to a Small One,* in 1773 bitterly protesting the injustices of its commercial policies, arbitrary taxes, and insolent military behavior.

The colonies protested the Stamp Act with riots and boycotts, and when London merchants complained that their businesses were suffering, Parliament repealed it. But when New York refused outright to obey the Quartering Act in 1766, the crown responded by suspending the colony's assembly. Subsequently, when John Hancock refused to pay duties on wine in 1768, British customs officials seized his ship. By now a spirit of independence was in the air, and colonists openly challenged the officials. America's prosperity had given the colonies a degree of power to stand up to British laws they thought unjust. They knew that England depended on America for its raw materials and manufacture as well as its market for British goods. Pennsylvania, New York, and New Jersey had more forges and furnaces in operation in 1775 than all of industrialized England and Wales; Philadelphia, with 40,000 people, was one of the biggest cities in the British Empire. One-seventh of all of England's trade was by then with the American colonies.

Another reason for the growing sense of national identity emerging in America was the growing unity of its people. In their first years, the colonies had more in common with London than they did with each other, but as British rule became more oppressive, they increasingly came to see their common interests. People of many nations were bound together in the colonies that had given them refuge, and those colonies were beginning to feel bound together into a nation. "The distinctions between Virginians, Pennsylvanians, New Yorkers, and New Englanders are no more," declared Patrick Henry in 1774. "I am not a Virginian, but an American." Benjamin Franklin was to make the point more forcefully when the colonies declared their independence from England in 1776: "We must all hang together, or assuredly we shall all hang separately."

They didn't all hang together—there were still bitter differences among the people of different colonies and among the immigrant groups within some of those colonies. America was far from an equal society; religious and national differences isolated people. The English looked down on the Scotch-Irish; the Germans remained separate in their own communities, distrusted by their neighbors; and everyone feared the paupers and criminals that they were compelled to accept. The involuntary immigrants from Africa, brought over as slaves and by then representing nearly 20 percent of the population, were not considered members of the society at all. Yet somehow, under the influence of circumstances unlike those of any other country in history, the many diverse peoples (with the exception of African slaves) were able to join their interests and work together for the common cause of national independence. Most of the colonists—English, Scottish, Irish, and European alike—were still loyal subjects of the English king. They were not seeking independence, but they were willing to fight for their rights as English citizens, equal in privilege to their countrymen across the Atlantic. Others felt that they could never have real freedom under a king and demanded a government of their own.

In 1775 the first open confrontation between the army of England and her rebellious children in the colonies took place: shots were fired in Lexington and Concord, Massachusetts. Within days, 15,000 volunteers rallied to march on Boston, the headquarters of the British forces. In time everyone—colonist and

Patrick Henry was a patriot who helped inspire colonists to revolt. *(From* The Pictorial Field Book of the Revolution, *2 vols., by B. J. Lossing. New York: Harper Brothers, 1851 and 1852)*

immigrant, Catholic and Protestant, plantation owner and indentured servant—was to be involved. A state of war was declared, and England suspended all immigration to North America.

As early as 1740, George II, himself of German birth, had signed the Naturalization Act, making all inhabitants of the colonies (excepting slaves and convicts) citizens of England. German Lutherans, French Huguenots, Scotch-Irish Presbyterians, Puritans, and Jews were members of a single national group. Now they were confronted with the choice of belonging to a new nation, one which they themselves could work together to form. Whether or not they could live together as one people remained to be seen.

Chronicle of Events

1701

- War breaks out between England and Spain. France is drawn into the conflict as Spain's ally. The next year it becomes known as Queen Anne's War.
- King William III of England dies. Anne, daughter of James II, becomes queen.
- Delaware, originally a part of Pennsylvania, becomes a separate colony.
- French colonist Antoine de la Mothe, sieur de Cadillac, founds Detroit.

1702

- East and West Jersey combine as the royal province of New Jersey.

1705

- Parliament passes Navigation Acts, adding rice, molasses, and naval supplies to the list of products that the colonies could export only to England.

1707

- Act of Union joins England and Scotland. Large-scale emigration of Scots begins, many coming as indentured servants to New York, New England, and the American South.
- Massachusetts troops unsuccessfully attack Port Royal, in Nova Scotia, to control privateers preying on New England fishermen.

1709

- War between France and Germany causes Palatine Germans to flee to the New World. Many settle in the Hudson Valley and Pennsylvania.

1710

- Colonial troops repeat their attack on Port Royal and occupy the city.

1713

- War between England and Spain ends. The Treaty of Utrecht gives Nova Scotia and Newfoundland, along with Gibraltar and Minorca, to England.

1714

- Queen Anne dies. George I, a German prince of the House of Hanover, ascends the throne of England.

1717

- Parliament passes an act initiating large-scale transportation of felons to Virginia.

1718

- High rents in Ireland cause extensive migration of Scotch-Irish to New England, Maryland, and Pennsylvania.
- Parliament enacts a bill prohibiting emigration of skilled artisans.
- *November*: Jean-Baptiste Le Moyne, sieur de Bienville, founds New Orleans, Louisiana, a strategic position for the control of Mississippi River traffic, as a French settlement. French immigrants establish trading stations and forts in the Mississippi Valley during the next seven years.

1719

- Carolina surrenders its proprietary status and accepts the rule of the king.

1720

- Extensive redemptioner trade begins as a means of recruiting servants for the New World. The redemtioner system is a harsher form of indentured service.

1722

- Pennsylvania passes an act imposing a tax on every convicted felon arriving in port and making the ship owner responsible for the good conduct of his passengers.

1727

- George I dies. George II becomes king of England.
- *September 21*: Pennsylvania passes an act requiring shipmasters bringing immigrants to give lists of their passengers' names and origins, and requiring non-English immigrants to swear allegiance to the British Crown.

1729

- Carolina is divided into North and South Carolina, which officially become Crown Colonies.
- A head tax is levied on all immigrants to Massachusetts, aimed at protecting the colonies from the arrival of "lewd, idle and ill-affected persons" who threaten to become public charges.
- *July*: A mob gathers at Boston harbor to prevent the landing of an immigrant ship from Ireland.

1730

- Rural settlements are founded by German religious sectarians in the Carolinas and Virginia.
- The religious revival known as the Great Awakening begins in the colonies.

1732

- The first non-English language newspaper in the colonies, the German *Philadelphische Zeitung,* appears in Pennsylvania.

1733

- The Molasses Act is passed by Parliament, imposing a high tax on sugar, molasses, and rum imported from non-British West Indies by the colonies.
- James Oglethorpe founds Georgia, a region until then a part of South Carolina. The last of the 13 British colonies, it serves as a protection from the Spanish in Florida and as a haven for convicts in prison for debt. The charter grants religious liberty and prohibits slavery, already widespread in the other colonies, and the importation of rum and brandy.

1735

- The principle of freedom of the press is established when John Peter Zenger is acquitted of libel after publishing articles opposing the royal governor of New York in his paper *New-York Weekly.*

1740

- The Naturalization Act, conferring British citizenship on immigrants from Europe, is passed.
- Maryland passes an act restricting the immigration of felons and paupers.

1744

- War breaks out between England and France. Massachusetts colonists capture Fort Louisberg, in Nova Scotia.

1745

- Rebellion in Scotland seeks to restore the House of Stuart to the throne. It fails, and many of its Scottish adherents are transported to the colonies in America.

1747

- The German Reformed Church is organized in Pennsylvania.

1749

- The Ohio Company grants land in Ohio territory to settlers from the Virginia and Pennsylvania colonies. French settlers in the region protest the expansion of British territory and establish forts. Iroquois and Delaware (Lenni Lenape) Indians join the French in opposing the English.

1750

- England passes the Iron Act, which prohibits the manufacture of finished iron products in the colonies but offers financial incentives for the development of iron as a raw material.
- The population of the 13 colonies is estimated at 1,260,000; that of England and Wales at 6,500,000.
- The legislative assembly of Georgia repeals its antislavery law and its prohibition on the importation of rum and brandy.

1752

- Georgia becomes a Crown Colony. In its 20 years as a proprietary venture, its population has reached only 2,084, of whom 349 are free African Americans.

1754

- French forces join with the Indians in a struggle with the English for control of North America. Known as the French and Indian War, the conflict becomes the North American theater of the Seven Years' War among England, France, Austria, Russia, and Sweden two years later and continues until 1763.

1755

- Colonial forces attack French forts in Canada and occupy the area of the Bay of Fundy, between New Brunswick and Nova Scotia, burning the French villages in the region.
- Six thousand Acadians are expelled from Nova Scotia to prevent their support of the French in the area. Many settle in Louisiana.
- *July 9*: British troops under General Braddock and Lieutenant Colonel George Washington of the Virginia militia are defeated by 900 French and Indian fighters in the battle of Fort Duquesne, on the site of present-day Pittsburgh, Pennsylvania. Braddock is killed, and Washington takes command of the retreating forces.

1756

- The Seven Years' War for domination of Europe breaks out between England and France, Austria, Russia, and Sweden.

1758

- *July 8*: British commander James Abercrombie attacks Fort Ticonderoga, New York, with 15,000 troops. They are defeated by French commander Louis Joseph, marquis de Montcalm, who inflicts 1,600 casualties.
- *August 27*: British defeat the French at Fort Frontenac on Lake Ontario.
- *November 24*: The English defeat the French at Fort Duquesne, Pennsylvania. The French are forced to destroy the fort.

1759

- *July 26*: The French blow up Fort Ticonderoga as the English invade it.
- *July 31*: The English defeat the French at Crown Point in New York.
- *September 12–13*: British forces under General Wolfe besiege Quebec. The French city, under Montcalm, surrenders on September 18.

1760

- George II dies. George III becomes king of Great Britain.
- *September 1*: British invade Montreal. Governor of Canada surrenders the province one week later.

1763

- *February 10*: The Seven Years' War in Europe, along with its North American phase, the French and Indian War, ends with the signing of the Treaty of Paris. France cedes Canada and eastern Louisiana to England and western Louisiana, including New Orleans, to Spain. Later in the year, former French territories are divided into East Florida, West Florida, and Quebec, and English law is established in Quebec.
- *May 16*: Indians, under Pontiac, attack settlements in Ohio. After five months, Pontiac accepts British rule.
- *October 7*: George III signs a proclamation forbidding settlement west of the Appalachian Mountains and orders settlers in upper Ohio to leave the territory.

1764

- The French found St. Louis, Missouri.
- *April 5*: Parliament passes the Sugar Act, rescinding the Molasses Act of 1733 and requiring colonies to pay revenue of sugar sales directly to the British government. It also passes the Currency Act, forbidding the southern colonies from issuing their own currency.

- *May 24*: Colonists protest taxation without representation at a Boston town meeting.
- *August*: Boston merchants initiate a boycott of British luxury goods, declaring that anyone buying British goods is to be considered "an open enemy to all civil and religious interests of their country." All colonies join the boycott within the next four months.

1765

- Parliament enacts the Quartering Act, requiring colonies to provide food, lodging, and supplies to British troops.
- *March 22*: Parliament passes its first direct tax on the colonies, the Stamp Act, requiring the purchase of tax stamps on paper. The act is scheduled to go into effect on November 1.
- *May 29*: Colonists protest the Stamp Act and organize the Sons of Liberty in Massachusetts, Rhode Island, Connecticut, New York, Pennsylvania, Maryland, and South Carolina to force the resignation of royal collection agents.
- *August*: Riots against the Stamp Act take place in Boston.
- *November 1*: The Stamp Act officially goes into effect, but businesses in the colonies openly defy it.

1766

- *January 17*: British merchants appeal to Parliament to revoke the Stamp Act because it reduces their market in the colonies.
- *March 18*: Parliament repeals the Stamp Act after hearing testimony of William Pitt and colonial representative Benjamin Franklin.
- *April 26*: Colonial boycott ends when the repeal of the Stamp Act is announced; the New York Assembly votes to erect a statue honoring George III and William Pitt.
- *August 11*: New York Assembly refuses to obey Quartering Act of 1765, leading to first skirmishes between British troops and colonists.

1767

- *March 24*: The New York Assembly is suspended by royal order for refusing to obey the Quartering Act.
- *June 29*: Parliament enacts Townshend Acts, charging duties on various imports to the colonies.
- *October 28*: Colonies revive their boycott in Boston; the other colonies join it in December.

1768

- Letters condemning the Townshend Acts and calling for united resistance to them are issued by the assemblies of Massachusetts, New Hampshire, Connecticut, New Jersey, and Virginia.
- *June 10*: British customs officials seize John Hancock's ship for refusing to pay duties on cargo of wine. Colonists attack the officials.
- *October 1*: British troops are stationed in Boston to defend customs officials.

1769

- First permanent European settlement in California is established by Spanish missionary Junípero Serra in San Diego. By 1784 he founds nine Franciscan missions in California.
- The Virginia House of Burgesses is dissolved for protesting Parliamentary acts.
- *December 27*: Samuel Wharton organizes the Grand Ohio Company, seeking a grant of 20 million acres. The grant is approved by the British Board of Trade in 1770 to establish a new proprietary colony, but the project ends as revolutionary activity increases.

1770

- The population of the British colonies in America is estimated at 2,312,000, almost double the number estimated for 1750. That of Great Britain has remained almost the same during the preceding 20 years.
- *January 31*: Lord North is appointed British Prime Minister.
- *March 5*: British troops quartered in Boston fire on colonists, killing five. The "Boston Massacre" outrages colonial society and results in removal of British troops.
- *April 12*: Townshend Acts are repealed, except for the duty imposed on tea. The Quartering Act lapses and is not renewed. Boycotts end, except in Boston.

1771

- Ulster, in Ireland, suffers a depression because of a falling market for linen. Scotch-Irish immigration increases, reaching about 10,000 per year for the next three years.

- *May 16*: An uprising in North Carolina pits 2,000 rebels against 1,200 British troops. The colonists are defeated, and seven executed for treason.

1772

- British customs ship *Gaspee* is burned in Rhode Island.

1773

- *December 16*: A group of Boston merchants disguised as Indians board a British ship and throw its cargo of tea into the bay to protest the tax imposed by the Tea Act. The "Boston Tea Party" outrages the British government and Board of Trade.

1774

- Virginia Governor John Murray seizes land in western Pennsylvania, leading to war with the Shawnee and Ottawa Indians. The Indians are defeated on October 10.
- *March 31*: Parliament passes the first of the Coercive Acts to punish Massachusetts for the Boston Tea Party. These laws, known in America as the "Intolerable Acts," prohibit the use of the Boston harbor until the tea is paid for. They include the Quebec Act (May 30), extending the Canadian boundary and reducing the territory of Massachusetts, Connecticut, and Virginia; and a new Quartering Act (June 2), requiring the lodging of troops in private homes as well as public buildings.
- *August 6*: The first members of the United Society of Believers of Christ's Second Appearing, known as the Shakers, arrive in New York harbor in flight from religious persecution. Led by Ann Lees, they establish a settlement in Watervliet.
- *September 5*: The first Continental Congress meets in Philadelphia to oppose the Intolerable Acts. It proposes severe trade embargoes on British goods and defiance of British law.

1775

- Battle between American militia and British at Lexington and Concord, Massachusetts, initiates the American Revolutionary war. The British government suspends all immigration to the colonies.

Eyewitness Testimony

The Humble Address of the People Called Quakers in the Province of New York . . . We are now forced to approach humbly the Governor with our complaint in a matter of the highest moment relating to our privileges as freeborn subjects being lately denied the undoubted right of choosing our own representation at an election in Queens county on the island of Nassau . . . because we could not (for conscience sake) swear we were freeholders although it was well known to the sheriff & judge too. . . .

We are also necessitated to lay before the Governor an oppression that we lye under being imposed upon by some of our neighbors. . . . Yet they have presumed to take away our substance . . . at their own will & pleasure, because we could not think it our duty to contribute with them to build their Nonconformist Preacher a dwelling house, & we do humbly conceive they have no legal [right] to impose any such tax upon us.

Petition by the Society of Friends to the royal governor of New York, November 11, 1702, (Gilder Lehrman Collection #2509.01) in Davis and Mintz, The Boisterous Sea of Liberty *(1998), p. 99.*

[The reports of Virginia described it as] a country so desirable; so pleasant, and plentiful; the Climate, and Air, so temperate, sweet, and wholesome; the Woods and Soil, so charming and fruitful; and all other Things so agreeable, that Paradice it self seem'd to be there, in its first Native Lustre.

And, to make it yet more desirable, they reported the Native *Indians* (which were then the only Inhabitants) so affable, kind, and good-natur'd; so uncultivated in Learning, Trades, and Fashions; so innocent, and ignorant of all manner of Politicks, Tricks, and Cunning; and so desirous of the Company of the *English*; That they seem'd rather to be like soft wax, ready to take any Impression, than any ways likely to oppose the Settling of the *English* near them: They represented it as a Scene laid open for the good and gracious *Q. Elizabeth,* to propagate the Gospel in, and extend her Dominions over: As if purposely reserv'd for her Majesty, by a peculiar Direction of Providence. . . .

Her Majesty accordingly took the Hint, and espoused the Project, . . . being so well pleased with the Account given, that as the greatest Mark of Honour she could do the Discovery, she call'd the Country by the Name of *Virginia*; as well, for that it was first discover'd in her Reign, a Virgin Queen; as that it did still seem to retain the Virgin Purity and Plenty of the first Creation, and the people their Primitive Innocence. . . .

Robert Beverley, clerk of the General Assembly and historian of Virginia, ca. 1705, The History and Present State of Virginia *(1947, first published 1705), pp. 16–17.*

. . . I have about a dozen acres of clear ground, the rest woods; in all 300 acres. Had I servants and money, I might live very comfortably upon it, raise good corn of all sorts, and cattle, without any great labor or charges, could it once be stocked; but for want thereof shall not make any advantage of my land. . . . I am forced to work hard with axe, hoe, and spade. I have not a stick to burn for any use but what I cut down with my own hands. I am forced to dig a garden, raise beans, peas, etc., with the assistance of a sorry wench my wife brought with her from England. Men are generally of all trades, and women the like within their spheres, except some who are the posterity of old planters and have great number of slaves, who understand most handicrafts. Men are generally carpenters, joiners, wheelwrights, coopers, butchers, tanners, shoemakers, tallow-chandlers, watermen, and what not; women soap-makers, starch-makers, dyers, etc. He or she that cannot do all these things, or has not slaves that can . . . will have but a bad time of it; for help is not to be had at any rate, everyone having business enough of his own.

Reverend John Urmstone, English missionary in North Carolina, letter of July 7, 1711, to the secretary of the Society for Propagating the Gospel, in Hawks, History of North Carolina, *Volume II (1858), p. 215.*

[The French will] find it a Matter of no great Difficulty, with the assistance of the *Indians,* to invade from [Louisiana] and *Canada, all the* English *Plantations at once, and drive the Inhabitants into the sea.* . . . His Majesty's Dominion on this Continent is canton'd into so many petty independent States or Common Wealths, whereof there is scarce one that can expect Relief or Assistance from another, in the most imminent Danger. . . . I think it naturally follows, that some time or other, the *Mississippi* will drown our Settlements on the Main of *America.*

Anonymous pamphleteer, in Some Considerations on the Consequences of the French Settling Colonies on the Mississippi . . . *(1720; reprinted by the Historical and Philosophical Society of Ohio, (1928), pp. 16, 28).*

The Muse, disgusted at an age and clime
    Barren of every glorious theme,
In distant lands now waits a better time,
    Producing subjects worthy fame:

There shall be sung another golden age,
    The rise of empire and of arts,
The good and great inspiring epic rage,
    The wisest heads and noblest hearts.

Not such as Europe breeds in her decay;
    Such as she bred when fresh and young,
When heavenly flame did animate her clay,
    By future poets shall be sung.

Westward the course of empire takes its way;
    The four first acts already past,
A fifth shall close the drama with the day;
    Time's noblest offspring is the last.

George Berkeley, Irish bishop, "On the Prospect of Planting Arts and Learning in America," 1726, in Untermeyer, ed., Treasury of Great Poems, English and American *(1955).*

The humour of going to America still continues, and the scarcity of provisions certainly makes many quit us. There are now seven ships at Belfast that are carrying off about 1000 passengers thither. And if we knew how to stop them, as most of them can get neither victuals nor work, it would be cruel not to do it.

Hugh Boulter, Archbishop of Armagh and Lord Primate of Ireland, letter of 1728 to the Duke of Newcastle, Letters Written by His Excellency Hugh Boulter . . . to Several Ministers of State *(1770), in Blumenthal and Ozer,* Coming to America *(1980), p. 34.*

The Trustees intend to relieve such unfortunate persons as cannot subsist here, and establish them in an orderly manner, so as to form a well-regulated town. As far as their fund goes, they will defray the charge of their passage to Georgia; giving them necessaries, cattle, land, and subsistence till such time as they can build their houses and clear some of their land.

By such a colony many families who would otherwise starve will be provided for, and made masters of houses and lands. The people in Great Britain, to whom these necessitous families were a burden, will be relieved. Numbers of manufacturers will be here employed for supplying them with clothes, working tools, and other necessities. And by giving refuge to the distressed Salzburgers, and other persecuted Protestants,

the power of Britain, as a reward for its hospitality, will be increased by the addition of so many religious and industrious subjects.

The colony of Georgia lying about the same latitude with part of China, Persia, Palestine, and the Madeiras, it is highly probable that when hereafter it shall be well peopled and rightly cultivated, England may be supplied from thence with raw silk, wine, oil, dyes, drugs, and many other materials for manufactures which she is obliged to purchase from southern countries. As towns are established and grow populous along the rivers Savannah and Altamaha, they will make such a barrier as will render the southern frontier of the British colonies on the continent of America safe from Indian and other enemies.

James Oglethorpe, in a pamphlet promoting the founding of Georgia, 1733, in Force, Tracts, *Volume I, (1836), pp. 2, 5, 6.*

My mother and we children were still in expectation that we were coming to an agreeable place. But when we arrived and saw nothing but a wilderness, and instead of a fine timbered house, nothing but a mean dirt house, our spirits quite sank.

Robert Witherspoon, a Scotch-Irish immigrant to South Carolina, 1734, in Hanna, The Scotch-Irish *(1902), p. 122.*

Our lives are uniform without any great variety, till the season brings in the ships. Then we tear open the letters they bring us from our friends as eagerly as a greedy heir tears open a rich father's will.

William Byrd II, letter to Anne Taylor Otway, June 30, 1736, on the cultural isolation felt by English colonists in Virginia, in Fischer, Albion's Seed *(1986), p. 253.*

Ye ken I had but sma Learning when I left ye, and now wad ye think it, I hea 20 Pund a Year for being a Clark to [New] York Meeting-House, and I keep a Skulle for wee Weans: Ah, dear Sir, there is braw Living in this same York for high learned Men: The young Foke in Ereland are aw but a Pack of Couards, for I will tell ye in short, this is a bonny Country, and aw Things grows here that ever I did see in Ereland; and wee hea Cows, and Sheep, and Horses plenty here, and Goats, and Deers, and Racoons, and Moles, and Bevers, and Fish, and Fouls of aw Sorts: Trades are aw good here, a Wabster gets 12 Pence a yeard, a Labourer gets 4 shillings and 6 Pence a Day, a Lass gets 4 Shillings and 6 Pence a Week for spinning on the wee Wheel, . . . Ye may get Lan here for 10 Pounds a

Hundred Acres for ever, and Ten Years Time tell ye get the Money, before they wull ask ye for it.

Scotch-Irish immigrant James Murray, letter to his minister in County Tyrone, Ireland, reprinted in Benjamin Franklin, Pennsylvania Gazette *November 3, 1737.*

An Act for naturalizing such foreign Protestants, and others therein mentioned, as are settled or shall settle in any of His Majesty's colonies in America.

Whereas the increase of people is a means of advancing the wealth and strength of any nation or country; *And whereas* many foreigners and strangers from the lenity of our government, the purity of our religion, the benefit of our laws, the advantages of our trade, and the security of our property might be induced to come and settle in some of His Majesty's colonies in America, if they were made partakers of the advantages and privileges which the natural-born subjects of this realm do enjoy; *Be it therefor enacted,* by the King's Most Excellent Majesty, by and with the advice and consent of the Lords spiritual and temporal, and Commons, in this present Parliament assembled . . . that from and after the first day of June in the year of Our Lord 1740, all persons born out of the legience of His Majesty, His Heirs, or Successors, who have inhabited and resided, or shall inhabit or reside for the space of seven years or more in any of His Majesty's colonies in America, and shall not have been absent out of some of the said colonies for a longer space than two months at any one time during the said seven years . . . and also make and subscribe the profession of his Christian belief . . . shall be deemed, adjudged, and taken to be His Majesty's natural-born subjects of this Kingdom, to all intents, constructions, and purposes, as if they and every of them had been or were born within this Kingdom. . . .

II. *Provided always and be it enacted,* . . . that no person, of whatever quality, condition, or place soever, other than and except such of the people called Quakers as shall qualify themselves and be naturalized by the ways and means hereinbefore mentioned, or such who profess the Jewish religion, shall be naturalized by virtue of this act, unless such persons shall have received the sacrament of the Lord's Supper in some Protestant and reformed congregation within this Kingdom of Great Britain, or within some of the said colonies in America, within three months next before his taking and subscribing such oaths. . . .

VI. *Provided always and it is hereby further enacted,* that no person who shall become a natural-born subject of the King by virtue of this act, shall be of the Privy Council, or a member of either House of Parliament, or capable of taking, having, or enjoying any office or place of trust within the Kingdom of Great Britain or Ireland, either civil or military, or taking any grant from the Crown to himself. . . .

King George II of England, an act conferring the rights of citizenship on Jews, Protestants, and Quakers in the colonies, 1740, in Publications of the American Jewish Historical Society, *No. 1 (1905), p. 94.*

WHEREAS, many persons trading into this government, have, for lucre and private gain, imported, sold, or disposed of, and do daily import passengers and servants into this government, who, by reason of age, impotence or indigence, have become a heavy burden and charge upon the inhabitants thereof, and likewise do frequently import divers persons convicted of heinous crimes, who soon after their coming into this government, do often commit many felonies, robberies, thefts and burglaries, to the great hurt of his Majesty's subjects. . . .

SEC. 4 *Therefore* to prevent such practices in the future, *Be it enacted,* . . . That if any such convict as aforesaid, or servant, or passenger, being poor and impotent persons, shall be imported into the river Delaware . . . then the Collector or Collectors, Or Justice of the Peace . . . shall demand and compel the persons, if convicts, immediately to comply with the directions of this act, by paying the duties hereby imposed on them, and giving the security hereby directed, in the case of convicts. . . .

SEC. 5. And, *Be it further enacted,* . . . That upon information given to any two Justices of the Peace within this government, that any old persons, infants, maimed, lunatick, or any vagabond or vagrant persons are imported, come or brought into this government, . . . it shall and may be lawful for the said justices . . . [to] compel said master, merchant, or other person who imported such infant, lunatick, aged, maimed, impotent or vagrant person or persons, to give sufficient security to carry and transport such infant, lunatick, maimed, aged, impotent or vagrant person or persons to the place or places from whence such person or persons were imported. . . .

"An Act Imposing a Duty on Persons Convicted of Heinous Crimes and to Prevent Poor and Impotent Persons being Imported," passed by the government of Delaware, 1740, in Laws of the State of Delaware, 1700–1797, *Volume I, pp. 166–170.*

This indenture Witnesseth that Hannah Toby Indian woman of So[uth] Kingstown of ye Colony of Rhode

Island . . . hath put her son Javin Toby, Molatto of her own free will & accord an apprentice or servant of John Steadman of South Kingstown yeoman & to Purthany his Wife . . . after the manner of an apprentice from of Day of ye date hereof for and during ye Term of fifteen years & five Months which Will be compleat on ye Seventh day of June 1763. During all which Term of apprentice or service his master & mistress faithfully shall serve their secrets keep their Lawful Commands of labor & every Where he shall do no damage to his s[ai]d Master & Mistress nor see it done by others. Without giving notice thereof to his s[ai]d Master & Mistress he shall not waste his Master & Mistresses goods nor lend them unlawfully to any. He shall not use any unlawful games nor contract matrimony nor commit Fornication. During s[ai]d term and his s[ai]d Master & Mistress . . . by their parts are to find and provide sufficient apparel meat Drink Washing & Lodging Suitable for Such an apprentice. During s[ai]d Term at ye Expiration thereof to Dismiss Him With one new suit of apparel fitting for his body besides his usual wearing Clothes.

Indenture between Hannah Toby and John Steadman apprenticing her son Javin Toby, January 9, 1747, (Gilder Lehman Collection #3002.01), in Davis and Mintz, Boisterous Sea of Liberty *(1998), p. 111.*

The country, especially all along the coasts, is inhabited by Europeans, who in some places are already so numerous that few parts of Europe are more populous. The Indians have sold the country to the Europeans, and have retired farther up; in most parts you may travel 20 Swedish miles, or about 120 English miles, from the seashore before you reach the first habitations of the Indians. . . .

Besides the different sects of Christians, there are many Jews settled in New York, who possess great privileges. They have a synagogue and houses, and great country seats of their own property, and are allowed to keep shops in town. They have likewise several ships, which they freight and send out with their own goods. In fine, they enjoy all the privileges common to the other inhabitants of this town and province. . . .

The servants which are made use of in the English American colonies are either free persons, or slaves, and the former are again of two different sorts.

1. Those who are quite free serve by the year; they are not only allowed to leave their service at the expiration of their year but may leave it at any time when they do not agree with their masters. However in that case they are in danger of losing their wages, which are very considerable. A man servant who has some abilities gets between sixteen and twenty pounds in Pennsylvania currency . . . A servant maids gets eight or ten pounds a year. These servants have their food besides their wages, but must buy their own clothes. . . .

2. A second kind of free servants consists of such person as annually come from Germany, England, and other country in order to settle here. These newcomers are very numerous every year; there are old and young ones, and of both sexes; some of them have fled from oppression, under which they supposed themselves to have labored. Others have been driven from their countries by persecution on account of religion; but most of them are poor, and have not money enough to pay their passage, which is between six and eight pounds sterling for each person; therefore they agree with the captain that they will suffer themselves to be sold for a few years, on their arrival. In that case, the person who buys them pays the freight for them. But frequently very old people come over who cannot pay their passage; they therefore sell their children. . . .

The English and Irish commonly sell themselves for four years, but the Germans frequently agree with the captain before they set out, to pay him a certain sum of money, for a certain number of persons; as soon as they arrive in America, they go about and try to get a man who will pay the passage for them. In return they give, according to the circumstances, one or several of their children to serve a certain number of years; at last they make their bargain with the highest bidder.

Swedish naturalist Peter Kalm, reporting a tour of New York, New Jersey, and Pennsylvania taken between 1748 and 1751, in Travels in North America *(1753–61), in Adler,* Annals of America, *Volume I (1968), pp. 472–478).*

Last autumn about twenty-five ships arrived here with Germans. The number of those who arrived alive was 1,049, among whom there were also about twelve who were in part regular schoolmasters in the old country, but on account of small pay, and in the hopes of improvement, moved into this, and in part they had been engaged in other pursuits. They would have better remained where they were. . . . The province is crowded full of people, and living becomes continually more expensive. Those who come in free—who had something in the old country, but consumed that which they had on an expensive voyage—and see that it is otherwise than it was represented to them, whine and cry. Woe on the immigrants who induced them to this! One of those in Germantown had wished to shoot himself recently from desperation. The newlanders, as they are here called, are such as do not work and still wish to become rich speedily, and for this reason they go out into Würtemberg and vicinity, and persuade the people to come into this country, alleging that everything was here that they could wish for, that such a country like this there was none in the world, and that everyone could become as rich as a nobleman, etc. These deceivers have this profit in it, that they with their merchandise are brought in free, and in addition for every head they bring to Amsterdam or to Rotterdam, they receive a certain sum from the merchants. The owners of these vessels derive much money herefrom in freightage. They pack them into the ships as if they were herring, and when they arrive there are so many sick and dying among them that it is pitiful to behold them. Those, however, who have nothing and are in debt also for their passage, are taken into small huts, where they lie upon straw and are corrupted like cattle, and in part half deprived of their reason, so that they can scarcely perceive anything of the parson's consolations.

Peter Brunnholtz, a German Lutheran pastor in Philadelphia, letter of May 21, 1750, published in Reports of the United German Evangelical Lutheran Congregations in North America *(1881), pp. 412–414.*

[W]hat really drove me to write this book was the sad and miserable conditions of those traveling from Germany to the New World, and the irresponsible and merciless proceedings of the Dutch traders in human beings and their manstealing emissaries—I mean the so-called Newlanders. For these at one and the same time steal German people under all sorts of fine pretexts, and deliver them into the hands of the great Dutch traffickers in human souls. From this business the latter make a huge profit, and the Newlanders a smaller one. . . .

In Rotterdam, . . . the people are packed into the big boats as closely as herring, so to speak. . . . The ships often take eight, nine, ten, or twelve weeks sailing to Philadelphia, if the wind is unfavorable. . . . During the journey the ship is full of distress—smells, fumes, horrors, vomiting, various kinds of sea sickness, fever, dysentery, headaches, heat, constipation, boils, scurvy, cancer, mouth-rot, and similar afflictions, all of them caused by the age and highly-salted condition of the food, especially

of the meat, as well as by the very bad and filthy water, which brings about the miserable death and destruction of many. Add to all that shortage of food, hunger, thirst, frost, heat, dampness, fear, misery, vexation, and lamentation as well as other troubles. . . .

Many parents in order to pay their fares . . . and get off the ships must barter and sell their children as if they were cattle. Since fathers and mothers often do not know where or to what masters their children are to be sent, it frequently happens that after leaving the vessel, parents and children do not see each other for years on end, or even for the rest of their lives.

Gottlieb Mittelberger, German teacher and organist, reporting his experiences as an immigrant, in Journey to Pennsylvania in the Year of 1750 and Return to Germany in the Year of 1754, *(1756), pp. 9, 11–12, 18.*

Our mother knows what is best for us. What is a little House-breaking, Shop-lifting, or Highway-robbing; what is a son now and then corrupted and hanged, a Daughter debauched, and Pox'd, a wife stabbed, a Husband's throat cut, or a child's brains beat out with an Axe, compared with this Improvement and Well peopling of the Colonies!

An anonymous American writer protesting the British practice of deporting felons to the New World, 1751, in the Pennsylvania Gazette, *in Geiser,* Redemptioners and Indentured Servants in the Colony and Commonwealth of Virginia, *(1901), p. 105.*

Whereas, Germans and other persons may be imported in so great numbers in one vessel, through want of necessary room and accommodations, they may often contract mortal and contagious distempers, and thereby occasion not only the death of great numbers of them in their passage, but also by such means on their arrival in this province, those who may survive, may be so infected as to spread the contagion, and be the cause of the death of many others; to the end, therefore, that such an evil practice may be prevented, and inconveniences thence arising avoided as much as may be—*Be it enacted by the Lieutenant-Governor, Council and House of Representatives:*

SECTION I. That from and after the publication of this act, no master or commander of any ship, or other vessel whatsoever, bound to the port of Boston, or into any other port within this province, any greater number of passengers, in any one ship or other vessel, than such only as shall be well provided with good and wholesome meat, drink and other necessaries for passengers and others, during the whole voyage; and shall have rooms therein to contain, for single freight or passengers of the age of fourteen years or upwards, at least six feet in length, and one foot and six inches in breadth for every two such passengers. . . . *Be it further enacted:*

SEC. 3. That the commissioner of impost . . . in going on board any ship or other vessel importing passengers, . . . shall, and is hereby required to, inform himself of the condition and circumstances of the passengers on board, and whether they have been provided for, and accommodated with the provisions, room and other necessaries herein directed; and where an any time a deficiency shall appear to him . . . he . . . shall forthwith give notice of the same to some one or more of the justices of the peace for the county where the offence is committed, to the end the person or persons delinquent may be sent for, or bound over, to the next court of general sessions of the peace, then and there to answer for such offenses. . . .

Extract from "An Act to Regulate the Importation of Germans and Other Passengers Coming to Settle in This Province, February 6, 1751," Acts and Resolves of the Province of Massachusetts Bay, Volume III *(1742–56), in Abbott,* Immigration: Select Documents and Case Records *(1924), p. 6.*

When we see our Papers fill'd continually with Accounts of the most audacious Robberies, the most cruel Murders, and infinite other Villanies perpetrated by Convicts transported from Europe, what terrible Reflections must it occasion! What will become of our Posterity? These are some of thy Favours, Britain! Thou are called our Mother Country; But what good Mother ever sent Thieves and Villains to accompany her children; to corrupt some with their infectious Vices and murder the rest? . . . In what can England show a more sovereign contempt for us than by emptying their Jails into our Settlements?

Editorial, Virginia Gazette, *May 24, 1751.*

Those who come hither are generally the most stupid of their own nation, and, as ignorance is often attended with credulity when knavery would mislead it, and with suspicion when honesty would set it right; . . . not being used to liberty, they know not how to make a modest use of it. . . .

In short, unless the stream of their importation could be turned from this to other colonies, . . . they will soon so outnumber us that all the advantages we have will, in my opinion, be not able to preserve our language and even our government will become precarious.

Benjamin Franklin, on the German immigration to Pennsylvania, May 9, 1753, in The Complete Works of Benjamin Franklin *Volume II, (1887–1888), p. 291.*

Old England, Old England, I never shall see you
    more,
If I do it's ten thousand to twenty;
My bones are quite rotten, my feet are quite sore,
I'm parched with fever and am at death's door,
But if ever I live to see seven years more,
Then I'll bid adieu to Virginia.

"The Lads of Virginia," nostalgic ballad popular among indentured servants in the mid-18th century, in Firth, The American Garland *(1915), pp. 72–73.*

For God's sake then let us Root the French blood out of America. . . . [I]t will be the Salvation of England for in 40 years this very America will absolutely take all the manufactory of England, a noble return for their assistance. . . . [W]hoever keeps America will in the end (whether French or English) have the Kingdom of England.

Thomas Hancock, uncle of John Hancock, letter to his agent Christopher Kilby, in England, 1755, in Baxter, The House of Hancock *(1945), p. 132.*

[S]hould our trade and plantations be exposed to the ravages of the French, a national bankruptcy would probably in a very few years ensue, which would render us unable to continue the war in Europe . . . or to prosecute the war by sea and in America, or even to defend ourselves here at home.

George Montagu, earl of Halifax, president of the British Board of Trade, in a speech to Parliament in 1755, quoted in Draper, A Struggle for Power *(1996), p. 157.*

Europe is generally full settled with Husbandmen, Manufacturers, &c. and therefore cannot now much increase in People: America is chiefly occupied by Indians, who subsist mostly by Hunting. But as the Hunter, of all Men, requires the greatest Quantity of Land from whence to draw his Subsistence, (the Husbandman subsisting on much less, the Gardener on still less, and the Manufacturer requiring least of all), the Europeans found America as fully settled as it well could bee by Hunters; yet these, having large Tracks, were easily prevail'd upon to part with Portions of Territory to the new Comers, who did not much interfere with Natives in Hunting, and furnish'd them with many Things they wanted.

Land being plenty in America, and so cheap as that a laboring Man, that understands Husbandry, can in a short Time save Money enough to purchase a Piece of new Land sufficient for a Plantation, whereon he may subsist a Family; such are not afraid to marry; for even if they look far enough forward to consider how their Children when grown up are to be provided for, they see that more Land is to be had at Rates equally easy, all Circumstances considered.

The importation of foreigners into a country that has as many inhabitants as the present employments and provisions for subsistence will bear, will be in the end no increase of people, unless the newcomers have more industry and frugality than the natives, and then they will provide more subsistence, and increase in the country; *but they will gradually eat the natives out.* . . .

. . . [W]e may here reckon 8 [births per marriage], of which if one half grow up, and our Marriages are made, reckoning one with another at 20 Years of Age, our People must be at least doubled every 20 Years.

But nothwithstanding this Increase, so vast is the Territory of North-America, that it will require many Ages to settle it fully; and till it is fully settled, Labour will never be cheap here, where no Man continues long a Labourer for others, but gets a Plantation of his own, no Man continues long a Journeyman to a trade but goes among those Settlers, and set up for himself, &c. Hence Labour is no cheaper now, in Pennsylvania, than it was 30 Years ago, tho' so many Thousand labouring People have been imported.

. . . There are suppos'd to be now upwards of One Million English Souls in North-America . . . and yet there is not one the fewer in Britain, but rather more, on Account of the Employment the Colonies afford to Manufacturers at Home. This Million doubling, suppose once in 25 years, will in another century be more than the People of England, and the greatest Number of Englishmen will be on this side of the Water. What an Accession of Power to the British Empire. . . . What an Increase in Trade and Navigation!. . . .

And since Detachments of English from Britain sent to America, will have their places at home so soon supply'd and increase so largely here; why should the Palatine Boors be suffered to swarm into the Settlements, and by herding together establish their Language and Manners to the Exclusion of ours? Why should Pennsylvania, founded by the English, become a Colony of *Aliens,* who will shortly be so numerous as to Germanize us instead of our Anglifying them, and will never adopt our Language or Customs, any more than they can acquire our Complexion.

Which leads me to add one remark: That the Number of purely white People in the World is proportionately very small. All Africa is black or tawny. Asia chiefly tawny. America (exclusive of the new Comers) wholly so. And in Europe, the Spaniards, Italians, French, Russians and Swedes, are generally of what we call a swarthy Complexion; as are the Germans also, the Saxons only excepted, who with the English make the principal Body of White People on the Face of the Earth. I would wish their Numbers were increased. And while we are, as I may call it, *Scouring* our Planet, by clearing America of Woods, and so making this Side of our Globe, reflecting a brighter Light to the Eyes of Inhabitants in Mars or Venus, why should we in the Sight of Superior Beings, darken its People. Why increase the sons of Africa, by planting them in America, where we have so fair an Opportunity, by excluding all Blacks and Tawneys, of increasing the lovely White and Red?

Benjamin Franklin, "Observations Concerning the Increasing of Mankind, Peopling of Countries, &c.," 1755, in The Complete Works of Benjamin Franklin *(1887–1888), Volume II, p. 231ff.*

Such is the British Empire in North America; which from Nova-Scotia to Georgia is a Tract of 1600 miles Sea-Coast; a Country productive of all the necessaries and Conveniences of Life; . . . America is become the Fountain of our Riches, for with America our greatest trade is carried on. . . .

This is the Country, which the French have many Years envied us, and which they have been long meditating to make themselves Masters of: They are at length come to a Resolution to attack us, in profound Peace, in one of the best of those Colonies, Virginia; and in that part of it which lies on the River Ohio, to which Country they never pretended before. Every one knows that the English were the first and only Europeans who settled Virginia. . . . The French, however, if they find their way to the Coast of Virginia, will easily over-run the provinces, because each Province considers itself as independent of the Rest, and the Invaders from Canada all act under one Governor; to unite 13 Provinces which fill an Extent of 1600 Miles is not easy. . . . Canada must be subdued.

Editorial, calling for unity in the colonies during the first year of the French and Indian War, The Maryland Gazette, May 22, 1755.

Last evening Captain Murray arrived and brought with him the instructions and letters. I consulted [with him on] methods for removing the whole inhabitants of the villages of Grand Pre, Mines, Rivers Cannard, Habbertong and Gaspereau, and agreed that it would be most convenient to cite all the male inhabitants of said villages to assemble at the Church in this place on the 5th of September next to hear the King's orders, and at the same time Captain Murray to collect the inhabitants of Piziquid, and the villages to Fort Edward for the same purpose. . . .

September 5th: At 3:00 in the afternoon the French inhabitants appeared, agreeable to their citation, at the Church in Grand Pre, amounting to 418 of their best men, upon which I ordered a table to be set in the center of the Church attended with those of my officers who were off guard. I delivered to them through interpreters the King's orders in the following words:

"Gentlemen—

"I have received from his Excellency Governor Lawrence the King's commission which I have in my hand and by whose orders you are convened together to manifest to you his Majesty's final resolution to the French inhabitants of this his province of Nova Scotia. . . .

"The part of my duty I am now upon is, though necessary, very disagreeable to my nature and temper as I know it must be grievous to you who are of the same kind. But it is not my business to criticize, but rather to obey such orders as I receive. . . .

"Your land and tenements, cattle of all kinds and livestock of all sorts are forfeited to the Crown with all other effects saving your money and household goods and you are to be removed from this province. . . .

"I must also inform you that it is his Majesty's pleasure that you remain in security under the inspection and direction of the troops that I have the honor to command."

I then declared them the King's prisoners.

I returned to my quarters and the French inhabitants soon moved by their elders that it was a great grief to them that they had incurred his Majesty's displeasure. . . .

The French people not having any provisions with them and pleading hunger begged for bread which I gave them.

Thus ended the memorable fifth of September, a day of great fatigue and trouble.

Colonel John Winslow, British officer, report of August 30–September 5, 1755, on the evacuation of the Acadians from Nova Scotia, in "Journal of Colonel John Winslow" in Colbert, Eyewitness to America *(1997), pp. 45–47.*

[New England]. In no part of the world are the ordinary sort so independent, or possess so many of the conveniences of life. . . . The most populous and flourishing parts of the mother country hardly make a better appearance.

[Pennsylvania]: The people free and flourishing.

[Philadelphia]: A splendid and wealthy city.

[Charleston]: The planters and merchants are rich and well bred; the people are showy and expensive in their dress and way of living. . . . much the liveliest and politest place, as it is one of the richest too, in all America.

William Burke, British traveler in America, 1757, in An Account of the European Settlements in America, *pp. 259, 275, 307.*

[Charleston]: The streets are straight, broad, and airy, the churches are handsome, the other places of worship are commodious, and many of the houses belonging to individuals are larger and handsome, having all the conveniences one sees at home.

[Williamsburg, Virginia]: Much resembles a good country town in England.

[Philadelphia]: The noble city of Philadelphia . . . is perhaps one of the wonders of the world, if you consider its size, the number of inhabitants, the regularity of its streets, their great breadth and length, . . . the magnificence and diversity of places of worship (for here all religions who profess the name of Christ are tolerated equally), the plenty of provisions brought to market, and the industry of all its inhabitants. One will not hesitate to call it the first town in America, but one that bids fair to rival almost any in Europe.

[Boston]: This is more like an English town than any in America.

Lord Adam Gordon, Scottish army officer and member of Parliament, in a description of his travels in America, 1764–65, in Peckham, Narratives of Colonial America, 1704–1765 *(1971), pp. 245, 249, 259, 290.*

The alleged reasons, namely a great burden of debt and insufficient food supplies, are not enough to justify the supplicants fleeing in such arbitrary manner from their hereditary sovereign and from the country in which they were born, brought up and hitherto nourished; on the contrary, it is their bounden duty to remain in the country and . . . to hope for the return of better and more blessed times.

Report by the Upper Hessian province of Giessen, banning emigration from the province, March 7, 1766, in Günter Moltmann, Germans to America: 300 Years of Immigration: 1683–1983 *(1982), p. 37.*

In order to accomplish their purposes the more readily, [the newlanders] resort to every conceivable trickery. They parade themselves in fine dress, display their watches, and in every way conduct themselves as men of opulence, in order to inspire the people with the desire to live in a country of such wealth and abundance. They would convince one that there are in America none but Elysian fields abounding in products which require no labor; that the mountains are full of gold and silver, the wells and springs gush forth milk and honey; that he goes there as a servant, becomes a lord; as a maid, a gracious lady; as a peasant, a nobleman; as a commoner or craftsman, a baron. . . . Now as everybody by nature desires to better his condition, who would not wish to go to such a country!

Letter from Germany, 1769, in Geiser, Redemptioners and Indentured Servants in the Colony and Commonwealth of Pennsylvania *(1901), pp. 18–19.*

In your frequent excursions about the great metropolis, you cannot but observe numerous advertisements, offering the most seducing encouragement to adventurers under every possible description; to those who are disgusted with the frowns of fortune in their native land, and to those of an enterprising disposition who are tempted to court her smiles in a distant region. These persons are referred to agents, or crimps, who represent the advantages to be obtained in America, in colours so alluring that it is almost impossible to resist their artifices. Unwary persons are accordingly induced to enter into articles by which they engage to become servants, agreeable to their respective qualifications, for the term of five years, every necessary accommodation being found them during the voyage, and every method taken that they may be treated with tenderness and humanity during the period of servitude, at the expiration of which they are taught to expect that opportunities will assuredly offer to secure to the honest and industrious a competent provision for the remainder of their days.

The generality of the inhabitants in this province are very little acquainted with those fallacious pretences, by which numbers are continually induced to embark for this continent. On the contrary, they too generally conceive an opinion that the difference is merely nominal between the indented servant and the convicted felon. . . .

The situation of the free-willer is, in almost every instance, more to be lamented than either that of the convict or the indented servant; the deception which is practiced on those of this description being attended with circumstances of greater duplicity and cruelty. . . . [They] meet with horror the moment which dooms them, under an appearance of equity, to a limited term of slavery. Character is of little importance; their abilities not being found of a superior nature, they are sold as soon as their term of election is expired, apparel and provision being their only compensation; till, on the expiration of five tedious, laborious years, they are restored to a dearly purchased freedom.

William Eddis, British traveler, Letters from America, Historical and Descriptive; Comprising Occurrences from 1769 to 1777, Inclusive *(1792), pp. 67–69.*

Twenty Dollars Reward for JOHN ECTON DUCRECT, a native of *Berne* in *Switzerland,* who speaks very good *French* and tolerable *English* and *Italian.* He is about 5 feet 9 inches high, pitted with the smallpox, and very swarthy, almost as dark as a mulatto; wears his own hair, with a false tail, and is generally powdered, being a barber by trade. I have heard, however, since he went off, that he intended to cut off his hair and wear a wig. He has been used to travel with gentlemen, and will probably try to get into employ that way, or with some of the barbers in *Williamsburg,* as he was seen at Doctor Todd's tavern, on the way there, the 22d ult. He took with him a suit of brown and a suit of green clothes, the brown pretty much wore, and has some rents on the back of the coat, the green almost new, a pair of new buckskin breeches, trousers that button down the legs, some white thread stockings and white shirts, a powder bag and some shaving materials, a prayer-book in *French,* and some old commissions for officers in the *Swiss* militia, by which he will probably try to pass. One of his testicles was swelled, which he says was occasioned by a kick he got on board the *Justitia,* capt. *Kidd,* the ship he came in. Whoever secures the said convict so that I can get him again, shall be paid the above sum. . . .

Advertisement for escaped indentured servant in Virginia Gazette, *July 21, 1775, in Roger Daniels,* Coming to America *(1990), p. 39.*

CHAPTER THREE

The American Revolution and After
1776–1813

Immigrants in the American Revolution

Revolution was in the air in the 13 colonies long before the war was declared, and for years colonists actually fought British soldiers without the formal support of the American government or a public proclamation of independence. By 1771 the poet Philip Freneau, New York–born son of a Huguenot immigrant, had written,

> Too long our patient country wears her chains,
> Too long our wealth all-grasping Britain drains:
> Why still a handmaid to that distant land?
> Why still subservient to their proud command?

In the first month of 1776, Thomas Paine, an English immigrant who had arrived in America only two years before, wrote a pamphlet that articulated the idea of revolution with passionate conviction. His *Common Sense* argued in ringing words that "everything that is right or reasonable pleads for separation. The blood of the slain, the weeping voice of nature cries, *'Tis time to part.'*" To Paine, America was destined to be free and to offer its freedom to the world. "O ye that love mankind!" he went on, "Ye that dare oppose not only tyranny but the tyrant, stand forth! Every spot of the old world is overrun with oppression. Freedom hath been hunted round the globe. Asia and Africa have long expelled her. Europe regards her like a stranger, and England hath given her warning to depart. O receive the fugitive, and prepare in time an asylum for mankind!"

However, although John Adams, a Massachusetts lawyer who was to become the second president of the United States, wrote two months later that "every post and every day rolls in upon us Independence like a torrent," not all the colonists were in favor of separating from England. There were people of every class and national background on both sides of the issue. Patriots like Paine and Adams were seen by many as agitators who were disloyal to their king and his lawful government. It was not easy to stir up resentment of the English among the merchants and the working class in America because it was a time of the greatest prosperity in the colonies' history. New England's imports had risen from £330,000 to £1,200,000 in a few brief years, and crop failures in Europe had created a huge market for American grain.

The employees of the crown, with a financial interest in preserving the social order as it was, were understandably unwilling to break their ties with the mother country. Long-established merchants and successful artisans felt the same way. But recent immigrants had mixed feelings about independence. Adams observed grimly in 1776, when the fighting had already begun, that only about a third of the American people really supported the Revolution, another third was against it, and the remainder either was not sure or frankly did not care. These divisions cut across all lines, both regional and ethnic. Even families were divided. As a loyal Connecticut citizen recalled the conflict, "Nabour was against Nabour, Father against the Son and the son against the father, and he that would not thrust his one blaid through his brothers heart was cald an Infimous fillon." Even famous families were split by the idea of war. Benjamin Franklin, one of the first and most passionate of American patriots, was on the opposite side of this debate from his son William, the royal governor of New Jersey and a devoted Loyalist. The revolutionary statesman James Otis was married to a Loyalist.

If even families were split by the issue of revolution, it followed that national communities within the country were equally divided among themselves. No immigrant group unanimously supported either side. In the last quarter of the 18th century, the English represented about half of the inhabitants of the colonies, and it was they who felt the call of loyalty to the home country most keenly. Still feeling themselves to be subjects of the king, they were torn between a desire for economic independence and patriotic devotion, and many wanted equal rights as Englishmen rather than independence from England. But most of the immigrants from other parts of the British Isles had no such conflict. The largest group of non-English Britons, the Scotch-Irish, brought with them memories of ancient wrongs that inclined them to oppose the English, and many of those on the frontier felt threatened by England's efforts to prevent further settlement in the interior. The Scotch-Irish of Pennsylvania were pro-revolution and contributed the majority of soldiers to that colony's armed force in the war, but even in Pennsylvania there were Loyalists whose sympathies were with the mother country. In the interior of the Carolinas, where the Scotch-Irish were often in conflict with the wealthier settlers of the coast, feelings were more divided. A good percentage of the frontiersmen supported the English because they were unwilling to join a movement led by the settlers of the coast, whose political dominance they resented and whom they saw as their enemies. By the time of the Revolutionary War, the interior of North Carolina was home to some 60,000 people; that of South Carolina to 80,000, and the majority of the inhabitants of the region were first- or second-generation Scotch-Irish.

Other things divided the Scotch-Irish on the issue of the revolution as well. Those who had recently arrived—and 40 percent of those in the Carolinas had come following the crop failures in Ireland in the 1770s—had received land grants from the British and were fearful of losing them if they joined the rebellion. Religious disunity also contributed to the divisiveness. In Pennsylvania the Scotch-Irish Presbyterians were hostile to the Quaker rule of the colony, which withheld the vote and proper representation in the Assembly from them. If this resentment did not bring about any particular support for the English, it worked against the desire for colonial independence.

The Irish were more uniformly pro-independence, having little reason for loyalty to the English. Victims of a series of severe laws discriminating against Catholics and non-Anglican Protestants, they were prohibited from holding government jobs, becoming lawyers, or advancing in other professions. Irish Quakers were particularly persecuted, and numerous Irish Catholics were transported to the British colonies. So it is not surprising that the Irish formed such military groups as the Volunteers of Ireland in Philadelphia, which contained both Catholics and Protestants and fought valiantly in the Continental army, or that four signers of the Declaration of Independence were born in Ireland. Nevertheless, as with all national groups, the Irish were not unanimous in their support of the struggle, and there were those who fought for the British against their neighbors in the Revolution.

The pattern of response to the Revolution was quite different among the Scots, who were much more uniform in their support of the British in the revolutionary period. Scotsmen in the Carolinas, in New York, and in Virginia fought loyally on the British side and formed Scottish units to support the British army. When the war ended in 1782, Scots probably represented a majority of the 80,000 Loyalists who emigrated from the newly established nation to Canada and England.

Scottish immigration to America was not so extensive in colonial times—estimates place their numbers in the New World at less than 8 percent of the white population in 1790—and much of it was not voluntary. Most Scots who chose to leave their country migrated to Ireland, England, or continental Europe. Many of those who did make the trip before 1707, when Scotland joined England in the United Kingdom, either came as indentured servants or were transported to America as political and religious dissenters. But as the majority of Scots in the colonies had come only within the previous decade, their ties with the Scottish economy were still close. They had not had enough time to develop any local affiliations and it was common for those who prospered to leave some of their money to schools and churches in their home country. Many of the Scottish immigrants had become successful merchants—they dominated the tobacco trade in Virginia—and wanted to maintain peaceful relations with England.

The Welsh formed a still smaller part of the American population—roughly 1 percent—and were almost entirely limited to Pennsylvania and its surroundings. Of the 21 Welsh churches in colonial America, including Baptist, Anglican, Presbyterian, and Quaker houses of worship, 18 were in Pennsylvania and two in neighboring Delaware. The first sizable Welsh settlement, in the Pennsylvania colony, soon lost its distinctive ethnic character and stopped using its own language as the English and Germans began to settle in the same area. Relatively prosperous and well assimilated, the Welsh had few grievances, but a majority supported the Revolution.

German immigrants—the largest non-British group in the colonies and the most clearly defined both regionally and culturally—had little ethnic solidarity and were by no means unanimous about the war for independence. The largest concentration, centered in Pennsylvania, were divided—as were the Scotch-Irish in the Carolinas—between the east and west part of the colony over the issue of eastern political dominance and aligned their political sympathies accordingly. In the Mohawk Valley of New York, the Germans had long been in conflict with their British landlords and so supported the revolutionary cause. The Germans of Georgia tended to support the British side because they depended on British protection from the Indians.

Most Germans, who continued speaking a different language and remained separate from American society, preferred to remain neutral on the subject. Because they did not drink tea, the tea tax did not bother them. However, like most English colonists, the Germans resented the Stamp Act, and, because most belonged to the Catholic, Lutheran, or German Reformed Church, they felt particularly bitter about the law requiring them to pay a tax to the Anglican diocese. Even those whose religious beliefs forbade them to fight often contributed supplies and equipment to the Colonial army. The famous Kentucky rifles used by the colonial artillery—described by a British soldier in 1775 as those "cursed twisted guns [that were] the most fatal widow-orphan-makers in the world"—were generally produced by Pennsylvania-German gunsmiths.

Religious differences among themselves also influenced the German response to the fight for national independence. There were many separatist movements among the German community, and their adherents often shared the same political positions. The Moravians, for example, were loyal to England because England had provided them with a haven from religious persecution and given them a special exemption from bearing arms because of their religion. The German Reformed Church, on the other hand, officially supported the Revolution and called upon its members to fight for it. The Lutherans had no official policy but generally favored the British side.

There were, however, notable exceptions even in these groupings. One of the best-known religious leaders of the time was Peter Mühlenberg, the son of the patriarch of German Lutheranism in America. Although his father remained a loyal subject of England and (as a good Lutheran) believed that the clergy should not be involved in politics, Peter Mühlenberg became a dedicated activist for the revolutionary cause. In 1774 he led a German group in Virginia that resolved, "We will

John Peter Gabriel Mühlenberg was a Lutheran minister who fought valiantly in the Revolutionary War. (From The Pictorial Field Book of the Revolution, 2 vols., by B. J. Lossing. New York: Harper Brothers, 1851 and 1852.)

most heartily and unanimously concur with our suffering brethren of Boston, and every other part of North America, who are the immediate victims of tyranny." In January 1776 Mühlenberg proclaimed from his Lutheran pulpit in Woodstock, Virginia, that "in the language of holy writ, there is a time for all things, a time to preach, and a time to pray, but those times have passed away; . . . there is a time to fight, and that time has now come!" Then he threw off his clerical robe to reveal a military uniform under it, and, walking down from the pulpit, he ordered drums to beat at the church door for recruits. The Lutheran pastor Mühlenberg led a German regiment in the Revolutionary War and became an important general in the Continental army.

The French were little represented in the colonies at the time of the Revolution, numbering fewer than 100,000 in 1790. The Protestant refugees called Huguenots, who arrived in small numbers after 1685, were quickly absorbed, and although they prospered and made many important contributions to the commercial and political life of the nation, they never established a separate cultural identity in the colonies. The Acadians, who became the Cajuns when they were exiled to America from Canada in 1755, settled mainly in Louisiana, which was French territory until 1762 and then Spanish territory until 1800, when it was ceded back to France; they therefore had no communal response to the Revolution. The Acadians were to become a distinctive ethnic group, maintaining their own language and social customs, and they had little influence on national policy during the formative years of the country.

Perhaps the most distinctive example of cultural identity surviving despite small numbers and geographic dispersion is that of the Jews. With no more than about 2,000 representatives at the time of the first census in 1790, the Jewish community of the United States was thinly spread from southern Georgia to New England but had important religious centers in New York, Newport, Philadelphia, Savannah, and Charleston. As they had come to North America from many areas—Europe, the Near East, and South America—the Jews were divided among themselves in their attitude toward the Revolution. There were ardent patriots who risked their lives and sacrificed much to support the American cause, and there were Loyalists who were no less ardent in their devotion to the crown.

Military Help from Europe

The Revolutionary War divided immigrant communities, as it did the population of the continent in general. It also polarized Europe. Although the conflict virtually ended the regular flow of immigrants at that time, it drew foreign adventurers and idealists from several countries eager to join in the American war effort. Germany, with its long military tradition and large representation among the populace of the American colonies, was a particularly fruitful source of manpower.

The most distinguished German to immigrate in order to fight in the American Revolution was Baron Friedrich Wilhelm von Steuben, a Prussian who had fought for Frederick the Great in the Seven Years' War in Europe. There is some question about whether his title was authentic and the accounts of his military exploits true, but he claimed that he had sacrificed a high rank in the Prussian army to fight for American freedom. In any event, when he arrived in 1777 he was appointed inspector-general and assigned to train the raw recruits that formed the beginnings of

Friedrich Wilhelm von Steuben, a German officer, became a general in the Continental army and later a citizen of the United States. *(From* The Pictorial Field Book of the Revolution, *2 vols., by B. J. Lossing, New York Harper Brothers, 1851 and 1852.)*

the Continental army. His experience with the highly disciplined Prussian military machine enabled him to turn a "rabble in arms" into a highly effective instrument of war. Steuben was commissioned a major general in 1778 and fought with valor throughout the war, sharing the hardships of the foot soldiers of the army he had helped make. In 1783 he was naturalized and became an American citizen, living in New York until his death in 1794.

Another German who chose to join the revolutionary cause in America was Johann Kalb, the son of a Franconian peasant who gave himself the title of baron in

Johann de Kalb came from Germany to join the American troops in their battle for independence. *(From* The Pictorial Field Book of the Revolution, *2 vols., by B. J. Lossing. New York: Harper Brothers, 1851 and 1852.)*

Thaddeus Kosciusko, a Polish engineer, served in the Revolutionary army and built the fortifications at West Point. *(From* The Pictorial Field Book of the Revolution, *2 vols., by B. J. Lossing. New York: Harper Brothers, 1851 and 1852.)*

order to gain a commission. After serving in the French army, where he earned the right to call himself "de Kalb," he came to America as Baron de Kalb and secured the military rank of major general. He served with distinction in New Jersey and Maryland, and in 1780 he was sent to aid General Gates in the Carolinas. There he fought in hand-to-hand combat against the armies of British general Cornwallis. When the armies of General Gates fled, de Kalb continued to fight, and after receiving 11 wounds he was killed in battle.

France, which recognized American independence in December 1777 and loaned the new country money in 1781, contributed military aid to the American cause as well. In 1777 the marquis de Lafayette, a nobleman only 19 years old, volunteered for the Continental army and performed important services. The comte de Rochambeau recruited more than 4,000 French volunteers to aid the American cause and, fighting alongside George Washington's troops, led them in the decisive battle of Yorktown that ended the war in 1781. The marquis de Chastellux came as a major-general in 1780 to serve with Rochambeau and later wrote an enthusiastic account of his travels in America. The comte de Grasse commanded the French fleet that prevented the English from giving aid to General Cornwallis in that battle. None of these men, though, remained to become American citizens, as Steuben did.

From Poland came the idealistic engineer Thaddeus Kosciusko, who built the fortifications in West Point from 1778 to 1780; and Count Casimir Pulaski, who joined the American army in 1777 after participating in the unsuccessful rebellion in Poland. Commissioned a general in 1778, Pulaski was killed in action in Savannah the next year.

The Hessians: From Enemy Soldiers to American Immigrants

One unexpected consequence of the Revolutionary War was an increase in the German population of the country. Immigration from the Palatinate, as well as from other parts of continental Europe, had become almost impossible, but a new source was opened with the addition of German troops to the British army. During the course of an increasingly unpopular war, England turned to the use of mercenary soldiers from Germany to supplement their own unwilling forces. Renting troops from Europe proved harder than Parliament had expected. Catherine the Great of Russia and the king of Holland flatly refused to hire soldiers out to England. Frederick the Great of Prussia not only forbade his subjects to serve in the British army but refused to allow any other German princes to send soldiers through territories for the purpose. Even George III, the German-born king of England, protested. But Parliament succeeded in finding six German states whose rulers were sufficiently in need of money to agree. As British statesman Edmund Burke wrote, they "snuffed the cadaverous taint of lucrative war" and rented the services of their subjects to the British army. The soldiers were paid about $1.25 a day, and the princes who had sold them into service pocketed a princely fee from England. As more than half of the 30,000 or so troops sent to America were furnished by the ruler of the small state of Hesse-Cassel, the term *Hessian* came to be applied to all German mercenary soldiers.

The evidence suggests that the Hessians were not much interested in the war and, although well trained, did not fight particularly well. Nevertheless, their sheer numbers alarmed the American army. From the beginning, the American government undertook to induce them to desert, printing broadsides to tempt them to join the American side. In August 1776 Congress passed a bill offering free land to any member of the British army who chose to change sides.

In December 1776 General George Washington undertook a daring maneuver. With his small army that had survived the harsh winter, he decided to cross the nearly frozen Delaware River on Christmas Eve and attack the Hessian stronghold in Trenton, New Jersey. Taking advantage of the Germans' Christmas celebration, the little American force attacked at 7:30 the next morning. In less than an hour of fighting, nearly the entire Hessian force was either killed or captured. Washington's troops suffered only five casualties—two men froze to death on the march and three were mortally wounded in the battle. More than 1,000 Hessians were taken prisoner.

The prisoners were treated very well, and a good percentage of them decided to accept the hospitality of the country they had come to fight. When peace came, many more chose to stay and joined their fellow immigrants. Welcomed by German settlers, most became farmers and blended into German communities in Virginia, Pennsylvania, and Maryland.

Post-Revolutionary Immigration

With the signing of the Treaty of Paris in 1783, immigration to the United States resumed on much the same pattern as before, though on a slightly smaller scale. Starting in 1776, colonists loyal to the British began fleeing to Canada, and their places were quickly filled by newcomers eager for the opportunities offered by the emerging nation. Once more the largest number of immigrants were Scotch-Irish, and they were almost as numerous as before. In 1789 the British consul in Philadelphia estimated that more than 20,000 Scotch-Irish immigrants had arrived in Philadelphia in the six years since the end of the war. The volume of immigration to the New World was reduced, but clearly America had lost none of its attraction

George Washington (1732–99), commander of Continental armies and first president of the United States, welcomed immigrants to the new nation. *(New York Public Library Print Collection)*

as an asylum for the oppressed. The Revolution, with its eloquent rhetoric about independence and equality, reinforced the image of America as a refuge from tyranny. George Washington expressed the idea clearly in 1783, the year the Treaty of Paris officially declared the United States a sovereign nation. "The Bosom of America is open to receive not only the Opulent and respectable Stranger," he said to a group of recently arrived Irish immigrants, "but the oppressed and persecuted of all Nations and Religions."

The generosity that the new nation showed in opening its bosom to all was not universal, however. From the beginning of the colonies there had been some suspicion and fear of "foreigners" among the English, and even the founding fathers had reservations about welcoming too many immigrants too quickly. During the war, Washington warned an officer against accepting "those who were not native who offer to enlist," and declined to have any who were not of English background in his personal guard. Benjamin Franklin feared concentrations of immigrants from the same country and found the large German-speaking communities in his native Pennsylvania a threat to national unity. Thomas Jefferson, who had written so movingly on the equality of mankind, was especially alarmed at the idea that Europeans were accustomed to tyranny and that their political opinions and experience would be inconsistent with the American spirit of liberty and freedom. Although he agreed that the new country needed to increase its population, he feared that the addition of large numbers of Europeans would turn the emerging society of America into "a heterogeneous, incoherent, distracted mass."

In the Constitutional Convention of 1787, there was a lively debate about what rights new arrivals should have. Many approved of admitting as many immigrants as could be attracted but felt that foreign-born citizens should not be eligible to hold office. George Mason, the delegate from Virginia who had drawn up the Declaration of Rights for that state, protested that he did not choose "to be governed by foreigners and adventurers." Many also called for a long period of residence before immigrants could apply for citizenship.

In the first Constitutional Congress of 1790, the issues were spelled out clearly and reflected the mixed feelings the public felt toward immigration. Some wanted to throw the doors open to all; others called for a more cautious approach. James Jackson of Georgia, for example, demanded that entry be denied "the common class of vagrants, paupers and other outcasts of Europe." But the majority stood by Washington's declaration that America was open to "the oppressed and persecuted of all Nations and religions." The first national immigration law, issued on March 26, 1790, offered a generous welcome, stating that "any alien, being a free white person, who shall have resided within the limits and under the jurisdiction of the United States for the term of two years, may be admitted to become a citizen thereof, on application to any common law court of record, in any one of the states wherein he shall have resided for the term of one year at least. . . ."

During the first decades of American independence, events abroad brought new sources of immigration. The French Revolution, inspired by the revolution of the United States, brought very different conditions in its wake. While America resolved its conflict peacefully, French society disintegrated into chaos following its revolution, and America became a haven for its royalist refugees. There are no exact records of the number of people who fled the Reign of Terror, but it is estimated at between 10,000 and 25,000. Unlike the waves of immigrants from the British Isles, the French were not seeking economic opportunity or freedom from religious persecution. The thousands of immigrants included royalty and aristocracy fleeing the guillotine, army officers and government officials who had fallen into disfavor, business people such as Eleuthère Irénée du Pont, whose companies had been appropriated by the new French government, and churchmen, including more than 100 Catholic priests. Unlike most other immigrants to the United States of the time, the French viewed their flight as temporary and made no provision for settling in the New World. Some, like du Pont, successfully reestablished their businesses in the United States and made new fortunes, but many did in fact return home as soon as social and political conditions permitted.

The violence generated by the French Revolution was not restricted entirely to its own borders and in some cases led to immigration from other countries. Some people in England who sympathized with the radical ideas of the French Revolution were subjected to such severe discrimination and harassment that they found it impossible to remain in their homes. Joseph Priestley, a clergyman and eminent chemist, favored the ideas of the Revolution so openly that he was hounded out of his house in Birmingham by an angry mob. The 61-year-old scientist immigrated to Pennsylvania in 1794 and never returned. Although he had given up his life work, he found his new home very much to his liking and wrote enthusiastically about it to friends back home in England.

Another wave of French immigration during the post-revolutionary period in America was from the Caribbean. The island of Hispaniola (now occupied by the Dominican Republic and Haiti)—the western third a French colony known as St-Domingue—experienced its own revolution beginning in 1791. St-Domingue was inhabited by 40,000 whites, 28,000 mulattoes (people of mixed African and white parentage) and free blacks, and 500,000 African slaves. When the post-revolution-ary French government granted mulattoes and free blacks some of the same rights as whites enjoyed, the result was a violent demonstration that soon escalated into a full-scale insurrection. Outnumbering whites by almost 10 to 1, the slaves, along with free blacks and others, overthrew the French colonial authorities and estab-lished their own government in 1801. When Napoleon took power the next year, he attempted to reestablish French control of St-Domingue, but the new govern-ment refused to submit. Renamed Haiti, it became the first free black republic in the world on January 1, 1804.

The old slave society of the island was demolished, and life for the whites and mulattoes was made impossible there. Almost the entire white population fled, and at least 10,000 former slave owners, businessmen, and artisans found their way to North America. A cross section of St-Domingue society, they were even more help-less than most immigrants, many of them unable to speak English and possessing no more than the clothes they wore. The majority found their way to Charleston, Norfolk, Baltimore, Philadelphia, or New York, where federal, state, and local gov-ernments contributed to their support. Congress voted $15,000 of relief monies to this new, unexpected wave of French immigrants in 1794.

A smaller stimulant to French immigration, and one with less significant inter-national consequences, was a land-development scheme that originated at about the same time. The so-called Scioto Company, operating in Paris, offered land for sale in the still undeveloped Ohio Valley in 1790, and its promotional literature described the region in glowing terms. They planned to build a town called Gal-lipolis (meaning "French City") and promised a paradise in which the settler could become rich in a short time and with little effort. But although the Scioto Company charged $1.20 an acre, the market value of the land was really no more than six or seven cents an acre, and life there was not nearly so easy as the brochures promised. Furthermore, there were legal disputes about the rights to the land, the Indians of the area treated the invading settlers with hostility, and many of the pioneers came down with fever. The Scioto Company went bankrupt, and the 500 or 600 hopeful adventurers who had set out from Paris five years before were left stranded in the wilderness with nothing but a lawsuit to show for their investment.

An enterprising group, the hapless victims of the Scioto Company's scheme, were welcome additions to America and found their way into society with few problems. The sudden influx of French immigrants in flight from the revolutions in France and St-Domingue, however, were more alarming. Even liberal legislators feared that a stream of Royalists might be a threat to the democratic institutions of the new nation. Pressure to protect the country from alien corruption grew, and in 1795 the Naturalization Act of 1790 was amended to require five years' residence

Toussaint Louverture (ca. 1743–1803) was a Haitian rebel leader whose overthrow of French colonial authority in St-Domingue ended slavery in his country and eventually sent a stream of immigrants to the United States. *(Photographs and Prints Division, Schomburg Center for Research in Black Culture, New York Public Library)*

to qualify an immigrant for citizenship. Even that did not satisfy all the conservatives. A nervous Congress added to the Naturalization Act of 1795 the requirement that any alien seeking citizenship "absolutely and entirely renounce and abjure all allegiance and fidelity to every foreign prince, potentate, state or sovereignty whatever, and particularly, by name, the prince, potentate, state or sovereignty, whereof he was before a citizen or subject." Furthermore, to make the United States's safety from European political ideas even more secure, the Act required that "in case the alien applying to be admitted to citizenship shall have borne any hereditary title, or been of any of the orders of nobility, in the kingdom or state from which he came, he shall . . . make an express renunciation of his title or order of nobility. . . ."

The Alien and Sedition Acts

The rejection of aristocrats reflected in the order that aliens renounce any titles or orders of nobility was only one part of the feeling of distrust and hostility Americans felt toward the French in the late 1790s. In 1798 a scandal generated powerful anti-French feelings. In that year the French foreign minister Talleyrand attempted to exact a bribe from an American trade mission in France to negotiate a treaty; when the story broke in the United States, the public was outraged, and its anger spread from the French to all foreign residents. At the point of going to war, the country made life very difficult for French refugees from the royalist revolutions in France and St-Domingue in particular and all foreign-born citizens in general. President John Adams, in response to what the public saw as a threat from aliens and alien ideas in the country, proposed a series of four laws that became known as the Alien and Sedition Acts. Congress willingly approved them.

These laws began with a new Naturalization Act on June 18, 1798, extending from five to 14 years the period an alien had to live in the United States before applying for citizenship. This prevented (for a while) any of the new arrivals—especially the French Royalists at whom it was directed—from becoming citizens and influencing American law with their vote for a while. Some wanted the law to be even stronger. Virginia politician Robert Goodloe Harper stated on the floor of the House of Representatives in 1798 that "the time is now come when it shall be proper to declare that nothing but birth shall entitle a man to citizenship in this country."

The second law, the Alien Act, passed June 25, gave the president wide powers over any resident alien, allowing him at his own discretion "to order all such aliens as he shall judge dangerous to the peace and safety of the United States, or shall have reasonable grounds to suspect are concerned in any treasonable or secret machinations against the government thereof, to depart out of the territory of the United States. . . . And in case any alien, so ordered to depart, shall be found at large within the United States after the time limited in such order for his departure . . . every such alien shall . . . be imprisoned for a term not exceeding three years, and shall never be admitted to become a citizen of the United States." This law, commonly referred to as the Alien Friends Act, gave the president powers that many felt to be those of a king, including the arbitrary authority to seize and expel a foreigner at will, without due process of law. The Act was never enforced, but it created a climate of such terror for immigrants, especially for French refugees, that several shiploads fled the country, preferring the dangers of France or St-Domingue to those of their new homes. Other French immigrants went into hiding.

On July 6 of that year, Congress passed the Alien Enemies Act, which stated that in time of war "all natives, citizens, denizens, or subjects of the hostile nation or government, being males of the age of fourteen years and upwards, who shall be within the United States, and not actually naturalized, shall be liable to be apprehended, restrained, secured and removed, as alien enemies. And the President of the United States shall be, and he is hereby authorized . . . to provide for the removal of those, who, not being permitted to reside within the United States, shall refuse or neglect to depart therefrom. . . ." The Alien Enemies Act was passed because everyone expected a war with France at any moment. However, the war never came, and consequently this law too was never enforced during Adams's administration.

The Sedition Act, passed on July 14, was perhaps the most controversial of all. That law made it a crime—punishable by a $2,000 fine and a two-year prison term—to "write, print, utter, or publish, or . . . cause or procure to be written, printed, uttered, or published, . . . any false, scandalous and malicious writing or writings against the government of the United States, . . . or the President of the United States, with intent to defame the said government, or the said President, or to bring them . . . into contempt or disrepute; or to excite against them . . . the hatred of the good people of the United States." This act was not directed specifically against immigrants, but most of the journalists and pamphleteers in the United States were foreign-born. The primary aim of this law was to silence the antigovernment press, but it resulted in the arrest of 25 editors and newspaper writers. Ten of those arrested, including patriot-poet Philip Freneau, were convicted and were sent to prison; many others were ruined professionally and many newspapers were closed down. The first victim of the Sedition Act was Matthew Lyon, an Irish-born congressman from Vermont, who went to prison for writing a letter criticizing President Adams to an opposition newspaper.

It wasn't only in the United States that the Alien and Sedition Acts had an effect; they influenced immigration from other countries, directly or indirectly. An attempted rebellion in Ireland in 1798 resulted in the creation of a large group of political prisoners, whom the British agreed to pardon if they went to America; many accepted this pardon, as they were eager to start their lives afresh in the New World. But the Alien and Sedition Acts, and the antiforeign climate they reflected, led to the prisoners' being rejected for entry to the United States on the grounds that the revolutionaries would not be "a desirable acquisition to any nation."

The Alien and Sedition Acts did little to strengthen American feeling against immigrants; on the contrary, they aroused so much antagonism against the government that in 1800 Adams's opponent Thomas Jefferson was elected president. The first of the unpopular acts was repealed in 1802 when the Naturalization Act of 1795 was reenacted; the remaining three were not renewed when they expired in 1801 and 1802.

Immigration Revives

The wave of anti-French sentiment following the French Revolution passed as the threat of war passed and it became apparent that the French refugees were not spies of Royalist agitators. In fact, when the post-revolutionary Reign of Terror ended in France, many French aristocrats went back home as soon as they could raise enough for the passage money; the rest generally remained aloof from American politics. The Alien and Sedition Acts had little effect on American immigration policy once they ceased to be in effect. The principal consequence of these laws, in fact, was the reverse of what was intended. Instead of increasing the power of President Adams's political party, the Federalists, they turned much of the country against them and helped secure the strength of Thomas Jefferson's Democratic-Republican Party. The German and French communities, which had been indifferent to what went on in the government until then, now became solidly opposed to the Federalists and supported Jefferson in his campaign for president in 1800.

Apart from the period of antiforeign agitation at the end of the 1790s, the rate of immigration remained relatively stable. The second census, taken in 1800, revealed a 35 percent increase in population, from about 4 million to 5.3 million, with about the same breakdown of national origins. Despite tensions between pro- and anti-immigration factions, the nation still looked to Europe to help populate its vast area. When the nine counties of the Northwest Territory were divided into an east part and a west part (called Indiana Territory) in 1800, the national government actively encouraged westward migration to develop it. At the recommendation of William Henry Harrison, governor of Indiana Territory and later ninth president of the United States, Congress passed the Land Act, offering public land on easier credit terms. Known as the Harrison Act, the law also established a lower minimum acreage requirement. In 1804 a second Land Act further reduced the acreage minimum, allowing the sale of 160-acre units, and lowered the price from $2.00 to $1.64 per acre. The public—native-born and immigrant—was quick to respond, though most of the purchases were by speculators rather than by pioneers.

Although immigration did not increase during the years following the Revolutionary War, the steady stream of arrivals took its toll on the population of Europe. The constant wars between 1790 and 1815 required manpower, and the flight to America of able-bodied men and women was a drain on the human resources of several countries. Great Britain had long banned emigration of skilled laborers from England, and in 1788 its government prohibited the departure of artisans from Ireland as well. By the end of the 1790s the depletion of the labor force from the British Isles had become critical, and the government passed its first restriction on the carrying of passengers to the New World. The Passenger Act of 1803—the first of several enacted during the 19th century—prohibited British ships from carrying more than one traveler or crew member for each two tons of unladen weight to any point in North America except Newfoundland and Labrador. Foreign ships leaving from English ports could take only one person for each five tons.

The official reason for the Passenger Act was to improve conditions on transatlantic voyages and eliminate the evils of overcrowding, but the principal objective was to restrict emigration and protect England from loss of skilled labor. Not only did the act diminish the actual number of people who could leave the country, it discouraged emigration by driving up the price of the voyage. In this it was very successful. Passengers on Irish ships leaving Londonderry and Belfast, which for years had averaged 400 to 500 per voyage, fell to about a total of only a thousand a year after 1803. Middle-class travel was not affected—businessmen and property-owners could afford the costly fares—but the business of importing servants through the indenture system became economically impossible to sustain and virtually disappeared overnight.

If 1803 marked a sharp drop in immigration to the United States with the Passenger Act, it also witnessed an event that would draw millions of new residents to the nation. President Jefferson, concerned about the threat to American security that a vast French territory sharing the continent posed, decided to purchase the port city of New Orleans in the French-held Louisiana Territory. With control of that city, the country would also be sure of access to the Mississippi River as a route for western commerce. In 1803 he sent an envoy to Paris to make Napoleon an offer for it.

France had acquired the Louisiana Territory when it defeated Spain just two years before, and although Napoleon wanted an empire in the New World, he realized that he had neither the money nor the manpower to maintain the territory. He had just lost Haiti, and without that strategic foothold in the Western Hemisphere, he was powerless to defend or exploit the land he commanded on the North American continent. Seeing the opportunity to rid himself of a responsibility he was unprepared to meet and make some sorely needed money at the same time, he offered to sell the entire Louisiana Territory.

The United States, a scant 20 years old, was hardly prepared to assimilate a huge tract of foreign property, but the modest price of 80 million francs (equivalent to about $15 million) was impossible to refuse. The territory was as large as the United States and several times the size of France; its 828,000 square miles stretched from the Mississippi River to the Rocky Mountains and from the Gulf of Mexico to Canada. With the Louisiana Purchase, the United States more than doubled in size. Its French-speaking residents—French citizens until the day later in that year when the territory became American soil—and the many Indian tribes inhabiting the Great Plains and the Rocky Mountains were an important addition to the populace.

When explorers had a chance to see something of the immense, rich territory the country had acquired, their descriptions of the fruitful fields and virgin forests of what was to become Iowa, Missouri, Arkansas, Minnesota, Kansas, Nebraska, the Dakotas, Colorado, Montana, and Oregon inspired dreams in land-hungry farmers throughout Europe. Drawn by their accounts, many others would cross the ocean in the years to come.

The Second War for Independence

Although the United States was prospering internally and discovering the almost infinite resources of its unmapped land, the Napoleonic Wars between England and France made international trade impossible and prevented any significant economic growth. As difficult as it was to break through the restrictions and elevated costs of immigration, England added another deterrent that increased the difficulty still further. English ships stopped American vessels to search for British-born seamen, whom they seized and forced to serve in their short-handed navy, and both France, under Napoleon, and England, under George III, took over any American vessel that did business with the other. American trade was on the verge of ruin. In 1806 Congress attempted a boycott, forbidding the sale of certain British products in the United States in hopes of putting enough pressure on England to force a treaty, but it had no success.

Determined to remain neutral, the United States avoided conflict, but in June 1807 an event occurred that drove even the most cautious to take a firm position for war: An English frigate fired on the United States Navy ship *Chesapeake.* Three American sailors were killed, and 18 were badly wounded. The English crew forcibly boarded her and removed four men they claimed were English deserters. Later it was discovered that one of the sailors taken was in fact guilty, but the other three were American citizens. The issue had gone beyond that of freedom of the seas; England had committed a violation of international law by seizing American citizens. Jefferson demanded an apology for the insult to the country's national sovereignty. The English responded that they intended to pursue the policy of search and seizure even more vigorously in the future.

Still, the young nation was determined not to provoke an open confrontation. In December 1807 Congress tried a stronger measure, establishing an embargo that prohibited all trade with any of the belligerent nations, a classification that included much of the continent. The next year Napoleon issued a decree ordering that any American ships in French or Italian ports be seized, on the grounds that since America had passed an embargo, such ships were in violation of American law.

The next year the Embargo Act was repealed because it had been so costly to the American shipping industry that it couldn't be sustained. As a final resort, Congress enacted a Non-Intercourse Act, which opened trade with all nations except England and France and authorized the president to resume trade with either of those powers if either agreed to respect America's maritime rights. The government hoped that their need for American supplies would make the two combatants come to terms. But this act was no more effective than the others had been.

In 1810, when the United States examined the results of its third census, the figures showed that the country's population had grown by almost 2 million, advancing by 36.4 percent over the previous decade. Clearly the young nation, now twice its former size with the addition of the Louisiana Territory, had become large enough to stand up for itself. National pride and frustration generated a spirit of defiance. The congressional election of 1810 reflected a growing desire for war as many young senators from the West and the South called for it. These "War Hawks" represented voters who were indignant at the treatment the country had received but also hungry for more land. Western farmers, looking for new territory to settle, found Canada tempting and saw a war with England as an opportunity to invade and appropriate it. Southerners eyed Florida, ruled by England's ally Spain, with the same idea.

Another ground for hostility was the belief that the English in Canada and the Spanish in Florida were conspiring with the Indians to raid American settlements. There was enough evidence of this to add fuel to the fire. Following a surprise attack by Indians in November 1811, General Harrison, the governor of Indiana Territory, led an assault on Shawnee Indian chief Tecumseh's village on the Tippecanoe River. There the American troops found a supply of British weapons. This was seen as proof that the British were supporting the Indian raids and as a justification for going to war.

The 12th Congress, meeting in November 1811, was led by War Hawks, and their voices were clear. America had been isolated from Europe by the Napoleonic Wars for nearly five years and decisive action could no longer be avoided. There was nothing to be gained from a war with France, but a war with England could bring rewards. In addition to the freedom of the seas and an end to Indian raids, it could justify the conquest of land in Canada and Florida. Accordingly, in June 1812 President James Madison asked Congress to declare war on England. When England learned of the plan, it lifted its blockade on American ships, but by then it was too late. Congress declared war on June 18.

The War of 1812 lasted for nearly three years, but neither its objectives nor its cause was ever very clearly defined. Many opposed it, especially those in New England. Neither side was fully committed to "The Second War for Independence," as it was called. The United States was poorly prepared and equipped and far from unanimous in its support of the war. Luckily for the Americans, however, England was busy fighting France and had little interest in challenging its former colonies over maritime rights. It was said that the war came to an end when both sides were too tired of it to continue. The British burned the White House and the Capitol building in Washington, but there were no great, decisive battles that turned the tide of the war. When England defeated the French in 1814, everyone involved had had enough. The combatants decided to bring it to an end on Christmas Eve of that year.

Neither side had gained any land or established any authority, but the battle helped define the relationship of the two countries. There were other conflicts to follow, but all differences between England and the United States were settled by law from that point on. Immigration, which had come to a complete end with the declaration of war, began to flow freely again. Now, with no obstacles from Europe and with almost limitless land to explore and exploit, the flow would soon turn into a flood.

Chronicle of Events

1776

- The Anglican church is disestablished in Virginia. By 1790 it has lost its official status in all colonies where it had been tax-supported.
- Trade relations with England are strained. American trade with Holland, France, and Spain increases.
- *January 10*: Thomas Paine's pamphlet *Common Sense* is published, attacking English colonialism and arousing a strong feeling for independence.
- *March 17*: American General Knox threatens to besiege Boston. British and Loyalist American residents evacuate the city and sail to Halifax, Nova Scotia.
- *April 6*: Congress opens ports to all nations except Britain.
- *April 9*: Congress passes a resolution prohibiting the importation of slaves into the colonies.
- *May 1–July 5*: American troops retreat from Canada after abandoning their siege of Quebec.
- *May 2*: France sends $1 million worth of munitions to America.
- *May 9–16*: American troops attack the Bahamas, capture Nassau, and seize a large quantity of military supplies.
- *June 10*: Spain provides the American army with arms.
- *June 28*: The Declaration of Independence, prepared by Thomas Jefferson, is presented to the Continental Congress. The British attack Charleston, South Carolina.
- *June 29*: British General Sir William Howe and his brother Admiral Lord Richard Howe arrive in New York harbor with a large fleet to begin an invasion of the colonies.
- *July 2*: General Howe transports an army of 10,000 British soldiers from Halifax to Staten Island, New York.
- *July 4*: Congress approves the Declaration of Independence.
- *July 12*: Reinforcements bring the total number of English troops and German mercenaries on Staten Island to 32,000.
- *August 12*: Congress passes a bill granting free land to deserters from the British army.
- *August 22*: In the Battle of Long Island, the British successfully besiege Brooklyn with 20,000 troops.
- *August 29*: The American army evacuates Long Island.
- *September 15*: The British occupy New York City.
- *September 21*: Fire destroys much of New York City. The population of the city, America's second largest after Philadelphia, is 22,000.
- *October 9*: Spanish Franciscan missionaries found the settlement of San Francisco de Asis, now San Francisco, California.
- *October 28*: George Washington inflicts heavy casualties on General Howe's army in the battle of White Plains.
- *December 11*: Washington retreats across the Delaware River into Pennsylvania.
- *December 26*: Washington recrosses the Delaware River and defeats the Hessians in a surprise attack at Trenton, New Jersey. Nearly 1,000 Hessians and a large supply of military supplies are captured, with a loss of only five American soldiers. Many Hessian soldiers elect to remain in the United States.

1777

- *January 3*: Washington defeats Cornwallis's troops at Princeton, New Jersey.
- *March 4*: Congress meets to solicit foreign aid. During the next few months it recruits Marquis de Lafayette and Count de Grasse from France, Baron de Kalb and Baron von Steuben from Germany, and Count Casimir Pulaski and Thaddeus Kosciusko from Poland.
- *June 17–October 17*: British general John Burgoyne leads an invasion from Canada, intending to join General Howe in New York.
- *September 11–26*: British General Howe defeats Washington's troops and occupies Philadelphia; Congress flees to Lancaster and then to York, Pennsylvania.
- *October 4*: Washington is defeated near Germantown, Pennsylvania, and later stations his army at Valley Forge.
- *October 7*: General John Burgoyne is defeated at Albany and retreats to Saratoga.
- *October 16*: British general Sir Henry Clinton marches north from New York City to meet and reinforce Burgoyne. He turns back after besieging and burning Kingston, New York.
- *October 17*: General Burgoyne surrenders with 5,700 men in Saratoga, New York. His army is sent back to England.
- *November 15*: Congress passes the Articles of Confederation and presents them to the states for ratification.
- *December 17*: France recognizes American independence.

1778

- *February 6*: France and the United States sign treaties of alliance and commerce, agreeing to support America's claim to any territory it conquers in Bermuda and Canada and France's claim to territory it conquers in the West Indies.

- *August 8*: The French and Americans jointly attack British forces in Newport, Rhode Island, but are turned back.
- *December 29*: The British capture Savannah, Georgia.

1779

- *January 29*: The British take Augusta, Georgia.
- *September 3*: The American army unsuccessfully attacks Savannah, Georgia. General Pulaski is killed.

1780

- *February 1*: A large British fleet arrives off the coast of the Carolinas to support an attack on Charleston. The attack begins on March 8.
- *May 12*: Charleston falls to the British under General Sir Henry Clinton, with a loss of 5,000 American troops, 300 cannons, five naval vessels, and a large store of military supplies.
- *August 16*: The British under General Cornwallis triumph at the Battle of Camden, South Carolina. Seven hundred of the 3,000 American troops, including General de Kalb, are killed.

1781

- *January 1*: Congress issues $191,000,000 in paper money.
- *March 1*: With ratification by Maryland, the Articles of Confederation are approved.
- *May 20*: France makes a large loan to the United States.
- *July*: Comte de Rochambeau brings French troops to support Washington's army at White Plains, New York.
- *August 30*: Admiral François de Grasse arrives with 28 ships off the Virginia coast; the next day he lands an army of French soldiers near Jamestown to join Lafayette in his blockade of Chesapeake Bay.
- *September 4*: Spanish Franciscan missionaries found the settlement of El Pueblo de Nuestra Señora la Reina de los Angeles de Porciuncula, now Los Angeles, California.
- *September 14–23*: The armies of Washington and Rochambeau move from the Chesapeake to Williamsburg, Virginia, to attack Cornwallis at Yorktown, nine miles away.
- *October 19*: General Cornwallis surrenders at Yorktown; the Revolutionary War comes to an end.
- *November 5*: The Netherlands approves a large financial loan to the United States.

1782

- *January 1*: The first wave of Loyalist emigration from the United States begins. Many leave New England and New York for Canada.
- *April 19*: The Netherlands recognizes United States independence.
- *October 8*: The United States and the Netherlands sign a treaty of commerce and friendship.

1783

- *February 3*: Spain recognizes United States independence.
- *April 26*: About 7,000 American Loyalists leave from New York harbor for Canada in the largest single emigration from the United States.
- *September 3*: The Treaty of Paris, officially ending the American Revolution, is signed by representatives of Great Britain and the United States. Immigration from the British Isles, suspended during the war, revives, the greatest increase being those of Scotch-Irish descent.
- *December 31*: All northern states and Maryland, Delaware, and Virginia prohibit the slave trade.

1784

- *February 22*: *The Empress of China* begins a six-month voyage from New York harbor to Canton to initiate trade with the Far East.
- *September 22*: A Russian settlement is established at Three Saints Bay on Kodiak Island, Alaska.
- *December 24*: The Virginia House of Delegates rejects a bill to support all churches equally by taxes.

1785

- *February 7*: Georgia annexes territory (most of it in the present-day states of Mississippi and Alabama) claimed by Spain as part of its Florida lands.
- *February 28*: The British refuse to evacuate posts on Lakes Ontario and Michigan and in western New York, in compliance with the Treaty of Paris, because America has failed to pay its prewar debts to British merchants.
- *May 15*: *The Empress of China* returns with valuable merchandise from Canton.
- *September 20*: John Adams negotiates a trade treaty with Russia.
- *October 10*: Spain demands restoration of land in Florida annexed by the state of Georgia.

1786

- *March 1*: The Ohio Company, a land speculating group, is founded in Boston to purchase 1.5 million acres of land north of the Ohio River to establish permanent settlements. The Northwest Territory ultimately composes five states.
- *August–September*: Several demonstrations to protest taxes and court costs disrupt court proceedings in Massachusetts.
- *December 26*: About 1,100 armed insurgents gather in Springfield, Massachusetts, under Daniel Shays to demand economic reforms. The troop prepares an attack on the federal arsenal.

1787

- *January 27–February 4*: Shays's Rebellion—protests by farmers against high taxation—is subdued by a federal militia, and the insurgents are scattered. One hundred fifty rebels are arrested and 14 of them are sentenced to death, but all are either pardoned or released after short prison terms.
- *July 13*: The Northwest Ordinance is passed, establishing a government for the Northwest Territory.
- *December 20*: The Shakers, or Shaking Quakers (United Society of Believers in Christ's Second Appearing), initiate a fervent religious revival that spreads to other denominations.

1788

- England extends to Ireland its ban on the emigration of skilled labor.

1789

- *February 4*: Washington is elected the first president of the United States; John Adams, with the second highest vote, becomes vice president.
- *May 7*: The Church of England in the United States is renamed the Protestant Episcopal Church.
- *July 14*: The French Revolution begins. Many French aristocrats and Royalists emigrate to America during the next decade.

1790

- The first census of the United States reports nearly 4 million inhabitants. The largest state is Virginia, with a population of more than 820,000. Nearly 20 percent of the national population is African or African American; 63.6 percent of the white population is from, or descended from natives of, the British Isles.

- *March 26*: Congress passes the Naturalization Act, the first national immigration law, requiring a two-year residence for naturalization.

1791

- A slave revolt in St-Domingue (present-day Haiti) leads to the widespread flight of French whites. Between 10,000 and 20,000 inhabitants, virtually the entire white population, seek refuge in the United States.

1792

- *December 5*: Washington and Adams are reelected.

1793

- *April 22*: The United States declares itself neutral in the war that has broken out between France and England.

1794

- *June 5*: Congress passes the Neutrality Act, forbidding U.S. citizens to enlist in the service of any other country.
- *August 20*: General Anthony Wayne defeats an Indian army at the Battle of Fallen Timbers in the northwestern Ohio territory, ending concerted Indian resistance in the area.
- *November 19*: The United States and Britain negotiate an agreement in which Britain promises to withdraw from its remaining posts in America by June 1, 1796, and America agrees to pay its remaining debts to British subjects.

1795

- *January 29*: Congress amends the 1790 Naturalization Act, extending the residence requirement to five years.
- *August 3*: The United States signs the treaty of Greenville, whereby Indians surrender a large area in present-day Ohio and Indiana.
- *October 27*: Spain and the United States sign the Treaty of San Lorenzo, defining the border between Spanish Florida and Georgia and granting free navigation of the Mississippi River.

1797

- *March 4*: John Adams is inaugurated as second president of the United States.

1798

- Unsuccessful rebellion in Ireland leads to a wave of Irish immigration. Fugitive rebels and impoverished workers look for safety and opportunity in America.

- *June 18–July 14*: Congress passes the four Alien and Sedition Acts. These highly unpopular laws make it more difficult for immigrants to become citizens, give the president discretionary power to deport, authorize the president to arrest and imprison aliens in time of war, and provide for the arrest of anyone who writes or speaks against the president, Congress, or the government.

1800

- Second national census shows a 35 percent increase in population, which has reached more than 5.3 million. More than 1 million inhabitants are African or African American, nine-tenths of them slaves. Virginia, with 900,000 inhabitants, remains the most populous state, followed by Pennsylvania, New York, and Massachusetts, with about 600,000 each.
- *May 10*: The Land Act of 1800 (Harrison Act) establishes easy credit terms and a lower minimum acreage requirement for purchase of public lands, stimulating widespread speculation and westward migration.

1801

- *January*: French immigrant businessman Eleuthère Irénée du Pont founds E. I. Du Pont de Nemours, a gunpowder plant, in Wilmington, Delaware.
- *March 4*: Thomas Jefferson is inaugurated the third president of the United States.

1803

- England passes the Passenger Act, its first restriction on carrying passengers from the British Isles to America, in order to discourage the emigration of skilled workers.
- *April 30*: France sells the United States the Louisiana Territory, comprising about 828,000 square miles, for 80 million francs (about $15 million). Ratified on October 21, the purchase more than doubles the size of the United States, adding land that was to become all or part of 13 states to the nation.

1804

- *March 26*: The Land Act reduces the minimum price per acre for public lands from $2.00 to $1.64 and authorizes the sale of 160-acre units.
- *May 14*: The Lewis and Clark Expedition to explore the Louisiana Territory begins by sailing up the Missouri River from St. Louis.

1805

- War between England and France continues to disrupt international trade and limit immigration to America.

Both countries forbid neutral vessels to touch at a port of an enemy or an enemy's ally, and England stops American ships to search for British-born seamen, who are seized and forced into British service.
- *March 4*: Thomas Jefferson is inaugurated for a second term as president.
- *November 8*: Lewis and Clark reach the Pacific Ocean, completing the first land crossing of the continent.

1806

- *April 18*: Congress passes the Non-Importation Act boycotting certain British products.

1807

- *March 2*: Congress prohibits the importation of slaves into the United States.
- *June 22*: The U.S.S. *Chesapeake* is forcibly boarded by an English ship, three American seamen are killed, and four are taken off as British deserters. It is later discovered that three of the four seized were American citizens.
- *July 2*: Jefferson orders all British warships out of American waters.
- *December 22*: Congress passes an Embargo Act forbidding all foreign trade into or out of the United States in response to Britain's seizure of American seamen.

1808

- *April 17*: Napoleon issues the Bayonne Decrees ordering the seizure of any American ship in French or Italian ports.
- *July 8*: German immigrant John Jacob Astor incorporates the American Fur Company in New York City.
- *September 8*: The Osage cede most of their lands in Louisiana Territory, constituting most of present-day Missouri and Arkansas, to the United States. They are removed to a reservation in present-day Oklahoma.

1809

- *March 1*: The Embargo Act of 1807 has proved so damaging to the American shipping industry that it is repealed. In its place Congress passes the Non-Intercourse Act prohibiting trade with either France or Great Britain until American rights are respected.
- *March 4*: James Madison is inaugurated as the fourth president of the United States.
- *July 2*: Tecumseh, a Shawnee chief, organizes an Indian Confederacy to oppose further white settlement. More than 30 million acres north of the Ohio River have been acquired from the Indians during the past seven years.

1810

- The third U.S. census shows a population of over 7,239,000, a gain of almost 2 million inhabitants, or 36.4 percent, in 10 years.
- *March 23*: Napoleon orders the seizure of all American ships in French waters.
- *August 5*: Napoleon imposes high duties on American goods.
- *October 27*: Madison declares the part of West Florida between New Orleans and the Pearl River, claimed by Spain, for the United States.

1811

- *April 12*: Fort Astoria, a fur trading post financed by John Jacob Astor, is established on the Pacific Coast.
- *November 8*: General William Henry Harrison, governor of the Indiana Territory, launches an attack on Tecumseh in response to an Indian ambush. Tecumseh's headquarters, an Indian village on the Tippecanoe River, is destroyed.

1812

- *June 1*: Madison asks Congress to declare war on Great Britain because of its policy of taking seamen from American ships.
- *June 18*: Congress declares war. All immigration to the United States comes to an end.
- *July 1*: A high tariff is enacted to support the war.
- *August 16*: Fort Dearborn (now Chicago, Illinois) is taken by the English, who massacre the garrison and burn the fort. The garrison at Detroit, Michigan, surrenders to the British without resistance.
- *August 19*: The U.S. frigate *Constitution* destroys the British ship *Guerrière* and takes its crew prisoner.
- *October 25*: The U.S.S. *United States* captures the British ship *Macedonian* off Connecticut.
- *December 29*: The U.S.S. *Constitution* destroys the British ship *Java* off the coast of Brazil.

Eyewitness Testimony

Jan. 23rd

This day I being reduced to the last shilling I had was obliged to engage to go to Virginia for four years as a schoolmaster for Bedd, Board, washing and five pounds during the whole time. . . .

May 2nd

At 2 pm Capt. Carried 5 servts ashore to Hampton in order to sell their Indentures, But returned again at Midnight without selling any more but one Boat Builder.

May 11th

This day severall came onbd. to purchase servts. Indentures and among them there were two Soul drivers. These are men who make it their business to go onbd. All ships who have either Servants or Convicts and buy sometimes the whole and sometimes a parcell of them as they can agree, and then they drive them through the Country like a parcell of Sheep untill they can sell them to advantage, but all went away without buying any.

May 17th

This day Mr. Anderson the Mercht. sent for me into the cabin and verry genteely told me that on my recommendations he would do his outmost to get me settled as a Clerk or bookkeeper if not as a schoolmaster which last he told me he thought wou'd turn out more to my advantage upon being settled in a good family.

May 23rd

This morning a great number of Gentlemen and Ladies driving into Town it being an annual Fair day and tomorrow the day of the Horse Races. At 11 am Mr. Anderson begged me to settle as a schoolmaster with a friend of his one Colonel Daingerfield and told me he was to be in Town tomorrow, or perhaps tonight, and how soon he came he shou'd acquant me. At same time all the rest of the servants were ordered ashore to a tent at Frederickbg. And brought to Colonel Daingerfield, when we immediately agreed and my Indenture for 4 years was then delivered him and he was to send for me the next day.

John Harrower, an indentured servant in the Virginia Colony, journal entries, 1774, in Sandler, Rozwenc, and Martin, The People Make a Nation *(1971), pp. 41–43.*

But Britain is the parent country, say some. Then the more shame upon her for her conduct. Even brutes do not devour their young nor savages make war upon their families; . . . Europe, and not England, is the parent country of America. This New World has been the asylum for the persecuted lovers of civil and religious liberty from *every part* of Europe. Hither have they fled, not from the tender embraces of the mother, but from the cruelty of the monster; and it is so far true of England that the same tyranny which drove the first emigrants from home pursues their descendants still.

Thomas Paine, British-born American patriot and pamphleteer, in Common Sense *(1953; first published 1776), p. 21.*

Americans are properly Britons. They have the manners, habits, and ideas of Britons; and have been accustomed to a similar form of government. . . .

America, till very lately, has been the happiest country in the universe. Blessed with all that nature could bestow with the profusest bounty, she enjoyed, besides, more liberty, greater privileges than any other land. . . .

But if America should now mistake her real interest—if her sons, infatuated with romantic notions of conquest and empire, ere things are rife, should adopt this republican's scheme—they will infallibly destroy this smiling prospect. They will dismember this happy

Thomas Paine's eloquent words describing America as a haven for European lovers of liberty helped spark the Revolutionary War. *(From* The Pictorial Field Book of the Revolution, *2 vols., by B. J. Lossing. New York: Harper Brothers, 1851 and 1852.)*

country, make it a scene of blood and slaughter, and entail wretchedness and misery on millions yet unborn.

Charles Inglis, Irish missionary, in The True Interest of America Impartially Stated, in Certain Strictures on a Pamphlet Intitled Common Sense, *a pamphlet opposing the American Revolution and disputing the conclusions in Thomas Paine's* Common Sense *(1776), in Bruno Leone,* Opposing Viewpoints in American History, *Volume 1 (1996), pp. 106, 108.*

[T]he residents are the friendliest and most courteous in America no matter what their standing and their opinion. Tories and [Whigs] are hospitable and obliging to everyone, especially strangers. The women are pretty, courteous, friendly and modest . . .; we enjoyed a great deal of civility from them and not-with-standing the fact that we are enemies, they gave us a great preference over their own men at balls and other occasions.

Andreas Wiederholdt, a Hessian officer taken prisoner by the American army describing his treatment in a journal entry of December 26, 1776, in Galicich, The German Americans *(1989), p. 42.*

Monday, January 6, 1777. News that Washington has taken 760 Hessian prisoners at Trenton. . . . Hope it is a lie. . . .

Tuesday, January 7, 1777. The news is confirmed. The minds of the people are much altered. A few days ago they had given up the cause for lost. Their late successes have turned the scale and now they are all liberty-mad again. Their recruiting parties could not get a man . . . no longer since than last week, and now the men are coming in by companies. Confound the turncoat scoundrels and Hessians together. . . . This has given them new spirits . . . and will prolong the war, perhaps for two years. . . .

January 17, 1777. . . . Poor General Howe [a British general] is ridiculed in all companies and all my countrymen abused. I am obliged to hear this daily and dare not speak a word in their favor. It is the . . . Hessians that have caused this, curse the scoundrel that first thought of sending them here.

Nicholas Cresswell, a Loyalist living near Alexandria, Virginia, diary entries of January 6–17, 1777, in Peck, Jantzen, and Rosen, American Adventures *(1983), pp. 97–98.*

You should be extremely cautious in your inquiries into the character of those who are not natives who offer to enlist. Desertions among men of that class have been so frequent that unless you find 'em on examination to be of good and unsuspicious conduct, they should not be taken by any means. Otherwise, most probably, they will deceive you—add no strength to our arms, but much expense to the Public account and upon first opportunity will join the Enemy.

George Washington, letter to an army officer of June 19, 1777, in Writings of George Washington, *Volume V, (1889), p. 441.*

The misery and distress which your ill-fated country has been so frequently exposed to, and has so often experienced, by such a combination of rapine, treachery, and violence, as would have disgraced the name of government, in the most arbitrary country in the world, has most sincerely affected your friends in America, and has engaged the most serious attention of congress; . . .

When I had the pleasure of residing in your capital some years ago, it gave me pain to observe such a debility and morbid langour in every department of your government, as would have disgraced anarchy itself; the laws are too weak to execute themselves, and vice and violence often reign with impunity; and even the military with you seem to claim an exemption from all civil restraint, or jurisdiction, and individuals are forced to trust to themselves for that security and protection which the government of the country can no longer afford them. We congratulate you however, on the bright prospect which the western hemisphere has afforded to you, and the oppressed of every nation, and we trust that the liberation of your country has been effected in America, and that you never will be called on for those painful, though necessary exertions, which the sacred love of liberty inspires, and which have enabled us to establish our freedom forever.

Benjamin Franklin, "To the Good People of Ireland," letter of October 4, 1778, from Versailles, France, in Niles, Principles and Acts of the Revolution in America: or, An Attempt to Collect and Preserve Some of the Speeches, Orations & Proceedings . . . Belonging to the Revolutionary Period in the United States *(1822), pp. 382–84.*

But are there no inconveniences to be thrown into the scale against the advantage expected from a multiplication of numbers by the importation of foreigners? . . . Suppose twenty millions of republican Americans thrown all of a sudden into France, what would be the condition of that kingdom? If it would be more turbulent, less happy, less strong, we may believe that the addition of half a million of foreigners to our present number would produce a similar effect here.

If they come of themselves they are entitled to all the rights of citizenship; but I doubt the expedience of inviting them by extraordinary encouragements.

Thomas Jefferson, in Notes on the State of Virginia *(1781–82), in Padover,* Thomas Jefferson on Democracy *(1967), pp. 107–108.*

We have no princes, for whom we toil, starve, and bleed: we are the most perfect society now existing in the world. Here man is free as he ought to be. . . .

In this great American asylum, the poor of Europe have by some means met together, and in consequence of various causes; to what purpose should they ask one another what countrymen they are? Alas, two thirds of them had no country. Can a wretch who wanders about, who works and starves, whose life is a continual scene of sore affliction or pinching penury; can that man call England, or any other kingdom, his country? A country that had no bread for him, whose fields procured him no harvest, who met with nothing but the frowns of the rich, the severity of the laws, with jails and punishments, who owned not a single foot of the extensive surface of this planet? No! Urged by a variety of motives, here they came. Everything has tended to regenerate them; new laws, a new mode of living, a new social system; here they are become men; in Europe they were so many useless plants, wanting vegetative mould, and refreshing showers; they withered, and were mowed down by want, hunger, and war; but now, by the power of transplantation, like all other plants they have taken root and flourished! . . .

What then is the American? He is either an European, or the descendant of an European, hence that strange mixture of blood, which you will find in no other country. I could point out to you a family whose grandfather was an Englishman, whose wife was Dutch, and whose present four sons have wives of different nations. *He* is an American who, leaving behind him all his ancient prejudices and manners, receives new ones from the new mode of life he has embraced. . . . Here individuals of all nations are melted into a new race of men, whose labours and posterity will one day cause great changes in the world. . . .

J. Hector St. Jean (Michel-Guillaume-Jean de Crèvecoeur), French consul to New York and later immigrant, in Letters of an American Farmer *(1782), pp. 58–60.*

Our interests and our laws teach us to receive strangers, from every quarter of the globe, with open arms. The poor, the unfortunate, the oppressed from every country, will find here a ready asylum;—and by uniting their interests with ours, enjoy in common with us, all the blessings of liberty and plenty. Neither difference of nation, of language, of manners, or of religion, will lessen the cordiality of their reception among a people whose religion teaches them to regard all mankind as their brethren.

Jonathon Trumbull, governor of Connecticut, letter to Baron Van der Capellen den Pol in Holland, 1782, in Smith, A New Age Now Begins, *Volume II (1976), p. 1819.*

The bosom of America is open to receive not only the opulent and respectable stranger but the oppressed and persecuted of all nations and religions: whom we shall welcome to a participation of all our rights and privileges, if by decency and propriety of conduct they appear to merit the enjoyment.

George Washington, December 2, 1783, in The Writings of George Washington, *Volume XXVII (1938), p. 254.*

We may all remember the time when our mother country, as a mark of her parental tenderness, emptied her gaols into our habitations, "for the better *peopling*," as she expressed it, *"of the colonies."* It is certain that no due returns have yet been made for these valuable consignments. We are therefor much in her debt on that account; and as she is of late clamorous for the payment of all we owe her, and some of our debts are of a kind not so easily discharged, I am for doing however what is in our power. It will show our good-will as to the rest. The felons she planted among us have produced such an amazing increase, that we are now enabled to make ample remittance in the same commodity. And since the wheelbarrow law is not found effectually to reform them, and many of our vessels are idle through her restraints in our trade, why should we not employ those vessels in transporting the felons to Britain?

Benjamin Franklin, "On Sending Felons to America," 1786, in Sparks, ed., The Works of Benjamin Franklin, *Volume II (1856), p. 495.*

The lesson we are taught is that we should be governed as much by our reason, and as little by our feelings, as possible. What is the language of reason on this subject? That we should not be polite at the expense of prudence. . . .

He ran over the privileges which emigrants would enjoy among us, though they should be deprived of that of being eligible to the great offices of Government; observing that they exceeded the privileges allowed to foreigners in any part of the world; and said that, as every society from a great Nation down to a Club had the right of declaring the conditions on which new members should be admitted, there could be no room for complaint. . . . [He said that] the men who can shake off their attachments to their own Country can never love any other. These attachments are the wholesome prejudices which uphold all Government. Admit a Frenchman into your Senate, and he will study to increase the commerce of France: An Englishman, he will feel an equal bias in favor of that of England.

Gouverneur Morris, Pennsylvania delegate to the Constitutional Convention of 1787, quoted by James Madison reporting the speeches in the convention, in Ferrand, The True Records of the Federal Convention of 1787 *(1937), pp. 235–238.*

I saw, for the first time, what I have since *observed* a hundred times; for in fact, whatever mountains I have climbed, whatever forests I have traversed, whatever bye-paths I have followed, I have never traveled three miles without meeting with a new settlement, either beginning to take form or already in cultivation. . . . [A pioneer's first habitation is the work] of eight and forty hours. I shall be asked, perhaps, how one man or one family can be so quickly lodged; I answer that in America a man is never alone, never an isolated being. The neighbors, for they are every where to be found, make it a point of hospitality to aid the new farmer. A cask of cider, drank in common, and with gaiety, or a gallon of rum, are the only recompense for such services. Such are the means by which North-America, which one hundred years ago was nothing but a vast forest, is peopled with three millions of inhabitants. . . .

François Jean, marquis de Chastellux, French general and diplomat who served in the American Revolutionary army, Travels in North America *(1787), in David B. Greenberg, ed.,* Land That Our Fathers Plowed: The Settlement of Our Country as Told by the Pioneers Themselves and Their Comtemporaries *(1969), p. 7.*

Providence has been pleased to give this one connected country to one united people—a people descended from the same ancestors, speaking the same language, professing the same religion, attached to the same principles of government, very similar in their manners and customs, and who, by their joint counsels, arms, and efforts, fighting side by side throughout a long and bloody war, have nobly established their general liberty and independence.

This country and this people seem to have been made for each other, and it appears as if it was the design of Providence that an inheritance so proper and convenient for a band of brethren, united to each other by the strongest ties, should never be split into a number of unsocial, jealous, and alien sovereignties.

John Jay, in Alexander Hamilton, James Madison, and John Jay, The Federalist Papers, *Number 2 (1787), p. 38.*

Permit me to hint whether it would not be wise and reasonable to provide a strong check to the admission of foreigners into the administration of our national government.

John Jay, first chief justice of the United States Supreme Court, in a letter of July 25, 1787, in The Correspondence and Public Papers of John Jay, *Volume III (1890–93), p. 250.*

As to the condition and treatment of the passengers . . . the legislature of Pennsylvania well aware of the consequence of encouraging migrations hither from Europe as the most speedy and effectual mode of contributing to the settlement and of increasing the strength of the country from time to time passed very salutary laws to regulate this trade and to secure the good treatment of the passengers; but these laws were formerly too often evaded—numbers were crowded in small vessels destitute of proper room and accommodations and abridged of the necessary allowance of proper food; by which means the unfortunate emigrants not only suffered greatly but contagious diseases were often introduced into the province—the terms too of paying the passage money were frequently departed from—passengers who embarked as redemptioners were often hurried from on shipboard before the limited time for their redemption was expired, and before their friends could have notice of their arrival. . . . In the list of German passengers which I have carefully perused I observe several instances of between 7 and 800 German passengers crowded in one vessel, and I should presume few of the vessels employed in this trade exceeded 250 or 300 tons burden. The Irish vessels were exceedingly crowded before the War, but lately the number in each vessel have been less, *only* because fewer passengers have offered. . . .

The practice of bringing passengers hither . . . independent of every consideration as to their personal convenience or inconvenience is detrimental in many respects to Great Britain and profitable to America—as an essential means of extending the population of America it adds to her strength and it diminishes ours by abridging us of so many industrious subjects of the benefit of their increase and of their useful labor.

Phineas Bond, British consul at Philadelphia, letter of 1789 to the British Foreign Office, in Annual Report of the American Historical Association, *Volume I (1896), pp. 643–645.*

A climate wholesome and delightful, frost, even in winter, almost entirely unknown, and a river called, by way of eminence, the *beautiful,* and abounding in excellent fish, of a vast size. Noble forests consisting of trees that spontaneously produce sugar (*the sugar maple*), and a plant that yields ready-made candles (*myrica cerifera*). Venison in plenty, the pursuit of which is uninterrupted by wolves, foxes, lions, or tigers. A couple of swine will multiply themselves a hundred fold in two or three years, without taking any care of them. No taxes to pay, no military service to be performed.

Prospectus of the Scioto Company, promoting the sale of land in Ohio, 1790, in C. F. Volney, A View of the Soil and Climate of the United States of America *in Abbott,* Historical Aspects of Immigration *(1926), p. 31.*

It is now no more that toleration is spoken of as if it were the indulgence of one class of people that another enjoyed the exercise of their inherent natural rights, for happily, the Government of the United States, which gives to bigotry no sanction, to persecution no assistance, requires only that they who live under its protection should demean themselves as good citizens in giving it on all occasions their effectual support. . . . May the children of the stock of Abraham who dwell in this land continue to merit and enjoy the good will of the other inhabitants' while every one shall sit in safety under his own vine and fig trees and there shall be none to make him afraid.

May the father of all mercies scatter light, and not darkness, upon our paths, and make us all in our several vocations useful here, and in His own due time and way everlastingly happy.

George Washington, letter to the Hebrew Congregation in Newport, Rhode Island, 1790, in Joseph L. Blau and Salo W. Baron, eds., The Jews of the United States, 1790–1840: A Documentary History, *Volume I (1963), p. xxiii.*

You seldom see a superior treat an inferior with haughtiness, but you see all, even to the lowest of the landholders, act with a certain air, that indicated that they are sensible that they are not in any degree dependent on you. . . . The truth is, every man seems to carry about with him

a consciousness that he is an independent citizen of an independent state.

Dr. Samuel Smith, describing American settlers in New England, in J. Long, Voyages of an Indian . . . Trader *(1791), p. 30.*

Here no beggarly monks and fryars, no princely ecclesiastes with their annual income of millions, no idle court-pensioners and titled mendicants, no spies watch and betray the unsuspecting citizen, no tyrant with his train of hounds, bastards and mistresses, those vultures of government, prey upon poor peasants and exhaust the public treasury of the nation.

Noah Webster, American lexicographer and writer, comparing the United States with Europe, in Morals *(1793), in Richard M. Rollins,* The Long Journey of Noah Webster *(1980), p. 75.*

Foreign influence is truly the Grecian horse to a republic. We cannot be too careful to exclude its entrance.

Alexander Hamilton, Secretary of Treasury, in a letter of July 17, 1793, in The Works of Alexander Hamilton *Volume IV (1904), p. 481.*

St. Domingo has expelled all its whites, has given freedom to all its blacks and coloured people, and seems now to have taken its ultimate form, and that to which all of the West Indian islands must come.

Thomas Jefferson, to his daughter Martha Jefferson Randolph, letter of December 1, 1793, in Davis and Mintz, The Boisterous Sea of Liberty *(1998), pp. 265–66.*

There is much to be apprehended from the great numbers of violent men who emigrate to this country from every part of Europe.

Oliver Wolcott, Revolutionary War general and governor of Connecticut, warning of the dangers of too liberal an immigration policy, 1794, in Jones, American Immigration *(1960), p. 82.*

If you come to NORFOLK for that boasted encouragement our countrymen are taught to expect in England, you will be most *miserably disappointed.* I have seen upwards of three hundred poor persons, chiefly from Ireland, landed from one ship bemoaning with tears their own credulity, and lamenting most pathetically their departure from their native homes. These poor creatures are marched in small bodies by persons employed for that purpose to the different plantations where they are forced to indent themselves for *so many years* to the planters, who pay the captains what is called the *redemption money* for them. You may be surprised that such transactions are permitted in what is called the *land of liberty*, but I assure you that this is thought nothing of here, and is actually the case. . . .

> *Letter from a carpenter in Norfolk, Virginia, dated August 16, 1794, warning potential emigrants, in* Look Before You Leap; or A Few Hints to Such Artizans, Mechanics, Labourers, Farmers, and Husbandmen, as Are Desirous of Emigrating to America. . . . *(1796), p. 85.*

My opinion, with respect to emigration, is that except of useful mechanics and some particular descriptions of men or professions, there is no need of encouragement, while the policy or advantage of its taking place in a body (I mean the settling of them in a body) may be much questioned; for, by so doing, they retain the Language, habits, and principles (good or bad) which they bring with them.

> *George Washington, journal note, November 15, 1794, in* The Writings of George Washington, *Volume XII, (1889–93), p. 489.*

Every account I have from England makes me think myself happy in this peaceful retirement, where I enjoy almost everything I can wish in this life, and where I hope to close it. . . .

The advantages we enjoy in this country are indeed very great. Here we have no poor, we never see a beggar, nor is there a family in want. We have no church establishment, and hardly any taxes. This particular state pays all its officers from a treasure in the public funds. There are very few crimes committed, and we travel without the least apprehension of danger. The press is perfectly free, and I hope we shall always keep out of war.

I do not think there ever was a country in a state of such rapid improvement as this at present. . . .

> *Joseph Priestley, English clergyman and chemist who emigrated to America in 1794, letter of October 4, 1796, to a friend in England, in Abbott,* Historical Aspects of Immigration *(1926), pp. 22–23.*

One Mile from St Genevieve, Down the [Ohio] River, is a Small Village called New *Bourbon* of about 20 Houses. At this place I was Introduced to The *Chevalier Pierre Charles De Hault De Lassus*, a French *Nobleman* Formerly of the Council of the late King of France. Chevalier De Lassus Told me he had an Estate in France of 30 thousand *Crowns*, but was oblig.d to make his Escape to America and leave all, Which has since been taken by the present government. *Madame* De Lassus had an Estate of half that sum per annum, so that the Yearly Income of the famely, besides the sumes allow.d him by the King, Amounted to 45 Thousand Crowns per annum. Madame De Lassus did not appear to support the Change of Situation so well as the *Chevalier*. I was examining a larg Piece of painting, which was in Madame De Lassus Bed Chamber, representing a grand Festival given by the Citizens of Paris to the Queen, on the birth of the Dauphin and a *Parade* of all the *Nobles* on the same Occasion. She came to me and puting her finger on the *Picture* pointing out a Coach "There," said she, "was I on that Happy Day. My situation is now strangly chang.d."

> *Moses Austin, miner and colonizer, journal entry of March 25, 1797, describing an encounter with a French refugee in the Ohio Valley, in* The American Historical Review, *Volume V, Number 3 (April 1900), p. 541.*

. . . the mass of vicious and disorganizing characters who can not live peaceably at home, and who, after unfurling the standard of rebellion in their own country, may come hither to revolutionize ours.

> *Harrison Gray Otis, member of the House of Representatives from Massachusetts, describing French refugees who have immigrated to the United States, May 1797, in Jones,* American Immigration *(1960), p. 86.*

Millions for defense but not a cent for tribute.

> *Robert Goodloe Harper, member of the House of Representatives from Virginia, in a toast, June 18, 1798, responding to France's demand for a bribe for approving a trade agreement, in Adler,* Annals of America, *Volume 4, (1968), p. 61.*

The state of things, if we are to judge from the complexion of this bill, must be that a number of aliens enjoying the protection of our government, were plotting its destruction; that they are engaged in treasonable machinations against a people who have given them an asylum and support; and that there are not provisions to provide for their expulsion and punishment. . . .

We must legislate upon facts, not on surmises; we must have evidence, not vague suspicions. . . . What facts have been produced? What evidence has been submitted to the House? I have heard, sir, of none. . . .

As far as my own observation goes, I have seen nothing like the state of things contemplated by the bill. Most of the aliens I have seen were either triumphant Englishmen or Frenchmen with dejection in their countenances and grief at their hearts, preparing to quit the country and seek another asylum. . . .

. . . If the same power that makes the law can construct it to suit [the executive's] interest, and apply it to gratify his vengeance; if he can go further and execute, according to his own passions, the judgment which he himself has pronounced, upon his own construction of laws which he alone has made, what other features are wanted to complete the features of tyranny? . . . [The president] is not only authorized to make this law for his own conduct but to vary it at pleasure, as every gust of passion, every cloud of suspicion, shall agitate or darken his mind. . . . This, then, comes completely within the definition of despotism—a union of legislative, executive, and judicial powers.

Edward Livingston, New York congressman, in a speech before Congress, June 21, 1798, opposing the Alien Act, in Gales, The Debates in the Congress of the United States. . . . , *Volume 5, (1834–56), pp. 2006–2007.*

Why should we take the bread out of the mouths of our own children and give it to strangers?

John Adams, warning against a liberal immigration policy, in a letter of August 14, 1800, in The Works of John Adams, *Volume IX, (1856), p. 77.*

Shall we refuse the unhappy fugitives from distress that hospitality which the savages of the wilderness extended to our fathers arriving in this land? Shall oppressed humanity find no asylum on this globe? . . . Might not the general character and capabilities of a citizen be safely communicated to every one manifesting a bona fide purpose of embarking his life and fortunes permanently with us?

Thomas Jefferson, 1801, referring to his opposition to the anti-immigration Alien Act of 1798, in Robbins, Coming to America *(1981), p. 62.*

The plan of our worthy friend, John Rutledge, relative to the admission of strangers to the privileges of citizens, as you explain it, was certainly prudent. Americans will find that their own experience will coincide with the experience of all other nations, and foreigners must be received with caution, or they will destroy all confidence in government.

John Adams, letter of April 16, 1801, in Works of John Adams, *Volume IX, (1856), p. 584.*

It is impossible not to look forward to distant times, when our rapid multiplication will expand itself . . . and cover the whole northern, if not the southern continent, with a people speaking the same language, government in similar forms, and by similar laws; nor can we contemplate with satisfaction either blot or mixture on that surface.

Thomas Jefferson, letter of November 24, 1801, in The Writings of Thomas Jefferson, *Volume VIII, (1892–99), p. 104.*

CHAPTER FOUR

Beginnings of Mass Immigration
1814–1860

The Flood Begins

The stream of immigration to the United States remained as steady as international affairs permitted between 1790 and 1814, and it was never extensive enough to worry the original settlers much. The best estimate places the average at about 6,000 newcomers per year until 1810, when unfriendly relations among England, France, and the United States brought it nearly to a halt. The effects of the hostilities between France and England were felt in other countries as well. Since the Germans generally sailed for the United States from Liverpool and the French port of Le Havre, passage was blocked at the source from about 1806. With the end of the War of 1812 and the resumption of trade, the flow of immigrants from the British Isles and northern Europe began again and soon swelled to unprecedented heights. Although exact records of immigration were not kept until 1820, custom-house documents show that in the year 1817 alone, 22,240 people arrived at U.S. ports from abroad—more than twice the number admitted in any previous year.

Of course the conditions of transit became worse as the numbers of immigrants increased. Overcrowding and lack of food and sanitary facilities in ships carrying human cargo soon became a problem for American society as wave after wave of immigrants staggered off the ships more dead than alive. Although the British Passenger Acts regulating conditions in emigrant ships were still in effect, they were not enforced, and until 1819 there was no American law stipulating either providing for the number of passengers a ship might carry or their health and comfort. In that year Congress enacted America's first passenger act, limiting the number of passengers on a vessel entering an American port to two per five tons of the ship's weight. A later act required that each passenger traveling on the lower deck be allowed "fourteen clear superficial feet of deck" and, for the more fortunate immigrants who traveled on the upper deck, "thirty such superficial feet in all cases." Subsequent passenger acts increased the space per traveler to 16 square feet, provided for proper ventilation, and prescribed the amount of food and water to be allotted to each passenger. "Health and strength are desirable elements in the character of immigration," the act of 1847 noted, "and immigrants, on reaching our shores, should not be wasted by sickness nor weakened by hunger." Unfortunately, these humane American passenger acts were no better enforced than the earlier British ones, and conditions on board these vessels, both British and American, continued to earn them the name "coffin ships" through the 19th century and beyond.

In the 45 years from 1815 to 1860, some 5 million people immigrated to the United States, more than the entire population of the country in 1790. In the years from 1845 to 1854 alone, more than 3 million arrived, representing 15 percent of the entire U.S. population, the highest percentage of foreign additions in its history before or since. The number increased from decade to decade: From 1820 to 1830, some 151,000 arrived, and from 1830 to 1840 immigration almost quadrupled to nearly 500,000. During the next decade immigration nearly trebled, to 1,713,251, and from 1850 to 1860 it went up again to 2,598,214. People came from every country in Europe—the records show immigration from Sardinia, Greece, Poland, Turkey, Malta, Persia, and Morocco as well as from England, France, and Germany—but 95 percent were born in northwestern Europe, more than half of them in the British Isles. Germany contributed the next largest number with 1.5 million.

Emigration from Europe was not exclusively to the United States. The political and financial upheavals that drove people from their homes most commonly sent them to closer havens, at least initially. It is estimated that some 250,000 Germans left their country for Russia in the decade following 1818, and more went to the newly independent state of Brazil than to the United States. The Irish found it more affordable to move to England than to America; when steamship travel was introduced, the fare across the Irish Sea was only 3d., while the lowest price to America was £3.10. Many English emigrants, preferring to stay within their empire, sailed for Australia or Canada. But the greatest draw for the displaced and impoverished remained the seemingly unlimited stretches of the United States, which received the largest number of people leaving their home countries in Europe. Many of the English and Irish who immigrated to Canada moved on to the United States, often immediately after arriving.

This huge migration was met with mixed feelings, both in the United States and in Europe. Some in the countries from which the immigrants came, generally suffering from widespread unemployment and political unrest, saw the exodus as a welcome relief from overpopulation and a good way to deal with the discontented and rebellious. Others saw it as a loss of their most energetic and skilled workers. Americans recognized the value of the new labor force in the country's expansion and development, but many viewed the flood of new arrivals as a threat to national unity and feared the introduction of foreign influences on the emerging country.

The enormous increase in immigration from Europe during the first half of the 19th century had several causes besides the obvious attractions of the New World and the long-deferred freedom to travel. The first was a population explosion unparalleled in history. During the hundred years following 1750, the number of inhabitants of Europe rose from 140 to 250 million. With the end of the great plagues of the Middle Ages and the improved health of the population, the death rate fell sharply. Improvements in the European diet also contributed to the continent's well-being. The potato, brought to Europe from the New World in the 17th century, fed more people per acre than grain. Better farming techniques increased the productivity of the land.

Improved means of transportation enabled food to be more efficiently distributed, so that local crop failures ceased to be a cause of famine.

Another explanation for the swelling tide of European emigration was the Industrial Revolution. The development of the factory system and of centralized means of production in the middle of the 18th century eliminated the need for many artisans and made their skills obsolete. Mechanization made large farms more efficient than small, independent holdings, and less manpower was necessary to maintain them. With the population increasing and the need for labor diminishing, unemployment reached its highest recorded levels throughout Europe. Governments that had opposed the exodus of their workers came to reverse their positions as social and economic pressures grew. In 1825 the British law prohibiting the emigration of artisans was repealed, and two years later all remaining restrictions on leaving the country were lifted. The German states withdrew their prohibitions on emigration in the 1840s, and in 1860 the Scandinavian countries abolished most passport regulations in response to the pressures of overpopulation. The numerous rebellions that took place during the 19th century in Ireland, France, Germany, Italy, Poland, and elsewhere in Europe added their share to the flow of exiles making their way to the New World. Religious dissension also continued to be a factor, inspiring groups from several countries to emigrate in flight from persecution.

All of these explanations for increased immigration during the first half of the 19th century would not have brought about the mass exodus that occurred without improvements in the means for accomplishing it: safer, faster, and cheaper transportation. As trade across the Atlantic increased with the establishment of peace after the War of 1812 and the end of the Napoleonic wars, such improvements were inevitable. Canada quickly became Europe's leading supplier of timber, and shipment of cotton and tobacco from the United States kept pace with it. From 1820 to 1840, the number of Canadian vessels carrying timber to Great Britain rose from 1,000 to 2,000, and the number carrying cotton from the American South to Liverpool increased from some 300 to more than 1,000. Trade with France and Germany grew at the same rate. Returning from Europe, the ships had room for the swelling ranks of emigrants waiting for passage, and soon a lively trade in human transport emerged, with agents in every major port in northwest Europe. Competition for business became so great that fares dropped yearly.

Travel technology improved during this period as well. In 1818 the Black Ball Line began sailing regularly from Liverpool to New York and succeeded in cutting the length of the voyage from 39 to 33 days. The next year steam was introduced as a source of power, and the transit from Savannah, Georgia, to Liverpool by steam-assisted sail was accomplished in the record time of 26 days. In 1838 full steamship service between England and the United States in as few as 15 days became available. Two years later the Cunard Line began regular voyages from England. In 1850 a rival American line opened offering steamship service between Liverpool and New York. The transportation of immigrants had become a major industry.

The vast majority of newcomers to the United States in the first half of the 19th century continued to be Europeans, but changing circumstances in the world—and new developments in North America—brought people from other regions as well. When gold was discovered in the Sacramento Valley in California in 1848, the news spread throughout the world. Adventurers flooded into the West Coast, not only from all parts of the United States but from countries as distant as Australia and China.

The impact of the discovery on China was particularly great. Conditions leading up to Chinese immigration had been mounting for some years. The Opium War of 1840 between China and England brought greatly increased taxes and inspired unrest throughout the country. With the report in China of limitless treasure on America's West Coast, the lure of *gam saan*—"mountain of gold," as they called California—worked on the hungry Chinese as it did on people all over the world. Those who could raise the passage money—often by selling their property and pooling contributions from members of their families—hurried to sign up for the 7,000-mile trip across the Pacific Ocean to California. When in 1850 a great rebellion broke out in Taiping, in southeastern China, it brought with it famine and social chaos. It took an estimated 20 million lives, paralyzed the economy of the region, and drove many farmers out of the country. By 1851 there were 25,000 Chinese working in California, and the numbers continued to grow from year to year.

British

Whole neighborhoods and parishes came from England and Ireland, and to a lesser extent Scotland and Wales, to found small colonies in the New World. In 1818 a prosperous English farmer named Morris Birkbeck invested his entire fortune in establishing an "English Settlement" in Illinois, buying 16,000 acres of public land to found a community he called Albion, an old poetic name for England. He began by constructing a blacksmith shop and a tavern, noting in his report home that "the two germs of civilization were now planted—one of the useful arts, the other a necessary institution of present civilization. Any man could now get his horse shod and get drunk in Albion, privileges which were soon enjoyed, the latter especially."

Birkbeck did not have enough cash left to transport many immigrants to his new village, but he had a gift for promotion. His *Notes on a Journey in America* and *Letters from Illinois*, both published in England in 1818, were best-sellers, the former appearing in 11 editions and the latter in seven during the next three years. These two brief volumes gave enticing, though not always realistic, accounts of life on the open plains of America and the hospitality of its residents, and they drew many followers to Albion. Even more effective were the letters the settlers themselves wrote home giving personal accounts of the prosperity awaiting their relatives and friends in the New World. As Birkbeck wrote later, such a letter "produced a greater impression in the limited circle of its readers than a printed publication had the power of doing."

Not every colonization project was as successful as Albion, and not all letters home were so enthusiastic about the new life to be found in America. Many warned of the dangers awaiting the emigrant unprepared for hard work and a simple life, and reminded their readers of the pains of separation from home. "Even if you have escaped from prisons and pauperism," wrote one Englishman in Indiana territory, "you will sometimes 'hang your harp on the willow and weep,' when you remember distant England. Very few emigrants, howsoever many have been their disgusts and evils in the old country, or their successes in the new, can forget their 'dear native land' . . . and as a much-loved, ungrateful mistress, her charms only are remembered and cherished."

The largest number—almost half—of all the immigrants to the United States between 1814 and 1860 were Irish Catholics and Presbyterian Ulstermen, lumped together as "Irish" in the customhouse records. Although arrivals from Ulster, the so-called Scotch-Irish, had represented the largest group of non-English immigrants in the 17th century, their numbers had not been great, and a large proportion of them had come as indentured servants or redemptioners. Others had been small farmers ruined by high rents and impossible taxes. In the 1830s, when many leases ran out and landlords began to clear their estates, evicting their tenants, many more were driven to seek homes elsewhere. In 1838 the British government enacted the Poor Law, requiring the owners of estates to help support those who were no longer able to earn a living. In many cases this added tax was more than the landlords could afford, and some went so far as to finance their evicted tenants' emigration, finding it cheaper to ship their tenants to America than to pay for their maintenance in Ireland. "The poor laws," according to an editorial in the *King's County Chronicle* some years later, "is the great and permanent depopulator of Ireland."

But emigration to America was not easy for the Irish. The English, in an effort at directing the flow of emigrants to its own territories, established laws making the trip to the United States more expensive than to British North America, as the provinces composing present-day Canada were known. Passage to New York ranged from £4 to £5, roughly equivalent to $20–25, while a voyage to Canada might cost as little as 15 shillings, or about $3.60. It was also much more convenient for the Irish to head for Canada; vessels bound for that country left from every port in Ireland while it was necessary to leave for America from England, a 14-hour trip across the Irish Sea. Nevertheless, the Irish choice, when any choice was possible, was clearly the United States. The prospects for work were much better in America than in Canada, and the Irish felt that their prospects for justice and opportunity

England tried to restrain the immigration of workers to the United States in the 1850s, but the attraction of a better life drew more than 2.5 million. Labor was needed in the United States before the Civil War, and women were needed to work in the textile mills, as depicted in this mid-19th-century cartoon entitled "The Lure of American Wages." *(New York Public Library Print Collection)*

were better there than under British rule in North America. When in 1816 the British government suspended the regulations that imposed higher fares to America, 92 percent of those leaving Ireland booked passage for the United States. When the law went back into effect later the same year, the number fell again to 33 percent.

Immigrants moving on from Canadian ports to America—sometimes on foot—headed into New England, and so regular a practice did this become that emigration agents used it as an argument for taking passage to Canada. The master of the ship *Ocean* included in his *Galway Free Press* advertisement in 1835 the assurance that "those living on that line of road [are] very kind to Strangers as they pass." Whether or not the farmers in Maine and New Hampshire were "very kind to Strangers" begging as they plodded southward, many a ragged Irishman found work on his way to Boston and settled down along the route. New England had need of labor in its lumber industry, and the Irish welcomed any chance to work. So many Irish immigrants made their homes in the region that their arrival has been described as "the second colonization of New England." One historian has asserted that New England owes its heavy Irish population primarily to the timber trade.

By 1840 a large percentage of the residents of New England—once populated by the purest English stock of any region in the country—was foreign-born. Of Boston's population of 136,881 in that year, 35 percent were from other countries, and of that foreign population, some 75 percent were Irish. More than half of the Irish immigrants in the United States had by this time settled in New England.

Most of the Irish who came to the United States in the 1820s and 1830s came alone. Families could not afford to come together, and an enterprising oldest son was usually sent first to earn enough to pay the passage of the rest. Without the responsibilities of wife and children, a worker was free to follow whatever path led to regular work, and for the Irish that usually meant the most strenuous and menial jobs.

In 1817 construction began on New York State's first canal, a waterway that was to connect the Atlantic Ocean with the Great Lakes. Stretching 363 miles from Albany to Buffalo, the Erie Canal gave New York City a connection with the interior of the United States and established it as the greatest trading center in the country. In 1825, the canal's first year of operation, almost a half-million dollars was collected in tolls, and an estimated 40,000 people traveled on freight and passenger boats. Impressed by how cheaply goods and people could be moved between the East Coast and the Midwest by canal, other communities began to demand them, and canal fever swept across the East Coast. Pennsylvania built almost 1,000 miles of canals in 15 years, and other states constructed canal systems to link themselves with the Atlantic.

The work was dreadful. Standing in dirty water all day, subject to malaria, cholera, and typhus, and threatened by collapsing riverbanks, the laborers endured worse conditions than miners, digging and blasting through tons of rock with spades and wagons as their only earthmoving equipment. Few Americans were tempted by the wages of 50 cents to $1.50 a day. The Irish, poorly prepared for any other work that was available and usually penniless, flocked to the canals as their only opportunity. According to one scholar, "Hardly a canal was built during [this] period that did not employ Irish workmen as its basic labor force."

When the canal era came to an end in the late 1850s with the advent of rail, the demand for hard and hazardous manual labor continued, and once again the Irish accepted jobs native-born Americans were unwilling to take. Most regularly

Starving Irish beg for food outside of a workhouse in the early 1850s, from a contemporary drawing. *(New York Public Library Print Collection)*

sent money home to help with the rent or, more often, to enable their families to join them. Often steamship tickets were sent instead of money; it is estimated that in 1848 about 40 percent of the total money sent back to Ireland by immigrants was in the form of prepaid passages to America.

In 1845 the flow of Irish immigration to the United States increased precipitously with the failure of the potato crop. That humble, nourishing tuber was the mainstay of Ireland's diet, and indeed of its economy. A third of Ireland's 9 million inhabitants ate almost nothing else. The stalks thatched their huts, the peels fed their chickens and pigs, farmers could store potatoes during the winter, and an acre of the easily grown vegetable could support a family. But the potato had certain disadvantages. It depleted the soil, it could not be stored for more than a few months, and the plant was a fragile one, subject to disease.

Ireland and the rest of Europe had seen "the potato disease" before—the fungus that destroyed potatoes was first identified in Germany in 1829 and had recurred here and there ever since—but the Irish potato blight lasting from 1845 to 1847 was like nothing that country had ever experienced. It killed nearly half of the 1845 crop and destroyed the potatoes in storage as well as the ones still underground. The famine and epidemic that resulted have been described as the worst national disaster to hit Europe since the bubonic plague of the 14th century.

The blight did not hit Ireland alone; it struck, though less disastrously, Germany and the Netherlands as well, and prevented those countries from offering Ireland any effective relief. The United States collected $1 million in public and private contributions to send grain, and England came to Ireland's aid with both food and public works projects, employing the Irish to build roads. Soup kitchens and work-houses were established for the completely destitute, but the help was insufficient and came too late for most of the victims. The workhouses were overcrowded and people who had lost their homes were turned away to beg from village to village. The soup kitchens did not have enough food for the throngs that crowded at their doors.

The next year, 1846, was worse than the first; almost the entire potato crop was lost. The farmers had to eat what few seed potatoes they had left to plant, so in 1847 only one-sixth of the available land was planted. The people were so weakened by hunger that they were unable to work effectively. The work reports of the British Board of Engineers of the time describes laborers as "too feeble to perform tasks, however willing," and records many instances of workers fainting on the job. As a result, the English government drastically cut the work projects and largely abandoned its relief programs, explaining that they were costing the country too much money. The official British policy was to allow business to follow its own course and to leave the Irish to cope with their own problems. All but able-bodied workers—a tiny minority in Ireland by that time—were dismissed from their work and were left with no income at a time when only expensive imported food was available.

To make matters worse, the winter of 1846–47 was a particularly severe one in Ireland, and much of the population had sold its clothes and bedding. The homeless slept in the fields or in crowded workhouses holding three times their legal limit. Unable to wash and with no change of clothes, the poor were crawling with lice. Inevitably disease followed. Dysentery and a form of typhus known as "famine fever" soon spread throughout the country, causing more deaths than starvation did. The papers of the time were filled with grisly details of the epidemic. In *The Times* of London published on Christmas Eve 1846, an Irish observer reported, "[T]he police opened a house, . . . and two frozen corpses were found, lying upon the mud floor, half devoured by rats. . . . In another house, . . . the dispensary doctor found seven wretches lying unable to move, under the same cloak. One had been dead many hours, but the others were unable to move either themselves or the corpse." The dead lay in the streets, sometimes unburied for weeks before being thrown, unrecorded, into pits. It is estimated that between 1845 and 1851, between 1 and 1.5 million Irish men, women, and children—nearly one-sixth of the entire population of the country—died of hunger or disease.

The Irish had always been reluctant emigrants, deeply attached to their own land despite their economic and religious problems there. But now, with almost certain death facing them, there was no choice but to leave the country, and emigration seemed a blessed escape rather than a painful exile. Between 1840 and 1860, some 2.5 million people left Ireland. Half of that number, almost 1.5 million, came to the United States and a third of a million to Canada, most of them finding their way south of the U.S.-Canadian border soon after.

The Irish did not find the United States as hospitable as other groups had, and the flood that poured in during the 1840s were under particular disadvantages. Generally poor, illiterate, and unskilled in anything but subsistence farming, many spoke only Gaelic. Unable to afford to go west, even though public land was freely available and cheap, they settled first in the port cities at which they arrived and took jobs digging sewers, paving roads, and laying gas and water pipes. Those who ventured farther afield became coal miners or worked in the railroad industry when canal construction came to an end, grading the roads, laying the rails, and tending the engines. The women generally took jobs as maids, washerwomen, and cooks. The men's labor was hard and often hazardous, and conditions were often so bad that workers rioted. This earned the Irish a reputation for violence, which made their adjustment to American society even harder. The suspicion and dislike they faced was nothing new in American immigration history, but it was probably the worst prejudice that any immigrant group had encountered yet. Because of their great numbers and their Catholic faith, Americans (even those who had themselves come as immigrants a few years before) feared that the country would be "overrun" by the Irish and that its Protestant English culture would be swamped. In fact, the Catholic Church was greatly strengthened in the United States by the addition of these millions of members and today ranks as the country's largest single religious organization.

Most Irish remained in the cities, where their poverty and lack of familiarity with American society condemned them to live in the slums. Clustering in the most

An anti-Catholic cartoon from the 1850s reflects nativist fears of Roman Catholic influence in the United States through Irish immigration. *(Library of Congress, Prints and Photographs Division [LC-USZ62-30815])*

ramshackle tenements, their lives were not much healthier than when they had been in Ireland. According to one sociologist's estimate, an Irish person in Boston at this time lived an average of only 14 years after arriving. Many Irish in the cities found work with local governments, where they were able to advance. Until 1859 it was not necessary to be a citizen or to be able to read or to write in order to work on the police force, and in Boston and New York City the Irish were well represented on the force. In fact, so many of the police were Irish that police vans came to be known as "paddy wagons" for the slang term *Paddy* by which Irishmen were often called.

Despite their record of success in city police and fire departments, the Irish continued to experience discrimination. Their reputation for brawling and drunkenness led to work barriers. Newspaper "help wanted" advertisements openly stated "No Irish need apply" after job descriptions. When a French wine company applied for a large land grant in the Alabama territory in 1817, it received 92,000 acres at the good price of $2.00 per acre. But when an Irish relief organization attempted to settle Irish paupers on a tract in the West the next year, Congress refused to sell because it disapproved of any national group settling in one place and forming a colony there. English, German, French, and Scandinavian immigrants wrote home enthusiastically about American equality; the Irish were not accepted so readily.

The Rise of Nativism

A thread of anger at and fear of foreigners had run through the fabric of American thought since early colonial days, but in the 1830s, 1840s, and 1850s the Irish brought that feeling to a head. Secret societies began to form to "protect" America from foreign (and especially Catholic) influence. Anti-immigration sentiment, while not new in American history—its first official expression was the Alien and Sedition Acts of 1798—reached new heights during this period. An Ursuline convent in Charlestown, Massachusetts, was burned down in 1834 by an angry mob, and priests and nuns were murdered on the streets of Philadelphia during the 1840s. The fears that inspired such acts were various and not always clearly defined. Some thought that the Pope was plotting to assume control of the country through secret Catholic agents or that American culture was in danger of being replaced by a foreign, "inferior" way of life. The most realistic fear was that foreigners would take jobs from Americans because they were willing to work for less. In 1835 the distinguished artist and inventor Samuel F. B. Morse, who built the first telegraph, wrote a passionate call for an end to immigration, which he saw as an international conspiracy to infiltrate the United States. The book's thesis was clearly stated in its title: *Imminent Danger to the Free Institutions of the United States Through Foreign Immigration.* It stated in part, "We have now to resist the momentous evil that threatens us from Foreign Conspiracy. . . . Up! Up! I beseech you. Awake! To your posts! . . . Fly to protect the vulnerable places of your Constitution and laws. Place your guards; you will need them, and quickly, too.—And first, shut your gates. Shut the open gates."

In 1830 there were 318,000 Roman Catholics in the United States; by 1860 the number had grown to over 3 million, almost two-thirds of them immigrants. It is not surprising that this flood of foreigners inspired fear and suspicion. Protestant groups employed every available means of stirring up the public in opposition. Sensational newspapers and books challenged the patriotism of Catholics, suggesting that their first loyalty was to the pope. Stories of corruption among priests were widely circulated, and a fraudulent document purporting to be a Vatican order to massacre all Protestants made the rounds.

This anti-Catholic and anti-immigrant feeling crystallized into a political philosophy in the 1830s. Because it favored native inhabitants over immigrants in employment and the holding of office, it was known as nativism, and at first it targeted the Roman Catholic Church rather than any particular foreign group. An anti-Catholic newspaper, *The Protestant*, was founded in New York in 1830, and the next year the New York Protestant Association openly called for a ban on the admission of Catholics to the country. By 1843 this feeling had become so widespread that a political party was formed in New York to stop, or at least retard, immigration. The American Republican Party opposed voting and office-holding privileges for Catholics and foreigners.

In 1845 the American Republican Party changed its name to the Native American Party, and in 1849 it became associated with a secret society known as the Order of the Star-Spangled Banner. During the years that followed, it created a powerful propaganda machine to combat foreign, and especially Catholic, influ-

An advertisement for the nativist newspaper *American Patriot* includes an anti-Catholic cartoon. *(Library of Congress, Prints and Photographs Division [LC-USZ62-96392])*

Major-General Zachary Taylor (1784–1850), president of the United States (1849–50), from an 1848 mezzotint by John Sartain. Despite widespread anti-immigration sentiment, Taylor approved the abolition of the head tax in 1849, facilitating the entry of new arrivals. *(Library of Congress, Prints and Photographs Division [LC-USZ62-7559])*

ence. Renewed after the national election of 1852, it took as its official name the American Party, but it was popularly known as the Know-Nothing Party because of its policy of replying to all questions about its activities with the words "I know nothing." It called for a 21-year waiting period before an immigrant could apply for citizenship and declared in its 1854 constitution that its objective was "to resist the insidious policy of the Church of Rome, and other foreign influence against the institutions of our country, by placing in all offices . . . none but native born Protestant citizens."

The Know-Nothing Party lasted only from 1853 to 1860 and was widely regarded as an irresponsible, extremist group, but it had considerable influence nonetheless. By 1855 it was powerful enough to win the office of governor in six states and to capture 75 seats in Congress. In the presidential election of the following year, it ran former President Millard Fillmore as its candidate. Fillmore, one of America's less distinguished heads of state, collected nearly 22 percent of the popular vote, but he won only the eight electoral votes of Maryland, and the party dissolved shortly afterward. The Know-Nothings did not have a major impact on American history, but the party was an expression of a sentiment that was beginning to matter deeply to many. The party's hostility was not directed specifically against the Irish; but, as the first large non-English group to appear on American soil, the Irish were the first immigrants to awaken powerful opposition to America's liberal immigration policy.

The Germans

The second great wave of immigration to the United States following the War of 1812 was from Germany. The Napoleonic Wars and the French Revolution produced military and economic instability throughout Europe and cut the continent off from the rest of the world. The American Revolution and the War of 1812 led to military blockades that prevented traffic across the Atlantic, and German immigration fell away to almost nothing. With the restoration of peace, Germany found itself both overpopulated and financially handicapped. The revenue on which it depended from small industry—home manufacture of clocks, tools, and textiles—fell off sharply with changed economic conditions on the continent and extensive foreign competition. A system of inheritance in Germany in which land had to be divided equally among all children of a landowner led to many farms too small to support their owners.

Germany was not a single country for most of the 19th century. Until its unification in 1871, the region now known as Germany was occupied by many independent states, each with its own government, its own army, and its own body of laws. Conflicts among them drained the populace of money and manpower and limited the chances for individual progress. Emigration was a natural solution. With no colonial empire like England's, Germany looked to the newly opened doors of the United States as an outlet for its excess population and as an opportunity for personal and professional advancement.

The United States was enjoying its highest level of prosperity. Land was plentiful, and the country was eager for settlers to fill it. Land speculators, transportation companies, and local governments of such new states as Kentucky, Tennessee, and Ohio promoted immigration eagerly and advertised in German newspapers. With the Louisiana Purchase of 1803, America's capacity to absorb newcomers had increased immensely. It was not until the second quarter of the century that the tide of German immigration reached great volume, but soon the United States was receiving more new residents from Germany than from any other country. By 1860 more than 30 percent of the foreign-born population of America was from one or another of the German states. German settlements were well established in Pennsylvania from the 18th century; within the first quarter of the 19th century, many new ones formed in Kentucky and Ohio. Such place names as Frankfort, Kentucky (the capital), and Berlin, Dresden, and Potsdam, Ohio, reflected the extent of German immigration in those states. Biblical names like Bethlehem and Nazareth were assigned to new towns founded by German Moravians in Pennsylvania.

"Settlement of Immigrants in Missouri," an 1850 lithograph, shows European pioneers adjusting to the New World. *(New York Public Library Print Collection)*

The large wave of German immigrants that began about 1830 was greatly influenced, as English immigration was, by the literature that came from the United States. American novelist James Fenimore Cooper, who wrote of frontiersmen who lived rugged, adventurous lives in close contact with nature, had a great appeal to Germans tired of their oppressive governments. Even more appealing, however, was a straightforward, factual account of life in the United States addressed specifically to them. In 1824 a wealthy German named Gottfried Duden purchased 270 acres of rich land in Missouri, and after a few years he concluded that life in the United States was the answer to all the Germans' problems. Since Duden was able to hire people to clear his land and plant his crops, he found the country to be a Garden of Eden. His account of life in America, *Report on a Journey to the Western States of North America and a Stay of Several Years Along the Missouri* (1829), became a bestseller, exhausting three editions in its first year and attracting thousands to follow him to the New World. It painted such a glowing picture that his countrymen back home found it irresistible. Of a typical day on the farm he wrote that he spent the mornings "shooting partridges, pigeons, or squirrels, and also turkeys." His day continued in the same idyllic vein. "After breakfast," he went on, "I take my books in hand [and] busy myself as peacefully with the sciences as I ever did in Germany. Shortly before dinner I put them down and wander in the garden . . . and after dinner I go for a ride, either to visit the neighbors, or alone in the woods, on the heights, and in the valleys, delighting in the beauties of nature."

Unfortunately, many of the Germans who followed his advice found life in the United States a little harder than Duden had led them to expect, and he earned the nickname of *der Lügenhund*, "the lying dog." But by then they were already too deeply invested in their immigration to go back to Germany. In the 10 years following the publication of Duden's influential book, more than 50,000 Germans made their way to America.

In 1833 the Giessen Emigration Society formed in southwest Germany to establish "a free German state, a rejuvenated Germany in North America," and they had little trouble recruiting 500 emigrants to undertake the project. The group broke up when they reached St. Louis, Missouri, but the idea continued to attract Germans, both at home and in America. In 1837 the German Philadelphia Settlement Society purchased 12,000 acres near Duden's farm and created a colony that became Hermann, Missouri. By 1840 the organization had dissolved, but the town remains a prosperous community.

Groups like the Giessen Society hoped not only to relieve the economic pressures of the immigrants they recruited but also to spread German culture, and they sought out educated people to send as settlers. These cultured pioneers were often unprepared for the demands of their new lives. They were known as "Latin farmers" because, as one modern scholar has observed, they were "more familiar with Virgil than with guiding a plow through a furrow in prairie soil." There were among them doctors, lawyers, and scholars, and their training had not fitted them to till the soil. Many failed as farmers and moved to cities, where they found jobs in the professions for which they had been educated. Some became journalists for the growing German press. Others became laborers for the canals and railroad lines or returned to Germany.

The dream of establishing a New Germany was never very successful in the United States, but it came close to fulfillment in Texas. German immigration to Texas began as early as 1823, when Texas was still a state of Mexico; in that year Baron von Bastrop founded a German settlement near Austin, which had been established as an American settlement just two years before. In 1831, when German immigration to the United States had begun to grow, the Mexican government gave a German developer a large land grant. He wrote a letter home describing his new holdings in rapturous terms, and by chance the letter found its way into a German newspaper. The effect was electric; like the writings of Birkbeck and Duden, it inspired thousands to come to America. Soon a society for promoting German colonization sent a group to settle in Texas under Prince Carl von Solms-Braunfels. Each immigrant paid $120 and agreed to develop 15 acres and live on them for three years. The society, the Mainzer Adelsverein (Mainz Nobleman's Club), agreed to provide passage from Germany, a certain amount of free land, a house, farming tools, and such community features as hospitals, schools, and churches.

From 1836 to 1845, Texas was an independent republic governed by American settlers, and it might well have accommodated an independent German colony. Between 1844 and 1846, the Adelsverein imported 7,380 Germans, enough to create a separate community. But Prince von Solms-Braunfels, who founded the town of New Braunfels, and his successor, Baron von Meusebach, were not very good administrators, and their mismanagement brought about the society's collapse. There was an unclear title to the land that tangled the group in legal negotiations. The United States had begun its war with Mexico over the annexation of Texas, and the Adelsverein ran into debt defending itself. When the Germans started to farm, they discovered that each family had only 10 acres in the country and half an acre in the town, instead of the 320 they had been promised in Germany. Their dissatisfaction, combined with the poor soil, hostile Indians, and the clouds of mosquitoes they found in Texas, finally convinced the settlers to abandon their holdings and declare bankruptcy in 1847. They moved to other states, enlisted in the Mexican army, or went back to Germany. The dream of creating a German colony in Texas had failed, but some 30,000 German-born immigrants found homes there, and in 1850 they represented more than 20 percent of the state's population.

Other German colonization societies were formed in Missouri and Wisconsin as well as in Texas. Some had the ambitious plan of building so large a German community that it could be admitted to the Union as a German state, to be known as Germania. Others aimed more modestly to transplant the home country's culture, or simply to make money in land investment, or to found religious communities isolated from the rest of society. Many succeeded as communities, but none survived as German colonies.

In 1848 a series of revolutions broke out in Europe against the tyranny of its feudal system. The German effort at uniting its 38 small states into a modern democracy failed, and its exiled leaders became a small but significant wave of German immigrants to the United States. These "Forty-Eighters" provided an infusion of intellectual leadership and European culture with strongly liberal ideas. Numbering only a few thousand, most of them came to this country between 1850 and 1852, after the final collapse of their revolutionary efforts in Europe. They were not really representative of the mass of German immigrants then pouring into the country, but they had a great influence on the cultural and political life of the German-American community, and they represented their countrymen in the American mind. Their democratic ideals were often radical—it was in 1848 that Karl Marx wrote the *Communist Manifesto*—and alarmed many Americans, who saw these college-educated aliens as a threat, and indeed the Forty-Eighters looked on themselves as international-minded revolutionaries who called for reform in their new country as they had in Germany. They aroused the particular anger of nativists with their vigorous assault on American traditions that they held to be undemocratic. Highly critical of their new country, many wrote contemptuously of its politics and culture and urged drastic reforms. For example, the Free Germans of Louisville, meeting in 1854, demanded the abolition of slavery, the right of women and African Americans to vote, the abolition of the presidency and the senate in favor of a single legislative body to be elected by direct vote of all the people, the end of the Know-Nothing Party, a department of the government to be set up for the protection of immigrants, and a host of other reforms. Other groups, more frankly communistic, advocated a complete change of the government to make America a "republic of the workers." It is not surprising that one nativist book accused the Germans of disloyalty. "The mass of foreigners who come to this country are incapable of appreciating the policies of our government, they do not sufficiently understand our institutions. . . .," wrote Samuel Busey in *Immigration: Its Evils and Consequences* in 1854. "The abjuration of the allegiance of the country of their birth has not divested them of their principles. The oath of allegiance to ours has not infused into them the spirit of our government."

Not surprisingly, the Forty-Eighters had difficulty adjusting to American life. Besides holding unpopular social views, few of them had money or spoke English,

Carl Schurz (1829–1906) was a German Forty-Eighter who became the U.S. secretary of the interior. *(Library of Congress, Prints and Photographs Division [LC-USZ62-15582])*

and like the Latin farmers they were unprepared for life on the frontier. As one of the more successful Forty-Eighters wrote later, "Learned professors, writers and artists . . . were forced to support themselves by making cigars, acting as waiters or house-servants, boot-blacks or street-sweepers." Many returned to Germany and others withdrew into the German communities to escape the attacks of the nativists. Some, however, remained in the battle for social and political reform and made significant contributions to American progressive thought. Carl Schurz, probably the most prominent of the Forty-Eighters, went on to publish a liberal newspaper in New York and campaigned for Abraham Lincoln in 1858 and 1860. Lincoln, who strongly opposed the Know-Nothing position, appointed him U.S. minister to Spain and later secretary of the interior. Schurz also served as a major general in the Civil War and was elected to the United States Senate from Missouri.

The Scandinavians

The conditions in Norway, Sweden, and Denmark—the Scandinavian countries—were much the same in the early 18th century as those in the rest of Europe. Improvements in health because of better nutrition had reduced the death rate, and the population more than doubled in the first two decades. Overpopulation and the poverty it brought made emigration a clear choice. Another motive for leaving Scandinavia was the growing dissatisfaction with the rigid policies of the countries' state religion. The Lutheran Church was the official faith, and the citizens of the three countries were required to follow its rules and support it with their taxes. Dissent was severely repressed, and Quakers, Mormons, and Baptists who had established missionary groups there were subject to prison. The religious freedom of America therefore exerted a strong appeal to the many converts in Scandinavia.

There had been little immigration to the United States from Scandinavia since the brief existence of New Sweden, on the Delaware River, in the 17th century. Almost two centuries were to pass before a group of 52 or 53 Norwegians—possibly Quakers seeking relief from religious intolerance—set sail in the *Restauration,* as important a vessel to Norwegian history as the *Mayflower* is to America. They left from the port of Stavenger in 1825, and after a painful 14-week voyage they landed in New York City, only to find themselves threatened with confiscation of their ship because of a technicality. After this inauspicious beginning, they had to sell the vessel for $400 to continue their journey to Rochester by way of the Erie Canal. These "Norwegian Pilgrims" did not find their adjustment to America easy, and their letters home are filled with warnings about the dangers of coming to a new land without money or the ability to speak the language. Still, the reports of freedom and opportunity—widely read and copied throughout Norway—were positive enough to encourage a small stream of followers during the next decade.

In 1836 a group of 84 farmers made the voyage that was to inspire the mania known as "America Fever" in Scandinavia. Led by Ole Rynning, the 28-year-old son of a Lutheran minister, the little band made its way to Detroit, where someone talked them into buying land in Illinois, 70 miles south of Chicago. Their settlement at Beaver Creek was a disaster from the beginning. The land was mostly swamp, an icefield in winter and a breeding ground for disease-carrying insects in summer. Rynning was trained for the ministry, but he worked as hard as any in the group to keep the settlement alive. During the group's second winter, however, his feet became so frozen that he was confined to bed. During that season he occupied himself by writing a book that opened the gates of Norwegian immigration to America: *A True Account of America for the Information and Help of Peasant and Commoner.*

This brief guidebook was unlike the enthusiastic tracts of Birkbeck and Duden, but it did for Norway what those volumes did for England and Germany.

Full of solid information and practical advice, it did not present a picture of a land of milk and honey but explained how to get along in the United States. It advised when to plant turnips and potatoes, warned the traveler to carry plenty of food and a change of linen for the trip, and suggested bringing "a little brandy, vinegar, and a couple of bottles of wine," along with some raisins and prunes to make "soup for the seasick." Above all, Rynning warned his readers to be realistic. "People whom I do not advise to go to America," he wrote, "are (1) *drunkards*, who will be detested, and will soon perish miserably; (2) those who can neither work nor have sufficient money to carry on business. . . . Of the professional classes, doctors and druggists are most likely to find employment; but I do not advise even such persons to go unless they understand at least how to use oxen, or have learned a trade, for example, that of a tailor." Of the people he met in

Emigrant ships from Scandinavia, carrying hundreds of passengers a week bound for the American Midwest, offered language instruction and employment agencies as well as transportation. *(New York Public Library Print Collection)*

America, he had nothing but good to say. "[T]he stranger can never be too careful," he admitted, "but it has been my experience that the American as a general rule is easier to get along with than the Norwegian, more accommodating, more obliging, more reliable in all things."

Known simply as the "America Book," Rynning's *True Account* was an immediate success and sold out three editions in Swedish and Danish as well as in Norwegian within a year. The public was so hungry for information about America that children learning to read used it as their first text. Unfortunately, Rynning did not live to see what his words had accomplished. He died before the book was published, and his ill-fated colony disbanded.

The flame Rynning's honest little text ignited soon spread throughout Scandinavia, and it was not long before the exodus grew to such proportions that his more conservative countrymen were attacking the America fever. The sermons and pamphlets urging people to stay home had little effect, though. A young Swedish government official named Gustav Unonius was less drawn to the New World by its economic opportunity or religious tolerance than by its political and social equality. Recalling his decision to emigrate, he wrote years later, "[America] realized . . . millions of hopes, had become a tomb for age-old prejudices, a cradle of true civil liberty, equality, and of such new social ideals as are destined to bring happiness to mankind." There he would put behind him the social caste system of feudal Sweden: "Work, in any industry that is honorable, in America is no shame. Every workman has there the same rights of citizenship as the nobles. Conventional judgments, class interest and narrowmindedness do not hang on your coat tail nor trample on your heels."

In 1840 Unonius left the university town of Uppsala and followed Rynning's path to Illinois. Finding that land speculators had already bought up all the good farms, he pushed on to Wisconsin, where public land could still be found at $1.25 an acre, and founded a small colony. The enthusiastic letters he wrote home about his "free and independent life" were as popular in Sweden as Rynning's *True Account* and soon attracted an assortment of ex-army officers, noblemen, merchants, and craftsmen to his New Uppsala. Despite the high ideals which had inspired its settlement, however, it didn't fare any better than Rynning's Beaver Creek, and after two or three years Unonius himself gave it up and went to New York to become an Episcopal minister. Later he gave up on the whole American adventure and returned to Stockholm. The colony didn't long outlast him; 10 years after it began, a visitor found only a handful of families there, living in their original log cabins.

There were many other failed communities begun with hope by Scandinavian immigrants. One of the best known was Oleana in Pennsylvania, established in 1852 with the noblest motives by the internationally famous Norwegian violinist Ole Bull. After a spectacularly successful concert tour of America, Bull invested his life savings in a 120,000-acre tract where he planned to build a utopian colony for the poor of Norway. He found the Pennsylvanians as accommodating and obliging as Rynning had found all Americans, and his little group of pioneers were warmly welcomed by the local farmers. Bull became a great hero in Norway for his generous plan, and people flocked to his colony. Unfortunately, it turned out that he was a better violinist than he was a businessman. The land in which he had already invested in improvements did not have a clear title, and the whole project fell through. Bull

Ole Bull (1810–88), Norwegian virtuoso and immigrant leader who attempted to found a Norwegian colony in Pennsylvania in 1852, poses with his violin in a picture taken by photographer Mathew Brady in the 1870s. *(Library of Congress, Prints and Photographs Division [LC-USZ62-102595])*

himself lost $70,000 on the transaction and had to go back to the concert stage to pay off his debts. Oleana, proudly named for him, fell apart before it ever got started and became the subject of ballads in Norway that mocked his unrealistic claims for America.

A people known for patience, diligence, and perseverance, the Scandinavians were not discouraged by the repeated failures of their pioneering efforts. Instead, they continued westward, pushing the frontier before them, throughout the 1840s and 1850s. Never competing for jobs in the big cities, they pursued the horizon, sending home an endless stream of encouraging "America letters" and money to help their families join them and so escaped most of the hostility and exploitation the Irish and Germans encountered.

Castle Garden

The abuses to which immigrants were subjected in the first half of the 19th century had long been a scandal in New York City, America's largest port by 1820 and the city to which the largest number of immigrants arrived. These abuses began with the deplorable conditions of the ships on which the immigrants came. Despite a series of Passenger Acts going back to 1819, which had tried to regulate the treatment of immigrants in transit to America, things had improved very little. The death toll among those coming to the United States averaged around 9 percent during the 1840s, and those who survived the trip were often so broken in health that they were unfit for work. Once on land, immigrants often fell victim to dishonest porters and money changers who met the boat to take advantage of the aliens' ignorance of American ways. Swindlers offered the newcomers food, lodging, and railway tickets despite all the city's efforts to keep them off the docks, and thieves picked pockets with confidence that their victims would be unable to complain. Until then, immigrants entered the city directly after going through customs.

Castle Garden, New York City's first immigrant depot, provided newcomers with an employment office. *(New York Public Library Print Collection)*

With the passage of the last national Passenger Act, in 1855, New York decided to establish a receiving station to afford immigrants some protection from fraud, change their money, and help them arrange for accommodations and buy railroad tickets. Castle Garden, an imposing structure at the southern tip of Manhattan, had been built in 1807 to protect the city from the British as the War of 1812 approached. It was named Fort Clinton and later Castle Clinton and leased to a private business as an amusement park. In the late 1830s it became a fashionable concert hall, but as the area around it began to deteriorate, the concerts ended, and the building stood vacant. When the city took it over as an immigration office, it was fenced off to control who came and went.

The installation had an office where each immigrant's name, birthplace, and destination were registered, and there was a clerk of the railway line who furnished each arrival with printed information on the price of the tickets needed. Immigrants were also able to exchange their money at fair rates, posted daily. During the 35 years of its operation, Castle Garden provided assistance and temporary shelter to thousands of bewildered aliens standing on American soil for the first time.

Chronicle of Events

1814

- Expenses of the War of 1812 raise the national debt from its 1811 total of $83 million to $127 million. Congress doubles land taxes and increases tariffs on imported goods.
- *August 24*: English troops burn the White House, the Capitol Building, and most of the government buildings in Washington, D.C.
- *November 7*: United States troops, under general Andrew Jackson, invade and capture Pensacola in Spanish-held Florida.
- *December 24*: The Treaty of Ghent officially ends the War of 1812 without resolving any of its issues. News of the treaty does not reach the United States until February 1815. The treaty is ratified February 16.

1815

- U.S. imports increase from $13 million in 1814 to an annual average of $100 million and exports from $7 million to an annual average of $70 million from 1815 to 1820.
- *January 1–8*: The British, not knowing that the war is officially over, launch a massive attack on New Orleans but suffer heavy losses, finally retreating January 27. The Battle of New Orleans costs the British over 2,000 men, while American casualties number only 13 killed and 58 wounded.
- *March 3*: President Madison proposes a standing army of 20,000; Congress approves a force of 10,000. Many immigrants enlist.
- *July 3*: The United States and Britain sign a trade agreement ending high duties imposed by Britain and allowing free U.S. trade with the East Indies.

1816

- *January 21*: The African Methodist Episcopal Church, the first independent African-American church, is founded in Philadelphia.
- *December 4*: James Monroe is elected the fifth president of the United States.
- *December 28*: The American Colonization Society is founded in Washington, D.C., to resettle free African Americans in Africa. Its work leads to the founding of the colony of Liberia in 1822.

1818

- Irish associations petition Congress for land on which to settle Irish paupers from Eastern cities. Congress refuses to sell land in large tracts to any national group.
- *May 30*: The Black Ball Line begins regular sailing-ship service between Liverpool and New York. New technology enables the ships to cut the transatlantic sailing time from 39 to 33 days.
- *October 20*: Britain and the United States sign a treaty granting Americans fishing rights off the coast of Newfoundland and establishing the 49th parallel of latitude as the boundary between Canada and the United States.

1819

- America's first financial panic, caused by a declining market for American products and excessive speculation in western lands, results in the failure of many banks early in the year.
- *February 22*: A treaty is signed between Spain and the United States in which Spain renounces all claims to the Oregon territory and cedes Florida to the United States.
- *March 2*: Congress passes an act limiting the number of passengers on any vessel entering the United States to two per five tons of the vessel's weight.
- *May 24–June 20*: The first transatlantic voyage by steam-assisted sail arrives from Savannah, Georgia, at Liverpool, England, in 26 days, a record for an Atlantic crossing.

1820

- The fourth national census shows a population of 9,638,453, of which more than 45 percent live in the North and about 23 percent live west of the Appalachian Mountains. The rate of increase continues at 33.5 percent per decade. Almost 90 percent of the African and African-American population, numbering 1,771,656, are slaves.
- The federal government begins recording the arrival of immigrants by country of origin, age, sex, occupation, etc.
- *March 30*: New England sends the first Protestant missionaries to the Hawaiian Islands.
- *April 24*: Congress passes a Public Land Act establishing a minimum price for public land at $1.25 per acre and reducing the minimum purchase from 160 to 80 acres.
- *December 6*: James Monroe is reelected president, defeating John Quincy Adams.

1821

- *January 17*: Moses Austin receives permission from the Spanish government to settle 300 American families in the province of Texas in northeastern Mexico. Following his death on June 10, his son Stephen F. Austin takes possession of the land on August 12.

1822

- *June 19*: The United States recognizes the Republic of Colombia, a region consisting of present-day Colombia, Venezuela, Ecuador, and Panama, newly freed from Spanish rule.
- *December 12*: The United States recognizes the independence of Mexico.

1823

- *January 27*: The United States recognizes Chile and Argentina.
- *April 14*: The Mexican government formally approves Stephen Austin's settlement as an American colony in Texas.
- *December 2*: President Monroe, in his annual message to Congress, presents Secretary of State John Quincy Adams's proposed policy of opposing foreign colonization in the Americas and involvement in American affairs and American interference with existing colonies or the internal affairs of foreign governments. The Monroe Doctrine, though never passed into law, becomes the basis of American policy in Latin America.

1824

- *April 17*: Russia and the United States settle their dispute over the southern portion of Alaska, including part of the Oregon territory, and establish the southern boundary of Alaska at the parallel of 54° 40' N.
- *May 26*: The United States recognizes Brazil.
- *August 4*: The United States recognizes the Central American Union, a state comprising present-day Costa Rica, Honduras, Guatemala, Nicaragua, and El Salvador.
- *October 4*: Mexico becomes a republic.

1825

- First wave of immigration from Norway begins.
- Great Britain repeals its anti-emigration law.
- *January 3*: Scottish textile-mill owner Robert Owen buys the 20,000-acre estate called Harmonie in Indiana and establishes the socialist colony of New Harmony. Although it fails three years later, the experiment inspires numerous other utopian colonies.

- *February 9*: John Quincy Adams is chosen by the U.S. House of Representatives the sixth president of the United States after the 1824 election failed to produce a clear winner.
- *March 24*: American colonization begins in the Mexican state of Texas-Coahuila.
- *October 26*: The Erie Canal, largely constructed by Irish immigrant labor, is officially opened in Buffalo, New York, connecting the Hudson River with Lake Erie.

1826

- *May 2*: The United States recognizes Peru.
- *April 26*: A treaty of commerce and mutual support between Denmark and the United States is signed.
- *December 16*: American colonists in the Mexican state of Texas declare their freedom; Stephen Austin helps the Mexican government put down the rebellion.

1827

- *August 6*: The United States and Great Britain sign a treaty agreeing to joint occupation of the Oregon territory.

1828

- *December 3*: Andrew Jackson is elected the seventh president of the United States.

1829

- *July 29*: The Chippewa, Potawatomi, and Ottawa Indians cede their land in the Michigan Territory to the United States.
- *August 25*: The American government opens negotiations for the purchase of part of the Mexican state of Texas-Coahuila, occupied by many American settlers. The negotiations break down on October 16, when the American minister to Mexico is recalled at the request of the Mexican government.

1830

- The fifth national census shows a population of 12,866,000, an increase of about one-third since 1820. The percentage living west of the Appalachians remains constant at about one-quarter.
- A revolution in Poland causes large-scale immigration to the United States.
- The Ursaline Convent at Charlestown, Massachusetts, is burned in an anti-Catholic demonstration.
- *April 6*: The Mexican government approves American laws prohibiting further colonization of Mexican terri-

tory by Americans; Joseph Smith founds the Church of Jesus Christ of Latter-day Saints, the Mormon Church, in Fayette, New York.

- *May 7*: A treaty of commerce and navigation is signed between the United States and the Ottoman Empire (Turkey).
- *May 28*: The Indian Removal Act, providing for the compulsory resettlement of all Indians in the east to lands west of the Mississippi River, is passed into law.
- *July 15*: The Sac, Fox, and Sioux (Dakota, Lakota, Nakota) Indians are compelled to cede all their land east of the Mississippi River to the United States. The territory constitutes most of the present states of Iowa, Missouri, and Minnesota.
- *September 15*: The Choctaw Indians cede all their land east of the Mississippi River to the United States.

1831

- *April 5*: Mexico and the United States sign a treaty of friendship and trade.

1832

- *May 9*: The Seminole Indians cede their tribal lands in Florida to the United States.
- *October 14*: The Chickasaw Indians cede their land in present-day Mississippi and Tennessee to the United States.
- *December 5*: Andrew Jackson is reelected the seventh president of the United States.
- *December 28*: St. Louis Academy, founded in St. Louis, Missouri, in 1818 as a French-language institution, receives a state charter as St. Louis College. The only Roman Catholic university west of the Appalachian Mountains, it changes its language of instruction to English.

1833

- *March 20*: The United States and Siam sign a treaty of friendship and commerce.
- *September 21*: The United States and the Sultanate of Muscat sign a treaty of friendship and commerce.

1834

- Congress allots 36 sections of land in Illinois to Polish refugees.
- *January 3*: Stephen Austin demands that the American colony in Texas be made a separate state of Mexico. Interpreted as a threat, the demand leads to Austin's arrest by the Mexican government.

1835

- *January–February*: Some 2,000 American settlers arrive in Mexico; by the end of the year, "Texas fever" has brought nearly 30,000 American home seekers, including a group of Germans and two shiploads of Irish peasants, to a region occupied by 3,500 Mexicans.
- *October 2*: A group of American settlers defeat a troop of Mexican soldiers, initiating the Mexican War.
- *December 29*: The Cherokee Indians surrender all their land east of the Mississippi River to the United States.

1836

- *February 23–March 6*: Mexican troops besiege an American garrison in the Alamo in San Antonio, Texas. Its 187 American defenders, including James Bowie and Davy Crockett, are all killed.
- *March 2*: American settlers in Texas adopt a declaration of independence.
- *April 21*: American settlers in Texas defeat the Mexican army.
- *May 14*: Mexico signs a treaty recognizing the independence of Texas.
- *July 1*: The U.S. Senate calls for the recognition of Texas. On July 4 the House of Representatives passes a resolution approving recognition, and on September 5 Sam Houston is elected president of the Republic of Texas.
- *September 16*: The United States and Morocco sign a treaty of friendship.
- *December 5*: Martin Van Buren is elected the eighth president of the United States.

1837

- A financial panic causes an increase of anti-immigration sentiment.
- *March 3*: The United States recognizes the Republic of Texas.

1838

- The Irish Poor Law Act "for the more effectual relief of the Poor" is passed, requiring landlords to support the destitute and leading to large-scale emigration of Irish farmers and laborers.
- *April 23*: Steamship service between England and the United States begins with the arrival in New York of two ships, one from London after a voyage of 17 days and one from Bristol that took 15 days.
- *October 30*: The government of Missouri declares the Mormons enemies and orders them "exterminated or

driven from the state." Mobs attack and kill 17, and some 15,000 Mormons flee to Illinois.

- *November 26*: The United States and the Kingdom of Sardinia sign a treaty of commerce.

1839

- *January 19*: The United States and the Netherlands sign a treaty of commerce.
- *September 23*: France is the first European country to recognize the Republic of Texas, with which it signs a treaty of commerce on September 25.

1840

- The Cunard Line is founded in London, beginning regular steamship transport between Europe and the United States.
- The Mormon Overseas Mission is founded in England.
- *August 26*: The United States and Portugal sign a treaty of commerce.
- *November 13*: Great Britain recognizes the Republic of Texas and signs a treaty of commerce.
- *December 2*: William Henry Harrison is elected the ninth president of the United States.

1841

- *April 4*: President Harrison dies of pneumonia; Vice President John Tyler becomes the 10th president of the United States.

1842

- The Society for the Protection of German Immigrants in Texas is founded.

1843

- *June*: The American Republican Party is founded to oppose immigration; it demands a 21-year residence requirement for naturalization.

1844

- *May 1*: Anti-Catholic demonstrations by the American Republican Party in the Irish section of Philadelphia result in 30 deaths and the burning of several churches.
- *April 12*: The United States and the Republic of Texas sign a treaty agreeing on the annexation of Texas as an American territory and the ceding of all Texas public lands to the United States.

- *July 1*: The United States and China sign a treaty giving the United States trading rights in China.
- *December 7*: James K. Polk is elected the 11th president of the United States.

1845

- An Irish potato famine begins, causing extensive immigration to the United States.
- *March 1*: Congress passes a joint resolution for the annexation of Texas. On March 28 diplomatic relations between Mexico and the United States are dissolved.
- *July 5–7*: The American Republican Party, renamed the Native American Party, holds its first national convention. Its members hold six seats in Congress.
- *November 10*: The United States and Belgium sign a treaty of commerce.
- *December 29*: Texas becomes the 28th state of the United States.

1846

- Crop failures in Germany and Holland lead to extensive emigration to the United States from those countries. By the end of the year, the German population of Texas reaches 5,247.
- *May 13*: The United States declares war on Mexico.
- *July 7–9*: U.S. forces seize and occupy Monterey and San Francisco, California, and declare it American territory. On August 13 American troops take possession of Los Angeles.
- *December 12*: The United States and New Granada (present-day Colombia) sign a treaty of friendship and commerce.

1847

- *July 22*: Mormons establish their first settlement in the valley of the Great Salt Lake in present-day Utah.

1848

- A revolution in Germany sends many refugees, known as "Forty-Eighters," to the United States.
- Emancipation of peasants in Germany and Austria-Hungary frees many to emigrate.
- *January 24*: Gold is discovered in California. The gold rush draws immigrants from many countries to the United States.
- *February 2*: Mexico and the United States sign a peace treaty in the village of Guadalupe Hidalgo, near Mexico City. In return for $15 million, Mexico cedes the present-

day states of Texas, California, Utah, Nevada, and New Mexico, along with large parts of Arizona, Oklahoma, Colorado, Kansas, and Wyoming, to the United States.

- *November 7*: Zachary Taylor is elected the 12th president of the United States.

1849

- "Passenger cases" are decided by the United States Supreme Court, which declares the head taxes on immigrants unconstitutional.
- The Native American Party is unofficially renamed the Know-Nothing Party.
- *February 28*: The gold rush begins in California with the arrival of the first shipload of prospectors. Stories of high wages in the mining camps draw many Chinese laborers fleeing the depression in China.
- *December 20*: The United States and the Hawaiian Islands sign a treaty of friendship and commerce.

1850

- The seventh U.S. census records a population of 23,191,876, representing a 35.9-percent increase between 1840 and 1850, the highest on record.
- The Taiping Rebellion in China paralyzes trade and industry. The economic failure and widespread famine that result cause extensive Chinese emigration to the United States. The rebellion continues to 1864.
- *April 7*: William Inman of Philadelphia initiates regular steamship service between Liverpool, England, and New York City, in competition with the Cunard Line.
- *July 9*: President Taylor dies of cholera; Vice President Millard Fillmore becomes the 13th president of the United States.
- *November 25*: The United States and Switzerland sign a treaty of friendship and commerce.

1852

- The first state commissioner of immigration is appointed in Wisconsin.
- *September*: Ole Bull founds Oleana in Pennsylvania. The Norwegian colony fails the next year.
- *November 2*: Franklin Pierce is elected the 14th president of the United States.
- *November 24*: Commodore Matthew C. Perry leaves for Japan at the head of a naval squadron to open the Pacific countries to U.S. trade and to end Japanese isolation from the West.

1853

- *December 30*: James Gadsden, U.S. minister to Mexico, secures a 29,640-square-mile strip of land near the southern boundary of New Mexico and Arizona for the United States for $10 million.

1854

- The Know-Nothing Party reaches the height of its influence.
- *March 31*: The United States and Japan sign a treaty of peace and friendship, allowing American ships to trade with Japan.
- *August 3*: Congress passes the Graduation Act, providing for sale of public land unsold for 10 years at $1 per acre and land unsold for 30 years for as little as 12.5 cents an acre.

1855

- Castle Garden, the first emigration depot in the United States, opens in New York City.
- *January 28*: A transcontinental water-rail route connecting New York and California is completed.
- *March 3*: Congress passes its fifth and last passenger act establishing conditions under which immigrants may be brought to the United States by boat.
- *August 4*: A consul general to Japan is appointed.

1856

- The Irish Catholic Colonization Convention in Buffalo, New York, fails to win support of Eastern bishops.
- *February 22*: The Know-Nothing Party nominates former President Millard Fillmore for president. He wins only Maryland's eight electoral votes.
- *November 4*: James Buchanan is elected the 15th president of the United States.

1857

- *May 20*: The Utah Territory is declared to be in a state of rebellion because of its treatment of migrants on their way to California. President Buchanan appoints a governor and authorizes the use of federal troops to enforce national law.

1858

- *March 18*: The Mormons abandon their capital in Salt Lake City and move south to Provo to avoid an open confrontation with federal troops.

- *June 14*: The "Mormon War" is settled as the governor of Utah proclaims that "peace is restored to our Territory." The Mormon leaders return to Salt Lake City on July 1.

1859

- *October 16*: Abolitionist John Brown and 18 followers attack the U.S. arsenal at Harpers Ferry, Virginia, in a move to liberate American slaves. On October 18 Brown and his men are captured, and Brown is hanged on December 2.

1860

- *November 6*: Abraham Lincoln is elected the 16th president of the United States.
- *December 20*: South Carolina votes to secede from the United States; on December 22 it proclaims its "independence, freedom, and sovereignty," and on December 30 the U.S. arsenal in Charleston is seized.

Eyewitness Testimony

The continued and increasing emigration from this country to America becomes every day more alarming. The immediate and earnest attention of government to this serious drain of the most useful part of the population of the United Kingdom, to the growing privation of its best hands in arts and manufactures, and to the almost daily accumulating loss of the mechanical means of the country's prosperity, is imperiously directed.

Editorial in a London newspaper, June 27, 1816, reprinted in Niles' Weekly Register *(1816).*

Col. Nicholas Gray, after having consulted with the governor of the Mississippi territory, is authorized to invite any number of industrious emigrants into that country, where they will be provided with lands *rent free,* for three years, and with cattle and corn at the usual rates.

Advertisement in Niles' Weekly Register, *November 9, 1816.*

I sincerely wish that your proposition to "purchase a tract of land in Illinois on favorable terms, for introducing a colony of English farmers," may encounter no difficulties. . . . For although as to other foreigners it is thought better to discourage their settling together in large masses, wherein . . . they preserve for a long time their own languages, habits, and principles of government, . . . English emigrants are without this inconvenience. They differ from us but little in their principles of government, and most of those (merchants excepted) who come here, are sufficiently disposed to adopt ours.

Thomas Jefferson, letter of September 12, 1817, in The Works of Thomas Jefferson, *Volume VII, (1882–1899), p. 83.*

Dear Brothers and Sisters:

. . . They say things are bad here, but I think they are good indeed. I have seen many from England; some have been here two and others three weeks, and got employ at from 10 to 14 dollars per month besides lodging and board. . . .

. . . The land is rich indeed, and every industrious farmer may become a freeholder of the United States, by paying eighty dollars, being the first installment for a quarter of a section of land; and though he has not a shilling left, he may easily gain as much off the land, as will pay the other installments as they become due. The land being his own, there is no limit to his prosperity; no proud tyrant can lord it over him; he has no rent to pay, no game, timber, or fishing laws to dread; few and small taxes to pay; no excise laws to harass him; no tythe nor poor's rate; so that the farmers are pros-

perous and happy. May the father of the human race pour down abundant blessings upon the authors and finishers of such a benevolent system. James has got rid of the English yoke, and is working at two pounds a week and paying 13s. 6d. for board and lodging. For breakfast he has coffee, beef, mutton, bacon, potatoes, butter, bread, pickles, &c., &c., and the rest of his living is as good. . . .

Matthew Farrar, English immigrant, letter of November 2, 1817, from Philadelphia, in Abbott, Historical Aspects of the Immigration Problem *(1926), p. 38.*

There prevails so much good sense and useful knowledge, joined to a genuine warmth of friendly feeling, a disposition to promote the happiness of each other, that the man who is lonely among them, is not formed for society. Such are the citizens of these new states, and my unaffected and well considered wish is to spend among them the remainder of my days. . . .

[W]hat is most at variance with English notions of the American people, is the urbanity and civilization that prevail in situations remote from large cities. In our journey from Norfolk, on the coast of Virginia, to this place, in the heart of the Allegheny mountains, we have not for a moment lost sight of the manners of polished life. Refinement is unquestionably far more rare than in our nation and highly cultivated state of society; but so is extreme vulgarity. In every department of common life, we here see employed persons superior in habits and education to the same class in England. . . .

Here, whatever their origin, whether English, Scotch, Irish, German, or French, all are Americans: and of all the imputations on the American character, jealousy of strangers is surely the most absurd and groundless. The Americans are sufficiently alive to their own interest. But they wish well to strangers; and they are not always satisfied with wishing, if they can promote their success by active services. . . .

Let a stranger make his way through England, in a course remote from the great roads, and going to no inns, take such entertainment only as he might find in the cottages of labourers, he would have as much cause to complain of the rudeness of the people, and far more of their drunkenness and profligacy than in these backwoods.

Morris Birkbeck, English immigrant and colonizer in Illinois, in Notes on a Journey in America *(1818), in Neidle,* The New Americans *(1967), pp. 85, 87–88.*

I am doing astonishingly well, thanks be to God, and was able on the 16th of this month to make a deposit of 100 dollars in the bank of the United States.

. . . [Here] a man is allowed to thrive and flourish without having a penny taken out of his pocket by government; no visit from tax gatherers, constables, or soldiers; everyone at liberty to act and speak as he likes, provided he does not hurt another; to slander and damn government, abuse public men in office to their faces. . . . Hundreds go unpunished for crimes for which they would surely be hanged in Ireland; in fact, they are so tender of life in this country, that a person should have [great difficulty] to get himself hanged for anything.

John Doyle, an Irish immigrant, letter to his wife in Ireland, January 1818, in Blumenthal and Ozer, Coming to America: Immigrants from the British Isles *(1980), pp. 89–90.*

Dear Friend:

. . . . I hope you will come over as I did, and I dare say you will be able to send for your wife, in three months. Never mind landing here without money, as all got work before we left the vessel. The sooner you come the better; you will never repent. . . .

John Redfern, English immigrant, letter of March 8, 1818, from Charleston, S. C., in Knight, Important Extracts from Original and Recent Letters Written by Englishmen. . . . *(1818), p. 7.*

In this country, the rich don't call the industrious people the "swinish multitude." The judge of the district, the justice of the peace, and the parson of our parish, are all pleased to pay, and receive visits from us.

Anyone may do well here, no matter what his trade be: if one does not do, another will. I never enjoyed the comforts of life so much as at present. . . .

There are poor people here, but no hungry children crying for bread in vain, they have all enough and to spare. This is the promised land, flowing with milk and honey.

If an honest man is set naked on the American shore, he may soon make an independence. . . .

I feel for all my acquaintance, inform them I will assist those of them who will come. Poor people live as well as the rich; they work when they please, and where they please. I wish my mother was here. Good fortune has attended me ever since I left England. My son James goes a hunting and shooting, and I can eat partridge as well as any knave in England. . . .

Luke Bentley, English immigrant, letter to his brother of March 27, 1818, from New York, in Knight, Important Extracts from Original and Recent Letters Written by Englishmen. . . . *(1818), p. 44.*

Dear Brother:

This is the country for a man to enjoy himself: I do not mean Virginia, but Ohio, Indiana, and the Missouri Territory; where you may see prairies 60 miles long and ten broad, not a stick nor a stone in them, at two dollars an acre, that will produce from seventy to one hundred bushels of Indian corn per acre: too rich for wheat or any other kind of grain. I measured Indian corn in Ohio State, last September, more than fifteen feet high, and some of the ears had from four to seven hundred grains. I believe I saw more peaches and apples rotting on the ground, than would sink the British fleet. . . . Good rye whiskey; apple and peach brandy, at forty cents per gallon, which I think equal to rum. . . .

There is enough to spare of everything a person can desire; I have not heard either man or woman speak a word against the government or the price of provisions

The poorest families adorn the table three times a day like a wedding dinner—tea, coffee, beef, fowls, pies, eggs, pickles, good bread; and their favorite beverage is peach brandy. Say, is it so in England?

If you knew the difference between this country and England you would need no persuading to leave it and come hither. . . .

Samuel Crabtree, English immigrant, letter to his brother in England from Wheeling, Virginia, of April 10, 1818, in Abbott, Historical Aspects of the Immigration Problem *(1926), p. 40.*

Among the splendid fooleries which have at times amused a portion of the American people, as well as their representatives in Congress, was that of granting, on most favorable terms, to certain emigrants from France, a large tract of land in the Alabama Territory to encourage the cultivation of the vine and olive, passed March 3, 1817.

This tract contains 92,000 acres, and was sold at $2 per acre, payable without interest, in fourteen years—. . . which could not, at this time, probably be purchased of the proprietors for less than $2 million.

. . . By the way, . . . I very much question the policy of any act of government that has a tendency to introduce and keep up among us a foreign national language or dialect, manners or character, as every large and compact settlement of emigrants from any particular country must necessarily occasion. . . . [T]he people of the United States are yet wretchedly deficient of a national character, though it is rapidly forming, and in a short time will be as the vanguard of the national strength. Its progress, however, is retarded by the influx of foreigners, with manners and prejudices favorable to a state of things repugnant to our rules and notions of right. . . .

Niles' Weekly Register, August 8, 1818.

Dear Mother:

I now sit down in a country, where fortune is within my reach. . . . Lands such as you never saw, which you may use for three years, and then it wants no manure. I have purchased one hundred and sixty acres, on a fine level plain, where there is not a tree to be seen, they are always covered with grass. . . . There are a great many thousands of acres of these lands in these parts. I intend purchasing eighty acres of woodland, then I shall have two hundred and forty acres.

. . . [The people here] will not work; they can live with the greatest ease and don't want to be rich; but they who come here and are industrious, make great fortunes in a short time.

. . . The people here want me to take the Oath and become an American, but I will not unless you will come, then I shall have no objection; the people here are very benevolent and obliging to Englishmen. Now my dear mother, I want you to send me word that you, my brothers and sister will come after me: this would be the most joyful news I could receive; a hundred pounds would bring you all comfortably.

I never experienced such health before, I am getting quite fat.

Letter from an English immigrant in Carmi, Illinois, to his mother in England, September 25, 1818, in Abbott, Historical Aspects of the Immigration Problem (1926), pp. 39–40.

As for general emigration, I imagine, by the time I reach England, it will have begun to subside. The voice of disappointment will certainly have risen above that of wild and romantic adventure, and made itself heard. At present, it is the height of folly. Such is the present state of things here that neither farmers nor merchants can succeed: the vast number of sheriffs' sales, are a sufficient proof of this. . . .

[B]ut, if such be the distress of England, and so gloomy its prospects, that emigration is (to anyone) an object of desire, I would certainly advise them to remove hither rather than to a new colony. The pioneers of civilization, those who advance first into an untrodden desert, and begin the work of culture and population, ought to be schooled to the office by a suitable education; they must be inured from childhood to a rude and desultory life, to every inconvenience of poverty and irregularity of climate, to struggle against difficulties which would daunt, and midst sufferings which would destroy all besides. The towns-man, the mechanic, and even the farmer, accustomed to regularity of life, must, in such a situation, become a wretched object. . . .

Emanuel Howitt, British visitor to the United States, warning of the hardships immigrants would encounter, in Selections from Letters Written during a Tour through the United States, in the Summer and Autumn of 1819 (1890), pp. 215–216.

It is, I regret to say, too true, that the writing of emigrants, however respectable, present a partial or unfaithful portraiture. . . .

To my countrymen disposed to emigrate, but who can . . . keep their unequalled comforts and honor unimpaired, I would say, in a voice which should be heard from shore to shore, Stay where you are; for neither America nor the world, have anything to offer you in exchange! But to those of decreasing means, and increasing families, uprooted, withering, and seeking a transplantation somewhere, full of hard, dirty-handed industry, and with means sufficient for location here, I would say, Haste away; you have no other refuge from poverty, which in England is crime, punishable with neglect, and contempt everlasting! But, if you come, come one, and all of you, male and female, in your working jackets, with axes, ploughshares, and pruning-hooks in your hands, prepared long to suffer many privations, expecting to be your own servants, no man's masters; to find liberty and independence, anything but soft indulgence, and America, a land only of everlasting, well-rewarded labour. . . .

I am now living on wild bucks and bears, mixed up, and barbarizing with men almost as wild as they; men systematically unprincipled, and in whom moral sense seems to have no existence; this is the lot of all coming here. . . .

Letter by William Faux, English traveler in Indiana, to the editor of the Stamford News, December 25, 1819, in Memorable Days in America (1823), pp. 329–331.

. . . The occasion has been judged proper for asserting, as a principle in which the rights and interests of the United States are involved, that the American continents, by the free and independent condition which they have assumed and maintain, are henceforth not to be considered as subjects for future colonization by any European powers. . . .

The citizens of the United States cherish sentiments the most friendly in favor of the liberty and happiness of their fellow-men on that side of the Atlantic. In the wars of the European powers in matters relating to themselves we have never taken any part, nor does it comport with our policy to do so. It is only when our rights are invaded or seriously menaced that we resent injuries or make preparation for our defense. With the movements in this hemisphere we are of necessity more immediately connected, and by causes which must be obvious to all enlightened and impartial observers. The political system of the allied powers is essentially different in this respect from that of America. . . We owe it, therefore, to candor and to the amicable relations existing between the United States and those powers to declare that we should consider any attempt on their part to extend their system to any portion of this hemisphere as dangerous to our peace and safety. With the existing colonies or dependencies of any European power we have not interfered and shall not interfere. But with the Governments who have declared their independence and maintained it, and whose independence we have, on great consideration and on just principles, acknowledged, we could not view any interposition for the purpose of oppressing them, or controlling in any other manner their destiny, by any European power in any other light than as the manifestation of an unfriendly disposition toward the United States. . . .

Our policy in regard to Europe, which we adopted at an early stage of the wars which have so long agitated that quarter of the globe, nevertheless, remains the same, which is not to interfere in the internal concerns of any of its powers, to consider the government de facto as the legitimate government for us; to cultivate friendly relations with it, and to preserve those relations by a frank, firm, and manly policy, meeting in all instances the just claims of every power, submitting to injuries from none.

James Monroe, fifth president of the United States, asserting America's opposition to European influence or control in the Americas ("the Monroe Doctrine"), Message to Congress, December 2, 1823, in Davis and Mintz, The Boisterous Sea of Liberty *(1998), pp. 349–350.*

I am convinced, that if several families, say ten or twenty, who are on friendly terms with one another, should spend a year here in the peaceful situation, such as the American is able to provide for himself so quickly in the midst of an unpeopled forest, they would never yearn again to return to Europe, to visit, yes, but never to stay.

Gottfried Duden, German immigrant to Missouri, letter of 1824, in Report on a Journey to the Western States of North America *(1829), in Stephenson,* A History of American Immigration *(1926), p. 47.*

The whole continent presents a scene of *scrambling* and roars with greedy hurry. Go ahead! Is the order of the day.

An English observer describing the United States after the opening of the first railroad to cross the Appalachians, 1829, in Cornelius, The English Americans *(1990), p. 91.*

Give my very kind love to Father, and tell him if he was here he could soon kill himself by drinking if he thought proper. . . . I can go into a store, and have as much brandy as I like to drink for three half-pence, and all other spirits in proportion.

Irish immigrant, letter home from Boston, 1830, in Marcus L. Hansen, "Immigration and Puritanism," in Norwegian-American Studies and Records, Volume IX, *(1935), p. 11.*

These impoverished and destitute beings, transported from the trans-Atlantic shores, are crowding themselves into every place of business and labor, and driving the poor colored American citizen out. Along the wharves where the colored man once done the whole business of shipping and unshipping—in stores where his services were once rendered, and in families where the chief places were filled by him, in all these situations there were substituted foreigners.

An African-American worker, complaining that Irish immigrants were taking jobs once held by blacks, 1830s, in Litwack, North of Slavery: The Negro in the Free States, 1790–1860 *(1965), p. 163.*

[I]t was known that a contractor on the 3rd division of the Baltimore and Ohio railroad, about 25 miles from the city, had absconded, leaving his laborers unpaid, and that they (as too often happens in Ireland, the country which, in general, they had recently left) had taken the law into their own hands, were wantonly destroying the property of the company, because their employer had wronged them! They were between 200 and 300 strong, and, with pick axes, hammers and sledges, made a most furious attack on the rails, sills, and whatever else they could destroy.

Niles' Weekly Register, *July 16, 1831.*

. . . There has been for many years past, and still continues, a large emigration from this port to different parts of the United States, and also to the British settlements in North America [Canada]; and from my knowledge of the subject, I have no hesitation in stating that the description of persons who generally embark for the United States from this port are of good character, in comfortable circumstances, and certainly many degrees removed from paupers.

On the contrary, the greater number of the persons who embark for the British settlements, on account of the cheap conveyance, are the evil and ill-disposed, who will not do well in their own country, and the landed proprietors are glad to get rid of them, which they do by paying their passages, and laying in sufficient provisions for the voyage, totally regardless of how they are to make out life on their arrival.

The reason why North America is preferred is on account of the cheapness of the passage.

Letter from the United States Consulate at Londonderry, Ireland, September 19, 1836, in "Report from the Secretary of the Treasury, Relative to the Deportation of Paupers from Great Britain. . . ." United States 24th Congress, 2d session, *Senate Document No. 5, in Abbott,* Immigration: Select Documents *(1924), p. 117.*

I am glad that I came here, though everything has not always gone according to my wishes. . . . I and others who have been accustomed to work since we were children think of this as a Canaan when we consider the fertile soil, which without the use of fertilizer brings forth fruits of every kind. Norway can no more be compared with America than a desolate waste with a garden in full blossom.

Norwegian immigrant Gjert G. Hovland, letter from Illinois to a friend in Norway, July 6, 1838, in Blegen, Norwegian Migration to America *(1931), pp. 196–197.*

What an impression it would make on a poor highlander's imagination to be told that someday he might eat wheat bread every day and pork at least three times a week! . . . Here even a tramp can enjoy a chicken dinner once in a while.

Norwegian immigrant Ole Munch Raeder, in America in the Forties: The Letters of Ole Munch Raeder *(1842), p. 74.*

I do not expect to "cut gold with jackknives." I am prepared to earn my daily bread by the sweat of my brow. . . . For this I am prepared, but I hope to be free and independent and to possess my own home, if ever so modest, and the happiness it confers.

Gustaf Unonius, Swedish Lutheran minister who founded New Uppsala, 1840s, in Forsbeck, "New Uppsala: The First Swedish Settlement in Wisconsin," in Wisconsin Magazine of History, *Volume XIX (1935), pp. 3–31.*

Without long deliberation we decided to settle on the shore of the little lake where both the natural beauty and the good soil promised us a pleasant home and where among oak, beech, and hickory trees, the evergreen pines, untouched by the axe, would always stand as a pleasant reminder of the pine forest of our old homeland. We needed to take no steps to insure our claim except to inform our neighbors that we were planning to make our home here, and as a sign of our intentions start some improvement to indicate that this part of the section had been occupied. . . . A Columbus on his first landing in the new world had raised the Castilian flag inscribed with F & I, the initials of his sovereigns, so we chopped down a few trees, and into the bark of a couple of others cut a big C, signifying "Claimed," a sign that we in our own name had taken possession . . . in hac altera mundi parte [in this other part of the world], with full and complete legal right of possession, to be inhabited, settled, and held by us and our descendants forever.

Gustave Unonius, A Pioneer in Northwest America, 1841–1858: The Memoirs of Gustave Unonius *(1950), in David B. Greenberg, ed.,* Land That Our Fathers Plowed: The Settlement of Our Country as Told by the Pioneers Themselves and Their Contemporaries *(1969), p. 137.*

The warm attachment of the Irish peasant to the locality where he was born and brought up will always make the best and most carefully conducted scheme of emigration a matter of painful sacrifice for the emigrant.

Lord Stanley, later earl of Derby, in an address before the British House of Lords, June 9, 1845, in Woodham-Smith, The Great Hunger *(1962), p. 206.*

It is not long since I was called in to prepare a poor fellow, whose mother lay beside him dead two days, and he was burning with rage to think she should have come to such an end, as to die of starvation. I was called in a few days after to a miserable object, beside whom lay a child dead. . . .; two others lay beside her just expiring and, horrible to relate, a famished cat got upon the bed, and was about to gnaw the corpse of the deceased infant, until I prevented it. . . .

Such is the mortality, that I do not think I exaggerate, when I give it as my opinion *that a third of the population has been already carried away.* Every morning *four or five corpses are to be found on the street,* dead, the victims of famine and disease.

Father John O'Sullivan, Catholic priest, reporting conditions in his parish in Ireland in a letter to the captain of a relief ship sent with supplies from the United States, in Forbes, The Voyage of the Jamestown on Her Errand of Mercy *(1847), pp. cviii–cix.*

Large numbers of these unfortunate emigrants, as soon as they quit the decks of the vessels, having no home to which to direct their movements, wander through the streets in a state of utter desolation, until some benevolent hand, appalled by the misery and wretchedness before him, guides their prostrated frames and tottering gait to the Park almshouse board; and here is exhibited so sickening a picture of human destitution and suffering as no pen, however eloquent in the sad gloom of misfortune's description, could well paint in illustration of the dark and solemn truth. The deplorable infirmity of their desolate unhappiness must be *seen and felt,* to be appreciated; and then, to often find amid the motley groups some with the last gasp of expiration issuing from their cold and blanched lips, forms a scene of dismay and distress too agonizing to look upon with any other than feelings of horror and overwhelming sympathy.

. . . "Leaving their homes," they say, "with the brightest prospects," alluring representations presented to them of the blessed state of American life, a few scanty coins in their pockets, though feeling in the enjoyment of rugged health and surrounded by their young and innocent offspring, little did they imagine the trials to which they would be exposed, but at length they discover to their sorrow, and very natural discontent, that the foul steerage of some ocean-tossed ship is to form the filthy receptacle of their persons, crowded too with hordes of human beings, with scarcely enough space to contain the half of them . . .; and thus huddled together *en masse,* they become the *emigrant passengers* destined to this country.

Numbers of them . . . fall victim to the destroying contagion, and the ocean wave becomes their silent tomb; and when at length our shores are reached, many of them had far better have been cast into the "deep sea," than linger in the pangs of hunger, sickness, and pain, to draw their last agonizing breath in the streets of New York.

Report to a committee of the Common Council of the City of New York from the Almshouse Commissioner of New York City, January 20, 1847, in United States 29th Congress, 2d session, House Document No. 54 *(1847), pp. 8–9.*

It is not well for those who are thinking of leaving their beloved homes in Ireland (wretched though they are) to think of Canada as a home. . . . The employment which grows from freedom are not to be found in Canada. It is a second edition of Ireland, with more room.

Letter from an Irishman in Boston, November 20, 1847, in The Boston Pilot.

Most of those who had died of ship-fever were delirious, some a day, others only a few hours previous to death. . . .

When we had been at sea a month, the steward discovered the four hogsheads, by oversight or neglect, had not been filled [with water]. On the following morning . . . our water was reduced from two quarts to one quart per day for an adult and one pint for a child. . . . My provisions were consumed, and I had nothing but ship allowances, . . . which was scarcely sufficient to keep us from perishing, being only a pound of sea-biscuit (full of maggots) and a pint of water. . . . I was seized with ship-fever, at first I was so dizzy that I could not walk without danger of falling; . . . my brains felt as if they were on fire, my tongue clove to the roof of my mouth and my lips were parched with excessive thirst. . . .

This disastrous voyage [came] to an end, after an absence of exactly eight weeks from the shores of my native land, (the day we arrived at Staten Island being Friday, the 21st of January, 1848). My whole lifetime did not seem so long as the last two months appeared to me.

William Smith, an English immigrant, describing his 1847– 1848 voyage from Liverpool, in An Emigrant's Narrative; or a Voice from the Steerage *(1850), pp. 33–34.*

. . . [A] crowded immigrant sailing ship . . . with fever on board—the crew sullen or brutal from very desperation or paralyzed with terror of the plague—the miserable passengers unable to help themselves or afford the least relief to each other; one-fourth, or one-third, or one-half of the entire number of the entire number in different stages of the disease; many dying, some dead; the fatal poison intensified by the indescribable foulness of the air breathed and rebreathed by the gasping sufferers—the wails of children, the raving of the delirious, the cries and groans of those in mortal agony! . . . [The] sheds [for their reception in Canada] were rapidly filled with the miserable people, the sick and the dying, and round their walls lay groups of half-naked men, women and children, in the same condition—sick or dying. Hundreds were literally flung on the beach, left amid the mud and stones, to crawl on the dry land how they could. "I have seen," says the priest who was chaplain of the quarantine, ". . . thirty-seven people lying on the beach, crawling in the mud, and dying like fish out of water." Many of these, and many more besides, gasped out their last breath on that fatal shore, not able to drag themselves from the slime in which they lay.

John T. Maguire, describing the voyage of an Irish immigrant ship to Canada, 1848, in The Irish in America *(1868), pp. 135–136.*

The people of Hor Lup Chui [a village in the Toishan district in southern China] knew there had been Foreign Barbarians, also known as White Devils, visiting the nearby city of Canton for centuries. But since the Emperor had been forced to create "treaty ports" for foreign trade, it seemed that White Devils were everywhere—huge, ugly, pasty-faced men, with big bellies and hair sprouting from all over their bodies. . . .

[T]hese White Devils, also known as Big Noses, told stories of gold—mountains of gold in a country called California, where one could go and become rich just by plucking the stuff off the ground. . . . The stories the White Devils told sounded good to hungry men and women. . . .

It was in . . . 1848 that two men and one woman first went aboard one of the alien ships and disappeared into the mists. Months went by. But eventually little packets of nuggets and gold dust started to arrive for their families. The following year, nearly eight hundred men and two women followed their compatriots. The year after that, more than three thousand men and five women—and finally by 1882, 27,000 Toi-Shan residents were seeking treasure beyond the sea.

Bruce Edward Hall, Chinese-American writer, describing his family's experiences in the 1840s, in The Tea That Burns: A Family Memoir of Chinatown *(1998), pp. 12–13.*

. . . [A]mong these sober Germans, my country counts the most orderly and valuable of her foreign population. It is they who have swelled the census of her Northwestern States. . . . There is something in the contemplation of the mode in which America has been settled, that, in a noble breast, should forever extinguish the prejudices of national dislikes.

Settled by people of all nations, all nations may claim her for their own. You can not spill a drop of American blood without spilling the blood of the whole world. Be he Englishman, Frenchman, German, Dane, or Scot; the European who scoffs at an American . . . stands in danger of the judgment. We are not a narrow tribe of men. . . . No: our blood is as the blood of the Amazon, made up of a thousand noble currents all pouring into one. We are not a nation, so much as a world; for unless we may claim all the world as our sire, . . . we are without father or mother.

For who was our father and our mother? . . . Our ancestry is lost in the universal paternity; and Caesar and Alfred, St. Paul and Luther, and Homer and Shakespeare are as much ours as Washington, who is as much the world's as our own. We are the heirs of time, and with all nations we divide our inheritance. On this Western Hemisphere all tribes and people are forming into one federated whole, and there is a future which shall see the estranged children of Adam restored as to the old hearthstone in Eden. . . . The seed is sown, and the harvest must come.

Herman Melville, American writer, in his autobiographical novel Redburn, His First Voyage *(1983; first published 1849), p. 183.*

Every man here is armed with a gun, pistols, and knives. My six-barreled pistols which I bought in New York for $12 I have sold here for $100. . . .

The work is extremely hard. I start at four o'clock in the morning and keep on till twelve noon. After that I rest for three or four hours, for at that time of day the heat is unbearable, and then I work again till eight o'clock in the evening. The nights here are exceedingly cold. The ground is our bed and a saddle or something like that our pillow. . . . We live a free life, and the best thing of all, that which I have always considered one of the supreme blessings of existence, is that no human being here sets himself up as your lord and master. It is true that we do not have many of the luxuries of life, but I do not miss them, with the exception of cigars, which are too expensive here, as you only get three for a dollar.

Letter from a Norwegian goldminer in California, July 15, 1849, to his family, in Blegen, Land of Their Choice *(1955), p. 227.*

I am living in God's noble and free soil. I have now been on American soil two and a half years, and I have not been compelled to pay a penny for the privilege of living. Neither is my cap worn out from lifting it in the presence of gentlemen.

Anonymous Swedish immigrant in Iowa, letter of 1850, in Taylor, The Distant Magnet *(1972), p. 88.*

My Dear Father:

. . . Any man or woman are fools that would not venture and come to this plentyful Country where no man or woman even hungered and where you will not be seen naked.

Margaret Clark, Irish immigrant in New York, letter home of 1850, in Schrier, Ireland and the Immigration *(1858), p. 24.*

I have crossed the ocean many a time and oft, and have since late years, acted as Doctor on board of several large American ships . . . and find it absolutely necessary that some sort of reform must be made to better the condition of the poorer class of emigrants.

In the health office at Liverpool where sometimes 1000 emigrants are examined per day from 10 in the morning till 3 o'clock in the afternoon, they are merely required to show their tongue: but no other notice is taken of their filthy condition, nor is the body which may be full of ulcers, itch, small pox, or other disagreeable disease properly examined. . . .

It has been, and is now, the practice of Ireland to send away a pauper (nay, hundreds of them) in the fall of the year to better his condition in the United States of America: for it costs the almshouse in Ireland £5 to feed a pauper through the winter, and a passage to New-York can be obtained for from £2 to £2 10s. in the steerage. Hence the almshouse is the gainer by this operation. . . .

Now if the present commutation money of $1.50 for each passenger was raised to $5 or $10 per head, I think the American vessels would obtain a better class of passengers at Liverpool and the poorer classes and the paupers would be shipped to Quebec or St. John: and after all it is but fair that her Majesty's poor subjects, who are starving in Great Britain, and particularly in Ireland, should first be sent to her Majesty's own colonies, than to fill the poorhouses of New-York and other American Atlantic cities.

Letter signed DOCTOR, to the editors of the New-York Daily Times, *October 15, 1851.*

Above all I warn old people who have no one but themselves to rely on against coming here. Only young, healthy people are fit to travel to California—I have seen many instances of that. It is strange to see how thoughtlessly some have created only misery for themselves. Old people at home who have got into straitened circumstances, either through their own fault or by bad luck, set out for California on the spur of the moment in the firm belief that they will find a land of milk and honey there to supply their wants. They do not stop to think that one has to work to acquire these riches. . . . Though young people may not have been accustomed to hard work, they at least can get into the habit of it; but it is physically impossible for aging people of fifty, sixty, or even sixty-five to stand regular day labor. They are to be pitied; at home they might have lived supported either by their family or friends. But here! I do not mean to imply that they starve to death here, but they have to beg their way among their countrymen and they live miserably.

A Norwegian immigrant in San Francisco, letter home of May 1, 1852, in Blegen, Land of Their Choice *(1955), p. 245.*

Fellow exiles! Claim your station
In the councils of the nation;
Be not aliens in the soil
Which exacts your sweat and toil.
For this land your fathers fought,
With their blood was freedom bought,
We can boast as brave a stock
As that which sprung from Plymouth Rock.

Anonymous poem addressed to Irish immigrants, in The Boston Pilot, *September 11, 1852, in Wittke,* We Who Built America *(1939), p. 160.*

Welcome the Norwegian band, a band so freely
    blest;
. . .You're welcome to our native land if it will give
    you rest;
You're welcome to our home so rude; you're welcome to its cheer;
We do not think it an intrude; you are all welcome
    here.

Miss R. E. Daniels, "To the Norwegians," welcoming the settlers of Oleana, November 29, 1852, in the Potter County, Pennsylvania, newspaper People's Journal.

I'm off to Oleana, I'm turning from my doorway,
    No chains for me, I'll say good-by to slavery in
    Norway.

Ole—Ole—Ole—oh! Oleana!
Ole—Ole—Ole—oh! Oleana!
They give you land for nothing in jolly Oleana,
And grain comes leaping from the ground in
    floods of golden manna.

    . . .

I'm off to Oleana, to lead a life of pleasure,
A beggar here, a count out there, with riches in
    full measure.

*Satirical ballad reflecting the optimistic hopes for the Norwegian
settlement in Pennsylvania founded by Ole Bull in 1852,
translated by Theodore C. Blegen, in* Norwegian-American
Studies and Records *(1944), pp. 1117–21.*

Moustached peasants in Tyrolese hats are arguing in unintelligible English with truck-drivers; runners from the German hotels are pulling the confused women hither and thither; peasant girls with bare heads, and the rich-flushed, nut brown faces you never see here, are carrying huge bundles to the heaps of baggage; children in doublets and hose, and queer little caps, are mounted on the trunks, or swung off amid the laughter of the crowd with ropes from the ship's sides. Some are just welcoming an old face, so dear in the strange land, some are letting down huge trunks, some swearing in very genuine low Dutch, at the endless noise and distractions. They bear the plain marks of the Old World. Healthy, stout frames, and low, degraded faces with many; stamps of inferiority, dependence, servitude on them; little graces of costume, too—a colored headdress or a fringed coat—which could never have originated here; . . .

It is a new world to them—oppression, bitter poverty behind—here, hope, freedom, and a chance for work, and food to the laboring man . . . to the dullest some thoughts come of the New Free World.

The New York Times, *June 23, 1853.*

All of us have suffered so much hardship and seen and heard so much evil during our passage from Liverpool to America on the English packets this year that we feel it is our duty, without delay, to inform you of all this. In particular, we wish to notify those of you who may already in good faith have heeded the shameless lies and frauds of the agents of this company. Least of all is the fact that *none* of the obligations of the company toward us was kept: we did not, for one thing, receive the supply of food and drink that we were entitled to by our contracts. But far worse than this, the crew treated the poor passengers in such an inhuman way that one

cannot listen to these descriptions (which are all alike) without shuddering. Several of us addressed ourselves to the Norwegian-Swedish consul here, but an indifferent shrug of the shoulder and something that sounded like "a private affair" and "go to a lawyer" were all the satisfaction we were able to obtain from him. And this despite the fact that when we arrived here, several of us had to be taken to the hospital. Some of us had been beaten so badly about the head that there was reason to fear for their lives.

*An open letter, dated November 30, 1853, from a group of
Norwegian immigrants, in the Oslo, Norway, newspaper*
Morgenbladet, *January 14, 1854, in Blegen,* Land of
Their Choice *(1955), p. 107.*

I believe the entire population of Wisconsin is on the way to the west now. Yesterday a young man stopped here with greetings from Pastor Preus. On his way he had passed more than three hundred wagons of Norwegians, most of whom were going to Minnesota. . . . There is no land to be had for them here now. Those who are thus traveling are either newcomers who have spent the winter in Wisconsin or else people who have sold their small farms to older Norwegians and are now going to regions where they can easily get land at low prices.

*Letter from the wife of a Norwegian clergyman in Iowa, 1854,
in Blegen,* Norwegian Migration *(1931), p. 368.*

Westward Ho! The great mistakes that emigrants, particularly Irish emigrants, make, on arriving in this country is, that they remain in New York, and other Atlantic cities, till they are ruined, instead of proceeding at once to the Western country, where a virgin soil, teeming with plenty, invites them to its bosom. Here . . . they become the easy prey of runners, boarding-house keepers and other swindlers; and, when their last cent is gone, they are thrown into the street, to beg, starve, or steal, for employment there is none. Many, who in their native land were strangers to drunkenness and other vices, are here seduced by acts of villains by whom they are surrounded, till they are steeped to their lips in infamy, their character is lost, their peace is gone, and the bright prospects, for which they encountered the perils of the ocean, have vanished like a vision. They sink into a pauper's grave.

What then is the duty of the unemployed or badly paid emigrants residing in New York, Philadelphia and Boston? To start at once for the West.

In "The Pitfalls Awaiting the New Arrivals in New York City" (1877), the humor magazine *Puck* warns immigrants of the dangers threatening them in their new home. *(New York Public Library Print Collection)*

. . . To the West, then, ye starving sons of toil—to the West! Where there is food for all, employment for all, and where for all there are happy homes and altars free.

Editorial in Citizen, *Volume II, February 3, 1855, p. 73.*

I'm a decent boy just landed from the town of
   Ballyfad;
I want a situation and I want it very bad.
I've seen employment advertised, "It's just the
   thing," says I,
But the dirty spalpeen [rascal] ended with "No
   Irish Need Apply."

"No Irish Need Apply," popular song in the 1850s,
in Adler, Annals of America, *Volume 7, (1968), p. 421.*

In eighteen hundred and forty-two
I left the Old World for the New.
Bed cess to the luck that brought me through
To work upon the railroad.
In eighteen hundred and forty-five

I found myself more dead than alive.
I found myself more dead than alive
From working on the railroad.
It's "Pat do this" and "Pat do that,"
Without a stocking or cravat,
Nothing but an old straw hat
While I worked on the railroad. . . .

"Pat Works on the Railroad," popular song of the 1850s,
about the experience of Irish Immigrants, in Adler, Annals of
America, *Volume 7, (1968), p. 391.*

I am not a Know-Nothing. How could I be? How can anyone who abhors the oppression of Negroes be in favor of degrading classes of white people? Our progress in degeneracy appears to me pretty rapid. As a nation we began by declaring *"all men are created equal."* We now practically read it, "all men are created equal, *except Negroes.*" When the Know-Nothings get control, it will read, "all men are created equal, except Negroes, *and foreigners, and Catholics,*" When it comes to this I should prefer emigrating to some country where they make no pretense of loving liberty—to Russia, for example, where despotism can be taken pure and without the base alloy of hypocrisy.

Abraham Lincoln, letter to Joshua F. Speed, August 24, 1855, in The Writings of Abraham Lincoln, *Volume II, (1905), p. 242.*

The German philosopher who . . . has here become a farmer, finds that the American axe is more difficult to wield than the pen, and that the plow and manure-fork are very matter-of-fact and stupid tools.

Karl Buchele, German visitor to America, commenting on Duden's romantic picture of pioneer life, in Land and People of the United States of North-America *(1855), in Galicich,* The German-Americans *(1989), p. 48.*

You are welcomed by a figure in blue flannel shirt and pendant beard, quoting Tacitus, having in one hand a long pipe, in the other a butcher's knife; Madonnas upon log walls; coffee in tin cups upon Dresden saucers; barrels for seats, to hear a Beethoven's symphony on the grand piano; . . . a book-case half filled with classics, half with sweet potatoes.

Frederick Law Olmsted, American landscape architect and writer, describing a visit to German immigrants in Texas, in A Journey Through Texas; or A Saddle Trip on the Southwestern Frontier *(1857), p. 430.*

There's freedom at thy gates, and rest
For earth's downtrodden and oppressed,
A shelter for the hunted head,
For the starved laborer toil and bread,
Power at thy bounds
Stops and calls back his baffled hounds.

William Cullen Bryant, "America," 1857, in Untermeyer, American Poetry from the Beginning to Whitman *(1931), p. 182.*

Many hundreds from my village [are leaving for America]. Fools! They could do much better at home. Sweden wants everyone now. But it is the cursed *läsere* ["readers," a religious sect] who turn everything upside down. They make disturbances, break the law. . . . They must be punished; and so they go to carry on their accursed doings in America. Damn them!

Swedish immigrant, quoted in Brace, The Norse Folk; or a Visit to the Homes of Norway and Sweden *(1857), pp. 406–407.*

They overwhelmed us with questions about our country, its government, laws, climate, products and geographical extent. . . . They all complained about the burdens which fall upon a poor man in Sweden, in the shape of government taxes, tithes, and the obligation of supporting a portion of the army, who are distrusted among them.

American travel writer Bayard Taylor, describing a trip to Sweden, in Northern Travel: Summer and Winter Pictures of Sweden, Denmark and Lapland *(1858), pp. 429–430.*

I, born in a foreign land, pay my tribute to Americanism? Yes, for to me the word "Americanism," *true* "Americanism," comprehends the noblest ideas which ever swelled a human heart with noble pride.

It is one of the earliest recollections of my boyhood that one summer night our whole village was stirred up by an uncommon occurrence. . . . That night our neighbors were pressing around a few wagons covered with linen sheets and loaded with household utensils and boxes and trunks to their utmost capacity. One of our neighboring families was moving far away across a great water, and it was said they would never again return. And I saw silent tears trickling down weather-beaten cheeks, and the hands of rough peasants firmly pressing each other, and some of the men and women hardly able to speak when they nodded to one another a last farewell. At last the train started into motion, they gave three cheers for *America,* and then in the first gray dawn of the morning I saw them wending their way over the hill until they disappeared in the shadow of the forest.

That was the first time that I heard of America, and my boyish imagination took possession of a land covered partly with majestic trees, partly with flowery prairies, immeasurable to the eye, and intersected with large rivers and broad lakes—a land where everybody could do what he thought best, and where nobody need be poor because everyone was free.

Carl Schurz, German Forty-Eighter influential in American politics, in a speech delivered in the presidential campaigns for Lincoln in 1858 and 1860, in Bancroft, Speeches, Correspondence, and Political Papers of Carl Schurz, *Volume I, pp. 49–50.*

CHAPTER FIVE

The Civil War and After
1861–1880

Immigration and the Civil War

The American Civil War (1861–65) affected immigration in several different ways. First, the social and political disturbances of the conflict brought about a temporary halt to the influx of Europeans. By the year 1861, the tide of immigration had ebbed to little more than 90,000, the fewest to enter the country for more than 20 years and the lowest number of immigrants to arrive in any one year for a century to come.

At the same time, the anti-immigration feelings that had flared up in the 1840s and 1850s began to subside. The diminished flow of aliens put to rest the fears that the country was being swamped by outsiders who would take American citizens' jobs and weaken their institutions. The Know-Nothing Party, as the anti-Catholic, anti-immigrant American Party was commonly called, became sharply divided over the more pressing issue of slavery and began to disintegrate as the conflict between the North and the South flared into open warfare. Another reason for the lessening of nativist hostility was the growing need for labor. As more and more men marched off to war, the loss of manpower was felt by farms, mines, and railroads, and foreigners arriving in the New World were actively recruited. Agents of shipping companies promoted immigration through much of Europe, promising free land and good jobs in the land of opportunity.

It was not only commercial interests that encouraged the coming of Europeans to American shores. As the Civil War spread, the need for troops prompted the national government to offer a bonus of several hundred dollars and to pass a new law guaranteeing automatic citizenship upon discharge to any soldier serving with the Union troops. The government saw to it that word of the tempting bait was spread by American diplomats and consular officials abroad. Secretary of State William Henry Seward denied that any soldiers had actually been recruited for the Union army overseas, but the government did all it could to make immigration attractive. Shipping agents were encouraged to publicize the high wages available in the United States, and representatives of immigrant ships were only too glad to cooperate. In New York, two large army-recruiting tents were set up a few yards from the exit of Castle Garden. There were recruitment officers who spoke most of the languages of the immigrants; so successful were their efforts that a great number of newcomers found themselves wearing the blue uniform of the Union army within days of their arrival.

In fact, foreign-born residents of the United States fought with equal valor and loyalty on both sides of the Civil War. The sympathies of the immigrant population were divided according to where the immigrants lived rather than where they had come from. Whatever the Germans or the Irish or the Scandinavians felt about slavery individually, as Americans they fought loyally for the section of the country in which they made their home. Lincoln's call to arms found as enthusiastic a response from the foreign-born—even those recent arrivals who did not yet speak English—as from the descendants of the earliest colonial settlers. Many whole regiments were made up of newcomers to America from Europe, chiefly from Ireland and Germany, and it is said that in 1861 the majority of the soldiers in the Union army in Missouri were German-born. Sympathizers with the Confederate states complained that the North would never have won the war if it had not been for its successful recruitment among immigrants and accused the government of enlisting men abroad.

Immigrants in the South fought as willingly for the Confederacy as those in the North did for the Union. Although there were fewer foreign-born in the Confederate states than in the North, there were tens of thousands of immigrants in the Southern army. Loyalty to the Southern cause surpassed that of original nationality in the South as in the North, and people from the same region in Europe were often opposed to each other on the battlefield. When the Union's Irish general Thomas Francis Meagher besieged Fredericksburg, Virginia, in 1862, it was an Irish regiment from Georgia that gallantly and successfully defended that Southern city. Only among the Texas Germans was there widespread resistance to the Confederate draft and, in some cases, enlistment on the Union side. But even in that state there were examples of heroic support of the Southern cause. German-born August Büchel organized a regiment of his countrymen in support of Robert E. Lee and as a Confederate general fought valiantly in the Louisiana campaign.

The Jewish population of the United States, by this time totaling about 150,000, was also divided in feelings between the North and the South. Many Jewish public figures, like Samuel M. Isaacs, editor of the *Jewish Messenger*, opposed any Jewish involvement in political affairs, arguing that as a minority they should remain neutral and avoid antagonizing either side in a controversy. But Jews were found in the ranks of both sides on the issue of slavery. The publishers of *Israel's Herald* and the *Kansas Post* were both powerful spokesmen for abolitionism, as were several prominent rabbis; on the other side, Jewish senators Judah Benjamin and David Levy Yulee left the national Senate in Washington to work for the Confederate government. Major Alfred Mordecai, a Jewish officer from the South in the Union army, resigned his commission rather than fight against people from his home region.

German Jews were so successfully assimilated into American society that they were not generally regarded as immigrants, but the Civil War aroused some anti-Semitic suspicions of disloyalty and corruption directed against them. Naturally there was extensive smuggling between the North and South at borders that were impossible to patrol, and Jewish merchants were accused of profiting from the war by selling southern cotton to northern mills. There was little official support for that charge, but in 1862 Union general Ulysses S. Grant believed it sufficient to cause what has been called "the principal nativist incident of the war years." In December of that year

General Ulysses S. Grant, commander of the Union forces, openly opposed Jewish participation in the Civil War. *(American Museum of Immigration, U.S. National Park Service)*

he issued the openly anti-Semitic "Order Number 11," expelling all Jews from his military jurisdiction in Tennessee for exploiting the war. The order was carried out, but it was generally unpopular and aroused considerable controversy. Three weeks after it was announced, President Lincoln ordered it revoked.

Indeed, Jews served with distinction in the army of the North, as well as in the war effort in the cities. Union troops included some 15,000 Jewish soldiers, and on the home front Jewish organizations supported the Union cause generously. A large part of Jews' Hospital (later renamed Mt. Sinai) in New York City was turned over to the army for military casualties, and Jewish financiers August Belmont and Joseph Seligman raised some $200,000,000 for the military and governmental expenses of the Union.

In Atlanta and other large Southern cities, the Jewish population was equally supportive of the Confederate cause, providing between 10,000 and 12,000 men to the armed forces and supplying food, money, and supplies to the war effort. Former U.S. senator Judah Benjamin became an important figure in the Confederate government and served as its secretary of state in the last years of the war.

Because the majority of immigrants to America had settled in the North, however, the feelings of most of the foreign-born were pro-Union, even among those who opposed the abolition of slavery. The Irish, who had long complained of freed slaves as competitors for work, bitterly opposed the idea of emancipation and resented being drafted to fight in a war aimed at freeing the people who threatened their employment. Their anger was increased by the fact that the 1863 Conscription Act permitted wealthier citizens to stay out of the army by a payment of $300. Since most immigrants could not afford that luxury, they felt the law was unfair, and four months after the act went into effect, they rioted in New York City. Most of the violence was directed against African Americans, who were felt to be the cause of the war, and a black orphanage was burned down. After the war, when the shipping lines and the railroad companies used black manpower to break the strikes of Irish workers in New York and the West, the hostility between the two groups was renewed.

Nevertheless, most immigrants put their political and social feelings aside to fight for the Union. Some people argued that it was the bonuses offered by the federal government for military service that inspired this loyalty, rather than any patriotism for their new country. The New York journalist Horace Greeley cynically observed in 1861 that foreign enlistees to the Union forces were less moved by a desire to preserve the union of the United States than by the desire to preserve "the union of their own bodies and souls." But many who had found sanctuary and opportunity in the United States were genuinely prompted to contribute to the national cause by gratitude for the benefits the nation had showered upon them. Germans in the Union army were among the strongest supporters of the Union, and the New York *Irish-American* in 1860 announced to the nation that the Irish in America would never permit "the destruction of the government that has naturalized, enfranchised, and protected them." The principal Boston Irish newspaper *The Pilot* spoke for the entire Catholic community in making the same point the following year: "We Catholics have only one course to adopt, one line to follow," an editor wrote on January 12, 1861. "Stand by the Union; fight for the Union; die by the Union." *The Pilot* was strongly proslavery, but it never wavered in its support of the Union in the Civil War. "The Irish adopted citizens," it stated in an editorial after the war had begun, "are true, to a man, to the Constitution." Of course, the

Immigrants poured into New York through Castle Garden from 1855 to 1892. *(New York Public Library Print Collection)*

fact that Britain openly favored the South in the conflict reinforced the Irish support of the North.

A bill passed on May 20, 1862, was particularly effective in inspiring the loyalty of the foreign-born to the government and attracting further immigration. On that day, Lincoln signed the Homestead Act, which offered a plot of 160 acres of public land to any citizen or anyone intending to become a citizen. The only requirement, besides a registration fee of from $26 to $34, was a promise to live on the homestead for five years. According to the act, 160 acres could be bought from the government for $1.25 an acre, or 80 acres or less for $2.50 an acre, with a promise of only six months of residence. In 1864 the terms were made more attractive still. Congress granted anyone who served in the Union army for two years a 160-acre homestead subject to only one year's residence.

Six weeks after passing the Homestead Act, Congress approved a bill authorizing the construction of a railroad line stretching from Nebraska to California, thus providing abundant work and opening up the country from the Atlantic to the Pacific. To land-hungry Europeans, the opportunity to find lucrative employment and to establish holdings of such size was irresistible. News of free land and available work spread rapidly, and immigration soon increased to pre–Civil War levels.

The Beginnings of Federal Regulation

Until the Civil War, immigration to the United States had been almost completely unrestricted by the federal government. States had the power to pass immigration laws, and since the Pennsylvania Head Tax was passed in 1729, many colonies and states required that some security be paid for every arrival who seemed likely to become a public charge. These statutes had authority only within their own territories, however, and were without effect beyond their boundaries; the national government imposed no restrictions on entry. The Alien and Sedition Acts of 1798 provided for the deportation of politically subversive foreigners but placed no limitations on those entering the country. The Passenger Acts of 1819, 1847, 1848, and 1855 were aimed at protecting immigrants from exploitation, overcrowding, and unsanitary conditions during the Atlantic crossing. In 1860 the last Passenger Act was amended to include protection for female passengers from "immoral conduct" by the crews of immigrant vessels, imposing a fine of $1,000 on anyone found guilty of such behavior. Essentially sympathetic to the immigrant, these laws reflected a welcoming attitude toward aliens seeking admission to the country.

During the Civil War, the need for labor on farms and factories and the shortage of military manpower made the arrival of immigrants more welcome to the general public, to business, and to the government. In 1863 President Lincoln urged the enactment of a law formally supporting it. The following year the Republican National Convention adopted a resolution asserting that "foreign immigration, which in the past has added so much to the wealth, development of resources, and increase of power to the Nation . . . should be fostered and encouraged."

On July 4, 1864, President Lincoln signed the first federal law intended to regulate the volume of immigration. Aimed at increasing the flow of foreign workers into the country, the act restored a version of the old indenture system by making contract labor once again legal, permitting immigrants to pledge the wages of their labor for up to a year in return for their passage. It also provided for the appointment by the president of a commissioner of immigration, under the direction of the Department of State, to process contract laborers and protect them from exploitation. The act further stipulated that no immigrant should be liable to military service in the Civil War unless he declared his intention to become a citizen. Finally, it established a federal immigration office in New York City to facilitate the arrival of immigrants and to arrange transportation for them with the railway companies.

This far-reaching bill was not intended to be a permanent one. Its approval in Congress was strongly influenced by pressure from employers in need for labor, and immediately after it was enacted, a corporation, the American Emigrant Company, was formed to import workers for businesses that paid their way to America.

The 1864 act was basically a war measure, intended to swell the ranks of the military or to replace the labor of those sent to the front. When the war ended and the servicemen returned to their work, the need for such encouragement to immigration came to an end, and the bill was repealed in March 1868. The U.S. government had no need of promotion to attract newcomers, however. Following a brief decline at the beginning of the Civil War, the flow of newcomers was quickly restored.

Immigration from Europe

The Germans

In the years after 1860, Germany and Ireland continued to be the principal sources of European immigration to the United States. From 1861 to 1870, Germany sent nearly 790,000 of its citizens to America and accounted for some 34 percent of the total immigration. In the following decade, the numbers fell off only slightly, totaling some 718,000. In 1860 the German population of the country was nearly one-third of all the foreign-born in the country, and until 1880 the numbers never fell below 25 percent. As in colonial times, Germans tended to form tightly knit communities in the United States, creating ethnic neighborhoods in cities and often holding onto their language. A high percentage of the German immigrants of the 1860s and 1870s were skilled craftsmen and came to dominate certain industries. German bakers, cabinetmakers, and machinists prospered, and many of the

In *Harper's Weekly,* in a cartoon entitled "Which Color Is to Be Tabooed Next?," March 25, 1872, Thomas Nast criticizes nativist hostility toward racial minorities when Congress banned Chinese immigration. The new law (text from which is shown in the cartoon) prompts a German immigrant to ask an Irishman, "If the Yankee Congress can keep the *yellow* man out, what is to hinder them from calling us *green* and keeping us out too?" *(New York Public Library Print Collection)*

breweries and distilleries of the time were both financed and operated by Germans. It is from their control of the beer and spirit industries that Germans acquired the stereotype of the heavy drinker who spent all his time in a beer hall. One German complained of his compatriots in America that "wherever three Germans congregated in the United States, one opened a saloon so that the other two might have a place to argue."

Only about one-quarter of the post–Civil War German immigrants went into agriculture, although there were solidly German farm communities throughout the Midwest and Texas. Most lived in smaller cities. Besides New York, the cities with the highest concentrations of German immigrants were Milwaukee, St. Louis, and Cincinnati, and a large majority of all Germans in America lived within the triangle formed by those three cities. Milwaukee, which became the beer capital of the country in the last half of the 19th century, was about one-third German.

The Irish

The second largest group, the Irish, followed a different pattern. From 1861 to 1880, about 870,000 came to this country from the Emerald Isle (compared to more than 900,000 in the decade from 1851 to 1860), and they accounted for an average of about 17 percent of the total immigration. More significant, however, is the percentage of the population of Ireland that these numbers represented. Nearly 14 percent of the entire population of Ireland came during the famine in the 1850s, and that percentage remained fairly constant into the 1880s. But while their numbers totaled more than a third of all the arrivals in the 1850s, they represented less than an eighth of the total immigration 30 years later.

After 1860, the Irish continued to congregate in large cities and stayed mostly in the Northeast. Except for a fair-sized community in San Francisco, the 10 largest concentrations of Irish-born residents in the 19th century were on the East Coast, seven of them in New England. Although most of them had come from rural areas in Ireland and had left because they could not keep their farms, they enjoyed the sociability of the crowded cities in America. Just as the Germans formed a Kleindeutschland—a "Little Germany"—in New York, the Irish created "Little Dublins" in Boston, usually in the poorest neighborhoods in the city.

Their concentration in cities gave the Irish an advantage and guided them into a distinct kind of adjustment to their new home. As the modern urban society was emerging in the last half of the 19th century, the Irish were in a position to make themselves an integral part of it, and their unified support of the Democratic Party gave them the chance to find work through the city government. The great numbers of Irish in the big cities of the Northeast, combined with their intense family loyalty, soon led to a network of mutual aid that assured help and work for relatives and friends who joined them from the old country. As one Irish-American worker wrote to a friend in Ireland, "Should your brother Paddy come to America, he can rely on his cousins to promote his interests in procuring work." This mutual support in time led to significant participation in city government. Many worked themselves up from minor party jobs to positions of influence and power in local politics, consolidating their ethnic support in the community by finding jobs for new immigrants, giving free turkeys to the poor at Thanksgiving, and providing legal representation to those in trouble. Although the Irish politician of the 19th century had a reputation for corruption, the political machines of the time provided real service for their voters and produced substantial reform in social welfare.

The predominantly Catholic Irish continued to exert a great influence on the growth of the Catholic Church in the United States after the Civil War. For many years the majority of the American priesthood was either Irish-born or descended from those who were, and it is to the Irish that the church owes the system of parochial schools. The Catholic education that these private schools administered was, in fact, one of the principal causes of anti-Irish sentiment during the 19th century. At a time when there was a lively fear that the pope intended to "colonize" America and extend his power over the nation, the establishment of separate schools to indoctrinate the young was viewed with grave suspicion. Many Protestant Americans felt that the schools of a country were an important instrument for instilling national loyalties. As the *Minnesota Chronicle and Register* argued in an 1850 editorial, public schools take "the child of the exile of Hungary, of the half-starved emigrant from the Emerald Isle, and of the hardy Norwegian, and places them on the same bench with the offspring of those whose ancestors' bones bleached upon the fields of Lexington. . . . [B]efore he leaves the school-desk for the plough, the anvil or the trowel, he is as sturdy a little republican as can be found in the land." Nevertheless, the Irish contribution to education in the United States, secular as well as religious, has been a significant one.

Not all Irish immigrants remained in the port cities where they arrived. Many were employed in the transportation industry, and Irish muscle and sinew provided much of the labor for the building of the railroads as it had earlier for the canals. In 1862 the Union Pacific Railroad began work on a line that stretched to meet the Central Pacific line in Utah and link the two coasts. Irish workers, who formed the largest part of the workforce on this vast project, earned $1.25 a day but found it difficult to survive in a system that required them to buy all their personal supplies at an overpriced company store. With no opportunity to negotiate for better conditions or higher pay, they were sometimes driven to violence in a series of what became known as the "Irish riots." Their strikes were seldom well organized, and they were seldom effective. The owners of the railways had the support of the state governments, and state militias were summoned to restore order. When that failed (often because the militiamen were in sympathy with the workers), the owners called on the federal government to send troops. In 1877 the newly elected President Rutherford B. Hayes, determined to take a firm stand, sent a regiment of soldiers to restore order. It was the first time the U.S. Army had been used to break a strike, and it was a controversial move, but it accomplished the owners' purpose.

The Irish also formed a large part of the workforce in the anthracite coal mines of western Pennsylvania, eastern Kentucky, and West Virginia. Here the conditions were, if anything, even worse than those on the railroad lines. Long hours, low pay, and dangerous work combined to make the job unbearable, and all attempts to organize and negotiate for improvements were sternly suppressed. In Ireland there had been a secret terrorist group called the Molly Maguires formed to address tenants' grievances against their landlords, and an American version sprang up among the miners to impress their demands on the owners. From the mid-1850s, the Molly

German and Irish immigrants arrive in New York in the 1860s. This sketch from *Harper's Weekly* shows the confusion and excitement of the event. *(New York Public Library Print Collection)*

Maguires were a powerful force in the mining districts, committing murder and arson when threats failed. The group accomplished some good for the workers, but it soon became a means of private gain for its members. All efforts to stamp out the organization failed. At last, in 1873, the president of the Philadelphia and Reading Coal and Iron Company hired the newly formed Pinkerton Detective Agency to investigate and learn the identities of the people in this secret organization. A young Irish detective joined the Molly Maguires and in time earned the confidence of its members. He drew up a full report of the groups' organization and activities and compiled a list of its members. When he gave testimony against them in court two years later, the organization was destroyed. Nineteen of its leaders were hanged and many other members were sentenced to long terms in prison.

In time the Irish were able to organize peaceable unions and made important contributions to the development of organized labor. But the "Irish riots" in the railways and the actions of the Molly Maguires in the mines brought discredit on the whole Irish community. They reinforced the unfortunate Irish stereotype of violence and brutality and contributed to a growing hostility toward immigrants. And as the Molly Maguires all identified themselves with the Catholic Church, their behavior added to the fear and suspicion that faith inspired in Protestant America.

The Scandinavians

The Norwegians, Swedes, and Danes had made small but significant appearances in the New World during the first half of the 19th century, and a steady stream of adventurous pioneers had found their way to the United States. Their agricultural settlements helped to open the western frontier, and their determination and faith in the face of hardship was an inspiration to both Europe and America, but their numbers were not great before the Civil War. In 1850 there were fewer than 20,000 Scandinavians in the United States, and 20 years later arrivals from Norway, Sweden, and Denmark amounted to little more than 7 percent of the total immigration. But the news of Lincoln's Homestead Act, passed in 1862, with the availability of free land it promised, created a sensation in those countries, and the attraction of immigration increased substantially. The offer of bonuses and land bounties for those willing to join the Union army raised so much excitement that an American consul in Sweden wrote in 1863, "I could take a quarter of the working population of this country to the United States next spring."

The middle of the 19th century saw a sudden worsening of conditions in Scandinavia. There was a war between Denmark and Prussia in 1864, and a financial depression affected all of Scandinavia from 1866 to 1870. In the mid-1860s there was a crop failure so severe it brought about what was known as "the Great Famine," and a change from wood to iron in shipbuilding affected the timber trade and led to widespread unemployment. All of this contributed to a dramatic upswing in immigration to the United States in the second half of the century. By 1880 more than 13 percent of all arrivals to America were from Scandinavia.

In addition, the "America letters," with their glowing accounts of the hospitality of the people, the fertility of the land, and the prosperity of the economy in the New World, continued to come, along with steamer tickets. "What a glorious new Scandinavia might not Minnesota become," wrote one traveler. "Here the Swede would find his clear, romantic lakes, the plains of Skane, rich in grain, and the valleys of Norrland. Here the Norwegian would find his rapid rivers, his lofty mountains. The Danes might there pasture their flocks and herds and lay out their farms on richer and less misty coasts than those of Denmark."

The frenzy of "America fever" met with opposition from the governments of the three countries, which tried to lure their subjects to stay with promises of better conditions, and the Lutheran clergy argued that it was wrong to desert one's native land because "God has placed us there." Reports of the difficulties immigrants encountered in America were circulated to counteract the favorable accounts that daily came in the mail. But the tide was not stemmed. By the end of the 19th century, 1.25 million Swedes, 850,000 Norwegians, and 350,000 Danes would come to the United States. These numbers did not represent a large share of the total immigration America received, but they constituted a huge percentage of the population of Scandinavia; in 1900, Sweden had 5 million inhabitants and Norway only 2 million.

As before, the great wave of Scandinavian immigrants headed west, pushing the frontier before it and establishing prosperous agricultural communities as they moved. Unlike the Irish, they formed no large part of the cities in which they first arrived. At the end of the Civil War, four states—Illinois, Wisconsin, Iowa, and Minnesota—held 94 percent of all the Norwegians in the country and 66 percent of the Swedes. The remainder of the Scandinavian community settled within the same region, all safely distant from the ports on the east coast. "These immigrants have gone straight across the country," as one social scientist noted admiringly in 1874, ". . . and have set at once to their chosen occupation, agriculture, in their chosen homes, . . . without loss of time, or injury to character by exposure, unemployed and unprovided, to the temptations of city life."

Scandinavian immigration has contributed much to the United States, but the mass exodus had profound effects on the home countries as well and has led to numerous reforms in Scandinavian life. Inspired by the success of the American model as reported by their countries' emigrants, the governments of Sweden and Norway have undertaken extensive programs of land reclamation and have liberalized the financial credit system to enable their citizens to buy land and build homes. All the countries have followed the American example in tax reform, voting rights, and free public education. As a Swedish prime minister noted years after the great wave of Scandinavian immigration to the United States, "Thanks to the Swedish immigrant, America became a living reality in almost every Swedish home and a challenge even to those who stayed in the old country."

Immigration from China

Until the middle of the 19th century, the story of voluntary American immigration has been essentially one of European settlement. Virtually no one came to the United States willingly from Africa, and there is little record of arrivals from south of the Mexican border. From Asia the statistics are equally scant. There is a documented case of a Chinese resident in the United States in the 18th century, but the first appearance of the Chinese in the immigration statistics is the admission of a single Chinese man in 1820. From 1820 to 1830, three were admitted, and in the next decade, eight more.

The beginnings of large-scale immigration from China began with the discovery of gold in California in 1848. By 1866 the wave of Chinese immigration was sufficient to justify the establishment of the Pacific Mail Steamship Company

An antialien scene portrays debased Chinese and Irish immigrants being introduced in America. Ironically signed Hunk E. Doré (hunky dory), this anonymous 1850 cartoon reflects American dismay at the racial mix being added to the U.S. population because of the nation's liberal immigration policy. *(New York Public Library Print Collection)*

to provide regular voyages from Hong Kong to San Francisco, and Chinese travel agents were soon promoting the trip as a sure means of getting rich. Of the 6,700 miners in Montana in 1880, according to one report, more than 1,400 were Chinese. By 1880 the number of Chinese residents in the United States had passed 100,000.

At first these newly arrived immigrants, many of whom were serious, sober, and hard-working, were welcomed in America. They patiently accepted strenuous and disagreeable tasks few natives wanted to undertake, and they often worked harder at them than whites. In 1852 the governor of California asked Congress for land grants to entice more Chinese to the state, calling them "one of the most worthy of our newly adopted citizens." In their mining, they were more careful, often taking over claims that whites had abandoned as unprofitable and making them pay.

But it was not long before they aroused the envy and suspicion of their white neighbors. Their peculiar clothes and strange customs, their incomprehensible language and seeming ability to live on nothing, all set them apart as mysterious aliens incapable of assimilation. In the mining camps they were subjected to unchecked abuse, and they obtained little protection from the authorities. The robbery or murder of a Chinese was almost never punished or even investigated. When they left the goldfields to work on farms or in factories, they were willing to work harder for less, and their presence became a labor issue. In good times, their enterprise and diligence were welcome, but when the economy failed, their willingness to take any job made them a serious threat to the white workingman in competition for jobs.

Popular sentiment soon influenced the government to pass state and local legislation to discourage Chinese competition. In 1855 the California legislature imposed a $55 head tax on every Chinese immigrant, and in 1860 a law was passed excluding Chinese children from the public schools of the state. City ordinances were passed requiring special licensing fees for laundries, and carrying baskets on a pole across the shoulders—the traditional Chinese manner of carrying merchandise—was declared a misdemeanor. Those convicted of any crime were required to have their hair cut to a length of one inch, a deliberate humiliation to the Chinese, who braided their hair in back.

Many Chinese went into domestic service, and those who had accumulated a little capital became entrepreneurs. Although there was no tradition of men working at cleaning clothes in China, a very small investment enabled the Chinese to open small one-man laundries where they were not dependent on exploitative employers or hostile coworkers, and they soon established a virtual monopoly in a service no one else wanted to perform. Their ability to stretch food supplies by

In its race with the Union Pacific, the Central Pacific Railroad bridged the Sierra chasms with timber trestles. Chinese laborers used picks and shovels, chisels, hammers, and wheelbarrows to do the work. *(1877, author's collection)*

blending a variety of elements naturally drew them to the restaurant business as well. Many had served as cooks in the mining camps and had learned how to provide savory mixed dishes for little money. Turning that talent to professional ends, they created a string of small restaurants to cater to the miners. Both of these businesses were independent and not in competition with whites.

The Chinese became the main workforce for the Central Pacific Railroad, which had found almost no white laborers willing to do the hard and often dangerous work of laying the tracks. It was well paid by the standards of the time—as much as $35 a month—and the Chinese accepted the work happily. Of the 14,000 laborers responsible for the project, nine-tenths were Chinese. When the line was completed in 1869, many turned to agricultural work, where their careful and tireless work made them very popular with farmers. In 1870 about one farmhand in 10 in California was Chinese; by the middle 1880s, the Chinese represented half of the state's farm labor. They became the major source of labor in other fields as well. In 1873 half the boots and shoes manufactured in San Francisco were made by Chinese workers, and many of the factories were Chinese-owned as well. Chinese accounted for four-fifths of the labor in canneries, and in 1877 it was reported that 5,500 of the 6,500 workers in the cigar factories in San Francisco were Chinese. Nevertheless, no labor union would admit them. Samuel Gompers, president of the American Federation of Labor (AFL) and himself an immigrant, was actively opposed to Chinese immigration and refused them membership in the AFL. Increasingly the Chinese were forced to resort to private businesses, and their restaurants, laundries, and small shops usually prospered.

The more prosperity their diligence and frugality brought them, the more bitterly the Chinese were resented by organized labor and the working class. Street gangs of unemployed workers—especially the Irish, who made up the largest share of the working class—often roughed up unoffending Chinese in the streets; sometimes it was reported that police stood by and watched with seeming approval. It was from such incidents that the phrase "not a Chinaman's chance" gained currency in the American vocabulary. A work detail of 30 Chinese repairing a street in San Francisco was attacked by a mob and severely beaten in 1870, and Chinese shops and homes were repeatedly vandalized and robbed. In a riot in 1871, 15 Chinese were hanged. In 1876 both political parties took an anti-Chinese stand in California, and the state legislature appointed a committee to investigate the social unrest. A 300-page report was presented to the congress in Sacramento and left no doubt about the sentiment of the people who had drawn it up. "The Chinese are inferior to any race God ever made," it stated in part. "These people have got the perfection of crimes of 4,000 years. . . . I believe the Chinese have no souls to save, and if they have, they are not worth saving."

Trade unions actively argued for the exclusion of the Chinese from the country. One particularly effective demagogue was Denis Kearney, an Irish immigrant who had worked as a teamster. Kearney blamed all of society's ills on the Chinese and ended every speech with "Whatever happens, the Chinese must go!" Presenting himself as a defender of the workingman, he spoke in a large open lot in San Francisco, drawing great crowds of angry citizens. In 1877 one of his "sandlot" speeches led to a riot in which 25 laundries were burned down. Later riots brought about physical assaults on Chinese. Many were killed and many of their homes were destroyed. In 1878 Kearney founded the Workingman's Party, dedicated to overthrowing the rich, abolishing the immigration of the Chinese, and ejecting those already in the country. His dreams of turning the mansions of millionaires into dormitories for the working class were never realized, but pressure from his party imposed a new state constitution on California the next year. It included laws barring Chinese from voting, forbidding their employment in public works, imposing complicated restrictions on their residence in the state, and ordering severe punishments for any company importing Chinese labor.

President Rutherford B. Hayes (1822–93) vetoed the first bill limiting Chinese immigration in 1879 but later compromised and approved another that had the same effect. *(Library of Congress, Prints and Photographs Division [LC-USZ62-98454])*

California was not alone in opposing the entry of Chinese. In Massachusetts and Pennsylvania, Asian labor was imported to break strikes and was seen as a potential threat to the American workingman. The federal government was receiving increasing pressure for action. In 1868 the United States signed a treaty, drawn up by former minister to China Anson Burlingame, authorizing the free passage of people between the two countries. It granted the Chinese rights equal to those of any other nation within American borders but did not give them the right of naturalization. Nevertheless, it was a powerful step toward opening China to U.S. trade and initiated an era of friendly and mutually supportive relations.

But mounting agitation against the Chinese forced the government to take some steps to satisfy the demands of labor. On May 3, 1875, Congress passed the country's first restrictive immigration act, the Page Law, prohibiting the importation of three classes of immigrant: foreign felons, women "for immoral purposes," and "coolies," defined for the purpose of the act as "men imported without free and voluntary consent for the purpose of holding them to a term of service." Clearly aimed at ending the trade in Chinese prostitutes, convicted felons, and cheap labor, it was the first step toward the exclusion of Asian immigration. The next year the government took another step toward placing responsibility for immigration in federal hands when the Supreme Court declared unconstitutional all state laws regulating immigration.

In 1879 a bill was introduced and passed in Congress calling for a limitation on the number of Chinese passengers to be admitted in our ports. It was supported by senators and representatives from the southern and western states, but President Hayes vetoed it. The country should do nothing to wound the pride of "a polite and sensitive people," he cautioned, and in his veto he stated that such a law would violate the terms of the Burlingame Treaty. He argued that Congress did not have the power to annul this treaty and explained that he feared the effect of doing so on the Chinese already in America and on the American missionaries and merchants in China. However, he was in a dilemma. He acknowledged the problems of working people in California and wanted to do something to placate them without submitting to their most extreme demands. In an effort to avoid either an open conflict with the senators from the west or an international incident with China, he promised to negotiate another treaty more appropriate to the needs of the time.

The next year a new treaty was drawn up offering a sort of compromise. The American government agreed not to "absolutely prohibit" immigration from China but claimed the right to "regulate, limit, or suspend" such immigration whenever the American government considered it necessary for the protection of the country's own interests. The document was wholly satisfactory to neither side. Although it specified that the limitation or suspension should be "reasonable,"the Chinese government consented only reluctantly, recognizing the new wording as a movement in the direction of exclusion. The western senators wanted something more decisive and continued campaigning for a new, stronger stand.

The Immigrant in the Postwar Era

As the Civil War introduced an era of industrial and agricultural expansion, the flood of new labor was generally welcome to man the new factories and develop the land opening in the West. The Know-Nothing Party, so divided on the issue of slavery that it had lost interest in the dangers of foreign and Catholic influence in the country, had virtually disappeared by the end of the war, and the country looked to Europe to help populate its wilderness. An editorial on "Our Country's Future" in the Chicago *Tribune* published in September 1864 enthusiastically stated, "Europe will open her gates like a conquered city. Her people will come forth to us subdued by admiration of our glory and envy of our perfect peace. On the Rocky Mountains and still over to the Pacific our mighty populations will spread. . . . Our thirty millions will be tripled in thirty years."

Business interests profited from the increase in population, not only for the construction of its railroads, labor in its mines, and manufacture of its products, but as a market for its goods and services. Everyone made money from the immigrants, from the shipping lines who transported them and the real estate agents who sold them land to the merchants who sold them tools and looked to them as customers. In 1870, according to one report, a third of all employees in manufacturing in the United States was foreign-born, and the ratio of immigrant to native in American industry increased from year to year well into the 20th century. In New England, factory owners sent agents into French Canada to recruit employees, and businesses in New York and Philadelphia actively sought workers in Europe. The value of the newcomers was calculated very precisely and assigned a dollar amount. An official report by the Commissioners of Emigration in New York City estimated that "German immigrants alone have for the past three years . . . brought into the country annually an average amount of about eleven millions of dollars," and a scholar added in 1870 that "the money is not the only property which immigrants bring with them. In addition to it, they have a certain amount of wearing apparel, tools, watches, books, and jewelry. Assuming that their cash amounts to only $100 a head, I do not think I exaggerate in estimating their other property at $50, thus making $150 the total of the personal property of each immigrant." More important, the report noted, "In order to obtain a proper idea of the importance of immigration to the United States, we must endeavor to capitalize, so to speak, the addition to the natural and intellectual resources of the country represented by each immigrant."

Although the failed economy of the Far West in the 1870s inspired an attitude of fear of and hostility toward the Chinese, this explosion of nativism was rather the exception than the rule in the post–Civil War era. Dubbed "The Age of Confidence," the times seemed to call for as much new blood as immigration could provide. Almost every state in the Middle West had a board of immigration established to draw newcomers from other countries. Michigan set up such an office as early as 1845, and, as one scholar wrote, "by the end of the Civil War the Northwestern states were competing with each other for Europeans to people their vacant lands and develop their economies."The South, its economy wrecked by the war and the loss of labor that resulted from the end of slavery, followed suit. South Carolina was so eager for newcomers to help rebuild its shattered society in the 1870s that it granted a five-year tax abatement on all real estate bought by immigrants.

Some nativism persisted, however. The South welcomed foreign labor but remained suspicious of alien ideas and blood. Following the war, a perceived threat to the "purity" of white, Protestant society led to the creation of secret terrorist groups that sought to establish white supremacy. Most famous of these was the Ku Klux Klan. Originally a social club of Confederate war veterans formed in Tennessee around 1866, it became a political group dedicated to restoring the white power structure in force before the war. Wearing long white robes and mysterious peaked masks to conceal their identities and frighten the superstitious freed slaves whom they saw as threatening their racial supremacy, they employed violence to

A pamphlet published soon after the founding of the Ku Klux Klan illustrates the secret society's methods of intimidating slaves, Catholics, and aliens. *(New York Public Library Picture Collection)*

undermine the growing political and economic power of the black populace. The organization worked to prevent blacks from voting and opposed the introduction of foreign elements into the South in an effort at regaining control of state governments. It was especially opposed to the mixture of races.

Other secret societies sprang up throughout the South during the period of postwar Reconstruction. The Knights of the White Camelia emerged in New Orleans in 1867, and the Invisible Empire and the White League appeared soon after, all with the same mission. They focused their hostilities on African Americans, but they all formally opposed the Roman Catholic Church and the influence of foreign interests in their region as well. As their terrorist campaigns grew more violent and disruptive of social order, these groups alienated the very societies they sought to preserve, and they lost much of their support. In 1869 the Imperial Wizard of the Klan formally dissolved the organization, and from 1870 to 1875 Congress passed four Force Acts to assure the rule of federal law in the South and the right of freed slaves to vote, as guaranteed by the Fourteenth Amendment. But the Klan and its various nativist imitators continued their activities more or less openly for many years afterward.

Such secret societies had little influence on the politics of the time, but reflected the persistent suspicion and fear of the foreign that existed in American society. With the attention of the nation centered on problems of reconstruction and rehabilitation, and the need for manpower and investment so great in a rapidly expanding economy, the nativist sentiments that had flared up in the 1850s and resurfaced so violently in the 1870s seemed forgotten. But a period of unprecedented immigration was approaching. In the 1880s a flood of foreign faces, not only from the familiar regions of the British Isles and northern Europe but from around the world, threatened to inundate the country. Unsettled industrial conditions made the public once more receptive to nativist propaganda, as demonstrated by the violent upsurge of nativism directed against the Chinese 20 years after the dissolution of the anti-immigrant Know-Nothing Party.

The 1880s would see an increase not only in the volume of immigration but in the range of its sources, and America's image as a haven for the oppressed of every nation would be put sorely to the test in the decades that followed. The pro-

"Uncle Sam's Thanksgiving Dinner," a political cartoon by Thomas Nast, illustrates that people of all races were treated equally in America. From *Harper's Weekly,* November 20, 1869. *(New York Public Library Print Collection)*

verbial open door creaked somewhat on its hinges and threatened to swing shut as the government added one piece of restrictive legislation to another. Poised on the threshold of a new era, the nation was divided in its feelings about the diverse threads that had combined and were continuing to combine to make up the fabric of its society.

Chronicle of Events

1861

- Immigration falls to 91,918, its lowest point since 1844.
- A law is passed in California forbidding anyone not a citizen to "take or extract gold, silver, or other metals from the mines of this state, or hold a mining claim therein unless he shall have a license therefor of four dollars a month." The act is formally directed at all immigrants but is enforced only against the Chinese.
- *January 9–February 1*: Mississippi, Florida, Alabama, Georgia, Louisiana, and Texas secede from the Union.
- *January 24–26*: Georgia seizes the federal arsenal at Augusta.
- *February 4*: Government is established for Confederate States of America. On February 9 Jefferson Davis is elected provisional president.
- *April 15*: Union president Abraham Lincoln proclaims a state of insurrection; on April 19 he establishes a blockade against the Confederate states.
- *May 6*: The Congress of the Confederate States declares that a state of war exists with the United States.
- *May 13*: England officially declares itself neutral in the conflict between the United States North and South, though British business interests favor the Confederacy and sell ships to the Confederate navy.
- *May 20*: North Carolina secedes from the Union, bringing the total of Confederate states to 11; the Confederate capital moves from Montgomery, Alabama, to Richmond, Virginia.
- *August 5*: A bill instituting the first national income tax, levying a 3-percent tax on incomes over $800, is passed.
- *October 24*: The first transcontinental telegraph begins operation.

1862

- California enacts a law requiring all Asians over 18 years of age except those engaged in the production of coffee, tea, sugar, and rice to pay a monthly head tax of $2.50. Along with other discriminatory acts, the law is declared unconstitutional by the U.S. Supreme Court in 1876.
- *February 19*: Congress passes an act prohibiting the importation of involuntary Asian laborers.
- *May 20*: Lincoln signs into law the Homestead Act, which offers a free grant of 160 acres to any adult citizen or prospective citizen who agrees to occupy and improve the land for five years. Land may be acquired after only six months' residence at $1.25 an acre. This act becomes a great incentive to emigration from Europe. From 1862 to 1904, 147,351,370 acres are distributed.
- *July 1*: The Pacific Railroad Act permits the Union Pacific Railroad to construct a line from Nebraska to Utah, where it will link up with the Central Pacific and complete the route to California. Irish immigrants provide most of the labor for the Union Pacific Railroad line; the Central Pacific is predominantly manned by Chinese.
- *July 14*: A law is passed establishing pensions for wounded Union soldiers and for the families of those killed in the war, a further incentive for immigrant enlistment.
- *September 17–18*: A battle is fought at Antietam Creek in Maryland, resulting in more than 26,000 casualties on both sides. One of the costliest encounters in the war, it results in a decisive victory for the Union forces.
- *December*: General Ulysses S. Grant issues an order (Order Number 11) expelling Jews from the section of Tennessee under his command, accusing them of illegal cotton trading with the South; the order is revoked by President Lincoln after three weeks.
- *December 11–15*: Union forces are defeated in Fredericksburg, Virginia, and sustain 12,653 casualties.

1863

- *January 1*: Lincoln signs the Emancipation Proclamation declaring all slaves in the Confederate States of America to be free. These slaves in rebelling states are invited to join the Union army.
- *March 3*: A national Conscription Act is passed drafting all married men between 20 and 45 years of age and all unmarried men between 18 and 45. Those drafted may hire substitutes to enlist for three years or may purchase exemption for $300. Mobs of laborers, including many Irish immigrants, riot to protest the first draft lists in New York City July 13–16, venting their anger on African Americans, who are seen as the cause of the war. Violent anti-Irish sentiment results, and the riots are suppressed by Union troops after hundreds are killed. Later in the month riots pitting Irish against African Americans take place in Detroit and other northern cities.
- *October*: Britain ceases providing ships to the Confederate states after a threat of war from the Union.

1864

- *March 14*: Lincoln calls for a Union military force of 200,000, to be filled by volunteers until April 15 and then by draft. Many immigrants volunteer.

- *March 21*: As a further incentive to enlistment in the Union army, Congress grants a homestead bonus for all soldiers with two years of service, subject to one year of residence.
- *July 2*: Congress charters the Northern Pacific Railroad to build a line from Lake Superior to Portland, Oregon, and open the area for settlement. Many Chinese laborers are employed in the construction.
- *July 4*: Congress passes the first federal law to regulate the volume of immigration. Called the Facilitating Act, it legalizes the importation of contract laborers and permits agreements whereby immigrants may guarantee a maximum of 12 months' labor in exchange for their passage. The statute also establishes the office of commissioner of immigration, under the direction of the Department of State.
- *November 8*: Lincoln is reelected president.
- *November 14*: Union general William Tecumseh Sherman burns Atlanta, Georgia, and begins a 60-mile march to Savannah, destroying everything on the way. On December 10 his army of 60,000 reaches Savannah, which surrenders 12 days later.
- *December 15*: The Union army takes Nashville, Tennessee.

1865

- *January–April*: General Sherman continues his destructive march through North and South Carolina.
- *April 2–3*: Confederate president Davis and his cabinet flee their capital, Richmond, Virginia, to reestablish the government in nearby Danville. On April 3 Richmond is occupied by Union troops.
- *April 9*: Confederate general Robert E. Lee surrenders to Union general Ulysses S. Grant at Appomattox, Virginia. Three days later Mobile, Alabama, the last city under Confederate control, surrenders peacefully.
- *April 14*: Abraham Lincoln is assassinated. The following day Vice President Andrew Johnson is inaugurated as the 17th president.
- *May 26*: Last Confederate forces surrender near New Orleans.
- *December 18*: The Thirteenth Amendment to the Constitution, declaring slavery illegal throughout the United States, is passed into law.

1866

- The Pacific Mail Steamship Company establishes direct passage between Hong Kong and San Francisco.
- The Ku Klux Klan is formed in Pulaski, Tennessee. Originally a social group of Confederate war veterans,

the secret organization seeks to establish and maintain white supremacy. It opposes African-American suffrage, Roman Catholic influence, and the rapid naturalization of foreign immigrants.
- *August 20*: The National Labor Union, the first national federation of unions, is organized in Baltimore, Maryland, and calls for an eight-hour work day.

1867

- Knights of the White Camelia, the White League, the Invisible Empire, and other white supremacist groups form throughout the South, all with programs similar to that of the Ku Klux Klan.
- *March 1*: Nebraska becomes the 37th state; due to the effects of the railroads on the settlement of the area, its population has reached 120,000, more than four times the number of inhabitants in 1860.
- *March 2*: Congress passes the First Reconstruction Act, calling for the readmission of 10 former Confederate states to the Union on condition of their establishment of black suffrage, over President Johnson's veto. When the South fails to comply, two supplementary Reconstruction Acts are passed, in March and July, empowering military commanders in the South to determine the eligibility of voters.

1868

- The number of Chinese immigrants in the United States is estimated at about 75,000, most of them employed in the construction of the transcontinental railroad. By the end of the year, nine-tenths of the laborers employed in building the Central Pacific Railroad are Chinese.
- *March*: The Facilitating Act of 1864, legalizing contract labor, is repealed.
- *May 16–28*: The Senate impeaches President Johnson on charges of violating federal law by dismissing Secretary of War Edwin M. Stanton, who opposed the president's position on Reconstruction in the southern states. Johnson is acquitted by one vote.
- *July 28*: Anson Burlingame, representing China, signs a treaty with Secretary of State Seward authorizing unlimited immigration between China and the United States.
- *November 3*: General Ulysses S. Grant is elected the 18th president of the United States.

1869

- *February 9*: Congress passes a second law forbidding the importation of involuntary Chinese laborers.

- *February 27*: Congress passes the Fifteenth Amendment to the Constitution, granting universal male suffrage in both the North and the South.
- *April 16*: The government appoints Ebenezer Don Carlos Bassett, the first African-American diplomat, consul general to Haiti.
- *May 10*: Union Pacific Railroad joins the Central Pacific in Utah, establishing a transcontinental route. Regular service from Boston to Oakland, California, begins the next year.

1870

- The national census reports a 22.5-percent increase in the United States population, from about 23,000,000 to 39,818,000, including more than 4,000,000 foreign-born inhabitants. Approximately 2,315,000 immigrants have arrived since 1860.
- *March 30*: Congress passes the Fifteenth Amendment to the Constitution, stating that "the right of citizens of the United States to vote shall not be denied or abridged by the United States or by any state on account of race, color, or previous condition of servitude."
- *March 13*: The Force Bill is passed, giving jurisdiction to federal courts to enforce the Fifteenth Amendment, in response to southern terrorism by such groups as the Ku Klux Klan.

1871

- Anti-Chinese feeling increases among laborers fearful of competition for work. Fifteen Chinese immigrants are hanged during a riot in Los Angeles.
- *February 28*: Congress passes a second Force Bill giving federal courts and marshals authority over national elections at the state and local level. From May 1870 to April 1871, the federal government arrests many members of secret societies in the South, convicting 1,250.

1872

- European Communists and Socialists split and the Socialists move their organization to New York City, where they form the Socialist Labor Party with American labor unions.
- *November 5*: Ulysses S. Grant is reelected president of the United States.
- *December 11*: Pinckney Benton Stewart Pinchbeck is elected governor of Louisiana. He is the first African-American state governor.

1873

- The highest immigration rate to date is reached; nearly 460,000 aliens enter the United States, one-third from Germany and the majority of the rest from England and Ireland.
- *March 3*: The Coal Lands Act permits the purchase of public coal fields for $10–20 per acre, up to 160 acres for individuals and 320 for corporations. The Timber Culture Act grants 160 acres of woodland to anyone who maintains 40 acres of it.
- *September 18*: The bank that financed the Northern Pacific Railroad fails, leading to a financial panic that causes more than 100 banks to fail.

1874

- A plague of locusts destroys grain crops from Texas to Canada.

1875

- Gold is discovered in the Black Hills Indian reservation in South Dakota. More than 15,000 prospectors flood into Indian territory, leading to a Sioux uprising.
- The Molly Maguires, a secret society of Irish miners using sabotage against mine owners in Pennsylvania, are brought to trial. In the next two years, 19 are hanged and many more are imprisoned.
- *March 3*: Congress passes its first restrictive immigration act, the Page Law, prohibiting the importation of alien convicts and prostitutes.

1876

- The U.S. Supreme Court, in *Henderson v. City of New York*, declares all state laws regulating immigration to be unconstitutional.
- *June 25*: General George Custer and a troop of cavalry attack the Sioux at Little Bighorn River in present-day Wyoming. Under chiefs Sitting Bull and Crazy Horse, 1,000 American Indians annihilate the U.S. soldiers, including Custer. The massacre results in severe reprisals from the United States until the two chiefs are captured in October.
- *August 1*: Colorado is admitted as the 38th state. By 1880 westward expansion has raised the number of Colorado's inhabitants to 194,000, more than five times its population 10 years earlier.
- *November 7*: A presidential race between New York governor Samuel Tilden and Ohio governor Rutherford B. Hayes ends indecisively, leaving the outcome to be decided by Congress.

1877

- Continued financial depression weakens labor unions, which have decreased in number from 30 to 9 and in membership from 300,000 to 50,000.

- *March 2*: The Electoral Commission declares Hayes the 19th president of the United States.
- *March 3*: Congress passes the Desert Land Act, permitting the purchase of 640 acres of publicly owned desert land at $1.25 an acre on condition that the purchaser agree to irrigate it within three years.
- *July*: Increased anti-Chinese feeling among the labor leaders in California leads to the Sandlot Riots in San Francisco.

1879

- The Workingman's Party, led by Denis Kearney, is founded in San Francisco to oppose Chinese immigration.
- *May 1*: Congress passes a bill prohibiting vessels from carrying more than 15 Chinese passengers at one time to the United States, but it is vetoed by President Hayes as a violation of the Burlingame Treaty. President Hayes appoints a commission to negotiate a new treaty.

- *May 7*: California passes a state law forbidding all corporations to employ Chinese workers, denying them the right to vote, and forbidding their employment in public work.

1880

- The 10th national census reveals the total population of the United States to be 50,189,209, an increase of 26 percent over 1870. Immigrants account for 2,812,195 of this number.
- *November 2*: James A. Garfield is elected the 20th president of the United States.
- *November 17*: Continued racial conflict and pressure from organized labor resulting from the competition of Chinese workers on the West Coast leads Congress to revoke the Burlingame Treaty of 1868, which allowed unlimited Chinese immigration. A new treaty is approved that permits the United States to "regulate, limit, or suspend" the immigration of Chinese laborers, but not "absolutely prohibit it."

Eyewitness Testimony

To the countrymen of Au Chan! There are laborers wanted in the land of Oregon, in the United States of America. There is much inducement to go to this new country, as they have many great works there which are not in our own country. They will supply good houses and plenty of food. They will pay you $28 a month after your arrival, and treat you considerately when you arrive. There is no fear of slavery. All is nice. The ship is now going and will take all who can pay their passage. The money required is $54. Persons having property can have it sold for them by correspondents, or borrow money of me upon security. I cannot take security on your children or your wife. Come to me in Hong-Kong and I will care for you until you start. The ship is substantial and convenient.

Au Chen, a Chinese immigration broker, in a circular recruiting labor in Hong Kong, 1862, in Conwell, Why the Chinese Emigrate and the Means They Adopt for the Purpose of Reaching America *(1871), p. 74.*

"The happiest people on the face of the earth, sir!" I had heard the assertion in almost all of the slave states, and knew something of the institution on which it was based: I was now listening to the familiar sentence at an epoch that has become historical. I sat in Charleston, South Carolina, during Secession time, December 1860.

"They are better fed and better treated than any peasantry in the civilized world. I've traveled in Europe and seen for myself, sir. What do you think of women—white women—working in the fields and living on nothing better than thin soup and vegetables, as they do in France, all the year round? . . . Such a thing couldn't happen in South Carolina—in all the South, Sir. . . . You are an Englishman . . . and therefor a born abolitionist—as a matter of sentiment, that is. You know nothing about the workings of our institutions, excepting what the d——d Yankees please to write about us, and the word *slavery* shocks you. . . .

". . . [You] were never in the Carolinas before, so you don't know how we old-fashioned folks live on our plantations. . . . I come of English blood myself; my grandfather was a Tory in the Revolution . . . and you'll find us a good deal more British than you think possible here in America. England and South Carolina are mother and daughter, you know; and under the influence of free trade, we're bound to be very intimate. All we of the South ask is that our institutions shall speak for themselves."

"An Englishman in South Carolina, December, 1860, and July, 1862," in Continental Monthly, *Volume 2, (1862), pp. 689–90.*

At this time life is not so pleasant in this so-called wonderful America. The country is full of danger, and at no time do we feel any security for our lives or property. A week ago in our county, the name of every citizen between eighteen and forty-five years of age was taken down, regardless of whether he, like myself, was married or not. Next month there is to be a levy of soldiers for military service. . . .

Last week we therefore all had to leave our harvesting work and our weeping wives and children and appear at the place of enlistment, downcast and worried. . . . To tempt people to enlist as volunteers, everybody who would volunteer was offered $225, out of which $125 is paid by the county and $100 by the state. Several men then enlisted, Yankees and Norwegians, and we others, who preferred to stay at home and work for our wives and children, were ordered to be ready at the next levy. . . . We are forbidden to leave the county without special permission and we were also told that no one would get a passport to leave the country. Dejected, we went home, and now we are in a mood of uncertainty and tension, almost like prisoners of war in this formerly so free country.

But this is not the worst of it. We have another and far more cruel enemy nearby, namely the Indians. . . . As yet they have not appeared in our fairly densely populated districts, but still they are not more than ten or fifteen Norwegian miles away. . . . Several Norwegians have been killed and many women have been captured. . . .

From this you can see how we live! On the one hand the prospect of being carried off as cannon fodder to the South, on the other the imminent danger of falling prey to the Indians . . . You are better off who can live at home in peaceful Norway. . . .

An unidentified Norwegian immigrant, letter to a friend in Norway from Dodge County, Minnesota, September, 1862, published in the Norwegian newspaper Morgenbladet, *November 22, 1862, in Blegen,* Land of Their Choice *(1955), pp. 425–426.*

I take my pen to write you a few words with my warmest greetings to all your relatives and friends. Thus far we are all in good health. I must also tell you that our family has been increased by the arrival of a little American, who was born on September 3. . . .

That which I suspected and wrote about in my last letter has come about. The Indians have begun attacking the farmers. They have already killed a great many people, and many are mutilated in the cruelest manner. Tomahawks and knives have already claimed many victims. Children, less able to defend themselves, are usually burned alive or hanged in the trees, and the destruction moves from house to house. The Indians burn everything on their way—houses, hay, grain, and so on. . . .

E. O., a Norwegian immigrant, letter from St. Peter, Minnesota, to friends in Norway, published in the Norwegian newspaper Stavenger Amtstidende og Adresseavis, *October 27, 1862, in Blegen,* Land of Their Choice *(1955), p. 427.*

Although the source of national wealth and strength is again flowing with greater freedom than for several years before the insurrection occurred, there is still great deficiency of laborers in every field of industry, especially in agriculture, and in our mines, as well of iron and coal as of the precious metals. While the demand for labor is thus increased here, tens of thousands of persons, destitute of remunerative occupation, are thronging our foreign consulates, and offering to emigrate to the United States if essential, but very cheap, assistance can be afforded them. It is easy to see that, under the sharp discipline of civil war, the nation is beginning a new life.

Abraham Lincoln, message to Congress, December 8, 1863, in Rhodes, History of the United States, 1850–1877 *(1899), p. 420.*

Resolved, That foreign immigration, which in the past has added so much to the wealth, development of resources and increase of power to the nation, the asylum of the oppressed of all nations, shall be fostered and encouraged by a liberal and just policy.

Platform of the Republican Party, formulated in part by Abraham Lincoln, 1864, in Cohen, Immigration and National Welfare *(1940), p. 32.*

The advantages which have accrued heretofore from immigration can scarcely be computed. The labor of immigrants has contributed vastly to the value of our cities, towns, and villages, our railroads, our farms, our manufactures, and our productions. Comparatively few of the race now predominant on this continent can trace their American ancestry more than a century back. Though a seeming paradox, it nevertheless approaches historical truth, that we are all immigrants. In 1790 the population of the United States was less than four millions; in 1860 it was little less than thirty-one millions and a half, showing an increase of twenty-seven millions and a half in seventy years. . . .

The advantages of foreign immigration, as between Europe and the United States and the people of Euro-pean countries, are mutual and reciprocal. If our prairies and mineral lands offer inducements to the immigrant and promise him requital for the pangs of severed family ties, and separation from the scenes of his early childhood, he, in his turn, contributes to the development of the resources of our country and adds to our material wealth. Such is the labor performed by the thrifty immigrant that he cannot enrich himself without contributing his full quota to the increase of the intrinsic greatness of the United States. This is equally true whether he work at mining, farming, or as a day laborer on one of our railroads.

The mutual interest of the United States and the immigrant being established, the next inquiry is, what facilities have been extended by the United States to promote immigration? And when we come to examine this subject, we find that very little is done by the government to promote this most desirable end.

Report from the Committee on . . . the Enactment of Suitable Laws for the Encouragement and Protection of Foreign Immigrants Arriving within Jurisdiction of the United States, February 18, 1864, *United States Thirty-Eighth Congress, first session, Senate Report No. 15, pp. 1–4.*

Instead of the indolent deportment, careless manner, and slouching gait, which characterized him at home, the young Hibernian receives the genteel inspiration of fashion, and speedily has himself tailored into external respectability; he learns to walk with his head erect, and assumes an air in keeping with his altered condition. That crouching servility and fawning sycophancy to people above his grade which made him a slave in all but the fetters, is cast aside, and he dons the character of a free citizen of the United States.

James Dawson Burn, British traveler, in Three Years Among the Working Classes in the United States During the War *(1865), pp. 15–16.*

After stating that the accommodations provided for emigrants at the depots, with one exception, are of the most shabby and insufficient character, Mr. Cumming [Castle Garden, New York, Superintendent of Emigration] gives a comparison of the rates charged between Chicago and Janesville, Wis., showing that between these two places emigrants are actually charged $6.50, being $3 more than a first-class and $3.50 more than a second-class passenger pays over the same road, yet one of the roads admitted to the privileges of the Garden advertises the second-class time to be less than half that of the emigrant time. . . .

There are so many instances of the emigrant being overcharged at Castle Garden for all or a portion of his ride that to note them all would be superfluous.

G. W. Daley, emigration officer at Castle Garden, New York, "How Emigrants Are Fleeced," letter to the New York Times, *May 29, 1866.*

Chicago is a large and splendid city. . . . But the location of the city is very unhealthful. . . . After a day's stay in Chicago I bought a ticket for La Crosse, the destination of my journey for the time being. . . . It is . . . still a small town of not over 8,000 inhabitants, of whom more than a third seem to be Norwegians. Here I met four clerks, all of whom I knew from Christiania. They had no good news for me, for they said it would be difficult to get a job just then. . . . These clerks had not had easy going during the first part of their stay in America. For a long time they had had to earn their living by manual labor. . . . An older clerk from Christiania, who arrived in La Crosse a couple of days after me, took service as a waiter in a boarding house, as he could not get a position in trade either in Chicago or La Crosse. After a few more days in La Crosse, I decided to go farther west.

Norwegian immigrant, letter to friends in Norway from Faribault, Minnesota, published in the Norwegian newspaper Aftenbladet, *September 28, 1866, in Blegen,* Land of Their Choice *(1955), p. 431.*

I do not seem to have been able to do so much to write to you, because during the time when the savages raged so fearfully here I was not able to think about anything except being murdered, with my whole family, by these terrible heathen. But God be praised, I escaped with my life, unharmed by them, and my four daughters also came through the danger unscathed.

Guri and Britha were carried off by the wild Indians, but they got a chance the next day to make their escape. . . . I myself wandered aimlessly around on my land with my youngest daughter, and I had to look on while they shot my precious husband dead, and in my sight my dear son Ole was shot through the shoulder. . . . We also found my oldest son Endre shot dead. . . . To be an eyewitness to these things and to see many others wounded and killed was almost too much for a poor woman; but God be thanked, I kept my life and my sanity, though all my movable property was torn away and stolen. . . .

COMING TO AMERICA. RETURNING FOR A VISIT.

A ragged pauper in Ireland preparing for immigration to the United States is contrasted with his prosperous condition afterward. *(New York Public Library Print Collection)*

I must also let you know that my daughter Gjaertru has land, which they received from the government under a law that has been passed, called in our language "the Homestead law," and for a quarter-section of land they have to pay $16, and after they have lived there five years they receive a deed and complete possession of the property and can sell it if they want to or keep it if they want to. She lives about twenty-four American miles from here and is doing well. . . .

. . . [O]ne or another has advised me to sell my land, but I would rather keep it for a time yet, in the hope that some of my people might come and use it . . . and if you, my dear daughter, would come here, you could buy it, and then it would not be necessary to let it fall into the hands of strangers.

Guri Endreden, Norwegian immigrant, letter to her mother and daughter in Norway, from Minnesota, December 2, 1866, in Theodore C. Blegen, "Immigrant Women and the American Frontier," in Norwegian-American Studies and Records, *Volume 5, (1930), pp. 14–29.*

Up to this time, our uncovenanted hospitality to immigration, our fearless liberality of citizenship, our equal and comprehensive justice to all inhabitants, whether they abjured their foreign nationality or not, our civil freedom, our religious toleration, our civil freedom, our religious tolerance had made all comers welcome, and under these protections the Chinese in considerable numbers have made their lodgment upon our soil.

President Hayes, in his veto of the 1868 bill to repeal the Burlingame Treaty, in Stephenson, A History of Immigration *(1926), p. 260.*

At the stations in Sweden we are grievously beset by lieutenants of emigration agents, and in Göteborg the situation was deplorable, to put it mildly. . . . I want to warn everybody who intends to emigrate not to take any stock in these agents, who talk and make promises as though they were angels of light, but do not know the least thing about what they promise.

A returned immigrant from Sweden, letter of 1868, in George Stephenson's "Hemlandet Letters" in Yearbook of the Swedish Historical Society of America, 1922–1923 *(p. 146).*

What Ireland has done for the American Church, every Bishop, every priest can tell. There is scarcely an ecclesiastical seminary for English-speaking students in which the great majority of those now preparing for the ser-

vice of the sanctuary do not belong, if not by birth, at least by blood, to that historic land to which the grateful Church of past ages accorded the proud title—Insula Sanctorum.

John T. Maguire, in The Irish in America *(1868), p. 540.*

The undersigned deemed it their duty to go on board the ill-fated ship "Liebnitz" and to inquire into the condition of her passengers transferred to the hospital ship "Illinois." . . .

Prior to our arrival on board, the ship had been cleansed and fumigated several times, but not sufficiently so to remove the dirt, which in some places covered the walls. . . . There was not a single emigrant who did not complain of the captain, as well as of the short allowance of provisions and water on board. As we know, from a long experience, that the passengers of emigrant ships, with a very few exceptions, are in the habit of claiming more than they are entitled to, we are far from putting implicit faith in all their statements. There is much falsehood and exaggeration among this class of people as among any other body of uneducated men. We have, therefore, taken their complaints with due allowance, and report only so much thereof as we believe to be well founded.

All the passengers concur in the complaint that their provisions were short, partly rotten, and that, especially, the supply of water was insufficient. . . . In quantity, the complaints of the passengers are too well founded; for they unanimously state . . . that they have never received more than half a pint of drinkable water per day, while by the laws of the United States they are entitled to receive three quarts. Some of the biscuits handed to us were rotten and old, and hardly eatable. . . . The butter . . . was rancid. . . . The beans and sauerkraut were often badly cooked, and, in spite of hunger, thrown overboard.

Annual Report of the Commissioners of Emigration, State of New York, January 21, 1868, pp. 124–26.

Teddy O'Flaherty votes. He has not been in the country six months. . . . He has hair on his teeth. He never knew an hour in civilized society. . . . He is a born savage—as brutal a ruffian as an untamed Indian. . . . Breaking heads for opinion's sake is his practice. The born criminal and pauper of the civilized world. . . . [A] wronged, abused, and pitiful spectacle of a man . . . pushed straight to hell by that abomination against common sense called the catholic religion. . . . To compare him with an intelligent man would be an insult to the latter. . . . The Irish fill our prisons, our poor houses. . . . Scratch a convict or a pauper, and the chances are that you tickle the skin of an Irish Catholic.

Anti-Irish editorial in The Chicago Post, *September 9, 1868, in Coleman,* The Election of 1868 *(1933), pp. 302–304.*

In December, 1868, . . . I set out alone on my first visit to Sweden, after an absence of nearly eighteen years. The chief object of the journey was recreation and pleasure; the second object was to make the resources of Minnesota better known among the farming and laboring classes, who had made up their minds to emigrate. . . .

I remember a conversation at an evening party at Näsby between a learned doctor and myself. He started with a proposition that it was wrong to leave one's country because God has placed us there, and, although the lot of the majority might be very hard, it was still their duty to remain to toil and pray, and even starve, if necessary. . . . My argument was of no avail; the doctor, otherwise a kind and humane man, would rather see his poor countrymen subsist on bread made partly out of bark, which hundreds of them actually did at that very time in one of the Swedish provinces, than have them go to America, where millions upon millions of acres of fertile lands only awaited the labor of their strong arms to yield an abundance, not only for themselves, but also for the poor millions of Europe.

. . . Here in America is found a civilization which is, to a large extent, built on equality and the recognition of personal merit. This, and the great natural resources of the country, the prospects of good wages which a new continent affords, and in many cases greater religious liberty, draws the people of Europe, at any rate from Sweden, to this country.

Hans Mattson, a Swedish emigrant who came to the United States in 1851 and later became secretary of state in Minnesota, in Reminiscences: The Story of an Emigrant *(1891), pp. 97–112.*

Since now most of the men I have met in these parts are old farmers . . . who have suffered many hardships and from nothing have worked themselves up to such a degree of prosperity that here they were able to take large farms and work with energy and insight for the benefit of themselves and their children, I draw the conclusion that their emigration from the native country has not only been useful to them economically, but also, and this is more important, morally. And this, ladies and gentlemen, is the great thing to note about emigration. If one could

not here attain prosperity without deteriorating morally, it would be better to live at home in the old country in the most miserable hovel. . . .

Therefore I say to you: Be agreed among yourselves, you Swedish, Norwegian, and Danish men and women, help and support one another. As the bearers of peace and harmony you must love one another. . . . But do not misunderstand me: I do not wish to say that the Scandinavians should form a power all to themselves or be a state within the state. . . . On the contrary, I believe it is the sacred duty of the emigrants who wish to make this country their future homes and who have taken the oath of allegiance to this society to become united and assimilated with the native population of the country, the Americans, to learn the English language and to familiarize themselves with and uphold the spirit and institutions of the Republic. The sooner this comes about, the better.

Paul Hjelm-Hansen, a Norwegian immigrant, in a speech to his countrymen in Alexandria, Minnesota, September 4, 1869, published in the Norwegian magazine Nordisk Folkblad, *September 22, 1869, in Blegen,* Land of Their Choice *(1955), pp. 445–446.*

A large proportion of emigrants are determined in their choice of locality by the communication of friends who had already settled there, and those who leave the decision till their arrival in America will receive every help and advice in the offices of the Emigration Commissioners, and at the "Labour Exchange" at the landing place in New York.

. . . Until a few years ago, the arrival of emigrants of the poorer classes was a scene of painful confusion and misery. Those who had no relatives or friends waiting to welcome them were at the mercy of New York's land-sharks and other devourers of body and soul, as well as of what little substance they brought with them. The hapless and helpless state of the large proportion of emigrants induced many benevolent people to form an association for their assistance, and the Government was induced to establish a Board of Emigration Commissioners. The old fort, with the surrounding area known as the Castle Gardens, was given over as a receiving house.

James Macauley, English physician and editor, reporting on his trip to America in 1870, in Across the Ferry *(1871), in Hoff,* America's Immigrants *(1867), pp. 79–80.*

These were all the arrangements for preparing meals for several hundred passengers. The result was that, except when they had nothing to cook or were sick, there was constant fighting for room near the caboose, and not one of the passengers could be sure of getting his food well-cooked. The sufferings which they endured in this way embittered the emigrants one against another, and their quarrels ended when in the evening the fires were extinguished, but only to revive in the morning.

Friedrich Kapp, New York State commissioner of emigration, describing a ship in Immigration and the Commissioners of Emigration of the State of New York *(1870), p. 25.*

It was a beautiful spring morning, and as I looked over the rail at the miles of straight streets, the green heights of Brooklyn, and the stir of ferryboats and pleasure craft on the river, my hopes rose high that somewhere in this teeming hive there would be a place for me. What kind of a place I had myself no notion of. I would let that work out as it could. . . . I had a pair of strong hands, and stubbornness enough to do for two; also a strong belief that in a free country, free from the dominion of custom, of caste, as well as of men, things would somehow come right in the end, and a man get shaken into the corner where he belonged if he took a hand in the game.

. . . By rights there ought to have been buffaloes and red Indians charging up and down Broadway. I am sorry to say that it is easier even to-day to make lots of people over there believe that, than that New York is paved and lighted with electric lights, and quite as civilized as Copenhagen. They will have it that it is in the wilds. . . .

. . . A missionary in Castle Garden was getting up a gang of men for the Brady's Bend Iron Works on the Allegheny River, and I went along. We started a full score, with tickets paid, but only two of us reached the Bend. The rest calmly deserted in Pittsburg and went their own way. . . . Not one of them would have thought of doing it on the other side. They would have carried out their contract as a matter of course. Here they broke it as a matter of course, the minute it didn't suit them to go on.

Danish immigrant Jacob A. Riis, photojournalist and reformer, recalling his arrival in New York, 1870, in The Making of an American *(1920, first published 1901), p. 21.*

Whereas, efforts are now being made to introduce into the manufactories of this state coolie labor from China in order to cheapen, and, if possible, degrade the intelligent, educated, loyal labor of Massachusetts; therefore, be it

Resolved, that while we welcome voluntary laborers from every clime, and pledge them the protection of our laws and the assurance of equal opportunities in every field of industry, still we cannot but deprecate all attempts to introduce into the manufactories of this state a servile class of laborers from China, or elsewhere, who come in fulfillment of contracts made on foreign soil . . . and we, therefore, declare our fixed and unalterable purpose to use the power of the ballot to secure the protection, safety, property, and happiness of the working people of this commonwealth as against this new attempt of capital to cheapen labor and degrade the working classes by importing coolie slaves for that purpose. . . .

Statement of a Boston labor organization protesting the use of Chinese immigrants to break a strike by the shoemakers of North Adams, Massachusetts, reported in the Boston Investigator *(July 6, 1870).*

Which I wish to remark,
    And my language is plain,
That for ways that are dark
    And for tricks that are vain,
The heathen Chinee is peculiar,
    Which the same I would rise to explain.

Bret Harte, "Plain Language from Truthful James," in The Overland Monthly *(September 1870).*

All I want in my business is muscle. I don't care whether it be obtained from a Chinaman or a white man—from a mule or a horse!

Anonymous labor leader in California, 1870s, quoted by the secretary of the Connecticut Board of Agriculture in the Board's Tenth Annual Report *(1876–1877), p. 48.*

The good of the country which receives the immigrant is quite as much to be considered as the good of the individual alien who, for one reason or another, comes to our shores. Immigration is by no means an unmixed blessing, and even in cases where it appears so in the end, it is often a blessing in disguise, to the country receiving an indiscriminate and unregulated immigration. It introduces youth, vigor, poverty and industry, but it also introduces disease, ignorance, crime, pauperism and idleness. There was a time when convicts and the sweepings of London streets were shipped over to the American colonies, just as they were afterward sent to Botany Bay [the British penal colony in Australia]. That was long ago, but even now we receive a great many persons of the same class—

True patriots they, for be it understood
They left their country for their country's good.

Report by Frank B. Sanborn, secretary of the Massachusetts State Board of Charities, to the National Conference of Charities and Correction, in Proceedings *(1876), p. 169.*

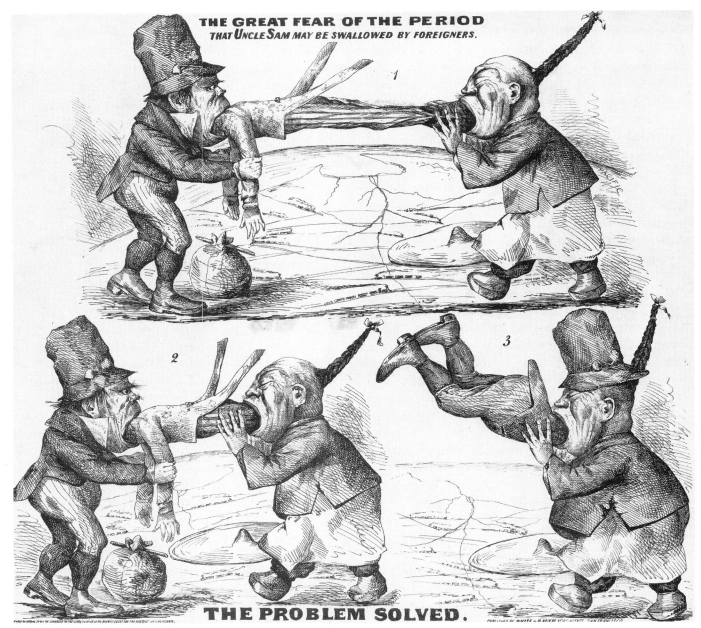

Nativist cartoon published in San Francisco in the 1860s shows an Irishman and a Chinese devouring Uncle Sam and then the Chinese consuming the Irishman. *(Library of Congress, Prints and Photographs Division [LC-USZ62-22399])*

There is scarcely a hamlet in all England which has not been invaded by the emissaries of one of the great steamship lines. Either in the tavern, the reading room, or the apothecary's shop, a bold red-and-black plaque is displayed, bearing the names of half a dozen vessels and the dates of their sailings. Honest Giles, sitting of an evening in his accustomed place by the fire-side of the village inn, has it constantly before him, and he makes it the text of many long chats with his neighbors about the wonderful land in the west. . . . Letters often come to the village [and] small amounts of money or photographs which represent the writers as brighter-looking and in better dress than they ever appeared at home.

Scribner's Monthly, *September 1877, p. 577.*

. . .[T]he Chinese should not, can not, will not go. I will show you that if they did, it would be so much the worse for you—aye, even the very classes who are clamorous for their removal. What are they doing here? In a word, they are pursuing a number of industries which, without them, would have no existence at all on this coast. . . .

. . .Now that the Chinamen have built up these trades, some of you would drive them away, hoping, no doubt, to fill their places, and perhaps fill them at higher wages. How mean! How stupid! . . . The Chinese are the labour-saving machines that render these industries possible. Banish them and the industries will perish. Then will your coast be deserted and your workingmen themselves be forced to flee from it. . . . May heaven guide them in their darkness. They have much need of light when they regard the poor Chinaman as being in their way; the truth being that without his aid in providing them with cheap food, clothing, services, etc., they would not be able to live here at all.

. . . No one has a deeper stake in the welfare of your working classes than the Chinese. . . . All I ask is that your workingmen will cease to look upon the Chinese as the source of their troubles. . . . It is not our business to discover the causes of your misfortunes. It is enough if we show that they do not spring from our presence here, and that, on the contrary, they would be aggravated were you unfortunately to forget what is due to honor, to justice, and to your own interests, and attempt to drive us away from your shores.

Kwang Chang Ling, letter to the San Francisco *[California]* Argonaut, *August 2, 1878.*

I am satisfied the present Chinese labor invasion (it is not in any proper sense immigration—women and children do not come) is pernicious and should be discouraged. Our experience in dealing with the weaker races—the negroes and Indians, for example—is not encouraging. We shall oppress the Chinamen, and their presence will make hoodlums and vagabonds of their oppressors. I therefore would consider with favor suitable measures to discourage the Chinese from coming to our shores. But I suspect that this bill is inconsistent with our treaty obligations. . . . If it violates the National faith, I must decline to sign it.

President Hayes, diary entry, February 20, 1879, in Charles Richard Williams, ed., Diary and Letters of Rutherford Birchard Hayes: Nineteenth President of the United States, *Vol. III* (1922–26), p. 52.

Among the number of immigrants [arriving at Castle Garden this week] were a number of Hungarians who arrived in a destitute condition. Thirty of these people came last week and had immediately to be taken charge of by the Castle Garden officers. Superintendent Jackson finally found employment for them at Lenhardtsville, Bucks County, in the lumber region of Pennsylvania. They were all wood-choppers and hardy forest laborers, hence the reason for sending them there. Today the [ship] Spain discharged 90 more of these people, equally destitute, on the Emigration Department. . . . It was not easy to communicate with the men, as they could not speak English, French, or German, but an interpreter was found . . . It was learned that they had come from the flooded districts of Hungary, where the crops have failed and long continued rains have caused the inundation of the country, sweeping away the subsistence of the people. . . . They are all lumbermen and farmers. It is likely that the steerage fare on the Spain was the best feeding they ever had in their lives. They were landed looking strong and hearty but without so much as a cent among the whole lot, and they had to get their breakfast from the department people. . . . Superintendent Jackson said they are honest, hard-working fellows and he thinks there will not be much difficulty to find work for them; but he says what he rather dreads is, that when they have got $15 or $20 together, each man will be sending for his family, and a long string of equally destitute Hungarian wives and children will trail through the department for a year or more.

"Destitute Immigrants, Arrival of Ninety Hungarians Without a Cent of Money," letter to the New York Times, *December 16, 1879.*

. . . The most familiar of the poorer class of the English people [emigrating to America] are from the towns, especially from the manufacturing towns, and with regard to them the impressions formed are for the most part unfavorable. They have much of the ignorance and stupidity, with none of the physique, of the agricultural laborer. Many of them cannot read, and still more know nothing of their destination or of what they are going to do. They are pitiful specimens of manhood, and England suffers as little by losing them as America gains by the acquisition. Indeed, few things have struck me more painfully than the deterioration which has taken place . . . in the character, stamina, and habits of the English working man. . . . Hence it comes to pass that the great proportion of the English steerage passengers—the limps, listless, pale-faced young fellows, with pipe in mouth and hands in pockets, and the slatternly young women who accompany them—must be

THEY ARE PRETTY SAFE THERE.

When Politicians do Agree, their Unanimity is Wonderful.

"GIVE IT TO HIM, HE'S GOT NO VOTE NOR NO FRIENDS!"

A sympathetic view of the immigrant's sorry lot in the United States shows politicians of all parties joining in victimizing him. *(New York Public Library Print Collection)*

regarded as a curse rather than a blessing to the country which acquires them.

*G. S., "Emigration from Europe, Its Character and Extent,"
Liverpool, England, May 15, in the New York Times,
May 28, 1880.*

One of the methods of recognizing passenger capacity is constantly in use at the present time, and is based on the avarice of owners of vessels and steamship companies. This method recognizes nothing else but to carry as many as can be put on board. It has no regard for the health or comfort of the emigrant, views him as supplying so many dollars to the bank account, and is a marine inheritance from the slave trade, with the horrors of the "middle passage." Although carrying an excess of passengers over that allowed by law renders a vessel liable to a penalty, official reports do not show that any prosecution has resulted in the recovery of such penalty from vessels reported as violating the provisions of any act to secure the emigrant from the evils of overcrowding. . . .

And yet these owners of large steamship lines, boasting of their superior accommodations and discipline, admitting the demonstrated facts of increased disease and death rates, of the disease-producing effects of overcrowding, of all the violations of the law, etc., . . . with a sublimity than to which impudence can rise no higher, suggests a rise in the rates of fare for the immigrant in their floating stockyards.

*Dr. Thomas J. Turner, medical director of the United States
Navy, in a treatise on the hygiene of emigrant ships, read before
the American Public Health Association December 1880, in
Abbott,* Immigration: Documents and Case Records
(1924), pp. 54–55.

CHAPTER SIX

The "New Immigration"
1881–1918

New Sources of Immigration

The 1880s marked a turning point in the history of American immigration, as well as in the American attitude toward it. In the first place, the annual rate rose dramatically: The number of arrivals from Europe went up more than 100 percent from 1879 to 1880. The volume of immigration from China more than doubled from 1880 to 1881, and it more than tripled during the next year, rising from 11,890 to 39,579, its highest point ever.

The first great wave of American immigration in the 19th century, from 1815 to 1860, and the second, from the end of the Civil War to about 1880, were primarily from England, Ireland, Germany, Scandinavia, and Holland—all countries with similar histories and cultures, speaking related languages. The immigrants pouring into the country from the 1880s to the beginning of the First World War, however, came increasingly from Italy, the former Austro-Hungarian Empire, Russia, Greece, and Turkey. The differences between these groups and earlier immigrants were more than geographic. The shift from northwest to southeast Europe as a source for immigration, which began about 1883 and increased rapidly until the first decades of the 20th century, brought unfamiliar cultures, in unprecedented numbers, to the New World.

If the longer-established Americans sometimes had trouble accommodating foreigners before, they found the hordes pouring in during the last decades of the century harder yet to understand and accept. The newcomers came increasingly from countries with absolute monarchies, little public education, high birth and death rates, and no traditions of social equality. Many were unskilled and illiterate, and a greater percentage than before of the new immigrants were "birds of passage"—single men who came to earn money and return, rather than to settle. Like the Asians, the Europeans of the "new immigration" were perceived as unwilling or unable to assimilate, and their competition for jobs made them unwelcome in many areas. Isolated into their own communities, they formed a patchwork quilt of small ethnic neighborhoods in the big cities of their new country. They clung defensively to their own languages, customs, and institutions, and they were often suspicious and highly critical of the American society from which they were excluded.

The change in nationality of the immigrant flow did not happen all at once, but it gathered momentum through the 1880s and 1890s, and its social and economic impact on the country accelerated rapidly. In 1882, of the 788,992 immigrants to the United States who arrived from Europe, 250,630 came from Germany, nearly 180,000 from the British Isles, and more than 105,000 from Scandinavia, totaling 87 percent. The countries of southern and eastern Europe—Italy, Spain, Russia, Poland, Romania, the Baltic States (Estonia, Latvia, and Lithuania), Finland, and Hungary—accounted for only about 13 percent. Twenty-five years later, in 1907, when immigration reached the highest numbers it had yet seen, the proportions were almost completely reversed. Of the total of 1,285,349 European immigrants to the United States arriving that year—the largest number to have arrived in a single year till then—80.7 percent were from countries in the southern and eastern part of the continent. Germany, the British Isles, Scandinavia, and Holland, from which virtually all immigrants to America had come until the mid-1870s, accounted for a mere 19.3 percent.

It was a period of unprecedented migration throughout the world. People were moving from one nation in Europe to another, from Europe to Australia and South America, and from Asia to both Europe and the Americas. In general, it was to the youngest countries that the greatest volume of newcomers came. In the first two decades of the 20th century, Canada received nearly 3 million people, Argentina admitted more than 2 million, and Brazil about 1 million. Australia and New

In "They Would Close to the New-Comer the Bridge That Carried Them and Their Fathers Over" (published in *Puck,* January 11, 1893), German-born cartoonist Joseph Keppler criticizes prosperous Americans who forget their immigrant origins and reject the next wave of foreigners. *(New York Public Library Print Collection)*

Zealand admitted some 900,000 European immigrants during the same period. But the United States remained by far the most popular destination; from 1906 to 1915, it saw the arrival of 9.4 million immigrants. They continued to come in ever-increasing numbers from the old sources: in 1882 some 250,000 Germans entered the United States, more than twice the number of English, and the Irish were still well represented with more than 76,000. But in that year Italian immigration, which had stood at fewer than 6,000 in 1879, increased to 32,159. The 5,041 Russians who had come to the United States in 1881 were joined the next year by 16,918 of their countrymen.

The Italians

No national group from southern Europe came over in greater numbers during the period of the new immigrations than the Italians. In 1881 the numbers arriving from Italy had risen (from 5,791 in 1879) to 15,401, while Germany sent more than 210,000 in that year. By 1895 the German immigration count had dropped to 32,173, and the Italian had passed it with 35,907. Five years later Germany had been completely passed as a source of new Americans. That year no more than 18,507 immigrants entered the United States from Germany, while 100,135 newcomers arrived in the United States from Italy. By 1905 the number of Italians had grown to 221,479. Although most of them were from rural areas, few went into farming. Most of them arrived with too little money to take advantage of the government's generous land offers and preferred to congregate with their countrymen in the cities. In New York City they formed neighborhoods that were divided by region of origin in Italy; a Sicilian street maintaining a distinct identity would be separate yet near one solidly populated by immigrants from northern Italy.

"The Modern Ark," a cartoon by E. S. Bisbee in *Harper's Weekly,* gives an unflattering picture of immigrants from many countries taking advantage of America's generosity. *(New York Public Library Print Collection)*

There are several reasons for the great increase in immigration from Italy at the end of the 19th and the beginning of the 20th century. The first, as with most waves of immigration, was overpopulation and poverty in the home country. The American consul in Palermo, the capital of Sicily, described the population of that city as living "in a manner not easily conceived by an American or other person not conversant with the poverty-stricken localities of Europe. The huts or hovels in which they live and sleep, together with their pigs, goats, and donkeys, and possibly any number of other living things, are not pleasant to look upon, nor is there any desire for a second inhalation of the odor which emanates from them." Historian John Rogers Commons wrote in *Races and Immigrants in America* (1907), "Of wheat and corn-meal together the Italian peasant eats in a year only three-fourths as much as the inmate of an English poorhouse. Of meat the peasant in Apulia gets no more than ten pounds a year, while the English workhouse pauper gets fifty-seven pounds a year."

The taxation system in Italy was oppressive, especially in the south, from which some 84 percent of the immigrants to America came. Centuries of deforestation and archaic farming methods had severely depleted the soil, and high rents and low wages added to the burden of life for the agricultural worker. One of the most densely populated countries in Europe, Italy was home to 349 people per square mile, a greater number than was to be found in either China or India. To make matters worse, France placed a high tariff on Italian wines at the end of the 1880s, and the United States stopped buying oranges and lemons when it developed its own citrus crops in Florida and California. With the loss of two of its principal markets, the tenant farmers of Italy could hardly feed their families, and by the end of the century it was said that population was Italy's principal export. The mayor of one town in southern Italy was quoted as saying that his community consisted of 8,000 people, "three thousand of whom are in America and the other five thousand preparing to follow them."

Although America was the favorite destination of Italian emigrants, it was not the only one. Since before 1870, Italians had been the largest group of immigrants to Argentina, constituting almost 50 percent of the total population. By the middle of the 20th century, it was estimated that almost one-third of the population of that country was Italian by birth or family. Like the United States, Brazil received its greatest number of immigrants from Italy at the turn of the century. Only when the coffee market suffered a crisis around 1900, and Brazil lost its capacity to support more agricultural workers, did the United States become the first choice for Italian immigrants.

Another reason for the huge wave of immigration from Italy during this period was the relative ease with which Italians were able to make the trip. Unlike the governments of Germany and the Scandinavian countries, Italian authorities recognized emigration as a positive solution to the country's economic ills and did what they could to encourage it. In 1901 Italy passed laws to protect emigrants from foreign exploitation, and philanthropic agencies were established to provide aid to Italians living abroad.

The combination of severe hardships in Italy and alluring economic prospects in the prosperous industrial society of America accounts for the extent of Italian immigration to the United States. The total number of Italians entering the country between 1820 and 1870 was 22,518; in the next half-century, 4,170,362 arrived. During its peak period, from 1901 to 1920, the Italian immigration to the United

States was considered the greatest movement of a single nationality in recorded world history.

The Slavs

The second largest group in the new immigration after the Italians were the various Slavic peoples of eastern Europe. It is difficult to classify these groups by nationality, because they came from many countries with shifting boundaries and the U.S. Department of Immigration identified them by different names at different times. Nationally, the second largest source of European immigrants was the Austro-Hungarian Empire, created in 1876 and ruled by the Habsburg family until the treaty ending the First World War in 1918 redrew the national boundaries of Europe. This loose federation of countries included Austria, Poland, Hungary, and parts of Romania and the nations later called Czechoslovakia and Yugoslavia. It comprised no fewer than 20 distinct ethnic groups and languages, and in its 42 years of existence it never knew either political unity or economic stability.

The majority of Slavs to emigrate from Austria-Hungary were Poles, whose homeland had been divided up in 1795 by Russia, Germany, and Austria and had no separate existence again until 1919. Therefore, by nationality, they were not truly Polish. Most of them came to the United States from Russia, Austria-Hungary, or Germany, and they were listed in the census as Poles only because they identified Polish as their mother tongue. These were not the first Polish immigrants in the United States. There had been Poles in the Jamestown colony in the beginning of the 17th century, and a few joined William Penn in his colony in the first half of the 18th century. Others, like Casimir Pulaski and Thaddeus Kosciuszko, came to the United States to fight in the American Revolution, and in the 1850s Poles accounted for some 10 percent of the pioneer population of Texas. But it was not until the beginning of the 19th century that Poles immigrated in sufficient numbers to establish a clear ethnic identity in America.

In 1910, the first year that immigrants were asked their native language, more than 13 million foreign-born white residents were recorded, of whom some 7 percent (a little more than 940,000) identified themselves as Polish speakers. About 45 percent (418,370) of these Polish speakers came from Russia, 35 percent (329,418) from Austria-Hungary, and 20 percent (190,096) from Germany. Like the Italians, they rarely had enough money to migrate beyond the big cities or take up farming. The largest settlements were in Chicago, where an estimated 250,000 lived in 1905; and New York City, which was home to more than 150,000. Buffalo, New York; Pittsburgh, Pennsylvania; and Detroit, Michigan, also had large Polish communities during the first decade of the 20th century. Many Poles were devout Catholics who strongly supported their own parochial schools and formed many social, political, and professional societies. In 1910 it was estimated that there were more than 7,000 Polish organizations in the United States and that two-thirds of the Polish-born in America belonged to at least one of them. Their solidarity was necessary for their survival, since they were met with the same social rejection as the Irish and the Italians and found it difficult to get any but the most menial work. As one Pole wrote home from Brooklyn around 1900, "[I]n America Poles work like cattle. Where a dog does not want to sit, there the Pole is made to sit."

Another Slavic group whose nationality is difficult to define is the Czechs. Formerly the residents of the ancient kingdom of Bohemia, a part of the Holy Roman

VOL. 42 NO. 1071·   APRIL 26 1902   PRICE 10 CENTS

Judge

ENTERED AT THE POST OFFICE AT NEW YORK AS SECOND CLASS MATTER. COPYRIGHT 1901 BY JUDGE COMPANY. TITLE REGISTERED AS A TRADE MARK.

COPYRIGHT 1901 BY JUDGE COMPANY OF NEW YORK.

Sackett & Wilhelms Litho & Ptg. Co. New York

THE MAGNET.
The only bad feature of our prosperity.

Dirt, disease, poverty, crime, and political agitation are among the negative results of foreign immigration according to this 1902 *Judge* cover by Eugene Zimmerman. Images of the Dutch, Germans, Chinese, English, Italians, Scots, Greeks, eastern Europeans, and Near Easterners are included among the insulting caricatures. *(American Museum of Immigration, U.S. National Park Service)*

Empire, they had been ruled by the Habsburgs since 1526 and were a part of the Austro-Hungarian Empire. Among the most educated of the Slavic immigrants, they began coming to the United States following a failed revolution in 1848. The gold rush of 1848–49 drew many more to the United States, and by the end of the American Civil War the Czech population of the United States was more than 40,000. When the Austro-Hungarian Empire permitted free emigration from Bohemia in 1867, the number of Czech arrivals increased, and soon large colonies grew up in several American cities. By 1920 Chicago held more than 100,000 Czechs, and nearly 50,000 lived in Cleveland, Ohio. But unlike the Poles, Czechs spread out into the American frontier. There was a sizable Bohemian community in Wisconsin by 1850, and in 1860 a Czech-language newspaper was published in Racine. Among the earliest pioneers of the upper Mississippi Valley, Czechs also settled in Iowa, Minnesota, and Kansas, and by the end of World War I there were eight Bohemian newspapers being published in Nebraska alone. There were towns named Prague in both Nebraska and Texas, where Bohemians were among the 19th-century immigrants from Germany and where the Czech language was taught in the public schools as late as 1930.

Closely related to the Czechs, in language and in history, are the Slovaks, whose original homeland in the southern Carpathian Mountains was ruled by

Czechoslovakian immigrants maintain their culture as they dance the Besada in Masaryktown, Florida. *(American Museum of Immigration, U.S. National Park Service)*

the Hungarians from the 10th century. Included in the immigration records with the Hungarians until 1899, they arrived in growing numbers, totaling more than 345,000 from 1899 to 1909. Many came to escape military service imposed by Hungary and were among the most patriotic of new Americans. The National Slovak Society of the United States, founded in 1890, required all its members to become citizens, and by the 1930s membership in Slovak organizations in America totaled some 300,000.

Records of the immigration of Russians from the 1880s to 1918 are complicated by the fact that the statistical reports did not distinguish between ethnic and national Russians, lumping together Russians with Ukrainians, Poles, Lithuanians, Latvians, Estonians, Finns, and Jews. Ethnic Russian immigration to America began before the Revolution, though never in large numbers. Russian fur traders crossed into Alaska as early as 1745, and when that territory was sold to the United States in 1867, the headquarters of the Russian Church were transferred to San Francisco. The U.S. immigration records in 1881 report 5,041 immigrants from "Russia and the Baltic States"—that is, all arrivals from Russia, Latvia, Lithuania, and Estonia. The next year, 16,918 more entered the United States. By 1887 that number had swollen to 30,766, and 1892 saw 81,511 arrive. The flood continued to swell until it reached its highest level in 1913, with 291,040. In that year the combined immigration of England, Ireland, Scotland, and Wales to the United States was a little more than 88,000; that of Germany was only 34,329.

Among the most unskilled and impoverished of the new arrivals, the Russians who came to the United States in the 1880s and 1890s were mostly former serfs—peasants tied to the land and owned by the gentry until their emancipation in the 1860s. Like the Poles, they were forced to take the most menial and unrewarding jobs in their new home. More than half stayed in New York or moved no farther than Pennsylvania, where they found work in factories and mines. They were often barred from craft unions, although they were admitted to the United Mine Workers and became active in such radical organizations as the Industrial Workers of the World. The Russians maintained their own Orthodox Church, which claimed 200 congregations by 1930. The Ukrainians, many of whom were Roman Catholic, settled in large numbers in Pennsylvania, where they formed a large part of the coal-mining workforce. Others formed colonies in Chicago and Detroit, where they found work in industry.

Other Slavic groups provided smaller streams of immigrants to the United States at the beginning of the 20th century. Bulgarians began arriving after a revolution in Macedonia in 1904 prevented expansion eastward, but they never reached large numbers. Not ethnically related to the Slavs but historically included in their number by American immigration officials, Finns first came to America as part of the New Sweden colony on the Delaware River in the mid-17th century. When Russia conquered Finland from Sweden in 1809, a small stream of refugees began immigrating to the United States; their immigration rates increased by the lure of the gold rush in 1849. Crop failures drove many more to emigrate between 1865 and 1870. Finland had been given the status of an autonomous grand duchy, but in 1899 the government in Moscow imposed the Russian language on the territory, abolished its native institutions, censored its press, suppressed its Lutheran churches, and disbanded its native army, initiating the largest exodus in the country's history. Finnish immigration to the United States reached its peak between 1900 and 1918. In the 1920 census the Finnish population of the United States was reported to number about 150,000, representing 1.1 percent of a total foreign-born population of 13.7 million.

The Baltic peoples, though technically not Slavs, are usually grouped with them statistically. Classified as Russians in U.S. immigration records until 1922, immigrants from Lithuania, Latvia, and Estonia came from a region ruled by Germans, Danes, Swedes, and Russians for centuries. The Baltic peoples were represented by a few settlers in colonial America but began to appear in substantial numbers only after 1900, usually in flight from political repression, economic exploitation, and military conscription by Russia. Lithuanians in America were estimated to number about 200,000 in 1920, more than half of them living in Chicago. Estonians totaled about 180,000, their largest settlements being in New York City and San Francisco. Latvians totaled fewer than 20,000, most of them in New York City, Chicago, and Boston. About equal numbers immigrated to Canada. During the interwar period of independence of these three countries, from 1918 to 1940, emigration from the Baltic states dropped to almost zero.

The Jews

The great majority—estimates run as high as 95 percent—of immigrants from Russia and its territories were not Russians but members of minorities living within Russian territory. Perhaps a quarter of them were Poles; Germans, Finns, and Baltic peoples made up another quarter. The largest number of Russian immigrants were Jews. More than 40 percent of those fleeing Russia for the United States and an equal percentage of those emigrating from Austria-Hungary and Romania were Jewish.

The Jews had long been the victims of oppression in eastern Europe. About 95 percent of the Jewish population of Russia was forced to live within a restricted territory called the Pale of Settlement in the west where Russia bordered Germany, Austria-Hungary, and Romania. Jews were drafted into the army at the age of 12, while other Russians were called up at 18. When Czar Alexander II was killed in 1882, things became worse. Although the czar's assassin was known to be non-Jewish, the government held the Jews responsible. Their residence within the crowded Pale was more strictly enforced than before, and they were prohibited from holding office or engaging in most professions and trades. Jews were subjected to special taxes and prevented from owning or renting land. Restrictions were placed on their worship. One observer reported that the Jews were blamed for all of Russia's problems. "By making the Jews the scapegoats," according to Abraham Cahan, the government "had confused the common people so that . . . the peasants were certain that the Jews and not the Czar were the cause of all their troubles." A wave of anti-Semitism swept across Russia. Violent assaults on Jewish homes and businesses were frequent, and wholesale slaughter of Jews by their Gentile neighbors was ignored, and even encouraged, by the authorities. These massacres, called pogroms, accounted for the deaths of many thousands and sometimes for whole villages being wiped out. The pogroms of 1882 were followed in 1903 by an even worse massacre in Kishinev, and another, following the Russo-Japanese War, in 1906.

The oppression of Russian Jews excited considerable sympathy in the United States. A large public meeting in New York City in February 1882 greeted the first Jewish refugees warmly, and one speaker was quoted as saying, "Let them all come! I would to heaven it were in our power to take the whole three million Jews of Russia. The valley of the Mississippi alone could throw her strong arms around them,

Jewish orphans whose parents were killed in a Russian pogrom pose for this photograph. *(American Museum of Immigration, U.S. National Park Service)*

and draw them all to her opulent bosom." The American government officially protested the pogroms, and speeches in Congress announced that in this country Jews would be treated with justice. Throughout Europe, America's reputation as a haven for the oppressed increased. Russia wanted to remain on good terms with the United States, and although it took no steps to improve its treatment of the Jews, it did nothing to prevent their emigration. In fact, the Russian government, recognizing a "Jewish problem," positively encouraged the departure of Jews. According to one report, the official goal of Russia was to kill one-third of its Jews, convert another third, and drive the rest out of the country.

Persecution was systematic and official, not only in Russia but throughout eastern Europe. Jews represented a large percentage of the emigration from other countries in the region as well, in about equal proportion to the populations of their countries. In the period between 1881 and the beginning of World War I, more than 1.5 million Jews entered the United States from eastern Europe; 1,119,950 of them came in flight from conditions in Russia, 281,150 came from Austria-Hungary, and 67,057 from Romania. They emigrated in numbers like the Irish in the early 19th century, and like the Irish came in large groups together. Sometimes whole villages transplanted themselves to America, most of them living in large cities in the Northeast. It is estimated that by 1920, the ratio of Jews to Gentiles in the United States had risen from five in 1,000 to three in 100.

America was not the only destination of Jews, but it was the only one that was able to accommodate the swelling wave of Jewish immigration. In the early 1890s the German-Jewish millionaire Baron Maurice de Hirsch gave about $55,000,000 to establish a Jewish colony in Argentina, hoping to transport the entire Jewish community of Russia to that country, but the project met with only limited success.

Efforts at resettlement in other countries had no better results. It was America that was seen as "the Golden Land," and enthusiastic letters from family members who had come to America had the same effect on Russian and Polish Jews as the Scandinavian "America letters" had. Some of the glowing reports of American opulence sound strange to a later ear, but in the context of their times they were impressive. Girls in a sewing school in Minsk received a letter reporting that the starting weekly wage for a seamstress in New York was $4—equivalent to a month's income for a Russian.

The social opportunities were even more astonishing. In America a large community of German Jews had already established itself and become assimilated successfully for the most part. In New York, families of Spanish Jews were among the longest-established residents of the city and had helped to found some of its best and most exclusive clubs. Such millionaires as August Belmont (who had translated his German-Jewish name Schönberg to the more elegant French form) was a leader in high society, and many Jews who had begun as peddlers when they arrived from Europe a few years before had become wealthy and respected merchants. In Cahan's popular novel *The Rise of David Levinsky*, the newly arrived Russian-Jewish immigrant hero observed the prosperity of the Jews of New York with amazement. "The poorest-looking man wore a hat . . . a stiff collar and a necktie," he marveled, "and the poorest woman wore a hat or bonnet."

Other Europeans: Armenians, Syrians, Greeks, Spanish, and Portuguese

People came from many parts of the world for other reasons besides overpopulation and poverty at the turn of the century. Religious persecution, an important motive for Jewish flight from eastern Europe, explained the exodus from Syria and Armenia, two small Christian nations surrounded by the Muslim empire of the Ottoman Turks. Long a victim of Turkish oppression, the Armenian community suffered large-scale massacres, as bloody as the Jewish pogroms in Russia, from 1894 to 1896, and as a result large numbers fled to the New World. An ancient kingdom south of the Black Sea, Armenia had been occupied at different times by Persians, Russians, and Turks, and its people were an object of worldwide sympathy for the brutal treatment the country had suffered. In 1894 there were an estimated 3,000 Armenians in the United States, but after the atrocities of the massacres during that and the next two years, the number increased rapidly. From 1894 to 1917, more than 70,000 Armenians, mostly peasants and artisans, came to America. Many found work in the textile mills and shoe factories of Massachusetts, while others became prominent in Boston as photoengravers. In Fresno, California, an Armenian farming colony was established to grow grapes. Many also became tradesmen, specializing in the sale of Oriental carpets.

Syrians were also victims of Turkish oppression, and from 1870 to 1900 almost a million left the country. Their first destinations were Egypt, South America, and India, but many were influenced by Protestant missionaries to continue their journey and settle in America, where they found a secure haven from persecution.

Greeks also suffered under the Turks but freed themselves after a long and bloody rebellion in the early 19th century. Greek immigration to the United States became extensive only after 1900. Greece was not experiencing any political or religious dissatisfaction at that time. The reasons for leaving their proud and historic country were largely economic. Overworked farms, poorly developed industry, low wages, and high prices led to widespread dissatisfaction. When the French market for currants, one of Greece's major crops, fell during the middle 1880s, unemployment led many to look beyond the nation's borders for a livelihood.

In U.S. immigration records, Greece was lumped together with Spain and Portugal under "Other Southern" countries in Europe, so no exact records were kept of the number of immigrants from there, but historians agree that between 1900 and 1918 more than 300,000 arrived. This does not seem a large number when compared with the figures for Italians, Slavs, and Jews, but it represented a large percentage of the population of their country. Most Greek immigrants were young, unattached men with few ties and no prospects at home. "America fever" swept through their country, increased by many "America letters" from Greeks in the United States, and when direct steamship service between Piraeus and New York began in 1902, whole villages were emptied of all but the aged. It has been estimated that when World War I began in 1914, one out of every four Greek men of working age was living in the United States.

Like the Armenians and Syrians, the Greeks found work in textile mills in New England at first, but they quickly adapted to their new country and found a specialty in confectioneries, coffee shops, and restaurants. A "Little Greece" sprang up in many large cities. By 1910 there were four Greek newspapers being published in New York City, and the Astoria section of Queens had a Greek population second only to that of Athens, Greece.

The influence of Spanish immigration has been very large in proportion to its numbers. In the entire history of American immigration, Spain accounts for fewer than 300,000 arrivals (less than two percent of the world total), yet at the end of the 20th century nearly 10 percent of the residents of the United States spoke Spanish. The Spanish dominated most of the Western hemisphere in the 16th and 17th centuries, controlling present-day Florida, Louisiana, Texas, California, New Mexico, and the western Great Plains as well as all of South and Central America. The first European settlement in California was the mission in San Diego, founded in 1769 by the Spanish missionary Junípero Serra. Spanish colonial architecture and Spanish-language place names throughout the Southwest bear witness to the impact Spain has had on American culture and the important influence it has had on the country's history.

Nevertheless, in 1781 there were fewer than 600 Spaniards living in California, and although Spain controlled vast territories, it ceded or sold much of its land to France and England during the 18th and 19th centuries. It was not until the beginning of the 20th century that a wave of "new immigration" from Spain to the United States began. From 1900 to 1924 more than 170,000 arrived, but many returned. Most of the millions of Spaniards emigrating from Europe during those years chose South and Central America as their destinations. Of the immigrants who came to the United States, many came from the provinces of Andalusia and Galicia. They gravitated to New York City and, by way of Cuba, to Florida. Those from the Basque region in northern Spain continued their traditional profession of herding sheep in Idaho, where the city of Boise has the largest concentration of Basques outside of Europe.

Less prominent but numerically greater has been the influx of Portuguese, who began immigrating to the United States, Canada, and Brazil in the early 17th century for both religious and economic reasons. The first Jewish community

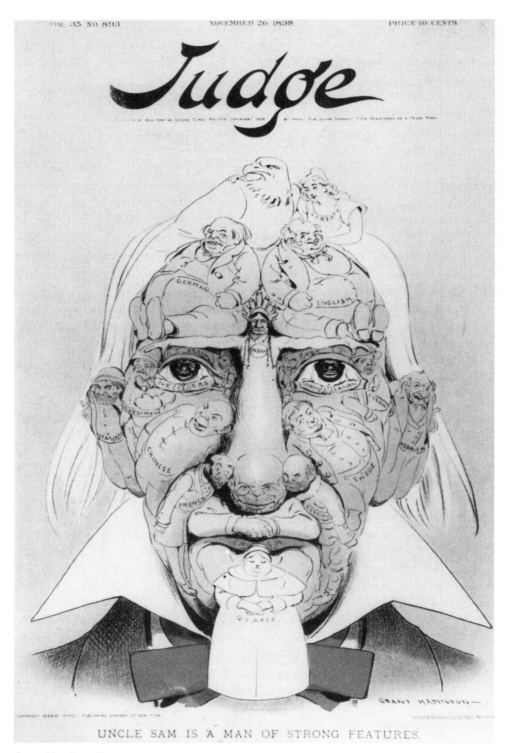

Grant Hamilton illustrates the mixture of races that gives America its unique character in this famous 1898 *Judge* cover. *(New York Public Library Print Collection)*

in America was composed of Portuguese refugees from Brazil, and Portuguese fishermen had established themselves in America well before the Revolutionary War. The main wave of immigration, however, began in the 1830s, mostly from the Azores, a group of nine islands in the Atlantic Ocean, 800 miles from Lisbon.

Many Portuguese settled in New Bedford, Massachusetts, where they followed their traditional occupation as fishermen. Others worked in mines or lumber camps in California. By 1850 there were two sizable settlements in Illinois populated by Protestant refugees from Madeira, another Portuguese island. Later, the Portuguese formed a large part of the population of Newark, New Jersey.

In 1890 the second and largest wave of Portuguese immigration began, and by 1920 more than 200,000 Azoreans, Madeirans, and Cape Verdeans had arrived from their islands in the Atlantic Ocean and established themselves as fishermen, farmers, or textile workers. By 1899 French-Canadians and Portuguese held most of the jobs in the cotton mills of New Bedford, Massachusetts. Others became prominent in the wine and dairy industries in New York, New Jersey, and Rhode Island.

Asians: Chinese, Japanese, Koreans, and Filipinos

Although small in comparison with the flood of newcomers from southern and eastern Europe, immigration from Asia began to assume significant proportions during the 1880s. The Chinese had already made such an impact that a powerful movement to exclude them from entry had begun. In 1882 their numbers reached an all-time high when 39,579 Chinese arrived, bringing the total Chinese to enter the United States since 1868 to more than 2 million. It was a turning point in Chinese immigration. The hostility caused by their competition for jobs came to a head, and a law was finally passed to prohibit the entry of all but a select few. In 1883 the number of Chinese to enter America was slightly more than 8,000; by 1887 the total had sunk to 10.

Only one Japanese is recorded as entering the United States in 1861, the first official entry from Japan in the government's files. The next listed arrival was of seven in 1866. Although in 1868 a group of 148 Japanese contract laborers landed in Hawaii, then still an independent kingdom, to work on the American sugar plantations, the annual number of Japanese arrivals in the United States stayed under 100 through 1882, the peak year for Chinese immigration. In that year five Japanese arrived. But with the conclusion of the "Chinese problem," the controversy over Asian immigration was renewed with increasing numbers coming from Japan. In 1869 some 20 Japanese arrived in San Francisco to explore the possibilities of growing tea and producing silk. Neither of these projects succeeded, but by the 1880s the Japanese were being actively recruited to work at the lower-paying jobs in the West. In 1891 a total of 1,136 were admitted; in 1900 the number reached 12,635, and in 1907 it grew to more than 30,000.

By that time the Japanese were suffering from the same discrimination as the Chinese had experienced 20 years before. Resented for taking jobs at lower wages than Americans would accept and feared for their mysterious and alien culture, they were ineligible for citizenship and denied most professional opportunities. In 1906 the school board of San Francisco segregated all Asian schoolchildren. President Theodore Roosevelt canceled that order the next year, but entered into what was delicately called a Gentlemen's Agreement with the Japanese government, guaranteeing that Tokyo would not issue any further passports to Japanese laborers attempting to come to the United States. In March 1906 Congress passed a formal act excluding the Japanese, as it had done to the Chinese in 1882. Other federal and state legislation made the lives of the Japanese already resident in America increasingly difficult.

Chinese immigrants arrive in San Francisco in an engraving from the 1830s. *(American Museum of Immigration, U.S. National Park Service)*

The island nation of Japan is smaller than the state of California, and much of its land is too rocky for agriculture. As the population increased during the last part of the 19th and the beginning of the 20th century, the pressure to emigrate grew. Australia, Brazil, and Canada received many Japanese immigrants, but none of those countries welcomed the new arrivals or provided them with much economic opportunity. America profited from their contribution to the workforce but was not much more hospitable. Nevertheless, the economic advantages of life in the United States were a powerful magnet to the Japanese. In 1890 the census reported a Japanese population in America of only 2,637, but between 1890 and 1900, more than 27,000 arrived. From 1901 to 1910, the country received some 58,000 more. The 1910 census reported a total of 72,157 Japanese in the United States. As other sources of cheap labor dried up, Japanese workers were able to find employment in the mines, canneries, farms, and lumber camps of the Pacific Coast, Washington, and Oregon. Others worked as domestic servants. Many who came as contract laborers to work in the sugar plantations of Hawaii moved on to the American mainland.

The Japanese government wanted those who immigrated to America to represent their native country honorably and contribute to good Japanese-American relations. A series of pamphlets was published in Tokyo during the first decade of the 20th century for those intending to go the United States. They urged that only honest and solid citizens should take that step. Emigrants were warned against acting like those provincial workers who "picked their teeth, picked their noses, scratched their heads, and undressed in public." Above all, the publications called on Japanese emigrants to behave as much as possible like Americans and adapt to American society. "We must seek to avoid clashes with customs," the *Guide to Success for Japanese in America* noted in 1908. "By striving to assimilate with white people relationships can be moderated. If our compatriots desire individual success, they must forget that they are Japanese."

Korea was known as the "hermit kingdom" until 1882 because it did not allow its citizens to travel. This isolation ended in that year when Korea declared itself independent of Japan and was officially recognized by the United States. The immigration statistics specified only China and Japan among Asian countries and included Korea under the general heading "Other Asia," so no records exist of its immigration numbers to the United States at the end of the 19th century. However, with the signing of a treaty of friendship and commerce between the two countries in 1882, America received 100 Korean students.

In 1903 the first group of Korean workers arrived at Hawaii. Japanese laborers there often protested the brutal conditions of their employment, and the Koreans, traditional enemies of the Japanese, were recruited to help break the frequent strikes among them. Unlike the Chinese and Japanese, Koreans considered themselves permanent immigrants and hoped to remain in the United States, even though their treatment was as harsh as that of other Asians. Most Americans could not distinguish Koreans from Japanese and treated them with the same cruelty the Japanese experienced.

Immigrants arrive with their luggage in Los Angeles in 1910. *(American Museum of Immigration, U.S. National Park Service)*

From 1570 until the end of the 19th century, the Philippine Islands were a colony of Spain. With the Spanish-American War of 1898, the Philippines gained their independence from Spain but were seized by the United States, which occupied the country for most of the next half-century. The first Filipinos to settle in America were seamen who deserted their ships in southern Louisiana in the 1830s. They founded a small colony, nostalgically named Manila Village, near New Orleans, in the 1890s. There they devoted themselves to fishing and fur trapping. The majority of Filipino immigrants to the United States, however, came as a result of the American conquest and occupation of their home islands. Since the Philippines were officially an American territory, Filipinos were freely admitted to the United States, but no exact records of their entry exist because, like the Koreans, their country was listed in the immigration files only under the heading "Other Asia."

In 1900 the United States formally annexed Hawaii, which had long been under American control, and beginning in 1906 the demand for cheap agricultural labor drew many Filipino laborers there. Travel between the two American territories was unrestricted, and by 1941, when the Second World War brought an end to all free movement in the Pacific, more than a quarter of a million Filipinos had taken the journey to Hawaii to make their homes. The second largest Asian-American population after the Chinese, the Filipino-American community settled mainly on the Pacific Rim, more than half of them in California. Hawaii and Chicago became the next largest centers of Filipino residence in the United States.

North Americans: The Canadians and the Mexicans

Not all of the "new immigration" came from distant places and necessitated long ocean voyages. The two countries with which the United States shares a border, Canada and Mexico, accounted for some of the new arrivals during the last decades of the 19th century. Canada, like its neighbor to the south, was a nation of immigrants from its inception. In the 40 years from 1850 to 1890, more than 1.5 million immigrants, from the same countries that provided the United States with new blood, arrived in Canada. However, many of those who entered the United States during that time came from Canada and thus might be counted as immigrants from that country. Since no records were kept of those entering the United States by land before 1908, there are no statistics on the arrivals from Mexico or Canada until then. We know, however, that many Canadians emigrated south and that many Europeans used Canada as a stopping-off place on their way to the United States.

A small but steady stream of Canadians had come to the United States for both economic and political reasons since the middle of the 19th century. Failed rebellions in 1837 and 1838, modeled on the American Revolution, impelled some to come as fugitives. American competition in the grain market, bad weather, bad harvests, and bad relations between the French and the English sent others across the border during the following decades. The promise of good jobs and free land drew people from what was then called British North America as it did people from Europe. The American Civil War attracted some Canadians who were opposed to British rule and wanted the chance to fight. According to American military records, more than 50,000 Canadian-born men served in the Union army. In 1865, the year the war ended, a record number of Canadians, totaling 21,586, left their country to make their homes in the United States. Between 1880 and 1882, Canadian immigration to the United States reached its peak, with 325,560 crossing their country's southern border. An estimated 825,150 native-born Canadians relocated permanently in America between 1899 and 1924.

Immigration from Mexico during the 19th century was like no other because most of those who became Americans did not enter the country but were absorbed by it. After the U.S.-Mexican War, the United States redrew the borders between the two countries and took over the northern half of Mexico. By the treaty of Guadalupe Hidalgo in 1848, the United States incorporated into its own territory what was to become the states of California, Nevada, Utah, New Mexico, Colorado, Wyoming, and parts of Arizona. The Mexicans living in those regions were given the choice of accepting a new nationality or returning to what was left of their former country to the south. Almost 80 percent chose to remain where they were and thus became citizens of the United States.

By 1886 there were approximately 80,000 formerly Mexican residents in the United States. They were for the most part agricultural workers and represented the poorest segment of a population by then predominantly Anglo. About 1 million more moved northward in search of work after 1900. According to the American census of 1930, the legal Mexican population of the United States was about 3 million, and many more entered illegally across the long and poorly guarded border to take unofficial jobs on the farms and in the cities of the Southwest. With the exclusion of Asian laborers, the influx was welcomed as a source of cheap labor and was treated accordingly. The Mexican newcomers, immigrating to an area that 50 years

Immigrant women from Guadeloupe, West Indies, pose for this photograph from April 6, 1911. *(American Museum of Immigration, U.S. National Park Service)*

before had been their own national land, were given as little opportunity, and shown as little respect, as their Chinese, Japanese, and Korean predecessors.

The causes of Mexican immigration were much the same as those of immigration from Europe and Asia. The country's population increased at an unprecedented rate from the 1880s to the 1900s, swelling from 9.4 million in 1877 to more than 15 million in 1910. During that time, a conservative government reversed many of the land reforms of the middle of the century and enabled foreign investors and a small Mexican propertied class to accumulate great fortunes. The country's economy blossomed, but its wealth benefited fewer and fewer people. The native tribes were dispossessed of their land and the Catholic Church was forced to sell its property. When the regime of Porfirio Díaz was overthrown in 1911, most of the industry, the mineral wealth, and the real estate belonged to just 900 families, while 9 million landless peasants worked in virtual slavery for them.

Thus by 1900 Mexico was overpopulated with displaced Indians and unemployed Mexicans all desperate for a better life. Railroad lines connecting the two countries had proliferated between 1880 and 1910, and there was a seemingly endless need for seasonal labor on the farms of the American Southwest. Contract labor supplied much of the workforce. In 1885 Congress passed the Foran Act, a law prohibiting the importation of contract labor, but neither the Mexican authorities nor the American employers obeyed it very rigorously, and it proved almost impossible to enforce.

Because Mexican laborers had no legal status in the United States, they were as cruelly exploited in America as they were in Mexico, but they continued to arrive in great numbers, both legally and illegally. No records were kept of the entry of Mexicans before 1908, and undocumented crossings of the border were common both before and after that date, so it is impossible to calculate precisely how many entered the United States during that period. The best estimate, however, is that more than 280,000 Mexican men, women, and children entered the United States between 1899 and 1914. By 1910 more than 12 percent of the population of the American Southwest was of Mexican birth.

Nativism Returns

Nativism, the preference for native inhabitants of a country over immigrants, has never been entirely absent from American society. In colonial America such patriots as Benjamin Franklin expressed a fear that Germans would dominate Pennsylvania, and the French were suspected of subversive ideas. The first major wave of nativism, which reached a peak from the 1830s to the 1850s, targeted Irish Catholics and expressed a fear that the pope intended to take over the American government. A second phase, prompted by competition for jobs, focused on Asians in the 1870s and produced Denis Kearney and the cry, "The Chinese must go!" Both of these outbreaks of fear and anger were directed at specific groups arriving in unprecedented numbers, and both diminished when the numbers of those groups fell off. From the middle 1880s to the 1920s, a third period of nativism flourished, and this time it was against all foreigners. The general antialien feeling of "native" Americans—many of whom were themselves either immigrants or the children of immigrants—became a mania as new and unfamiliar groups began to flood America's shores.

Like the Chinese before them, the new arrivals were resented by the trade unions for their impact on the job market. Unions felt that foreign-born workers willing to

The American policy of admitting paupers from Ireland was controversial for many years after the potato famine had ended, as reflected in this 1883 cartoon entitled "The Balance of Trade with Great Britain Seems to Be Still Against Us." *(Library of Congress, Prints and Photographs Division [LC-USZ62-118126])*

work for lower wages than Americans threatened the American worker's standard of living. Unsettled industrial conditions and a growing supply of labor in the 1880s created a social climate that bred anti-immigrant sentiment. Unions worked to protect the workman from the danger of foreign competition. The American Federation of Labor (AFL), founded by the London-born labor leader Samuel Gompers in 1886, announced that the principle of a protective tariff on low-priced imported merchandise should apply to laborers as well. "We keep out pauper-made goods," an AFL advertisement read in the 1890s, "why not keep out the pauper?"

Objections to the new immigration were not based only on economic grounds. There were religious and political fears as well. The old mistrust of the Catholics resurfaced as thousands of members of that church poured in from Italy. A "Committee of One Hundred" in Boston published anti-Catholic pamphlets in the early 1880s, and many newspapers sprang up accusing the Church of sinister plots against America.

In 1887 these fears were crystallized in the American Protective Association, an organization dedicated to the suppression of Catholic influence in America. Inspired by the pre–Civil War Know-Nothing Party, it demanded of its members that they neither vote for nor employ Catholics and urged legislation to restrict their immigration. Although the group claimed 500,000 members by 1893, it was not much more influential than the Know-Nothing Party had been. Like its predecessor, it was torn with internal dissension—some members wanted to establish a third political party, others supported the presidential candidacy of McKinley in 1896—and its irresponsible charges against the Catholic Church had too little substance to be believed. But also like the Know-Nothing Party, it was a symptom of the unfocused alarm that the flood of new arrivals was causing among Americans.

Economic, cultural, and religious objections to unlimited immigration were a familiar element of American thought, but new fears were beginning to make themselves felt at the end of the century. One concern was that immigrants endangered the political stability of the country because of their radicalism. Anarchism, a political philosophy that calls for the abolition of government, was associated

Thomas Nast illustrated America's horror of international communism as early as 1874 in this drawing published in *Harper's Weekly. (New York Public Library Print Collection)*

Police attack rioters in Haymarket Square, Chicago, in "The Anarchist Troubles," published in *Frank Leslie's Illustrated Newspaper* in 1886. *(Library of Congress, Prints and Photographs Division [LC-USZ62-75192])*

with German and Russian immigrants active in the labor movement, and the image was reinforced by the repeated involvement of immigrants with labor unrest. A small body of German anarchists in Chicago actually published newspapers calling for armed insurrection by the working class and instructing their readers on the construction of bombs for the purpose.

It was in Chicago that the most dramatic event in the history of immigrant radicalism, and of nativist reaction to it, occurred. On May 4, 1886, during a series of strikes for an eight-hour working day, Chicago's anarchist group organized a protest meeting at Haymarket Square to demonstrate against police intervention. The demonstration was peaceful, but the Chicago police were called in to disperse it, and they advanced threateningly on the demonstrators. Suddenly a bomb exploded, killing one of the policemen. At once the police began firing into the crowd, and in the riot that followed, 17 people were killed. The bomb-thrower was never identified, but the police, the newspapers, and the general public were eager to lay the blame on the anarchist group that had called for the meeting. The police arrested all of the members of the group they could locate, and the courts summarily sentenced seven of them to death. One of the condemned men was an American; the other six were immigrants, five of them German.

The national press seized on the Haymarket Affair as a proof that foreign immigrants were dangerous. One Chicago paper described them as "long-haired, wild-eyed, bad-smelling, atheistic, reckless foreign wretches, who never did an honest day's work in their lives" and called on the country to "crush such snakes . . . before they have time to bite." Another paper observed, "These people are not Americans, but the very scum and offal of Europe." The image of the immigrant as a lawless, violent social outcast was to become fixed in the American mind, and was greatly to influence immigration policy in the coming years.

The Italians inspired a different fear among Americans. If the Germans and the Russians brought to mind wild-eyed revolutionaries, the Italians were associated with organized crime, secret societies, and merciless vendettas. "The disposition to assassinate in revenge for a fancied wrong," the Baltimore News wrote, "is a marked trait of this impulsive and inexorable race." Any unsolved murder was blamed on Italians, whose reputation for violence was widely believed. In 1891 the superintendent of police of New Orleans was murdered. As he had been investigating a group of Sicilian immigrants whom he suspected of a crime, many Sicilians were arrested, more or less at random, and hastily brought to trial for murder. The mayor of the city publicly announced, "We must teach these people a lesson they will not forget for all time," but, as there was no evidence of their guilt, the jury acquitted them. A mob was so enraged at what they were sure was a failure of justice that they broke into the jailhouse and lynched eleven of the suspects. The police did nothing to interfere.

The event caused a national uproar, not against the mob but against the Italian community. When the government in Rome protested and demanded that the lynch mob be brought to justice, the American government ignored the complaint. Italy then recalled its ambassador, which made matters worse. Already objects of suspicion and contempt, Italian Americans were accused of being unpatriotic and planning to start a war.

The Jewish population had experienced hostility and suspicion in America since Peter Stuyvesant tried to bar them from New Amsterdam in the 17th century, but the new wave of eastern European Jews experienced more trouble than the German Jews that had preceded them. The first wave had come in smaller numbers and had dispersed, many of them finding work or starting businesses in small towns. The Russian and Polish Jews of the second wave, flooding in by the thousands, clung together in the big cities as they had lived in small Jewish settlements in eastern Europe. The German Jews, relatively assimilated in their German homeland, found it easy to assimilate in America and were often thought of as Germans rather than as Jews. But though the wealthy were accepted socially, some degree of anti-Semitism persisted.

This was dramatically demonstrated when Joseph Seligman, the head of America's largest banking group, was refused a room at the fashionable Grand Union Hotel in Saratoga, New York, in 1877. The bitterness the event caused resulted in a boycott of the hotel and of the store owned by A. T. Stewart, its owner, and led ultimately to the sale of the hotel. As the first widely publicized example of anti-Semitism among the wealthy and powerful, the incident highlighted an almost unconscious rejection of Jews in America, and many bars, social clubs, college fraternities, and hotels followed the Grand Union's example and closed their doors to Jews. The hostility revealed by the Seligman incident became what one historian has called "an epidemic that rapidly and calamitously infected much of the country."

When the Jews of the new immigration joined their coreligionists in America in the 1880s, the division between Jew and Gentile in America became wider. The earlier immigrants, themselves suffering discrimination, tended to reject the eastern Europeans, more culturally different from them than the Americans were. "Native" Americans, suspicious of and hostile to the older Jews, were even more so to the exotic and clannish newcomers. As the new wave of Jews settled into New York,

"Where the Blame Lies," a cartoon in *Judge* (1891), places the blame for "anarchy, socialism, the Mafia, and such kindred evils" on the liberal immigration policy of the time. *(Library of Congress, Prints and Photographs Division [LC-USZ62-75192])*

they made it the largest Jewish city in history and developed a distinct identity that their German predecessors had never had. Their shop signs in the Hebrew script of Yiddish, their strange clothes and long beards, and their rigid and archaic religious observances, set them apart and intensified the suspicion and dislike that the German Jews had begun to overcome.

The fear that immigrants inspired was clear enough, but under it lay something more subtle—a deep-rooted racism that dreaded the pollution of the American people more than it feared economic, spiritual, or political danger. The threat of unemployment, plots involving the pope, and imported anarchy was nothing to the fear of what one social scientist of the time called "racial suicide," the dilution of the "pure" American stock by intermarriage with inferior peoples. Good Americans feared that these wild, uncivilized foreigners might not only take their jobs, challenge their religion, and disrupt their society, but marry into their families. The popular writer Thomas Bailey Aldrich published a widely quoted poem in the *Atlantic Monthly* in 1882, the year of the highest number of both German and Chinese immigrants to the United States. It voiced the concern shared by many Americans that the country's open door policy was letting in too many of the wrong kind of people. Called "The Unguarded Gates," it warns:

Wide open and unguarded stand our gates,
And through them presses a wild motley throng—
Men from the Volga and the Tartar steppes, . . .

These bringing with them unknown gods and rites,
Those, tiger passions loud, here to stretch their claws.
In street and alley, what strange tongues are loud,
Accents of menace alien to our air. . . .

The attitude reflected in Aldrich's poem was to spread during the next decades and to spread through all classes. Respected and influential people were to lend it their support, and eventually it was to bring about profound changes in the pattern of american immigration. The generous welcome that George Washington expressed in 1783 when he stated, "The bosom of America is open to receive not only the Opulent and Respectable Stranger, but the oppressed and persecuted of all Nations and Religions" was giving way to a new spirit, not only in popular sentiment but in federal law.

Chronicle of Events

1881

- Beginning of the peak decade for German and Scandinavian immigration. German arrivals total 1,452,970 between 1881 and 1890, and Scandinavian immigration reaches 656,494.
- The assassination of Czar Alexander II initiates widespread anti-Semitism in Russia. A wave of Jewish immigration begins.
- *September 19*: President Garfield dies of an assassin's bullet fired on July 2.
- *September 20*: Vice President Chester A. Arthur takes office as the 21st president of the United States.

1882

- German immigration reaches 250,630, its highest number in a single year to date.
- German-language newspapers and magazines published in the United States number about 550.
- Chinese immigration totals nearly 40,000, its all-time highest number. Since 1868 more than 2 million Chinese have entered the United States.
- *May 6*: Over President Arthur's veto, Congress passes the first restrictive federal immigration law in American history, the Chinese Exclusion Act, prohibiting the immigration of all Chinese laborers for a period of 10 years.
- *May 22*: The United States recognizes the independence of Korea. The two countries sign a treaty of friendship and commerce. Approximately 100 Korean students enter the United States.
- *August 3*: Congress passes an act prohibiting the entry of "undesirables," including paupers, criminals, and the insane, and fixes a head tax of 50 cents on all immigrants. This tax is increased to $2 in 1903 and to $4 in 1907.

"Expulsion of the Jews from St. Petersburg: Scene at the Baltic Railway Station," an engraving made June 1891. Russia began deporting Jews in the 1880s. *(American Museum of Immigration, U.S. National Park Service)*

The New Colossus.

Not like the brazen giant of Greek fame,
With conquering limbs astride from land to land
Here at our sea-washed, sunset-gates shall stand
A mighty woman with a torch, whose flame
Is the imprisoned lightning, and her name
Mother of Exiles. From her beacon-hand
Glows world-wide welcome, her mild eyes command
The air-bridged harbor that twin-cities frame.

"Keep, ancient lands, your storied pomp!" cries she
With silent lips. "Give me your tired, your poor,
Your huddled masses yearning to breathe free,
The wretched refuse of your teeming shore,
Send these, the homeless, tempest-tost to me,
I lift my lamp beside the golden door!"

Emma Lazarus.

November 2nd 1883.

Poet Emma Lazarus worked and wrote to support her fellow Jews persecuted in Russia during the 1880s. Her eloquent sonnet, shown here in her own handwriting, was engraved on a plaque placed on the base of the Statue of Liberty in 1885. *(New York Public Library Print Collection)*

1883
- Northern Pacific Railway completes a line from Lake Superior to Portland, Oregon.
- The Brooklyn Bridge, designed by German immigrant Augustus John Roebling, opens. It is the largest suspension bridge in the world.

1884
- The Supreme Court decides against the Ku Klux Klan, determining that interference with a citizen's right to vote in a federal election is a federal offense.
- *November 4*: Grover Cleveland, governor of New York, is elected the 22nd president of the United States.

1885
- *February 26*: Congress passes the Alien Contract Labor Law, an act prohibiting the immigration of laborers under contract to work for the cost of their passage. Skilled, professional, and domestic workers are excepted.

1886
- First American settlement house opens in New York City.
- *May 4*: A bomb explodes in Haymarket Square in Chicago during a union protest. The seventeen deaths in the resulting riot lead to numerous arrests and general anger at organized labor and the German "anarchists" believed guilty of the crime. Seven are sentenced to death and four hanged in November 1887. The remaining three are pardoned by the governor of Illinois in 1893.
- *October 28*: President Cleveland dedicates the Statue of Liberty, erected on Bedloe's (now Liberty) Island in New York Harbor.
- *December 8*: The American Federation of Labor is founded in Columbus, Ohio, incorporating 25 trade unions. Samuel Gompers is elected president.

1887
- The American Protective Association, an anti-Catholic organization, is founded by Henry F. Bowers. It is the first major successor of the Know-Nothing Party and a predecessor of the revived Ku Klux Klan of the 1920s.

1888
- *November 6*: Benjamin Harrison is elected the 23rd president of the United States.

1889

- *April 22*: The United States declares the Oklahoma Indian Territory open to white settlement. Within 24 hours more than 2 million acres are claimed.

1890

- The 11th U.S. census shows 62,947,714, including 5,246,613 immigrants added since 1880. More than 72 percent of the immigrants arriving since the last census have come from northern and western Europe. The settled area of the country is so widely distributed that the census reports that the frontier no longer exists.
- Danish immigrant Jacob Riis publishes *How the Other Half Lives,* an exposé of the conditions of the urban poor revealing that one percent of the population in America owns more than the total of the remaining 99 percent. The account of immigrant life in the slums inspires widespread economic reforms.
- Large-scale immigration from eastern and southern Europe (known as the "New Immigration") begins.

1891

- *March 3*: Congress passes a law banning the immigration of "all idiots, insane persons, paupers or persons likely to become a public charge, persons suffering from a contagious or loathsome disease, persons who have been convicted of a felony or other infamous crime or misdemeanor involving moral turpitude, and polygamists." The Immigration Act also establishes the Bureau of Immigration, forerunner of the Immigration and Naturalization Service (INS), within the Department of the Treasury, to inspect arrivals at all 24 ports of entry to the United States.
- *March 14*: A mob storms a New Orleans jail and lynches 11 Sicilian immigrants. Seven of the victims had just been acquitted of the murder of the New Orleans police chief investigating Italian secret societies suspected of engaging in organized crime.

1892

- *May 5*: The Geary Law extends the 1882 Chinese Exclusion Act for another 10 years and requires all Chinese to register.
- *July 6*: Strikers at the Carnegie steel mill in Homestead, Pennsylvania, protesting wage cuts and demanding recognition of their unions, fire on Pinkerton detectives hired by management to break the strike.

- *July 9*: The governor of Pennsylvania sends state troops to restore order. The strike is broken on November 20, and the steel union is stripped of its power.
- *October 15*: President Harrison opens 1,800,000 acres in the Crow Indian reservation to white settlement.
- *November 8*: Grover Cleveland is elected the 24th president of the United States.

1893

- The United States and Canada agree to prevent illegal immigration across their border.
- *January 17*: The United States envoy to the kingdom of Hawaii lands marines, without the authorization of the federal government, to protect the lives and property of American planters there. They set up a provisional government declaring Hawaii a U.S. protectorate and seeking annexation.
- *September 16*: A 6 million-acre tract in the Cherokee Strip of Oklahoma Territory is opened to white settlement.

1894

- The Immigrant Restriction League is founded by a group of Harvard graduates under Massachusetts senator Henry Cabot Lodge. Its avowed purpose is to support a law requiring a literacy test for immigrants.
- *January 17*: The United States and China sign a treaty excluding Chinese laborers from entry into America.
- *May 11–August 6*: Employees of the Pullman Palace Car Company in Chicago strike. The American Railway Company declares a boycott and many union workers walk out. President Cleveland sends federal troops, and union president Eugene V. Debs is arrested for criminal conspiracy. The power of the union is broken and the troops are withdrawn on August 6.
- *July 4*: Hawaii is proclaimed an independent republic under an American president. The United States recognizes it on August 7.

1896

- *March 2*: The Immigration Restriction League influences Congress to pass an act requiring a literacy test for immigrants. President Cleveland vetoes the bill.
- *November 3*: William McKinley is elected the 25th president of the United States.

1897

- The *Jewish Daily Forward,* a Yiddish-language newspaper, is founded in New York City. It becomes the largest

The Spanish-American War opened America to immigration from the Philippine Islands, which were seized by the United States after the conflict. The official reason for the war was the liberation of Cuba, as shown in this C. B. Bush cartoon published in the *New York World* in April 1898. In the background is the U.S. battleship *Maine*, whose unexplained sinking in February triggered the war. *(New York Public Library Print Collection)*

foreign-language newspaper in the country before World War I.

1898
- The U.S. Supreme Court decides that children born of Chinese parents in the United States are American citizens and may not be deported under the Chinese Exclusion Act.

- *February 15*: The U.S. battleship *Maine* explodes in Havana Harbor, bringing about the death of 260 of its crew.
- *April 19*: Congress adopts a resolution declaring that Cuba should be free of Spanish rule and authorizes the president to use whatever force is necessary to enable Cuba to achieve sovereignty. A blockade of Cuban ports is declared on April 22 and war is declared against Spain on April 25.

- *May 1*: The U.S. Navy destroys or disables all ships in the Spanish Pacific fleet at Manila. Three hundred Spanish are killed and seven Americans are wounded in the battle.
- *May 29*: An American fleet blocks the entrance of Santiago Harbor in Cuba, restricting movement of the Spanish Atlantic fleet.
- *June 20*: American troops capture the Spanish-held island of Guam.
- *July 7*: The United States annexes Hawaii, over the protest of the Japanese. It becomes a U.S. territory in 1900.
- *July 17*: Cuban troops surrender to the United States.
- *July 25*: U.S. troops invade Porto Rico (spelled Puerto Rico from 1932).
- *August 13*: Spanish troops in Manila, the Philippine capital, surrender to U.S. forces.
- *December 10*: The Treaty of Paris, formally bringing the Spanish-American War to an end, is signed. By its terms Spain surrenders all claims to Cuba and cedes Porto Rico, the Philippine Islands (for a payment of $20 million), and Guam to the United States. Filipinos are declared "wards" of the United States and allowed to enter without visas. Filipino wives of Spanish-American War veterans are admitted as war brides.

1899

- *February 17*: The Anti-Imperialist League is founded to oppose American expansion, including U.S. occupation of the Philippines.
- *September 6*: The United States proposes the Open Door Policy for China, calling for maintaining free trade relations between that country and the United States, Britain, Germany, Japan, and other major world powers.

1900

- The 12th national census discloses a population of 76,212,168, reflecting an increase during the previous decade of more than 20 percent. Immigration since 1890 totals 3,688,000, a reduction of some 1.5 million from the previous decade. Railroad lines have increased from 37,000 miles to 193,000 miles since the Civil War. Literacy of people more than 10 years old, estimated at about 80 percent in 1870, has increased to almost 90 percent. In the same 30 years, 430 million acres of land have been occupied, more than all the territory settled between 1607 and 1870.

- *April 7*: Congress creates a civil government for Porto Rico, establishing the island's status as an American territory without all the rights of American citizenship.
- *May 14*: Hawaii becomes a U.S. territory. Sanford Dole, its American president, is appointed its first governor. All U.S. laws go into effect in Hawaii, bringing contract labor to an end.
- *June*: The Boxer Rebellion, protesting foreign intrusion in China, breaks out in Peking. It lasts until August 14, when an international expeditionary force occupies the Chinese capital and defeats the rebels.
- *August*: The United States and Japan enter into the first Gentlemen's Agreement, in which Japan agrees to limit emigration by refusing to issue passports to laborers.
- *November 6*: President McKinley is reelected with New York governor Theodore Roosevelt as his vice president.

1901

- Beginning of the decade with the highest number of immigrants to the United States. Between 1901 and 1910, the total is 8,795,386.
- *February 25*: Ten companies, including railroads and coal and iron mines, merge to form the United States Steel Corporation, the largest industrial organization in the world.
- *September 6*: A Polish-American anarchist shoots President McKinley.
- *September 7*: The Chinese sign a treaty agreeing to pay $333 million for deaths and losses caused by the Boxer Rebellion. The United States forgives its $24.5-million share in 1908 by granting its equivalent in scholarships for Chinese students in America.
- *September 14*: President McKinley dies. Vice President Theodore Roosevelt is sworn in as the 26th president of the United States.

1902

- Congress extends the Chinese Exclusion Act for another 10 years.
- *July 1*: The Philippine Islands are officially made an American territory by the Philippine Government Act. U.S. solicitor-general William Howard Taft is made governor.

1903

- Ninety-three Korean contract laborers enter Hawaii to work in the American-owned sugar plantations. In the

next two years, approximately 7,000 Koreans immigrate to Hawaii.
- Congress passes an act permitting Filipinos to come to the United States to study.
- *March 3*: Congress passes an act authorizing inspection of emigrants bound for the United States at all European ports of departure and prohibiting the admission of the "insane," "beggars," anarchists, and prostitutes.

1904
- Chinese exclusion is made indefinite and the law is extended to all overseas possessions.
- *November 8*: Theodore Roosevelt is elected president.

1905
- For the first time, more than 1 million immigrants enter the United States in one year.
- Japan establishes a protectorate over Korea and prohibits emigration.
- The Industrial Workers of the World (IWW) is organized. It is strongly supportive of immigrant workers.
- *May 7*: The Japanese and Korean Exclusion League (also called the Asiatic Exclusion League) is organized in San Francisco.

1906
- The National Liberal Immigration League is founded to oppose the passage of a law requiring a literacy test for immigrants.
- *October 11*: The San Francisco school board segregates Chinese, Japanese, and Korean children into a separate school.

1907
- A congressional bill adds the tubercular, the "feeble-minded," and those with mental or physical defects affecting their ability to earn a living to the list of those barred from entry to the United States.
- *March 13*: A sharp drop of the stock market initiates a financial panic. Many banks fail and unemployment is widespread.
- The San Francisco school board cancels the order segregating Asiatic students, at the request of President Roosevelt.
- *March 14*: Congress authorizes the exclusion of Japanese laborers from the United States.

1908
- Israel Zangwill's play *The Melting Pot* opens in New York, popularizing the image of America as a melting pot in which all races are fused.
- *November 3*: William Howard Taft is elected the 27th president of the United States.

1910
- The United States's 13th census reports a population of 92,228,496, of whom about 8,795,000 are immigrants who have entered the country since 1900. This represents an increase of more than 5 million since the decade from 1900 to 1910. In contrast with the immigration of that decade, about 71 percent of the arrivals to the United States between 1900 and 1910 have come from countries in southern or eastern Europe, predominantly Italians, Slavs, and Jews.
- Japan annexes Korea.
- A revolution in Mexico initiates a large wave of immigration to the United States.

1911
- The Dillingham Commission reports that the "new" immigration since the beginning of the century was dominated by "less desirable" groups that were less able to assimilate. It argues that the United States no longer benefits from a liberal immigration policy and recommends restrictive legislation.
- *May 15*: The Supreme Court orders the Standard Oil Company dissolved as being in violation of the Sherman Antitrust Act. On May 29 it applies the same law in a finding against the American Tobacco Company.

1912
- Italian, French-Canadian, and Irish workers in the textile mills of Lawrence, Massachusetts, unite to strike under the leadership of the IWW.
- Alaska becomes a U.S. territory.
- *November 5*: New Jersey governor [Thomas] Woodrow Wilson is elected the 28th president of the United States.

1913
- *February 14*: President Taft vetoes a bill imposing a literacy test on immigrants.

1914
- Mass immigration to the United States from Europe is halted by the outbreak of World War I.

- *July 28*: Austria-Hungary declares war on Serbia.
- *August 1*: Germany declares war on Russia. On August 3 it declares war on France.
- *August 4*: Great Britain declares war on Germany. President Wilson calls for American neutrality.
- *August 15*: The Panama Canal officially opens.

1915

- *May 7*: The Germans sink the British steamer Lusitania off Ireland, killing almost 1,200 people including 100 Americans.
- *December 4*: Georgia grants a new charter to a revived Ku Klux Klan.

1916

- Fiorello La Guardia is elected to Congress from New York City. He is the first Italian American to hold a major office in national politics in America.
- Madison Grant's influential anti-immigration book *The Passing of the Great Race* is published.
- *May 24*: A German submarine torpedoes the French ship *Sussex* in the English Channel, injuring two Americans. President Wilson threatens to break diplomatic relations with Germany.
- *July 30*: German saboteurs blow up a munitions dump in New Jersey. On January 11, 1917, a similar explosion destroys a foundry in the same state. A commission proves German responsibility for the two acts of sabotage and awards America $55 million in damages, but Germany does not pay.
- *August 4*: Denmark and the United States sign a treaty for the American purchase of the Virgin Islands (Danish West Indies) for $25 million. Residents become U.S. citizens in 1927.

1917

- *January 16*: Plans by the German government to make an alliance with Mexico if the United States enters the war are revealed. Germany promises to help Mexico regain territory comprising Texas, Arizona, and New Mexico.
- *January 29*: A bill requiring immigrants over the age of 16 years to prove ability to read "not less than 30 nor more than 80 words in ordinary use" in any language passes over President Wilson's veto. The act also designates Asia a "barred zone" and orders the deportation of any immigrant who preaches revolution or sabotage.
- *February 3*: A German submarine sinks the U.S. ship *Housatonic*. President Wilson breaks off diplomatic relations with Germany.
- *March 2*: Porto Rico is formally made a U.S. territory and its residents become American citizens.
- *March 5*: President Wilson is inaugurated for a second term as president of the United States.
- *March 15*: A revolution in Russia forces Czar Nicolas II to abdicate. In November a communist government is established, and in December Russia signs an armistice with Germany.
- *April 2*: President Wilson asks Congress for a declaration of war against Germany because "the world must be made safe for democracy." The declaration is signed April 6.
- *May 9*: Congress passes an act extending the right of naturalization to anyone who has enlisted and served in the U.S. armed forces, regardless of race.
- *May 18*: The Selective Service Act is passed calling for a draft of all able-bodied men aged 18 to 45.
- *June 15*: Congress passes the Epionage Act, calling for severe punishment for any action that aids the enemy.

1918

- *May 16*: The Sedition Act is passed to extend the Espionage Act of 1917. It provides strong penalties for any criticism of the war effort and is used to silence socialists and pacifists. Under its provisions, Socialist Party leader Eugene V. Debs is sentenced to 10 years in prison.
- *October 3*: The chancellor of Germany calls for an armistice in a note to President Wilson. On October 30 the chancellor of Austria also asks for peace.
- *October 16*: Congress passes a bill excluding alien anarchists and others advocating the overthrow of the government from entering the United States.
- *November 9*: Kaiser Wilhelm of Germany abdicates, the chancellor resigns, and Germany becomes a republic.
- *November 11*: World War I ends with the signing of an armistice at Compiègne, France. Emigration from Europe, which had fallen from 1,218,480 in 1914 to an average of about 250,000 during the war years, resumes.

Eyewitness Testimony

My father gave me $100, and I went to Hong Kong with five other boys and we got steerage passage on a steamer, paying $50 each. All my life I had been used to sleeping on a board bed with a wooden pillow, and I found the steamer's bunk very uncomfortable, because it was so soft. The food was different from that which I had been used to, and I did not like it at all. I was afraid of the stews, for the thought of what they might be made of by the wicked wizards of the ship made me ill. Of the great power of these people I saw many signs. The engines that moved the ship were wonderful monsters, strong enough to lift mountains. When I got to San Francisco . . . I was half starved, because I was afraid to eat the provisions of the barbarians. . . .

The rat which is eaten by the Chinese is a field animal which lives on rice, grain and sugar cane. Its flesh is delicious. Many Americans who have tasted shark's fin and bird's nest soup . . . are firm friends of Chinese cookery. If they could enjoy one of our fine rats they would go to China to live, so as to get some more.

American people eat ground hogs, which are very like these Chinese rats, and they also eat many sorts of food that our people would not touch. Those who have dined with us know that we understand how to live well.

. . . There is no reason for the prejudice against the Chinese. . . . It was the jealousy of laboring men of other nationalities—especially the Irish—that raised all the outcry against the Chinese. No one would hire an Irishman, German, Englishman or Italian when he could get a Chinese, because our countrymen are so much more honest, industrious, steady, sober and painstaking. Chinese were persecuted, not for their vices but for their virtues.

Lee Chew, Chinese immigrant recalling his early days in San Francisco during the 1880s in "Biography of a Chinaman: Lee Chew" in the Independent, *Volume LV, (February 19, 1903), pp. 417–423.*

We eat here every day what we got only for Easter in our country.

Polish immigrant, 1880s, in Bailey, Voices of America *(1976), p. 123.*

The school teacher said, why in the world anybody would want to go to America. . . . You know, we have all these resources in Sweden. We have iron. We have coal. We have forests. We have land. And he gave quite a dissertation on this. I went home and told my father. And I always

remember this. It's the only time I heard him swear. And he said, "You go back and tell that teacher if I can have one of those resources, I'll stay in Sweden."

Edward Myrbeck, Swedish immigrant, 1880s, in the Ellis Island Oral History Collection, in Yans-McLaughlin and Lightman, Ellis Island and the Peopling of America *(1997), p. 22.*

The emigrants this year are, without exception, of the best agricultural and industrial classes, taking money with them, the savings of years, the proceeds of their little tenements sold here, etc. My own inquiry and observation confirm the truth of the statement of the German journals, that Germany has never before lost such numbers of worthy and industrious people as are this year emigrating to the United States.

American consul at Bremen, Germany, in a report to the Department of Immigration in Washington, April 1, 1881, in Abbott, Immigration: Select Documents *(1924), p. 55.*

In Munster . . . people are living together in such crowded conditions. . . . They do not have as much and as fine fresh air as we have. I also see many people who are much poorer or who are doing rough work, and they are, of course, clothed much more poorly and wear wooden shoes and work much harder. Better society is just as it is with us, only they don't have anything to do with craftsmen and workmen, and those who have government positions are then really the masters, and they live with their ladies very comfortably.

Jette Bruns, German immigrant, in a letter written in 1882 during a visit to Germany, comparing it to her home in Missouri, in Hold Dear, As Always: Jette *(1988), p. 245.*

The emigrants who leave European countries nowadays belong mostly to the agricultural class. They come here and buy and settle our lands; they convert the wilderness into green pastures and productive fields, and thereby add so vastly to our national wealth. . . .

The countries of Europe look upon this emigration with jealous eyes. It is the marrow-bone that leaves them. It is not to be presumed that the law-making powers of these countries will exert themselves to any great extent in favor of these people. On the contrary, they look upon the privations which the emigrants have to undergo with a sort of grim satisfaction.

But we, the representatives of the American people, who receive the benefits of this immigration, a people which is ever ready to stand by those who need our help, always willing to correct all abuses of human beings, should not now hesitate to pass a law which is so urgently required. . . .

Congressman Richard William Guenther, from the debate in Congress of April 18, 1882, in support of "A Bill to Regulate the Carriage of Passengers by Sea," in Congressional Record, *47th Congress, 1st session, pp. 3013–3022.*

Not like the brazen giant of Greek fame,
With conquering limbs astride from land to land;
Here at our sea-washed sunset gate shall stand
A mighty woman with a torch, whose flame
Is the imprisoned lightning, and her name
Mother of Exiles. From her beacon-hand
Glows world-wide welcome; her mild eyes command
The air-bridged harbor that twin cities frame.
"Keep, ancient land, your stories pomp," cries she
With silent lips. "Give me your tired, your poor,
Your huddled masses yearning to breathe free,
The wretched refuse of your teeming shore.
Send these, the homeless, tempest-tost to me,
I lift my lamp beside the golden door!"

Emma Lazarus, "The New Colossus," 1883, sonnet carved on the base of the Statue of Liberty, 1886, in The Poems of Emma Lazarus *(1889), volume I, pp. 202–203.*

When I saw that beautiful pink glass lamp shade in a million pieces on the floor I fell over in a faint. I thought I would be put in jail! I thought I would be killed! Miss May and one other . . . they came running in to see what had happened. When they saw me there on the floor without my senses they woke me up and carried me into the kitchen and made me drink hot tea with sugar in it. "Rosa, Rosa," they said. "Where are you hurt? Where did it hit you?" And when they learned that I had only fainted from scare because I had broken the pink glass lamp they started to laugh. . . . How can I *not* love America! In the old country I would have been killed for breaking a lamp like that!

Rosa Cavalleri, Italian immigrant (1884), recalling her first job as a servant in Chicago, in Ets, Rosa: The Life of an Italian Immigrant *(1971), p. 221.*

Our population of foreign extraction is sadly conspicuous in our criminal records. This element constituted in 1870 twenty per cent of the population of New England, and furnished seventy-five per cent of the crime. That is, it was twelve times as much disposed to crime as the native

stock. The hoodlums and roughs of our cities are, most of them, American-born of foreign parentage. . . .

Moreover, immigration not only furnishes the greater portion of our criminals, it is also seriously affecting the morals of the native population. It is disease and not health which is contagious. Most foreigners bring with them continental ideas of the Sabbath, and the result is sadly manifest in all our cities, where it is being transformed from a holy day into a holiday. But by far the most effective instrument for debauching popular morals is the liquor traffic, and this is chiefly carried on by foreigners. . . .

We have seen that immigration is detrimental to popular morals. It has a like influence on popular intelligence, for the percentage of illiteracy among the foreign-born populace is thirty-eight per cent greater than among the native-born whites. . . .

. . .Our safety demands the assimilation of these strange populations, and the process of assimilation will become slower and more difficult as the proportion of foreigners increases.

Josiah Strong, Congregationalist clergyman and advocate of immigration restriction, in Our Country: Its Possible Future and Its Present Crisis *(1885), pp. 55–60.*

The German ragpicker of thirty years ago, quite as low in the scale as his Italian successor, is the thrifty tradesman or prosperous farmer of today.

The Italian scavenger of our time is fast graduating into exclusive control of the corner fruit stands, while his black-eyed boy monopolizes the bootblacking industry in which a few years ago he was an intruder. The Irish hod carrier in the second generation has become a bricklayer, if not the alderman of his ward, while the Chinese coolie is in almost exclusive possession of the laundry business. The reason is obvious. The poorest immigrant comes here with the purpose and ambition to better himself and, given half a chance, might be reasonably expected to make the most of it. To the false pleas that he prefers the squalid homes in which his kind are housed there could be no better answer. The truth is his half-chance has too long been wanting, and for the bad result he has been unjustly blamed. . . .

Were the question raised who makes the most of life thus mortgaged, who resists most stubbornly its leveling tendency, . . . the palm must be unhesitatingly awarded the Teuton. The Italian and the poor Jew rise only by compulsion. The Chinaman does not rise at all; here, as at home, he remains stationary. The Irishman's genius runs to public affairs rather than to domestic life; wherever he is mustered in force, the saloon is the gorgeous center of political activity. The German struggles vainly to learn his trick; his Teutonic wit is too heavy, and the political ladder he raises from his saloon usually too short or too clumsy to reach the desired goal. The best part of his life is lived at home, and he makes himself a home independent of the surroundings, giving the lie to the saying, unhappily become a maxim of social truth, that pauperism and drunkenness naturally grow in the tenements. He makes the most of his tenement, and it should be added that whenever and as soon as he can save up money enough, he gets out and never crosses the threshold of one again.

Danish immigrant Jacob A. Riis, describing the immigrant populace of New York City, in How the Other Half Lives *(1890), pp. 23–25.*

The flood gates are open. The bars are down. The sally-ports are unguarded. The dam is washed away. The sewer is choked. . . . The scum of immigration is viscerating upon our shores. The horde of $9.60 steerage slime is being siphoned upon us from Continental mud tanks.

Editorial in a New York City newspaper, early 1890s, in Foerster, The Italian Emigration of Our Times *(1917), pp. 41–68.*

A throng of foreign paupers are swarming to our
    shore
Who seek to serve the Romish church and papacy
    restore
They must learn that in America his power can be
    no more.
Our country must be free.

Anti-Catholic song sung in the 1890s by the American Protective Association to the tune of "The Battle Hymn of the Republic," in Bailey, Voices of America *(1976), p. 245.*

[A fellow immigrant and I] began to make inquiries about jobs and were promptly informed that there was plenty of work at "pick and shovel." We were also given to understand by our fellow-boarders that "pick and shovel" was practically the only work available to Italians. Now these were the first two English words I had heard and they possessed great charm. Moreover if I were to earn money to return home and this was the only work available to Italians, they were very weighty words for me, and I must master them as soon and as well as possible and then set out to find their hidden

meaning. I practiced for a day or two until I could say "peek" and "shuvle" to perfection. Then I asked a fellow boarder to take me to see what the work was like. He did. He led me to Washington Street, not far from the colony [in Boston], where some excavation work was going on, and there I did see, with my own eyes, what the "peek" and "shuvle" were about. My heart sank within me, for I had thought it some form of office work; but I was game and since this was the only work available to Italians, and since I must have money to return home, I would take it up.

Italian immigrant Constantine Panunzio, on his first days in America in the 1890s, in The Soul of an Immigrant *(1921), pp. 75–77.*

Much has been said of the causes of immigration. These are numerous but the chief cause I have found to be that the people of the Old World are now being aroused to the facts that the social conditions of Europe with its aristocracy and other inherited privileges, are not founded on just principles, but that the way to success ought to be equally open for all, and determined, not by privileges of birth, but by the inherent worth of man. And here in America is found a civilization which is, to a large extent, built on equality and the recognition of personal merit. This, and the great natural resources of the country, the prospects for good wages, which a new condition affords, and in many cases greater religious liberty, draws the people of Europe to this country.

German immigrant Hans Mattson, in Reminiscences: The Story of an Emigrant *(1891), p. 296.*

We got only so much as would keep us from starvation. Things cost us more than three times their regular price. Our daily fare was coffee and bread for breakfast, rice with lard or soup at dinner-time, and cheese or sausage for supper. Yet we were not able to pay off our debt; so after a while we were given only bread, and with this only to sustain us we had to go through our daily work. By and by we became exhausted, and some of us got sick. Then we decided to try, at the risk of our lives, to escape. Some of us ran away, eluding the guards. We were, however, soon surprised by the appearance of the bosses and two guards. They thrust guns in our faces and ordered us to return to work or they would shoot us down. . . . We went before a judge, who was sitting in a barroom. . . . [T]he bosses, the policemen, and the judge . . . held a short consultation, and the result was that the bosses paid some money (I believe it was forty-five dollars), the policemen put the manacles on our wrists, and we were marched off.

An Italian immigrant, forced to work in a mine to pay his padrone for his railroad fare in 1891, quoted in Moquin and Van Doren, A Documentary History of the Italian Americans *(1975), p. 103.*

We heartily approve all legitimate efforts to prevent the United States from being used as the dumping ground for known criminals and professional paupers of Europe.

The Democratic national platform in the election of 1892, in Bailey, Voices of America *(1976), p. 245.*

Of all stupid ill-feelings, the sentiment of my fellow-Caucasians towards our companions in the Chinese car was the most stupid and the worst. They seemed never to have looked at them, listened to them, or thought of them, but hated them *a priori*. The Mongols were their enemies in that cruel and treacherous battle-field of money. They could work better and cheaper in half a hundred industries, and hence there was no calumny too idle for the Caucasian to repeat, and even to believe. They declared them hideous vermin. . . . Again, my emigrants declared that the Chinese were dirty. I cannot say they were clean, for that was impossible upon the journey; but in their efforts at cleanliness they put the rest of us to shame. . . .

These judgments are typical of the feeling in all Western America. The Chinese are considered stupid, because they are imperfectly acquainted with English. They are held to be base, because their dexterity and frugality enable them to underbid the lazy, luxurious Caucasians. They are said to be thieves; I am sure they have no monopoly on that. They are called cruel; the Anglo-Saxon and the cheerful Irishman may each reflect before he bears the accusation. . . .

Awhile ago it was the Irish, now it is the Chinese that must go. Such is the cry . . . yet we may regret the free tradition of the republic, which loved to depict herself with open arms, welcoming all unfortunates. And certainly, as a man who loves freedom, I may be excused some bitterness when I find her sacred name abused in the connection. It was but the other day that I heard a vulgar fellow . . . roaring for arms and butchery. "At the call of Abraham Lincoln," said the orator, "ye rose in the name of freedom to set free the negroes; can ye not rise and liberate yourselves from a few dhirty Mongolians?"

Robert Louis Stevenson, Scottish writer, reporting a visit taken to the American West, in Across the Plains *(1892), pp. 62–63.*

"'Hands Off, Gentlemen' America Means Fair Play for All Men." Thomas Nast, in this February 15, 1887, cartoon in *Harper's Magazine,* shows the spirit of Liberty protecting the Chinese immigrant from a mob of immigrants from other countries. *(author's collection)*

The Mongolian race should no more be allowed to come here and displace our labor, to lower our civilization, to contaminate our people with disease and to build up a brotherhood of murderers and criminals than should we welcome an armed mob of Fiji Islanders bent only on spoil and plunder. The Chinese must stay in their own country. Our experience with the Chinese has not been pleasing. They have added nothing to our wealth, given nothing to science, been concerned in no enterprises and only in rare instances embraced the Christian religion or donned the garb of civilization.

"Chinese Immigration Again—A Plea for Severe Restrictions," an excerpt from the Toledo Blade *calling for the reenactment of the Chinese Exclusion Act due to expire on May 6 of that year,* Literary Digest, *January 30, 1892.*

Even in his diversions the American is too active and too self-willed. Unlike the Latin, who amuses himself by relaxation, he amuses himself by intensity, and this is the case whatever be the nature of his amusements, for he has very coarse and very refined ones.

Paul Bourget, French traveler recounting his observations of America on a visit in 1893, in Outre-Mer: Impressions of America *(1895), p. 326.*

So at last I was going to America! Really, really going, at last! The boundaries burst. The arch of heaven soared. A million suns shone out for every star. The winds rushed in from outer space, roaring in my ears, "America! America!"

. . . As we moved along in a little procession I was delighted with the illumination of the streets. So many lamps, and they burned until morning, my father said, and so people did not need to carry lanterns. In America, then, everything was free, as we had heard in Russia. Light was free; the streets were as bright as a synagogue on a holy day. Music was free; we had been serenaded, to our gaping delight, by a brass band of many pieces, soon after our installation on Union Place.

Education was free. That subject that my father had written about repeatedly, as comprising his chief hope for us children, the essence of American opportunity, the treasure that no thief could touch, not even misfortune or poverty. It was the one thing that he was able to promise us when he sent for us; surer, safer than bread or shelter. On our second day I was thrilled with the realization of what this freedom of education meant. A little girl from across the alley came and offered to conduct us to school. My father was out, but we five between us had a few words of English by this time. We knew the word school. This child, who had never seen us till yesterday, who could not pronounce our names, who was not much better dressed than we, was able to offer us the freedom of the schools of Boston! No applications made, no questions asked, no examinations, rulings, exclusions; no machinations, no fees. The doors stood open for every one of us. The smallest child could show us the way.

This incident impressed me more than anything I had heard in advance of the freedom of education in America. It was concrete proof—almost the thing itself.

Russian immigrant Mary Antin, who arrived in Boston in 1894, in The Promised Land *(1911), pp. 162, 185–186.*

Common labor, white $1.30 to $1.50
Common labor, colored $1.25 to $1.40
Common labor, Italian $1.15 to $1.25

Help Wanted notice for workers on New York's Croton Reservoir appearing in New York newspapers and handbills, 1895, quoted in Gambino, Blood of My Blood *(1974), p. 71.*

I came from Wilkes-Barre on a Monday . . . and came via Harrisburg, Hagerstown, and Roanoke. . . . Being beastly tired of the train, I got into a large dining saloon. Presently two niggar young women came to me: they were about eighteen years old and they had delightfully melodious sweet voices and spoke in most guarded and beautiful English. "By Jove," says I to myself, "if all the niggars are like these girls, I am jolly glad I came down here." Talking about modest and respectful behavior, why every other place I have ever been to both at home and America, were not in it.

I came in contact with several of them, men this time, while waiting at Poco and found them all extremely well-behaved and enlightened people. I am extremely fond of them. . . .

The poor niggar has been shamefully abused and ill-treated by white men, more the shame to them. Even the niggar children when you meet them on the road are different to white children; the former are polite and thoroughly well-behaved, with no coarse language, the white children, quite the reverse, a filthy low set.

The white man of this state and adjoining states is about the most contemptible person on the face of God's earth. He is unbearably ignorant and does not know it. He has generally been brought up on the mountains, hog fashion, and when they come to the mines and earn a lot of money they swell out and don't know themselves.

John R. Williams, Welsh immigrant coal miner, letter to his friend in Wales from West Virginia, November 10, 1895, in Conway, The Welsh in America *(1961), pp. 206–208.*

Mr. President, this bill is intended to amend the existing law so as to restrict still further immigration to the Untied States. Paupers, diseased persons, convicts, and contract laborers are now excluded. By this bill it is proposed to make a new class of excluded immigrants and add to those which have just been named the totally ignorant. The bill is of the simplest kind. The first section excludes from the country all immigrants who cannot read or write. . . .

Anti-immigrant activist Henry Cabot Lodge (1850–1924), U.S. senator from Massachusetts (1893–1924), posed for this photograph in his last year. *(Library of Congress, Prints and Photographs Division [LC-USZ62-97848])*

The illiteracy test will bear most heavily upon the Italians, Russians, Poles, Hungarians, Greeks, and Asiatics, and very lightly, or not at all, upon English-speaking emigrants or Germans, Scandinavians, and French. In other words, the races most affected by the illiteracy test are those whose emigration to this country had begun within the last twenty years and swelled to enormous proportions, races with which the English-speaking people have never hitherto assimilated, and who are most alien to the great body of the people of the United States.

[This "new immigration"] carries with it further consequences far deeper than any other event of our times. It involves, in a word, nothing less than the possibility of a great and perilous change in the very fabric of our race.

Senator Henry Cabot Lodge, in a speech to Congress supporting the use of a literacy test to restrict immigration proposed March 2, 1896, in Congressional Record, *March 16, 1896, 54th Congress, last session, pp. 2817–2820.*

I herewith return, without approval, House bill numbered 7864, entitled "An Act to Amend the Immigration Laws of the Untied States. . . ."

A radical departure from our national policy relating to immigration is here presented. Heretofore we have welcomed all who came to us from other lands, except those who whose moral or physical condition or history threatened danger to our national welfare and safety. Relying upon the jealous watchfulness of our people to prevent injury to our political and social fabric, we have encouraged those coming from foreign countries to cast their lot with us and join in the development of our vast domain, securing in return a share in the blessings of American citizenship.

A century's stupendous growth, largely due to the assimilation and thrift of millions of sturdy and patriotic adopted citizens, attests the success of this generous and free-handed policy. . . .

The best reason that could be given for this radical restriction of immigration is the necessity of protecting our

President Grover Cleveland (1837–1908) vetoed the first bill requiring a literacy test for immigrants in his last year of office, 1897. *(Library of Congress, Prints and Photographs Division [LC-USZ62-95675])*

population against degeneration and saving our national peace and quiet from imported turbulence and disorder.

I can not believe that we would be protected against these evils by limiting immigration to those who can read and write in any language twenty-five words of our Constitution. In my opinion it is infinitely more safe to admit a hundred thousand immigrants who, though unable to read and write, seek among us only a home and opportunity to work, than to admit one of those unruly agitators and enemies of governmental control, who can not only read and write but delights in arousing by inflammatory speech the illiterate and peacefully inclined to discontent and tumult.

President Cleveland, the first presidential veto of a literacy test act, in a message returning the Immigration Bill of 1897 to the House of Representatives, March 2, 1897, United States 54th Congress, 2nd session, Senate Document Number 185.

Americans feel a violent need to paralyze cerebral activity with external aids. Or perhaps the source of the invincible seductiveness of alcohol that steadily leads them to the ultimate stupor lies in their impatience for extreme sensations; they love to save time, to get there all at once. . . .

In New York, toward evening, when the working day ends, miles of carriages scatter the innumerable crowd, which all day long conduct their affairs downtown, to all parts of the upper city. The six parallel elevated railway lines each run trains of five or six enormous coaches every five minutes, all jammed to overflowing with people. There the millionaire sits beside the porter. . . . Some elegant Wall Street bankers are marked by special clothes of English cut. But with that exception, no European would be able to pick out by eye who there represents the infinite variety of professions, trades, states, fortune, culture, education that may be encountered among the whole people.

The gentleman who sits at your side and can scarcely edge himself into the tiny space available while he nonchalantly reads his immense newspaper might with equal likelihood be the attorney of the richest railroad in the world, a shoe clerk, or a cab driver. . . . At most, some hands might betray the exercise of the more menial trades, and some odors, peculiar industries. But the shape and texture of the clothing in all shows the same care, the same cut, and almost the same easy circumstances; and in manners and speech all display the same vigorous sentiments of an egalitarian society and of personal dignity.

Giuseppe Giacosa, Italian playwright, recalling his visit to the United States in 1898 in Impressioni d'America (1908), *in* Handlin, This Was America (1949), pp. 398–399.

Before long my office was crowded with Italians, Chinese, Greeks and Syrians. Each nationality had its own quarter—the Italians on Mulberry Street and its immediate neighborhood, the Greeks and Syrians on lower Washington Street, the Chinese on Doyer and Pell Streets, and the Hungarians on Second Avenue. In these linguistic islands one heard no word of English. Each group kept to itself, adhering strictly to its own religious beliefs and traditions, preferring to settle their own difficulties among themselves. The Italians had brought with them their inherited distrust of all government, and even the friends of a murdered man would shelter his assailant rather than have his guilt litigated in an American court of justice.

Arthur Train, American author and lawyer, writing of New York City around 1900, in Yankee Lawyer, the Autobiography of Ephraim Tutt (1944), pp. 101–102.

The steerage cooks and stewards served "biscuits" and coffee. The latter was what might be expected. The first named was a disk of dough, three-quarters of an inch thick, and a hand-length broad. It was hard as a landlord's heart, and as tasteless as a bit of carpet. . . . Half the biscuits were moldy. About some 3,000 were served out, and for the next half hour disks went sailing high in the air over the sides and into the sea. . . . If conditions aboard the *Lahn* and the *Prinzessin* were so bad, what must it be like aboard the cheaper ships running from Mediterranean ports?

Broughton Brandenburg, Ellis Island inspector, in Imported Americans (1904), p. 184.

Wide open and unguarded stand our gates,
Named of the four winds, North, South, East, and
    West;
Portals that lead to an enchanted land
Of cities, forests, fields of living gold,
Vast prairies, lordly summits touched with snow,

      . . . .

Wide open and unguarded stand our gates,
And through them presses a wild, motley throng—

      . . . . . .

Malayan, Scythian, Teuton, Kelt, and Slav,
Flying the Old World's poverty and scorn;
These bringing with them unknown gods and
    rites,—
Those, tiger passions, here to stretch their claws.
In street and alley, what strange tongues are loud,
Accents of menace alien to our air,
Voices that once the Tower of Babel knew!

O Liberty, white Goddess! Is it well
To leave the gates unguarded? On thy breast
Fold Sorrow's children, soothe the hurts of fate
Lift the downtrodden, but with hand of steel
Stay those who to thy sacred portals come
To waste the gifts of freedom. Have a care
Lest from thy brow the clustered stars be torn
And trampled in the dust. . . .

Thomas Bailey Aldrich, "Unguarded Gates," 1822,
Unguarded Gates and Other Poems (1895),
pp. 16–17.

I remember the food was so bad that many times my mother would say, "Don't eat it," or "Eat a little." She herself was very sick. She was confined to her bed actually the whole trip through, and we three kids were standing there around her. We were allowed to go out on the deck and people from the upstairs, first and second class, would look down on us and they would feel sorry for us and many times they would throw down an orange or apples or some food. And we, the children, would all stand by . . . and this one would catch this and this one would catch that and you were lucky to get something. And, of course, being that my mother was sick, if it was an orange or so we'd bring it in to her. . . .

Immigrants travel to the "Land of Promise," 1902. *(Library of Congress, Prints and Photographs Division [LC-USZ62-7307])*

Once it happened . . . that a few people came down from upstairs and spoke to the children and gave us some candy the first time we really saw any kind of candy or sweets and how we were so happy to get it. . . .

. . . And then all of a sudden we heard a big commotion and we came to America and everybody started yelling they see the Lady, the Statue of Liberty, and we all ran upstairs and everybody started screaming and crying. We were kissing each other. People that you don't even know before that were along side of you and you never paid any attention. Everybody was so excited that you see America and see the Lady with her hand up, you know. . . .

. . . My mother held us to her hands and then when we got to the end, they sent us to another large room and they had a meal for us. Well, that room I remember distinctly because it was immense. To me it looked like it was everything. And they gave us some kind of meat and we looked at my mother whether we can eat it because it might not be kosher. And my mother just smiled and said, "eat it" because we didn't have a good piece of meat all the way there and we were just starting, we ate some of it, some of the food, and everybody was busy running around . . . and as we were eating they were calling people out that had to be called. . . . People came to pick somebody up. . . . And finally they called our name. . . . We were in the middle of eating and when they called our name we looked at our mother. Should we go or should we eat? Well, anyhow we went and, in fact, my brother took a napkin and put the meat into it. You can't leave it when you get meat so there was a napkin there; he took it and put the meat in there. My mother hollered at him but he took it anyway. . . .

Estelle Schwartz Belford, born 1900, an immigrant from Romania (1905), in interview #E147, conducted May 14, 1941, by the Ellis Island Oral History Project.

Well, the new year of 1905 had barely begun when the inevitable happened. Papa lost his business. Another failure.

Meanwhile, word of the new land across the ocean was spreading through Europe like wildfire. America was on every tongue. And talk of the "Golden Land" eventually reached Brod, that remote corner of Serbia where my parents lived.

Suddenly, to save his pride, my father announced that he was going to America. In America lay his future, he said. People had been known to make their fortunes there. One only needed the courage to break away.

Mama told him he was insane. Never would she leave her homeland. But my father, always the adventurer, could not be dissuaded. He was going to America.

. . . My father did his best, but all his days, here in New York, he remained a working man. He found, as did so many thousands who came before and after him, that in golden America, money did not grow on trees.

Serbian immigrant Marie Jastrow, in A Time to Remember: Growing Up in New York Before the Great War *(1979), pp. 16–17.*

[Lincoln] Steffens made one good point in his book [*The Shame of the Cities,* published in 1904]. He said that he found that Philadelphia, ruled almost entirely by Americans, was more corrupt than New York, where the Irish do almost all the governin'. I could have told him that before he did any investigatin' if he had come to me. The Irish was born to rule, and they're the honestest people in the world. . . . One reason why the Irishman is more honest in politics than many Sons of the Revolution is that he is grateful to the country and the city that gave him protection and prosperity when he was driven by oppression from the Emerald Isle. . . . Yes, the Irishman is grateful. His one thought is to serve the city which gave him a home. He has this thought even before he lands in New York, for his friends here often have a good place in one of the city departments picked out for him while he is still in the old country. Is it any wonder that he has a tender spot in his heart for old New York when he is on its salary list the mornin' after he lands?

George Washington Plunkitt, New York Democratic politician, in William L. Riordon, Plunkitt of Tammany Hall *(1905), pp. 30–31.*

The Chinaman is a man. I have nothing against the Chinaman as a Chinaman, but there is a great deal of difference between a Chinaman and an American. I am not in favor of excluding the Chinaman from our shores because he is a Chinaman, but because his ideas and his civilization are absolutely opposed to the ideals and civilization of the American people. Never in the history of the world have the Chinese been admitted into a land save to dominate or to be driven out. The Chinese is a cheap man. . . .

It is true now, as it has always been, that self-protection is the first law of nature, and it is of the utmost importance that the American workman should do all in

Labor leader Samuel Gompers (1850–1924), president of the AFL, casts his ballot at a union election. *(Library of Congress, Prints and Photographs Division [LC-USZ62-117862])*

his power to prohibit the importation of those who would still further press him down.

Samuel Gompers, president of the American Federation of Labor, in a speech delivered at the National Conference on Immigration, New York, December 7, 1905, in the New York Times, December 8, 1905.

I had landed that morning in New York and was on my way to spend the day with friends. I found myself on a streetcar somewhere in Brooklyn. A huge furniture van had got stuck in front of the car; the horses were balky and refused to move. The car stopped and a large crowd gathered while the driver of the van tried various ways of starting his balky horse. The suggestions from the crowd didn't improve his temper. The street was absolutely tied up; the horses had decided to stay right where they were.

All the while our motorman was clanging his bell impatiently. At last he couldn't stand it any longer. He turned on the power, brought his car up behind the van, and began to shove. By George, those horses had to move! He shoved them for nearly two blocks, van and all, while the crowd cheered and the bell clanged. . . .

And all the while I sat there in the car thrilled to the core of my being. Something had come over me like a wave. This was America—hurry and rush, clang, clang, over the top—if you can't do it one way, try another! Such a thing as that would never have happened on a European street; such a thing as that would never have been done by a European motorman, and I liked it. Tears came into my eyes. This was America, my country. I had come home.

> *O. E. Rölvaag, Norwegian novelist who immigrated to America in 1896, recalling an experience in New York after returning from his first visit to Norway in 1906, in Cavanah,* We Came to America *(1954), pp. 204–205.*

"'Tis time we done something to make th' immigration laws sthronger," says he. "Thrue f'r ye, Miles Standish," says I, "but what wud ye do?" "I'd keep out the out-scourins iv Europe," says he. . . . "But what ar-re th' immigrants doin' that's roonous to us?" I says. "Well," says he, "they're arnychists," he says; "they don't assymilate with th' counthry," he says. "Maybe the counthry's digestion has gone wrong fr'm too much rich food," says I; "perhaps now if we'd lave off thryin' to digest Rockefeller an' thry a simple diet like Schwartzmeister, we wudden't feel th' effects iv our vittels," I says. "Maybe if we'd season th' immygrants a little or cook them thurly, they'd go down betther," I says.

> *Finlay Peter Dunne, mocking the restrictionist position of the descendants of immigrants, in* Observations of Mr. Dooley *(1906), pp. 51–52.*

Dear Mr. Editor:

I am a greenhorn. I have only been five weeks in the country. I am a jewelry maker. I left a blind father and stepmother in Russia. Before my departure my father begged me not to forget him. I promised that I would send him the first money I should earn. I walked around two weeks and looked for work. But at the end of the third week I succeeded in getting a job. I worked a week and received eight dollars for the week. I am working the third week now, I paid for my board and bought certain necessities, such as a hat, shoes, and some small items and I have a few dollars too. Now, Mr. Editor, I want to ask you to give me some advice, as to what to do. Should I send my father a few dollars for Passover, or should I keep them for myself? Because the work at our place is at an end and I may have to be without work. . . . I hope that

you will give me some advice and I shall obey you just as you tell me.

> Your constant reader,
> Youah Mednikoff
> *Letter to the editor of the Yiddish-language newspaper,* Jewish Daily Forward *(New York), March 16, 1906.*

What [Italian immigrants in America] need is a teacher, someone who will make them realize that they are missing the greatest of all blessings this country affords, equal rights. If you tell them casually that any one of them before the law of the land is as good as the richest and the proudest of the native born they will laugh at you. They must be instructed so that the humble organ grinder, the shopkeeper and even the laborer on the tracks of the Subway will know that when the Black Hand picks him out for blackmail and possible destruction, the Black Hand is not only attacking him but is also seeking to break down and destroy the laws built by Americans to protect their sacred rights in which he shares equally.

> *Joseph Petrosino, Italian-born detective famous for under cover work exposing Italian crime in New York, in "Petrosino, Detective and Sociologist,"* The New York Times, *December 30, 1906.*

America is God's Crucible, the great Melting Pot where all the races of Europe are melting and reforming! Here you stand, good folk, think I, here you stand in your fifty groups with your fifty languages and histories, and your fifty blood hatreds and rivalries, but you won't be long like that, brothers, for these are the fires of God you've come to—these are the fires of God. . . . Germans and Frenchmen, Irishman and Englishman, Jews and Russians—into the Crucible with you all! God is making the American.

> *David Quixano, a Russian-Jewish immigrant in New York, in Israel Zangwill's play* The Melting Pot *(1909), p. 37.*

Men wanted. Tinners, catchers, and helpers, to work in open shops. Syrians, Poles, and Roumanians preferred. Steady employment and good wages to men willing to work. Fare paid and no fees charged.

> *Advertisement in Pittsburgh newspapers, 1909, quoted by John Mitchell, president of the American Federation of Labor, in* American Federationist *(October 1909), in O'Neill,* Immigration *(1992), p. 155.*

Two years in America! Two years in the golden country! What had I accomplished?—a weak stomach, headaches every other day, a pale face, inflamed eyes. . . . I wanted a doctor and I could not afford one. . . . I always got headaches traveling on the subways. In Russia no more passengers than seats are allowed. Here in free America the people are free to choke themselves with the suffocating subway air. They are thrown together like cattle and carried down to the industrial market. . . . If I could forget all my humiliations and return to my old days, which, though very unhappy because of the Government brutality . . . still after . . . American life, seemed the happiest.

Elizabeth Hassanovitz, Russian immigrant, recalling her first years in America, about 1910, in One of Them: Chapters from a Passionate Autobiography *(1918), pp. 193–194, 308–309.*

We were in steerage, and [my mother] was so sick. She was too sick to even get up and walk around. I'd bring a big bowl, a wooden bowl with sauerkraut and pork, and she couldn't take that. Also don't forget, she was a lady. She worked for very fine people all her life as a cook. Not a cleaning woman, as a cook. The boat trip took three weeks. We were down in that hole for three weeks. We couldn't see nothing. My mother didn't eat.

When we got to America, we saw the Statue of Liberty and Mother said to me in German, "That means we are free." And I didn't know what she meant by being "free." I only learned that after. And to this day I think I'm a better American than a lot of them born here, because when I sing "God Bless America" I'm in tears. You see, I feel I've been very blessed to live to be over ninety and be healthy.

Margaret Wertle, Hungarian immigrant, remembering her voyage to America at the age of seven, in 1910, in Coan, Ellis Island Interviews *(1997), p. 310.*

Something had grown in me during my stay in America. Something was keeping me in this wonderful, perilous land where I had suffered so much and where I had so much more to suffer. Should I quit this great America without a chance to really know it? . . . There was a lingering suspicion that somewhere in this vast country an opening existed, that somewhere I would strike the light. I could not remain in the darkness perpetually.

Pascal D'Angelo, recalling his experiences soon after his arrival from Italy in 1910, in Son of Italy *(1975; first published, 1924), p. 115.*

A considerable proportion of immigrants now coming are from races and countries, or parts of countries, which have not progressed, but have been backward, downtrodden, and relatively useless for centuries. If these immigrants "have not had the opportunities," it is because their races have not made the opportunities; for they have had all the time that any races have had.

Statement of the Immigration Restriction League in U.S. Congress, Statements and Recommendations Submitted by Societies and Organizations Interested in the Subject of Immigration *(1911), p. 107.*

[Steerage] is the poorest possible introduction to, and preparation for, America. It inevitably lowers the standard of decency, even of the immigrants, and too often breaks down their moral and physical stamina. It shatters their bright vision of American life, and lands them cynical and embittered. . . . The ventilation is almost always inadequate, and the air soon becomes foul. The unattended vomit of the seasick, the odors of not too clean bodies, the reek of food and the awful stench of nearby toilet rooms make the atmosphere of the steerage such that it is a marvel that human flesh can endure it.

Senator William P. Dillingham, in the U.S. Immigration Commission, Reports of the Immigration Commission, *1911, quoted in Gambino,* Blood of My Blood *(1974), pp. 109–110.*

Here at home [in Hungary] the savings of the American emigrant practically works miracles. It makes the villages bloom, covers the lovely thatched houses with tile roofs, brings machinery to an agricultural production that earlier had subsisted on the most primitive tools.

Bertalan Nemenya, Hungarian sociologist, 1911, in Puskas, From Hungary to the United States, *(1982), p. 79.*

Everyone was hungry, and they started examinations on Ellis Island. I had twenty-five dollars in my pocket. I knew to bring money, otherwise they keep you there. They wouldn't let you go to shore without money. Because if you were hungry, you might steal. And I was alongside Gus, and I noticed he had a chalk mark on his back. I couldn't reach or see my back, so I asked him, "Do I have a chalk mark on my back?" So he looked, he say, "No." I say, "You've got one. Your father too." And I'm thinking, either they go back to Greece or I go back to Greece. So what happened, the one with the chalk mark went back to Greece. Gus and his father had to go back. I don't know why.

Scottish naturalist John Muir (1838–1914), observes the landscape after immigrating to the United States. *(Library of Congress, Prints and Photographs Division [LC-USZ62-72111])*

I just thank God. To this day, I pray, dear Lord, and thank God, that I was admitted to the United States, that they didn't put a chalk mark on my back.

Greek immigrant Theodore Spako, recalling his arrival at Ellis Island in 1911 at the age of 16, in Coan, Ellis Island Interviews *(1997), p. 278.*

In another of our reading lessons some of the American forests were described. The most interesting of the trees to us boys was the sugar maple, and soon after we had learned this story we heard everybody talking about the discovery of gold in the same wonder-filled country.

One night . . . my father come in with the news, the most wonderful, the most glorious, that wild boys ever heard. "Bairns," he said, "you needna learn your lessons the nicht, for we're gan to America the morn!" No more lessons, but boundless woods full of mysterious good things; trees full of sugar, growing in ground full of gold. . . . And when we in fullness of young joy spoke of what we were going to do, . . . the sugar and gold,

etc., and promised to send him a big box full of that tree sugar packed in gold from the glorious paradise over the sea, poor lonely grandfather, about to be forsaken, looked with downcast eyes on the floor and said in a low, trembling, troubled voice, "Ah, poor laddies, poor laddies, you'll find something else ower the sea forbye gold and sugar. . . . You'll find plenty hard, hard work." And so we did.

Scottish naturalist John Muir, in The Story of My Boyhood and Youth *(1913), pp. 53–54.*

I was having luncheon when a very pleasant Swede came down the road . . . Mr. G. B. Olsen, bossing a gang of workers on the highway. . . .

"Have you ever been back to Sweden?" I asked.

"No, sirr, never."

"Are you content with America?"

"Yes, sirr; it's the finest country under the sun. It gives the working-man a show."

"The Americans speak very kindly of your countrymen. They like them."

"Yes. We gave the Americans a good lift, we Swedes, Norwegians, Danes, and Germans, by settling the land when the rest of the colonists were running to the towns. We came in and did the rough pioneer work that had to be done if America was going to be more than a mushroom growth. Where would America be today if it were not for us in Minnesota, Wisconsin, Iowa? You can't keep up big cities unless you've got plenty of men working in the background on the land."

Stephen Graham, English journalist reporting a walking tour of America in 1913, in With Poor Immigrants to America *(1914), pp. 130–131.*

. . . [W]ithout any exception, I have found that illiterate laborers make far better diggers than immigrants of higher standard, because, first, in their native land they have done nothing else, therefor are well accustomed to hard work, and, second, the laborer's mind, not being trained in other channels, lacks the nerve to branch off in other field, and remains what it is trained to be, a common laborer, a common digger, if you wish, but the most vital part and the most perfect of the whole machine which makes the country what it should be.

The heavens of the United States are bright enough without the need of foreign stars, but the hand of this glorious Republic does need the bone and brawn of the foreigner, whether or not he can read and write.

An "employer of . . . foreign laborers" in a letter to the New York Times, *January 23, 1915.*

TO THE HOUSE OF REPRESENTATIVES; It is with unaffected regret that I find myself constrained by clear conviction to return this bill (H.R. 6060, "An act to regulate the immigration of aliens to and the residence of aliens in the United States") without my signature. . . .

Restrictions like these, adopted earlier in our history as a Nation, would very materially have altered the course and cooled the humane ardors of our politics. The right of political asylum has brought to this country many a man of noble character and elevated purpose who was marked as an outlaw in his own less fortunate land, and who has yet become an ornament to our own citizenship and to our councils. The children and the compatriots of these illustrious Americans must stand amazed to see the representatives of their Nation now resolved, in the fullness of our national strength and at the maturity of our great institutions, to risk turning such men back from our shores without test of quality or purpose.

. . . Does this bill rest upon the conscience and universal assent and desire of the American people? I doubt it. It is because I doubt it that I make bold to dissent from it. . . .

Woodrow Wilson, "Message to the House of Representatives," January 28, 1915, vetoing the House bill to establish a literacy test for immigrants, in Dollar and Reichard, American Issues *(1994), pp. 305–306.*

Well, we're off for America. Where it is I don't know. I only know it's far. You have to ride and ride until you get there. . . .

"So you're going, really going to America?" says our neighbor Pesi. "May God bring you there safe and sound, and help you strike luck. With God everything is possible. Just last year our Rivele went to America with her husband, Hillel. The first months we heard nothing from them. We thought they had fallen, God forbid, into the sea. Finally they write us, 'America is a free country where everyone is miserable making a living.'"

Sholom Aleichem, Russian Jewish writer, in The World *(1916), quoted in Howe and Libo,* How We Lived *(1979), p. 20.*

The language was full of mysteries and adventure. Every new word I learned brought to me something new and exciting. Since my contact with America and its people was necessarily limited, through the language I sought to link myself with them. If I mastered the speech, I felt certain I would come nearer attaining my American ideal. I knew then as I know now that the language was the passport to my America.

The track hands who came to Montana for the summers and returned East for the winters to live in colonies made up of their own countrymen had little in common with America. Many had been in America ten years and still they were strangers in this country. They thought old-country thoughts, spoke only their native tongues. All of them were interested in making money, and that was their only contact with America. I was fortunate to see the tragedy of these people. And I did not want the same thing to happen to me.

I was now, after five years, on the eve of a second journey to America. I was ready and eager to return to the East, but not to the colony. America was not there. My America was elsewhere. No train or steamship could take me to it. I alone must find it.

Stoyan Christowe, Bulgarian immigrant (1911), recalling his study of English in Montana, around 1916, in This Is My Country *(1938), in Cavanah,* We Came to America *(1954), p. 30.*

As the immigrant approaches the officer gives him a quick glance. Experience enables him in that one glance to take in six details, namely the scalp, face, neck, hands, gait, and general condition, both mental and physical. Should any of these details not come into view, the alien is halted and the officer satisfies himself that no suspicious sign or symptom exists regarding that particular detail. For instance, if the immigrant is wearing a high collar, the officer opens the collar or unbuttons the upper shirt button and sees whether a goiter, tumor, or other abnormality exists. . . . Likewise, if the alien approaches the officer with hat on he must be halted, hat removed, and scalp observed in order to exclude the presence of favus, ringworm, or other skin disease of this region of the body. Pompadours are always a suspicious sign. Beneath such long growth of hair are frequently seen areas of favus. . . .

Many inattentive and stupid-looking aliens are questioned by the medical officer in the various languages as to their age, destination, and nationality. Often simple questions in addition and multiplication are propounded. Should an immigrant appear stupid and inattentive to such an extent that mental defect is suspected, an X is made with chalk on his coat at the anterior aspect of his right shoulder. Should definite signs of mental disease be observed, a circle X would be used instead of plain X. In like manner a chalk mark is placed on the anterior aspect of the right shoulder in all cases where physical abnormality or disease is suspected.

In this connection, B would indicate back; C, conjunctivitis; Ct, trachoma; E, eyes; F, face; Ft, feet; G, goiter; H, heart; K, hernia; L, lameness; N, neck; P, physical and lungs; Pg, pregnancy; Sc, scalp; S, senility. . . .

E. H. Mullen, U.S. Public Health official, "Mental Examination of Immigrants: Administration and Line Inspection at Ellis Island," in Public Health Reports, 33, *No. 20 (May 18, 1917), pp. 733–746.*

We Americans must realize that the altruistic ideals which have controlled our social development during the past century and the maudlin sentimentalism that has made America "an asylum for the oppressed," are sweeping the nation toward a racial abyss. If the Melting Pot is allowed to boil without control and we continue to follow our national motto and deliberately blind ourselves to "all distinctions of race, creed or color," the type of native American of Colonial descent will become as extinct as the Athenian of the age of Pericles and the Vikings of the days of Rollo.

Madison Grant, a proponent of immigration restriction, in The Passing of the Great Race *(1918), p. 263.*

[The deportees] were brought under guards and in special trains with instructions to get them away from the country with as little delay as possible. Most of the aliens had been picked up in raids on labor headquarters; they had been given a drum-head trial by an inspector with no chance for defense; they were held incommunicado and often were not permitted to see either friends or attorneys, before being shipped to Ellis Island.

In these proceedings the inspector who made the arrest was prosecutor, witness, judge, jury, and executioner. He was clerk and interpreter as well. This was all the trial the alien could demand under the law. . . . I was advised by the commissioner-general to mind my own business and carry out orders, no matter what they might be, yet such obvious injustice was being done that I could not sit quiet.

Frederick C. Howe, U.S. Commissioner of Immigration at the Port of New York, 1914–19, describing the treatment of aliens suspected of being anarchists, around 1918, in The Confessions of a Reformer *(1925), p. 327.*

CHAPTER SEVEN

The "Immigrant Problem" and the Federal Government
1890-1921

Castle Garden Closes

The elegantly named Castle Garden—neither a castle nor a garden but New York's somewhat grim first immigration depot—did heroic service for many years, but it had its critics from the beginning. Although the commissioners of emigration tried to fence it in to protect the residents of lower Manhattan from the immigrants, and to protect the immigrants from the residents of lower Manhattan, they were never able to do so effectively. Many New Yorkers complained of the facility's presence and of the people swarming into the city from it. Chronic shortage of funds led to the deterioration of the physical plant over the years, and when a fire broke out in 1876, destroying most of the old fort, critics of the facility urged that another receiving station be built somewhere else, preferably at a distance from the city. But the increasing volume of immigration made the need for such an installation too urgent for its restoration to be postponed, and in four months Castle Garden was once more in operation.

The demands on it grew with every passing year, however. In 1881 more than 455,600 immigrants were processed there. The next year the number rose to 476,000. It was not the only state immigration depot in the country—there were others at ports in Portland, Boston, Philadelphia, Baltimore, Key West, New Orleans, Galveston, and San Francisco—but it was by far the busiest, receiving nearly 70 percent of all immigrants arriving in the United States. Of the 5,250,000 arrivals from 1880 to 1890, more than 3,780,000 arrived in New York and passed through the crumbling portals of Castle Garden. Intended to protect the newcomers from exploitation, the facility was powerless to stop thieves and swindlers from taking advantage of the helpless arrivals.

There were also complaints about the way the depot was run—the commissioners were accused of collusion with the railroad companies and profiting from ticket sales, receiving kickbacks from contractors and failing to provide sufficient care for their wards. The New York *World*, in an 1887 exposé, described the establishment as "a place for tyranny and whimsical rule, a place for the abuse and insult of helpless mothers and children, for the plunder of the poor, for the lecherous pursuits of shielded employees, for the disgrace of the nation in the eyes of those who desire to become citizens." New York governor (and later U.S. president) Grover Cleveland called the management of Castle Garden "a scandal and a reproach to civilization."

A federal investigation found the facilities inadequate and the operation inefficient; Secretary of the Treasury William Windom proposed that the business of admitting immigrants be taken away from individual states and handed over to the federal government. With the number of arrivals increasing every year, the job of processing the newcomers had simply become too great for any city or state to manage. The policy of federal control of immigration was adopted in 1890, New York's

Immigrants on an Atlantic liner crowd the deck for their first view of America, around 1900. *(American Museum of Immigration, U.S. National Park Service)*

Emigration Commission was abolished, and Castle Garden was officially closed. The newly formed Federal Bureau of Immigration, the commission's successor, replaced the term *emigration* with *immigration* to emphasize the focus on its subjects' arrival to their new country rather than their departure from their old ones. The new bureau was housed, for the time being, in the barge office, a nearby landing place in Battery Park. The derelict Castle Garden building remained empty for six years and then opened again as a municipal aquarium. When construction began on the Brooklyn-Battery Tunnel in 1940, it closed for the last time, and 10 years later the building was declared a national monument.

Officials from the Treasury Department, of which the Federal Bureau of Immigration was a part, explored New York's harbor for a new and better site for a receiving station. Secretary Windom first proposed Governor's Island at the mouth of the East River, but that site was being used as a military base, and the War Department objected to sharing it. Windom's second choice was Bedloe's (now Liberty) Island, a full 12 acres in size and conveniently located between New York and New Jersey in the harbor, but the public was outraged at the idea. In 1886 the French government had presented the United States with the monument *Liberty Enlightening the World*, erected on Bedloe's Island.

The idea of giving part of the same island to an immigrant-receiving station, though, raised a storm of protest throughout the country. Even Auguste Bartholdi, the creator of the statue, wrote in Paris that such an establishment sharing the island with his work would be "a desecration."

The third and least popular choice was a much smaller island to the north of Bedloe's. Described contemptuously as "a tiny low-lying islet of mud and sand," Ellis Island measured only three acres, and the surrounding water was so shallow that boats could not dock there. The navy was using it to store gunpowder, but people in New Jersey considered a large deposit of explosives near their shore to be so dangerous that they had petitioned the federal government to clear the island. Like Governor's and Bedloe's Island, Ellis Island already belonged to the government and apparently no other department had any other use for it. Thus, on April 11, 1890, President Benjamin Harrison signed a bill naming Ellis Island as America's first national immigration depot.

Ellis Island Opens

Known as Kioshk ("Gull Island") to the native Indians of the region, Ellis Island had never had much value. In Dutch times it was part of the large land holding of the patroon Michel Paaw, along with Bedloe's Island, Staten Island, and a long stretch of the west bank of the Hudson River. It was called Little Oyster Island then (the much larger Bedloe's Island was called Oyster Island), for the abundant oyster beds around it, and the Dutch used it as a picnic ground. When New Amsterdam became New York, the property was ceded to William Dyre, a city customs inspector and later mayor. As Dyre's Island, it was sold, along with some land along Broadway, to Thomas Lloyd, who sold it to Enoch Story in 1696. The island changed both hands and names many times in the 18th century—for a while it was called Gibbet Island because pirates were hanged there—but by the 1770s it belonged to a merchant named Samuel Ellis, and his was the name that stuck. Ellis had no use for the site and tried to sell it for years, but though it was still famous for its fat oysters, it had no buyers. When Ellis died in 1794, the little island went to his family.

Ellis Island provided immigrant children with amusement and an introduction to patriotism in the rooftop playground while their parents were being examined for entry. *(New York Public Library Print Collection)*

The Ellises argued over the possession of the property until 1807, when the federal government, seeing the need for a fort to defend the harbor in case of attack, instructed the state to acquire it. New York State paid $10,000—considered exorbitant at the time—to the descendents of Samuel Ellis and then sold the island for the same price to the nation. A small fort was built there, but for more than 80 years the land was used only as a munitions dump. When it was selected as the site of a receiving station in 1890, the gunpowder was removed and $75,000 was allotted "for improving Ellis Island for immigration purposes."

It was a major operation. Government engineers examined the land and proposed "improvements" necessary before work on the clearing station was possible. The first thing they did was to increase the island's scanty three acres to 27 with landfill. Then they dredged a channel—12 feet deep, 200 feet wide, and 1,250 feet long—so that ferries could dock there and land passengers. Wells had to be dug and pipes laid to provide fresh water before any construction could begin.

The original structure erected for the facility was an impressive edifice, larger than the entire original island. Built of Georgia pine, it was two stories high and measured some 400 by 150 feet. A contemporary magazine said it looked like a resort hotel and noted that its amenities included hospital facilities, doctors' quarters, a bathhouse, a laundry, an electric power plant, several kitchens, and an ample dining hall. Costs for the construction and furnishing of the main building were estimated at over $200,000. By the time Ellis Island opened its doors to new arrivals on January 1, 1892, outfitting it had cost the government more than half a million dollars.

The opening of the receiving station at Ellis Island was a turning point in American immigration policy. It came about at the crest of the largest period of new arrivals in the country's history, and it marked the effective beginning of federal control of the process. The period of unrestricted immigration was coming to an end as nativist sentiment grew in response to the unregulated flow of newcomers. Shadowed by the colossal bronze figure of Lady Liberty holding her beacon out to arriving vessels, the facility reflected American hospitality and prosperity during the country's peak era of immigration, and Ellis Island became known to many Europeans as "the isle of hope."

However, it also represented some of the worst aspects of American society. Like its predecessor, Castle Garden, it was the subject of charges of corruption and brutality. As author Pamela Reeves noted in *Ellis Island: Gateway to the American Dream*, "Its very existence was a testimony to a class system—immigrants who could afford a first- or second-class ticket aboard the big ocean liners were briefly inspected aboard ship and allowed, in most cases, to pass directly into the United States. Only the poor were required to undergo an inspection at Ellis Island, and the poor comprised, by far, the majority of immigrants." Some, following a grueling passage that had cost them everything they owned, were turned away when they arrived, often arbitrarily and cruelly. For them, the site was called, in many languages, "the isle of tears."

During its 62 years of service, Ellis Island processed more than half of all immigrants arriving in the United States. In 1892, its first year, a total of 579,663 immigrants entered the country. Of that number, 445,987 came through the new facility at the Port of New York. From 1892 to 1924, the country admitted a total of 20,003,041 aliens, and more than 71 percent of them—14,277,144—came through Ellis Island.

The unprecedented volume of traffic inevitably led to problems. Five years after Ellis Island opened its doors, a fire swept through the main building, completely destroying the wooden structure. The barge office once more took over the job of registering immigrants while workmen cleared the ruins of the old edifice. In two years an imposing new building of brick, stone, and steel stood in its place. The stately new main building, built at a cost of $1.5 million and capable of processing as many as 8,000 people a day, opened on December 17, 1900. Designed to impress the incoming aliens with the prosperity and opulence of their new country, it was both larger and more elegant than its predecessor had been. The *New York Times* described the new building as "magnificent and admirably arranged."

The treatment of the arrivals did not always come in for such praise, however. Many of the old employees from Castle Garden remained with the bureau, and the new facility soon had the same reputation for corruption and abuse. Immigrants were herded like cattle; bribes were openly solicited; the one restaurant on the island overcharged the newcomers, who were unable to go elsewhere for food; relatives who came to escort immigrants to their new homes were illegally charged a fee to enter the island; and people were cheated at the money exchange. One German immigrant who understood what was happening reported in 1906, "I knew that the money changers were 'crooked,' so I passed a 20 mark piece to one of them for exchange, and was cheated out of nearly 75 percent of my money. My change was largely composed of new pennies, whose brightness was well calculated to deceive any newcomer."

In 1901 the recently elected president Theodore Roosevelt shook up the station's administration by firing many of the officials. In time the problems of corruption and inefficiency were corrected, or at least improved, but the reputation for harsh and unsympathetic treatment persisted. Even when the officials were honest, efficient, and sympathetic, they were often unable to cope with the swelling tide of immigrants that flowed through. In 1907—the year with the all-time record for volume—as many as 10,000 immigrants, speaking more than 100 languages, arrived daily to be examined and recorded. Those who had traveled first or second class were often questioned briefly on board their ships and sent directly into the city; if they could afford the luxury of cabins and free movement on the upper decks, they seemed to pose no threat to the country. But passengers in third class—known as "steerage" because those traveling in that class were assigned to the lowest deck of the ship, near the steering mechanism—were not always received with such courtesy. Fearful that such poor people might bring infectious diseases into the country or be unable to support themselves, immigration officials subjected them to rigorous and often humiliating examinations for mental or physical disorders.

Although over the years fewer than 2 percent of the immigrants applying for admission at Ellis Island were rejected and sent home again, the process of selection was terrifying, and the harried officials who examined the arrivals were often insensitive to the pain they occasioned. Some immigrants were passed quickly, but a full 20 percent had to spend long periods of detainment before being approved and released. The process was painful, and the suspense was sometimes unbearable. In the course of its operation as a receiving station, more than 3,000 people committed suicide on Ellis Island rather than face the prospect of deportation. Families

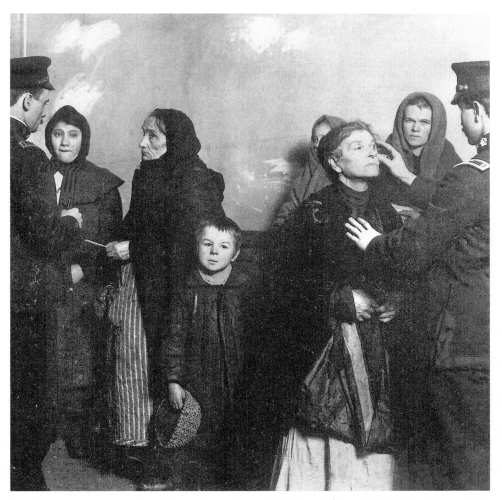

Immigrants undergo the dreaded trachoma test on Ellis Island. *(New York Public Library Print Collection)*

were broken up—a child might be returned and its parents allowed to stay. It is no wonder that the fear of being turned away after the fearful voyage figured so prominently in immigrants' recollections of the ordeal, or that Ellis was known as the "isle of tears" by so many. Overworked doctors and clerks were often careless and unfair in their decisions. Fiorello La Guardia, who worked as an interpreter on Ellis Island before becoming a judge and later mayor of New York City, recalled one case that, as he reported, haunted him for years. "A young girl in her teens from the mountains of northern Italy turned up," he recorded in his memoirs. "No one understood her particular dialect very well, and because of her hesitancy in replying to questions she did not understand, she was sent to the hospital for observation. . . . The child rebelled—and how! It was the cruelest case I ever witnessed on the island. In two weeks' time that child was a raving manic, although she had been sound and normal when she arrived at Ellis Island."

In addition to the medical and psychological examinations intended to weed out the ill and the insane, each arrival was questioned about his or her background in an effort to detect criminals. They were asked their names, ages, professions, financial conditions, places of origin, intended destinations, and whether they had been in a prison, an almshouse, or a mental institution. The first and most obvious of the questions—the immigrant's name—often posed a major problem. Those who came from Asian countries, or whose languages used the Russian, Hebrew, or

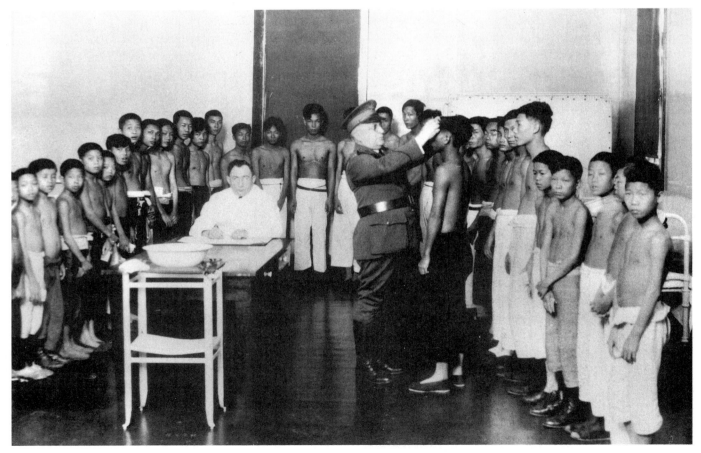

People from every part of the world flooded into the United States. Here a group of South Pacific Islanders are being examined by a doctor at Ellis Island in the first years of the 20th century. *(American Museum of Immigration, U.S. National Park Service)*

Greek alphabet, were often unable to spell their names, and family names in some languages were virtually unpronounceable to American officials at Ellis Island. Although not verified, it was said that many immigrants simply invented names, chose names they saw on signs at the immigration depot, or had names arbitrarily assigned to them by clerks who could not spell or could not be bothered to figure out what the immigrants said. A widely circulated story tells of a Chinese man with the unusual name Carl Olson, who explained, "When I arrived at Ellis Island, they asked the Swede ahead of me for his name and he answered 'Carl Olson.' When they asked me the same question I gave them my name, Sem Ting, and they've had me down as Carl Olson ever since."

In fact, this incident could never have happened, because the names recorded for immigrants were taken not from what they said but from the ships' manifests that they brought with them. Immigration agents at the receiving station asked their names to ascertain that the applicants were the people described on the passenger lists of the ships. Only when the spelling was impossible to preserve did the immigration officials make changes. Thus the common German name Müller became Muller, Miller, or Mueller according to the wishes of the immigrant or the random decision of the official. Changes or simplifications of names most often took place when immigrants booked passage from countries whose shipping agents accepted for the record whatever a client said. And changing a name, officially or unofficially, was relatively easy once immigrants arrived in the country. Thus, many Vladimirs became Walter; Pedros, Pierres, and Pietros became Peter; and Juans, Jans, Johans, Giovannis, Seans, Ivans, and Ions became John after they landed.

Entry on the West Coast: Angel Island

While Ellis Island was the port of entry for the great majority of immigrants to the United States from the 1890s to the 1920s, it was not the only one, and passage through it was not the most difficult. On the West Coast, Asian immigrants were subjected to more intense investigations and closer scrutiny. The purpose of the procedure at Ellis Island, and at such smaller installations as those in Philadelphia, Boston, and Baltimore, was to record the flow of immigrants. But after the passage of the Chinese Exclusion Act of 1882, the main objective of the receiving stations on the West Coast was to restrict the number of Asians and to prevent the fraudulent entry of those who were not eligible. When the government established federal control of immigration in 1891, the arrival of Asians in California was handled differently from that of others. Chinese, Koreans, Filipinos, and Japanese were sent immediately to a quarantine station, where they were fumigated and detained for lengthy interrogations. In 1904 Angel Island, the largest island in San Francisco Bay and a U.S. Army base since 1863, was selected as the site for the process.

The Chinese Exclusion Act of 1882, which prohibited the entry of all Chinese laborers, skilled and unskilled, for 10 years, specifically exempted merchants, teachers, students, and tourists from the prohibition. According to Section 6 of that act, however, people claiming eligibility had to obtain certificates from the Chinese government establishing their claims as members of those privileged classes. While the applicants were in quarantine, the federal immigration inspectors collected these Section 6 certificates to compare them with the information in the government files at the Chinese bureau.

Many Chinese with this exempt status were unable to produce documents to prove their claims. In those cases, the only evidence that could be presented was personal identification by witnesses. These witnesses were often suspected of being in league with Chinese trying to enter the country illegally. As one secret service agent reported to the Department of the Treasury in 1899, "San Francisco is full of old men, that will, for $5, identify ANY Chinaman as his son." To prevent and expose such fraud, the immigration officials developed an elaborate system of questioning and cross-checking.

First, inspectors interrogated the witnesses and the applicants separately, asking detailed questions about the aliens' backgrounds. They asked such minute points as how many steps there were out of a family's back door, where an applicant had sat in the village schoolhouse, what an applicant's mother looked like, and where the rice bin was kept in the family home. Often the answers of the applicant and those of the witness disagreed on small points, and that was sufficient grounds for rejecting an application to enter the country. The procedure was deliberately intimidating, and many legitimate immigrants were turned away because they became confused or frightened.

One Chinese woman, identified as Mrs. Chin, recalled her arrival at Angel Island in 1927 as bewildering. "I was interrogated one day for several hours," she reported. "They asked me so much, I broke out in a sweat. Sometimes they would try to trip you: 'Your husband said such-and-such and now you say this?' But the answer was out already and it was too late to take it back, so I couldn't say anything about it. If they said you were wrong, then it was up to them whether to land you or not." Sometimes, as one immigrant noted, the result was that illegal aliens, who had coached their witness carefully, were allowed to enter while legal ones, who were unprepared for so minute an interrogation, were rejected. Chinese minister Wu Ting-fang, in a letter to the U.S. secretary of state published in the records of the 57th Congress in 1901, protested this "inquisition" bitterly. "The manner of these examinations is reprehensible," he wrote. "Men and women are examined alone, neither their friends nor a lawyer in their behalf being allowed to be present, and the interpreter is generally a foreigner. There are so many dialects of the Chinese language that one interpreter can not understand them all, hence misunderstandings often arise and injustice is inflicted."

The Government Takes Control: Federal Legislation

There was little federal legislation dealing with immigration for the first hundred years of American history. There were two reasons for this: first, the U.S. Constitution was unclear about whether the federal government had the authority to regulate immigration; and second, new arrivals were welcomed in the young nation, and few people felt any need to regulate their entry. As individual colonies had had the power to determine the eligibility of new residents, individual states made their own laws on the subject. It was not until 1819 that Congress passed what has been called the first significant federal legislation on the subject of immigration. In that year, a law was passed requiring that a full report be made of all new arrivals, recording their names, ages, and occupations. As a result of this law, we have a complete record of all legal immigrants from 1820. The law—the first of the "passenger acts"—also provided for the comfort and safety of steerage passengers at sea by limiting the number permitted on any one vessel arriving from abroad. Four other passenger acts were passed during the succeeding four decades to remedy overcrowding and other abuses on immigrant ships.

The western frontier and the need for labor in the cities kept the United States's door open to immigrants until after the Civil War, and in fact the government openly supported immigration with a law, passed in 1864, establishing the legality of contract labor. By this statute, aliens were permitted to pledge their labor for a term of up to one year to pay for their passage. The bill also made the first move toward federal control by providing for a commissioner of immigration. Signed by President Abraham Lincoln, it was the first and only U.S. law specifically encouraging immigration. It was passed without much difficulty in response to a clear need for laborers on the railroad and soldiers in the Civil War.

As the war ended, the law was no longer felt to be necessary, and it was repealed in 1868. However, the government's support of a liberal immigration policy did not change. That same year, the committee on foreign affairs in the House of Representatives strongly urged passage of a bill in favor of opening the doors of the nation still wider, stating in its report, "We want people to fill up these States and Territories; we want land cultivated, that wealth and plenty may abound. . . . We desire . . . to let the toiling and almost starving millions of foreign lands know, that in America there are free homes, where every citizen, be he native or naturalized, is guaranteed protection in his right to life, liberty, and property. . . ."

That was the position of the federal government, but the public was already beginning to oppose it. Increasing pressure from organized labor resulted in the bill being defeated. Laws excluding immigrants for various reasons followed. In general, they were similar to laws that had been in force in individual colonies, and later states, and were based on "quality control"—a desire to maintain a high physical, social, and moral character in the populace. On March 3, 1875, the government enacted a law closing the door to three further classes of applicant. Section 5 of that act declared, "That it shall be unlawful for aliens of the following classes to immigrate into the United States, namely, persons who are undergoing a sentence for conviction in their own country of felonious crimes. . . . women imported for purposes of prostitution." In Section 4 the act declared it a felony to import any "coolie," as Chinese laborers were called, into the United States.

Quality-control statutes increased during the 1880s to include other "undesirable classes," serving both to upgrade the level of newcomer and to limit the flow of arrivals. In 1882 immigration reached the unprecedented total of 788,992—a number it did not reach again until 1903—and organized labor redoubled its efforts at blocking the competition of foreign workers. On August 3 of that year, Congress submitted to public pressure in passing what has been called "the first inclusive federal immigration act."

The law began by levying a duty on every passenger not a citizen of the United States who came from a foreign port. This head tax was officially to help "to defray the expense of regulating immigration into the United States," but its principal objective was to prevent the entry of the poor. The duty stipulated in Section 1 of the act was 50 cents, but the amount was to increase in several amendments over the next few years.

Section 2 placed the supervision of foreign immigration in the hands of the secretary of the treasury and directed that department to designate the state

President Chester A. Arthur (1881–85) vetoes the Chinese Exclusion Act in 1882. His courageous effort failed, and the act was passed over his veto. *(New York Public Library Print Collection)*

boards or commissions to take charge of immigration through their ports. The state commissioners were authorized to examine all incoming aliens. "[I]f on such examination," the law stated, "there shall be found among such passengers any convict, lunatic, idiot or any person unable to take care of himself or herself without becoming a public charge, they shall report the same in writing . . . and such persons shall not be permitted to land."

In 1885 there was a marked increase in the influence of organized labor, and employers began to import large numbers of unskilled workers from Europe under contract to work for substantially lower wages than U.S. laborers demanded. To meet this problem, Congress further tightened its restrictive legislation with the Alien Contract Labor Law of 1885, amended and tightened in 1887 and 1888, prohibiting such contracts. "All persons included in this prohibition," according to the law of 1887, "upon arrival, shall be sent back to the nations to which they belong and from whence they came. . . . The expense of such return . . . shall be borne by the owners of the vessels in which they came." The next year, the last loophole in this law was closed by requiring that those imported under contract from Mexico or Canada (and thus not by vessels) be returned "at the expense of the person previously contracting for his services." These laws effectively diminished the flow of immigrant labor and added the threat of deportation to the growing body of laws restricting or excluding immigration.

In 1891 the law establishing the Bureau of Immigration and Naturalization (the forerunner of the Immigration and Naturalization Service, or INS) added to the list of those denied entry "persons suffering from a loathsome or dangerous contagious disease," paupers, polygamists, and persons whose passage had been paid for by others. By the act of March 3, 1891 (26 Stat. 1084), the number of excluded classes was increased to seven, besides Chinese laborers. The law also required all new arrivals to take medical examinations to make sure that they were not "diseased." Twenty-four ports of entry were officially established, and the federal bureau assumed the responsibility of inspecting all arrivals at these ports. Section 6 of the law stated that bringing into the United States or aiding another to bring in any alien not entitled to enter was a misdemeanor punishable by a fine of up to $1,000 or imprisonment of up to a year, or both. The law further made provision for inspection stations along the borders of Canada and Mexico. The act of 1891 was the most comprehensive immigration law made until that time.

The next year, the Chinese Exclusion Act, which had barred Chinese laborers from entry for 10 years, expired. In a presidential election year, both parties agreed to its renewal for another decade, and an extension of the act was passed in 1892. The only debate in Congress was the means of preventing the illegal entry of the Chinese. The solution to that problem was the passage of the Geary Act, authored by California Democrat Thomas Geary and supported by a great majority of his colleagues in the Senate. The act extended Chinese exclusion for another 10 years and required that all Chinese laborers entitled to residence in the United States obtain a certificate establishing their eligibility. To get such a certificate, Chinese workers had to be fingerprinted and had to present the testimony of one credible white witness. Those who did not register were subject to a one-year prison sentence and then deportation to China. The credibility of witnesses was often challenged. Like the immigrants seeking admission at Angel Island, many people who were entitled to live in the country because they were born in the United States or were the spouses or children of American citizens found it difficult to obtain such a document. Unregistered Chinese were denied bail or the right to a trial. The law ordered that any Chinese charged with being without a valid certificate be taken before a U.S. judge, who had the authority to order his immediate deportation.

The act was very controversial and deeply offended the Chinese. The Chinese vice consul in San Francisco protested that requiring a license to remain in the United States put his countrymen "on the level of your dogs." Asian businessmen also complained that the requirement subjected nonlaborers to harassment. As a letter reprinted in the *Congressional Record* in 1893 noted, "A Chinese merchant who has resided in San Francisco for many years and who may desire to go to New York on business can be stopped at every little hamlet, village, and town on the line of the railroad and arrested on the charge of being a laborer who has failed to register." The law was challenged in the courts, but without success. Lawyers acting for the Chinese argued that while the government had the right to exclude Chinese entry to the United States, it did not have the right to expel those already legally in the country. The case failed in the lower courts and was appealed. In 1893 the Supreme Court, in a 5-3 decision, upheld the constitutionality of the Geary Act. It was not until World War II that the ban on Chinese immigration to the United States was brought to an end, in recognition of China's contribution to America's battle in the pacific against Japan, the common enemy. The repeal of the last special restrictions to Chinese immigration was passed by Congress, after long debate, in 1943.

Further regulations were passed into law in 1893, 1894, and 1895 to clarify and strengthen the growing list of restrictive statutes. By the end of the century, the effort seemed to have succeeded; the total immigration into the United States during the 1890s was some 3.6 million, about 1.5 million fewer than in the decade before. But even with these exclusionary policies, the turn of the century saw a sizable increase in new arrivals. Strict anti-immigrationists were alarmed by the quantity, but many were more concerned about the quality of the newcomers. Theodore Roosevelt put it clearly in 1902: "We cannot have too much immigration of the right kind, and we should have none at all of the wrong kind." There were three classes of immigrants that worried Roosevelt: the poor, the uneducated, and, above all, the subversive. As he announced in his first message to Congress after assuming the presidency in 1901, "First, we should aim to exclude absolutely . . . all persons who are known to believe in anarchistic principles. . . . The second object of a proper immigration law ought to be to secure by a careful . . . educational test some intelligent capacity to appreciate American institutions. . . . Finally, all persons should be excluded who are below a certain standard of economic fitness. . . . This would stop the influx of cheap labor."

Roosevelt's views reflected a growing national desire for "quality control" legislation. In 1902 a meeting was called of the immigration commissioners of all the American ports of entry. Their report summarized the general feeling of what was needed to keep out "the wrong kind" of immigrant. The result was the comprehensive Act of March 3, 1903, whose 39 detailed sections attempted to seal any loophole by which undesirables might gain entry into the country. It added substantially to the list of excluded classes, barring "all idiots," epileptics, and the "insane" (defined as "insane persons, persons who have been insane within five years previous, and persons who have had two or more attacks of insanity at any time previously"). It also barred prostitutes, paupers and professional beggars, "persons afflicted with a loathsome or with a dangerous contagious disease, and those convicted of a felony or other crime or misdemeanor involving moral turpitude." Other classes of undesirables included polygamists and "anarchists, or persons who believe in or advocate the overthrow by force or violence of the government of the United States or of all government or of all forms of law, or the assassination of public officials." The addition of anarchists to the list was a response to the assassination, in 1901, of President McKinley by an American-born anarchist, Leon Czolgosz.

The new law also reinforced the earlier statute prohibiting contract labor by rejecting "any person whose ticket or passage is paid for with the money of another, or who is assisted by others to come." The head tax, applicable to "every passenger not a citizen of the United States, the Dominion of Canada, the Republic of Cuba, or the Republic of Mexico," was raised to $2.

From year to year, it became harder and harder to get into the country. On February 20, 1907, a law was passed that raised the head tax to $4 and further increased the number of excluded classes of immigrant. This law contained 42 sections, repeating the prohibitions of prostitutes, polygamists, anarchists, felons, etc. In case the exclusion of idiots and the insane was not clear enough in the 1903 law, the new statute added "imbeciles," the "feebleminded," and those "with a mental or physical defect which may affect their ability to earn a living" to the list. Tuberculosis was specified among the "loathsome or dangerous contagious diseases." With only 1,200 employees in 1907, the bureau was not well equipped to enforce these often vaguely defined restrictions with much precision or consistency.

The Literacy Test

Probably no element of restrictive legislation in the body of immigration law was as controversial as the literacy test, an idea that had been proposed repeatedly since the 1880s. Anti-immigrationists—especially those in favor of diminishing the "new immigration"—supported Roosevelt's idea of adding an educational qualification to the various mental, moral, and physical requirements that previous immigration acts included. The people of the poor countries that fed the new immigration were unlikely to pass a literacy test (given in their own language). The countries of northern and western Europe had languages and cultures much closer to those of the United States, and their educational systems were more advanced than those of the countries of the new immigration. According to statistics compiled by the Immigration Commission in 1909, the percentage of illiteracy among Scandinavian immigrants from 1899 to 1909 was .4, among the English 1.1, among the Irish 2.7, and among Germans 5.1, while the rate among Polish immigrants was 35.4, among Italians 54.2, and among Portuguese 68.2. It was estimated that such a test would exclude as many as 25 percent of the applicants, heavily weighted in favor of the old immigration but without being obviously racist.

The reasoning behind the proposed test was stated clearly by Elihu Root, senator from New York and former secretary of state. In 1912 Senator Root told Congress: "I think there is a general and well-founded feeling that we have been taking in immigrants . . . in recent years rather more rapidly than we have been assimilating them. . . . The specific reason why I think this educational requirement will, as a whole, be a great advantage is that it will especially effect a very large immigration from southeastern Europe, which has in recent years furnished the unassimilated element. . . . It is manifest that the imposition of the literacy test will bar practically one-half of this class of immigration. It will bar that part which by and large is the least intelligent, the least capable of being manufactured into good American citizens, and the most dangerous as a new and unassimilated element in our body politic."

The idea of a literacy test appeared before Congress 39 times over a period of more than a quarter of a century before it passed into law. During the decade that followed the Geary Act of 1893, bills excluding people unable to read had passed one or the other house of Congress seven times. Three times such a proposed law was approved by a large majority of both houses and failed to pass only because of presidential vetoes. In 1897 President Cleveland rejected the proposal, which he called "illiberal, narrow, and un-American," because he considered it counter to the country's tradition of hospitality to the oppressed.

In 1907, after several more unsuccessful attempts to pass a literacy bill, Congress organized a joint congressional-presidential commission to study the impact of immigration on the country. In 1911 the commission issued a detailed report outlining its recommendations. They included, of course, exclusion of all the familiar classes of "undesirables" and added a few more. Specifically, the report noted "an over supply of unskilled labor in the industries of the country as a whole" and

Britain's White Star Line advertises "the completeness and comfort" of its ships' accommodations, with fares to the United States from about $30 to $100. *(American Museum of Immigration, U.S. National Park Service)*

urged legislation to restrict "further admission of such unskilled labor." The first of its recommendations to bring about that restriction was "the exclusion of those unable to read or write in some language."

A bill based on that report was proposed on February 14, 1913. It was approved by both the Senate and the House of Representatives but was vetoed by President Taft, who quoted a letter from Charles Nagel, his secretary of commerce and labor, in his explanation. Among other criticisms of the law, Nagel commented, "No doubt the law would exclude a considerable percentage of immigrations from southern Italy, among the Poles, the Mexicans, and the Greeks. This exclusion would embrace probably in large part undesirable but also a great many desirable people. . . . The people who come from the countries named are frequently illiterate because opportunities have been denied them. The oppression with which these people have to contend in modern times . . . consists of a denial of the opportunity to acquire reading and writing . . . and these immigrants in coming to our shore are really striving to free themselves from the conditions under which they have been compelled to live."

President William Howard Taft (1909–13) vetoed the literacy test for immigrants in 1913. *(New York Public Library Print Collection)*

Two years later, another bill including the literacy test was passed in both houses and was again vetoed, this time by President Woodrow Wilson. Wilson's message focused on the principal objective of the test and, like Cleveland's veto, condemned the test as inconsistent with American policy. "Hitherto we have gen-

President Woodrow Wilson vetoed a bill that required immigrants to pass a literacy test before being granted admission to the United States. *(Library of Congress, Prints and Photographs Division [LC-USZ62-107577])*

erously kept our doors open to all who were not unfitted by reason of disease or incapacity for self-support," Wilson observed. "In this bill it is proposed to turn away from tests of character and of quality and to impose tests which exclude and restrict; for the new tests here embodied are not tests of quality or of character or of personal fitness, but tests of opportunity. Those who come seeking opportunity are not to be admitted unless they have already had one of the chief opportunities they seek—the opportunity of education."

Wilson's veto did not discourage the proponents of the literacy test, however, and on February 5, 1917, a new act incorporating it was presented to Congress. World War I had already reduced immigration from Europe; the numbers from July 15, 1915, to June 30, 1916, were less than a third of those during the preceding year. But as America prepared to enter the conflict, nationalist feeling grew, and Europe was viewed with distrust and fear. Again, the restrictionist legislation was passed by a large majority. The president vetoed it again, but this time the two houses mustered enough support to override his veto, and the bill became law, known as the Asia Barred Zone and Literary Act. It increased the head tax to $8—a considerable barrier to many—and further increased the excluded classes by adding "persons of constitutional psychopath inferiority, persons with chronic alcoholism, vagrants, [and] stowaways," among others. The law also contained a clause closing the door to almost all Asiatic immigration not already included in the Chinese Exclusion Act and the Gentlemen's Agreement with Japan, effectively barring entry from India, Siam (modern-day Thailand), Indochina, Afghanistan, and Arabia, as well as New Guinea, Borneo, Sumatra, and Java. Containing 38 sections, it was the strictest immigration act yet passed.

Although it reflected widespread American sentiment, the 1917 law received criticism, both for its selective nature, targeting the least advantaged applicants for entry, and for the way in which it was administered. Its most important addition to excluded classes, the literacy test, was viewed by many as both unjust and ineffective. It specified that "all aliens over sixteen years of age, physically capable of reading," be able to read "not less than thirty nor more than forty words in ordinary use," in the language he or she chose. But it also required the reading of a passage from the Old Testament of the Bible. The selection widely used was from Psalm 7: 13–15: "He hath also prepared for him the instruments of death; he ordaineth his arrows against his persecutors. Behold, he travaileth with iniquity and hath conceived mischief, and brought forth falsehood. He made a pit, and digged it, and is fallen into the ditch which he made." These were not exactly "words in ordinary use."

The Red Scare

Drastic as the new law was, it did not greatly reduce the number of immigrants. For one thing, the literacy test proved very difficult to administer, since it was virtually impossible to find interpreters to administer it in all the many languages of the thousands of immigrants. It is reported that in 1922 only 1,249 people—384 of them Mexicans—were refused admission to the United States because of an inability to read, while 10,743 who could neither read nor write were admitted. The next year 11,356 illiterates got in and only 2,095, including 602 Mexicans and 672 Finns, were turned away. Clearly the law was not doing the job it was intended for.

Organized labor, concerned with the competition of foreign workers willing to work for lower wages, continued to press for reduced immigration, and so did a growing body of people fearful of political subversion. Immigration was naturally limited by the war, which made shipping difficult, but the numbers increased rapidly after the armistice in 1918. The country, fearing both the effect of postwar refugees on the labor force and the danger of radical foreign ideas, renewed its prewar isolationist spirit. As an article in the *Literary Digest* (December 18, 1920) put it, "In addition to citing our already existing unemployment problem as a reason for checking the inrush of foreigners, . . . a considerable number of newcomers are revolutionary radicals who add to the ominous forces of social unrest; . . . and failure to recognize this fact may result in the loss of the 'American type.'"

The fear of "revolutionary radicals"—political dissidents inspired by the recent Russian Revolution, seen as advocating the violent overthrow of the government— also played an important role in anti-immigration feeling as postwar immigration resumed. Although the number of communists in the United States after the war was estimated at no more than 100,000, they seemed to pose a threat of repeating the Russian experience. Associated with the militant fringe of organized labor, they were active in a wave of strikes, and the image of wild-eyed, bomb-throwing anarchists became a stock figure in political cartoons. According to one businessman in a letter written to Wilson's attorney general A. Mitchell Palmer in 1919, "There is hardly a respectable citizen of my acquaintance who does not believe that we are on the verge of armed conflict in this country."

The fact that most of the radicals were immigrants added to the wartime fear of foreign saboteurs in increasing nativist sentiment. Palmer was convinced that the Jew, the Slav, and the Italian were bent on revolution. "Out of the sly and crafty eyes of many of them leap cupidity, cruelty, insanity, and crime," he stated; "from their lopsided faces, sloping brows, and misshapen features may be recognized the unmistakable criminal type." In August 1919 he established the General Intelligence Division of the Department of Justice (renamed the Federal Bureau of Investigation in 1924) under J. Edgar Hoover to investigate radical activities. In November of that year, Palmer (who had presidential ambitions) ordered raids on the anarchist organization known as the Union of Russian Workers in a dozen cities. Sudden and sensational, they resulted in 650 arrests, and although only 43 Russians were ever convicted, the impact on the public was electric. Two months later, armed with 3,000 warrants, Palmer repeated the attack on the offices and homes of suspected foreign agitators in 33 cities. These raids (which became known as Palmer raids) netted about 6,000 suspects, but most of them were citizens and thus not subject to deportation. Public opinion began to turn against Palmer, and the hysteria of this first Red Scare soon faded.

Nevertheless, suspicion and fear of immigrant radicalism remained widespread. No event so dramatically demonstrated this national paranoia as the controversial Sacco-Vanzetti case. In 1920, two naturalized Italian immigrants, Nicola Sacco, a shoemaker, and Bartolomeo Vanzetti, a fish peddler, were accused of killing two employees of a Braintree, Massachusetts, shoe factory during a robbery. They were both anarchists, though neither had any record of violence or political agitation. There was little evidence against them—the $16,000 stolen from the factory was never found—but so great was the antiforeign feeling of the time that they were quickly convicted and sentenced to death. There is still some question about their guilt or innocence of the crime, but there is no doubt of the injustice of the trial. Their judge, Webster Thayer, reportedly referred to them as "anarchist bastards" and virtually directed the jury to find them guilty. Despite a wave of liberal protest that attracted worldwide attention and sympathy, they were executed in 1927.

The Cleveland, Ohio, Board of Education offers free classes to its immigrants to prepare them for citizenship. *(American Museum of Immigration, U.S. National Park Service)*

Whether or not they were guilty, most historians agree that they were put to death because they were radicals and Italians.

"Race Suicide"

Arguments in favor of restricting immigration during the late 19th and early 20th centuries had been largely based on economics, religion, health, and politics.

Foreigners, it was felt, competed for jobs, threatened Protestant traditions, carried diseases, and fomented revolution. By the first decades of the new century, however, another and more deeply disturbing argument had surfaced: that the new immigrants were racially inferior.

The idea that moral character and intellectual ability were determined by race was not new, of course. It had been raised as an argument against the "Yellow Peril" of Chinese and Japanese immigration in the middle of the 19th century. But it was essentially the poverty, the Catholic infiltration, the threat of crime, and the radical political ideas of immigrants that had frightened the American public. It was not until about 1890 that the pseudoscientific theory of hereditary racial types became a weapon in the battle against open immigration. Basing their thinking on the new science of physical anthropology, scholars divided Europeans into a northern Teutonic race, a central Alpine race, and a southern Mediterranean race with fixed physical and mental characteristics. It was the Teutonic, or Nordic race, the argument went, that had made the United States great, and by allowing inferior strains to infiltrate its pure stock, the country would be committing "race suicide."

One of the theory's most prestigious proponents, lawyer, naturalist, and social leader Madison Grant, wrote in *The Passing of the Great Race* (1916), "The Nordics are, all over the world, a race of soldiers, sailors, adventurers and explorers, but above all of rulers, organizers, and aristocrats." Using the language of stock breeders, he pointed out that when different races mate, the "lower traits" always dominated in the offspring. Thus, he warned, if the government continued to allow the inferior Alpine and the Mediterranean peoples—and, still worse, the Slav, the Jew, the African, and the Asian—to enter the country, we would dilute and debase the aristocratic Nordic strain. A psychologist claimed "scientific" evidence that the "intellectual superiority of our Nordic group over the Alpine, Mediterranean and Negro groups has been demonstrated." One of Grant's followers described the inevitable result of continued indiscriminate immigration as "a hybrid race of people as worthless and futile as the good-for-nothing mongrels of Central America and southeastern Europe."

Grant went on to become a leader of the Immigration Restriction League and to have a profound influence on both the thought and the legislation of the 1920s. He was a close friend of Theodore Roosevelt, came from a prominent family, and had the support of several notable scientists and academics, as well as of such distinguished political figures as Massachusetts senator Henry Cabot Lodge. Together, such people lent authority and respectability to racism, and the country was ready to embrace their flattering picture of America as a stronghold of pure Nordic blood and genes threatened by the barbarian hordes of Europe, Asia, Africa, and Latin America. After the war the Ku Klux Klan resurfaced and eagerly accepted their theories. Originally based in the South and violently opposed to African Americans and Catholics, the Klan became a powerful national force and added immigrants to its list of targets. In the 1920s it claimed to have millions of members throughout the country.

Anti-Semitism also took on new life in the United States after World War I, when the ugly image of the Jew as a sinister financial manipulator was darkened still further by a reputation for political radicalism. The Klan had always taken an anti-Semitic stand, and others eagerly joined in the assault, socially, professionally, and politically. Automobile manufacturer Henry Ford contributed to the evil reputation of Jews through his newspaper the *Dearborn* (Michigan) *Independent*, which printed a series of editorials accusing the Jews of an international conspiracy to topple the American government and dominate the world. The newspaper campaign, the longest and most intense in American history, lasted from 1920 to 1922, was resumed in 1924, and was dropped only when business pressures prevented Ford from continuing it. The essays appearing under his name were collected in a book, *The International Jew* (1920), that had considerable influence on U.S. immigration policy and later found a wide audience within the emerging Nazi Party in Germany.

Despite the literacy test and the ever-expanding list of exclusionary statutes, immigrants continued to pour into the country. In 1921 more than 800,000 arrived, and it was obvious that many more were preparing to follow them. A

Henry Ford (1863–1947) opposed immigration in various anti-Semitic publications. *(Library of Congress, Prints and Photographs Division [LC-USZ62-111278])*

congressional committee reported grimly, "If there were in existence a ship that could hold 3,000,000 human beings, the 3,000,000 Jews of Poland would board it to escape to America." The Red Scare, the threat of racial pollution, and the wave of renewed anti-Semitism had set the stage for profound changes in U.S. immigration law. The quality-control statutes had failed and legislators of both parties were ready to try different means to solve what was now universally described as "the immigrant problem." As historians Leonard Dinnerstein and David M. Reimers noted in *Ethnic Americans* (1988), "Given the intense nativism of the 1920s, the issue was not *whether* there would be immigration restriction but *what form* it would take."

In 1921 a new formula was devised for stemming the tide of immigration, one not based on selection but on simple numerical limitation. With the quota laws, America entered an entirely new phase of immigration legislation.

Chronicle of Events

1890

- *April 18*: Castle Garden, long considered inadequate to the volume of immigrants entering through it, is closed. It remains vacant for six years and in 1896 reopens as a municipal aquarium. The Bureau of Immigration processes immigrants until 1892 in the barge office, a landing place in Battery Park close to Castle Garden.

1892

- *January 1*: The Bureau of Immigration opens a federal immigrant receiving station on Ellis Island in New York Harbor.

1897

- President Cleveland vetoes an immigration act containing a literacy test.

1904

- Angel Island immigrant receiving station is opened in San Francisco, California.

1907

- Congress establishes the United States Immigration Commission—popularly known as the Dillingham Commission for its director, Senator William Paul Dillingham—to study the impact of immigration on the country.
- *February 24*: In a second Gentlemen's Agreement, Japan promises to withhold passports to Japanese and Korean laborers seeking to come to the United States.

1908

- *November 30:* The United States and Japan sign the Root-Takahira Agreement, signed by U.S. secretary of state Elihu Root and Japanese ambassador Takahira Kogoro, reaffirming recognition of the territorial sovereignty of China (the "Open Door Policy"), Japan's recognition of the U.S. right to annex Hawaii and the Philippines, and Japan's right to annex Korea and southern Manchuria.

1909

- *March 4:* William Howard Taft is inaugurated president of the United States.

1910

- The U.S. Immigration Commission initiates an investigation of the "white slave" traffic in response to complaints that girls are being imported from Europe for purposes of prostitution.

1913

- The California Alien Land Act bars noncitizens from owning land. The law is directed at Japanese farmers.

The reception building on Ellis Island after 1903. This splendid structure was the first building to hold arrivals from Europe after their long, painful voyage. *(American Museum of Immigration, U.S. National Park Service)*

1915

- *January 28*: President Wilson vetoes a new bill requiring a literacy test for immigrants.

1917

- *November 6:* Alexander Kerensky, prime minister of Russia, is forced from office by Vladimir Lenin, Leon Trotsky, and Joseph Stalin, who form a communist government.

1919

- *January 29*: The 18th Amendment to the Constitution, prohibiting the sale of alcohol, is ratified. The law goes into effect January 29, 1920.
- *June 28*: The Treaty of Versailles is signed, bringing World War I to an end.
- *August 31*: A radical faction of the Socialist Party forms a separate group in sympathy with the Russian government. In the 1920s this groups organizes as the U.S. Communist Party.
- *September 22*: U.S. steelworkers, organized by William Z. Foster, a founder of the U.S. Communist Party, strike for shorter hours. Joined by other workers, the total number of strikers reaches 365,000 before the U.S. Army crushes the strike four months later.
- *December 22*: In response to a wave of anti-communist hysteria, Attorney General A. Mitchell Palmer orders a series of raids on groups suspected of including or encouraging alien anarchists. About 250 people are deported to Russia.

1920

- The 14th census of the United States reports a population of 106,021,537, nearly 15 percent larger than that of a decade before. It is estimated that 5,736,000, roughly 5 percent of the population, are foreign-born, showing a slight decline since the previous census. The iliteracy rate for those more than 10 years of age has shrunk from 7.7 percent to 6 percent. For the first time, the urban population of the United States is larger than the rural.
- A bill to suspend all immigration is introduced by Republican representative Albert Johnson, the chairman of the House Committee on Immigration and Naturalization. It is approved by the House of Representatives but voted down in the Senate.
- *January 2*: Federal agents make a second sweep of suspected anarchists, arresting 2,700 nationwide. The raids continue for five months.
- *May 5*: Nicola Sacco and Bartolomeo Vanzetti, Italian immigrants and political radicals, are charged with the murder of an employee of a shoe factory in Braintree, Massachusetts, during a payroll robbery.
- *May 8*: The American Socialist Party meets and nominates labor leader Eugene V. Debs for president. Debs has been in prison since 1918 for a violation of the Sedition Act of that year prohibiting pacifist opposition to World War I. Debs later polls almost 1 million votes in November.
- *May 20*: Congress officially declares U.S. involvement in World War I against Germany to be ended, but President Wilson vetoes the resolution.
- *June 5*: An act is approved ordering the exclusion and expulsion of "members of the anarchistic and similar classes." The law defines such classes as "aliens who advise, advocate, or teach, or who are members of or affiliated with any organization, association, society or group, that advises, advocates, or teaches, opposition to all organized government."
- *August 26*: The 19th Amendment to the Constitution, granting women the right to vote, is ratified.
- *December 26*: Congress passes a bill providing for "the treatment in hospitals of diseased alien seamen," charging all expenses for such treatment to the owners, agents, consignees, or masters of the vessels.

1921

- A revived version of the Ku Klux Klan surfaces in the South. Its terrorist activities against African Americans, Catholics, and aliens spread to the Middle West and the North.
- *March 4*: Warren G. Harding is inaugurated the 29th president of the United States.
- *May 19*: Congress approves the Emergency Quota Act ("the Johnson Bill"), setting immigration quotas of three percent for each country represented of the population from that country resident in the United States in 1910. The total limit per year is 357,803, deliberately weighted in favor of those from northern and western Europe. With this act, the "new immigration" comes to an end.
- *July 2*: By a joint resolution, Congress ratifies the terms of the Versailles Treaty ending World War I.
- *July 14*: Sacco and Vanzetti are convicted of murder, initiating a worldwide controversy about whether they were convicted because they were aliens and radicals rather than on substantial evidence.
- *November 12*: A Conference in Washington, D.C., that includes representatives of the United States, Great Britain, France, Italy, and Japan establishes several treaties of mutual support, agreeing on military limitations, rights to Pacific Island territories, and an Open Door policy in China.

Eyewitness Testimony

We born in Russia, who left that land during the pogroms, had our full share of troubles till we got here. But even here we did not find the peace and quiet we were seeking. In Branford [Connecticut], there are twenty Jewish families. All work in the factories and earn from seven and a half to nine dollars a week.

The work we do in the factories may be compared to the labor of our ancestors in Egypt—hard drudge toil. . . . In America, the life of a laborer is regulated by his work schedule. If he comes a few minutes late to work, he finds the doors closed and he loses a day's wages. The same happens to the worker who stops work a minute before the designated time. The worker spends his days and years running to work and working. Even when he is ill, he pushes himself to work, fearing that his absence will be used as a cause for dismissal.

Even after six days of toil, on the American sabbath, which is on Sunday, we have no respite. No sooner does the Jew appear on the street—even if elegantly dressed—the cry goes up from all sides, "Here comes the sheeny!" Sometimes, the boys run after him and throw stones. Only in one way is it better here than in Russia—our homes are not attacked, the window panes are not smashed. . . .

Description of the conditions of life for Jews in Connecticut, published in the Yiddish periodical Ha-Magid, *February 11, 1889, in Karp,* Golden Door to America *(1976), pp. 169–170.*

Jewish refugees from Russia get their first view of the Statue of Liberty in this 1892 engraving in *Frank Leslie's Illustrated Weekly. (American Museum of Immigration, U.S. National Park Service)*

To close the avenues of this free and liberty-loving country, that has always opened its gates to the downtrodden and unjustly persecuted, would be against the underlying genius and theory of our glorious and beloved Constitution.

Neither the letter nor the spirit of the laws of our country require us to "close the gates of mercy on mankind.". . .

[A]bout ten years since, in consequence of enforcement of the cruel edicts recently again being carried out, a very large number of Russian Hebrews sought this land of liberty as a haven of rest. . . . To refuse asylum to such people by reason of misfortune would give the right to deny rescue of a shipwrecked crew cast on our shores by dire disaster. . . .

The Russian Hebrews are wrecked on their voyage of life; cast out on tempestuous oceans by inhuman machinations. National and international law should not interfere when humanity throws them life-preservers to save them from being engulfed by the waves, even of a sea of despair.

Simon Wolf, spokesman for four American Jewish organizations, July 27, 1891, an appeal to Secretary of the Treasury Charles Foster protesting the Congressional act excluding "paupers or persons likely to become a public charge" from immigration, in Karp, Golden Door to America *(1976), p. 92.*

Anyone who is desirous of knowing in practical detail the degrading effect of this constant importation of the lowest forms of labor can find a vivid picture of its results in the very interesting book just published by Mr. [Jacob] Riis, entitled *How the Other Half Lives.* The story which he tells of the condition of a large mass of the laboring population of New York is enough to alarm every thinking man; and this dreadful condition of things is intensified everyday by the steady inflow of immigration, which is constantly pulling down the wage of the working people of New York and affecting in a similar way the entire labor force of the United States.

Senator Henry Cabot Lodge, anti-immigration activist, in "The Restriction of Immigration," in North American Review, *Volume 152, (January 1892), p. 28.*

It is charged that immigrants furnish a larger percentage of paupers and criminals than the native element. This is probably true, but it is hardly because they are foreigners, but because they are the poorer half of society, and consequentially less able to cope with misfortune or to withstand temptation. It is not so creditable to a rich man to refrain from stealing a loaf of bread as a hungry one.

John B. Weber, commissioner of immigration at Ellis Island, in "Our National Dumping Ground: A Study of Immigration," in North American Review *(April 1892), p. 424.*

Our people had the worst possible jobs—jobs that paid little and were very uncertain. A stonemason worked ten hours a day for a dollar and a half—if there was work. When there was snow or rain or ice there was no work at all. During slack periods the men just hung around the house or played "boccie" in the vacant lot. . . . They did not talk about their troubles, but their games did not have their usual gusto. The children especially could sense their feeling of helplessness in this land which offered them little more than strangeness and hardship. . . .

Very early the essential difference between working hard in Italy and working hard in America became apparent to us who were young. In Italy it was work and work hard with no hope of any future. . . . But here in America we began to understand—faintly at first, without full comprehension—that there was a chance that another world existed beyond the tenements in which we lived and that it was just possible to reach out into that world and one day become a part of it. The possibility of going to high school, maybe even college, opened the vista of another life to us.

. . . Even I, as close as I was to the older people, could only imagine what it meant to them to leave "the golden years" behind to seek the elusive pot of gold at the end of the rainbow. No wonder the shrinking within themselves. No wonder the "living burial" in the graveyard filled with kindred spirits known as the slum area. Who but the few really bold and reckless and the strong could survive? For the others, what was left of their bubble but the water which came at the turn of a tap, the toilet in the hall, the electric light, the subway that rattled them to work for a nickel—and their children? Their children! That was it. The rewards for all this sacrifice would come through the children.

Leonard Covello, Italian-born high school teacher and principal who arrived in 1896 at the age of nine, recalling his early days in New York City, in The Heart Is the Teacher *(1958), pp. 246–247.*

The entrance into our political, social and industrial life of such vast masses of peasantry, degraded below our utmost conceptions, is a matter which no intelligent patriot can look upon without the gravest apprehension and alarm. These people have no history behind them which is of a nature to give encouragement.

Francis Walker, a Yale professor of economics and anti-immigration activist, in "Restriction of Immigration," in Atlantic Monthly *(June 1896), p. 822.*

A man with filthy hands filled our hats or handkerchiefs with moldy prunes. Another thrust two lumps of bread into our hands. Supervising the distribution was a foul-mouthed Bowery tough who danced upon the table and poured forth upon us torrents of abuse, blasphemous abuse. I saw him drag one old man, a long-bearded Polish Jew, past the barrel of prunes by the hair of his face. I saw him kick another emigrant, a German, on the head with a heavy boot.

An account by a reporter disguised as an immigrant of the treatment given immigrants at the barge office, in The London Express, *quoted in the* New York Times, *July 29, 1900.*

Two years ago I came to this place, Brownsville [in Brooklyn], where so many of my people are, and where I have friends. I got work in a factory making underskirts—all sorts of cheap underskirts like cotton and calico for summer and woolen for the winter, but never silk, satin or velvet underskirts. I earned $4.20 a week and lived on $2 a week. . . .

I got a room in the house of some friends who lived near the factory. I pay $1 a week for the room and am allowed to do light housekeeping—that is, cook my meals in it. . . . My food for a week costs a dollar, and I have the rest of the money to do as I like with. I am earning $5.50 a week now and will probably get another increase soon.

Sadie Frowne, a Jewish immigrant from Poland, in "Sweatshop Girl," in Independent, *Volume LIV (September 25, 1902), pp. 2281–2282.*

Now and then I had heard things about America—that it was a far-off country where everybody was rich and that Italians went there and made plenty of money, so that they could return to Italy and live in pleasure ever after. One day I met a young man who pulled out a handful of gold and told me he had made that in America in a few days.

. . . We came to Brooklyn to a wooden house . . . that was full of Italians from Naples. Bartolo had a room on the third floor and there were fifteen men in the room, all boarding with Bartolo. . . .

Bartolo told us to go out and pick rags and get bottles. He gave us bags and hooks and showed us the ash barrels. On the streets where the fine houses are the people are very careless and put out good things, like mattresses and umbrellas, clothes, hats and boots. We brought all these to Bartolo and he made them new again and sold them on the sidewalk; but mostly we brought rags and bones. . . . Most of the men in our room worked at digging the sewer. Bartolo got them the work and they paid him about one quarter of their wages. Then he charged them for board and he bought the clothes for them, too. So they got little money after all. . . . [Bartolo] was what they call a padrone and is now a very rich man. The men that were living with him had just come to the country and could not speak English. . . . Bartolo told us all that we must work for him and that if we did not the police would come and put us in prison.

He gave us very little money, and our clothes were some of those that we found in the street. Still we had enough to eat and we had meat quite often, which we never had in Italy.

Rocco Corresca, an immigrant from Naples, recalling his first days in the United States, in "The Biography of a Bootblack," in Independent, *Volume LIV (December 4, 1902), pp. 2865–2866.*

It is impossible to understand the Lower East Side . . . or the attitudes of the people there toward American institutions without knowing the conditions from which these people came in eastern Europe. For instance, the average Russian Jew of the Lower East Side will declare that there is more religious liberty in Russia than in America. . . . As a matter of fact, there is perfect liberty in Russia as far as the exercise of his religion is concerned. The Jew is never interfered with in his religious observances. He simply loses, on account of them, all civic and economic rights. . . .

You can imagine the confusion in the immigrant's mind when he reaches America. He finds his church of no account whatever. No one cares what church he belongs to or whether he belongs to any church or not. . . . In place of finding the congregation all powerful and all embracing, he finds when he joins a congregation that he has simply joined a liberal society.

There are 332 little congregations east of Broadway and south of Houston Street. They are founded not on differing shades of belief but merely on the fact that the members came from different towns or villages in eastern Europe.

Dr. David Blaustein, director of the Educational Alliance, one of the leading New York settlement houses, in an interview in the New York Tribune, *August 16, 1903.*

This grim building was an immigration depot in Boston, 1905. *(American Museum of Immigration, U.S. National Park Service)*

Here [at the stairway in the main building of Ellis Island, known as the "stairs of separation"] families with different destinations are separated without a minute's warnings, and often never to see each other again. It seems heartless, but it is the only practical system, for if allowance was made for good-byes the examination and distribution process would be blocked then and there by a dreadful crush. Special officers would be necessary to tear relatives forcibly from each other's arms.

Broughton Brandenburg, describing part of the immigrant inspection procedure at Ellis Island, in Imported Americans *(1904), p. 220.*

All that I had heard of sugar was true. . . . There was lots of it, and it was cheap, and its use in the accepted form was no special extravagance. . . . True also were the stories of white bread. . . . Magnificently true were the stories of handkerchiefs and shoes. Here even I had to have a handkerchief, and not only on the Sabbath and on holidays but on weekdays. . . . Most true was the story of cigarette paper, too true. Nobody used wrapping paper, copybook paper, newspaper, for the rolling of cigarettes, and what was more hardly anybody made his own anyway. . . .

Russian-born journalist Maurice Hindus, who came to America at the age of 15 in 1905, in Green Worlds *(1938), in Neidle,* The New Americans *(1967), pp. 263–264.*

Clean they are, but there is neither breathing space below nor deck room above, and the 900 steerage passengers crowded into the hold of so elegant and roomy a steamer as the *Kaiser Wilhelm II*, of the North German Lloyd line, are positively packed like cattle, making a walk on deck when the weather is good, absolutely impossible, while to breathe clean air below in rough weather, when the hatches are down is an equal impossibility. . . .

On the whole, the steerage of the modern ship ought to be condemned as unfit for the transportation of human beings; and I do not hesitate to say that the German companies, and they provide best for their cabin passengers, are unjust if not dishonest towards the steerage.

The steerage ought to be and could be abolished by law. It is true that the Italian and Polish peasant may not be accustomed to better things at home and might not be happier in better surroundings or know how to use them;

but it is a bad introduction to our way of life to treat him as an animal when he is coming to us.

Edward A. Steiner, an Austrian immigrant who became a professor of Applied Christianity in Iowa, reporting on the conditions in steerage on a German immigrant ship, in On the Trail of the Immigrant *(1906), pp. 35–36.*

My first impressions of the new world will always remain etched in my memory, particularly that hazy October when I first saw Ellis Island.

The steamer *Florida*, fourteen days out of Naples, filled to capacity with 1,600 natives of Italy, weathered one of the worst storms in our captain's memory. . . . My mother, my stepfather, my brother Giuseppe, and my two sisters, Liberta and Helvetia, all of us together, happy that we had come through the storm safely, clustered on the foredeck for fear of separation and looked with wonder on this miraculous land of our dreams.

Passengers all about us were crowding against the rail. Jabbered conversation, sharp cries, laughs and cheers—a steady rising din filled the air. Mothers and fathers lifted up the babies so that they too could see, off to the left, the Statue of Liberty . . . looming shadowy through the mist, it brought silence to the decks of the *Florida*.

This symbol of America, this enormous expression of what we had all been taught was the inner meaning of this new country we were coming to—inspired awe in the hopeful immigrants.

Edward Corsi, Italian immigrant and later immigration commissioner at Ellis Island, recalling his arrival to the United States in 1907, in In the Shadow of Liberty *(1935), quoted in Reeves,* Ellis Island: Gateway to the American Dream *(1991), p. 52.*

. . . Nearly any hour on the East Side of New York City you can see them—pallid boy or spindling girl—their faces dulled, their backs bent under a heavy load of garments piled on head and shoulders, the muscles of the whole frame in a long strain. The boy always has bowlegs and walks with feet wide apart and wobbling. . . . Once at home, the little worker sits close to the inadequate window, struggling with the snarls of thread or shoving the needle through unyielding cloth. . . . And for this lifting of burdens, this giving of youth and strength, this sacrifice of all that should make childhood radiant, a child may add to the family purse from 50 cents to $1.50 a week. . . .

In New York City alone, 60,000 children are shut up in home sweatshops. This is a conservative estimate, based upon a recent investigation of the Lower East Side of Manhattan Island, south of 14th Street and east of the Bowery. Many of this immense host will never sit on a school bench. Is it not a cruel civilization that allows little hearts and little shoulders to strain under these grown-up responsibilities, while in the same city a pet cur is jeweled and pampered and aired on a fine lady's velvet lap on the beautiful boulevards?

American poet and journalist Edwin Markham, describing the life of children in the Jewish ghetto in "60,000 Children in Sweatshops," in Cosmopolitan Magazine *(January 1907).*

[My mother] loved quiet, and hated noise and confusion. Here [in New York's Little Italy] she never left the house unless she had to. She spent her days, and the waking hours of the nights, sitting at that one outside window staring up at the little patch of sky above the tenements. She was never happy here and, though she tried, could not adjust herself to the poverty and despair in which we had to live. . . . At the end of three years my mother, who had become ill, went back to Italy. . . . She lived only one year after returning to Sulmona.

An Italian immigrant recalling life in New York's Italian neighborhood around 1910, in Novatny, Ellis Island, Castle Garden, and the Great Migration to America *(1971), p. 88.*

The American-born wage earners and the foreign wage earners who have been here long enough to aspire to American standards are subject to the ruinous competition of an unending stream of men freshly arriving from foreign lands who are accustomed to so low a grade of living that they can underbid the wage earners established in this country and still save money. Whole communities, in fact whole regions, have witnessed a rapid deterioration in the mode of living of their working classes consequent on the incoming of the swarms of lifelong poverty-stricken aliens. Entire industries have seen the percentage of newly arrived laborers rising, until in certain regions few American men can at present be found among the unskilled.

. . . It is not on account of their assumed inferiority, or though any pusillanimous contempt for their abject poverty, that, most reluctantly, the lines have been drawn by America's workingmen against the indiscriminate admission of aliens to this country. It is simply a case of the self-preservation of the American working classes.

Samuel Gompers, president of the American Federation of Labor, in the AFL journal The American Federationist, *January 1911.*

I was told while in Syria that in America money could be picked up everywhere. That was not true. But I found that infinitely better things than money—knowledge, freedom, self-reliance, order, cleanliness, sovereign human rights, self-government, and all that these great accomplishments imply—can be picked up everywhere in America by whosoever earnestly seeks them. . . .

It was in that little town [in Ohio] . . . that I first heard "America" sung. The line "Land where my fathers died" stuck in my throat. I envied every person in the audience who could sing it truthfully. For years afterward, whenever I tried to sing those words, I seemed to myself to be an intruder. At last a new light broke upon my understanding. At last I was led to realize that the fathers of my new and higher self did live and die in America. I was born in Syria as a child, but I was born in America as a man. All those who fought for the freedom I enjoy, for the civic ideals I cherish, for the simple but lofty virtues of the typical American home which I love, were *my fathers!* . . .

Now, do you wish to know what riches I have gathered in the New World? I will tell you. These are my riches, which neither moth nor rust can corrupt. I have traveled from the primitive social life of a Syrian village to a great city which embodies the noblest traditions of the most enlightened country in the world. I have come from the bondage of Turkish rule to the priceless heritage of American citizenship.

Abraham Mitrie Rihbany, Protestant clergyman who immigrated from Syria in 1891 at the age of 22, in his autobiography A Far Journey *(1913), in Neidle,* The New Americans *(1967), pp. 223–224.*

At long last we had arrived in America! . . . There may be better fare than the American breakfast to justify God's ways to man. If so, it has not been my good fortune to ingest it. . . . As much as we could eat of anything. All for one price. *Just ask for it!* So that was America! Just ask for it! Or, *just reach for it!*

Angelo Pellegrini, Italian immigrant recalling his first reaction to America when he arrived in 1913 at the age of nine, in Immigrant's Return *(1953), p. 289.*

As long as the warm weather lasts, the enclosed porch overlooking the city makes a capital social room. They have magazines and pictures here to look at and excellent concerts every Sunday, besides a gramophone to play cheerful tunes for them. Now we want to take down the wire netting from around the examination rooms, which makes them feel like animals in a cage, and then we'll hang maps and pictures on the walls.

The only thing that is lacking over here is imagination. No one ever seemed to try to imagine what a detained immigrant must be feeling.

Frederick C. Howe, director of the immigrant depot on Ellis Island, recalling the reforms he instituted when he took office in 1914, in The Confessions of a Reformer *(1925), pp. 273–274.*

It is unthinkable that so many persons with crooked faces, coarse mouths, bad noses, heavy jaws, and low foreheads can mingle their heredity with ours without making personal beauty yet more rare among us than it actually is. So much ugliness is at least bound to work to the surface.

Edward A. Ross, professor of sociology at the University of Wisconsin, warning of the dangerous effects of the new immigration, in The Old World in the New: The Significance of Past and Present Immigration to the American People *(1914), pp. 287–288.*

Now when I meet italians, russians, jews here in America I see the great meaning of that country for us. We who in Castle Garden were still the same poor, desolate emigrants of Europe after a struggle with life, became winner of the battle, we have new ideas of freedom, we think with pride that in seven years we will be "Americans" and citizens and we are proud of our new country . . . because it is so much better than our old country and that it wellkomed us, and we try to be worth it and go to schools to study civics and all do hard work which makes our country just a little better. America means something to an American it means more to us immigrants for this meaning is new and holly and wonderfully dear to us.

When I meet American children in white dresses and pink ribbons going to school to teachers whom they love and who love them and try to make their studies as interesting as possible, I see myself and my chums going to school as to a trial, in gray uniforms, black aprons, coming there to repeat words of a strange catechism which was forced into our heads. While young Americans learn in school how to love and respect your people and your government, 'so wise, so free,' so practical, we were forced to devine our kings who are so cruel so dull and so unsensible. But trying to force us into seeds of patriotism, they raised hatred in them, for teachers who offend us, calling us "zudovka" (dirty jew) such teachers are unfit to stand as tutors of growing minds and certainly mislead more than one of the young generation.

In about five month after I came to America, I entered a hospital to take up training for a nurse. I could not speak English at all for some time, but when in a month I aske questions America opened to me through my patients. There were immigrants unable to speak, even to each other because of the mixture of all different nationalities and languages. . . . America opened to me through the Irishmen and Italians hurt in a saloon fight and others their countrymen who were sick because they worked a whole day at hard labor in factories and outside and then went to school to study civics in night school, for their ambition told them, that they ought know their civil duties to a country in which they worke with a shovel diging sewers and laying tracks.

Anonymous Russian Jewish immigrant in an essay submitted to a contest entitled "What America Means," printed in The Immigrants in America Review 1 *(June 1915), pp. 70–71.*

And then, suddenly, in spite of the fact that we had anticipated it for days, there was America, the Statue of Liberty and New York's wonderful towers. How could it be, I wondered, that after having been so impatient to get there, I suddenly seemed almost frightened by America now that we had arrived. Was it because our uncertain future was only becoming concrete and unescapable . . .? We had left home behind; we were not approaching a new home, only an indefinite spot in an unknown vacuum. . . .

. . . And even if our early hopes had lasted only a few hours, the miseries of Ellis Island would have wiped them out efficiently. We were shunted here and there, handled and mishandled, kicked about and torn apart, in a way no farmer would allow his cattle to be treated. "From here on," father predicted with some strange insight, "we are no longer men created in the image of God, but less than dumb beasts."

[After arriving in Michigan] we started out for . . . our first house in America, which was situated in a Christian neighborhood composed entirely of Hollanders, all of the same faith we were. . . . We were outcasts. . . . Whenever we stirred outdoors we heard the singsong ditty shouted at us:

Dutchman, Dutchman, belly fulla straw,
Can't say nothin' but, ja, ja, ja. . . .

. . . [Two years later] Mother asked: "And now, when are we going back to Holland?" Father said calmly: "We are not going back." "I don't want to stay here where we've had nothing but grief, humiliation, poverty and suffering," she cried. "That's why we're staying here," he answered. "Now that we've had all that, it's time to see what America can really offer us."

Dutch poet and novelist David Cornel De Jong, recalling his arrival at Ellis Island in 1917, in With a Dutch Accent *(1944), in Neidle,* The New Americans *(1967), pp. 292–294.*

The cross between a white man and an Indian is an Indian; the cross between a white man and a Negro is a Negro; the cross between a white man and a Hindu is a Hindu; and the cross between any of the three European races and a Jew is a Jew."

Madison Grant, advocate of immigration restriction, in The Passing of the Great Race *(second edition, 1918), p. 18.*

I have no land of my own. I am not a craftsman and it is very difficult for me to live here. I rent some . . . land from an estate-owner. . . . And now I cannot pay the rent to the proprietor; therefor I must soon leave this place. But where can I find a piece of bread with a wife and two children? Because of this difficulty, having no work, I address myself to the respected directors with the request that they advise and protect me in my journey to America. . . . I do not intend to go with my whole family because I have too little money. I am merely looking for work for some time.

Polish peasant, letter to a protective association in Warsaw written before the outbreak of World War I, explaining the need to immigrate to the United States, in Thomas and Znaniecki, The Polish Peasant in Europe and America, *Volume V, (1920), p. 27.*

I wonder whether, after all, the foreign-born does not make in some sense a better American—whether he is not able to get a truer perspective; whether his is not the deeper desire to see America greater; whether he is not less content to let its faulty institutions be as they are.

Edward Bok, Dutch immigrant, in The Americanization of Edward Bok *(1920), p. 451.*

When I came to this country, and saw the Statue of Liberty, I tipped my hat to it and I was happy. During my stay in this country, I could not find any understanding from the American people toward myself, and have been frowned upon all the time as a "Polack" in public places. When my wife came, here, both of us went to work, and my wife also came to the conclusion that Americans did not treat her as they treated one another, but always

called her "Polack." The final result is that the wife is in the hospital and I am arrested by the government which I tried to understand and obey.

A Polish immigrant, deported as a subversive during the Red Scare in 1920, in Shapiro, Gateway to Liberty *(1986), p. 237.*

Sanitary conditions aboard this ship were not fit for a pig. There were aboard this vessel 1,931 steerage passengers, of whom nine were stowaways, forty-seven were diseased and 687 were detained. Three hundred and nineteen of these people had no money and a total of 1,138 had less than $20. One woman with three children had $1.09 on which to support them, and a woman with five children, who soon expected to give birth to another, had $5.07.

These people had been crowded on the boat for seventeen days—they ate from buckets, seated on the deck, amid frightful odors, and there was no provision for bathing.

Frederick A. Wallis, commissioner of immigration, in a report on an Italian ship arriving from Palermo, quoted by "Investigator" in the New York Daily News, *December 7, 1920.*

The intellectual standards of Americans, we observed, were very low. . . . Who ever heard of a nation whose newspapers headlined ball players, printed on their front pages stories about mothers-in-law, and called their president "Cal," as if he were a dog! It was manifest that such people could have no real, serious literature; of this we were certain. America, we knew, had produced a few good writers, but Russians were better acquainted with them than Americans. Whenever we met a native, we invariably asked him, had he read Bret Harte? (There is no *h* in the Russian language, and we pronounced it "Bret Garte.") He had not, of course. Had he read Jack London? Had he read Mark Twain's immortal story about the boy Gookelberry Finn? No American ever heard of Gookelberry Finn—a fact we used to point out triumphantly and venomously whenever we discussed the glaring shortcomings of American cultural life.

M. K. Argus, recalling the Russian immigrant community in New York City during the 1920s, in Moscow-on-the-Hudson *(1951), in Greenleaf,* America Fever *(1970), pp. 153–154.*

. . . [T]hey put all the women in a room. My sister and I were with mother; the boys were in a separate room. They took off all our clothes and deloused them, and they gave us showers to take with certain medication, I guess a disinfectant or something.

Then we went before the inspectors—you could not get off without the doctor's examination. The only thing is that my mother had trouble with her eyes. You see, my sister took sick on the way—she had some kind of childhood sickness, measles or something. My mother was very concerned and here we were on the boat. She said, "I left Europe with five children, I promised your father five children, and I am going to bring him five children!" She was only worried that my sister would die. You know, you get into such a depressive mood. She was very worried, so every night she would sit and cry. My sister got better on the boat, but when we got off, my mother's eyes were very red from crying. So when she got to the doctor at Ellis Island, he wouldn't pass her. They thought she had some trouble with the eyes. . . . That is what kept us three more days.

A Russian immigrant recalling her arrival at Ellis Island in the 1920s, in Brownstone, Franck, and Brownstone, Island of Hope, Island of Tears *(1979), p. 207.*

I inform you that I intend to emigrate to America. I know only one handicraft, carpenter's. I practiced it with a country carpenter, but at the present time it is very difficult to find material, and therefor difficult to earn. We have little land, and I have a sister and two brothers. I am eighteen years old; so if I can go to America and get work . . . before the call to the army I could earn still more money.

A Polish immigrant, letter written in the 1920s to the Emigrants Protective Association in Warsaw, in Thomas and Znaniecki, The Polish Peasant in Europe and America *(1927), p. 1505.*

I arrived here with a complete English vocabulary. That is, not that I knew English so well; it was the dictionary that I carried with me that knew English well. But not I. As soon as I stepped on board that ship I realized that no one understood a word of my English, and that I didn't understand a word of anybody else's. And this hurt me. It hurt me very much that when I asked a waiter for water he brought me butter.

I ask you to imagine the situation of an intelligent man who finds himself in a strange country where the language is not familiar to him. While I was *en route,* and during the few days I spent in hotels—well, not too bad. In a good many places people are accustomed to foreigners. And aboard ship, who is a foreigner anyway? It's not a country. It's not a state. It's a place that hovers between heaven and earth, where every individual is thinking only about the journey, and where other people don't concern him, least of all the language they speak.

Jonah Rosenfeld, a Jewish immigrant from Russia, in "Vreplamrendn," 1921, in Rosenfeld, Pushcarts and Dreamers *(1967), p. 176.*

The day before we were to disembark [on Ellis Island, April 15, 1921], a few of the French and German sailors had instructed all the passengers about their clothing. "You can't take any dirty clothes with you or they will send you back." The horror of being sent back frightened us, and very dutifully we did as the sailors instructed, discarding our beautiful but unwashed clothing into their boxes. My prize possessions were a white fur boa that I wore around my neck with a smart navy blue coat and a white turtle-neck sweater that I had worn for ice-skating. All the fancy embroidered lingerie which we had worked hours to make was slowly deposited in the box. It wasn't until we had arrived in America that we were made aware of this hoax. How crazy we were to believe them! The seamen had probably taken all our clothes home to their families or sweethearts—perhaps had even sold them for money. We very promptly cursed the sailors in our very best Slovenian.

Slovenian immigrant Irene M. Planinsek Odorizzi, in Footsteps Through Time *(1978), p. 17.*

The true spirit of American democracy that *all men are born with equal rights and duties* has been confused with the political sophistry that *all men are born with equal character and ability to govern themselves and others,* and with the educational sophistry that education and environment will offset the handicap of heredity. In the United States we are slowly waking to the consciousness that education and environment do not fundamentally alter racial values. We are engaged in a serious struggle to maintain our historic republican institutions through barring the entrance of those who are unfit to share the duties and responsibilities of our well-founded government.

Henry Fairfield Osborn, president of the American Museum of Natural History, welcoming address to the Second International Congress of Eugenics, of which he was the president, New York, September 22, 1921, in Eugenics, Genetics and the Family, *Volume 1, (1923), p. 2.*

Severe restriction of immigration is essential to prevent the deterioration of American civilization, according to students of race and biology, now taking part in the Second International Eugenics Congress at the American Museum of Natural History.

The "melting pot" theory is a complete fallacy, according to eugenists, because it suggests that impurities and baser qualities are eliminated by the intermingling of races, whereas they are as likely to be increased, if not more likely to be increased. Speakers who touched on the subject were all on one side, holding that the mixture of poor stock with a good one does as much harm to the good stock as it does benefit to the poor.

"Eugenists Dread Tainted Aliens," The New York Times
September 25, 1921.

I say the class of immigrants coming to the shores of the United States at this time are not the kind of people we want as citizens of this country.

Representative James V. McClintock (D-Okla.) in an address to Congress, Congressional Record, *December 10, 1921, p. 177.*

Motherwell [Scotland] was a nice little town, but after the war I wasn't too content there. I just knew there was something better. . . . I felt I was at an age where I had to start earning money and making a career for myself, and I didn't see any possibilities in Scotland.

My whole idea was to get to the United States, and work, and help to bring my family. Eventually each one would come, because there were many people migrating, so I was very insistent and, of course, much to my parents' dislike, they were afraid to let me go at a young age. . . .

It wasn't easy for me to convince my parents that I was capable of going over and taking care of myself. But I was determined. No matter what obstacle came up I always found a way out of it. For instance, a professional man—a priest or doctor—had to sign certain papers, and the expression that my mother got from our Catholic priest was, "You're daft." My mother said, "You don't know this girl, what a determined person she is." So I said, "Don't worry. I know another Baptist minister, and he will sign for me."

It was a ten-day journey. . . . The journey over, I began to have regrets about leaving home. I was feeling very lonesome, feeling sorry for myself, crying all the time. . . . I was always afraid of Ellis Island. I had heard stories that if they keep you at Ellis Island they go through your hair looking for bugs. My mother was always scaring me with that. . . . I remember that they took all my clothes off and made me shower, and wrapped all my beautiful clothes in a duffel bag, which hurt me so much to see

them being rolled up, you know, and put in a duffel bag and put away.

Marge Glasgow, who immigrated alone from Scotland at the age of fifteen in 1922, in Coan, Ellis Island Interviews: In Their Own Words *(1997), pp. 136–137.*

. . . I can still remember my first Christmas tree. There was a school assembly for Christmas. What an elaborate thing it was! And all the children got down and sang Christmas carols, and it was just beautiful. Of course we had trees in Czechoslovakia. . . . But they were little conifers with a couple of candles stuck on them. They celebrated Christmas very simply there. And so this was my first real American lit-up Christmas tree, with all the tinsel and all the electric lights and everything you could imagine. That left quite an impression on me.

The other was bigotry. It was an inhospitable neighborhood is all I can remember. There was a grumpy lady living next door who would not associate with us. The Germans ignored us. But I think the people who were the most bigoted to us were the Irish. They seemed to go out of their way to make life miserable for us. To them we were the dumb Polacks. They had only two terms for any foreigners. You were either a dumb Polack or you were a dumb Hunky, meaning Hungarian. And there was no other distinction. And after I became older and read a lot about the history of Ireland, it always amazed me how the Irish, who were so persecuted over the years, would not be more understanding or compassionate or considerate.

George Banovert, a Czech immigrant who arrived at the age of six in 1922, in Coan, Ellis Island Interviews *(1997), p. 294.*

I can't live with the old world, and I'm yet too green for the new. I don't belong with those who gave me birth or to those with whom I was educated. . . . I'm one of the millions of immigrant children, children of loneliness, wandering between worlds that are at once too old and too new to live in.

Russian immigrant Anzia Yezierska in Children of Loneliness *(1923), pp. 122–123.*

Another absolutely unblendable element is the Jew. For ages, ever since his ejection from Judea, he has been a wanderer upon the face of the earth. In speaking of him, there is never a reference to the country whence he came, because throughout the centuries there has been no country he would or could call his home. Into his life there has come no national attachment. To him, patriotism as the Anglo-Saxon feels it is impossible.

. . . They are a people apart from all other peoples. They always will be. . . . By every patriotic test, he is an alien and unassimilable. Not in a thousand years of continuous residence would he form basic attachments comparable to those the older type of immigrant would form within a year.

. . . [A]s a class, the Jews are mercenary minded, money mad. "To get, to have and to hold," is their materialistic motto, and always, always do you find them seeking some tangible, quickly convertible, easily movable, kind of wealth which is in no vital way related to and dependent upon social and national values.

Hiram W. Evans, Imperial Wizard of the Ku Klux Klan, in a speech in Dallas, Texas, October 24, 1923, in "75,000 Klansmen Gather in Dallas to Impress Nation," quoted in the New York Times, *October 25, 1923.*

[M]y cousin said that she had invited some of the ladies of the town to meet her cousin from Paris. I was not to worry. Whenever anyone asked me a question, I was just to answer "yes" to everything.

. . . My cousin introduced me to each in turn. . . . One woman said, "Is that what they're wearing in Paris?"

I smiled and said, "Yes."

"Much shorter than we are wearing here."

"Yes."

"I hear you are a milliner. What are the newest hats in Paris?"

"Yes."

"I mean, are they going to be bigger this fall, or smaller? With feathers or without?"

"Yes."

I could see this lady was growing angry. "Do you think I'm stupid, asking all these questions?"

"Yes."

Lily Daché, French milliner, recalling her first day in America at the age of 18, in 1924, in Talking Through My Hats *(1946), in Cavanah,* We Came to America *(1954), pp. 85–86.*

I believe that our particular ideas, social, moral, religious, and political, have demonstrated, by virtue of the progress we have made and the character of people that we are, that we have the highest ideals of any member of the human family or any nation. We have demonstrated the fact that the human family, certainly the predominant breed in America, can govern themselves by a direct government of the people. . . . Those who come from the nations which from time immemorial have been under the dictation of a master fall more easily by the law of inheritance and the inertia of habit into a condition of political servitude than the descendants of those who cleared the forests, conquered the savages, stood at arms and won their liberty from their mother country, England.

I think we now have a sufficient population in our country for us to shut the door and to breed up a pure, unadulterated American citizenship. I recognize that there is a dangerous lack of distinction between people of a certain nationality and the breed of a dog. . . . Thank God we have in America perhaps the largest percentage of any country in the world of pure unadulterated Anglo Saxon stock. . . . It is for the preservation of that splendid stock that has characterized us that I would make this not an asylum for the oppressed of all countries, but a country to assimilate and perfect that splendid type of manhood that has made the American the foremost nation in her progress and her power, and yet the youngest of all the nations. . . .

Without offense, but with regard to the salvation of our own, let us shut the door. . . .

Senator Ellison D. Smith of South Carolina, speech before Congress, April 9, 1924, Congressional Record, *LXV, part 6, p. 5961.*

To the war-weary, overcrowded and underfed denizens of Europe and Asia, the United States, peaceful, opulent and roomy, looks like "the last place in the sun." They are crowding into our place in the sun as much as we will permit, and, failing in that, they are sneaking in by the tens of thousands in addition to the regularly admitted immigrants.

The time is not far distant, in the opinion of some statesmen, that we shall have to station a soldier every hundred yards on our borders to keep out the hordes pressing to share our advantages, or to adopt a drastic policy of registration of lawfully admitted immigrants and expulsion or punishment of unregistered aliens.

Fully alive to this situation, Congress has determined that it is time to safeguard our place in the sun for the benefit of posterity, to bar out unassimilable races and to halt the dilution of the Nordic strain in the blood of the American people.

Henning, "U.S. Firm in Excluding Japanese," New York Daily News, *April 21, 1924.*

Ellis Island is barred to visitors, women are said to be unlawfully detained there, and employees have been forbidden to communicate with newspaper representatives. . . .

. . . Although the U.S. Court of Appeals has ruled that four months is a reasonable time in which to effect the deportation of any alien and detention thereafter is "unlawful imprisonment," several persons are now said to be on the island who have been detained for longer periods.

"Alien Police Head Charges Island Beating: U.S. Detention Pen Called Worse Than Criminal's Prison," New York Daily News *in the second of a series of articles on conditions on Ellis Island, November 6, 1924.*

If you came back, you wanted to leave again; if you went away, you longed to come back. Wherever you were, you could hear the call of the home-land, like the note of a herdsman's horn far away in the hills. You had one home out there, and one over here, and yet you were an alien in both places. Your true abiding place was the vision of something very far off, and your soul was like the waves, always restless, forever in motion.

Johan Bojer, Norwegian immigrant, in The Emigrants *(1925), p. 351.*

The first direct messages from the United States of America to me, written in white letters as high as a house, possibly loaded with awesome significance, was peremptorily sibylline. It reached me early one morning in August, 1925 (I was then a bookish sixteen-year-old). The Italian liner *Duilio,* on which my mother, brothers, sister, and I had crossed the ocean to join my father in New York, had arrived at the Narrows. The ship had stopped shivering and throbbing; the sea no longer rushed by its flanks with the roar of a waterfall. I peered through the porthole. In the gray-pink pearly light of a hot summer dawn I saw a low green cliff rising from the still brownish waters. On its flat top, at equal intervals, like teacups arranged on a tidy table, sat small wooden white houses. They were the dwellings of the Americans, as typical as the igloos of the Eskimos or the tents of the nomad Arabs. We had arrived in the New World. This was the rising of the curtain, the turning point of my life, the moment I had been expecting for months, my first contract with the unknown, awe-inspiring country where I would finish my studies and possibly live forever. . . . The immense white letters forming the cryptic message ran along the grass embankment, between the water and the houses. Were the words meant for me, and what exactly was their meaning?

. . . I reached no conclusions then. It took me years, five to be exact, to formulate a possible explanation. The message said: "Do not anchor. Cable crossing." After the stock market crash, after my graduation from Columbia,

after I had decided to give up my at best dubious chances of glory and wealth in the United States, the country I had come to know, commiserate with, and love, and after I had returned to Italy, I suspected the words "Do not anchor" had imperiously tried to warn me in time not to sink roots in the New World, not to let myself be deluded like so many others by its stupendous but often treacherous promises.

Italian author Luigi Barzini, recalling his arrival in the United States in 1925, in O America: When You and I Were Young *(1977), pp. 19–23.*

High grade germplasm often leads to better results than a high per capita school expenditure. Definite limits are set by heredity, and immigrants of low innate ability cannot by any amount of Americanization be made into intelligent American citizens capable of appropriating and advancing a complex culture.

Clifford Kirkpatrick, in Intelligence and Immigration *(1926), p. 2.*

I was a man and stronger than most men. Yet my second childhood began the day I entered my new country [1906]. I had to learn life over in a brand-new world. And I could not talk. My first desire was for chocolate drops, and I pointed my finger at them. My second was for fishing tackle, and I pointed my finger at a wrapping cord and heaved up an imaginary fish. I used baby talk. "Price?" I asked. And later in the day, "Vatsprice?" Saleswomen answered me with motherly grimaces.

I never quite got over my second childhood. I doubt that any immigrant does—with his hasty, often harsh attuning to the new world. My first birth was distant and dim and unreal, for I was almost three years old when I awoke, and most of the shock had disappeared. The old world and I grew up together. We just grew in blissful ignorance of one another's growing pains. And my first childhood stole upon me softly.

Not so my second childhood. I was born full-grown, so to speak, and therefore was aware of my new birth. I regressed to the greed of infancy. My curiosity was that of a child. My manners lacked the poise of adulthood. My angers, fears, and joys were fleeting and childish and divided the new world into absolute categories—into good and evil. The new world cut into my clay and chronicled something which was not there before—another code of thought and feelings. . . .

I hoarded words like a coin-collector, and the language of my second childhood grew. Every day I found new words; for all the things and acts that I beheld in the new world had a name, and every name had many modifiers. . . . My childish response to the new world uttered themselves in my emotions. A bartender giving me a plate of corned beef and cabbage filled my heart with rare joy. A park cop poking my ribs with his club made me angry enough to kill. A watchman pointing his gun at me gave me a fear that literally tasted salty.

Danish immigrant Carl Christian Jensen, recalling his first days in America, in An American Saga *(1927), pp. 64–65, 78.*

. . . [C]ertain Irish in South Boston and in Charleston . . . have allied themselves with the most corrupting gang of grafters that ever held political office, . . . send ex-convicts to office and place on a sacred pedestal a vulgarian with the ideals of a bartender and the mentality of a ferrygate tender. . . .

Editorial in the Italian-American newspaper United America, *January 29, 1927, in Wittke,* We Who Built America *(1939), p. 445.*

What I say is that I am innocent . . . of the Braintree crime. . . . [T]hat not only have I not been . . . in Braintree to steal and kill and have never steal or kill or spilt blood in all my life, not only have I struggled hard against crimes, but I have refused myself the commodity or glory of life, the pride of life of a good position, because in my consideration it is not right to exploit man. I have refused to go in business because I understand that business is a speculation on profit upon certain people that must depend upon the businessman, and I do not consider that is right and therefore I refuse to do that. . . .

This is what I say: I would not wish to a dog or to a snake, to the most low and misfortunate creature of the earth—I would not wish to any of them what I have had to suffer for things that I am not guilty of. But my conviction is that I have suffered for things that I am guilty of. I am suffering because I am a radical and indeed I am a radical; I have suffered because I was an Italian and indeed I am an Italian; I have suffered more for my family and for my beloved than for myself; but I am so convinced to be right that if you could execute me two times, and if I could be reborn two other times, I would live again to do what I have done already.

I have finished. Thank you.

Bartolomeo Vanzetti, Italian fish peddler who, with fellow Italian immigrant Nicola Sacco, was convicted of murder, in his last statement in court, April 9, 1927, in The Sacco-Vanzetti Case *(1929), pp. 4896–4904.*

CHAPTER EIGHT

The Door Closes
1922–1945

The Quota Laws

William Paul Dillingham was a distinguished statesman, highly respected as a law-yer and public servant. The son of the governor of Vermont, he served as a state senator and tax commissioner and like his father became governor of his state. He was elected to the U.S. Senate in 1903, 1909, 1914, and 1920, and he served with distinction until his death, at the age of 79, in 1923. But what he is principally remembered for is his work as the chairman of the Senate Committee on Immi-gration created in 1907. This group, consisting of three members of the House of Representatives, three senators, and three others appointed by President Theodore Roosevelt, was assigned the job of making a study of "the immigration problem" and submitting recommendations for solving it.

They labored on the task for more than two years and produced the most exhaustive survey of the subject ever written. It not only investigated every aspect of immigration in the United States, it explored the conditions in other countries leading their citizens to emigrate, the character of the various national groups that came to the United States, and the foreign legislation that governed their depar-ture. It examined the differences between the "old" and the "new" immigration and judged their consequences to the country. Published in 1911, it ran to 41 large volumes and profoundly affected the pattern of immigration to the United States for the next half-century.

The famous (some called it "infamous") Dillingham Report reflected the grow-ing isolationism and racism of the country. Senator Dillingham introduced the 1913 immigration bill noted in the last chapter, vetoed by President Taft because it contained a literacy test. His report was also the basis for the proposed bill of 1915 vetoed by President Wilson for the same reason and the 1917 bill that finally passed over Wilson's veto. This law has been described as marking "a definite end to our traditional immigration policy."

But in the light of later legislation, Dillingham has entered the history books as "a moderate restrictionist." By 1917 national feelings against the entry of aliens had already grown so strong that even the fine mesh through which immigrants were forced to pass was deemed inadequate, and new legislation was repeatedly proposed to narrow the passage still further. The public at all levels was worried about the influx of aliens. Henry Fairchild, professor of social economics at New York University, was particularly alarmed about the effects of immigration on postwar society. "The injection of a new mass of undigested human material into the present turbulent and feverish situation," he wrote in a *New York Times* article on "the immigration crisis" in 1919, "would be immeasurably disastrous." Others continued to be terrified by the specter of wild-eyed, bomb-throwing radicals or by the threatened "mongrelization" of the "American race." Perhaps the most strident anti-immigration voice was that of organized labor. The American Federation of Labor and other union organizations feared the competition of foreign workers flooding in from European countries whose economies had been shattered by the war, and it strongly opposed any and all immigration during what was termed "the present emergency."

In 1919 a bill was introduced to suspend all immigration entirely while Congress worked out a permanent plan for a more tightly restrictive policy. This bill was the work of Albert Johnson, a Republican member of the House of Representatives, who had just become chairman of the House Committee on Immigration and Naturalization. Described as "an unusually energetic and vehement racist and nativist," Johnson was especially concerned for the racial purity of the country—in 1923 he became the president of the Eugenics Research Institute, which opposed interracial marriage—and made no secret of his anti-Semitism. In support of his bill he included in his committee's report a quote from a State Department official referring to Jews as "abnormally twisted" and "unassimilable" and describing them as "filthy, un-American, and often dangerous in their habits."

Representative Johnson's bill passed the House but was rejected in the Senate, although most senators agreed with the general public that immigration should at least be reduced. One reason the bill failed was that most senators knew that it would not receive executive approval from Wilson, as indeed it did not. In 1921, however, Wilson was out of the White House, and President Warren G. Harding was far more responsive to restrictionist sentiment. In that year the Dillingham bill that Wilson had rejected in 1913 was reintroduced, with no modification except for the date. Johnson gave up his advocacy of total suspension of immigration and presented the bill, which proved very popular with the general public. The unions, which had approved Johnson's idea of banning all immigration, accepted it as a good compromise, and the *New York Daily News* applauded it for its protection of the American job market from a flood of aliens willing to work for low wages. "Cheap labor is not cheap in reality," the popular newspaper warned in a 1921 editorial. "It will cost American industry its prosperity."

Both houses of Congress, as before, approved the Johnson Bill overwhelmingly within hours. It passed the Senate with a vote of 78–1 and was signed by President Harding on May 19, 1921. Called "the most important turning-point in American immigration history," the new law was formally entitled "An Act to limit the immigration of aliens into the United States." It introduced two new elements into American immigration legislation: absolute numerical limits on how many Europeans could enter the country and national quotas based on previous immigration statistics. The idea of limiting how many members of each race or nationality could enter the country was not a new one—Dillingham had suggested a percentage system in his report published in 1911—but it had never been passed into law before, except in the case of the Chinese and the Japanese. Strongly favoring the "old immigration," the Quota Law of 1921 changed the composition of the national population, and the policy it embodied was to remain in effect through many changes of legislation.

Previous requirements for admission had been based on "quality control"— anyone could enter the United States who met certain moral, financial, educational, and political standards, which, if they were often harsh and arbitrary, applied democratically to all (except Asians). The Immigration Act of 1921 (42 Stat. 5) imposed

This family of Serbian Gypsies was turned back at Ellis Island as ineligible for entry to the United States. *(American Museum of Immigration, U.S. National Park Service)*

a total limit of 357,000 immigrants per year, and for the first time it also imposed a quota from each country, based on the population from that country already in the United States according to the census of 1910. Immigration was limited to 3 percent of the number of foreign-born persons from each country living in the United States according to the census of 1910. Senator Dillingham made no secret of the fact that the law favored the "Nordic race" and specifically targeted the "new immigration" from southeastern Europe. The largest quotas were open to people from the European countries in the North and West. The total number of entries permitted from the new immigrant groups was 45,000 less than that from the older sources of immigration, and Germany, England, the Netherlands, and Scandinavia did not even fill their quotas under the new law. Total immigration for 1922 was 309,556, down from 805,228 in 1921.

The act also specified that only 20 percent of any nation's quota was to be admitted in any one month. Anyone arriving too late, even if the delay was caused by bad weather at sea, was deported. This resulted in a panic among the hopeful crowds of would-be immigrants and the shipping lines that carried them to the New World. During the last weeks before the law went into effect on June 3, 1921, there was a mad dash to get in, and the American ports were crammed with ships trying to beat the deadline. Edward Corsi, who later became an immigration commissioner at Ellis Island, described the scene in his book *In the Shadow of Liberty:* "Imagine the ships, bulging with human cargo, racing through the Narrows and into New York harbor, actually colliding with one another in their hurry to be at Ellis Island before the last minute." When the *Saxonia,* one of the last vessels of the Cunard line bringing immigrants in before the law closed the door, arrived at Ellis Island, the depot was too full to admit anyone. Its 800 passengers were herded ashore by detectives at Manhattan's West 13th Street pier and had to camp out on the floor for four days before anyone could attend to them. Many whole shiploads were refused admission. One Public Health Service doctor recalled a group of 500 immigrants from southeastern Europe who had sold all their possessions and broken all ties with their countries but arrived at Ellis Island too late to be admitted. "They screamed and bawled and beat about like wild animals," she reported, "breaking the waiting room furniture and attacking the attendants, several of whom were hurt. It was a pitiful spectacle."

One of the most painful results of the new quota restrictions was that they made no distinctions for personal relationships and often separated families. Henry Curran, a sympathetic commissioner at Ellis Island, was especially moved by these cases. He recalled in his 1941 memoir *Pillar to Post,* "When part of a family had been born in a country with a quota still open, while the other part had been born in a country whose quota was exhausted, the law let in the first part and deported the other part. Mothers were torn from children, husbands from wives. The law came down like a sword between them, the wide ocean suddenly separated them. And there were other foot trips in the quota law, to work unexpected and exquisite cruelty on these innocent wayfarers. When the cases were reported in the papers, there were waves of public rage that fairly lapped the shores of the little island. I could do nothing about the separated unfortunates save plead with Washington to 'find a way.'"

The law was intended to be a temporary one, to meet what was seen as a crisis, and was set to expire in one year. It was frankly an uneasy compromise, and no one was entirely satisfied with it. Some members of Congress still wanted immigration suspended altogether; most felt that the bill did not go far enough in either reducing the total number of entries or in discriminating in favor of the more desirable groups that were admitted. Everyone agreed that one year was not enough time to frame a bill that would answer the country's needs. Accordingly on May 11, 1922, Congress passed a new law entitled "Joint Resolution Extending the operation of the Immigration Act of May 19, 1921," putting the date of its expiration off to June 30, 1924. During the next two years, Congress busied itself with the creation of a permanent measure. There was no doubt in anyone's mind that the new legislation would be even more restrictive. The question was not whether immigration was to be further curtailed, but how much and in what statistical proportions.

The bill that was presented to the House by Johnson and Republican Senator David Reed of Pennsylvania was structured along the same lines as the Dillingham bill, but it was a good deal tougher. The main differences were that the basis for percentage calculations was set back from the census records of 1910 to those of 1890, and the percentage was reduced from three to two. The new bill also cut the total of immigrants admitted annually from 357,000 to 164,667 until July 1, 1927, at which time the total was to drop to 150,000. It further contained the provision that in 1929 a new quota system would take effect. This was the "national origins formula," using the ethnic background of the current U.S. population, native-born as well as foreign-born, based on the number descended from the people of each country according to the census of 1920. Because the population was still predominantly Anglo-Saxon in 1920, the national origins quotas would effectively restrict the newer immigrant groups even more than the former quotas, which were based on only the population of foreign-born residents. The national origins quotas allotted to countries from northern and western Europe were 85 percent of the total 150,000 admissible to the United States. Thus, only about 22,500 immigrants from southeastern Europe would be permitted entry. A provision excluding Japan aroused such distress in that country that 7,000 Japanese staged a protest in Tokyo, and there was a rash of suicides throughout the country.

The immigrant quotas, corrected to July 1, 1935, produced some ludicrous results, partly because tracing the ancestry of people in the United States proved almost impossible. The first U.S. census was not taken until 1790, and no records of nationality were kept until 1820. The recording of the country of origin of persons born in the United States was not begun until 1890, and by then millions of people of mixed stock had entered. Furthermore, many countries had changed their borders in Europe, and intermarriage had blurred the ethnic definition of much of the nation's population. As the minimum allotted for each nation was 100, many countries were assigned quotas completely out of proportion to their populations or to their needs. Thus, a quota of 100 was allotted to the principality of Andorra, whose total population was scarcely 5,000 and which had virtually no applicants for entry. The tiny countries of Bhutan, Nepal, Liechtenstein, San Marino, and the Pacific islands of Yap and Western Samoa also got quotas of 100 each, while Norway was assigned a quota of 2,377. The Netherlands was allotted 3,153 entries, while China had a quota of 100. Not surprisingly, the largest quota was granted to Great Britain, which received permission to send 65,721 immigrants per year. Germany ranked second, with 25,957, and the Irish Free State was third with 17,853. The total came to 153,774. Of these, the number of immigrants admissible from Europe was 150,275. The remaining 3,499 openings were divided between two continental groups: Africa, Australia (with a quota of only 100) and the Pacific islands were permitted 1,850, while Asia was allotted a total of 1,649.

Of course, the foreign-born population, especially those from the new immigration groups, opposed the Johnson-Reed bill. The governments of southeastern Europe also responded bitterly, noting the insult to their people in its discrimination against those from their region, and the Italian, Jewish, and Slavic press in the United States condemned the bill loudly. Japan was so outraged by its virtual exclusion that there were riots. But the House passed the bill without trouble by 323 to 71. Of the negative votes, all but a few came from the eastern states, where the foreign-born vote was highest—New York, New Jersey, Massachusetts, Connecticut, Rhode Island, Pennsylvania, and Maryland.

When the bill reached the Senate, opinion was not so uniform. Senator Le Baron Bradford Colt of Rhode Island spoke eloquently against the revised quotas. "For what reason is it proposed to go back to the census of 1890?" he demanded. "The reason is the desire to exclude southern and eastern Europeans. If you are going to do that, do it openly. . . . We have 6,000,000 of southern and eastern Europeans living among us who are just as proud of their race as we are of our race. . . . It is now proposed to divide our 12,000,000 of alien population into two groups of 6,000,000 each. We are in effect saying to one of these groups of 6,000,000, 'We wish you had never come here; you Italians are on a lower level than are the Prussians.' Italy replies, 'We fought by your side; will you now admit five of our enemies to one loyal Italian?'" But the South, where the Ku Klux Klan was once again active, voted together in support of the Johnson-Reed Act. Senator Morris Sheppard of Texas argued that the foreign-born population of America "forms the main source and breeding ground of revolutionary and anarchistic propaganda in this country . . . countenancing violence and disorder." Others raised once more the specter of "racial pollution" and the threat to American institutions. Senator Heflin of Alabama demanded, "Have we enough Americans here to speak the American spirit, to talk the American language, to vote for the benefit of America, to take a positive American stand on this question now?" Others from the West, with its long tradition of antiforeign sentiment, spoke just as forcefully. On May 26, 1924, the Johnson-Reed Act (43 Stat. 153) was passed by a vote of 47–32.

One restrictive feature of the bill, however, did not pass. That was the proposal that Canada, Newfoundland (which was then separate from Canada), Mexico, Haiti, the Dominican Republic, the countries of South and Central America, and the Caribbean be included in the quota limitations. There was already concern about the illegal entry of aliens across the Canadian and Mexican borders, but the Senate did not want to antagonize U.S. neighbors in the Western Hemisphere. In any event, there was at that time little fear of a large migration from these countries. Canadians had always passed without much trouble across the border and posed no threat of "racial pollution," and Mexicans were too valuable as laborers on railways and in the cotton fields to restrict. "Mexico is a very sparsely settled country, much more than any portion of the United States," Senator Holm Olaf Bursum of New Mexico argued in April 1924. "The time is not far distant when Mexico will be a very desirable field for Americans to settle in. . . . Through [allowing immigration] we can hope to obtain a large measure of benefit, but to close the door against our neighbors, first, it is impracticable and, second, it is offensive."

Although the law kept the door open to neighbors in the New World, it barred all Asian immigration, which soon led to a shortage of farm and sugar plantation workers. Filipinos satisfied much of the need, since, as an American possession, the Philippines did not come under the immigration quota laws. However, when the islands became independent in 1934, the new nation was assigned an immigration quota of only 50 and Philippine immigration virtually disappeared. The need for agricultural workers soon became pressing. One of the results of this was the new problem of illegal entry, especially across the Mexican-American border. Before 1924, few of the immigrants who had been unable to enter officially tried to get in secretly. Stowaways were almost never successful, and it was seldom necessary to cross the Canadian or Mexican borders illegally. But with the new laws the number of undocumented immigrants increased dramatically. In response to the growing problem, Congress created the Border Patrol in 1924 (43 Stat. 240), hiring 45 men to oversee the country's 8,000 miles of land and sea border. The number was and was to remain woefully inadequate.

It is impossible to measure the effect of the national origins quota laws exactly, because soon after it went into effect immigration fell off drastically in response to the greatest economic crisis in U.S. history. The stock market collapsed in October 1929, bringing about the Great Depression. This disaster had worldwide reverberations. Immigration dropped to new lows. During the 1930s the annual quota was never completely filled, the total numbering less than 100,000 a year, and many emigrated out of the country. In 1932 only 35,576 aliens arrived, and more than 100,000 left, since there was no more employment available in the United States than elsewhere in the world. In 1933 only 23,068 immigrants arrived from Europe, the smallest number since 1831.

Refugees

Most of the immigrants in the beginning of the 1930s were relatives of previous immigrants, but from 1933 onward an increasing number of people sought entry as refugees from Nazi Germany. One of the most tragic elements of the Johnson-Reed Bill was its inflexibility in the face of the desperate need for sanctuary before and during World War II. The need became increasingly urgent after 1938, when Adolf Hitler intensified his anti-Semitic policies in Europe. Because Congress was unwilling to open the doors wider during the depression, many refugees were turned away. In 1934 President Roosevelt instructed American consulates to be as liberal as possible with special visas, but the laws provided little latitude, and few were helped by it. In 1939 Congress refused to pass a bill that would have admitted 20,000 children fleeing from Germany, even though the children had willing sponsors in the United States, because they would have exceeded the German quota. Most of the public supported the decision; the American Coalition of Patriotic Societies, the American Legion, and the Daughters of the American Revolution all strongly opposed the bill. It was not until 1940 that the State Department made a special concession to permit consuls outside of Germany to issue visas to German refugees when the German quota was unfilled, but the regulation provided little help. During the period from 1934 to 1941, only 250,000 refugees were admitted to the United States, and all came within the limits of the existing laws.

Fear of subversion made the situation even worse, and in 1940 Congress passed the Alien Registration Act (54 Stat. 670) to safeguard the country from possible espionage and sabotage. This act required all aliens to register and those over the age of 14 to be fingerprinted. Surveillance of aliens was no longer a question of

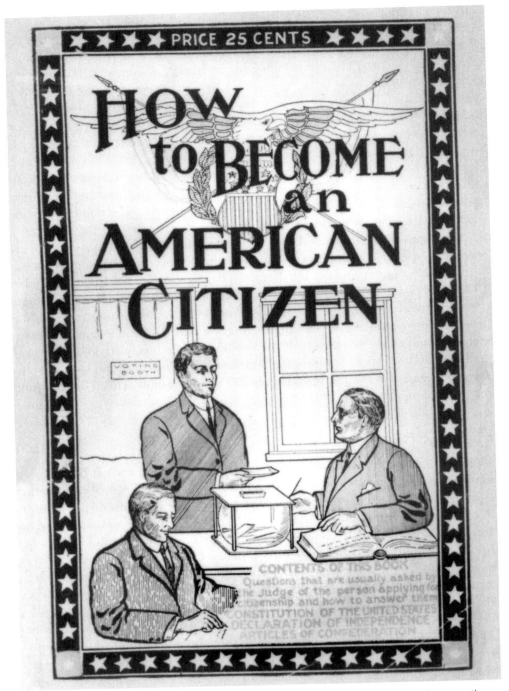

The United States provided aid to the new arrivals with language instruction and preparation for citizenship. *(American Museum of Immigration, U.S. National Park Service)*

the numbers to be admitted; the fear of war made it a matter of national security. Accordingly, that year the Bureau of Immigration was transferred from the Department of Labor to the Department of Justice. The job of the bureau changed from that of judging who got in and keeping undesirables out, as it had been during the 1920s and 1930s, to that of dealing with enemy infiltration, and immigration officials worked closely with the Federal Bureau of Investigation (FBI) and the U.S. attorney general.

The flow of refugees from Europe was different from the waves of immigrants during the preceding century. Driven by their fugitive status in their own countries rather than by poverty, they were mostly from a different background than their predecessors. Mainly Jewish, they were usually of professional or white-collar background, and the number included many who had been highly successful in business, science, and the arts. Among them were Henry Kissinger, America's first foreign-born secretary of state; physicists Albert Einstein, Leo Szilard, Edward Teller, and Enrico Fermi; architect Walther Gropius; psychologist Erik H. Erikson; theologian Paul Tillich; playwright Bertolt Brecht; novelists Thomas Mann, Franz Werfel, and Stefan Zweig; composers Béla Bartók, Paul Hindemith, and Arnold Schoenberg; and orchestra leaders Bruno Walter, Fritz Reiner, and Arturo Toscanini. Refugees fleeing the Nazis from Germany, Italy, Hungary, and other countries included 12 Nobel laureates. Some distinguished newcomers, like Brecht, found the problem of learning the language too much for them and returned to Europe as soon as the war ended. Some, like Bartók, lived obscurely in poverty, isolated from the American cultural scene. Others, like Einstein, Toscanini, and Kissinger, adjusted well, became American citizens, and made valuable contributions to the society of their new home.

Although refugees were usually better qualified to earn a good living than the immigrants who had come during the 19th and early 20th century, jobs of any sort were hard to get during the Great Depression, and in fact unskilled laborers were usually able to find work more easily than the flood of highly educated Europeans who came during the war. Many states protected their native professionals—doctors, lawyers, teachers, accountants, even plumbers—by barring aliens from practice, and people were forced to take such jobs as they could find. As Maldwyn Allen Jones wrote in *American Immigration* (1960), "It was by no means uncommon in the thirties to find refugee judges working as dishwashers, businessmen as hospital orderlies, factory managers as elevator operators, and engineers as night watchmen." The wartime refugees, even the most qualified ones, often found it equally difficult to find work in their fields, and many had to settle for low-paying jobs.

Japanese Americans during the War

The Japanese had prospered in the United States despite the discriminatory laws and practices to which they had been almost continuously subjected. A few native-born people of Japanese ancestry lived in Hawaii in the 19th century before there was any significant number on the mainland, and by 1930 native-born Japanese Americans outnumbered those born in Japan by 80 percent in Hawaii, while on the mainland Japanese born in Japan still outnumbered the second generation. According to the census report, there were some 85,000 Japanese in the United States in 1900, nearly two-thirds of them in Hawaii. By 1920 the number exceeded 220,000, more than half of them on the mainland. Immigration from Japan virtually disappeared with the exclusionary law of 1924, but the Japanese community continued to thrive. The ratio of American-born Japanese grew steadily and at a faster rate than that of other immigrant groups. In 1920 only 26.7 percent of Japanese Americans were born in the United States. By 1930 the percentage had risen to 49.2, and the census of 1940 records that the American-born children of Japanese immigrants totaled 62.7 percent.

Most first-generation Japanese began their American lives as either agricultural laborers or domestic servants. Like the Chinese, they were usually paid less for their work and forced to pay more for land than whites, but by diligence and thrift they often surpassed whites in earnings. As a result, nearly three-fifths of them eventually bought farms or started businesses of their own before World War II. This was despite the Alien Land Laws that barred "aliens ineligible for citizenship" (all Asians) from owning land in California, where the majority of mainland Japanese lived. But as Thomas Sowell reports in *Migrations and Cultures* (1996), "A variety of evasions developed, followed by a tightening of the legal loopholes, followed by more evasions." Because American-born children of the Japanese (known as Nisei) were automatically U.S. citizens, however, these discriminatory laws did not apply to second-generation Japanese, and the amount of land owned by Japanese more than doubled in the 1930s. Japanese farmers produced about a third of the garden crops sold in California by 1940.

America's entry in World War II began with Japan's attack on Pearl Harbor, in Hawaii, on December 7, 1941. Of course anti-Japanese feelings were sharply intensified at once, and the first official response was the arrest and detention of many Japanese Americans of both the first and second generation. Curiously, fewer than 1,500 Japanese Americans were taken into custody in Hawaii (where a considerable number of people had been killed in the bombing attack), but some 120,000 were arrested as enemy aliens on the mainland. Rumors flew of a plot among Japanese Americans to sabotage the war effort. Secretary of the Navy Frank Knox announced to the press, "I think the most effective fifth column work of the entire war was done in Hawaii, with the possible exception of Norway." The report was later proved by naval intelligence and the FBI to be false, and General Delos Emmons, military governor of Hawaii, asserted emphatically, "There have been no known acts of sabotage committed in Hawaii." In fact, in the whole course of World War II only 10 people were ever convicted of spying for the Japanese in the United States, and all of them were white. But military alarmists and racists combined to pressure the government to "relocate" all people of Japanese ancestry to internment camps.

Farmers on the West Coast, competing for a share of the vegetable market, were especially articulate in their support of internment. By February 1942 the California Farm Bureau Federation and the Western Growers Protective Association had come out strongly in favor of it, and the Grower-Shipper Vegetable Association admitted frankly in the *Saturday Evening Post* in May, "We've been charged with wanting to get rid of the Japs for selfish reasons. We might as well be honest. We do. It's a question of whether the white man lives on the Pacific Coast or the brown man. They came into this valley to work, and they stayed to take over. . . . If all the Japs were removed tomorrow, we'd never miss them in two weeks, because the white farmers can take over and produce everything the Jap grows."

The press was not uniformly in favor of the decision. The *Honolulu Star Bulletin* described the rumors of Japanese subversion as "weird, amazing, and damaging untruths," and another Hawaiian newspaper accused the government of "an invasion of the rights of the Japanese people on the Pacific coast." Even J. Edgar Hoover, the FBI director generally known for his antialien sentiment, opposed the move, describing the decision as reflecting "hysteria and lack of judgment" and asserting that the military decision was based "primarily upon public and political pressure rather than on factual data." But the newspapers of California widely supported the move. The *Los Angeles Times* stated emphatically that loyalty to their mother country was an inherited trait of the Japanese. "A viper is nonetheless a viper wherever the egg is hatched," it wrote, "so a Japanese American, born of Japanese parents, grows up to be a Japanese, not an American."

Many members of the government were also in favor of internment. One senator stated emphatically at a Congressional session, "A Jap born on our soil is a subject of Japan under Japanese law; therefore he owes allegiance to Japan. . . . The Japanese are among our worst enemies. They are cowardly and immoral. They are different from Americans in every conceivable way, and no Japanese . . . should have a right to claim American citizenship. A Jap is a Jap everywhere you find him. . . . They do not believe in God and have no respect for an oath. They have been plotting for years against the Americans and their democracies."

Such rhetoric carried the day in the face of all evidence of Japanese-American loyalty, and on February 19, 1942, President Roosevelt signed the notorious Executive Order 9066, directing all Japanese Americans to evacuate the West Coast. The government set up 10 internment camps in California, Utah, Idaho, Arizona, Colorado, Arkansas, and Wyoming, in the most barren regions. Surrounded with barbed wire and patrolled by military police, in some cases armed with machine guns, these camps lacked even the amenities of most American prisons.

Not surprisingly, the Japanese in America were outraged by their treatment, and 5,589 indignant Nisei renounced their American citizenship, though a federal judge refused to accept the gesture, ruling that renunciation made from behind barbed wire was void. But many second-generation Japanese chose to defend "their" country and enlisted in the American armed forces. Some 3,600 Nisei entered the service from internment camps, and more than 22,000 from Hawaii or outside the relocation zone joined them. Thousands of them became members of the Military Intelligence Service, working as interpreters and translators in the Pacific campaign. Many Nisei also served on the European Front with great valor. The famous 442nd all-Japanese Regimental Combat Team won a total of 18,143 decorations, including a Congressional Medal of Honor, 47 Distinguished Service Crosses, 350 Silver Stars, 810 Bronze Stars, and more than 3,600 Purple Hearts, for their fighting in Germany and Italy. Military historians have named the 442nd the most decorated unit in U.S. military history.

The relocation of nearly 120,000 Japanese Americans to internment camps, without charges or trial, has been called one of the most flagrant violations of civil liberties in American history. It was challenged during the war all the way to the Supreme Court, but without success. When the cases of *Hirayabashi v. U.S.* (1943) and *Korematsu v. U.S.* (1944) were heard in Washington, the justices upheld the internment of these immigrants and their American-born children as "serving the national interest in wartime." Shortly before the defeat of Japan, early in 1945, some Japanese Americans were permitted to return to the West Coast after being carefully sifted for loyalty, but the last camp was not closed until March 1946. Two years later, much of the nation had repented and urged the government to make up for its treatment of its Japanese-American citizens, many of whom had been ruined financially by the interruption in their lives. Reimbursement for property losses was paid to internees in 1948. Forty years later, Congress made a more concrete apology to the survivors of America's first and only concentration camps by awarding them $20,000 each as "restitution" for their ordeal. In 1998–99, the federal Ellis Island Immigration Museum mounted an exhibition to remind America of the experience of Japanese Americans in World War II, "in the hopes that the more people who

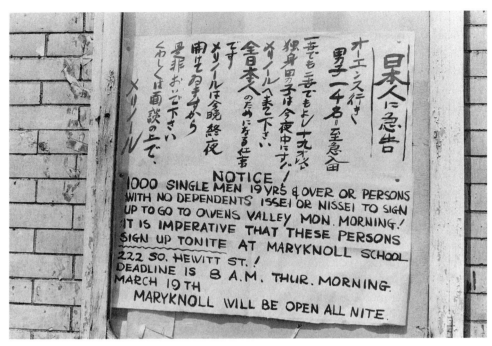

Japanese citizens, including those born in the United States, were evacuated from the West Coast under U.S. Army war emergency orders in 1942. This sign directs them to report for construction work in California. *(American Museum of Immigration, U.S. National Park Service)*

learn about what happened over fifty years ago, the less likely such an injustice will happen again to other people."

Both the Germans and the Italians had much longer histories of immigration to the United States and better-established communities than the Japanese. Thus, although these groups were objects of some fear and suspicion, there was little of the spy and sabotage hysteria that surrounded the Japanese. Rocks were thrown through windows, the music of German composer Richard Wagner was barred from the Metropolitan Opera in New York, and the government arrested a few Nazi agents and harassed a few German-American groups suspected of sympathy with the enemy, but nothing like wholesale internment was applied to people of German or Italian ancestry.

Many of the more recent immigrants were not yet American citizens, however, and these lived under the threat of detention unless they satisfied the authorities of their loyalty. German noncitizens and the more than 600,000 Italians who had not yet been naturalized were reclassified as "aliens of enemy nationality" and required to register with the government. They could not leave their official cities of residence, travel by airplane, or buy cameras, shortwave radios, or other equipment that could be used in espionage without government permission. Italians were never viewed with the same alarm as Germans and Japanese, and the restrictions on them were neither as severe nor as long-lasting. In some cases, the authorities detained Italians whose sons were serving in the U.S. Army. "Potentially dangerous" foreign-born residents, according to the official FBI profile, included employees of Italian-language newspapers or radio stations, teachers of Italian in schools sponsored by the Italian consulate, and members of the Federation of Italian Veterans, a social group made up of former soldiers in the Italian army who had fought in World War I as allies of the United States. On Columbus Day 1942, the restrictions imposed on Italians as enemy aliens were lifted, and their rights were restored, while many German and Japanese noncitizens were interned on Ellis Island for the duration of the war.

Germans and Italians, both first- and second-generation, citizens and noncitizens, had a high rate of enlistment in the armed forces during the war, and unlike the Japanese they were included in integrated troops with servicemen of other ethnic backgrounds. Indeed, both wars contributed to the assimilation of many national groups and to ending ethnic isolation in the United States, an end strongly promoted by the government in an effort to unify the nation in a common cause.

American novels and movies frequently pictured military units as microcosms of the national population—small models of the American dream of the melting pot—working together in harmony. The military experience of fighting side by side enabled men—especially those from neighborhoods such as the lower east side of Manhattan, which had long held separate and often hostile communities protective of their own national languages, customs, and diets—to find a new solidarity in the 1940s. There was a significant drop in foreign-language newspapers in the United States during and after World War II, and the number of radio stations broadcasting in immigrant languages was reduced by 40 percent between 1942 and 1948. There was also a great increase in applications for citizenship among aliens, with over 1,750,000 taking the pledge of allegiance during that period.

Immigrants have continued to make significant contributions to the U.S. military. All branches of the armed forces include disproportionate shares of the foreign-born, in part because those seeking naturalization receive significant advantages in return for their voluntary service. Between 2000 and 2006 Congress amended the rules for applying for citizenship in favor of those who enlist, providing greater benefits for immigrants and their families to encourage recruitment of immigrants, just as the Union army did during the Civil War. Without immigrant service, in fact, the armed forces would not have been able to meet its recruitment needs during the conflicts in Korea, Vietnam, Afghanistan, and Iraq. The country would have been especially handicapped in its need for translators, interpreters, and cultural analysts during these more recent combats.

There were nearly 70,000 foreign-born in the U.S. armed forces in 2004, roughly 57 percent of them citizens. After the terrorist attack of 2001, the immigrants in the military became immediately eligible for naturalization. "As of October 2006," Stock writes, "25,000 immigrants had taken advantage of this provision to become U.S. citizens, and another 40,000 were thought to be eligible to apply."[1] To help meet the new demand, immigrants who were able to act as translators while serving in Iraq were given special visas.

Mexicans and the Bracero Program

Because present-day California, New Mexico, Arizona, Texas, and Colorado were originally Mexican territory, Mexicans have had a history of residence in what is now the United States since before the country existed. With the treaty that ended the Mexican-American War in 1848 and the Gadsden Purchase of 1853, the United States acquired more than half of the territory of that nation, and its inhabitants became U.S. citizens without, technically, immigrating to another country. As mining, logging, and railroad interests grew in the Southwest, Mexican labor was needed, and unsettled conditions following the Mexican Revolution of 1910–17 sent many north to provide it. An estimated 1 million Mexicans had crossed the Rio Grande in search of work by 1920. Most came to take temporary jobs, but 220,000 remained.

World War I created a great need in the United States for labor on farms and in factories to provide the goods necessary for the Allies, and the end of the war introduced a period of great prosperity in the country. Jobs continued to be plentiful, and although a border patrol had been established in 1921, it was easy for Mexicans to enter to fill them. Exempt from the quota laws, they had only to pay a small head tax. Workers were recruited by enticing ads promising high wages and personal liberty. But when the Stock Market crashed in 1929, the work dried up. Farmers were subsidized to cut down on production, Mexican labor was no longer needed, and immigration fell drastically. The competition for work became fierce, and Mexicans were seen as a threat to American labor. The border was closed, and as many as 500,000 Mexican-Americans—more than one-third of the Mexican-American population in 1930—were deported. About one half of these people were American-born and thus U.S. citizens. Those who remained worked under the worst conditions, if they found work at all. Agricultural wages in the Southwest dropped from 35 to 15 cents an hour, and migratory Mexican families averaged $254 a year. In 1940 it was estimated that 25 percent of Mexican children between six and nine years of age worked full-time in the fields with their families, as did 80 percent of those from 10 to 14.

The 1930s had witnessed the lowest rate of Mexican immigration in U.S. history, but when World War II broke out in 1939, the situation changed abruptly. With the United States's entry into the conflict, things changed dramatically. As young men went off to war and as the nation recovered from the depression with the introduction of war industry, jobs came open all over the country. Workers left the farms for work in airplane plants, shipyards, steel mills, foundries, and automobile factories. Now, instead of deporting Mexicans, the United States returned to trying to recruit them.

In 1942 the two countries negotiated a treaty permitting the entry of Mexican farmworkers on a temporary basis to work under contract for U.S. employers on farms and railroads and then return to Mexico after a fixed term. These workers were called braceros (from the Spanish word *brazo*, "arm," meaning manual laborer). On September 29, 1942, the first trainload, numbering some 1,500 braceros, was transported across the border to California; by the end of the year the total had mounted to 4,203. The following year saw the stream swell to 52,098, and in 1944 it reached 62,170. The program was originally scheduled to end in 1947, but there were temporary extensions as need arose, and it ultimately lasted 22 years. When it was finally discontinued in 1964, the total number of Mexican workers who had participated in it was approximately 4.9 million; in 1959, its peak year, 437,643 braceros entered the United States under the contract.

The program was originally designed to provide farm labor, and it was administered by the Department of Agriculture. Workers were sent to help grow and harvest sugar beets, tomatoes, peaches, plums, and cotton. Women took jobs as domestic servants and in time some of the men were assigned to jobs as section hands and maintenance laborers on railroads transporting military personnel and freight. Braceros worked in 21 states across the Southwest and the South, but the

Mexican government stipulated that none were to be sent to Texas, because of that state's long history of discrimination toward Mexicans.

The treaty provided that the braceros were to receive decent care; adequate pay, housing, and food; and transportation both ways, and generally the workers were glad to get the work. Many observers in the United States, however, were horrified at the conditions under which the Mexicans were forced to work and live. They earned only 30 cents an hour, some were lodged in converted chicken coops, abandoned railroad cars, or decrepit shanties; and there were seldom proper sanitary facilities. But the program was still so attractive to Mexican laborers that it was almost always oversubscribed. As one historian noted, "Although [it] offered an alternative to illegal immigration, it probably contributed to it. Far more Mexicans wanted to participate in the program than there were openings. Many who had traveled to the Mexican-American border to find contract labor simply continued across the border illegally when they could not enter the program." It was not difficult to sneak across the river into the United States, as the patrol was always understaffed.

Not all American farmers liked the bracero program, because it provided some measure of protection and assurance to the Mexican workers and actually sought out illegal immigrants. This was especially so in Texas, where the program did not operate. Texas farmers frequently sent agents to the border to help "wetbacks" (Spanish *mojados*, so called because they allegedly swam or waded across the Rio Grande, which separates Mexico from Texas). It is estimated that more than 50 percent of all Mexican farm labor entered the United States illegally during the operation of the program.

The government of neither the United States nor Mexico was ever wholly satisfied with the bracero program, because it both permitted the exploitation of the workers and undercut American labor. The Mexican government felt the program put its countrymen in a position of inferiority—one grower in the American South remarked cynically, "We used to own slaves but now we rent them from the government"—and American labor organizations opposed the program because it kept wages low, competed with native workers, and permitted inhumane living conditions. The program was finally brought to an end in 1964 following a bitter conflict between American farmers in the Southwest, who wanted to maintain their supply of cheap labor, and labor organizers, who protested the treatment of domestic workers.

The braceros were contract laborers and were not eligible to serve in the armed forces, but many Mexican Americans enlisted and fought valiantly. Members of the 200th and 515th Coast Guard artillery units of the New Mexico National Guard had been stationed in the Philippines before the United States entered the war because they spoke Spanish; they therefore took part in the bloody battle of Bataan. California congressman Jerry Voorhis praised them for their valor and their sacrifice. "As I read the casualty list from my state," he wrote, "I find anywhere from one-fourth to one-third of those names are names such as Gonzales or Sanchez, names indicating that the very lifeblood of our citizens of Latin-American descent in the uniform of the armed forces of the United States is being poured out to win victory in the war." In all, some 500,000 Mexican Americans fought for the United States and lost more than their share of life and limb. Although Mexican Americans constituted one-tenth of the population of Los Angeles, they suffered one-fifth of the casualties.

Not all Americans concurred with Voorhis's admiration of Mexican Americans during the war, however. Despite their war record, they continued to experience discrimination and exploitation on the home front. "In many parts of Texas," the Mexican foreign minister complained, "Mexicans cannot attend public gatherings without being subject to vexations, complaints and protests. There are towns where my fellow countrymen are forced to live in separate districts." In 1943 the hostility erupted in violence when hundreds of servicemen assaulted young Mexicans wearing the "zoot suits" then in fashion.

Years later, the plight of Mexican immigrants in the Southwest has scarcely improved. Still predominantly limited to agricultural labor, they began to organize in the 1950s when Mexican-American civil rights activist César Chávez formed the National Farm Workers Association (NFWA). Renamed and expanded as the United Farm Workers (UFW) in 1966, the organization entered the civil rights struggle, seeking to legalize undocumented Mexican farm laborers and protect the rights of immigrants. The UFW has taken a strong stand against temporary guest-worker plans such as the bracero program and has been a powerful force in promoting immigrant rights legislation.

Ellis Island Changes

Immigration resumed after World War I as shipping lanes reopened and America's largest reception station was again thronged with people in flight from Europe. The process now took longer than before, since the Immigration Act of 1917 imposed a more complicated procedure, including a thorough medical examination and the terrifying literacy test that had finally been instituted. The time it took to get through the reopened doors to America was more than doubled, and soon thousands of hopeful immigrants were once more crowding tiny Ellis Island. In 1919 only 26,731 immigrants arrived at the island, still by far the largest depot in the United States; the following year the number had grown to 225,206, and in 1921 it more than doubled, reaching 560,971. And since the postwar economy had tightened the purse strings, and the island was understaffed, the inspectors were able to process only 2,000 a day. Many had to remain on board their ships for several days before being admitted.

When the first quota law was put into effect, permitting only 20 percent of any nation's quota to land in a given month, those who missed the deadline were sent back to begin the process of application over. This greatly reduced the overcrowding of Ellis Island, and when the laws became stricter yet in 1924, the numbers fell still farther. When Secretary of Labor James J. Davis inspected the installation in July 1924, he observed that it looked like a deserted village. He expressed his "gratification" in seeing "all that was expected in relieving congestion." After that year, the island was never to receive more than 190,000 immigrants in any single year. From the year it opened to 1924, Ellis Island had been the point of entry for 71 percent of all aliens entering the United States officially; from that year until it closed in 1954, it processed an average of only 54 percent, and often much less.

With the chaos and overcrowding relieved, living conditions on Ellis Island underwent some improvement. Commissioner Curran, who had taken charge in July 1923, set up recreation areas, a nursery, and a library, and reorganized the living space to provide the immigrants with a measure of privacy. The notorious dormitories in which 2,000 immigrants slept each night while they awaited word of whether they were to be admitted—Curran described their three-layered iron cots in wire cages as contraptions that would make a sardine sick—were reconfigured and the cots replaced by real beds. "I have seen many jails," he later reported, "some pretty bad, but I never saw a jail as bad as the dormitories at Ellis Island, where nine out of ten of the immigrants had never committed any crime at all."

An important feature of the National Origins Act of 1924 was the stipulation that immigrants receive visas from American consulates in their countries before leaving, which entailed their medical, psychological, and political examination; the process of admission was therefore greatly simplified. Beginning in 1926, American Public Health Service doctors were stationed at American consulates throughout Europe, and the visas they issued were almost enough to assure immigrants of admission. It is estimated that only about 1 percent of those arriving required any further examination once they reached the United States. In 1924, the last year of heavy immigration through Ellis Island, from 40 to 60 surgical procedures (such as pulling teeth, setting bones, stitching cuts, etc.) were performed a day; by 1926 the need for medical personnel had almost vanished, and the entire staff of the island was greatly reduced. In time, medical examinations and inspection of all immigration papers were instituted on board ships before they landed, and there was little reason to hold immigrants at Ellis Island. The major purpose of the station had ended, and an article in *The Forum* magazine of March 1927 posed the question "Is it time to scrap this Ellis Island, to make the hard benches of the United States Immigration Station gruesome relics of an Inquisition?"

When the Great Depression struck, immigration fell off still further, because there was little reason for the poor of Europe to seek admission to a country just as poor as their own. In the fiscal year ending June 30, 1933, the total immigration to the United States was 23,068—the lowest number since 1829—and of these, 12,944 entered through the Port of New York. The number of aliens, including immigrants and visitors, held at Ellis Island that year totaled only 4,488, most detained for only one or two days.

But the purpose of the station was changing. During that same year, some 7,037 outgoing aliens had passed through its great halls. Many of them were willing returnees, discouraged with conditions in their new country and unable to make a living during the depression, but others were being expelled from the country. The main business of Ellis Island, as Commissioner Corsi noted when he took office in 1931, was deportations rather than admissions. Now, while entry was usually immediate or took only a few days, the process of expulsion was as lengthy as the process of admission had been. Many deportees had to wait weeks or even months for their original countries to issue them passports. Others postponed their departure as long as they could with lengthy appeals. Secretary of Labor William N. Doak, whose department was then still in charge of the Bureau of Immigration, had cracked down on "undesirable foreigners" and, as Corsi wrote, "in some instances he employed the 'anarchist' or radical clause of the law, but he also made a drive against vagrants and the unemployed, as well as those here illegally."

This new class of Ellis Island detainee required different treatment, and the Department of Labor recommended the construction of another building to keep the immigrants away from those being deported. The new structure, built to house arriving immigrants and protect them from "undesirables," took two years to finish and cost $1.1 million, but it was never used for its original purpose. By the time it was finished, immigration had fallen off so greatly that it did not pay to maintain it, and it was kept empty.

When war broke out in Europe in 1939, the fear of foreign infiltration grew rapidly in the United States. Immigrants were seen as a threat no longer to the American labor force but to the political security of the country. It was for that reason that the Bureau of Immigration was transferred to the Department of Justice in 1940 and the attorney general was made responsible for Ellis Island. Originally purchased to hold a fort, and from 1810 to 1890 used as a munitions dump, Ellis Island became a prison when the United States entered World War II. As in World War I, it was used to detain enemy aliens and their families, and it also housed seamen from captured enemy ships. The immigrant station was almost deserted, but the island once again thronged with people. The main building was officially renamed a "detention facility," and the new building, at last opened, was put to use, along with the baggage room and the dormitory building, to house new recruits to the coast guard, who trained on the island. Enemy aliens from Germany, Italy, Japan, Hungary, Romania, and Bulgaria flooded in to fill the almost empty buildings. In time the island became so overcrowded that some of its unhappy inhabitants had to be transferred to Riker's Island, the New York City prison in the East River. But its days as the gateway to America were past for good.

The total number of immigrants to the United States during World War I (1914–18) was somewhat over 1,200,000. The number for World War II (1942–45) was less than 200,000. The two conflicts, making travel between continents almost impossible and increasing the national sentiment of isolationism and racism, naturally reduced the influx of immigrants. The depression had a still greater impact, lowering the figure from 241,700 in 1930 to 29,470 in 1934. But it was the legislation of the 1920s that most effectively stemmed the tide of immigration to the United States. It was not until the late 1980s, under very different world conditions, that the annual numbers were to pass the million mark again.

Chronicle of Events

1922

- *February 9*: World Foreign Debt Commission is organized to renegotiate international war debt and postwar loans. American insistence on payment creates anti-U.S. sentiment in Europe and consequent isolationist feeling in the United States.
- *May 11*: Congress extends the expiration of the Immigration Act of 1921 to June 30, 1924.
- *May 23*: Anne Nichols play *Abie's Irish Rose* celebrating religious intermarriage begins a five-year run in New York City.

1923

- More than 13 million automobiles are registered in the United States, tripling the number recorded in 1917; there are about 15 million telephones in use.
- *January 10*: The last United States occupation troops are withdrawn from Germany.

- *March*: Bill to transfer American Indian lands to white settlers without payment is defeated in Congress.
- *August 2*: President Warren G. Harding dies of a heart attack.
- *August 3*: Vice President Calvin Coolidge takes the oath of office as the 30th president of the United States.
- *September 15*: Violence by the Ku Klux Klan leads Governor J. C. Walton of Oklahoma to declare martial law.
- *October 25*: A U.S. Senate subcommittee begins investigation of the Teapot Dome oil lease scandal.
- *December 6*: President Coolidge delivers his first address to Congress, supporting the World Court but opposing United States membership in the League of Nations.

1924

- Congress creates the Border Patrol to oversee the nation's 8,000 miles of border with Canada and Mexico. The initial staff is 45 men.
- Ku Klux Klan membership is estimated at 4 million, its highest level.

President Warren G. Harding (1865–1923) (center, no hat) vetoed the immigration restriction bill. *(Library of Congress, Prints and Photographs Division [LC-USZ62-102540])*

- *February 8*: Congress finds former Secretary of the Interior Albert Fall guilty of issuing false contracts and leases in the Teapot Dome case.
- *May 26*: The Johnson-Reed Act, amending the Immigration Bill of 1921, is passed, limiting annual immigration to 2 percent of the number of people from each country present in the United States in 1910, establishing national quotas, excluding Japanese immigration altogether, and fixing a maximum of 357,000 immigrants. The bill does not include Canada or the Americas. The bill is to be in effect until July 1, 1927, when the maximum number of immigrants admitted to the United States will be set at 150,000, and the quota will be based on the national origins of the people in the United States recorded in the census.
- *June 15*: Congress enacts a bill making all native-born Indians U.S. citizens.
- *July 1*: Japan reacts strongly against the exclusion clause in the May 26 Immigration Act, declares this date Humiliation Day, and calls "Hate America" meetings.
- *November 30*: The Bureau of Investigation is renamed Federal Bureau of Investigation and J. Edgar Hoover is appointed its director.

1925
- *March 4*: Calvin Coolidge is inaugurated.
- *November 14*: The United States agrees to a strong reduction in payments of war debts.

1926
- Congress approves U.S. participation in the World Court at The Hague, founded by the League of Nations in 1920. Isolationist propaganda results in the country's withdrawal, and the United States does not join until 1935.
- *January 14*: The United States and Cuba sign an extradition treaty.

1927
- Ole Rolvaag publishes *Giants in the Earth*, his classic novel of Swedish immigrants on the Great Plains.
- *October 10*: The Supreme Court rules that the lease of the Teapot Dome oil reserve was fraudulent.
- *November 17*: Mexican Congress grants unlimited concessions on U.S. development of oil lands in use before 1917.

1928
- *January 6*: The first Pan-American Conference opens; President Coolidge pledges peace and cooperation among the nations of North America.

- *March 10*: President Coolidge approves the Alien Property Act compensating German nationals and companies for property seized from them at the beginning of World War I.

1929
- Automobile manufacture becomes the leading industry in the United States, with 3 million cars produced. In the census of 1930 it is reported that one person in five in America owns an automobile.
- *March 4*: Herbert Hoover is inaugurated 31st president of the United States.
- *October 24–28*: The U.S. Stock Market collapses, bringing on the Great Depression.

1930
- The census records a population of 122,775,000, including 4,107,000 immigrants who have arrived since 1920. Illiteracy is shown to be at an all-time low of 4.3 percent.
- *September 9*: The State Department orders restrictions on immigrant labor.

1931
- *January*: Unemployment is estimated at between 4 and 5 million. The number reaches 9 million by the end of the year.
- *June 20*: President Hoover declares a moratorium on war debts and reparations because of the worldwide depression.
- *September–October*: More than 800 U.S. banks close.
- *October 1*: U.S. Steel cuts wages of 220,000 employees by 10 percent.

1932
- Immigration falls to 35,576. More than 100,000 aliens leave the country.
- *March 3*: Japan occupies Shanghai, China. Under League of Nations pressure it withdraws on March 11 but remains in Manchuria.
- *July*: The depression reaches its low point: average wages are about 60 percent of their 1929 level, dividends 57 percent, while industry operates at half its 1929 production. More than 5,000 banks have closed since 1930, and the average monthly unemployment is about 12 million.
- *November*: Franklin Delano Roosevelt is elected the 32nd president of the United States.

1933

- Immigration reaches a new low, numbering only 23,068, the smallest number since 1831. A record low of 12,944 enter through Ellis Island, which is partially converted to a detention station for enemy aliens and a training ground for the coast guard.
- *March*: Japan withdraws from the League of Nations.
- *March 4*: Franklin Delano Roosevelt is inaugurated as president of the United States.
- *March 9*: Congress approves the Emergency Banking Relief Act, which restores confidence. Banks, about half of which have failed or suspended payments since 1930, begin to reopen. By the end of the month, about three-quarters of United States banks are operating normally.
- *May 12*: The government creates the Federal Emergency Relief Administration to fund state relief agencies with grants.
- *June 16*: Congress passes the National Recovery Act to reduce unemployment and stimulate business, the Farm Credit Act is passed to refinance farm mortgages, and the Federal Deposit Insurance Corporation is established to guarantee individual bank deposits up to $5,000.
- *November 16*: United States establishes diplomatic relations with the Soviet Union, which it has not recognized since 1917.
- *December 5*: The 21st Amendment, repealing the Prohibition amendment to the Constitution, is ratified. Alcohol may now be legally sold and drunk.

1934

- *March 24*: The Philippines rejects the independence act of 1933 and is established as a commonwealth. The act provides for complete independence in 1944 and suspension of U.S. supervision in 1946.
- *June 28*: The Federal Housing Administration is established to permit housing loans by private institutions. The U.S. Housing Authority is established in 1937 to provide loans by local governments for public housing.

1935

- *August 14*: The Social Security Act is passed, establishing a federal payroll tax to provide funds for old-age and survivor pensions, unemployment insurance, and maternity and infant care.
- *November 9*: The Committee for Industrial Organization (CIO) is established to organize workers by industry rather than by employer and to include clerical and unskilled workers.

1936

- Civil War breaks out in Spain. The State Department warns all Americans to leave Spain in August.

1937

- *January 20*: President Roosevelt is inaugurated for a second term.
- *October*: The Committee of Industrial Organizations is expelled from the American Federation of Labor (AFL).

1938

- *March*: The depression reaches its lowest point in four years; the number of unemployed has risen by 2 million during the past year.
- *November 18*: The Committee of Industrial Organizations changes its name to the Congress of Industrial Organizations (CIO) and chooses John L. Lewis, president of the United Mine Workers, as its leader.

1939

- Congress rejects a bill extending the quota for German immigrants to rescue 20,000 German children seeking refuge from the Nazi government.
- *March 15*: Germany invades Czechoslovakia.
- *April 7*: Italy invades Albania. Anti-immigration sentiment mounts in the United States, but the country remains officially neutral in the face of German and Italian aggression.
- *May 5–13*: John L. Lewis leads the United Mine Workers in a strike of coal miners.
- *May 22*: Italy and Germany sign a military alliance.
- *August 23*: Germany and the Soviet Union sign a nonaggression pact.
- *September 1*: Germany invades Poland without declaring war. England and France declare war on Germany on September 3, initiating World War II.
- *September 17*: Germany takes Warsaw, and the Soviet Union invades Poland. Eleven days later Germany and the Soviet Union divide the country into two areas of control, and Polish forces surrender.
- *November 2*: Congress authorizes arms sales to warring countries. All sales must be for cash, which favors those at war against Germany.

1940

- The census reports a population of 131,669,000, of whom 528,000 are immigrants who have arrived since

1930. This reflects the lowest immigration rate in more than a century. Illiteracy is down to 2.9 percent, a drop of 1.4 percent since the last census.

- *January 26*: The United States refuses to renew its trade agreement with Japan.
- *June 3*: The United States begins shipping armaments to Great Britain.
- *June 14*: The Immigration Bureau is transferred from the Department of Labor to the Department of Justice.
- *June 15*: Germany invades Lithuania, Latvia, and Estonia, which are made part of the Soviet Union in August.
- *June 29*: The Alien Registration Act (Smith Act), requiring all aliens to register and those over the age of 14 to be fingerprinted, is passed as a form of protection from espionage and subversion. The act affects about 5 million people in the United States.
- *September 14*: Congress approves the first U.S. peacetime draft, calling for registration of all men between the ages of 21 and 35 years and training of up to 900,000.
- *September 27*: Japan signs a military and economic pact with Germany.
- *October*: Germany occupies Romania, and Italy invades Greece.

1941

- *January 20*: President Roosevelt is inaugurated for a third term.
- *April 6*: Germany attacks Yugoslavia and Greece; both surrender within the next three weeks.
- *April 13*: The Soviet Union and Japan sign a nonaggression pact.
- *June 18*: The United States suspends diplomatic relations with Germany and Italy and seizes all their assets.
- *June 22*: Germany invades the Soviet Union. All Italian consulates in the United States are closed. President Roosevelt pledges financial aid to the Soviet Union two days later.
- *July 25*: The United States and Britain end all trade with Japan.
- *July 26*: The United States calls up all Philippine troops into its service and impounds all Japanese credits in the country.
- *October 17*: German submarine torpedoes an American destroyer near Iceland, causing 11 deaths.
- *December 7*: Japanese planes attack a U.S. naval base at Pearl Harbor, Hawaii, resulting in the loss of 2,300 lives, 140 U.S. planes, eight battleships, and three destroyers.

- *December 8*: The United States declares war on Japan.
- *December 11*: Germany and Italy declare war on the United States.
- *December 12*: Japanese troops occupy Guam, a U.S. possession.
- *December 22*: Japanese troops occupy Wake Island, a U.S. possession.

1942

- *January 1*: Twenty-six nations agree to mutual support against Germany, Italy, and Japan.
- *February 19*: President Roosevelt signs Executive Order 9066, requiring the internment of all Japanese Americans, including American-born Japanese, on the West Coast, as a wartime security measure. In all, over 110,000, of which more than 75,000 were American-born, are detained in isolated camps under military guard for the duration of the war.
- *February 27*: U.S. fleet begins a three-day battle with the Japanese in the Java Sea.
- *April 9*: The Japanese take the Bataan Peninsula in the Philippines.
- *August 7*: The United States takes Guadalcanal in the Solomon Islands, its first major offensive against Japan.
- *September 29*: Bracero program of Mexican contract laborers hired to work in the American South and West begins. The numbers hired mount from 4,203 in 1942 to 437,643 in 1952.
- *November 13*: Draft age is lowered to 18.
- *December 4*: The United States makes its first air strike on Italy.

1943

- *June 4–8*: White servicemen attack African Americans and Mexican Americans wearing the fashionable "zoot" suits of the time in Los Angeles. The riot is finally quelled by military authorities.
- *July 10–14*: U.S. troops invade Italy.
- *July 25*: Italian premier Mussolini and his cabinet resign; Italian Fascist Party is dissolved on July 28.
- *September 8*: Italy surrenders.
- *November 23*: The United States takes Tarawa and Makin in the Gilbert Islands.
- *December 17*: Congress passes a bill repealing the Chinese Exclusion Acts, setting an annual Chinese quota at 105, and authorizing naturalization of Chinese immigrants as U.S. citizens.

1944

- *January 11*: Allies begin air attacks on Germany from England.
- *March 20*: German forces occupy Hungary.
- *June 6*: Allied invasion of Europe begins along Normandy coastline.
- *June 15–19*: U.S. Marines take Saipan in the Marianas.
- *June 19–20*: The Battle of the Philippine Sea ends in victory for the Allies.
- *September 11*: U.S. troops enter Germany through Luxembourg.
- *December 16–27*: Germans are defeated in the Battle of the Bulge, the last German counteroffensive of World War II, with heavy losses on both sides.
- *December 17*: The U.S. Army declares that as of January 2, 1945, Japanese Americans can no longer be excluded from the West Coast.

1945

- *January 20*: President Roosevelt is inaugurated for a fourth term.
- *February 19–March 14*: Iwo Jima, a strategic island 750 miles from Tokyo, falls to U.S. troops, with more than 20,000 American casualties.
- *April 1–July 2*: U.S. forces capture Okinawa in the Ryukyu Islands, 350 miles from Japan's main islands.
- *April 12*: President Roosevelt dies. Harry S. Truman becomes president.
- *May 1*: Adolf Hitler commits suicide in Berlin, which falls to the Allies the following day.
- *May 7*: Germany signs an unconditional surrender, ending World War II.
- *August 6*: The United States drops an atomic bomb on Hiroshima, Japan, and invades Manchuria. The second atomic bomb is dropped on Nagasaki, Japan, three days later.
- *August 8*: The Soviet Union declares war on Japan and invades Manchuria.
- *September 2*: Japan surrenders unconditionally. On the 9th Japan formally surrenders its forces in China. The war, fought by 57 Allied and Axis countries, has cost the lives of more than 15 million military personnel and an equal number of civilians. At the end of the war, an estimated 10 million European civilians have been displaced from their own countries as refugees, prisoners, or slave laborers.
- *December 22*: Special orders are issued for admission of displaced persons to the United States.

Eyewitness Testimony

Gradually I got used to it. I lived there [Lowell, Massachusetts] for three years. I found a job in a fabric mill. Then I went home each night with food to cook for the boys, and then wash the dishes and then wash the clothes. Each boy brought me underwear to wash. "I didn't come here to wash them clothes," I said to my brother. "You better buy me a ticket home. . . ."

. . . America was not a paradise. The minute I moved to Lowell . . . after a couple of days, a couple of weeks, working in the factory, preparing my lunch every morning, washing the underwear of strangers every night, and slipping and sliding on the wintery streets—this was no paradise. It was suffering. But at that time I didn't know it was suffering because I said I wanted to come here.

Now I'm the happiest woman in the world, and I always said to my friends, "Kneel down and kiss the ground, and say, 'God bless America,'" . . . I don't want to go back home anymore. I don't find anybody. . . . I'm a stranger there. I'm happy here. So I want to die here.

Maria Tovas, an immigrant who arrived from Greece in 1920, recalling her first years in America, in Coan, Ellis Island Interviews *(1997), p. 287.*

Something more like a panic than enthusiasm is manifested by our growing army of idle workers, which already numbers two million, according to the American Federation of Labor, over the promise of vast reinforcements from war-broken countries of Europe.

Through its leaders it entreats Congress to put a two-year ban on all immigration and insists that "no other question is of such vital importance to the workers" as that of protection from "the menace of excess of immigration." . . . Nor is labor, we gather from the news and editorial columns of the daily press, the only element of the community that sees cause for alarm in recent official announcements that "at this moment all records of immigration are being broken" and that behind the men and women now crowding through our gates at the rate of 125,000 a month are countless others—estimates range from 15,000,000 to 25,000,000—either clamoring for immediate passage or planning to leave their native lands at the earliest opportunity. . . . In addition to citing our already existing employment problems as a reason for checking the inrush of foreigners, many editorial observers warn us that a considerable number of the newcomers are revolutionary radicals who add to the ominous forces of social unrest; that the United States has reached a "point of saturation" where it cannot properly assimilate the foreign elements already here; and that failure to recognize this fact may result in the loss of the "American type."

Literary Digest, *December 18, 1920, p. 7.*

One reason I hated Greek school was because it gave me little time to play or do the things I wanted to do as

. . . sville, Texas, poses for a photograph. *(U.S. Citizenship and Immigration Services)*

a youngster. Imagine a grade school youngster coming home from the public school in late afternoon, then having to ready himself for a school he had no desire to attend, and which he attended often under protest, haunted with the thought he would be reprimanded by the teacher for coming to school unprepared, taking with him often a piece of Greek bread or some other edible to curb his growing appetite, often sitting in bleak, uncomfortable and sometimes cold surroundings totally different from what he knew in the public school, and forced to have a late supper. . . . For a youngster, the Greek language school was a nightmare. I felt incarcerated in it, and I hated it, but I had little choice in the matter as long as the parental will reigned supreme.

Theodore Saloutos, describing his experience in the early 1920s, in "The Greeks of Milwaukee," in Wisconsin Magazine, *Vol. 53, No. 3, (Spring 1970), p. 176.*

The tenants in our building were from Palermo, Naples, Minsk, Bucharest, and Warsaw, with a number of unidentifiables thrown in. How did we communicate? In Yiddish, partly. . . . My father, [an Italian] tailor, mastered conversational Yiddish in the needle trades; conversed in Italian with his compatriots; and spoke English at home. My [American] mother spoke enough Italian and Yiddish to shop and communicate with in-laws and neighbors.

Milton Catapano, recalling the fusion of cultures in his neighborhood on the Lower East Side of Manhattan in the 1920s, in 46 Eldridge/P.S. 65. A Memoir *(1988), p. 7.*

I feel profoundly sorry for some of the temporarily detained, a mother waiting for a delayed child, or a father with his children anxiously watching for his wife to come to him. . . .

Large numbers of immigrants have to go before a board to determine whether or not they may be admitted. I saw five or six of these boards at work. The proceedings were decorous and seemly; the arrangements for witnesses who come to speak for or against the admission of an immigrant are good. Every immigrant rejected by the board is told of his right to appeal before the Secretary of Labour in Washington.

This arrangement, the theory of which is probably right, is in practice nothing short of diabolic. For days some wretched creature is kept in suspense. The appeal board at Washington, which advises the Secretary of Labour, works on paper records, tempered, I have heard it said, by political pressure. The Secretary of Labour may be busy, overwhelmed perhaps, with work in connection with some labour dispute, or anything. Days slip by, into weeks sometimes, before a decision is reached. When the doubt affects one member of a family, perhaps a child, the mental anguish must be excruciating.

Sir Auckland Geddes, British ambassador to the United States, in Dispatch from H. M. Ambassador at Washington Reporting on Conditions at Ellis Island Immigration Station *(London, 1921), pp. 1–12.*

There is no shadow of an excuse for refusing to close the national gates in this emergency . . . The scheme to keep them open while Congress delays and debates is treachery to the nation, nothing else.

. . . What these opponents of the immigration bill want is plenty of cheap labor on whose groaning backs profits may be piled up, profits to themselves at the cost of American labor and the American nation.

The DAILY NEWS would say to these gentlemen that from this cheap labor they seek today will be recruited the Bolshevists of tomorrow. The great industries rest upon foundations of peace and social health or they are rotten at their base. Cheap labor is not cheap in reality. It will cost American industry its prosperity—to say nothing of the cost to the nation which these interests are so ready to betray. . . .

Selection in immigrations is a difficult problem. In time it may be solved. But at this moment the tide of unsettled immigration is pouring in. If we have any care for our own people, if we have any care for the integrity of America, we will dam it without delay.

Editorial supporting the bill to suspend immigration, New York Daily News, *February 3, 1921.*

"[F]irst an Irish reel, very zippy, see, and when I am good and warmed up in the middle of the Irish jig, . . . I wants the music to slip into a Jewish wedding *Kazzatzka* with a barrel of snap. . . . But the hard part is the windup, when you gotta get a medley of the Irish jig and the Russian *Kazzatzka*. . . ." [They] keep it up, patiently, for over an hour until the desired Irish-Russian-Jewish potpourri is accomplished.

A street musician describing the blend of ethnic melodies he presented on the Lower East Side of Manhattan in the 1920s, in Ornitz, Haunch, Paunch, and Jowl: An Anonymous Autobiography *(1923), pp. 116–118.*

It is not the failure of Jews to be assimilated into undergraduate society which troubles [President Lowell of Harvard and the supporters of his policy of limiting Jewish enrollment]. They do not want Jews to be assimilated into undergraduate society. What troubles them is the completeness with which the Jews want to and have been assimilated.

Horace Kallan, 1923, in Steinberg, The Ethnic Myth: Race, Ethnicity, and Class in America *(1981), p. 246.*

Motorcycles and cars, that's what really got me going on coming to the United States. Because to have a motorcycle or a car, at least at that time, was almost impossible. You had to be very well off in Denmark, and I think it was the same in most of Europe. I had no family here. But my cousin had a friend who went to the United States, and he was back to Denmark on a trip. He was going to be in Copenhagen a couple of months, and then go back to the United States. So I went with him.

My mother didn't like it too much, because it was another helper that had to leave. But she accepted it. I told her that just as soon as I could get a job, and earn some money, I would send her help, which I did. I sent her ten dollars a month, and that was a help.

. . . I remember how frustrating it was not to be able to understand what people were saying. I'll tell you, if somebody would have said, "I'll give you the money and you can take the boat back to Denmark," I would have done it, because you get so disgusted, and you don't feel good. It took me about a year before I conquered that.

Garth Svenson, Danish immigrant recalling his immigration to the United States in 1923 at the age of 24, in Coan, Ellis Island Interviews *(1997), pp. 344, 346.*

[In] New England a century has witnessed the passage of a many-child family to a one-child family. The purest New England stock is not holding its own. The next stage is the no-child marriage and the extinction of the stock which laid the foundations of the republican institutions of this country.

It is questions of this kind which are being set forth before this congress so that they may be disseminated among our people. Let us endeavor to discard all prejudices and to courageously face the facts. . . . I regard an optimist as one who faces the facts but is never discouraged by them. The optimist in science is one who delves afresh into nature to restore disordered and shattered society. . . . To know the worst as well as the best in heredity: to preserve and to select the best—these are the most essential forces in the future evolution of human society.

Henry Fairfield Osborn, anti-immigrationist and president of the American Museum of Natural History, in Eugenics, Genetics and the Family, *Volume I, (1923), p. 2.*

The Polish wife of a Pennsylvania coal miner—both good Poles, admitted a year before—had gone back suddenly to Poland to visit her old father and mother, who had taken sick and might soon die. The visit over, she returned quickly to America. She would be admitted at once, for little visits do not count against quotas. . . . On the day before the ship made port, out on the high seas, a baby Pole had been born to the returning mother. The expected had happened, "mother and child both doing well" in Ellis Island hospital, everybody delighted, until—the inspector admitted the mother but excluded the baby Pole.

"Why?" asked the father trembling.

"Polish quota exhausted," pronounced the helpless inspector.

"The baby was not born in Poland," I ruled, "but on a British ship. She is chargeable to the British quota."

"British quota exhausted yesterday," replied the inspector.

"Come to think of it, the *Lapland* hails from Antwerp," I remarked. "That's Belgium. . . . The baby is a Belgian. . . ."

"Belgian quota ran out a week ago." . . .

"Oh, look here," I began wildly. "I've got it! . . . [W]ith children it's the way it is with wills. We follow the intention. . . . Under the law . . . the baby by intention, was born in America. It is an American baby—no foreign baby at all—no British, no Belgian—just good American. That's the way I rule. Run up the flag!"

Henry H. Curran, a lawyer and former judge appointed immigration commissioner at Ellis Island in 1923, recalling the hardships of families separated under the 1921 Quota Law, in his memoir Pillar to Post *(1941), pp. 299–300.*

We were shipped first to Ellis Island and that was not very pleasant. It was rough, very rough. Years ago, they called it a cattle farm. Oh, it was just like a barn. Millions of people standing around with bundles. You were just a big herd. And they fed us with a wagon full of that cattle food. They slapped it on the plates.

You were just a number. Over 5,000 a day were arriving from all over—Russia, Romania, Poland, from Germany, from France, and naturally I couldn't speak one word of

English. . . . I was detained for two weeks. I talked with the directors every day but I couldn't explain anything.

Greta Wagner, a young German immigrant, recalling her arrival at Ellis Island in 1923, in Reeves, Ellis Island: Gateway to the American Dream *(1991), pp. 107–108.*

[A]mong all racial misconceptions none is more vigorously absurd than the belief that the Minnesota Scandinavians are, no matter how long they remain here, like the characters of that estimable old stock-company play "Yon Yonson"—a tribe humorous, inferior, and unassimilable. To generalize, any popular generalization about Scandinavians in America is completely and ingeniously and always wrong.

In Minnesota itself one does not hear . . . that the Scandinavians are a comic people, but rather that they are surly, that they are socialistic, that they "won't Americanize." Manufacturers and employing lumbermen speak of their Swedish employees precisely as wealthy Seattleites speak of the Japs, Bostonians of the Irish, Southwesterners of the Mexicans, New Yorkers of the Jews, Marine officers of the Haitians, and Mr. Rudyard Kipling of the nationalist Hindus—or nationalist Americans. Unconsciously, all of them give away the Inferior Race Theory, which is this—An inferior race is one whose members work for me. They are treacherous, ungrateful, ignorant, lazy, and agitator-ridden, because they ask for higher wages and thus seek to rob me of the dollars which I desire for my wife's frocks and for the charities which glorify me. This inferiority is inherent. Never can they become good Americans (or English Gentlemen, or Highwellborn Prussians). I know that this is so because all my university classmates and bridge partners agree with me.

Sinclair Lewis, Nobel Prize–winning American novelist, in "Minnesota: The Norse State," The Nation, *May 30, 1923.*

America's pantry door swung open an inch or two yesterday at Ellis Island and 1,600 lucky European children of toil squeezed in breathlessly to clutch at her shelves. Another 9,000, racing shoreward in swift liners, sweating in the steerage at the piers, or palpitant in the immigrant pens, prayed in alternate hope and despair that the door would not be slammed in their faces.

Several thousand prayed in vain. Already, as they still stared, with restrained smiles at their first American sunset, adding unneeded glamour to Manhattan's skyline, the dreaded and little understood quota law had operated to mark them losers in the 1923 race for the square meal which they sought in the melting pot.

Twelve steamers crossed the finish line during the night and were anchored in the harbor's Sabbath calm.

On five of those ships at dawn were 2,074 steerage immigrants who knew that they, due to the superior skill of their vessel's captain, would be the first to enter on the first day under the new year's quota.

These five winners in the dramatic trans-Atlantic race of the immigrant armada were the President Wilson, the Washington, the Canada, the Polonia, and the King Alexander.

Editorial in the New York Daily News, *July 2, 1923.*

These six months had been spent in curing their eyes of trachoma. When they had first gone for their visas, they had been told by the consul that they would have to obtain clearance from a Greek doctor in Piraeus. . . . he had suspected that their eyes might be *"no bono,"* as the condition had come to be described in immigration circles. In fact, few had escaped this endemic eye disease that was caused by lack of water, common washbasins, and communal towels. . . . Slowly, slowly the cure took effect, and although the doctor had finally given them the necessary papers, it was clear that the old lady had scarring on the cornea.

"Perhaps it won't matter," Aram said to Veron. "As long as she isn't blind, what difference should it make to the authorities?"

This worry was soon put aside when it became apparent that they were not going to be included in the June quota. Mike had learned in America that the immigration laws were being rewritten and that there would be a curtailment in the number of immigrants allowed from eastern Europe. . . . When Veron suggested that Aram attempt to bribe the officials by offering them $100 for each visa instead of the regulated fee of $10, Mike quickly gathered the money together and mailed a bank check to his mother.

. . . It was a tearful parting, for there was little hope that they would meet again in this life. . . . In a state of anxiety and fear, mingled with the pain of separation and loss, Veron, Aram, and the old lady walked up the gangplank and boarded the ship that would carry them on the first leg of their journey from the Old World to the New.

David Kherdian, American poet, in his account of his parents' immigration from Armenia around 1924, in Finding Home *(1981), pp. 19–20.*

Never again is there to be an unlimited influx of cheap alien labor; a numerical limitation of labor is here to stay, and there must be careful selection of our immigrants within the fixed limits.

Since there were fewer southeastern Europeans here in 1890 than in 1910, a percentage provision based on the former census would decidedly cut down on the number of such immigrants. This provision would change the character of immigration, and hence of our future population, by bringing about a preponderance of immigration of the stock which originally settled this country.

On the whole, immigrants from northwestern Europe furnish us the best material for American citizenship and for the future upbuilding of the American race. They have higher living standards than the bulk of the immigrants from other lands; average higher in intelligence, are better educated, more skilled, and are, on the whole, better to understand, appreciate and support our form of government.

. . . It is simply a question as to which of these two groups of aliens as a whole is best fitted by tradition, political background, customs, social organization, education and habits of thought to adjust itself to American institutions and to American economic and social conditions; to become, in short, an adaptable, homogeneous and helpful element in our American national life.

. . . If our future population is to be prevented from deteriorating, physically and mentally, higher physical standards must be required of all immigrants. In addition, no alien should be admitted who has not an intellectual capacity superior to the American average. . . . Further, aliens whose family history indicates that they come of unsound stock should be debarred.

Irving Fisher, professor at Yale University and chairman of the Eugenics Committee, in a statement of the Committee on Selective Immigration of the United States, January 6, 1924, reported in the New York Times, *January 7, 1924.*

This is the first time in the history of American legislation that there has been an attempt to discriminate in respect to European immigration between those who come from different parts of the continent. It is not only a differentiation between different countries of origin, but also of racial stocks and religious beliefs. Those coming from northern and western Europe are supposed to be Anglo-Saxon or mythical Nordics, and to a large extent Protestant. Those coming from Southern and eastern Europe are of different racial stocks and of a different faith. There are today in this country millions of citizens, both native-born and naturalized, descended from those racial stocks and entertaining those religious beliefs against which this bill deliberately discriminates. There is no mincing of the matter.

To add insult to injury, the effort has been made to justify this class legislation by charging that those who are sought to be excluded are inferior types and not assimilable. There is no justification in fact for such a contention. In common with all other immigrants, those who have come from the countries sought to be tabooed have been industrious and law-abiding and have made valuable contributions to our industrial, commercial and social development. They have done the hard manual work which is indispensable to normal economic growth. Their children, educated in our public schools, are as American in their outlook as those of the immigrants of earlier periods. Some of the intellectual leaders of the nation have sprung from this decried origin.

Louis Marshall, chairman of the American Jewish Relief Committee, in a letter to President Calvin Coolidge urging him to reject the National Origins Act then being considered, May 22, 1924, in Reznikoff, Louis Marshall, Champion of Liberty: Selected Papers and Addresses *(1957), Volume I, p. 210.*

Tokyo, June 4—There were three more suicides of Japanese yesterday in protest against the passage of the United States legislation excluding Japanese immigrants from the United States. Two threw themselves from trains, one at Hamamatsu and the other at Choshi, another hanged himself.

. . . The victim at Choshi was an unidentified boy of about twenty who was dressed like a student. He left a note saying:

"I sacrifice myself for the sake of the nation. . . ."

. . . The news of the suicides is prominently displayed by the press and it is likely to lead to an epidemic of such.

"3 Japanese Die as Protest Against U.S. Exclusion Act," New York Daily News, *June 5, 1924.*

The new selective law is just beginning to function. It is more pleasant now for the immigrants. There is no pulling and hauling. It is more pleasure for the mother or her child and for the brother and sister. Fathers do not greet me now as they did under the old law. The hangman's job used to be a pleasant one compared to mine.

Secretary of Labor James J. Davis reporting on a visit to Ellis Island after the Immigration Act of 1924 had reduced the number of immigrants crowding the depot, in the New York Times, *July 20, 1924.*

[I have tried to be] as American as possible. But now they come to me and say, I am no longer an American citizen. . . . What have I made of myself and my children?

We cannot exercise our rights, we cannot leave this country. Humility and insults, who are responsible for all this? I do not choose to live a life of an interned person. . . . Is life worth living in a gilded cage? Obstacles this way, blockades that way, and the bridges burnt behind.

Vaisnho Das Bagai, naturalized immigrant from India deprived of his citizenship by a 1923 Supreme Court decision ruling that Asian Indians were ineligible for naturalization, in a 1928 suicide note in Takaki, Strangers from a Different Shore *(1998), pp. 299–300.*

. . . We were seven people in this small apartment. Just two bedrooms. And, you know, Williamsburg [in Brooklyn, New York] was not a pretty place to come to after Jerusalem, which was a beautiful city, and it was sort of countrylike, and it was quiet, and the air was clean and fresh. This [Williamsburg] was a noisy slum. So the transition was difficult for me.

I was very angry at being uprooted. The adjustment was difficult for me. I had to learn a new language. I was put into a grade with young children until I learned the language and arrived at my right grade for my age level. But I remember being angry at being uprooted. I didn't know the reason for it. In 1929, it was not one of the times when many immigrants came. We were the only ones who came from that part of the world. They were accustomed to eastern European immigrants. We were well-treated, but it was uncomfortable being with little children. I was as tall as the teacher. I was given the name June.

June Gusoff, who immigrated from Palestine at the age of 12 in 1929, in Coan, Ellis Island Interviews *(1997), p. 410.*

We cannot make a heavy draft horse into a trotter by keeping him in a racing stable. We cannot make a well-bred dog out of a mongrel by teaching him tricks. . . .

What goes into the Melting Pot determines what must come out of it. If we put into it sound, sturdy stock, akin to the pioneer breed which first peopled this country and founded its institutions, if these new stocks are not only sound physically but alert mentally, then we shall develop a race here worthy to carry on the ideals and traditions of the founders of our country. But if the material fed into the Melting Pot is a polyglot assortment of nationalities, physically, mentally and morally below par, then there can be no hope of producing anything but an inferior race.

Robert De C. Ward, professor of history at Harvard University, in "Fallacies of the Melting-Pot Idea and America's Traditional Immigration Policy," in Grant and Davison, The Alien in Our Midst *(1930), pp. 231–232.*

Senator Patrick McCarran (1876–1954) was an influential proponent of immigration restriction throughout his career in the Senate (1932–54). *(Library of Congress, Prints and Photographs Division [LC-USZ62-110930])*

The Mexicans can no more blend into our race than can the Chinaman or the Negro, any biological [sic] scientist to the contrary notwithstanding. The blood of a game cock and that of a dorking may mix in a test tube but the birds will not fight alike in the pit or even crow alike. . . . Mexican labor, if they but knew it, is the dearest labor ever brought into our country. Every year, like that other evil importation from Mexico, the boll-weevil, this creeping blight goes further afield and robs more of our own people of the chance to live on a civilized plane.

Major Frederick Russell Burnham, anti-immigration activist, in "The Howl for Cheap Mexican Labor," in Grant and Davison, The Alien in Our Midst *(1930), pp. 45–46.*

America is not a land of one race or one class of men. We are all Americans who have toiled and suffered and known oppression and defeat, from the first Indian that offered peace in Manhattan to the last Filipino pea pickers. . . . America is also the nameless foreigner, the homeless refugee, the hungry boy begging on the street for a job and the black body dangling on a tree. America is the illiterate immigrant who is ashamed that the world of books and intellectual opportunities is closed to him.

Carlos Bulosan, Filipino immigrant who arrived in 1930, in America Is in the Heart *(1946), p. 189.*

As a boy of nine, and even younger, in my native village of Blato, in Carniola—then a Slovenian duchy of Austria and later a part of Yugoslavia—I experienced a thrill every time one of the men of the little community returned from America.

Five or six years before, as I heard people tell, the man had quietly left the village for the United States, a poor peasant clad in homespun, with a mustache under his nose and a bundle on his back; now a clean-shaven *Americanec,* he sported a blue-serge suit, buttoned shoes very large in the toes and with India-rubber heels, a black derby, a shiny celluloid collar, and a loud necktie made even louder by a dazzling horseshoe pin, which, rumor had it, was made of gold, while his two suitcases of imitation leather, tied with strips, bulged with gifts from America for his relatives and friends in the village. . . .

My notion of the United States, then, and for a few years after, was that it was a grand, amazing, somewhat fantastic place—the Golden Country—a sort of Paradise—the Land of Promise in more ways than one—huge beyond conception, thousands of miles across the ocean, untellably exciting, explosive, . . . a place full of movement and turmoil, wherein things that were unimaginable and impossible in Blato happened daily as a matter of course.

In America one could make pots of money in a short time, acquire immense holdings, wear a white collar, and have polish on one's boots like a *gospod*—one of the gentry—and eat white bread, soup, and meat on weekdays as well as on Sundays, even if one were an ordinary workman to begin with. In Blato no one ate white bread or soup and meat, except on Sundays and holidays, and very few then.

Louis Adamič, Yugoslavian immigrant, in Laughing in the Jungle *(1932), pp. 69–71.*

This country was founded with a very splendid dream in the minds of its founders. It was to be a country where the oppressed and the valiant from everywhere could find refuge and tear a living out of the generous earth without restrictions imposed by anybody.

As long as we could, we clung to that ideal. We let in anybody and everybody, almost without qualification. Then we excluded Orientals, largely because American labor did not want to have to compete on home territory with cheaper labor from the East. Later we set up the quota system, in an attempt to let in only the national strains the law-makers considered desirable and keep the others out or much reduced in volume. Now we have hardly any immigration at all.

We don't suppose the process can be reversed; aren't sure that it should be. There are too many forces in favor of little or no immigration, labor being among the strongest of those forces, as it is in Australia and New Zealand.

But we do feel a bit sad about it, and we do wonder whether it doesn't mean that the United States has passed its first exciting youth and is on the way to quieter middle age, nationally speaking.

It seems to us that the years of the immigration tide were in many ways the best years the country ever saw. There was a lift and an excitement in those years that seems somehow missing now. Things boiled and fermented, the country grew like a youngster in his early teens. The Irish came in on the 1848 potato famine wave and stormed the trenches of the earlier arrivals; the Italians arrived later, and the Jews; there was nothing stable or settled about the country because too many bold and more or less piratical fellows were forever arriving to challenge those who were already here.

. . . [I]t will be a different country by a long shot from the country it was, say, in 1886, when the Statue of Liberty was erected in New York harbor and really meant something. . . .

"End of the Melting Pot," editorial in the New York Daily News, *July 5, 1933.*

Within its population of one hundred and twenty-five million, the United States has about thirty million new citizens—the overwhelming majority of them young citizens—who are the American-born children of various nationalities. . . . The chief and most important fact . . . about the New Americans is that the majority of them are oppressed by feelings of inferiority in relation to their fellow citizens of older stock, to the mainstream of American life, and to the problem of life as a whole; which, of course, is bad for them as individuals, but, since there are so many of them and their number is still rapidly increasing, even worse for the country.

These feelings of inferiority are to some degree extensions of their parents' feelings of inferiority as immigrants in a country so drastically different from their native lands. The fathers and mothers of these New Americans were naturally at a disadvantage even in the most friendly surroundings, and the surroundings were seldom wholly and continually friendly.

. . . And these widespread personal inferiority feelings are producing in a large section of this New American element *actual* inferiority in character, mind, and physique. There is no doubt, that, by and large, in bodily and other personal qualities, many of the immigrants' children do not favorably compare with their parents. They cannot look one in the eye. They are shy. Their limp handshakes gave me creepy feelings all the way from New York to the Iron Range in Minnesota. Those handshakes symbolized for me the distressing tendency on the part of this vast and growing section of America's population toward characterlessness, lack of force and spirit, and other inferior personal qualities.

Louis Adamic, Yugoslavian immigrant, "Thirty Million New Americans," in Harper's *(November 1934).*

I dreamed once that [Atlantis] had not disappeared, after all, . . . and that it was happier and freer and finer than ever. . . . I dreamed that America had got itself in such trouble that thousands of people were leaving to live in Atlantis. . . .

But it wasn't at all easy to emigrate and give up America. . . . [W]e were fond of our country. And we knew if we went to another we mightn't come back. You can imagine how it would feel if you yourself were leaving America, and looking for the last time at all the little things in your room, and walking for the last time in the streets or the fields you knew best. . . .

But you'd find at the start that Atlantis was busy and rough, and parts of the city would be dirty and have a bad smell. And then you would find that the [Americans] mostly lived in those parts, and had to work at pretty nearly anything to pay for their lodging. You'd see Americans that you knew; an ex-senator, perhaps, sewing shirts; and a prominent bishop would be standing in the street peddling shoe-strings. . . . [T]hey would look to a native like cheap, outlandish peddlers. Even their own fellow-immigrants would try to exploit them. And instead of finding it easy to get rich, as they'd hoped, they would be so hard up they'd have to fight like wolves for each nickel.

. . . [Y]our most polite ways would seem rude in Atlantis, or silly; so you'd have to learn *their* rules of politeness, which would strike *you* as silly. And you'd have to learn habits of living which would often amaze you; and if you were slow to adopt them, they'd class you as stupid. . . .

You'd have to change yourself in so many ways, your old friends wouldn't know you. Pretty soon you wouldn't be an American at all any longer. And yet you would never feel wholly an Atlantisan either. Your children would look down on you as a greenhorn, and laugh at your slips. They would seem unsympathetic, or different,—not quite your own children. . . .

American writer Clarence Day, imagining the experience of an immigrant, in "From Noah to Now," in After All *(1936), pp. 157–161.*

If . . . it be assumed that one of our values should be a type of racism which excludes certain races from citizenship, then the plan of execution should provide for the annihilation, deportation, or sterilization of the excluded race.

Lawrence Dennis, in The Coming American Fascism *(1936), p. 109.*

[Immigrants] brought to us strength and moral fiber developed in a civilization centuries old but fired anew by the dream of a better life in America.

They brought to one new country the cultures of a hundred old ones. . . . They adopted this homeland because in this land they found a home in which the things they most desired could be theirs—freedom of opportunity, freedom of thought, freedom to worship God. Here they found life because here there was freedom to live. It is the memory of all these eager seeking millions that makes this one of America's places of romance. Looking down on this great harbor I like to think of the countless number of inbound vessels that have made this port. I like to think of the men and women who—with the break of dawn off Sandy Hook [Brooklyn]—have strained their eyes to the west for a first glimpse of the New World.

Franklin D. Roosevelt, public address on the 50th anniversary of the unveiling of the Statue of Liberty, reported in the New York Herald Tribune, *October 29, 1936.*

[Pak] was a typical Korean, an exile only in body, not in soul. Western civilization had rolled over him as water over a rock. He was a very strong nationalist; so he always sat in at the Korean Christian services, because they had something to do with nationalism. With his hard-earned money, he supported all the societies for Korean revolution against Japan. Most of his relations had moved out of Korea since the Japanese occupation . . . but Pak still lived believing that the time must come to go back, and even now, with a little money sent in care of a brother-in-law, he had bought a minute piece of land to the north of Seoul. For fifteen years his single ambition had been to get back there and settle down. On Korean land, he wanted to raise 100 percent Korean children, who would be just as patriotic as himself.

Younghill Kang, Korean immigrant novelist, in East Goes West *(1937), p. 58.*

I say if we are going to keep this country as it is and not lose our liberty in the future, we have to keep not only these children out of it but the whole damned Europe.

A witness during the Congressional hearings on a proposed bill to allow 20,000 children in flight from Nazi Germany to enter the United States outside the quota in 1939, in Divine, American Immigration Policy, 1924–1952 *(1957), p. 101.*

Once we were in camp, owing the employer for the ride to the job, having no means to get back to town except by walking and no money for the next meal, arguments over working conditions were settled in favor of the boss. I learned firsthand the chiseling techniques of the contractors—how they knocked off two or three lugs of grapes from the daily record of each member of the crew, or the way they had of turning the face of the scales away from you when you weighed your work in.

There was never any doubt about the contractor and his power over us. He could fire a man and his family on the spot and make them wait days for their wages. . . . Lord of a rag-tag labor camp of Mexicans, the contractor, a Mexican himself, knew that few men would let their anger blow, even when he stung them with curses.

Mexican immigrant Ernesto Galarza, recalling his experience as a farm laborer in California during the 1930s, in Barrio Boy *(1971), quoted in Meltzer,* The Hispanic Americans *(1982), pp. 66–67.*

Then a lot of times in the show you see Mussolini on the screen and they all start to razz him. Then I feel, "How the hell do I stand?"

Comment by an Italian American in the late 1930s, in Child, Italian or American? The Second Generation in Conflict *(1943), p. 88.*

Going down the ship's gangplank to the Custom's Office on the pier was a dream-like walk. To think that I had arrived safely in the New World! America meant a new life in safety, meant no more bombs, no more Gestapo terror, no more threat of Nazi cruelty. . . .

For the first time I felt how badly prepared we European intellectuals were for living in "another world." Why had I not learned to keep house, to cook, to sew? I could find a job immediately if only I knew what every other woman in the world was supposed to know! . . .

Here for the first time I came across a serious problem, which puzzles me even now, once in a while. What are the standards by which American employers . . . measure the suitability of an applicant? In Europe . . . a pleasant appearance, a slim figure, a charming personality are of little or no importance. I know of some very successful woman professors and social workers to whom the term "charming personality" could never be applied. Who cared? Careful grooming, on the other hand, might be considered by a prospective European employer as suspicious, as an indication of other than scholarly interests, of "worldly inclinations," interest in hunting for a husband instead of hunting for a job.

Erna Barschak, German psychologist and professor who fled the Nazis in 1940, in My American Adventure *(1945), in Neidle,* The New Americans *(1967), p. 323.*

I'm for catching every Japanese in America, Alaska and Hawaii and putting them in concentration camps.

Congressman John Rankin, Congressional Record, *December 15, 1941.*

I'd rather do business with a Jap than with an American.

Anti-Japanese sign in a funeral parlor, around 1942, in Patterson, America in the Twentieth Century *(1976), p. 310.*

The Japanese race is an enemy race. The very fact that no sabotage has taken place to date is a disturbing and confirming indication that such action will be taken.

Lieutenant General John L. Dewitt, U.S. Army, in defense of the internment of the Japanese in 1942, which he administered, quoted in Mark C. Carnes and John A. Garraty, American Destiny: Narrative of a Nation *(2003), p. 918.*

When we first arrived here we almost cried and thought that this was a land that God had forgotten. The vast expanse of sagebrush and dust, a landscape so alien to our eyes, and a desolate woe-begone feeling of being so far removed from home and fireside bogged us down mentally, as well as physically.

A Japanese-American woman interned at Camp Minidoka, north of Twin Falls, Idaho, in 1942, in Dinnerstein and Reimers, Ethnic Americans *(1988), p. 83.*

A Japanese family awaits forced relocation to an internment camp in 1942. *(New York Public Library Picture Collection)*

Their guards march them to breakfast in the big dining room at 7:30, Germans and Italians together, Japs separately. Dinner is at 12, outdoor exercise begins at 3 if they want it, supper is at 5:15, and taps at 10. It leaves a good deal of time to be got through somehow, and the immigration officials do their best to keep the time from hanging too heavily.

The guests are allowed all the newspapers and magazines they want. They draw on the island library as often as they like. The American Tract Society has stocked it with some 20,000 volumes in about 30 languages. Subject to censorship they write and receive letters. They telephone under strict supervision. They receive visits from wives, business partners, lawyers, and others whom they have a legitimate reason for seeing.

> *Clair Price, "Harbor Camp for Enemy Aliens," the* New York Times Magazine, *January 25, 1942, p. 29.*

Ysaacs, a Syrian, sat on the bench and smoked brown paper cigarettes. . . . He was from our cabin, and I knew he was worried about the money to show the examiners. But now . . . Ysaacs explained a way to get me by the examiners—a good way.

Such a good way, in fact, that when the inspector looked over my passport and entry permit I was ready.

"Do you have friends meeting you?" he asked me. "Do you have money to support yourself?"

I pulled out a round fat roll of green American money—tens, twenties—a nice thick pile with a rubber band around.

"O.K.," he said, "Go ahead." He stamped my papers.

I got my baggage and took the money roll back again to Ysaacs' friend, Arapouleopolus, so he could rent it over again to another man. One dollar was all he charged to use it for each landing. Really a bargain.

> *Georgian immigrant George Papashvily, recounting his arrival from Russia at Ellis Island, in George and Helen Waite Papashvily,* Anything Can Happen *(1945), pp. 3–4.*

I wanted to show something, to contribute to America. My parents could not become citizens but they told me, 'You fight for your country.'

> *Minoru Hinahara, Nisei Japanese-language interpreter in the U.S. 27th Army Division who participated in the 1945 invasion of Okinawa during World War II, in an interview (1988) reported in Takaki,* Strangers from a Different Shore *(1989), p. 385.*

My friends and my family—they mean everything to me. They are the most important reason why I am giving up my education and my happiness to go to fight a war that we never asked for. But our Country is involved in it. Not only that. By virtue of the Japanese attack on our nation, we as American citizens of Japanese ancestry have been mercilessly flogged with criticism and accusations. But I'm not going to take it sitting down! I may not be able to come back. But that means little. My family and friends—they are the ones who will be able to back their arguments with facts. They are the ones who will be proud. In fact, it is better that we are sent to the front and that a few of us do not return, for the testimony will be stronger in favor of the folks back home.

> *A Japanese-American soldier writing home from the European battle front during World War II, in Lind,* Hawaii's Japanese: An Experiment in Democracy *(1946), pp. 161–162.*

The two world wars in which the United States was arrayed against Germany were painful experiences for German-Americans. They hated to be obliged to fight against their racial cousins, but they did so, and it is significant that of the millions of German descendants in the United States during those dreadful wars there was not one case of treason.

The Germans, while loving the country of their origin, did not approve of Kaiser Wilhelm II and his warlords, nor Hitler and his wretched Nazis. Their sympathies were with England, and their adoption of the culture of England determined their attitudes. When England was in trouble in 1917, and again in 1941, the German-Americans rallied to her support against the Fatherland. This is a phenomenon little remarked upon.

John Rauch, Indianapolis lawyer and distant relative of novelist Kurt Vonnegut, "An Account of the Ancestry of Kurt Vonnegut, Jr., by an Ancient Friend of His Family," in Vonnegut, Palm Sunday: An Autobiographical Collage, (1981), pp. 20–21.

What if I were killed? . . . All the horrible thoughts imaginable would grip me, and before I could find the answers, other thoughts would begin to swirl in. I remembered about us, the Mexican-Americans . . . how the Anglo had pushed and held back our people in the Southwest . . .

Why fight for America when you have not been treated as an American? . . . . [But] all we wanted was a chance to prove how loyal and American we were.

A Mexican-American soldier in a letter written as he was traveling to the European front during World War II, in Takaki, A Different Mirror (1993), p. 393.

Our liberties, our homes, and our lives directly threatened by fascism demand our greatest unity. . . . We as Latinos have had centuries of gloriously fighting for freedom; we shall not abandon this historic tradition in these days of crisis. . . . We are also children of the United States. We will defend her.

Statement of the Congreso del Pueblo de Habla Española (the Spanish-Speaking Congress) calling on Mexican Americans to serve in the United States war effort during World War II, in García, Mexican Americans: Leadership, Ideology & Identity, 1930–1960 (1989), p. 166.

Notes

1. Margaret D. Stock, "Essential to the Fight: Immigrants in the Military, Five Years after 9/11," Immigration Policy Center, November 3, 2006. Available online. URL: http://http://www.ailf.org/ipc/infocus/infocus_11206.shtml.

CHAPTER NINE

Some Windows Open
1946–1954

Postwar Immigration

The restrictive acts of 1921 and 1924 and the depression beginning in 1929 had a drastic effect on immigration: The numbers admitted annually dropped sharply for twenty-five years. Between 1921 and 1930, more than four million immigrants entered the United States. The number fell to slightly more than half a million during the 1930s, and from 1931 to 1946 it never reached 100,000 in any one year. But although the quota laws and the collapse of the stock market stemmed the flood of immigration to the United States, World War II had the same unifying effects as World War I on the country, and reports of the Nazi holocaust brought about a marked reduction of American anti-Semitism. Hostility to Catholics, long a source of profound anti-immigrant sentiment in America, also dropped as Catholics, Protestants, and Jews formed many alliances.

When shipping lanes reopened after the war, immigration surged upward again, at least from the countries with quotas that allowed it, and newcomers met with far less opposition than they had before the war. In 1945, the final year of the international conflict, only 38,119 immigrants entered the country. The following year, the number rose to 108,721, and it continued to mount through the remainder of the decade, reaching almost a quarter of a million by 1950.

Changes in the law reflected the changing attitudes of the public. In the years immediately following World War II, racial and religious discrimination was banned in public accommodations, education, and employment. Although ethnic prejudices did not altogether disappear, they ceased to be supported by law, and the generally improved relationships between races, nationalities, and religions in the United States allowed for an improvement in some of the more discriminatory aspects of immigration law. There was no change in the small quota allotments governing admission to the United States, but the application of these laws became less strict. Nevertheless, the lists of those seeking visas in Europe continued to grow disproportionately. In one year there were nearly 104,000 applicants for the 308 visas allotted to Greece.

However, despite such obstacles, some windows began to open, and new patterns of immigration began to emerge.

Emergency Relief Legislation

The war had altered national boundaries, disrupted families, and shattered economies throughout Europe, and the resulting chaos had made it impossible for many to find or return to their homes. Survivors of the Nazi concentration camps, as well as forced laborers transported to Germany from Nazi-occupied countries, had no homes to return to. Others had fled from the Soviet advances into Germany and abandoned their property. The first American gesture in response to these tragic conditions was an order signed by President Truman on December 22, 1945, just months after the war ended, directing American consulates to give preference to displaced persons in granting visas to enter the United States. This was a humane recognition of the hardships suffered by the victims of war, but it was cautiously framed and did little to extend American hospitality. Since the directive specified that all new admissions be counted against the quotas granted for each country, and since most of the homeless were from countries with low quotas, only about 41,000 people were able to enter under its provisions. When more refugees needed asylum than the quotas allowed, the numbers were charged to future allotments, thus "mortgaging" their countries' quotas. As a result, some nations used up their full quotas for several years to come in the first years after the new policy went into effect. By the end of the period the act remained in force, Poland's allotment was half used up until the year 2000, and Latvia's until 2274.

The directive became a formal law three years later with the passage of the Displaced Persons Act of 1948. This was the first U.S. statute to establish a distinct refugee policy. It provided for the admission of 250,000 refugees over a period of two years. When the law expired in 1950, it was renewed for another two years, and the total number of displaced persons allowed to enter was raised to 415,000. During these years, the total number of people seeking refuge in the United States increased as anti-Semitic riots in Poland and Romania sent Jews once more running for their lives and as Czech, Polish, Yugoslavian, and Baltic refugees fled postwar Communist domination.

The border patrol examines all incoming ships. *(U.S. Citizenship and Immigration Services)*

An Immigration Service attorney presents certificates of citizenship to foreign-born children of U.S. Army personnel after World War II in San Francisco. *(U.S. Citizenship and Immigration Services)*

The sympathy of the American people for these victims of war was not unanimous, and the emergency relief measures aimed at their rescue were uneasy compromises. The amended Displaced Persons Act of 1950 specified that three-quarters of those admitted from Europe were to be displaced persons as defined by the International Refugee Organization and the rest to be those of German ancestry living in the Baltic States. When it ran out in June 1952, a new law, the Refugee Relief Act of 1953, allowed another 214,000 homeless persons to enter the United States during the next 41 months. The new laws applying to both displaced persons and refugees met with considerable opposition and were passed only because intensive lobbying secured strict adherence to the quota system of the 1924 immigration act. The laws strongly favored people of Germanic background and exiles from the Baltic States, and the 1948 bill specifically stipulated that more than 80 percent of those admitted under its provisions be Christian. President Truman signed the bill with great reluctance, objecting especially to the religious provision as discriminating "in callous fashion against displaced persons of the Jewish faith." Only after most of the Jewish refugees had been accommodated in the newly formed state of Israel did an amendment to the 1950 act eliminate that provision.

Less controversial was an emergency bill enabling wives, husbands, and children of members of the armed forces to join their families in the United States. The War Brides Act of 1946, followed in a few months by the Fiancées Act, lifted quota requirements for some 150,000 wives and fiancées, a few hundred husbands, and some 25,000 children of United States servicemen and women in Europe by

1950. The law was amended in 1947 to allow the entry of nearly 5,000 Chinese and some 800 Japanese wives as well.

Internal Security Legislation

Because tension between the United States and the Soviet Union mounted after World War II, American immigration policy reflected the fears and suspicions of the cold war. The fear of Communist "infiltration" spread as the fear of "anarchists" had done in the 1920s, and the onset of the Korean War intensified it. Legislation prohibiting the entry of those who advocated the violent overthrow of the government was already in place, but public sentiment, inspired by this new "Red Scare," called for stricter laws. FBI director J. Edgar Hoover clearly articulated the national terror as early as 1947 when he testified before the House Un-American Activities Committee. "The Communist Party of the United States is a fifth column if ever there was one," he announced. "It is far better organized than were the Nazis in occupied countries prior to their capitulation. They are seeking to weaken America just as they did in their era of obstruction when they were aligned with the Nazis. Their goal is the overthrow of our government. There is no doubt as to where a real Communist's loyalty rests. Their allegiance is to Russia, not the United States. . . . Communism, in reality, is not a political party. It is a way of life—an evil and malignant way of life. It reveals a condition akin to disease that spreads like an epidemic, and like an epidemic, a quarantine is necessary to keep it from infecting the nation." Such a quarantine was not long in coming. In 1948 several leaders of the American Communist Party were imprisoned for "conspiring to advocate seditious acts."

Congress passed several laws limiting the growth and activities of the American Communist Party during the late 1940s and making it more difficult for immigrants likely to "infect" the nation with communist ideas to enter. Fear of such infection was stimulated by political agitation. Wisconsin senator Joseph McCarthy announced on February 9, 1950, that he had the names of 205 persons working in the State Department who were "card-carrying" members of the Communist Party. The report was later proved to be a hoax, and Senator McCarthy was censured by the Senate, but the impact of such announcements remained powerful and moved Congress to act. On September 20 of that year, Congress approved its strongest and most sweeping anticommunist law, and the one to have the most direct bearing on immigration.

The Internal Security Act was proposed by Nevada senator Patrick A. McCarran, a strong opponent of the open-door policy for American immigration, even though he was himself the son of two Irish immigrants. The law required all organizations listed as either fascist or communist by the attorney general, and all members of such organizations, to register with the Justice Department. It also banned the employment in national defense work of communists or communist sympathizers, prevented them from acquiring passports, and authorized their deportation. Any group the Justice Department listed as a "Communist front" organization was ordered to report all its members and disclose all its finances. The law prohibited anyone who had been a member of "a totalitarian organization" from becoming a citizen. It required legal resident aliens to report their addresses annually and made reading, writing, and speaking English a requirement for naturalization. Finally, it barred the entry of anyone suspected of being a communist or being "likely to engage in subversive activity."

Basically a revision of the 1918 Anarchists Act, the McCarran Internal Security Act of 1950 was much stricter and gave the government broader powers to exclude aliens whose backgrounds gave the slightest reason for suspicion. Many considered the law a violation of civil liberties and felt that it gave powers to immigration officials that were too sweeping and too vaguely defined. Among those who opposed the law was President Truman, who vetoed it the day after Congress passed it. His reasons included his belief that the act "would antagonize friendly governments," that "it would put the government of the United States in the thought-control business," and that "it would give government officials vast powers to harass all of our citizens in the exercise of their right of free speech." Such a bill, he argued in his veto, "would strike blows at our position in the forefront of those working for freedom in the world."

Congress was not persuaded. The next day, September 23, it passed the bill over the president's veto, and the McCarran Internal Security Act became law.

The McCarran-Walter Act

The patchwork of acts and amendments related to immigrants, refugees, and displaced persons had been unsatisfactory to both liberals and conservatives since the war, and by the early 1950s the public was calling for an all-encompassing law consolidating the previous statutes into one comprehensive regulation. The result was the Immigration and Naturalization Act of 1952, a massive document whose 164 separate sections, some with more than 40 subdivisions, revised and codified all prior immigration laws. The act was the work of Senator McCarran, and Pennsylvania congressman Francis E. Walter, another influential opponent of a liberal immigration policy, and, with minor amendments during the following years, it was to remain the basic law governing American immigration for many years.

Popularly known as the McCarran-Walter Act, the new law was in reality an update of the Johnson-Reed Act of 1924. It closed up some loopholes in that legislation but retained as its principal feature the structure of the quota system based on national origins. There were some changes in numbers—it determined the annual quota of national groups on a flat rate of one-sixth of 1 percent of the population according to the 1920 census and established a limit of about 160,000 entries per year—but the act made no fundamental changes in the principle of selection.

Within its rigid and rather narrow quotas, the law established four levels of preference for applicants. The first group to be allowed into the country was those with skills or professional training that the nation needed. Doctors, engineers, research scientists, and educators were among those favored by this provision. Lower levels of preference were accorded to those with close family relations to U.S. citizens and to relatives of legal resident aliens. Husbands and wives of U.S. citizens were allowed to enter outside of both the quota and the preference system.

The Immigration and Nationality Act of 1952 had one relatively liberal new provision: it removed the ban on Asian immigrants. But even this did little to open the door, since the law set a quota of only 2,000 for people of the Asia-Pacific triangle. Apart from this token gesture to Asia and the Pacific islands, the act basically repeated the early pattern of favoring England and Germany and establishing low allotments for southern and eastern Europe.

The central feature of the new legislation, however, was its many provisions to exclude possible subversives and to permit the expulsion of aliens, and even of naturalized citizens, whose behavior was seen as potentially "prejudicial to the public interest." The act kept all the "quality control" features of previous legislation—exclusion on the basis of medical, psychological, moral, and ideological grounds—and even added a few new ones. In all, the act established 31 distinct "classes of aliens ineligible to receive visas and excluded from admission." These included all the old familiar groups—the feebleminded, the insane, the tubercular, the epileptic, the "psychopathic"; paupers, prostitutes, polygamists, beggars, stowaways, criminals, narcotics addicts and dealers, etc.—and added such new categories as "aliens seeking to enter the United States for the purpose of performing skilled or unskilled labor, if the Secretary of Labor has determined and certified . . . that . . . sufficient workers in the United States who are able, willing, and qualified are available at the time. . . ." Thus, under the new law organized labor was not threatened with competition from immigrants willing to work for lower wages than natives.

Many of the new provisions specifically targeted the communists and communist sympathizers by whom America had felt so threatened during the Red Scare of the 1950s. The wording of the McCarran-Walter Act took no chances of omitting any kind of subversive alien from its list. It barred "anarchists," as previous laws had done, and, in Section 212 (a), (28), (C), (i–vi), it hammers the point home by specifying among those denied entry "aliens who are members of or affiliated with the Communist Party of the United States, . . . the Communist or any other totalitarian party of any state of the United States, of any foreign state, or of any political or geographical subdivision of any foreign state, any section, subsidiary, branch, affiliate, or subdivision of any such association or party, or the direct predecessors or successors of any such association or party . . ." and so on for several pages. Over all, the Immigration and Naturalization Act of 1952 was the most rigorously restrictionist immigration law in American history, and many people considered it the most discriminatory.

The press was generally hostile to the act. Pulitzer Prize–winning historian Oscar Handlin attacked it in an *Atlantic Monthly* article unambiguously entitled "We Need More Immigrants" (May 1953) for keeping the national origins quotas of the 1924 act, with all of "[their] racist consequences." The liberal publication *The Nation* condemned the McCarran-Walter Act even more fiercely, calling it "obnoxious, dangerous, un-American, formidably exclusive, cruelly suspicious, and offensively arrogant." Its purpose in using quotas, the anonymous writer asserted, was to retain "the archaic and baseless ideas that some races are superior to others." [1]

President Truman opposed the bill as unequivocally as he had opposed the Internal Security Act two years earlier, calling it inconsistent with the country's democratic ideals. In his veto message of June 25, 1952, he emphasized the importance of the issue. "What we do in the field of immigration and naturalization," he stated, "is vital to the continued growth and internal development of the United States—to the economic and social strength of our country—which is the core of the defense of the free world." But, he argued, the Immigration and Naturalization Act did not contribute to that strength. Instead, by perpetuating the system of national-origin quotas, it reinforced the racist policies of the Johnson-Reed Bill. "The greatest vice of the present quota system," Truman wrote, ". . . is that it discriminates, deliberately and intentionally, against many of the peoples of the world. The purpose of it was to cut down and virtually eliminate immigration to this country from Southern and eastern Europe."

Truman admitted that the bill took a step to improve the nation's immigration law by granting "at least some minimum immigration quota" to the countries of Asia, but he noted that "this most desirable provision comes before me embedded in a mass of legislation which would perpetuate injustices of long standing against many other nations of the world, hamper the efforts we are making to rally the men of the East and West alike to the cause of freedom, and intensify the repressive and inhumane aspects of our immigration procedures. The price is too high and, in good conscience, I cannot agree to pay it."

Truman could not agree to pay it, but the U.S. Congress could. The House of Representatives overrode the president's veto on June 26, and the Senate did the same the following day.

Some elements of the McCarran-Walter Act drew heavy criticism in American newspapers for what one critic called its "blatant racial and ethnic discrimination." Foreign press coverage was even more negative. The influential French journalist Jean-Jacques Servan-Schreiber wrote in 1952 that the new immigration law "is stupid, inefficacious and does more harm to the United States than all the Soviet propaganda." In the same year England's *Manchester Guardian* observed that the bill "is doing the United States incalculable harm and is undoing all the lavish propaganda about its noble leadership in the free world. . . . Most countries have their immigration absurdities, but there are aspects of the McCarran Act that go beyond mere bureaucratic arbitrariness and are repugnant to civilized intercourse."

Truman urged in his veto that Congress undertake "a careful re-examination of this entire matter" and suggested "the creation of a representative commission of outstanding Americans to examine the basic assumptions of our immigration policy." Despite the failure of his veto, he did appoint such a commission, which issued a 319-page report on January 1, 1953. The report, *Whom We Shall Welcome,* took its name from George Washington's famous 1783 statement "The bosom of America is open to receive not only the Opulent and Respectable Stranger, but the oppressed and persecuted of all Nations and Religions; whom we shall welcome to a participation of all our rights and privileges, if by decency and propriety of conduct they appear to merit the enjoyment." As the title suggests, the document was highly critical of the McCarran-Walter Act and urged Congress to end the national-origins system of quotas in favor of a policy welcoming immigrants regardless of race, creed, color, or place of origin. The commission recommended raising the number of people eligible to enter the country annually to 251,162 and urged that within the quotas "there should be a statutory priority, implementing the Right of Asylum, for the admission annually of 100,000 refugees, expellees, escapees, and remaining displaced persons."

The report was issued shortly before Truman left the White House and had no influence on the policies of Dwight Eisenhower, his successor. It was largely ignored by both the government and the public, and although during the next few years Congress passed several acts making minor revisions in the bill, America's laws governing immigration, as spelled out in the McCarran-Walter Act, remained in force for the next 13 years essentially unchanged.

Despite the strictness of the new law, however, more than 2.5 million immigrants entered the United States during the 1950s. The previous decade (including the war years) had seen a total of only 1,035,039. The upswing in new arrivals, and especially the great increase in illegal entries, posed a problem for the always-understaffed Immigration and Naturalization Service (INS). Faced with new and almost incomprehensibly complicated laws, the INS pleaded with Congress for more personnel and funds for its work, but with little success. The border patrol, guarding the thousands of miles of the United States's frontiers with Mexico and Canada, still numbered only about 1,000 agents. Even so, in 1952 the patrol was responsible for the arrest of 800,000 deportable aliens, and two years later the total number apprehended was more than a million. Ninety percent of the illegal aliens deported by the United States during those years were Mexicans.

New Sources of Immigration

In 1820, the first year in which immigration to the United States was recorded, a total of 8,385 aliens entered the country. Of them, 7,690, or about 92 percent, were from Europe. The vast majority of newcomers continued to be from Europe throughout the century; the ratio of European immigrants to arrivals from other regions was never less than nine to one in any year until 1911. But European immigration naturally diminished as a result of the quota laws of the 1920s, and the numbers entering from areas not restricted by quotas grew proportionately. In the decade from 1921 to 1930—a period that witnessed the arrival of more than 4 million immigrants—fewer than 60 percent of the newcomers to America were from Europe. By the 1950s, only a little more than half of those entering the country were Europeans.

The two regions that provided the greatest increase in immigration to the United States from the 1920s onward were Asia and the Americas, but the growth was far from equal between them until the 1970s. Only 30 immigrants from Asia entered the United States in the 10 years following 1820: two from China, eight from India, and 20 from Turkey. The numbers grew steadily until laws prohibiting entry from Asia cut them back. When the McCarran-Walter Act cracked the door slightly to Asians after World War II, the numbers grew slowly, since the new law granted them small quotas. In the 1920s, a scant 2 percent of the immigrants to the United States were from Asia; in the next decade the total rose to only about 3 percent. China sent fewer than 5,000 immigrants to America in the 1930s, but the number grew to 16,709 in the 1940s. India's numbers rose from 195 to 1,380 during the same period, and Japan's fell from 1,948 to 1,555.

The Philippines

The largest increase in immigration of any Asian country after World War II was from the Philippine Islands. From 1924 until that nation was granted independence 10 years later, its residents were classed as American nationals and were therefore free to enter the United States, although they were not eligible for citizenship until 1946. The need for agricultural labor in Hawaii brought great numbers of Filipinos during the first decade of the 20th century, but in 1920 there were still no more than 5,000 living on the mainland. By 1930 there were an estimated 30,000 Filipinos living in California and perhaps 15,000 elsewhere in the continental United States, while Hawaii held more than 60,000. There were a few students and professionals among them, but almost all the Philippine immigrants were migratory agricultural workers. Males outnumbered females by as much as 15 to 1 on the mainland.

Like the Chinese and Japanese, immigrants from the Philippines suffered severe discrimination. A powerful movement for Philippine exclusion grew in the 1930s. Organized labor on the West Coast, supported by numerous patriotic societies, fought their entry, as it had fought for Chinese exclusion in the previous century, and competition for work in fruit and vegetable picking led to violent anti-Filipino demonstrations in California and Washington State. The American Federation of Labor passed a resolution in 1928 declaring that the number of Filipino laborers coming to the United States was sufficient "to create a race problem" and formally urging "exclusion of the Filipino race." California and other Western states passed laws against intermarriage of Americans and "members of the Malay race." In 1930 a California judge wrote, "It is a dreadful thing when these Filipinos, scarcely more than savages, come to San Francisco, work for practically nothing and obtain the society of white girls." Although most arrivals spoke at least two European languages, Spanish and English, they were regarded, like the Chinese and Japanese, as too alien ever to be able to assimilate to American society. One Filipino immigrant, Carlos Bulosan, wrote in 1943, "Do you know what a Filipino feels in America? . . . He is the loneliest thing on earth. There is much to be appreciated . . . beauty, wealth, power, grandeur. But is he part of these luxuries? . . . He is enchained, damnably, to his race, his heritage." Filipino Americans suffered many restrictions; they were not permitted to practice law, medicine, and other professions, and when World War II began they were exempted from the draft and prohibited from volunteering for military service. However, during the war some 30,000 Filipinos in their own country were taken into the U.S. Army to fight the Japanese. When the war ended, General Douglas MacArthur and President Franklin Roosevelt promised these fighters that they would be welcomed to the United States and granted citizenship. The U.S. government retracted the offer nine months before the deadline, however, and the Filipinos were unable to emigrate until the Immigration Act of 1990 granted them the opportunity 45 years later. Few of the veterans were still alive to accept the offer by then.

Philippine immigration, like all other immigration to the United States, was reduced by the depression in the 1930s, but the number nevertheless grew from 4,690 in the 1940s to 19,307 in the following 10 years. By the 1960s Filipinos represented the largest group of Asian immigrants to the United States. The number entering the country from the Philippine Islands in that decade reached 98,376.

The 1990 census counted 1.4 million Filipino Americans, a number second only to that of the Chinese among Asian immigrants to the United States.

The Americas

The McCarran-Walter Act did not spare the Western Hemisphere from quota restrictions for humanitarian reasons, but rather for two strictly practical ones: the need for low-priced labor to work on the farms and ranches of the Southwest and the growing solidarity of the Western Hemisphere. The strategic importance of close ties with America's neighbors to the north and south was partly an expression of the country's growing rejection of Europe and partly a recognition of the importance of trade with Canada and Latin America. Isolationists continued to oppose open borders in the New World, but all proposals to restrict immigration to the United States from other countries in the Americas were defeated as violating what was known as the "Good Neighbor Policy." In the decade following 1911, Europe accounted for 75 percent of the arrivals to the United States

Immigration agents at Champlain, New York, inspect bus and highway passengers. *(U.S. Citizenship and Immigration Services)*

and the Americas for less than 20 percent; by the 1950s the balance had shifted to less than 53 percent from Europe and nearly 40 percent from the Western Hemisphere.

The first great wave came from Canada, a country whose populace had never met with any very serious opposition in coming to the United States. Racially and linguistically similar to their neighbors south of the 49th parallel, Canadians had little trouble crossing the long border that separated the two countries, and during the 1920s nearly a million poured through Ontario into the American Midwest, outnumbering the immigrants from all the rest of the Western Hemisphere. In the following decade, total immigration to the United States was reduced due to the depression, but Canada continued to account for more than the combined influx from Mexico, the Caribbean, and South and Central America by more than two to one.

Most of the arrivals from the North were English-speaking descendants of British families, although a few French-speaking Canadians came to join the close little French-Canadian communities already established in the mill towns of New England. Neither political nor religious pressure accounted for this brief tide of Canadian immigration; the impetus was entirely economic, and when industrial development began to flourish in Canada after World War II, Canadian immigration fell off sharply. By the 1950s, arrivals from Canada accounted for considerably less than half of the total immigration from the Americas.

A longer-lasting increase in postwar immigration to the United States came from the Caribbean and from South and Central America. At the beginning of the 20th century, a steady stream of new arrivals from the West Indies began, accounting for an average of more than 100,000 per decade. Like all immigration, it dropped off because of the depression in the 1930s and the war from 1942 to 1945, but it resumed after World War II. Until then it was largely composed of blacks from the British West Indies. From the end of the war, the numbers from the French West Indies, Cuba, and Haiti grew. Cubans—a total of 26,313—accounted for more than half of the newcomers from the Caribbean during the 1950s, and the number nearly tripled during the next 10 years.

The British West Indian immigrants arrived with certain advantages over most aliens. They spoke English, and many were highly skilled. As British nationals they were able to enter under the unfilled portion of the British quota. They tended to settle in the large cities along the East Coast, especially New York and Boston, and formed a large and distinct community separate from the African Americans already established in those cities. Under the terms of the McCarran-Walter Act, however, the situation of people from the West Indies changed: they were allotted a small quota of their own, and the stream came to an abrupt end. After 1952, most of those leaving Trinidad and Jamaica made their way to England, where they settled in London and other large industrial centers.

From the end of World War II, the vast majority of those entering the United States from the Caribbean were from the American territory of Puerto Rico. Since the annexation of the island following the Spanish-American War of 1898, Puerto Ricans have been American nationals, and by the Jones Act of 1917 they were declared citizens. Thus, their entry into the continental United States is not technically immigration, but they have experienced many of the same problems of adjustment as aliens entering the country. Like Europeans, West Indians, and Asians before them, they encountered racial discrimination and were relegated to the lowest-paying jobs, in addition to having to cope with communicating in a foreign language. For the first quarter of the 20th century, Puerto Rican migration was small: in 1910 the total number of Puerto Ricans living on the mainland was estimated to be 1,500.

Although economic opportunities were limited on their home island, and no legal difficulties prevented their migration to the mainland of the United States, the cost of the boat trip was usually prohibitive, amounting to more than the average Puerto Rican earned in a year. In 1930 the American census reported a total of 53,000 Puerto Ricans living in the continental United States. Ten years later the number had grown to only 70,000.

However, World War II made the trip both more attractive and more affordable. Overpopulation and poverty at home drove many to seek their fortunes elsewhere, and new jobs became available in the United States as native laborers either entered the armed forces or left their regular jobs to work in defense plants or factories. More significant, perhaps, was the availability of air travel. Commercial airlines made the trip from San Juan to New York in a few hours, and at prices as low as $50, initiating what has been called "the first airborne migration in history." In 1945 the net migration from Puerto Rico (the total arrivals minus the total returns) was a little more than 13,000; the following year the number rose to 40,000. When the Korean War began in 1950, the need for labor stimulated another surge of Puerto Rican migrants to the mainland. In that year, 35,000 arrived. In 1951 the figure was more than 53,000, and in 1953 it mounted to 69,000. An estimated 675,000 Puerto Ricans were living in the continental United States in 1955, more than 90 percent of them in New York City.

Immigration from South and Central America increased following World War II at the same rate as that from the rest of the hemisphere. From a total of 13,664 during the 1930s, the figures mounted to 43,496 from 1941 to 1950, and the next decade saw the entry of 136,379 from South and Central America. From Argentina the number of arrivals grew from 1,349 during the 1930s to 19,486 between 1950 and 1959. Immigration from Colombia increased almost as much, rising from 1,223 to more than 18,000 during those same years.

Of all increases in American immigration from the New World, however, none was to grow more impressively or to represent a larger percentage of the total than that from Mexico. Mexican immigrants had been arriving steadily since the turn of the century, when the construction of railroads and the growth of agriculture in the southwestern states created a great demand for cheap labor. As the region developed, so did the need for workers, and the number grew from 49,642 during the years between 1901 and 1910 to 219,000 in the next decade, and to 459,000 in the 1920s. During World War II, labor shortages in California caused by the internment of Japanese Americans led to temporary admissions from Mexico under the bracero program, but legal immigration—entry of Mexicans as resident aliens with

Braceros undergo customs inspection at the Mexican border in 1955. *(U.S. Citizenship and Immigration Services)*

permanent status—increased significantly after the war. The numbers fell during the depression, but from 1941 to 1950, a total of 60,589 immigrants from Mexico came to the United States. During the next 10 years, the number swelled to 299,811 and continued to grow. By 1980 the census reported that there were some 2.2 million Mexican-born residents of the United States, and that they represented nearly 15 percent of all foreign-born Americans.

The range of Mexican settlement began to expand as well. Originally limited to the cotton-, fruit-, and vegetable-growing region of the Southwest, Mexican immigrants soon spread to the Rocky Mountains and the Middle West in their search for work. By the 1970s Mexicans had begun to enter industry and were firmly established in Chicago, Detroit, and New York.

A distinctive feature of the huge wave of Mexican immigration that emerged after the war is the high percentage of the total believed to be in the country illegally. The Census Bureau reported in 1980 that the number of those Mexicans it politely calls "undocumented" may have been as much as 50 percent. It also believed that from 50 to 60 percent of all illegal aliens in the United States were from Mexico, despite continued efforts at patrolling the border. The Mexican illegal immigrant has not always been the traditional "wetback" who has sneaked across the border under cover of darkness; in many cases the undocumented alien is a legal visitor who has simply outstayed his or her visa and melted into the general population. Estimates of the number of such illegal aliens vary widely, but by the end of the 20th century many experts believed that there were as many as 12 million living in the United States.

Ellis Island Closes

For more than six decades, American immigration was almost synonymous with Ellis Island, the country's largest depot. The majority of all immigrants to enter the country during those years landed on that 27.5-acre island in New York harbor. But by the end of the war, in the summer of 1945, airplanes began to rival ships as a means of transportation, and hundreds of thousands of war brides, refugees, and displaced persons arrived at La Guardia Airport exempt from the national quota laws. Less than 1 percent of the new arrivals had to go to Ellis Island to be processed. The station continued examining aliens thought to have contagious diseases, investigating those suspected of carrying false documents, and deporting illegal aliens, but the average population of the island from 1945 to 1950 was only about 600. In 1950 the hospital was closed because the facility's budget was not sufficient to maintain it.

When the Internal Security Act went into effect at the beginning of the Korean War, there was a flurry of activity on the island because the depot was briefly used as a detention center for suspected illegal aliens already resident in the country. In June 1951 a dragnet of foreigners—most of them arrested in New York restaurants and hotels—brought some 1,500 more suspects to Ellis Island. The next year the number of detainees fell to about 10 until Christmas Eve, when the McCarran-Walter Act required that foreign sailors be examined for their political views before receiving shore leave. The island was once more crowded for a time, but the sojourn of most of these unhappy residents was brief.

Clearly the facility was costing more money to operate than it was worth to the country. In 1953 the average number of residents on Ellis Island was 230, and the staff employed to process them numbered 250. The following year the government decided to close the station, along with five smaller immigrant depots in Massachusetts, Washington, California, and Hawaii. In November 1954 Attorney General Herbert Brownell announced that the services that had been performed on Ellis Island since 1892 would be handled from then on at the Immigration Service's office at 70 Columbus Avenue in Manhattan. Only about 10 people were being held on Ellis Island by then. On its last day, November 12, the number had fallen to one, a Norwegian sailor who had missed his boat.

Chronicle of Events

1946

- Unemployment falls below 4 percent. Postwar inflation reaches new highs.
- Immigration to the United States almost triples from the preceding year, totaling 108,721. In 1947 the number mounts to 249,187, and the following year to 265,520.
- *January 10*: The first meeting of the United Nations takes place in London with 51 countries participating. The League of Nations disbands and transfers its properties to the United Nations on April 18. On December 14 a site for the United Nations is established in New York City on land donated by John D. Rockefeller.
- *March 20*: The last Japanese-American internment camp, at Tule Lake, California, closes; some 5,000 internees have been removed during the preceding month and the remaining 554 internees are relocated or freed. The final 302 are released on September 6, 1947 but ordered deported.
- *April 1–May 29*: The United Mine Workers go on strike, ending all coal production in the United States. The striking workers total over 400,000. President Truman orders the military to seize the mines on May 21, and the miners return to work May 29.
- *May 17–28*: Railway workers announce a strike. President Truman orders the seizure of the railroads, and the conflict is settled without a strike.
- *June 4*: Trial for war crimes of high-ranking Japanese military and political leaders begins. Seven are condemned to death, including Prime Minister Hideki Tojo, and 16 to life imprisonment. Later trials, running until October 19, 1949, result in 4,200 convictions and 720 executions.
- *July 4*: The United States grants full independence to the Philippine Islands. The Philippine Trade Act establishes nonquota immigrant status to all Philippine citizens and their spouses and children who have lived in the United States for a period of three years.
- *August 1*: President Truman approves a bill introduced by Arkansas Senator William J. Fulbright to establish a fund for international exchange of students and teachers.
- *August 2*: The United States accepts the jurisdiction of the World Court, a branch of the United Nations.
- *August 19*: Congress passes the War Brides Act, granting spouses and minor children of American servicemen and women nonquota immigration status if married before March 19, 1952. Later a Fiancées Act is added. The two acts allow some 150,000 wives and fiancées, a few hundred husbands, and 25,000 children to enter the country between 1946 and 1950.
- *October 1*: War crimes trial at Nürnberg, Germany, ends after 10 months. Of the 24 major Nazi defendants on trial for "crimes against peace, humanity, and the laws of war," 12 are sentenced to death. By April 14, 1949, United States war crimes tribunals in Europe have tried 1,873, of which 1,569 have been convicted and 459 condemned to death.

1947

- Great Britain grants independence to India, which separates into Hindu India in the south and Muslim Pakistan in the north.
- *March 14*: The United States establishes military and naval bases on the Philippine Islands on a 99-year lease.
- *March 22*: A program to investigate the loyalty of government employees begins. By 1951 more than 3 million people have come under scrutiny but only 212 have been dismissed from their jobs.
- *October*: The United Nations assigns to the United States the trusteeship of the Caroline, Marshall, and Mariana Islands, all former Japanese possessions in the Pacific Ocean.

1948

- *January 23*: The Soviet Union refuses to permit United Nations Commission representatives to enter Soviet-occupied North Korea, leading to that region's separation from United States–occupied South Korea.
- *April*: The federal district court in San Francisco reverses an order for the deportation of the 302 Japanese Americans interned at Tule Lake who had renounced their citizenship and later appealed for its restoration. The federal government appeals the district court's decision, but the appeal is denied, although the Japanese appellants do not regain their citizenship.
- *April 3*: The Economic Cooperation Act, providing $5.6 billion in foreign aid for 16 countries, is passed.
- *April 30*: The Organization of American States (OAS) involving America and 20 other nations of the Western Hemisphere, is established in Bogotá, Colombia, to provide mutual aid and defense.
- *May 14*: The United States recognizes the state of Israel, established earlier in the year. The neighboring Arab states refuse to accept the existence of the new nation.

- *June 25*: President Truman signs the Displaced Persons Act, authorizing the admission of 205,000 stateless persons from Europe, including 3,000 nonquota orphans. Renewed and amended in 1950 to run to 1952, this act enables a total of 393,542 immigrants to enter the United States.
- *July 2*: President Truman signs into law a bill to compensate Japanese Americans for losses occasioned by their internment. A total of $38 million is paid.
- *July 15*: President Truman receives the all-Japanese 442nd Regimental Combat Team at the White House to honor them for their military service in World War II.
- *August 15*: South Korea establishes the Republic of Korea, under Syngman Rhee, in Seoul, and North Korea establishes the People's Republic of Korea, under Kim Il Sung, in Pyongyang.
- *September 9*: North Korea declares itself an independent nation as the Democratic People's Republic of Korea in Pyongyang. The new nation claims sovereignty over the entire country.
- *October 1*: The U.S. Supreme Court rules unconstitutional a California law prohibiting interracial marriage.
- *November 10*: A series of strikes by the longshoremen's union begins. It spreads through the East Coast but is settled on November 27.

1949

- The People's Republic of China (PRC) is established in Beijing (Peking) under Mao Tse-tung. The nationalist government under Chiang Kai-shek forms an independent nation on the island of Taiwan, which is not recognized by the PRC. The United States later passes refugee acts to encourage the immigration of Taiwan's politically oppressed, its professionally trained, and relatives of American citizens.
- *January 20*: Harry S. Truman is inaugurated as the 33rd president of the United States.
- *April 4*: The North Atlantic Treaty is signed in Washington by ministers of the United States, Great Britain, Canada, France, Belgium, the Netherlands, Luxembourg, Italy, Denmark, Norway, Iceland, and Portugal. As a result of the treaty, the North Atlantic Treaty Organization (NATO) agrees to rearm and provide mutual military support in case of attack. Greece and Turkey join NATO in February 1952.
- *October 1–November 11*: U.S. steel production is closed down by strikes over who should pay pensions.
- *October 11*: Eleven leaders of the American Communist Party are convicted of conspiracy to overthrow the federal government by force and sentenced to fines or imprisonment.
- *October 26*: The national minimum wage is raised from 40 to 75 cents an hour.
- *December 1*: The United Mine Workers return to work three days a week until the conflict with the mine owners is settled.

1950

- The census records the United States population as 150,325,798, including 1,035,000 immigrants admitted since 1940. Immigration from Asia and the Americas has more than doubled since the last census, reaching 249,187, an increase of more than 60,000 over 1949. The total population of the country has increased by more than 14 percent since the last census.
- *February 7*: The United States recognizes the state of Vietnam, which is anticommunist.
- *June 16*: Congress passes a bill authorizing an increase of visas to 341,000, to be issued by June 30, 1951. The new law adds additional categories of expellees and war orphans.
- *June 25*: Communist forces from North Korea invade South Korea.
- *June 27*: The United Nations demands that the North Korean army withdraw and calls on its members to provide military support for South Korea. President Truman sends American air and naval forces into Korea.
- *June 28*: North Korea conquers Seoul. President Truman sends U.S. ground forces into battle on June 30 without consulting Congress.
- *September 23*: The Internal Security Act is passed over President Truman's veto. Known as the McCarran Act, it provides for the registration and strict control of communist organizations in the United States and prohibits the entry of anyone who has belonged to such organizations. The act is later amended to permit admission of people forced into communist organizations before they were 14 years of age.
- *September 30*: Chinese foreign minister Zhou Enlai announces that the communist government of his country would intervene in support of North Korea. On November 26 Chinese troops open a large-scale offensive against United Nations troops.

1951

- *June 28*: The issuance of visas to displaced persons is extended to December 31, 1951.

- *September 1*: The United States signs a mutual security pact with Australia and New Zealand.

1952

- The Immigration and Naturalization Service apprehends some 800,000 deportable aliens, 90 percent of them from Mexico. In 1954 the number reaches 1 million.
- *February 27*: The United States and Japan sign a treaty authorizing American military bases in Japan.
- *April 8*: The federal government seizes steel mills in order to prevent a strike threatened by 600,000 steelworkers.
- *June 27*: Congress passes the Immigration and Nationality Act, proposed by Senators McCarran and Walter, over President Truman's veto. The McCarran-Walter Act codifies all previous immigration legislation, retaining the national-origins quotas but removing the ban on immigration from Asia and the Pacific Islands, establishing token quotas, and allowing naturalization for first-generation Japanese. The act includes strict provisions to prohibit the entry of "subversives" and enables the attorney general to deport immigrants, even after they have acquired citizenship, for communist affiliations. The bill goes into effect on December 24.

1953

- The average number of detainees on Ellis Island falls to 230.
- Republican senator Joseph R. McCarthy, chairman of the Senate Permanent Investigating Subcommittee, begins a two-year series of public and private hearings into communist subversion in the U.S. government and U.S. Army, accusing the Democratic Party of "twenty years of treason." His accusations become increasingly controversial until the Senate officially condemns him for Contempt of the Privileges and Elections Subcommittee on December 2, 1954.
- *January 20*: Dwight D. Eisenhower is inaugurated as the 34th president of the United States.
- *March 3*: President Eisenhower signs a congressional resolution declaring Puerto Rico a free self-governing commonwealth voluntarily associated with the United States. The status becomes effective July 25 and is recognized by the United Nations General Assembly on November 27.
- *April 20*: The Communist Party of the United States of America (CPUSA) is required to register with the Department of Justice as being controlled by the Soviet Union.

The bracero program brought hundreds of thousands of Mexicans to the United States to work on farms and ranches. *(U.S. Citizenship and Immigration Services)*

- *July 27*: North and South Korea sign an armistice, ending hostilities between the two countries. The Korean War, fought by UN forces from 16 countries, has resulted in 39,000 deaths among forces of the United States and other UN countries. South Korea has suffered losses of 70,000 military and 500,000 civilian personnel. Communist military losses (predominantly Chinese) are estimated at more than 1.6 million.
- *August 7*: President Eisenhower signs the Refugee Relief Act, authorizing admission to the United States of 214,000 refugees from communist persecution during the next 41 months. The act provokes controversy because it stipulates that 80 percent of those admitted be Christian.
- *September 26*: The Spanish government signs a treaty authorizing the United States to station military forces in Spain.
- *October 12*: The Greek government signs a treaty authorizing the United States to station military forces in Greece.

1954

- *March 8*: The United States signs a mutual defense agreement with Japan promising to help restore Japan's defense forces.
- *May 13*: The United States begins work on the St. Lawrence Seaway with Canada, linking Montreal to Lake Ontario and enabling oceangoing ships to travel 2,300 miles inland from the Atlantic Ocean.
- *May 17*: In *Brown v. the Board of Education of Topeka, Kansas* the Supreme Court rules that racial segregation in public education is unconstitutional. Aimed primarily at discriminatory treatment of African Americans in the South, the ruling affirms the right of all races to equal protection under law.
- *June 27*: An anticommunist group overthrows the procommunist government in Guatemala. On September 1, the United States signs an agreement promising technical assistance to Guatemala.
- *July 21*: The French war in Indochina ends with an armistice granting Vietnamese independence. Vietnam is divided at the 17th parallel into a communist northern part and a noncommunist southern part.
- *August 24*: Congress passes the Communist Control Act, outlawing the Communist Party in the United States and limiting the civil rights of registered communists.
- *September 8*: The Southeast Asia Treaty Organization (SEATO) is formed, comprising the United States, Great Britain, Australia, New Zealand, France, Pakistan, the Philippines, and Thailand. The eight nations pledge mutual military defense and economic development.
- *November 13*: Six immigration stations, including Ellis Island, the nation's largest, are closed.

Eyewitness Testimony

I was first of all impressed by your general fearlessness. Children are not afraid of their parents, students are not afraid of their teachers, men of their bosses. Women don't seem to be afraid of anything. Nobody closes doors here, or erects fences and walls that might serve as a hostile or discriminating gesture. Even your houses look inviting. . . . People keep their shades up for everybody to look in, and nobody seems disturbed by the fact that his privacy can be violated at any time on the slightest pretext.

In the United States dreams are made to come true. The gap between dream and reality is narrow, and while Europeans are often unwilling to bridge it because they feel the result might not live up to their expectations, Americans seem to know no such hesitancy.

If you make mistakes in America, your life isn't ruined. You have tremendous reserves and tremendous room. Americans will greet a new idea or experiment with "why not try it" and, strange to say, it does not kill them.

A European refugee reporting her observations of America after World War II, in Shippen, Passage to America: The Story of the Great Migration *(1950), pp. 194–195.*

One time we had Jimmy Durante here. He gave a show for the aliens. He was the only celebrity that came to Ellis Island and gave a show. But otherwise the aliens supplied their own entertainment. They had radios. I don't remember television. There was no entertainment at all in the Great Hall except at Christmas, we put up a tree. Somebody would buy little gifts. For the Jewish people we had menorahs for Hanukkah. We used to try to make it as pleasant as possible for the holidays. It's not easy to be locked up during the holidays, especially for children. When I say "locked up," I mean they couldn't go anywhere, but they were not in jail. "Detained" was the word we used. Of course, for them it felt like jail.

. . . We had a big influx of war brides after 1947 to maybe 1950. While the GIs were in Europe, they married everything and everyone. The British, French, Italian, everyone. And these girls used that as a way to get into the country, because that was the fastest way to get into the country, because you didn't have a quota. You were the bride of a GI.

. . . And they used to come in, we used to hold them here until the GI would call and say, "Mr. Gallo, you got Mrs. So-and-so?" And I'd look in my file and I'd say, "Yeah, she's here. She's waiting to be picked up." They come out to Ellis Island, they'd have to identify themselves as a GI, the husband on the marriage certificate, and take them home, these beautiful girls. I mean, these were outrageously beautiful girls. All different types. . . . And I used to talk to these girls and say, "You know, by law you're supposed to live with this GI." I think at that time it was mandatory that they had to live with the GI for at least a year. And then they scat. They leave. That was the fastest way to get here. Nine out of ten brides ended up on Ellis Island, just to be processed and to be picked up by the groom.

Joseph Gallo, Immigration and Naturalization Service employee recalling his work on Ellis Island after World War II, in Coan, Ellis Island Interviews *(1997), pp. 30–31.*

I just took a suitcase with a few nightgowns and underwears, just clothes. My mother gave me a couple of sheets. That's all I had. I had to go to the consulate for a passport, vaccinations, and the paperwork. In Palermo they had a consulate. Just in case [my boyfriend] didn't marry me when I got to America, my parents deposited $500 so I could come back to Italy. That was the law then.

My father paid for my passage from Vittoria to Messina across the straits to the mainland. I went by train to Rome. . . . Then I flew from Rome to Lisbon to New York. . . . There were fifty girls coming here, all on the same plane. All a similar age. Going to marry or meet their boyfriends who were soldiers or in the navy. Nobody else was in the plane. Just us fifty girls.

. . . Then I was taken with all those girls to Ellis Island, but we didn't know where we were going to end up. We started crying. We got in the ferry. Suitcase all ripped up, three days being up and down. We carry everything, and we got to this big place. And there was a big, big room with all the beds and they say, "This is your bed, this is your bed." Oh, my God, we started to cry. . . . In the morning, a breakfast like I never saw in my life. The dining room was full of all kinds of foods. Pancakes, French toast, sausage, bacon, and all kinds of Danish. Unbelievable! But me, I didn't want to eat because the black men, they served and I was scared. I never saw any black people. So I didn't want to have nothing. A lady who worked there said, "You know, you'll be here for a couple of days, you should eat." I said, "I don't care. I just want my boyfriend. I want to get out of here."

Elda Torini, Italian immigrant, describing her trip to America at the age of 20 in 1947, in Coan, Ellis Island Interviews *(1997), pp. 59–60.*

The [Communist] party for the past eighteen months has been giving special attention to foreign-language groups and has called for a sweeping self-critical examination of its work in this field. As long ago as 1945, in urging the importance of penetrating these groups, party leaders said, "We need only mention the Polish, Italian, Yugoslav, and Greek questions," and in characteristic party double talk observed that they occupied an important relationship "to the entire democratic camp and to the broader peoples movements." In other words, the Communists now seek strength from foreign groups who may have relatives in countries which Russia seeks to influence.

. . . The Communist Party of the United States is a fifth column if there ever was one. It is far better organized that were the Nazis in occupied countries prior to their capitulation. Their goal is to overthrow our government. . . .

. . . Communists and fellow travelers . . . can teach our youth a way of life that eventually will destroy the sanctity of the home, that undermines faith in God, that causes them to scorn respect for constituted authority and sabotage our revered constitution.

. . . The Communists have been, still are, and always will be a menace to freedom, to democratic ideals, to the worship of God and to America's way of life.

J. Edgar Hoover, director of the Federal Bureau of Investigation, testimony before Congress, March 26, 1947, in Investigation of Un-American Propaganda Activities in the United States. Hearings Before the Committee on Un-American Activities, House of Representatives, *80th Congress. 1 Session, 1947, pp. 33–50.*

The next time I went as an *alembrista* [one who crosses the border illegally], over the fence, with some relatives. . . . And two in the morning we crossed. We were about to get on the bus when the immigration caught us. . . . They told us, "You're going to your Mexico, and if you return we'll really give it to you."

Well, the next day a relative and I crossed again. We walked a little way and they caught us again. "Where are you from," they asked us.

"From Guadalajara," we replied.

. . . They sent us back, but we came back singing.

We entered again. This time some mechanics, who had a garage on the border, let us pass over their fence. . . . A man from Zacoalco . . . told us to get on a bus on the other side of the bridge. We did, but again they caught us as we were arriving in San Clemente. "How many times have you passed? What is your name? We've seen this shirt before." They put some in jail and others they sent back to Tijuana.

[After succeeding in crossing the border and working for three years], I was with a friend. . . . He was a little drunk, and he went through a red light. The police stopped us. When they asked, I said I was Mexican and to send me back to Mexico. First they put me in jail in the basement, then later, on the top floor. . . . They kept me for eighteen days and then sent me to Sacramento. I was there one day and they put us on a bus to Mexico. . . .

I came back [to Mexico] with all the money I had saved, and we bought several parcels of land and animals—horses, cows, and pigs.

Ezekiel Perez, Mexican rancher, recalling his illegal entry from Mexico in 1948, in Davis, Mexican Voices/American Dreams, *(1990), pp. 18–21.*

I was scared to death. There were two other women who had similar visa problems, and one man who was a criminal. He was taken away. The two ladies were also scared to death. I almost fainted, because in Europe at that time the reputation of Ellis Island was terrible; that it's a dungeon and they beat people up. It was a horror even to hear the name.

I remember a woman, a matron, in a white robe with a big bunch of keys at her side coming toward me, and I was trembling. I didn't see the other ladies anymore. And this matron suddenly said, "Are you hungry?"

I said, "Yes, I am."

"The cafeteria is closed, but I can get you something."

I said to myself, "This is Ellis Island? They are so nice to me?"

"Eat whatever you want." And I did.

. . . The matron came back and guided me to a room where there were other women sleeping. She lifted up the cover of the bed and she looked at the sheet and said, "That's not clean." She changed the sheets, and said, "Would you like to have a shower? We have hot water." She showed me the bathroom. I had a shower. It was unbelievable. Where was this horrible Ellis Island?

Harriet Kovak, Hungarian immigrant, recounting her arrival in the United States in 1948 at the age of 22, in Coan, Ellis Island Interviews *(1997), p. 319.*

The parents of some of our splendid citizens went through a life of hardship and sacrifice. It is no wonder that some of their children have made valuable contributions to American life, for they valued what they and their parents got after such effort. . . . Look around you in any part of this country: the immigrants have contributed more than their share to its power and its wealth.

> *Fiorello H. La Guardia, second-generation Italian-American mayor of New York City, 1948, recalling his work as an interpreter on Ellis Island, in* The Making of an Insurgent: An Autobiography, 1882–1919 *(1948), p. 68.*

I see women bite into huge sandwiches or whole apples, peel and all, drink champagne at restaurants late at night after the theater or opera, converse with their husbands or male friends with frankness. . . . That kind of happiness was never shown by . . . my mother.

> *Nagai Kafu, Japanese immigrant, commenting on the freedom of American women, in* Amerika Monogatari, *(1949), p. 262, in Sawada,* Tokyo Life, New York Dreams *(1996), p. 172.*

. . . We got into New York on New Year's Eve, about three o'clock in the afternoon. It was Brooklyn on one side and New York on the other side. There was snow. Brooklyn was white. I never saw snow. I heard people say, "That's snow, that's snow!"

. . . We were there [Rhode Island] for a month until I got a job. I worked for a rubber company. I worked on the press making heels, rubber heels for shoes . . . The first year when we got here, it was wintertime, with the clothes I brought from the old country. I said to my wife a few times, you know, "This is the last winter. Next winter we're going back to the old country." But you know, you raise the kids, you have another girl. . . . The first baby we had over here lived nine hours and she died. So we made another girl, and a little boy, and we kept staying, and soon we stopped thinking about going back no more. Now I don't want to go back there no more.

> *Jose Martinez, Portuguese immigrant from the Azores, describing his first impressions of America when he arrived at the age of 22 in 1949, in Coan,* Ellis Island Interviews *(1997), pp. 381–382.*

One who has grown up in an environment takes much for granted. On the other hand, one who has come to this country may have a keen eye for everything peculiar and characteristic. I believe he should speak out on what he sees and feels. . . .

What soon makes the new arrival devoted to this country is the democratic trait among the people. I am not thinking so much of the democratic political constitution of this country, however highly it must be praised. I am thinking of the relationship between individual people and the attitude they maintain toward one another.

In the United States everyone feels assured of his worth as an individual. No one humbles himself before another person or class. Even the great difference in wealth, the superior power of a few, cannot undermine this healthy self-confidence and natural respect for the dignity of one's fellow-man.

> *Albert Einstein, German physicist who left Europe in 1933 to escape Nazi persecution, in his autobiography* Out of My Later Years, *(1950), in Neidle,* The New Americans *(1967), p. 308.*

When I departed Naha Harbor [in Okinawa], my mother sang loudly and danced with other women relatives until our ship went out of sight. Her song went like this: "My beloved child, on this auspicious ship, may your journey be as safe and straight as if linked by a silk thread."

> *A Japanese immigrant recalling the journey to America in the early 1950s, in Takaki,* Strangers from a Different Shore *(1998), p. 66.*

Mr. Bayswater put down a copy of the Rolls-Royce monthly bulletin . . . and snorted, ". . . Wait until you come up against the United States Immigration Inspectors—they'll put you through it. I'll never forget the first time I came over. It was after the war. They had me sweating. You never heard of Ellis Island? It's a kind of gaol where they can pop you if they don't like the look of your face. Wait 'til you sit down with those lads. If there's so much as a bit of a blur on your passport, or a comma misplaced, you're for it."

[Mrs. Harris] said to Mrs. Tidder, "Garn, I don't believe it. It's just people talking. It's a free country, ain't it?"

"Not when you're trying to get into it," Mr. Bayswater observed. "Proper Spanish Inquisition, that's what it is. How much have you got? Who are you with? Where are you going? When? Why? For how long? Have you ever committed a crime? Are you a Communist? If not, then what are you? Why? Haven't you got a home in England— what are you coming over here for? Then they start in on your papers. Heaven 'elp you if there's anything wrong

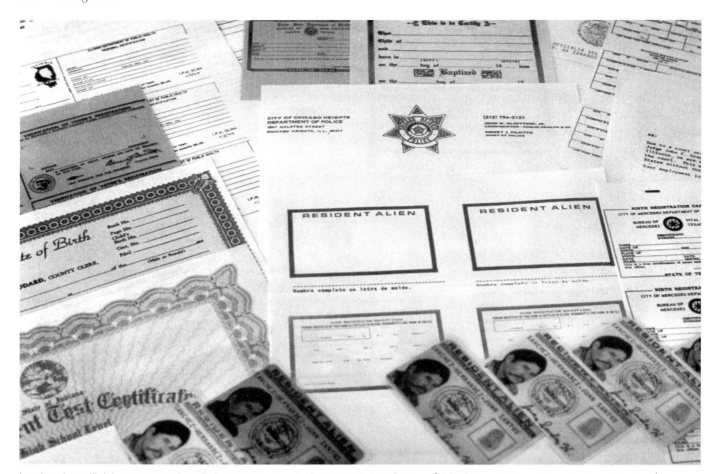

Immigration officials must examine all documents of arrivals to the United States. *(U.S. Citizenship and Immigration Services)*

with them. You can cool your heels behind bars on their ruddy island until someone comes and fetches you out."

The stone at the pit of Mrs. Harris's tum grew a little larger. . . . She asked . . ., "Are they like that with kids, too? The Americans I knew in London were always good with kids."

"Ha!" snorted Mr. Bayswater again. "Not these chaps. . . . They eats kids. A baby in arms is like a bomb to them. If they don't see the name and birth certificate and proper papers for them they don't get through. When the time comes they herd you into the main lounge, and there you are. Queue up until you sit at a desk with a chap in uniform like a prison warder on the other side, with eyes that look right through you, and you'd better give the right answers. I saw one family held up for three hours because some clerk . . . had made a mistake in one kid's papers. That's the kind of thing they *love* to catch you out on."

Paul Gallico, reporting a conversation taking place on a voyage from London to New York in the early 1950s, in "Mrs. 'Arris Goes to New York," Gallico Magic, *(1960), pp. 141–142.*

As you are no doubt aware, the Russians have long made heavy propaganda use of Ellis Island. They call it a concentration camp, which, of course, is outrageous. No one mistreats us here. Our jailers—nearly all of them, anyway—are very kindly people, who go to extraordinary lengths, within the system, for which they don't pretend to be responsible, to make our stay here as little like a nightmare as they can. There is a movie every Tuesday and Thursday night; the children get milk six times a day. We are kept warm and fed generously—nothing like the Colony [one of New York City's most luxurious restaurants], I assure you, but more than enough. And, as people are always pointing out to us, it doesn't cost us anything.

George Voskovec, Czech playwright and actor, recalling his detention on Ellis Island, 1951, in Andy Logan, "A Reporter at Large: It Doesn't Cost Them a Cent," The New Yorker, *May 12, 1951, pp. 56–77.*

But my greatest shock was when I came off the ship and wound up at Ellis Island. When you're young and you're alone and you have a lot of unknown things awaiting you, you really don't fall apart so fast. But it was a scary experience, because when I arrived at Ellis Island, I saw the same guard stands with guards I remembered at [the Nazi concentration camp] Bergen-Belsen. It brought back terrible memories, and I really didn't know what the outcome of my stay would be. . . . I was very turned off by the Bronx. I saw clotheslines hanging, and cats running around garbage cans. Coming from a progressive country like Sweden that's so clean and so neat, and everybody does the right thing, and then to come to the Bronx, well, let's just say it was an adjustment. But I didn't jump to conclusions. I was the one who wanted to be here and I was determined that things were going to be all right.

> *Estelle Zeller, Czech immigrant, recalling her arrival in the United States at the age of 23 in 1952, in Coan,* Ellis Island Interviews *(1997), pp. 300–301.*

Americans are free to enter the countries of Western Europe without even being required to have a visa. They are heartily welcome here. But it is a shame that Europeans who would visit America in return should have to undergo a political investigation extending over many months by officials without any knowledge of European affairs and should be eventually rejected by such persons with a blast of libelous accusations against their political honesty. This is bound to poison the friendship between Americans and Europeans.

The remedy lies in a simple act of imagination. Let any American go carefully through the whole list of conditions imposed upon western European visitors to the United States and imagine himself to be subjected to the same conditions when he travels to Europe—while at the same time western Europeans could visit the United States without let or hindrance.

A European immigrant receives her naturalization certificate from a U.S. District judge. *(U.S. Citizenship and Immigration Services)*

He would be horrified to realize that such a position exists today in reverse.

> *Michael Polanyi, British chemist, social scientist, and anticommunist activist, June 1952, on being refused a visa to the United States because of an unfounded charge of "certain political beliefs . . . membership in, or affiliation with, certain organizations," in Bruce,* The Golden Door *(1954), pp. 163–164.*

In all but a few cases, these aliens whose admissibility or deportation is under study will be detained. Only those deemed likely to abscond or those whose freedom of movement could be adverse to the national security or the public safety will be detained. . . .

The new detention policy is so far-reaching in scope and effect that the Department of Justice is discontinuing its six seaport facilities at New York, Boston, Seattle, San Francisco, San Pedro, and Honolulu.

> *Attorney General Herbert Brownell, November 12, 1954, in the* New York Times, *November 13, 1954.*

Notes

1. "Ministry of fear," editorial, March 29, 1952, in Rita J. Simon and Susan H. Alexander, *The Ambivalent Welcome* (1993), p. 142.

CHAPTER TEN

After Ellis Island
1955-1999

New Legislation

The closing of Ellis Island marked the passing of an era. The *New York Times* noted the end of this legendary institution, and in an editorial on November 13, 1954, wrote of the millions of immigrants who had poured through its gates since 1892. "They make part of what is now the American temperament—a livelier and richer national personality than could have existed without them," the editorial concluded. "Perhaps some day a monument to them will go up on Ellis Island. The memory of this episode in our national history should never be allowed to fade."

For more than 10 years, however, it appeared unlikely that such a monument would be erected. From March 1955, when Ellis Island was formally declared "surplus property," the government tried to sell the land, offering it as "a perfect location and facilities for oil storage depot, import and export processing, warehousing, manufacture, private institutions, etc.," but none of the private developers who bid on it satisfied the government's General Services Administration. The installation had cost $6.5 million to build, but it could have been bought for far less if anyone had met the government's requirements for an appropriate use. There were 21 offers in 1956, ranging from 5 cents, bid by someone who wanted to build a private home there, to $201,000 from an entrepreneur who hoped to put up a luxury hotel. Later bids were higher and included suggestions for a gambling casino, a Bible college, a hospital for the mentally retarded, an amusement park, and a woman's prison. The architect Frank Lloyd Wright designed a small super-modern city to be constructed there, and a New York firm proposed to invest more than $2 billion to build it. But the government turned them all down, some because the bids were too low and some because the proposed use did not seem appropriate to a site that had become an important historic symbol. At last the National Park Service took the island over, and on May 11, 1965, President Lyndon B. Johnson officially declared Ellis Island a part of the Statue of Liberty National Monument.

By then the facility was in terrible shape. The National Park Service had no money to maintain the buildings, which were falling apart. Thieves stripped them of their copper roofing, light fixtures, and machinery, and vandals broke their windows and defaced their walls. What people did not destroy, nature invaded. Weeds grew through the pavement, plaster crumbled, floors rotted, and mattresses were soaked with rain coming through holes in the roofs.

In 1982, as the 100th anniversary of the Statue of Liberty approached in 1986 and that of Ellis Island in 1992, the Park Service organized a foundation to raise funds for a proposed museum of immigration on the island. There were 35 structures there—including 14 office buildings, 11 storage areas, a laundry, a cafeteria, dormitories, and a school—and their restoration was a tremendous job, the largest and most expensive renovation project in American history. In all it cost some $160 million and took almost 10 years to finish. When the Ellis Island Immigration Museum opened in 1990, the refurbished Great Hall of the main building gleamed as it had not since January 1, 1892. It contains more than 30 separate galleries displaying artifacts, documents, photos, and maps. There are two theaters, an oral history room, a library, and an interactive learning center for children, where visitors can study the experience of the more than 16 million people who landed there. A stately symbol of America's rich immigrant history, the restored facility once known as both "the isle of hope" and "the isle of tears" is one of the most moving public monuments in the country.

Controversy over Ellis Island did not end with the opening of the long-awaited immigration museum, however. For years there had been a dispute about which state held the site. Since the island is situated more than a mile southwest of Manhattan and large areas of the landfill that composes it lie to the west of the original three-acre island, New Jersey repeatedly introduced bills in the Senate during the 1970s and 1980s claiming the territory. At last, to the great chagrin of New York City, the U.S. Supreme Court resolved the border dispute on May 26, 1998, by decreeing that the historic gateway to the nation is mainly in New Jersey. The federal government actually owns the island, so its official location has no economic consequence to either state, but the decision was a great blow to the pride of New York. As George Pataki, that state's governor at the time, observed, "Ellis Island will always be a part of New York in the hearts and minds of the millions of immigrants who came to America seeking freedom and liberty."

The Immigrant Museum notes in its brochure that the facility on Ellis Island "processed the greatest tide of incoming humanity in the nation's history," and this is true—through the time it was in operation. Of the 24,178,469 immigrants to enter the United States during the facility's 62 years of service, nearly three-quarters landed at Ellis Island in the country's largest harbor. The greatest number of immigrants to enter the country in any single year before the Great Hall closed its massive doors in 1954 arrived in 1907. In that year the United States received 1,285,349 newcomers—almost all of them from Europe. Of these, 1,004,756 arrived at Ellis Island.

Historians have called the closing of Ellis Island "the official end of the period of mass immigration to the United States," but the flow—interrupted by war, depression, and restrictionist legislation—did not end in 1954. The number of annual entries to the country, scarcely a half million in the 1930s, grew to more than twice that between 1941 and 1950, doubled again in the next 10 years, and continued to increase in each succeeding decade in the 20th century. The record set in 1907 was passed in 1990, when more than 1.5 million newcomers arrived, and the number went up again the next year. World events and new American laws changed the patterns and the sources of American immigration, but the tide continued to swell through the end of the century. And with it, new challenges, and new "immigrant problems," emerged.

The golden door to America, once thought to have slammed shut with the closing of Ellis Island in 1954, has swung on its creaking hinges in both directions since. Periods of recession, international hostilities, and racial prejudices have blown it almost closed; humanitarian concerns and a need for labor, both unskilled and professional, have exerted pressure from the other direction. What has remained constant is the legal mechanism for change. The nation's immigration policies have fluctuated with the will and the needs of the population as well as with world conditions, and at the beginning of the 21st century these policies were as controversial and as fluid as they had been in the 1920s.

The Johnson-Reed Act of 1924, which established the basic principles of American immigration policy for the next 41 years, marked the end of centuries of open admission by setting yearly limits for all entrants and assigning quotas for each country. It underwent numerous amendments, but within a few years the Great Depression and World War II rendered most of its restrictionist provisions meaningless as immigration fell off sharply. With the war, new changes became necessary. The Chinese Exclusion Act of 1882 was repealed as China became an ally, and a flood of nonquota war brides, refugees, and displaced persons were allowed into the country under special legislation. The need for farm labor in the Southwest drew a flood of newcomers from south of the border. A failed revolution against the communist government in Hungary in 1956 sent 38,000 refugees to the United States. As this number exceeded the refugee limits permitted by the law, special provisions were enacted to admit them outside the quota, and Congress passed legislation to grant them resident or refugee status. These special arrangements were used to admit some 15,000 refugees from Hong Kong outside of the quota allotments in 1962 and to accommodate escapees after the unsuccessful revolution in Czechoslovakia 1968, as well as people fleeing the dictatorship in Uganda in the 1970s and Lebanese displaced by their civil war in the 1980s.

In addition to those needing asylum and work, the immigration laws made exceptions for a stream of professionals attracted by the prospect of higher incomes and a higher living standard than they could find in their home countries. It is estimated that between 1956 and 1965, more than 18,000 physicians, 38,000 nurses, and 35,000 engineers came to the United States to live. Some 16 percent of Great Britain's Ph.D.s left their country during the 1950s, half of them for the United States. Countries in Asia and the Western Hemisphere lost even greater percentages of their most educated and capable citizens in what was known as a worldwide "brain drain." The McCarran-Walter Act was amended so often, for so many special circumstances, that its basic principles became impossible to define.

The element of both the 1924 Johnson-Reed Act and 1952 McCarran-Walter Act that most offended an increasingly liberal public was the frankly racist national-origins formula. The quota system had never worked as it was intended, and the numerous new laws amending it to allow victims of the war to enter had made it almost meaningless. John F. Kennedy, as a member of the House of Representatives from 1947 and a senator from 1953, worked actively for immigration reform from his first years in government. He sponsored the Displaced Persons Act, signed by President Truman in 1948, and later promoted the 1953 Refugee Relief Act. In 1958 he published a brief book, *A Nation of Immigrants,* outlining his ideas for change in America's discriminatory immigration policies.

Kennedy was the great-grandson of poor immigrants from Ireland, and for 14 years he represented Massachusetts, at that time the state with the country's highest percentage of foreign nationalities. When he became president in 1961, he continued to work for the interests of the foreign-born and those seeking to join them. Just four months before his assassination in 1963, he presented Congress with a formal proposal to liberalize immigration statutes, calling for a complete revision of the McCarran-Walter Act and an end to the national-origins formula for admission to the United States.

The president's ideas met with general approval from both sides of the fence, among both the government and the general public. Democrats had long been in favor of immigration reform, and members of that party supported Kennedy's proposal warmly. Congressman Emmanuel Celler of New York described it as "a broad and firm basis for a long overdue revision of our policies and practices in this most important area of domestic and foreign human relations." Franklin D. Roosevelt's son James, a congressman from California, called them "sorely needed changes in our immigration laws." Republicans such as Senator Kenneth Keating of New York also spoke out in favor of the proposals, and so did the national press. The *Washington Post*, on the day after the message was delivered to Congress, called it "the best immigration law within living memory to bear a White House endorsement."

The Hart-Celler Act, 1965

The White House continued to endorse Kennedy's proposal in the voice of his successor, Lyndon Baines Johnson, and after two years both houses of Congress approved an act that embodied sweeping reforms in immigration policy. In October 1965 President Johnson, in a ceremony at the Statue of Liberty, signed Public Law 89–236, considered a landmark of immigration legislation. Known as the Hart-Celler Act for the two congressmen who formally proposed it, the far-reaching Immigration Act of 1965 essentially followed Kennedy's proposals, to which Johnson gave full credit. It abolished national origins as a basis for admission, replacing them with a limit of 20,000 for each country in the Eastern Hemisphere and an overall limit of 170,000 from that hemisphere. The Western Hemisphere was allotted a quota of 120,000 with no preferences or country limits. The statute became effective July 1, 1968.

The Hart-Celler Act also abolished the system of preferences for the Eastern Hemisphere, which had established four levels, and in its place instituted a system of seven. First preference was given to unmarried children of U.S. citizens. The next level was allotted to unmarried adult children of permanent residents, followed by people with "exceptional ability," scientific, artistic, or professional. Other relatives of citizens were assigned to levels four and five in the preference system. Unskilled laborers in trades needed by the United States came in sixth. The final level of preference was reserved for displaced persons or refugees from religious, racial, or political discrimination. Parents, spouses, and children under 21 years of age of U.S. citizens were allowed to enter outside of the quota and the preference system.

Like all new immigration laws, the 1965 act was something of a compromise. Although hostility to Jews, Catholics, and Asians had diminished in the country as a result of the war and the civil rights movements of the 1960s, there was still considerable prejudice against the wave of Mexican and South and Central American newcomers beginning to dominate the immigration picture. The McCarran-Walter Act had permitted unlimited immigration from the Western Hemisphere, but the new law imposed a quota on these regions as a trade-off for the abolition of the national-origins system. The system established in 1952 had had problems from the beginning. Based on the nationalities of Americans already in the country in 1920, the quotas required the Census Bureau to determine the number of people descended from countries that had changed their borders drastically during the preceding half century. Poland, for instance, had not existed between 1795 and 1918, so people listed as being of "Polish" descent had come from either Germany, Austria, or Russia. Many Irish immigrants who could not afford to come directly to the United States had sailed to Canada and then crossed that country's southern border. They were listed in the immigration records, and consequently in the census, as Canadians.

All of these problems of classification were at last eliminated by the legislation of 1965, substituting individual skills or relationship with U.S. citizens as the basis for admission. As President Johnson noted when he signed the 1965 bill, "From now on, those who can contribute most to this country—to its growth, to its strength, to its spirit—will be the first that are admitted to this land. . . . The days of unlimited immigration are past. But those who come will come because of what they are—not because of the land from which they sprung."

The new law did not solve all the problems, however. The 1953 Refugee Relief Act had functioned badly from the beginning, sometimes delaying entry for years despite repeated efforts at liberalizing and streamlining it, and new sources of immigration strained the nation's resources. When Fidel Castro assumed control of Cuba and instituted a communist government in 1959, an unprecedented stream of arrivals claimed refugee status. The numbers entering the country swelled to new highs and continued to grow. With the fall of Saigon in 1976, Vietnam soon became a second major source of refugees. In the decade from 1951 to 1960, a total of 335 Vietnamese entered the United States; from 1971 to 1980 the number had grown to 172,820, and the next 10 years saw 280,782 arrive. By 1985, more than 700,000 refugees from Vietnam and nearby Laos and Cambodia had found asylum in the United States.

The laws required endless adjustment and amendment. In 1976 a revision of the 1965 act was established. The policy in use for the Eastern Hemisphere—the seven-level system of preferences that decided the order in which applicants were admitted, and the limit of 20,000 from each country—was applied to the countries of the New World as well. The separate annual limits—120,000 from the Western Hemisphere and 170,000 from the rest of the world—remained in place. Two years later, an additional amendment erased the last vestige of difference in the treatment of the two hemispheres, establishing a worldwide quota of 290,000, with the same per-country limit of 20,000 and the same seven-rung ladder of preference.

The 1976 legislation addressed problems of disproportionate immigration from Latin America but left untouched the growing need for a correction in the many statutes governing the admission of refugees. In 1980 a new Refugee Act was passed that clarified and enlarged the definition of refugees, including anyone persecuted "on account of race, religion, nationality, membership in a particular social group, or political opinion." It set an annual limit of 50,000 through 1982 but reduced the worldwide quota from 290,000 to 270,000 to offset the flow of refugees.

The new law proved almost impossible to enforce as world conditions increased the need for sanctuary in the United States. Within months of the bill's passage, a flood of Haitians, protesting their despotic government and claiming refuge as its victims, arrived. They were denied entry, but the federal courts overruled the INS and allowed their claim. In spring of that year, Cuba allowed some 130,000 of its poorest citizens and inmates of its prisons and mental institutions to leave the country through the port of Mariel; this flood of "Marielitos" poured into Miami, Florida. The strain that this unexpected influx of newcomers imposed on that city's social order aroused howls of protest and claims of a new Cuban-based crime wave, but the federal government felt bound to honor its commitment to provide a haven for refugees, especially those in flight from communist countries.

The country's generous position did not last, however. In 1991 the newly elected president of Haiti, Jean-Bertrand Aristide, was overthrown, and a new flood of refugees began to stream toward U.S. waters from that Caribbean country, often in dangerously small boats. If they were able to reach the United States, these "boat people," as they were called, had the opportunity to petition for asylum. If the U.S. Coast Guard rescued them in the water, they were taken to the U.S. naval base at Guantánamo Bay, Cuba, where they had the same chance. But when the U.S. base became overcrowded in 1992—the population passed 13,000 at one point—President George H. W. Bush ordered the Coast Guard to return those picked up at sea to their country, where they were usually arrested and subjected to severe punishment. Nearly 3,000 Haitians were repatriated in one month. The U.N. high commissioner for refugees, many humanitarian groups, and most Democrats in the U.S. Congress objected strongly to this policy, but it was supported in 1993 by the U.S. Supreme Court in the case of *McNary v. Haitian Centers Council* on the grounds that the United States' commitment to providing asylum "extends only to refugees who reach U.S. soil or territorial waters."

Haitian refugees crowd a boat while attempting to leave Haiti in February 2004. *(AP Photo/ United States Coast Guard)*

The Immigration Reform and Control Act (IRCA), 1986

While the number of refugees seeking admission grew from year to year, the incidence of illegal entry, especially from Mexico, also continued to swell. Many people began to feel serious alarm and to fear that America had lost control of its borders. By 1986, when the INS reported a 40-percent increase in illegal aliens during the previous year, Congress was ready to do something about it. There had been several bills—proposed over a five-year period and to three consecutive Congresses—to tighten the laws against entering or staying in the country illegally. In 1986 both houses of Congress finally approved the Simpson-Mazzoli Act, officially termed the Immigration Reform and Control Act and popularly known as IRCA.

The new law, signed by President Reagan on November 6, 1986, was seen as both generous and repressive. It imposed severe penalties on employers who knowingly hired illegal aliens—up to six months in jail and a fine of $10,000—but it also provided amnesty for undocumented immigrants who had entered before 1982 or engaged in agricultural work for 90 days during 1985–86. This amnesty enabled aliens living in the country illegally to become legal residents and ultimately apply for full citizenship. To help stem the tide of illegal entry, the law called for a 50-percent increase in personnel for the border patrol, to take effect in 1987 and 1988. Since such new regulations would certainly cost the states a great deal, the Simpson-Mazzoli Act sought to offset some of the expense by disqualifying newly legalized aliens from receiving most federal welfare benefits for five years.

One of the sponsors of IRCA, Republican senator Alan Simpson of Wyoming, wrote of it in 1990, "The purpose of the bill for me was to avoid exploitation of human beings. It was not a jobs bill; I didn't care about numbers. I cared about the fact that if people were coming to the United States to go to work like dogs, that they ought to have a legal status so that they would not be exploited by their fellow man." Nevertheless, IRCA met with mixed reactions from the public. Many found the exclusion of legal immigrants from welfare services cruel. Employers were unhappy with their obligations under the new law, which required them to establish the legal status of their employees, and they were often unable to understand the statute. A survey revealed that a majority did not comply with the law, and some even reported that they did not intend to. The response to the amnesty provision was similarly disappointing. Because of the high application fee, the aliens' fear of the INS, and the complicated documentation required, fewer than one-third of the expected number of illegal aliens actually asked for permanent residency under the amnesty. Some 50,000 applied on the last day, May 4, 1988, but the total taking advantage of the offer during the six months it was open amounted to only about 1.4 million. The INS estimate of those eligible for it was nearly 4 million.

IRCA was felt by many to be too loose in some regards. One of its loopholes was that it permitted would-be immigrants to obtain entry visas by marriage to U.S. citizens; people entered into sham marriages for the purpose of obtaining immigrant privileges. So widespread was the practice of contracting marriages arranged by agencies for that purpose that Congress was compelled to pass another bill the same year, the Immigration Marriage Fraud Amendment of 1986 (IMFA), which established rigorous criteria for valid marriages. It required that alien spouses—husbands or wives—live in the country for two years before they could get permanent residency. The penalties for immigration-related marriage fraud were even harsher than those for hiring illegal aliens—up to five years in prison, a $250,000 fine, and permanent deportation.

The Immigration Act, 1990 (IMMACT 90)

The last major immigration reform of the 20th century, the Immigration Act of 1990, known as IMMACT 90, was the work of Senator Simpson and Democratic senator Edward Kennedy of Massachusetts. A reform of the 1952 Immigration Act, it made changes in many provisions relating to the legal entry of aliens. Its most prominent features were the changes it dictated in the total number of immigrants allowed into the country and in the preference system that determined the priorities in granting visas. The annual limit it set was an increase of 35 percent, from 500,000 to 700,000, to continue for three years. Beginning in 1995, it was to go down to 675,000.

IMMACT 90 also increased the number of family-related immigrants permitted to enter and refined the preference system, creating five new categories of professional and skilled applicants. More significantly, it established a three-year program for the admission of "diversity immigrants" to accommodate people from "adversely affected" countries that were considered underrepresented. In a historic reversal that earlier immigrants would have found surprising, this class referred mainly to countries of northern and western Europe, originally the major source of newcomers to America. Some 40 percent of the 40,000 diversity visas granted during the three years were issued to immigrants from Ireland. Others coming in for special consideration were 1,000 displaced Tibetans living in exile in India and Nepal. Immigrants with diversity visas were permitted to enter without relatives to sponsor them or jobs for which there was a labor shortage. In all, 34 "adversely affected" countries were represented.

Another new category established by IMMACT 90 was that of "Temporary Protected Status" (TPS) to aid people from countries suffering from natural disaster or internal conflict. This status allows the victims of such conditions to work in the United States for a limited period of time but does not provide the benefits of permanent residence or eligibility for most forms of public assistance. A group of Liberians, Lebanese, and Kuwaitis were granted TPS in 1991, and later that year Somalis were added to the list of those qualifying. Bosnians joined the number in 1992 and Rwandans in 1994. Among the national groups that have benefited most from TPS have been natives of El Salvador, of whom more than 187,000 had received Temporary Protected Status by 1993.

The 1990 act also created a lottery in which immigrant applications were approved more or less by chance. In its first year, 1992, visas were granted in the order in which their applications were received. The INS received 9.3 million applications in seven days, plus an additional 7.5 million that arrived early and 2 million that came after the deadline. They came from all over the world, but the highest number of visas—about 20,000—were awarded to Ireland; Poland came in second with 12,060. In 1993 and 1994, the selection was made at random, and again Ireland and Poland had the highest number of winners, totaling about 87 percent.

After 1995, the diversity program was established on a permanent basis, with 55,000 visas available to people from countries with fewer than 50,000 immigrants to the United States during the preceding five years. Its provisions currently include a limit of seven percent to be granted to any one country. Applicants must have a high school education or its equivalent or at least two years of experience in a specialized occupation.

Immigration was a major issue in the presidential election of 1992. Republican hopeful Patrick J. Buchanan, one of the most outspoken opponents of a liberal immigration policy, focused on the subject in his campaign for the Republican presidential nomination, arguing for the termination of all foreign entry, legal and illegal. By the next election, in 1996, immigration had become even more controversial, and Buchanan was even more strident in his opposition to it. In his second unsuccessful bid for the nomination, he announced that he would "stop immigration . . . cold" within six months if elected. "I would supply a security fence along those areas where huge amounts of illegal immigrants run into this country at will," he promised in a speech in Tucson, Arizona, as reported in *Insight on the News* (March 18, 1996, p. 11).[1] In 2002 he published a book with the alarming title *The Death of the West: How Dying Populations and Immigrant Invasions Imperil Our Country and Civilization.* Four years later he followed it with another, even more threatening, volume, *State of Siege: How Illegal Immigration Is Destroying America.*

Immigration law in the United States has never been static, and no act remains unchanged for long. As Doris Meissner, commissioner of the Immigration and Naturalization Service from 1993 to 2000, observed wryly after her retirement, "Immigration has been an area given to wild swings."[2] It was a standing joke among employees of the service that INS stands for "I'm Not Sure." In 1996 Congress passed an amended version of IRCA, the 1986 Immigration Reform and Control Act, addressing the same issues of illegal entry but tightening up both the restrictions and the penalties. The Illegal Immigration Reform and Immigrant Responsibility Act (IIRIRA) doubled the number of border patrol agents to 10,000 by 2001 and ordered the erection of new fences and the construction of an additional 2,700 detention cells for illegal aliens apprehended at the borders. The act also attacked the growing problem of immigrant smuggling, which had become a scandal

Pat Buchanan maintained a strong anti-immigration platform as a Republican Party nominee during the 1992 presidential election. *(AP Photo/Eric Draper)*

by the early 1990s, by increasing the punishment for it to 10 years in prison, and those found guilty of document fraud were threatened with sentences of up to 15 years. IIRIRA called on employers to verify the immigrant status of job applicants, simplified the procedure for immediate deportation of undocumented aliens, and required immigrant sponsors to provide binding commitments of support and evidence that they were paying incomes of at least 125 percent of the poverty level.

Like most legislation related to immigration, IIRIRA had its opponents, who feared that it gave INS agents too much power. Some objected that, as one critic put it, "Businesses should not be responsible for being immigration policemen," and that such a requirement "would lead to great discrimination against foreigners." Others protested that the new bill was not strong enough and that America was still "losing control of its borders."

In 1994 the United States entered into an agreement with the other two countries on the continent, Canada and Mexico, which was to have far-reaching consequences for the immigration from both. The North American Free Trade Agreement (NAFTA), which took effect on January 1 of that year, established the world's largest free trade area. It eliminated duties on one-half of all U.S. goods shipped to Canada and Mexico, gradually phased out tariffs among the three countries on certain products over a period of 14 years, and lifted restrictions on sales of many items, including motor vehicles and parts, computers, textiles, and agricultural products. A very controversial agreement, it was opposed by conservatives, who feared, among other things, that it would draw jobs away from the United States. It specifically allows temporary entry for business visitors, intra-company transferees, professionals, traders, and investors, but in facilitating the international movement of goods and services, it has also greatly increased the movement of labor across the two national frontiers. Migrant labor from Mexico, in particular, has been attracted to the better prospects north of their border.

To help stem that flood of legal and illegal immigration, the United States passed another restrictive bill in 1996, when President Bill Clinton signed the Personal Responsibility and Work Opportunity Reconciliation Act. Intended to prevent immigrants from applying for welfare immediately after arriving, this law denied most public assistance to legal immigrants for their first five years in the country and gave individual states the authority to establish their own welfare policies. Illegal aliens were made ineligible for food stamps, Medicaid, and Supplemental Security Income by this law.

The debate on these issues, begun in the 19th century, continued through the end of the 20th between those who feared the impact of a flood of aliens and those who valued the contributions the newcomers make to the workforce and to the culture. As the 21st century began, "the immigrant problem" in the United States was perhaps as troubling as ever, but the controversy focused on new and unforeseen problems.

Chronicle of Events

1955

- By the end of 1955 more than 400,000 displaced persons have entered the United States under the 1948 bill.
- *April 1*: West Germany becomes independent as the United States ends its occupation.
- *May*: West Germany joins NATO.
- *May 27*: President Eisenhower proposes a series of amendments to liberalize the Refugee Relief Act of 1953.
- *September 26*: The stock market shows its greatest loss since 1929 in response to a heart attack suffered by President Eisenhower on September 24. The dollar loss is more than $14 billion.
- *December*: An African-American boycott protesting segregated buses begins in Montgomery, Alabama. It lasts almost a year and results in the U.S. Supreme Court declaring segregation of local transportation facilities unconstitutional.
- *December 5*: The American Federation of Labor and the Congress of Industrial Organizations merge. Membership in the combined labor unions (AFL-CIO) is more than 16 million.

1956

- A failed revolution against the communist government of Hungary results in the flight of more than 38,000 "freedom fighters" to the United States. Of these, 6,000 are admitted under the Refugee Relief Act and 32,000 are granted temporary admission, which may lead to permanent residence or immigrant status.
- Immigration figures reach 326,687, the highest number since 1924.

1957

- *January 20:* Eisenhower is inaugurated for his second term as president.
- *September 24*: President Eisenhower sends 2,000 National Guard and army troops to enforce school desegregation in Little Rock, Arkansas.
- A communist rebellion, led by Ho Chi Minh and his force, the Vietcong, breaks out in South Vietnam. The United States supports the nationalist South Vietnamese government.

Fidel Castro, whose 1959 takeover of Cuba resulted in a large wave of emigration from his island nation to the United States *(New York Public Library Print Collection)*

1958

- *April*: Vice President Richard Nixon begins a goodwill tour of Latin America and is met with violent public hostility in Uruguay, Peru, and Venezuela.

1959

- Alaska and Hawaii are admitted as the 49th and 50th states of the United States. Hawaii's Asian-American majority has delayed its long efforts to join the union.
- *January 1*: Rebels under Fidel Castro overthrow the government of Fulgencio Batista in Cuba. Within six months Castro establishes a communist-leaning dictatorship and begins making anti-American public statements. A large-scale immigration of Cuban refugees totaling some 200,000 mostly of the upper-middle and upper class, begins.

1960

- The national census records the population of the United States as 179,323,175, representing an 18.5-percent growth since the last census, the highest in half a century. Immigration in this year totals 265,398, the fourth highest number since 1929.
- *February*: The Soviet Union signs an agreement to purchase Cuban sugar and grants Cuba a $100 million credit.

1961

- *January 3*: The United States breaks off diplomatic relations with Cuba.
- *January 20*: John F. Kennedy is inaugurated as the 35th president of the United States.
- *April 20*: The anti-Castro invasion at the Bay of Pigs is defeated.

1962

- The United States takes a strong stand against Soviet missiles in Cuba, and the missiles are withdrawn.
- *May 28*: The New York Stock Exchange loses $20.8 billion, its greatest drop since 1929.

1963

- The Immigration and Naturalization Service consolidates duties at ports of entry with several other government agencies, including customs, the U.S. Public Health Service, and the Bureau of Plant Quarantine at the Mexican border.
- *July 23*: President Kennedy issues a Proposal to Liberalize Immigration Statutes, urging Congress to eliminate "discrimination based on national origins."
- *November 22*: President Kennedy is assassinated in Dallas, Texas. Later that day Lyndon B. Johnson is sworn in as the 36th president of the United States.

1964

- The INS makes 178 million inspections at more than 400 ports of entry, almost twice the number for 1949; in 1966 the number grows to about 200 million and in 1973 to more than 250 million at about 1,000 ports of entry. The service's total staff in 1964 has increased from 6,900 in the 1950s to 7,048.
- Congress passes the Civil Rights Act prohibiting racial discrimination.

A member of the border patrol uses binoculars as he scans the international border in the Florida Keys for illegal aliens. *(U.S. Citizenship and Immigration Services)*

1965

- A second wave of Cuban refugees to the United States begins, totaling some 360,000.
- *January 20*: Lyndon Baines Johnson is inaugurated as president after completing John F. Kennedy's term and winning the 1964 election.
- *October*: President Johnson signs into law an immigration act, to take effect in 1968, based on President Kennedy's 1963 proposal. The new law replaces the national-origins formula with a limit of 20,000 for each country in the Eastern Hemisphere, an overall limit of 170,000 for quota immigrants, and an annual limit of 20,000 for natives of any single nation. The Western Hemisphere is granted a quota of 120,000, without preferences or country limits. The four-level preference system is amplified to one based on seven levels.

1966

- *October 30–31*: The National Education Association, at a conference in Tucson, Arizona, introduces the bilingual-education movement.

1967

- *November 20*: The Census Bureau reports that the population of the United States has reached 200 million.

1968

- Congress passes the Bilingual Education Act, Title VII of the Elementary and Secondary Education Act, to counteract the high dropout rate among Hispanics. In 1984 the act is extended through 1988 and creates programs to help students maintain their native languages after learning English.

1969

- *January 20*: Richard M. Nixon is inaugurated as the 37th president of the United States.

1970

- The United States census reports a total population of 203,211,926, an increase of 13.3 percent over 1960. The rate of increase has dropped by more than 5 percent.
- *April 30*: The United States invades Cambodia to eliminate North Vietnamese sanctuaries, leading to widespread antiwar demonstrators nationwide and bringing 100,000 protesters to Washington, D.C., on May 9. Ground troops are withdrawn from Cambodia on June 19.

1971

- *February 8*: South Vietnamese troops invade Laos to attack North Vietnamese supply lines. The United States renders air and artillery support.
- *March 15*: The United States lifts its ban on travel to the People's Republic of China.
- *June 14*: A riot breaks out in an 11-block Puerto Rican neighborhood, East Harlem, New York.
- *October 25*: The People's Republic of China is admitted to the United Nations, and Taiwan is expelled.
- *December 3*: Indian troops invade Pakistan in support of Bengali rebels. The United States and China support Pakistan and the Soviet Union supports India. Bengalis are victorious on December 16 and proclaim an independent state of Bangladesh.

1972

- A half-million deportable aliens are apprehended; the figure doubles by 1977. The border patrol now employs 2,400.
- *June 17*: Five men are arrested during a break-in at Democratic National Headquarters in Washington, initiating the Watergate investigation. The trial of seven defendants in the case begins on January 8, 1973.

1973

- *January 20*: Richard Nixon is inaugurated for his second term as president.
- *January 27*: A cease-fire agreement ending the Vietnam War is signed in Paris. Exchange of prisoners begins February 12.
- *February 21*: Civil war in Laos ends after 20 years.
- *March 23*: The United States denies former Beatle John Lennon permanent resident status because of a 1968 conviction for possession of hashish in Great Britain.
- *October 6*: War breaks out in the Middle East as Syria attacks Israel in the Golan Heights and Egypt attacks in the Sinai desert. Hostilities end with Egypt's surrender on October 25. The first of many peace conferences between Israel and the Arab states begins on December 21.

1974

- *January 21*: The U.S. Supreme Court rules in favor of bilingual education. In *Lau v. Nichols* it declares that denying special instruction to "limited English proficiency" (LEP) students violates the 1964 Civil Rights Act.

- *August 9*: President Nixon resigns his office as president. Vice President Gerald R. Ford takes office as the 38th president of the United States.

1975

- The United States withdraws its support of South Vietnam, whose capital, Saigon, falls to the Vietcong. The United States accepts 130,000 Vietnamese refugees, making Indochina the second largest source of refugees after 1965. By 1985 more than 700,000 refugees from Vietnam, Cambodia, and Laos have entered the United States, the majority of them settling in California.
- *June 30*: The Supreme Court rules that the border patrol cannot stop cars at traffic checkpoints near the Mexican borders to stop illegal immigrants without a warrant.

1976

- In *Wong v. Hampton*, the Supreme Court rules that the Civil Service Commission regulation barring resident aliens from federal jobs violates the Constitution's Fifth Amendment.
- A new law is passed unifying the limits and the preference system of each hemisphere. Annual limits for each hemisphere remain separate: 170,000 for the Eastern, 120,000 for the Western, and a special ceiling of 600 visas for colonies and dependencies.

1977

- *January 20*: Jimmy Carter is inaugurated as the 39th president of the United States.
- *August 17*: President Carter signs a bill lifting the ban on communist aliens entering the United States.
- *October 28*: President Carter signs a bill extending federal aid for refugees entering the United States following the communist takeover in Vietnam, Cambodia, and Laos.

1978

- An amendment to the 1976 immigration law establishes a world quota of 290,000.
- Immigration totals 601,442, the highest number since 1924.
- *November 11*: Cuban Premier Fidel Castro announces that he will free 3,600 remaining political prisoners if the United States will admit them as immigrants.
- *November 28*: The U.S. attorney general announces that he plans to admit 21,875 Indo-Chinese refugees from Cambodia in addition to the established annual allowance of 25,000.

- *December 20*: The House of Representatives Committee on Population proposes a major change in the United States immigration policy to reduce the number of illegal aliens entering the country.

1979

- *February 11*: The INS reports a record number of Mexican and Central American illegal aliens. The border patrol now employs almost 11,000 personnel and has a budget of more than $300 million. Inspections total 274 million, and the patrol apprehends about one million deportable aliens.
- *February 12*: The United States, Canada, and Australia agree to admit almost 2,000 Vietnamese refugees from the Philippines.
- *August 3*: Conflict breaks out between immigrant Vietnamese fishermen and Texas crab fishermen. One Vietnamese fisherman is killed.
- *August 25*: The Centers for Disease Control reports that Vietnamese refugees show a high rate of tuberculosis and skin and intestinal parasites.

1980

- The national census reports a total population of 226,545,805, a 9.8 percent increase on the 1970 figures. Of these, 3,500,439, or 1.5 percent, are of Asian or Pacific Island origin, and 14,608,673, or 6.4 percent, are of "Hispanic" origin of any race. The Census Bureau records 2,047,000 undocumented aliens but estimates that there are 5,965,000 actually resident in the country on census day, April 1.
- Congress passes a Refugee Act that broadens the definition of refugees to include not only people fleeing communism but those "with a well founded fear of persecution" based on race, religion, nationality, or membership in a political organization. The act sets an annual limit of 50,000 refugees to be admitted through 1982, leaving it to Congress to set limits after that year, and reduces the worldwide quota of immigrants from 290,000 to 270,000.
- About 130,000 Cuban refugees arrive in Florida through the port of Mariel in Cuba when Castro allows many inmates of Cuban prisons and working-class citizens to emigrate. By the end of 1980, Cuban Americans represent the largest national group of post–World War II refugees in the United States.
- *July 2*: A federal judge confirms the political claim to refuge of thousands of Haitians seeking asylum in the

United States and rules that the INS has violated their legal rights in denying them entry.

1981

- New legislation eliminates the permanent exclusion of people previously deported, permitting them to return after five years. Other changes include new provisions for investment and exchange visitors.
- *January 20*: Ronald Reagan is inaugurated as the 40th president of the United States.
- *January 30*: The INS moves to expel 3,500 Haitians entering since October 11, 1980.

1982

- President Reagan sets a ceiling of 10,000 Southeast Asian admissions.
- *April 26–30*: The INS arrests 5,635 illegal aliens arrested in nine cities. Of these, 4,908 (87 percent) are Mexicans.

1983

- *August 27*: Dario Fo and Franca Rame, Italian playwrights, are denied visas because of their political satires. The controversial decision is based on the McCarran-Walter Act prohibition of visas for "aliens who are members of or support anarchist or Communist and terrorist organizations."

1984

- Dade County, Florida, the county that includes Miami, makes English its official language in an effort to discourage the growing use of Spanish in the schools. The ordinance is repealed in 1993.

1985

- *January 20*: Ronald Reagan is inaugurated for his second term as president.

1986

- Marriage Fraud Amendments are passed later this year, requiring a two-year conditional residency for alien spouses before they can obtain permanent residency and imposing a criminal penalty of up to five years in prison and a $250,000 fine for immigration-related marriage fraud. The bill also makes such fraud grounds for permanent deportation and a bar to future immigration.
- California passes Proposition 63, making English the state's official language, by a 73 percent majority.

- *February 20*: The INS reports a "startling" increase in illegal aliens from Mexico. The total of apprehended aliens is up nearly 40 percent over 1985, reaching a record number of 1.2 million.
- *November 6*: After three unsuccessful tries over a five-year period, President Ronald Reagan signs into law the Immigration Reform and Control Act (Public Law 99-603). The bill, known as IRCA, is aimed at solving the problem of illegal entry by imposing sanctions on employers who knowingly hire illegal aliens, calling for penalties of up to six months in jail and a $10,000 fine for each illegal alien hired. The law legalizes the status of undocumented entrants who have arrived before January 1, 1982, and creates a program to grant permanent resident status to qualified agricultural workers. It also calls for increasing the border patrol in 1987 and 1988 by 50 percent over the 1986 level and offers a broad amnesty for many undocumented aliens already in the country.

1987

- *January 20*: The INS rules that employers must ascertain the citizenship or immigrant status of all new workers within 24 hours of hiring them.
- *May 5*: About 50,000 immigrants apply at 107 special offices for amnesty offered under the Immigration Reform and Control Act of 1986. The Service estimates that there are 3.9 million illegal aliens eligible for amnesty.
- *October 8*: The INS allows children not eligible for amnesty to remain with their parents.

1988

- *August 10*: Congress passes a bill providing $1.25 million in reparations to Japanese Americans interned during World War II; $20,000 is given to each surviving internee.
- *November 15*: President Reagan signs into law an amendment to the 1986 IRCA law, allowing more visas for Irish citizens to enter the United States.

1989

- Immigration figures pass one million for the first time since 1914.
- *January 20*: George H. W. Bush is inaugurated as the 41st president of the United States.

1990

- The census shows a population of 248,709,873, a 9.8-percent increase over the 1980 count. Asians and

Pacific Islanders comprise 7,273,662, reflecting 2.9 percent of the total. The total Asian-Pacific Islander population of the United States has increased by 107.8 percent since 1980. People of Hispanic origin in the United States—Spanish-speaking people from the Caribbean and Latin America of any race—now total 22,354,059, representing 9 percent of the total population. This marks a 53-percent increase since 1980. More than half of the Hispanics in the United States (13,495,938) are Mexican. For the first time, the census questionnaire is distributed in both English and Spanish.

- *October 9*: The first nine reparation payments to Japanese-American World War II internees are made at a ceremony in Washington, D.C.
- *November 29*: Congress passes the Immigration Act of 1990 (IMMACT, Public Law 101-649), increasing the numerical limits of immigrants by 35 percent and changing the preference system by giving higher priority to relatives of U.S. citizens and more highly skilled workers. It increases the annual limit of 500,000 immigrants worldwide to 700,000 for three years, after which it is to be decreased to 675,000.

1991
- Immigration figures reach 1,827,167, the highest number in U.S. history.

1992
- *April 29*: Four white police officers in Los Angeles, California, are acquitted of charges connected with the beating of black motorist Rodney G. King 13 months earlier. Within two hours, riots break out among blacks and Hispanics protesting the decision. The violence continues for five days, resulting in 58 deaths, 2,000 injuries, and $717 million in damages, and requiring the National Guard and federal troops to enter and quell the riots. Among the principal targets of the rioters are Korean businesses.

1993
- *January 20*: William J. Clinton is inaugurated as the 42nd president of the United States.
- *February 26*: A car bomb explodes in the underground parking lot of the World Trade Center in New York City, killing six and injuring 1,042 people. The attack is believed to have been financed by the Islamic organization al-Qaeda, whose officially stated purpose is to eliminate foreign influence in Islamic countries. Eng-

land, Canada, Australia, and the United States classify al-Qaeda as a terrorist group.

1994
- California passes Proposition 187, denying many government services to illegal aliens. In November 1995 the federal court rules that the state could not withhold public education or other services from resident children.
- *November 24*: The House of Representatives approves the free trade treaty (General Agreement on Tariffs and Trade, or GATT), cutting tariffs. The Senate confirms the treaty December 1.
- *December 13*: Russia invades the rebellious province of Chechnya.

1995
- Growing opposition to bilingual education results in the introduction of six bills in Congress to make English the official language of the United States. On October 5 the 9th Circuit Court of Appeals rules in *Yniguez v. Mofford* that Arizona's Official English law violates the right to free speech guaranteed in the First Amendment of the Constitution.
- *January 29*: Congress approves sending 6,000 troops as peacekeepers to Haiti. The troops withdraw, transferring peacekeeping responsibilities to a United Nations mission, at the end of March.
- *May 2*: The United States changes its Cuban refugee policy; boat people seeking refuge are to be returned to Cuba.
- *July 11*: Diplomatic relations between the United States and Vietnam are restored, and a U.S. embassy is opened in Hanoi.
- *October 1*: Ten Muslims, under the leadership of Sheik Omar Abdel Rahman, are convicted of a terrorist plot in New York City to force the United States to withdraw its support for Israel.
- *December*: The United States sends 8,000 troops to Bosnia for a peacekeeping mission.

1996
- *August 22*: President Clinton signs into law the Personal Responsibility and Work Opportunity Reconciliation Act (Public Law 104-193) allowing individual states to restrict public assistance to legal immigrants. This law cuts spending on food-stamp programs by $23.3 billion by making illegal aliens ineligible for most major welfare benefits, including food stamps, Medicaid, and

Supplemental Security Income, a cash benefit for low-income, aged, blind, and disabled citizens.

- Congress passes the Illegal Immigration Reform and Immigrant Responsibility Act (Public Law 104-208), authorizing funds for more personnel of the border patrol and increasing penalties for those who smuggle illegal aliens into the United States or use fraudulent documentation. It also streamlines deportation procedures.

1997

- Congress sets a cap of 78,000 on the number of refugees who can be admitted to the United States, down from 90,000 in 1996 and 110,000 the year before.
- The Census Bureau reports that California has admitted the largest number of immigrants of any state this year, a total of 170,126. New York, with 96,559 has received the second largest number, followed by Florida (59,965), Texas (44,428), and Illinois (33,163).
- A record 1.6 million applications for naturalization are received. The annual average from 1990 to 1995 was 600,000.
- *January 20*: Clinton is inaugurated for his second term as president.

1998

- The total number of legal immigrants admitted to the United States reaches its lowest in 10 years, totaling only 660,477.
- *January 1*: The North American Free Trade Agreement (NAFTA) takes effect. It allows free movement of goods and services among the United States, Canada, and Mexico.
- *March 17*: A California district court declares invalid most of the remaining provisions of Proposition 187, passed in 1994 denying many government services to illegal aliens. The American Civil Liberties Union calls the ruling a major victory.
- *March 26*: The Immigration and Naturalization Service releases a plan proposing its division into two separate agencies, one to guard the borders and the other to process legal immigration.
- *August 7*: The INS announces extensive modernization measures to speed up citizenship applications, including a centralized computer system, a national telephone information center, and application instructions to be printed in 14 languages.

- Terrorists bomb the U.S. embassy in Nairobi, Kenya, and Dar es Salaam, Tanzania, killing 257 and injuring more than 4,000. The attacks are linked to Osama bin Laden, leader of al-Qaeda.
- *August 20*: The United States launches missile attacks on al-Qaeda training bases in Sudan and Afghanistan in response to the August 7 bombings.
- *October 13*: The INS institutes higher fees for most immigration services to help defray the costs of modernizing the immigration process. The agency reports that some 1.9 million immigrants are currently engaged in the complicated procedure, which takes as long as two years to complete. Services for which fees are raised include registration for permanent residence and issuance of applications for naturalization.
- *October 24*: The INS reports that an estimated 100,000 Chinese have been arriving illegally in the United States annually for several years despite increased border precaution.
- *December 4*: The U.S. Department of Labor announces that unemployment is at 4.4 percent. About 64 percent of working-age Americans hold jobs, the highest percentage on record.
- *December 16*: The United States and Britain launch air attacks on weapon sites in Iraq.

1999

- *January 1*: President Clinton proposes a defense spending increase of $100 billion over the next six years.
- *February 1*: President Clinton submits a budget for the fiscal year 2000 of $1.77 trillion. The proposal increases the INS budget to $4.3 billion.
- *February 28*: Israel launches an air strike on southern Lebanon in retaliation for weeks of attacks by militant Islamic organization Hezbollah.
- *May 3*: The Supreme Court, in *INS v. Aguirre*. rules unanimously that foreigners convicted of "serious, non-political crimes" in their own countries are ineligible for refugee protection in the United States regardless of the risk of persecution they face if deported.
- *September 13*: Muslim terrorists detonate a bomb in Moscow, killing at least 95 people. It is the third attack by Islamic militants in Moscow in two weeks.
- *November 23*: A small aluminum boat carrying 14 Cubans seeking asylum sinks on the way to Florida. Six-year-old Elián González is saved although his mother and 10 others drown. After treatment, the boy is released to relatives in Miami on November 26.

A political cartoon portrays Elián González's return to Cuba as a victory for President Fidel Castro. *(Copley News Service/Marshall Ramsey)*

- *December 5*: Cuban president Fidel Castro demands the return of Elián González to his father's custody in Havana within 72 hours, but the U.S. Department of State rejects the demand. This initiates an international custody dispute.

- *December 19*: The sovereignty of Macao, situated partly on the Chinese mainland and partly on two islands off the China coast, returns to China after 442 years of Portuguese rule. Macao was the last European colony in Asia.

Eyewitness Testimony

For almost ten years now the Voice of America has been exhorting freedom-loving people from behind the Iron Curtain to escape to freedom. We have been describing the glories and advantages of the free world. . . .

But how do we treat those who flee from Soviet tyranny and Communist brutality? Ask those who have been to Europe and have visited the refugee camps in Austria, Western Germany and Italy. Hear their descriptions of the barbed wire entanglements, the cells, hovels and barracks where hundreds of thousands of men, women, and children live lives of savage desperation.

The refugees from war and postwar upheaval and the escapees from behind the Iron Curtain find a cold hospitality in the facilities set aside for them. . . . [T]he number of refugees and escapees who have been admitted to the United States are precious few indeed.

More than half the life span of the Refugee Relief program is over. But only about one tenth of the number authorized to be admitted have actually been permitted to come to the United States.

. . . The Refugee Relief Act, as passed in 1953, contained so many restrictions and booby-traps, that entry into the United States under the refugee program has become a challenge which relatively few could meet.

[I]t is necessary that the Congress and the Administration show a clear appreciation of the high importance—in terms of our foreign policy, our humanitarian principles, and our own national origin and traditions—of serving as an example, before the world, of hospitality and haven for the oppressed and persecuted.

Herbert H. Lehman, Democratic senator from New York, defending a proposed bill to repeal the McCarran-Walter Act and liberalize United States immigration policy, in the New York Journal-American, *July 28, 1955.*

Ever since I was a kid, I have been talking to statues person-to-statue, pretty much the way I talk to people person-to-person. Like people, some statues talk back to me, while others merely turn their back.

No wonder that soon after December 20, 1957, the day I landed in the United States (and one I consider my second birthday and a prelude to my coming-of-spiritual-age), and soon after I got my first job—parking cars—I went to talk to the Statue of Liberty, the colossus of the New World.

. . . Imposing, the Statue of Liberty greets me with a smile. I smile back. It's a lovely scene: the two of us—two exiles, she from France and I from Poland—facing each other on this warm, though rainy, day on Bedloe's Island (renamed the Island of Liberty).

"Welcome to the land of the free. What's your origin, if you don't mind my asking?" says the Statue.

"I was born a Jew and I come from Poland," I declare, no longer afraid I might be overheard by someone who's not Jewish, or someone who does not like the Poles.

Jerzy Kosinski, Polish novelist, recalling his arrival from Poland in 1957, in "Being There," in New York, *May 12, 1986, p. 71.*

I don't know why [I left Sweden]. I didn't leave it because I was in misery. I didn't leave it because I didn't see any future in it. I didn't leave it because I didn't have anybody there. I left it to come back to it because I just wanted, maybe part of my Viking blood, you know, takes me out on adventures, and I just simply wanted to see something else. . . .

I cannot say I feel at home in a sense. I probably will not feel at home anywhere anymore. Once you have left someplace that actually was home, you took up something there, you tried to settle down here, but you can't—I can't completely feel that I didn't really pull up my roots completely there and I can't therefore plant it completely down here, so I feel I have one foot here, one foot there. . . .

I was more Americanized the first three years I was in this country than I am now. I wanted to fit in more at that time. I didn't want to seem so foreign. . . . Once I realized I probably would live here most of my life, I realized how important my Swedish background was to me and that I, in no way, wanted to lose it. I started to cultivate my traditions.

Margaret Maryk, Swedish immigrant, 1958, in Robbins, Coming to America: Immigrants from Northern Europe *(1981), pp. 185–186.*

This monster of a land, this mightiest of nations, this spawn of the future, turns out to be the macrocosm of microcosm me. If an Englishman or a Frenchman or an Italian should travel my route, see what I saw, hear what I heard, their stored pictures would be not only different from mine but equally different from one another. . .

From start to finish I found no strangers. . . . [T]hese are my people and this is my country. . . . If I were to prepare one immaculate inspected generality it would be this: For all of our interwoven breeds drawn from every part of the ethnic world, we are a nation, a new breed. Americans are much more Americans than they are Northerners, Southerners, Westerners, or Easterners. And descendants of English, Irish, Italian, Jewish, German, Polish are essentially American. . . . California Chinese, Boston Irish, Wisconsin German, yes, and Alabama Negroes, have more in common than they have apart. And this is the more remarkable because it has happened so quickly. It is a fact that Americans from all sections and of all racial extractions are more alike than the Welsh are like the English, the Lancashireman like the Cockney, or for that matter the Lowland Scot like the Highlander. It is astonishing that this has happened in less than two hundred years and most of it in the last fifty. The American identity is an exact and provable thing.

John Steinbeck, American novelist, describing his observations while touring America in 1961–62, in Travels with Charlie *(1962), pp. 185–186.*

When my great-grandfather left here to become a cooper in East Boston, he carried nothing with him except a strong religious faith and a strong desire for liberty. If he hadn't left New Ross, I would be working over there [at the Albatross Fertilizer Company plant across the street].

John F. Kennedy, 35th president of the United States, in a speech made on a visit to New Ross, Ireland, the town from which his great-grandfather emigrated, June 1963, in Reeves, President Kennedy: Profile of Power *(1993), pp. 537–558.*

Adoption of the President's wise recommendations would be an act of justice and wisdom, as well as evidence that we fully understand the true nature of the changed world—now grown so small—in which all humanity lives.

Editorial on President Kennedy's proposal to amend the immigration law in the New York Times, *July 25, 1963.*

Fresh off the boat from England in August 1964, we went into our first North American restaurant and ordered a hamburger. We had planned this event in advance—it was to be our first direct contact with the reality behind images we had known through movies, through television, through novels, through myth and fantasy, desire and suspicion and dread. . . . The waiter had come and gone, and had understood every word we said. It was very hot; enormous cars drifted past in the street. So far, so good. We could handle this. We were not surprised to be given glasses of water with ice in them, almost as

A team of INS investigators searches a ship's hold for stowaways. *(U.S. Citizenship and Immigration Services)*

soon as we sat down. We were delighted; this is what we had been told would happen in New York, and it had happened.

The hamburger came, and with it a plastic squeeze bottle full of tomato ketchup. . . . I decided I would prefer mustard, and asked for some. About a minute later, the air moved slightly near my cheek, and there was a light thump as packet of mustard hit the tabletop. After a moment's panic I turned, but the waiter was already gone. The mustard lay, yellow in its transparent covering, on the table between us. It was an individual serving, just for me and not for Colin, who had not asked for any. . . . You were expected to tear the packet open and squeeze the mustard out with your fingers—but I could not bring myself to do that yet. We sat and looked at the mustard missile, and knew that we had reached a foreign place, an unpredictable and infinitely weird environment, which we had not come from, and into which we would slot ourselves only eventually and with the utmost difficulty. That packet of mustard was my introduction to North America.

Margaret Visser, English writer, in The Way We Are *(1994), pp. xvii–xviii.*

It was never easy to get into the Promised Land. It certainly was no picnic for me. Half of all Americans living today have someone who came through Ellis Island. They waited here to find out if they would be held, deported, or let in. They washed over the island in waves, millions and millions of them, all of them done with the Old World, ready to be reborn. Steins to become Stones, Rosens Rosses, Cardarellas Cards, Witkevieczes Vicks, Codrescus Corkscrews.

Immigration officers walked glumly among them, looking for anarchists like Emma Goldman and poets like me to send back. I fought them for ten years to get my citizenship. They thought I was a Communist poet spy. But that was progress: in Romania just "poet" was enough to get you noticed by the police. . . .

So many of us, so much hunger! So much flag waving! Eyes looking out on promises and deceptions. . . .

Andrei Codrescu, Romanian poet and essayist, describing his arrival in the United States during the 1970s, in Road Scholar *(1993), pp. 36–37.*

Spanish mass in my neighborhood was held in the basement. They had to fight to bring it up into the Church, but they eventually got it. The parish there was anti-Spanish. They wanted Puerto Rican parents to stop teaching their children Spanish because it confused the children in the early grades. I was proof that it wasn't true because I was bilingual as a child—more so than I am now. And I was doing very well. So I was resented by the whole parish.

. . . The children of white immigrant groups, the groups that I've met and dealt with in the city, we could understand each other. Because there was a struggle in the family. There's just no link at all with the other group, the middle-class children. They seem to have no concept of struggle. That's what used to amaze us. Life was like applesauce for them, smooth and tasty.

José Ramirez, American-born Puerto Rican, recalling his youth in New York City in the 1970s, in Morse, Pride Against Prejudice *(1980), pp. 168–69.*

These people [illegal Mexican immigrants] are not coming here with any sense of shame. They feel they have a moral right to migrate to the United States for work. If the Southwest still belonged to Mexico, it would have been a major economic power in the world today.

Alberto Juárez, legal-aid attorney with One-Stop Immigration, Los Angeles, California, in Holgar Jensen, "Flood of Illegal Aliens," Fort Worth [*Texas*] Star-Telegram, *June 28, 1976, p. 1.*

Part of the problem is that many Puerto Ricans have always identified themselves with whoever has been ruling them. Spain was the mother country and some people had a ritualistic feeling about Spain. Anything that Spain did was right. Other Puerto Ricans would question this, but they would have to go along with it anyway because they had no power. . . .

The same thing happened when the Americans first came into Puerto Rico. I think that accounts for the fact that some Puerto Ricans are on the side of "they." I may be wrong, but I feel that for some reason a lot of Puerto Rican people are in this position. For instance, my mother will never question authority. And that attitude stems from things that went on in Puerto Rico even before the Americans came. There was *La Ley, La Autoridad,* the law and the authority. You keep quiet and you bow your head down and you don't say anything. You don't talk back. Many older people have that attitude. . . . I can understand that because that is the way I was reared. But then again I learned something different from the American culture. This was to challenge and to talk back and to look people straight in the eye when you had something to say.

Maria Diaz, a Puerto Rican attending college in New York City in the late 1970s, in Morse, Pride Against Prejudice *(1980), p. 195.*

An illegal alien is fingerprinted before being returned to Mexico. *(U.S. Citizenship and Immigration Services)*

Nobody in Arthur Bobowicz's family really liked turkey. Certainly the kids didn't like it as much as chicken or duck. They suspected that Momma and Poppa didn't like it very much either. Still, they had a turkey every Thanksgiving. "Thanksgiving is an important American holiday," Poppa would say. "You kids are Americans. Would you want people to think we were ungrateful?" Poppa came from Poland, and he was very big on holidays and being an American. There was no arguing with him. . . .

Most of the kids in the neighborhood [in Hoboken, New Jersey] had the same scene at home. Some of them liked turkey, some of them didn't—but they all had it on Thanksgiving. They all had fathers like Arthur Bobowicz's father—they came from Italy, and the Ukraine, and Puerto Rico, and Hong Kong. The kids were all being raised to be Americans, and everyone's father knew that Americans ate turkey on Thanksgiving.

> *D. Manus Pinkwater, in his 1977 novel* The Hoboken Chicken Emergency, *pp. 1–2.*

[How much fear do these undocumented employees have that they're going to be turned in?]

I think [illegal immigrants] live a life of fear around the clock, every one of them. It's indicated to us when we walk into a factory and they run helter-skelter. And naturally they don't want to be caught. They don't want to go back. They've made a—may have given several hundred dollars just to get here, maybe their life savings, and when we catch them, their dreams go down the drain.

> *Ralph Raimond, U.S. Immigration and Naturalization Service official, on the CBS television program* 60 Minutes, *November 4, 1979, in CBS News,* 60 Minutes Verbatim: Who Said What to Whom, *p. 107.*

They bring everybody to Miami: Nicaraguans, Cubans, Haitians. And we're still on the bottom.

> *A black rioter during the Mariel boatlift from Cuba, 1980, in John Sullivan, "Immigration's Effects on Blacks,"* The Social Contract, *Fall 1993, p. 40.*

Of course, I'm an American. And at the same time I'm Irish, and this is something I can never deny—my birthright. Now the way I face it is—you love your mother. Yet get married. You love your wife. Does this mean you do not any longer love your mother? Not at all. They are two entirely different things. So I'm a citizen of America. I love the country, I respect all its laws. And at the same time I can't get away from the fact that I was born an

Irishman. And the fact is that I would not have come to America if I could have lived in my own country, in any capacity at all tolerable.

> *Sean Lyons, Irish immigrant who came to the United States in 1927 at the age of 24, commenting on his Irish-American identity in 1980, in Blumenthal and Ozer,* Coming to America: Immigrants from the British Isles *(1980), p. 165.*

I used to be a real man like any other, but not now any longer. Things I used to do, now I can't do here. I feel like a thing which they say drops in the fire but won't burn and drops in the river but won't flow. . . . We only live day by day, just like the baby birds who are only staying in the nest opening their mouths and waiting for the mother bird to bring the worms. Because we are now like those baby birds who cannot fly yet.

> *A middle-aged Hmong refugee from Laos, in the 1980s, in Portes and Rumbaut,* Immigrant America *(1996), pp. 143–144.*

We don't recognize the border. Our country was taken from us by the U.S. and the only way we can reclaim it is to wage war against the U.S.

> *Ricardo Romero, leader of the Chicano/Mexicano Commission of the MLN (National Liberation Movement), a group linked with the Puerto Rican FALN (Armed Forces of National Liberation), at a rally on November 15, 1981, in Stacy and Lutton,* The Immigration Time Bomb, *(1985), p. 111.*

There has never been anything like it in our history. They are the most ruthless criminals I have seen in 31 years as a cop. Castro dumped his most hardcore, murderous criminals on us, all at one time, and one place. Castro exported a crime wave that will be with us into the next generation.

> *Mike Gonzales, sergeant of the Miami, Florida, Police Department Homicide Squad, describing the effect of the wave of Cuban immigrants arriving through the port of Mariel in 1982, in Stacy and Lutton,* The Immigration Time Bomb *(1985), p. 104.*

Los Angeles—A massive influx of immigrants from Asia and Latin America has sharply increased the tuberculosis rate here and in other cities, a change so drastic it has reversed what was a steady decline in tuberculosis nationwide.

> The Washington Post, *January 4, 1982.*

Leprosy is a bacterial disease that attacks tissue, particularly skin and nervous tissue. Its more than 13-fold increase in the past 20 years is entirely due to immigration, said Dr. Thomas Rea, chief of dermatology at County-USC Medical Center and a professor of medicine at USC Medical School.

Los Angeles Times, *October 14, 1983.*

We have to find a way to gain control of our borders. . . . The economy within the United States can never keep up with the fertility pressure outside of the United States.

Richard D. Lamm, governor of Colorado, on Face the Nation, *CBS-TV, May 20, 1984.*

During the next 125 years, assuming a persistently strong economy, the United States will create about 30 million new jobs. Can we afford to set aside more than 20 percent of them for foreign workers? No. It would be a disservice to our own poor and unfortunate.

Father Theodore M. Hesburgh, president of Notre Dame University and chairman of the Select Commission on Immigration and Refugee Policy of Congress, in "Enough Delays on Immigration," in the New York Times, *March 20, 1986.*

Our youngest son, Christopher, recently asked me why everyone was making such a fuss over the Statue of Liberty. I tried to explain it to him the way my parents explained it to me.

My mother and father came from another country. My mother came here by ship from Italy, and her first glimpse of this great country was when she sighted the Lady of Opportunity, steadfastly lifting her torch.

My mother understood immediately the meaning of that beautiful symbol. To her the statue meant freedom and opportunity, a chance to earn one's own bread with dignity. The Statue told my mother that if she and my father were willing to work hard and care about this nation, they would be able to share in its incredible bounties. And this new country would not ask them, or force them, to give up the culture of their parents. Lady Liberty said, "Welcome. You are welcome, and the culture you bring with you is welcome, to blend with all the others into this beautiful mosaic that is America."

. . . . What's all the fuss about, Chris? It's about a struggle by millions who came before us to create a new society of opportunity and tolerance. It reminds us how, beginning with nothing but their hands and their hearts

The mosaic of America welcomes people from all nations. Two young citizens salute their new home in 1974. *(U.S. Citizenship and Immigration Services)*

and their minds, they built this beautiful country and gave it to us and left us the obligation to make it a better one.

Mario Cuomo, governor of New York, commenting on the centenary of the Statue of Liberty, in "Family-Style," New York, *May 12, 1986, p. 84.*

When you pull a plant out of the ground without any soil around its roots—soil from where it was grown—and transplant it, the plant will have trouble surviving. The Hmong people never really thought about coming to America, never really believed they would have to leave Asia. Then suddenly we were here. . . . The technology and the Latin languages of European and Mexican immigrants are much closer to America's. They have some dirt on their roots.

Dang Moua, Hmong farmer in California, in Frank Viviano, "Strangers in the Promised Land," San Francisco Chronicle, *May 31, 1986, p. 18.*

Perhaps the most acute challenge confronting an immigrant on arrival in the United States is a fear of legal authorities. This has nothing to do with violation of the law. Immigrants are generally careful to ensure that they don't end up on the wrong side of the law. What most immigrants fear most is the Immigration and Naturalization Service. . . . There are frequent news reports about immigration officials raiding restaurants and factories looking to deport undocumented immigrants. However, there are never reports about such raids on offices of large corporations, simply because they don't occur. Therefore, undocumented immigrants who work in prestigious environments, do so with confidence because they don't fear they will be hunted like those with menial jobs. To believe, as some do, that large corporation never hire undocumented immigrants to positions of responsibility is a mistake.

. . . Many people think they know who the undocumented immigrant is and what he looks like. They think that he is the Jamaican who picks apples on a farm, the Mexican family that lives down the road, the Honduran and Asian families who work in sweatshops across America, or the Haitian who works three jobs to make ends meet. They almost never think that the undocumented immigrant may be the English, German or French gentleman who works in a Fortune 500 company, drives a fancy car and owns a beautiful home on the beach.

Ohiro D. Oni-Eseleh, Nigerian psychotherapist who immigranted to the United States in 1988, in In Pursuit of Dreams: The Truth About Immigration, *Baltimore: Erica House Book Publishers (1999), pp. 70–71.*

Nowadays, sometimes I feel like a frog jumping from one world to the other: school, my family, being American, being Khmer. In a way to be assimilated in another culture, you have to give up your own culture. With one foot in each culture, the wider you have to spread your legs, the more you could lose your balance.

Sathaya Tor, Cambodian refugee who arrived in the United States at the age of 14 in 1981, reflecting on his adjustment as the only Cambodian student in Stanford University in 1988, in Takaki, Strangers from a Different Shore *(1998), p. 470.*

A hundred thousand Chinese here, more or less, no one had an accurate count, and more of them arriving every day of the week. Cost an immigrant five thousand bucks for "key money" to a one-room apartment in a sleazy tenement. Twenty years ago all your Chinese here were from only two counties in Guangdong province. Today, you had maybe twenty provinces represented here.

No to mention all the Chinese immigrants from Southeast Asia. Chinatown had become a distant province of China, a third-world city right here in New York. A city unto itself, spilling over into southeast Manhattan, bursting its long-ago boundaries, displacing the Puerto Ricans, spreading like a vaporous cloud over Little Italy and what used to be the Jewish tenements on Henry Street, drifting all the way to Houston Street, moving restlessly, growing all the time.

Ed McBain, describing New York's Chinatown in the novel Another Part of the City *(1986), p. 136.*

My cousin, who is fifteen, dresses all punk and goes skateboarding everywhere. He can't decide if he is Hmong or American. He's going to get in a lot of trouble that way, because he can't be either one. . . .

I don't feel confused about who I am. Being American is great. I enjoy going to football games, eating hot dogs, and cheering the team on. But with my relatives I go to ceremonies at the farm. I know that I am Hmong. I have black hair and speak a certain dialect. But my ideals are American.

Shoua Vang, 43-year-old Hmong refugee from Laos who arrived in the United States in the late 1980s, in Santoli, New Americans *(1988), p. 332.*

The school was so big! There was no one who could speak Mien and explain to me. My uncle had told me if I needed any help to go to the Dean. My teacher asked me something and I didn't understand her. So I just said, "Dean, Dean" because I needed help. That is how I got my American name. She was asking me, "What is your name?" Now everybody calls me Dean. Now it is funny, but it is also sad. My name comes from not knowing what was going on.

A twelfth-grade boy from the Mien people in Laos, who had immigrated to America at the age of fourteen, in an interview conducted in a California public school by the National Coalition of Advocates for Students in the late 1980s, in Olsen, Crossing the Schoolhouse Border *(1988), p. 89.*

If you catch 'em, you ought to clean 'em and fry 'em.

Harold Ezell, western regional commissioner of the INS in charge of border enforcement, speaking of illegal aliens, quoted in George Ramos, "Even If Days Are Numbered, Ezell Is Making Them Count," Los Angeles Times, May 29, 1989.

We are like animals from a zoo suddenly freed. . . . Imagine you were born in prison and lived in it all your life and then were set free and you don't know what to do and where to go—you are in the jungle of freedom.

Yevgeny Rubin, Soviet-Jewish journalist describing his experience of immigrating to the United States in 1992, in Daniels, Coming to America *(1990), p. 386.*

We are a nation of immigrants. But where do we draw the line? We have to stop being the 911 of the world.

Bette Hammond, president of STOPIT (Stop the Out-of-Control Problems of Immigration Today), 1992, in Reimers, Unwelcome Strangers *(1998), p. 25.*

In the two-and-a-half years since I arrived in Washington from Ghana, I've come a long way from the sense of alienation I felt when I got here. Some of this alienation was the usual confusion surrounding initiation into a different society—trying futilely to dilute a different accent, learning the true meaning of "daily weather forecast" in a city whose weather can change drastically in a few hours—all the normal adjustments that come with deciding to live in someone else's country.

But the deeper cause of my sense of separateness from the America I found was the shock of discovering the racial realities that underlie life here. . . .

My first encounter with America's complexities came soon after my arrival when, like so many other immigrants, I had to go job-hunting. . . .

The first page of my job application booklet declared in flowery language the American ideal of equal employment and explained that for statistical purposes only, and this of my own volition, I should fill out the questionnaire on the next page. . . .

I remembered a friend's advice: "To play it safe, always choose neutral responses. That way they know you are not an extremist." This would be simpler than I thought. There was, for example, the matter of gender: "M( ) F( ) OTHER( )." Thinking, "There must be a catch somewhere," I put an "x" in the third box.

The next question asked my racial self-identification. The options were: African American, American Indian, Asian, Caucasian, Hispanic, Other. None applied to me, and I was loath to classify myself again as "Other."

Was I in the middle of an identity crisis? No way!

I tore out the page.

Maria Kwami, Ghanaian immigrant, recalling her arrival in the United States in 1989, in "An African in America" in the Washington Post National Weekly Edition, *January 6–12, 1992.*

The students, as diverse as their America is diverse, are gathered around a conference table. And their visitor asks: suppose they were to grade the American civilization, grade it just as their professor grades them? How would they grade America?

It is Freshman Jona Goong, a Hawaiian of Chinese ancestry, who says it best.

"If I were to grade America," she says, softly, "I would give it an incomplete."

Dennis Farney, "Mosaic of Hope: Ethnic Identities Clash with Student Idealism at a California College," a report of an interview at Occidental College, Los Angeles, California, in the Wall Street Journal, *December 2, 1992.*

My first name is José. But I was born an American citizen. I resent having to prove I am a citizen. And if you ask me for papers right now, I cannot prove I am a citizen, and neither can any of you. But most of you will never be asked whether you are a citizen or not. I will because of my first name, and I resent it.

José Serrano, member of the House of Representatives, at a House hearing on proposed changes in the employment verification system, in Congressional Record, *July 28, 1993, p. 5403.*

Even today, much of America is a patchwork quilt of ethnic enclaves. On the North Side, for example, . . . one passes the offices of *India Weekly* and, a bit further on, of the Seoul Travel Service, before coming to a distinctly Polish, and then a Jewish, neighborhood. . . . A bicyclist in Chicago can easily have a multi-cultural experience, overhearing conversations in rapidly alternating Spanish, German, Swedish, Greek and African-American street English, as he crosses a series of intersections. The dividing lines may be as stark as an expressway or as imperceptible as the beginning of a school-district zone, but everyone who lives in each neighborhood knows where the boundaries are.

Sanford J. Ungar, commenting on the ethnic diversity of the United States in 1995, Fresh Blood *(1995), p. 222.*

When people come over here [from Korea], the father, the head of the household, often loses his status and his stature. That causes a lot of tension in the family circle. He begins to feel inadequate because he can't provide for his family like he used to and now he has to send his wife to work. Often, though, the women adjust more quickly. They learn English faster, and that's another source of frustration for the man. He's too proud to take these low-

A three-year-old immigrant embraces the American flag in Cleveland as he is naturalized in 1972. *(U.S. Citizenship and Immigration Services)*

principle there is no problem. But your travel permit has expired. Where do you want me to put the visa?" He advised me to ask the French consulate to revalidate the permit.

At the consulate, a less than amiable secretary informed me that this was impossible, explaining that according to regulations this kind of document could be validated only in France. . . .

. . . I didn't have enough money to go back to France. Taxis had already cost me a small fortune, and in any case my doctors would have forbidden an Atlantic crossing. As I stood there wondering whether I would be deported or placed on some sort of blacklist, the official leaned toward me, smiled, and said, "For God's sake, why don't you become a U.S. resident? Then later you can apply for citizenship." I stared at him. Could I actually become an American citizen? His smile gave me my answer. . . .

In 1981, after François Mitterand was elected President of France, a high official asked whether I would like to have French nationality. Though I thanked him—and not without some emotion—I declined the offer. When I needed a passport, it was America that gave me one.

Elie Wiesel, Nobel Prize–winning writer and political activist, adapted from his 1995 memoir All Rivers Run to the Sea, *quoted in* Parade Magazine, *November 5, 1995, p. 5.*

paying jobs. And so his wife is passing him up in terms of gaining newfound freedom and experiences and friends and language acquisition. And then you lose control over your kids, because nobody's home to watch them; they're prone to join gangs. You begin to lose touch with your family. You're discriminated against because you don't speak English or you speak English with a foreign accent. You're treated as less than human by the rest of the world.

Marcia Choo, Korean immigrant, in an interview with Sanford J. Ungar in 1995, in Fresh Blood *(1995), p. 288.*

In the 1950s my American visa expired. I had recently been struck by a car and severely injured while crossing a New York street, where I was working as a correspondent for a French newspaper. Equipped with my crutches and wheelchair, I headed for the Immigration office, where an amiable official took a long look at my stateless person's French travel permit and handed it back to me. "Since you have press accreditation at the United Nations, in

When Senator Simpson came to talk to me recently about the immigration legislation that he has worked on judiciously . . . he noticed a grouping of photographs on the wall. . . . So I introduced him to my mother's father, Mordecai Shanin, who came from a small town on the Russian border when my mother was 5 and settled in St. Jo, Mo. And I reintroduced Senator Simpson to my father, Harry Specter, who was in his uniform, and I recounted that he emigrated from Ukraine, walking across Europe with barely a ruble in his pockets. . . . My sense is that America is a big, broad, growing country and that we do have room for immigrants.

Arlen Specter, senator from Pennsylvania, in Congressional Record, *April 25, 1996, p. 4135.*

New Chinese immigrants in California have acculturated and assimilated into welfare and have evolved an understanding that [Supplemental Security Income, a federal welfare program] is part of a family entitlement. . . . We

A Vietnamese-American parishioner prays at a Buddhist temple altar in San Jose, California. About 90,000 Vietnamese immigrants have come to live in the San Jose area since the 1970s. *(AP/Wideworld)*

cannot be the retirement home for the world's indigent elderly.

Daniel Stein, executive director of the Federation for American Immigration Reform, in Christopher Conte, "Welfare, Work and the States: Reforms Target Food Stamp Users, Immigrants," CQ Researcher, *December 6, 1996, p. 1063.*

Walk into any Latino neighborhood and you see all the American icons, from Dallas Cowboys posters to the New York Yankees to rock and roll. Hispanics are learning English faster than previously, and there are 50,000 waiting for night classes in Los Angeles alone. Latinos are hard-working and patriotic, and in the armed forces they win more medals proportionately than their numbers.

Raul Yzaguirre, president of the National Council of La Raza, America's largest Latino civil rights group, in Charles S. Clark, "The New Immigrants," CQ Researcher, *January 24, 1997, p. 54.*

We've hired a pretty good number of Asian people here. We've hired some people from other countries, too. Those people . . . they come to this country, and man, it's the American dream. They go to work. These people will give you sixteen hours a day. Not that I'm looking for that, but I'll tell you what. They train themselves. They teach themselves. . . . And why? Because they left a war-torn country, or they left where the opportunities weren't there for them. What that is going to show other Americans I would hope eventually is that, jeez, this ain't all that bad.

George Slade, general manager at a tool production plant in Cobb County, Georgia, in 1998, in Wolfe, One Nation, After All *(1998), pp. 144–145.*

[I]t's the people who come to this nation with very little and worked their butts off which have created . . . the greatest economic benefit for us all. I have nothing but admiration for these Vietnamese boat people who came over here in rags, couldn't speak a word of English, and now own chains of restaurants.

> *Joseph Palumbo, physicist in Medford, Massachusetts, in 1998, in Wolfe,* One Nation, After All *(1998), p. 145.*

They're still not going to convince me that my grandfather, when he was sitting in Italy thinking of coming to the United States, was saying to himself, "I'm coming to New Jersey."

> *Rudolph Giuliani, mayor of New York City, on learning of the U.S. Supreme Court decision that most of Ellis Island, in New York Harbor, is in New Jersey, Associated Press report, in the Middletown, N.Y.,* Times Herald-Record, *May 27, 1998.*

[In the United States] you can go out and bad-mouth Clinton all you want; nothing is going to happen to you.

> *Florence Moise-Stone, New York lawyer who immigrated from Haiti around 1968, in David Chen, "What Would You Like in Your Welcome Package: Immigrants Offer Tips for an Official Guide to America," the* New York Times, *July 4, 1998, p. B2.*

We had to begin from zero. I tell you, this is the best country in the world, because from zero you can have whatever you want. There is no limit.

> *Nancy Lledes, Cuban immigrant (1994) living in Miami, in David Foster, "Refugees Find Uneasy Peace in America," Associated Press report in the Middletown, New York,* Sunday Record, *April 11, 1999, p. 29.*

Notes

1. Patrick J. Buchanan, quoted in *Insights in the News,* March 18, 1996, 11.
2. Doris Meissner, "After the Attacks: Protecting Borders and Liberties." *Policy Brief* #8, Carnegie Endowment for International Peace, November 2000, 2.

CHAPTER ELEVEN

Immigration in the New Century: 2000 and Beyond

Immigration Today

In 1753 Benjamin Franklin expressed the fear that Germans would become so numerous in the New World that "Americans"—that is, the English stock that first colonized the country—would not be able to maintain their language and government. A hundred years later, it was the Catholics from Ireland that seemed most threatening to the national unity. At different times, Chinese, Jews, Italians, and Slavs were seen as incapable of assimilating to American life and posing a threat to the "racial purity" of the country's Anglo-Saxon stock. The best hope was that the country would be a "melting pot" in which the different strains of many races and cultures would lose their identity and produce a new and superior breed. The French aristocrat Michel-Guillaume-Jean de Crèvecoeur asked in 1782, "What then is the American, this new man?" and answered himself with the words "here, individuals of all nations are melted into a new race of men." These sturdy, self-reliant, independent-minded citizens of the New World, he predicted, would "one day cause great changes in the world." His prediction has proved true, but by the middle of the 20th century the image of melting pot had been largely abandoned for that of a salad bowl, containing a mixture in which each ingredient remains distinct but contributes its own flavor and texture. And some of the elements that have become a part of the American salad are peoples that Crèvecoeur could never have imagined.

No country in the world has absorbed more different races and languages than the United States, and at no time in its history have the newcomers been more diverse or more determined to retain their diversity. As the 21st century began, America contained some 23 million foreign-born inhabitants, representing about 8.4 percent of the entire population. According to the 2000 U.S. Census, about 44 percent of the inhabitants of Los Angeles are Hispanic or Asian, and more than 70 percent of the population of Miami. A third of those living in New York City are foreign-born. These 2.6 million residents come from a bewildering assortment of places. At least 114 languages are spoken in New York City's schools. One high school in Queens has signs in English, Spanish, Chinese, and Korean.

Despite the many accommodations America has offered the newcomer in recent years, the nativism of the 19th century has not entirely disappeared. Only its targets have changed. To critics of a liberal immigration policy, Asians and Hispanics have replaced the Irish and Italians as a threat to the cultural identity of the country. But the nature of the threat has also changed somewhat. Recent waves of immigration from countries as remote and exotic as Laos have seemed impossible to absorb, and their numbers have been so great that large isolated communities have formed. And where the 19th- and early 20th-century notion of immigrants has evoked an image of huddled masses of starving peasants, many of the modern groups have been educated and prosperous. Professionals and skilled technicians compete for highly paid jobs rather than for subsistence wages on farms or in coal mines.

Immigrants and Crime

Another source of perceived danger from immigrants has always been the belief that they brought with them inferior social or moral standards and thus increased the crime rate in America. High rates of immigration, especially illegal immigration, have traditionally been accompanied by the image of foreigners as undermining the social order as well as the economy and the cultural integrity of the country. Irish Catholics in the 19th century and then Chinese, Jewish, and Italian immigrants have variously been seen as violent or sinister or devious, and by the last decades of the 20th century the focus of the threat had shifted to Cuban, Colombian, and Mexican immigrants. The belief is more than a popular myth among the uneducated; it has the official standing of legislative sanction, having been written into the law in California's Proposition 187, which passed with 59 percent of the public vote in 1994 before it was overthrown by a federal court. Proposition 187 states explicitly in Section 1 that "The People of California find and declare . . . that they have suffered and are suffering personal injury and damage caused by the criminal conduct of illegal aliens in this state." President George W. Bush was even more explicit in his speech of May 15, 2006, when he stated that "illegal immigration . . . strains state and local budgets and brings crime to our communities." A 2000 General Social Survey revealed that 73 percent of the public believed that increased levels of immigration caused an increase in crime, while only 60 percent thought that immigrants caused Americans to lose jobs and 56 percent feared that they disunited the country.

In fact, the statistics contradict the notion that crime goes up when more immigrants enter the country. As far back as the Dillingham Immigration Commission report of 1911, in a time when crime was increasing generally, it was noted that the foreign-born committed fewer crimes in the United States than the native-born. The 2000 U.S. census shows that the rate of incarceration of native-born Americans, 3.51 percent of the national population, was more than four times that of the foreign-born, .86 percent. As Rumbaut and his colleagues point out, "[I]mmigrants have the lowest rates of imprisonment for criminal convictions in American society. . . . In every ethnic group without exception, the census data show an *increase* in rates of criminal incarceration among young men from the foreign-born to the US-born generations, and over time in the United States among the foreign born— exactly the opposite of what is typically assumed both by standard theories and by public opinion on immigration and crime. . . . What is more, these patterns have now been observed consistently over the last three decennial censuses, a period that spans precisely the eras of mass immigration and mass imprisonment."[1]

Immigrants and Welfare Assistance

It is not merely immigrants' competition for jobs—high or low end—that seems to pose an economic threat to many Americans. Much of the concern about the large numbers entering the United States has focused on their cost to the taxpayers. In the 19th century, it was sink or swim; the poor, native as well as alien, received little or no aid from the government in their struggle for survival and had to depend on private or church-sponsored charity in time of need. But by the start of the 20th century, immigrants were absorbing a large share of public welfare. In 1906 the New York Board of Health reported that the immigrant poor received nearly half of the treatment in the city hospitals, and in Chicago in 1909 immigrants represented four out of five of the city's welfare recipients. The outcry against foreigners putting a strain on public assistance has become louder in more recent years. Palmer Stacy and Wayne Lutton, in their 1985 book *The Immigration Time Bomb*, include a chapter entitled "Aliens Raid the Welfare System," citing such statistics as "Nearly 80 percent of the infants born at the hospital nursery of the . . . University of California Medical Center are born to mothers who are illegal aliens." They also note that "in Arlington, Virginia, 26 percent of the students speak 40 different languages and nearly $2 million a year is required to run special English programs in the public schools." The 1990 census revealed that the poverty rate of immigrants was 42.8 percent higher than that of native-born Americans and that they received 44.2 percent more public assistance than natives.

These figures are disputed, however. The Urban Institute in Washington, D.C., has argued that the complaint does not take into account the positive contribution to the economy. "Immigrant businesses pay over $70 million in taxes," the institute reports, and therefore "immigrants incur no overall net fiscal deficit." The issue has been controversial for decades. Special provisions were written into the Immigration Reform and Control Act disqualifying immigrants from any but the most basic welfare relief, but many thought the act still too liberal. In 1994 California—the primary destination for immigrants since 1976—went IRCA one better with Proposition 187, prohibiting illegal aliens from receiving any welfare, schooling, or emergency health care. The proposition went so far as to require doctors and teachers to report to the INS anyone they even suspected of being undocumented. Although the voters supported the law by a large majority, a federal court struck it down the next year as denying equal protection "by creating classes and sub-classes without any rational basis and encouraging rampant discrimination against persons who appear or sound foreign."

The issue of immigrant use of the American welfare system goes to the heart of much nativist protest. Despite the Urban Institute's statistics, opponents of a liberal policy have argued that immigrants—especially the undocumented—consume more by receiving such public services as Aid to Families with Dependent Children (AFDC), food stamps, Social Security, Medicare, and Medicaid than they contribute in taxes, and that the benefits of such programs serve as a "welfare magnet" for immigrants. The several restrictive acts such as IIRIRA and the Personal Responsibility and Work Opportunity Reconciliation Act, both of 1996, clearly reflect the concern expressed in California's Proposition 187.

In fact, much research has found that immigrants use public services less than the native population, and most of those who do use them are refugee groups such as Russians, Cubans, and Southeast Asians. According to a paper published by the American Immigration Law Foundation on August 1, 2005, "Studies that focus specifically on undocumented immigrants suggest they use public services at rates far below those of legal immigrants. A 1987 study, for example, found that just 2 percent of illegal Mexican immigrants had ever received welfare or Social Security payments and just 3 percent had ever accepted food stamps. In contrast, 84 percent paid taxes."[2] The article further notes that of 6,000 undocumented Mexican migrants surveyed, 66 percent reported the withholding of Social Security taxes from their income in the United States and 62 percent stated that their employers withheld income taxes; only 10 percent had ever sent a child to a public school, only seven percent had ever received Supplemental Security Income, and five percent or less had ever received food stamps, AFDC, or unemployment compensation. As the Carnegie Endowment for International Peace stated in its paper "Immigrants and Welfare" in 1996, "There is no reputable evidence that prospective immigrants are drawn to the U.S. because of its public assistance program."[3]

Bilingual Education

Problems of assimilation have always been one of the root issues of the immigration question, and another controversy with deep roots in history that flared up in the last half of the 20th century and early 21st century concerns language. Benjamin Franklin was afraid of German replacing English in the English colonies, and in fact shortly after the adoption of the Constitution there was a proposal to print the federal laws in German as well as English. It was defeated by one vote in the House of Representatives. The display of signs in foreign languages in cities with large immigrant populations has angered many, who feel that it is against the interests of national unity and retards the assimilation of the newcomers. A common language, some have argued, is necessary to hold a nation together.

Efforts have been made over the years to make English the official language of the United States (six proposals were formally presented to Congress in 1995 alone), but they have all failed. To many the idea is insensitive to cultural differences and a return to nativism and the outmoded idea of America as a melting pot. Nevertheless, Dade County, Florida, found it necessary, in the face of Miami's huge Spanish-speaking populace, to declare English its official language in 1984. The law was repealed in 1993, but California—always among the first to propose anti-immigrant legislation—made English the state language in 1986, and 16 other states have followed its example. Some of the statutes have been repealed by the federal courts, as Dade County's was. In 1995 a circuit court of appeals ruled that Arizona's Official English law was unconstitutional because it violated the First Amendment guarantee of free speech. In any event, multilingual signs and announcements are often a practical necessity, and, law or no law, Los Angeles has continued to print the instructions in its telephone directories in no fewer than 14 languages. In the national census of 2000, questionnaires were distributed in Spanish, Chinese, Korean, Vietnamese, and the national language of the Philippines, Tagalog. Almost 2 million of the Spanish-language forms were used.

A more significant issue, and one that has provoked bitter conflict, is the use of bilingual education in the public schools. Former Senate majority leader Bob Dole dismissed the idea of teaching foreign elementary students in their

An immigration agent scrutinizes a Colombian's visa for evidence of fraud. *(U.S. Citizenship and Immigration Services)*

own language as "a means of instilling ethnic pride or . . . a therapy for low self-esteem," and historian Arthur Schlesinger concludes that "it promotes segregation more than it does integration." Bilingual education, he has stated, "nourishes self-ghettoization and racial antagonism." Some from the immigrant community agree with him. Hispanic civil leader Alfredo Mathew, Jr., observed that it "encourages concentrations of Hispanics to stay together and not be integrated."

A *Washington Post* writer, on the other hand, compared those who backed English as the sole means of instruction in American schools to "Nazis, the Klan, skin-heads, and other boosters of the master race." The opponents of multilingualism, the 1995 article continued, send a message to immigrants "that they are not wanted here until they have ceased to discomfit the rest of us with their strangeness."

The bilingual education movement began as a method of keeping foreign children in schools where they were helpless to keep up with their classmates because they did not speak the language. Dade County began employing it as a program for Cuban refugees in 1963, and Texas, California, and Arizona followed suit. The National Education Association proposed providing federal funds for bilingual programs at a conference in Arizona in 1966, and two years later Congress passed the Bilingual Education Act supporting the idea. With arguments that it fragmented the nation and retarded the assimilation of young people, the practice was fought bitterly, but in 1974 the Supreme Court decided in favor of it. In *Lau v. Nichols,* the high court ruled that denying instruction in another language to those unable to communicate in English was a violation of students' civil rights. In time, the original purpose of helping students to learn English faded. In 1984 the Bilingual Education Act of 1968 was extended through 1988, and the government added programs to help students maintain and improve their use of their native languages after learning English. The decision was a triumph for those who believed in a diverse culture and the celebration of that diversity; those who found the practice divisive thought it a tragedy.

With the growing hostility to immigration in the 1990s, bilingual education became a more divisive issue, and the government withdrew much of its support in the face of increased public protest. According to Craig Donegan, more than 20 percent of the federal bilingual education budget—$38.5 million of $192.2 million—was cut in 1995, and several bills were proposed in Congress to eliminate the government's Office of Bilingual Education and Minority Language Affairs altogether.[4] By the next year, English had been declared the official language in 22 states. In California, a bill was passed by referendum in 1998 ending most bilingual education programs in the schools.

Illegal Immigration

Perhaps the most widespread concern about immigration at the end of the 20th century was the thought that the country was being overrun by illegal aliens. A Gallup poll taken in March 1992 showed that two-thirds of Americans believed that the country was overburdened with foreigners. Most of those entering the country illegally are from Mexico, whose porous border with the United States is almost impossible to patrol effectively. In later years, the number of Asians willing to incur the great expense and face the terrible risk of sneaking into

A group of immigrants protect their belongings in plastic bags as they cross the New River from Mexico to Calexico, California, in June 2006. *(AP Photo/Jae C. Hong)*

The United States accommodates foreign cultures, as bilingual signs at a customs inspection station in Laredo, Texas, show in this 1980 photo. *(U.S. Citizenship and Immigration Services)*

the country increased significantly, and terrible tragedies occurred as entire boatloads drowned in the effort. More than 1 million Mexicans are arrested and detained at the border every year, and about half of them are deported. Some of them are in flight from political oppression, but most come for the reason that has drawn immigrants to the United States since the 17th century: the chance to make a decent living. They accept the worst jobs and the lowest wages, and they risk their lives for the chance to fill the jobs that Americans are unwilling to fill.

The Mexican ambassador to the United States has expressed himself as frankly puzzled at the rigor with which Mexico's neighbor to the north strives to exclude his countrymen. "If they stopped [illegal immigration]," he remarked in 1997, "there would be a state of emergency in California, in the state of Texas, and in a good number of regional places in the United States."

Yet it is because Mexicans are willing to work for wages that no American would accept that many in the country oppose their entry. The low-paid labor of Chinese railroad workers and Mexican fruit and vegetable pickers is a boon to employers, but to their fellow workers it means the loss of jobs for which they cannot compete at the same rate of pay. The incidence of illegal entry—or at least the number of those caught at the border trying to get in without papers—fell off sharply after the passage of IRCA, which legalized some aliens already in the country and made it harder to cross the border. That 1986 act also made businesses responsible for examination and verification of an employee's papers. But within a couple of years, the numbers rose again and soared to new heights. It has been suggested that all aliens be required to carry official identification and produce it on demand, but that idea failed because people thought it discriminatory and insulting, and because false papers and cards are so easy to obtain that it would just add to the income of the counterfeiters.

Despite all efforts, the problem has escalated through the end of the century. In 1996 Congress passed a law increasing the personnel of the border patrol, authorizing more sophisticated methods of prevention and detection, and increasing the penalties of those caught sneaking in or helping others to sneak in, but the number of illegal aliens has continued to grow. As one Mexican has admitted, "It doesn't matter how many people, horses, bicycles, helicopters, or planes they use, people will go. It doesn't matter if the fence is electric."

Terrorism and Legislation to Combat It

On September 11, 2001, an event occurred that radically altered America's view of the world, and was to have a great impact on the country's immigration policies. On that day members of an Afghanistan-based terrorist group called al-Qaeda hijacked four American airplanes, crashing two into the World Trade Center in New York City and one into the Pentagon in Arlington, Virginia, outside Washington, D.C., killing more than 3,000 people and destroying the New York buildings. The fourth plane crashed in Pennsylvania. The nation was stunned, and within days it mobilized against the threat of future attacks. To the many concerns for the country's unity and economy was added a new, and far more frightening one, a concern for its physical safety.

As the terrorists had succeeded in entering the United States on valid visas, it was apparent that the security of the country was compromised, and the Immigration and Naturalization Service (INS) was called upon to tighten its regulations. Attorney General John Ashcroft announced on September 18 that the authority of the INS was to be enlarged and that it would now have the power to detain any immigrant suspected of a link to terrorism for twice the 24-hour period that had been permitted. This was the first of a long series of controversial government policies affecting the nation's treatment of immigrants, beginning with the establishment of the Office of Homeland Security, whose first director was Thomas Ridge, former governor of Pennsylvania. In

Tom Ridge, the onetime governor of Pennsylvania, became the first secretary of the Department of Homeland Security. *(AP Photo/Doug Mills)*

January 2002 the House of Representatives approved the elevation of the office to the status of a cabinet department, and Ridge was named its secretary. In March of that year, Ridge announced a system of color-coded terrorist alerts, which kept the country in a state of alarm as the reported level of peril fluctuated from day to day.

The USA PATRIOT Act

On October 26, 2001, six weeks after the event that had become known by the abbreviation of its date as "9/11," President Bush signed one of the most sweeping legislative decisions in U.S. history. Awkwardly named the Uniting and Strengthening America by Providing Appropriate Tools Required to Intercept and Obstruct Terrorism Act, a title devised to provide the lofty acronym USA PATRIOT Act, Public Law 107-56 was passed in the Senate by a vote of 98 to 1. It was not so widely welcomed by the country, however. If the new power bestowed on the INS to hold foreigners for two days without formal charges or counsel disturbed some civil rights advocates, the greatly expanded authority of the government written into law by "the Patriot Act," as it came to be known, was considerably more disturbing to many.

First introduced in the House of Representatives as H.R. 3162 by Wisconsin Republican F. James Sensenbrenner, a long-time advocate of a tighter immigration policy, the Patriot Act amended provisions in banking, foreign intelligence surveillance, and immigration law. It authorized the government to conduct secret searches without warrants, use electronic surveillance, and examine personal records, including medical and financial history and even library usage. Intended as a protection from terrorists, it was seen by many as an invasion of privacy and a violation of civil liberties, but it was nevertheless renewed on March 2, 2006, in a vote of 89 to 10 in the Senate, and on March 7 of the same year with a vote of 280 to 138 in the House of Representatives.

Two weeks after the president signed the Patriot Act, he approved an executive order authorizing the trial of foreigners suspected of affiliation with terrorist organizations by military tribunals and without the legal protections afforded to citizens. Five days later he signed a bill tightening security measures at airports and allowing guards to arrest and detain anyone seen as having a "link to terrorism," and on November 19 he created the Transportation Security Administration to oversee security for railroads, buses, mass transit systems, ports, and the 450 U.S. airports. Before this order, security had been maintained by private companies, but now it was placed under the control of a government agency that within the year employed 50,000

Republican F. James Sensenbrenner of Wisconsin was responsible for introducing the USA PATRIOT Act in the House of Representatives in 2001. (AP Photo/Lawrence Jackson)

people from Alaska to Puerto Rico. The series of security measures taken in the days immediately following 9/11 culminated in December 2001 with the signing of the Canada–U.S. Smart Border Declaration, a 30-point agreement described as an "Action Plan for Creating a Secure and Smart Border." Signed by Thomas Ridge and the deputy prime minister of Canada, it called for permanent resident cards, advance passenger information checks, closer scrutiny of visas between the two countries, and tighter security at the U.S.–Canada border.

As terrorism increased throughout the world during the following months, the American fear of it grew, and the government passed a seemingly endless series of new bills focusing on national security from foreign terrorism. The bill that had the most immediate impact on American immigration, however, was the Barbara Jordan Immigration Reform and Accountability Act of 2002, H.R. 3231. A sweeping reform of the entire immigration system, it was sponsored by James Sensenbrenner, the Republican representative who introduced the Patriot Act. It was first presented on November 6, 2001, and passed almost unanimously (the vote was 405 to 9) on April 25, 2002. Its official title was "To replace the Immigration and Naturalization Service with the Office of the Associate Attorney General for Immigration Affairs, the Bureau of Citizenship and Immigration Service, and the Bureau of Immigration Enforcement, and for other purposes." In effect the bill eliminated the INS, replacing it with two new bureaus that divided its functions, one to deal with processing immigrants—the job that had occupied such depots as Ellis Island and Angel Island—and the other to deal with border security and enforcement, both under a new associate attorney general for immigration affairs in the Department of Justice. The dismembered INS was to function under the Department of Justice as two separate entities, the Bureau of Citizen and Immigration Services (BCIS) and the Bureau of Immigration Enforcement (BIE), until March 1, 2003, when it was reunited as the U.S. Citizenship and Immigration Services (USCIS) and its functions transferred to the Department of Homeland Security.

The Border Protection, Antiterrorism, and Illegal Immigration Control Act

By 2005 public opinion on immigration (or anti-immigration) legislation had become quite polarized, and the major bill of 2005, the Border Protection, Antiterrorism, and Illegal Immigration Control Act, sparked widespread protest. It was passed by the House of Representatives as H.R. 4437 on December 16, 2005, by a vote of 239 to 182—a sizable majority, but far below that of the almost unanimously approved Patriot Act. Like the Barbara Jordan Immigration Reform and Accountability Act of 2002, it was sponsored by James Sensenbrenner and became known as the Sensenbrenner Bill. It was like his former bill, but tougher. Humanitarian, religious, and civil rights groups called it the harshest anti-immigration bill in nearly a century.

The Sensenbrenner Bill's stated its purpose as "to amend the Immigration and Nationality Act to strengthen enforcement of the immigration laws, to enhance border security, and for other purposes." It makes undocumented presence in the country a felony, requires employers to verify their employees' residential status, and eliminates the diversity visa lottery program. Among the provisions that disturbed many were its demand for the construction of a fence up to 700 miles long at the U.S.-Mexican border; its mandate that the federal government, rather than the more lenient local authorities, take custody of undocumented aliens; and its redefinition of illegal immigrants as criminals, which makes providing them with any assistance a felony and thus subjects social workers, public school teachers, and church groups to the threat of criminal prosecution.

The Border Protection Bill was strongly opposed by organized labor, though unions were divided on the subject of its provisions for a guest-worker program and amnesty for those already in the country—two elements proposed for the Senate version of the legislation. Most church groups condemned the bill as inhumane. An editorial in *Catholic New York* for example, stated that the United States Conference of Catholic Bishops "decried, in the strongest terms, provisions . . . which would make it a federal offense—punishable by up to five years in prison—to 'assist an illegal immigrant in any way.' Even offering a bowl of soup to a hungry man or first aid to an injured child would count as a crime." The National Immigration Forum described the bill as "unworkable and punitive."[5]

The public reaction was dramatic. During April 2006 protest marches and job and school walkouts protesting the new laws, which were approved by the House and expected to pass in the Senate, took place all over the country. On April 5 thousands of immigrants stormed City Hall in New York City in support of the Voting Rights Restoration Act, a proposed bill giving permanent residents who have lived in the city for more than six months the right to vote in city elections. In other cities schools closed when students walked out of classes chanting slogans of Latino pride and waving their countries' flags. On April 10 an even larger wave of demonstrations took place, with more than 100,000 people gathering in Washington, D.C., similar numbers in New York City, and Phoenix, and more than 50,000 each in Houston and Atlanta, all protesting repressive immigration legislation. The government responded with a roundup of illegal workers. The action involved more than 200 federal agents and dozens of raids nationwide and marked the country's largest single interior immigration sweep on record, according to Michael Chertoff, the secretary of the Homeland Security Department. "We arrested more people [on April 19] than all of last year," Chertoff stated.[6]

On May 1 a national boycott was declared; more than a million illegal immigrants and their supporters around the country paraded in cities large and small. The crowds in Los Angeles numbered more than 600,000, the city's ports virtually shut down, and the wholesale produce market was deserted; Chicago reported 400,000 marchers, Denver 75,000, Houston 15,000. May 1 was designated "A Day without Immigrants," and participants were urged to stay home from work and school and not to buy anything, to dramatize how important the immigrant population is to the American economy. Major corporations closed their plants because of absenteeism, and Latino-owned shops and restaurants closed in support all over the country. It was a festival of ethnic pride and a powerful demonstration of support for immigrants' rights by the native and foreign-born alike.

The fearfully awaited Senate bill intended to match the House's Border Protection, Antiterrorism, and Illegal Immigration Control Act of 2005 came soon after. Senate Bill 2611 is named the Comprehensive Immigration Reform Act of 2006 (CIRA). Sponsored by Arlen Specter, a liberal Republican senator from Pennsylvania, it follows H.R. 4437 in calling for an increase in security on the U.S.–Mexican border and declares it unlawful to "hire, recruit, or refer for a fee an unauthorized alien," but it is more lenient with regard to illegal immigrants' collecting social security benefits and mandates an agreement with the Mexican government before any work is begun on a fence on the U.S. side of the border. The Senate bill provides for 200,000 new temporary guest-worker visas a year and creates a special guest-worker program for the estimated 1.5 million immigrant farm workers, who would be able to earn permanent legal status. It is this "path to citizenship" program that proved the most controversial element in the Senate bill.

The Senate bill met with strong criticism from both sides of the issue. The Federation for American Immigration Reform (FAIR online statement of May 25, 2006) described the Comprehensive Immigration Reform Act as "neither comprehensive nor in any sense a true reform," and the Heritage Foundation said that if enacted, CIRA would be the most dramatic change in immigration law in 80 years. It would add 66 million more immigrants to the United States over 20 years—or more than one-fifth of the current population of the country—and would "open the spigot" on visas for skilled workers, driving up unemployment and driving down wages. These are among many questions the two bills raise, but the major difference between them is that CIRA proposes an opportunity for illegal immigrants who have been in the country for five years to apply for citizenship after paying fines and back taxes. No temporary or guest-worker program exists in H.R. 4437, the Sensenbrenner Bill. As of 2007, the two houses of Congress had not yet come to an agreement on the subject, and committees were being formed to work out a compromise between the two competing reform bills.

Members of the Utah National Guard work on extending a border fence in Arizona in June 2006. *(AP Photo/Khampha Bouaphanh)*

Before congress adjourned in October 2006 for the November elections, it made a last effort to pass some positive legislation, and on September 14 both houses agreed on H.R. 6061, the Secure Fence Act, authorizing the construction of an additional 700 miles of double-layered fencing between the United State and Mexico. The Department of Homeland Security is to install a complex system of surveillance cameras and employ aerial vehicles, ground-based sensors, satellites, radar, and cameras to guard against any unlawful entry to the country. Congress approved $1.2 billion to finance the operation, but the estimated cost for the whole project was in excess of $6 billion, and critics argued that such a fence would work no better than the Great Wall of China had worked in keeping out the Mongol hordes. The fence was widely viewed as virtually impossible to construct across the many rivers, steep ravines, and high mountains that would have to be traversed. Environmentalists opposed it as dangerous to wildlife migration patterns, and American Indians in Arizona opposed it as a violation of their tribal lands and threatened to bring legal action against it.

Two weeks later, on September 28, 2006, the Senate passed S. 3930, the Military Commissions Act of 2006, permitting the continuation of the secret CIA interrogation program, suspending the writ of habeas corpus for detainees who are not U.S. citizens, and authorizing torture and permanent detention without charge. The bill was widely denounced: Amnesty International said the act "contravenes human rights principles,"[7] and the *New York Times* said in an editorial on September 28 that the act was "a tyrannical law that will be ranked with the low points in American democracy, our generation's version of the Alien and Sedition Acts." Nevertheless, on September 29, the House of Representatives approved the bill as H.R. 6054. On October 17 President Bush signed the bill, and the Military Commissions Act went into effect.

In the meantime, while the federal government was fiercely debating the massive immigration reform bill that was being hammered out, individual states were vigorously pursuing their own immigration-reform projects. During 2006, 570 bills were introduced in state legislatures relating to immigration, and the number soared still further in 2007. In that year, governments in every one of the 50 states introduced legislation aimed at correcting perceived flaws in immigration policy. In the first three-and-a-half months of the year, 169 bills and resolutions were introduced nationwide. Not all of them were passed, but 18 states adopted new legislation on the subject between January 1 and April 13.

The new acts included changes in the law on such things as voting, driver's licenses, health benefits, and employment. Forty-one states tightened restrictions on hiring of "unauthorized" workers, tightened eligibility requirements for workers' benefits, and 31 passed new laws restricting driver's licenses to citizens and legal immigrants. In 22 states, legislation was passed that required proof of citizenship or identity to vote and redefined acceptable forms of identification. Almost no state passed legislation during that period making life easier for immigrants or would-be immigrants.

By the beginning of 2007, the two houses of Congress had not yet agreed on a comprehensive immigration reform bill. Committees had been formed to work out a compromise between the two competing bills proposed in 2005 and 2006 to produce what some ironically referred to as a "comprehensible immigration reform bill." At last, on May 9, a new version, The Secure Borders, Economic Opportunity and Immigration Reform Act of 2007 (S. 1348, commonly known by the more familiar and slightly less cumbersome name Comprehensive Immigration Reform Act, or CIRA, of 2007) was presented by Senate majority leader Harry Reid. Mainly authored by Senators Ted Kennedy, John McCain, and Jon Kyl, and strongly supported by President Bush, the complex 326-page document addressed all of the controversial immigration issues that had been dividing the country. It proposed a path to citizenship for the estimated 12 million illegal aliens in the United States, offering them amnesty after the payment of fines and fees. It provided for increased border security and tighter monitoring of immigrants. It proposed a guest-worker program similar to the bracero program that operated from 1942 to 1964. It redefined eligibility for visas and proposed two new classes of visa—a "Y visa," permitting a guest worker to stay in the country two years, and a "Z visa," permitting an illegal immigrant who had been in the United States on January 1, 2007, to stay permanently. Finally, it included all the provisions of the DREAM Act, a bill that had been voted down in Congress repeatedly, granting illegal immigrant minors in either college or the military a path to citizenship.

The Senate agreed to consider the bill and did so at length but could not come to an agreement. On June 7, 2007, it voted three times on cloture—an agreement to end the debate and vote on the bill—but could not agree on that either. On June 15, President Bush convinced the Senate to reconsider the bill, but again no decision was reached. After intense dispute, the Senate failed again on June 28 to agree to end the debate, and, to the great disappointment of the president and much of the public, the immigration reform plan was given up, with little hope of its being reconsidered before 2008.

Issues such as welfare assistance, bilingual education, and illegal entry are relatively new elements of the eternal "immigrant problem," but they reflect the same underlying division in the American attitude toward the admission of foreigners to their shores. The arguments against free immigration—an "open door policy"—have been much the same since the beginning of the country's history: People dread the foreign and unknown. They fear cultural fragmentation, overcrowding in the cities, and the debasement of their standard of living. They fear the Bolshevik's bomb, the Papist plot, the Yellow Peril. They fear that foreigners will take their jobs, marry their daughters, undermine their religions and their government, and ruin their neighborhoods. They fear that open borders will lead to crime, drugs, civil unrest, and unemployment. Their sense of territoriality is violated by the fear that the country is "losing control of its borders."

Defenders of the open immigration policy, on the other hand, argue that American history has shown that the country has always absorbed foreigners and incorporated their foreignness into its own vital culture. They point out that the country owes its strength and flexibility to its diversity, and that it is big and rich enough to give room to any number of newcomers. Economic growth depends on social growth, and rather than take jobs needed by others, immigrants increase the market for the goods and services those jobs provide, in addition to performing the jobs most Americans do not want. Finally, supporters of this position have noted that the efforts at blocking the country's borders are futile anyway; tougher immigration laws, tighter enforcement of them, and harsher punishments for those caught breaking them have all failed. If Americans really want to keep foreigners out, it is argued, they should do something for the countries whose conditions drive people to emigrate.

Probably the strongest argument for a liberal immigration policy is the moral one. America is a nation of immigrants; its roots are in all nations of the world. No one (except the aboriginal inhabitants from whom the first settlers took the land by trickery or force) can claim America as a birthright. The founding fathers defined the new country as a haven for the world's needy, and those who have accepted its welcome have richly rewarded the hospitality they have received.

History has shown that there is some truth in the isolationists' fears, but it has also shown that these fears are vastly exaggerated. There is as little danger that the nation will disintegrate like the Balkans as that Americans will fuse into some homogeneous alloy in the melting pot. New foods, new ideas, new languages, new art, and new blood will continue to enrich the mix, as it has from the beginning, as America moves on into the new century.

Chronicle of Events

2000

- The 22nd U.S. Census reports a population of 281,421,906, an increase of 13.2 percent over the 1990 total. Asians and Pacific Islanders compose some 11 million, or 4 percent of the population, and Hispanics total about 32 million, a 3-percent increase over the past decade, representing 12 percent of the population of the United States. Census questionnaires are printed in five languages—Spanish, Chinese, Korean, Vietnamese, and Tagalog, the native language of the Philippines—as well as in English. Nearly 2 million of the forms are filled out in Spanish.
- *January 5*: The INS orders Elián González to be returned to his father in Cuba.
- *January 31*: The United States government announces that the country has had the longest economic boom in history, experiencing 107 straight months of economic expansion since March 1991.
- *February 10*: President Clinton requests the outlay of $5 billion for the INS, $320 million more than in fiscal 2000, to be used to hire new border patrol agents and to modernize the processing procedure.
- *February 16*: The AFL-CIO reverses its long-standing policy of opposition to immigration as a source of cheap labor that competed with native workers. In an executive council action, the organization announces its support of immigrant labor and recommends amnesty for undocumented workers.
- *February 27*: President Clinton approves the Child Citizenship Act, granting automatic U.S. citizenship to foreign-born adopted children under age 18 with at least one adoptive parent or legal guardian who is a U.S. citizen.
- *March 21*: The Elián González decision is confirmed by a federal district court, after prolonged protest and litigation.
- *April 10*: A federal appeals court in California rules that the INS may not detain immigrants convicted of crimes indefinitely when federal officials are unable to reach deportation agreements with their native countries; instead, these immigrants must be released when their sentences have been served. The decision is appealed to the Supreme Court, which upholds it on June 28, 2001.
- *April 22*: Elián González is forcibly taken from his relatives in Miami, in a raid that provokes much national

A 14-year-old illegal immigrant is detained in Brownsville, Texas, at a U.S. Citizenship and Immigration Services office. *(AP Photo/ LM Otero)*

and international controversy, and is sent back to Cuba on June 28.
- *May 11*: President Clinton proposes raising the number of skilled workers allowed to enter and work in the United States to 200,000 for three years. The 1998 figure was 65,000, increased to 115,000 in 1999 and 2000 and scheduled to be cut back to 65,000 in 2001. Half the skilled-worker visas are to be reserved for applicants with master's degrees.
- *October 12*: A terrorist bomb kills 17 U.S. seamen and injures 39 others on the warship *USS Cole* in the Yemeni port of Aden. It is later established that the attack was carried out by Osama bin Laden's terrorist organization al-Qaeda.

2001

- *January 2*: The INS reports that national standards for the treatment of detainees are to take effect at all detention centers. Approximately 20,000 undocumented immigrants are being held in jails and prisons pending the results of deportation hearings. Until this date the state and local institutions have followed their own rules.
- *January 20*: George W. Bush is inaugurated as the 43rd president of the United States.
- *March 7*: The U.S. Census Bureau reports that the population of Hispanics in the country has grown 60 percent

since 1991; it is now about equal in size to that of African Americans, previously the largest U.S. minority.

• *April 27*: Senate sergeant-at-arms James W. Ziglar, the Senate's chief law-enforcement officer, is named commissioner of the Immigration and Naturalization Service.

• *May 23–24*: The bodies of 14 Mexican immigrants are found in Arizona after being abandoned by smugglers on May 19. Immigrants' rights groups protest the border patrol's treatment of those attempting to enter the United States.

• *June 1*: The INS institutes the Premium Processing Program, in which influential foreign applicants for admission to the country, such as celebrities, athletes, business executives, and scientists, may pay $1,000 to have their visa applications processed in 15 days rather than the usual three months or more. Many citizens protest that the program unfairly favors the wealthy.

• *June 25*: The U.S. Supreme Court, in *INS v. St. Cyr*, rules 5-4 that immigrants who had pleaded guilty to crimes in the U.S. before 1996 will not automatically face deportation.

• *June 28*: The U.S. Supreme Court, in *Zadvydas v. Davis et al.*, rules 5-4 that the indefinite detention of deportable immigrants is unconstitutional.

• *August 21*: INS Commissioner Ziglar announces that he will begin a major reorganization of the agency, dividing it into two branches: one to process legal immigrants and one to guard the country's borders.

• *September 11*: Middle Eastern terrorists, members of the Afghanistan-based group al-Qaeda, crash two hijacked planes into the World Trade Center in New York City and one into the Pentagon in Arlington, Virginia. Another plane crashes in Pennsylvania. More than 3,000 people are killed, and the World Trade Center is destroyed. The anger and fear that result bring about a wave of antiforeign feeling in the United States.

• *September 18*: In response to the September 11 attack, attorney general John Ashcroft announces that henceforth the Immigration and Naturalization Service (INS) will be allowed to detain immigrants suspected of links to terrorism for 48 hours without charges, twice the period permitted until this time.

• *October 7*: The United States and Britain begin air attacks on Afghanistan, whose government, controlled by the Islamic fundamentalist group known as Taliban, refuses to surrender Osama bin Laden, presumed organizer of the September 11 terrorist attacks. Afghanistan is believed to be offering a safe haven to bin Laden and al-Qaeda.

• *October 24*: The Department of Labor reports that unemployment, at 5.4 percent, is at its highest point in five years and that the nation is officially in a recession. During this month 400,000 Americans lose their jobs. Competition for employment prompts widespread anti-immigrant sentiment.

• *October 26*: President Bush signs into law the Uniting and Strengthening America by Providing Tools Required to Intercept and Obstruct Terrorism Act, commonly known by the acronym USA PATRIOT Act, after it is passed in the Senate on October 25 by a vote of 98 to 1. A very controversial law, it greatly enlarges the government's authority to conduct secret searches, perform electronic surveillance, and access medical, financial, and personal records. The act is intended as a response to the threat of terrorism but is also used to investigate other potential crimes as well.

• *November 13*: President Bush signs an executive order authorizing the trial of foreigners suspected of terrorism to be held in military tribunals.

• *November 19*: President Bush signs a bill tightening security measures at airports. By the end of the month, more than 1,200 people have been detained on suspicion of links to terrorism.

• *December 12*: Thomas Ridge, director of the U.S. Office of Homeland Security, and the deputy prime minister of Canada sign a 30-point agreement to protect America's northern border. The Canada–U.S. Smart Border Declaration, an "Action Plan for Creating a Secure and Smart Border," proposes counterterrorism legislation, permanent resident cards, visa policy coordination between the two countries, passenger identification verification, and a secure flow of goods.

2002

• *January 11*: Taliban and al-Qaeda fighters captured in Afghanistan are sent to the U.S. prison at the naval base in Guantánamo Bay, Cuba. Defined as "unlawful combatants" rather than prisoners of war, they are denied the rights of prisoners guaranteed by the Geneva Convention, despite the protests of international human rights organizations.

• *January 23*: The House of Representatives passes the Homeland Security Act of 2002 (H.R. 5005), establishing an executive Department of Homeland Security, devoted to internal security against terrorism and incorporating 22 government agencies. The bill is signed into law on November 25.

- *March 12*: Tom Ridge, the director of Homeland Security, announces the office's system of color-coded terrorist alerts. Public fear of foreigners increases as the announced levels of threat continue.
- *April 25*: The House of Representatives passes (by a vote of 405 to 9) the Barbara Jordan Immigration Reform and Accountability Act, H.R. 3231, authorizing the abolition of the Immigration and Naturalization Service and the division of its functions between two new bureaus in the Department of Justice.
- *May 3*: The U.S. Department of Labor reports that unemployment has reached six percent, the country's highest rate in nearly eight years.
- *September 24*: The Census Bureau reports that the number of people living below the poverty line in the United States increased during the previous year for the first time in eight years.
- *October 29*: Two hundred Haitians seeking asylum are detained by U.S. police when their boat founders on the coast of Florida.
- *November 25*: President Bush signs legislation creating a cabinet-level Department of Homeland Security, as he had proposed June 6. Pennsylvania governor Tom Ridge, coordinator of the national security program since the terrorist attack on September 11, 2001, is named director. He is sworn in on January 24, 2003.

2003

- *March 1*: The functions of immigration services and enforcement are formally transferred from the Justice Department to the Department of Homeland Security. The bureau is renamed U.S. Citizenship and Immigration Services (USCIS).
- *March 19*: U.S. and British forces initiate military strikes against Iraq in an effort to oust its leader, Saddam Hussein.
- *April*: The last organized Iraqi resistance ends. Major Iraqi government buildings are occupied by U.S. and British troops by April 8. President Bush declares the war ended May 1. United States and British losses number 140, and 548 are wounded in action; Iraqi civilian losses are estimated at more than 3,000. Violent civil disorder ensues.
- *June 16*: A Honduran immigrant smuggler, Karla Chavez, is charged with responsibility for the deaths of 19 undocumented Hondurans attempting to enter the U.S. in a sealed trailer.

- *July*: A system of electronic monitoring of illegal aliens who have been released while awaiting trial is tested by federal officials in Michigan.
- *July 3*: The Department of Labor reports a 6.4 percent unemployment rate in the United States, the country's highest since 1994.
- *August 1*: The Department of Labor announces that the United States lost 44,000 jobs in July.
- *September 5*: The Department of Labor announces that the United States lost 93,000 jobs in August.
- *October*: The Development, Relief and Education for Alien Minors Act (the DREAM Act), originally introduced during the 107th Congress in 2001 as H.R. 1918, is reintroduced by Senator Orrin Hatch in the Senate as S. 1545. It is a bipartisan bill that would provide a path to citizenship for illegal immigrant students. It is passed by the Senate Judiciary Committee but never voted on in the Senate.
- *November 3*: The U.S. Senate approves President Bush's request for $87.5 billion for emergency spending in Iraq.

2004

- The U.S. Census Bureau announces that Hispanics, the largest and fastest-growing minority in the country, now number 41.3 million. Including Latinos of any race, they represent more than one-half of the national population growth (about 2.9 million) between July 1, 2003, and July 1, 2004, with a growth rate of 3.68 percent, more than three times that of the total population. Of the entire foreign-born population of the country, 52.4 percent are from Latin America, 27 percent from Asia, and 14 percent from Europe; in 1920 more than 50 percent were from Europe.
- *January 5*: U.S. immigration officers initiate the US-VIS-IT Act requiring the fingerprinting and photographing of all foreign visitors with visas at 115 American airports.
- *January 7*: President Bush proposes a major overhaul of U.S. immigration laws, providing a path to legal status for millions of illegal aliens now in the country.
- *January 12*: The U.S. Supreme Court approves the secrecy of the arrest and detention of hundreds of Muslims following the September 11, 2001, attack.
- *February 29*: An insurrection in Haiti forces president Jean-Bertrand Aristide to resign. The number of Haitians seeking refugee status in the U.S. increases sharply.
- *November 2*: George W. Bush defeats the Democratic Party candidate John Kerry and is reelected president.

- *November 30*: Homeland Security secretary Tom Ridge resigns from office.

2005

- *January 11*: President Bush appoints U.S. circuit court of appeals judge Michael Chertoff, former head of the criminal division of the Justice Department, as secretary of Homeland Security.
- *January 20*: George W. Bush is inaugurated for his second term as president of the United States.
- *February 3*: Alberto Gonzales is appointed attorney general. Gonzales is the first Latino to hold that office in the United States.
- *May 17*: Antonio Villaraigosa, a Democrat, is elected mayor of Los Angeles, California. He is the first Latino mayor of that city since 1872.
- *July 7*: A group claiming to be affiliated with al-Qaeda detonates bombs in the London, England, underground transit system and on a bus, killing 52 people.
- *August 2*: President Bush signs the Central America Free Trade Agreement (CAFTA). This will make about one half of U.S. farm products and 80 percent of manufactured goods tariff-free and will reduce other tariffs gradually. The agreement is opposed by environmentalists and organized labor.
- *November 17*: The DREAM Act is reintroduced in the Senate.
- *December 16*: Border Protection, Antiterrorism, and Illegal Immigration Control Act of 2005 (H.R. 4437) is passed 239 to 182 in the House of Representatives. Known as the Sensenbrenner Bill after its sponsor, Wisconsin Republican F. James Sensenbrenner, it calls for the construction of an extended fence along the U.S. border with Mexico and requires federal officers to take custody of all undocumented aliens. The bill is protested by various social justice, religious, and humanitarian groups as the harshest anti-immigration law of recent times.

2006

- *April 10*: Huge immigration demonstrations occurs throughout the country with Washington, D.C.; New

A political cartoon from the *San Diego Union Tribune* satirizes President George W. Bush's plan to combat illegal immigration by building a fence along the U.S.-Mexico border. *(Copley News Service/Steve Breen)*

The agricultural industry's dependence on the labor of illegal immigrants is highlighted in this political cartoon. *(Copley News Service/ Michael Ramirez)*

York City; and Phoenix, Arizona, each witnessing more than 100,000 protestors demanding immigrant rights.

- *May 15*: President Bush speaks on the need for immigration reform, calling for a policy that will enable illegal aliens working in the United States to obtain citizenship, urging a temporary guest-worker program, and recommending the addition of 6,000 National Guard troops to patrol the U.S.-Mexican border.
- *May 25*: The Comprehensive Immigrant Reform Act (CIRA), S. 2611, is passed by the U.S. Senate. It is intended to increase security at the United States' border with Mexico, to increase the number of authorized guest workers, and to enable illegal immigrants who have been in the United States five years or longer to gain citizenship. The act severely restricts access to federal courts for people in deportation proceedings. The bill is later voted down in the House of Representatives.
- *July 10*: Colorado passes an immigration bill that denies the state's estimated 1 million illegal immigrants the right to public housing and welfare benefits.

- *August 15*: The Census Bureau reports that between 2000 and 2005 the foreign-born population of the United States increased by 4.9 million, 12.4 percent of the 288.4 million total population. The majority still settle in California, New York, Texas, and Florida, but new destinations in the South are increasingly being chosen. Immigrants account for more than 15 percent of the population in California, Texas, Florida, New Jersey, New York, and Hawaii.
- *September 14*: The House of Representatives passes H.R. 6061, the Secure Fence Act of 2006, "to establish operational control over the international land and maritime borders of the United States." The act authorizes the construction of an additional 700 miles of double-layered fencing along the U.S.-Mexico border and gives the secretary of Homeland Security additional authority to stop unlawful entry of immigrants.
- *September 29*: The Senate passes the Secure Fence Act, authorizing the construction of a 700-mile double-layered fence on the U.S.-Mexico border by May 30, 2007.

- *October 4*: President Bush signs the Homeland Security Appropriations Bill, providing $34.8 billion in funding for the Department of Homeland Security in 2007.
- *October 17*: President Bush signs into law the Military Commissions Act of 2006, establishing commissions to try people suspected of links with terrorism. It allows, under certain conditions, suspension of habeas corpus, permanent detention without charge, and "harsh interrogation methods" that violate a ban on cruel, inhuman, or degrading treatment as defined by the Geneva Convention. Many Democrats vigorously oppose the law.
- *October 18*: The New York Stock Exchange reports that the Dow-Jones Industrial Average passes 12,000 for the first time.
- *October 26*: President Vicente Fox of Mexico, along with representatives of 27 other members of the OAS (Organization of American States), signs a statement opposing the Secure Fence Act of 2006 as "a unilateral measure that goes against the spirit of understanding that should characterize how shared problems between neighboring countries are handled and that affects cooperation in the hemisphere."
- *October 27*: President Bush signs into law the Secure Fence Act of 2006, authorizing the construction of a 700-mile fence on the U.S.-Mexica border.
- *November 1*: The American Civil Liberties Union (ACLU) and The AFL-CIO join with other civil- and labor-rights groups in a suit against the federal government charging that it deprives undocumented immigrants of their rights according to international law.
- *December 12*: The Immigration and Customs Enforcement (ICE) unit of the Department of Homeland Security (DHS) raids six Swift & Co. meatpacking plants in six states, arresting almost 1,300 undocumented aliens. It is the largest government raid on record and results in 148 indictments of illegal immigrants.
- *December 15*: The Department of Homeland Security suspends parts of the US-VISIT program, which provides for the fingerprinting and photographing of everyone entering and leaving the country, because it has proved too expensive.

2007

- *January 8:* Pizza Patrón, a Texas restaurant chain with a mainly Hispanic market, initiates the policy of accepting Mexican pesos as well as U.S. dollars. The decision arouses violent opposition and results in death threats.

- *January 31*: The United States Citizenship and Immigration Services (USCIS) announces a decision to increase fees for visa and citizenship documents by an average of 66 percent. The plan is criticized as unfair to immigrants.
- *February 8*: The Secretary of the Department of Homeland Security (DHS), Michael Chertoff, reports to a House of Representatives committee that violence along the U.S.-Mexican border has increased as a result of United States efforts to stop illegal immigration.
- *February 28:* A study by the nonpartisan Public Policy Institute of California reports that the increased flow of immigrants to California since 1990 has brought about an average 4 percent increase in the wages of native workers because natives have been promoted to higher-paying jobs as immigrant labor filled lower-paying jobs.
- *March*: The Coalition for Comprehensive Immigration Reform (CCIR), a national umbrella group of local and national immigrant advocacy groups, labor unions, and policy organizations, is formed in Washington, D.C.
- *March 14*: President Bush announces during a visit to Mexico that he will approve a bill providing for a guest worker program for Mexicans and for potential citizenship for immigrants now working in the United States. He promises Mexican president Felipe Calderón that he will try to pass a comprehensive immigration reform bill within the year.
- *April 3*: Representatives Luis Gutierrez of Illinois and Jeff Flake of Arizona introduce the Security Through Regularized Immigration and a Vibrant Economy Act of 2007 (STRIVE Act of 2007) to the House Judiciary Committee and the Homeland Security Committee to submit to the House of Representatives. The bill proposes to toughen border security, increase penalties for illegal immigration, create a system to verify the identity of aliens working in the United States, and present new programs for immigrants to become citizens.
- *April 14:* The USCIS holds its first lottery for work visas issued to highly skilled workers (H-1B visas). These visas allow workers with a bachelor's or higher college degree to work in the United States for three years.
- *May 1:* An immigration rally in Los Angeles, California, results in violent clashes with the police. Fifteen civilians and eight police officers are injured. The FBI announces on May 4 that it will initiate a civil rights investigation into the incident.

- *May 9:* The Secure Borders, Economic Opportunity and Immigration Reform Act of 2007, better known as the Comprehensive Immigration Reform Act of 2007 (S. 1348) is introduced in the U.S. Senate, but not voted on. Called by its chief architect, Democratic senator Edward M. Kennedy of Massachusetts, "a compromise," the bill would grant legal status to almost all the estimated 12 million undocumented workers in the United States and create a temporary-worker program, tighten border controls, and create a point system for future immigrants to favor education rather than family ties.
- *May 21:* The Senate votes 69 to 23 to proceed with the overhaul of immigration laws embodied in S. 1348. Dozens of amendments are planned for the controversial bill.
- *May 25:* Congress approves a large increase in visas for Iraqi and Afghan interpreters, in special danger from enemy forces for working with the U.S. military. The number of permitted visas is raised from 50 to 500.
- *June 7:* The Senate holds three votes on cloture—a move to end discussion—on the Comprehensive Immigration Reform Act of 2007, but all three fail. This is seen as a sign that the bill will fail.
- *June 14:* The government of the city of New Haven, Connecticut, votes to issue municipal identification cards to illegal immigrants. It is the first program of its kind in the United States.
- *June 15:* S. 1348 is returned to the Senate for discussion at the urging of President Bush.
- *June 28:* After 13 days of vehement dispute, S. 1348 (the Comprehensive Immigration Reform Act) fails to get the 60 votes necessary for cloture and an end to debate. The Senate concludes that this effectively ends the bill's chances of passage, at least for the next year and a half.

Eyewitness Testimony

People think that cities like [Los Angeles] are going to be so Mexican that they'll secede from the union. But L.A. is going to be Mexican in the same way that Boston is Irish or Milwaukee is German.

Frank Sharry, executive director of the National Immigration Forum, in David Nasci, "Debate Over Immigration," CQ Researcher, *July 14, 2000, p. 580.*

If over one million Mexican soldiers crossed the border Americans would treat it as a major threat to their national security and react accordingly. The invasion of over one million Mexican civilians. . . . would be a comparable threat to American societal security, and Americans should react against it with comparable anger.

Harvard professor Samuel P. Huntington, "Is Mexico a Special Case?" Center for Immigration Studies Backgrounder, *November 2000, p. 5.*

There were no characteristics to single me out as a noncitizen. I speak English without an accent.

It was my parents who pushed me to make the change. . . .

"You have no voice in this country," they warned.

But I never wanted it so bad for myself until this past November. The election especially showcased the power of one vote. But not mine. I had no vote. I had no voice.

That all changed as I stood in the courtroom with 264 other citizens-to-be.

. . . As I waited to sign my naturalization certificate, I looked at my neighbors. From India to Ireland, there was a face to represent every part of the world. This was truly America.

With my right hand cupped over my heart I recited the Pledge of Allegiance with a voice that would now be heard by all.

My Jamaican heritage will always be a part of me. And I'll make sure my future children know about it, too. But they will never be voiceless.

Roberta T. McCulloch, Jamaican immigrant who came to the United States as a child, "A New Voice Heard from a New American," Middletown, New York, *Times Herald-Record, February 2, 2001, p. 4.*

In this political cartoon the United States is portrayed as being unable to stem the influx of illegal immigrants. *(Copley News Service/ Scott Stantis)*

Spectators wave flags on New York's Fifth Avenue during the 1997 Puerto Rican Day Parade. *(AP/Wideworld)*

Once I started school and I got the hang of English, I wouldn't speak my language in the house, and I remember my father was always mad. He used to tell us, "Speak Ga, speak Ga. You shouldn't speak English in the house. You have to speak your language." I regret that now, because now it's hard for me to communicate in my language. I got stuck on certain words. We wanted to speak English. We wanted to be like everyone else in school.

. . . When I went back [to Ghana] this summer I saw where I grew up 'til I was eight years old. And I remember the house, the layout of the place and everything, but I really forgot how the everyday living was, and I had a hard time adjusting.

Here you can have soda anytime you want; the fridge is stocked with juice. There you drink water. I don't like water. I always have some kind of juice or soda, so I couldn't have that there. I have American dollars. For people living there, it's expensive, and I couldn't really just buy it just for myself. . . .

. . . Last summer, people would laugh at me sometimes because it was hard for me to be understood since I stopped speaking my language when we came to the states. I wasn't as fluent as I could have been, and it was hard for me to communicate. Sometimes I wouldn't use the exact, correct word. Sometimes they would laugh at me because the English there is British English, so they are pronouncing every little "t," every little "d." Sometimes they would laugh at me when I'm speaking English because I say a word differently.

. . . Everybody in America is considered wealthy over there. As soon as they know that you are an American, there's a big pot of money right there walking around—then the prices triple, quadruple. They even treat me that way. I'm Ghanaian, but I've been in the States for so long that when I go there, when they look at my skin, they know that I haven't been there for a long time, that I've been out of that African sun. I guess I could say that my skin has become Americanized just like the rest of me. Refrigerated drinks, soft beds, and a lukewarm sun have turned me into a guest in my motherland.

Rosemund Reimmer, Ghanaian American of the Ga tribe, recalling the difficulties of readjusting on visits to her homeland, in Ellen Alexander Conley, The Chosen Shores: Stories of Immigrants *(2004), pp. 150, 153, 155, 156.*

Working in government you get a lot of animosity because you come from another country. What was interesting to me was that when you work with construction people, they think that there are only two other nationalities: Mexicans or Chinese. Since my hair is very black they thought I was Chinese or Mexican. People do not know where Bolivia is. . . . There is some discrimination, and some subjective animosity is an everyday event. I had the opportunity to be promoted from an onsite doctor at a local nuclear plant to be an area supervisor. Instead they hired a brand-new African-American who had no experience. When I questioned them they could not give me an explanation.

I have no regrets coming to the United States. Occasionally I missed my family, especially my mother and sisters. . . . I never went back because of political instability. There were two factions, pro-American and pro-Russian. . . . Fifty-five percent of the population was pro-Russian. Anybody who comes from the American establishment is suspected. For instance, if I went back, I wouldn't be perceived as a private citizen; the perception would be that I am a spy. . .

My mother discouraged me from coming home, and she never came here. Another perception of the cold war—everybody over here is a hippie who abuses drugs. That was the type of American people she saw visiting Bolivia, so her perception was that if she came here she would be mugged.

My son was born here in Chattanooga, and he grew up in this community. He speaks Spanish with an American accent. . . . I have my wife and I have my son. This is the only family I have, so this is my country now. . . .

Sam Lizarraga, Bolivian physician working for a U.S. nuclear plant, in Ellen Alexander Conley, The Chosen Shores: Stories of Immigrants *(2004) pp. 238–239.*

On September 11 [2001] my son had just started his first day at school, and he came home and said, "I want you to go to Pakistan and ask Grandfather to kill all the Muslims."

I said, "Killing is not a good thing. You should not kill anybody. You know what? I am Muslim, too. And Grandfather is Muslim, too, and partly you are Muslim, too." I felt bad because obviously it's very confusing because I have never talked to my children about religion. Also his first fieldtrip was to walk into a neighborhood and find the largest American flag. After

that he would come from school and make statements like, "I want you to kill them." He precisely used the words "us and them."

I said, "Who are them?" and he couldn't explain it.

Friday of last week he said, "Afghanistan is our enemy." So obviously he is American. He lives here. This is his country. This is his language. This is his culture. But these should not be his values, and this is what he is getting.

My son will be six tomorrow. He is trying to make sense out of it himself. He loves his grandfather. He wanted Grandfather to take care of the situation. Culturally I cannot deny that I am Muslim. I am a product of that culture.

Irfan Malik, Pakistani writer who immigrated to America in his 30s, in Ellen Alexander Conley, The Chosen Shores: Stories of Immigrants *(2004) pp. 282–283.*

In our country, we think America is a dream country. But our dreams are broken. There are no dreams come true here.

Nishat Islam, Bangladeshi immigrant whose father and husband were deported for remaining in the United States after their visas had expired, quoted in Rachel L. Swarns, "Program's Value in Dispute As a Tool to Fight Terrorism," the New York Times, *December 21, 2004.*

You know what? America is built on that: struggle. I understand what these kids are saying. You shouldn't have to be born here to get an opportunity here.

Charles Kimbrough, African-American merchant in Newburgh, N.Y., commenting about the March 31, 2006 student protest for immigrant rights, in John Doherty, "Latino Students March, Middletown, N.Y.," Times Herald-Record, *April 12, 2006.*

America has a way of bringing us in, welcoming us and allowing us to become a part of the whole.

Mel Martinez, Republican senator from Florida who fled Cuba in 1962 at age 15, in a Senate debate on U.S. immigration policy, quoted in the New York Times, *April 4, 2006.*

I have this fear always, I fear being deported every day, I fear being sent back. I have a good life in America. I want to keep it.

Juan Carlos Wolochianez, undocumented Honduran immigrant who works as a short-order cook, after an April 10, 2006, protest march, in New York Daily News, *April 11, 2006.*

The number one message here today is we are America. We're here and we're here to make America strong.

Chung Wha Hong, Executive Director of the New York Immigration Coalition, one of the groups sponsoring the pro-immigration demonstration on April 10, 2006, as reported in "Immigrants Rally for Rights," New York Daily News, *April 11, 2006.*

Massive deportation of the people here is unrealistic. It's just not going to work. You can hear people out there hollering it's going to work. It's not going to work. What I do think makes sense is that a person ought to be allowed to get in line. In other words, pay a penalty for being here illegally, commit him- or herself to learn English . . . and get in the back of the line.

President George W. Bush, April 24, 2006, in a speech delivered in Southern California, reported in Deborah Orin, "Booting All Illegals Is Just Loco, Bush Says," New York Post, *April 25, 2006.*

We are the backbone of what America is, legal or illegal, it doesn't matter. We butter each other's bread. They need us as much as we need them.

Melanie Lugo, one of 75,000 rallying for a nationwide "Day without Immigrants" boycott in Denver, Colorado, May 1, 2006, quoted in Associated Press, "Boycott Makes Impact," May 2, 2006.

On May Day a persistent rumble came from Market Street in San Francisco, but it was not the oft-predicted earthquake, or at least not in the geologic sense. Thousands of people were marching down the thoroughfare, from the Embarcadero to city hall, holding signs. NO HUMAN BEING IS ILLEGAL. I AM A WORKER, NOT A CRIMINAL. TODAY I MARCH, TOMORROW I VOTE. I PAY TAXES.

. . . Americans who are really incensed by millions of undocumented immigrants can take action, just as

Demonstrators march on May 1, 2006, in Los Angeles, as part of the nationwide "A Day Without Immigrants" protest in support of immigrants' rights. *(AP Photo/Ric Francis)*

those marching in the streets did. They can refuse to eat fruits and vegetables picked by those immigrants. They can refuse to buy homes on which they worked. After all, if Cesar Chavez could organize a national boycott of grapes, then opponents of immigration could organize something similar. But they won't; we like our cheap houses and our fresh fruit. And our government likes the bait-and-switch, taking taxes from workers whose existence it will not recognize.

Anna Quindlen, syndicated columnist, reporting the May 1, 2006, march protesting H.R. 4437, in Newsweek, *May 15, 2006, p. 78.*

Almost half [of the illegal immigrants in the United States] enter legally, then overstay their visas. And—unlike in Europe, where many immigrants come for the welfare system—they come here for one reason: to work.

Carlos Gutierrez, Cuban-born U.S. Secretary of Commerce, quoted in Lyric Wallwork Winik, "An Insider's View: Immigration," Parade, *August 13, 2006, p. 8.*

Immigrants are not only our history but our destiny.

Marcelo Suarez-Orozco, founder of Harvard Immigration Project and codirector of immigration studies at New York University, reported in Lisa L. Colangelo, "Melting Pot Hot, Hot, Hot!," New York Daily News, *August 15, 2006.*

No more excuses. You're drunk. You're driving. You're illegal. You're deported. Period.

Republican representative Sue Myrick, after a July 2005 truck crash caused by an illegal alien with a blood alcohol level above the legal limit, defending the new laws authorizing deportation for driving while drunk, reported in Peter Whoriskey, "States, Counties Begin to Enforce Immigration Law," Washington Post, *September 27, 2006.*

When any of them cross that border without proper documentation, they've violated the law—however insignificant that may seem to some people. I've heard stories about folks wanting to come up here to have a better life and earn money for their family. I've arrested bank robbers who've had the same excuse.

Mecklenburg County, N.C., sheriff Jim Prendergraph, reported in Peter Whoriskey, "States, Counties Begin to Enforce Immigration Law," Washington Post, *September 27, 2006.*

It's tense, very tense. It used to be everybody here loved the Latinos. They would say, "We like you better than the blacks." Now we're like the Big Bad Wolf.

Angeles Ortega-Moore, director of the Latin American Coalition in Charlotte, N.C., reported in Peter Whoriskey, "States, Counties Begin to Enforce Immigration Law," Washington Post, *September 27, 2006.*

Fortifying our borders is an integral component of national security. We can't afford to wait.

Republican Senate majority leader Bill Frist, in support of the Secure Fence Act passed September 29, 2006, reported in Jonathan Weisman, "With Senate Vote, Congress Passes Border Fence Bill," Washington Post, *September 30, 2006.*

This is not a sign of strength and engagement, but a sign of weakness and fear. And frankly, speaking as an American, it's an embarrassment.

Kevin Appleby, director of migration and refugee policy at the United States Conference of Catholic Bishops, speaking in opposition to the Secure Fence Act, Reported in Jonathan Weisman, "With Senate Vote, Congress Passes Border Fence Bill," Washington Post, *September 30, 2006.*

We cannot criminalize people who are working, people who are contributing to our economy and contributing to the nation.

Antonio Villaraigosa, first Hispanic mayor of Los Angeles, California, addressing the crowd demonstrating against the Illegal Immigration Control Act of 2005, quoted in Dan Baum, "Arriba!: A Latino Radio Scold Gets Out the Vote," New Yorker, *October 23, 2006, p. 42.*

Don't forget to march with us! People! We'll be leaving from Broadway and Olympic, and end up in front of the City Hall of Los Angeles, the first day of spring, to protest this terrible law, HR 4437, that practically turns the undocumented into criminals.

We will be totally united in a day of action . . . to say no to the anti-immigrant laws and yes to the legalization of 12 million of our undocumented countrymen. Wear your white shirt, carry your American flag. . . . We are the working class. We are in the United States to work. And also the students—go to school, and afterward support us! All united, we will make the difference.

Renán Almendárez Coello, Mexican-American talk-show host ("El Cucuy de la Mañana") in Los Angeles, California, speaking on the air in support of a protest march, quoted by Dan Baum, "Arriba!: A Latino Radio Scold Gets Out the Vote," New Yorker, October 23, 2006, p. 42.

They treat you better here than in Mexico. Living here without papers is still better than living there.

Veronica Rodriguez, pseudonym of a 31-year-old Mexican illegal immigrant in San Antonio, Texas, who entered the United States on a tourist visa and remained after it expired, quoted in Lizette Alvarez, "Fear and Hope in Immigrants' Furtive Existence," New York Times, December 20, 2006, p. A26.

[Nonimmigrants] think we have it easy, that we don't pay taxes. They don't know how hard it is to get ahead here.

Fernanda, a 19-year-old Mexican whose parents were deported in an April, 2007, immigration raid at a meatpacking plant in Beardsville, Illinois, quoted in Nathan Thornburgh, "The Case For Amnesty," Time, June 18, 2007, p. 42.

Legal immigration is one of the top concerns of the American people, and Congress's failure to act on it is a disappointment. A lot of us worked hard to see if we couldn't find common ground. It didn't work.

President Bush, at an appearance in Newport, R.I., after the failure of the Comprehensive Immigration Reform Act of 2007 (S. 1348) to pass in the Senate on June 28, reported in the Associated Press, "Immigration Plan Collapses in Senate," June 29, 2007.

Notes

1. Rubén G. Rumbaut et al., "Debunking the Myth of Immigrant Criminality," Migration Information Source, June 1, 2006. Available online. URL: http://www.migrationinformation.org/Feature/display.cfm?id=403.
2. Douglas S. Massey, "Five Myths about Immigration," American Immigration Law Foundation, August 1, 2005. Available online. URL: http://www.ailf.org/policy_reports_2005_fivemyths.shtml.
3. "Immigrants and Welfare," Carnegie Endowment for International Peace, *Research Perspectives on Migration.* 1 (1996): 1.
4. Craig Donegan, "Debate over Bilingualism," *CQ Researcher* 6 (January 9, 1996): 51–64.
5. Editorial, *Catholic New York,* April 2006, 10.
6. Quoted in Brendan Lyons, "Illegal Worker Sweep Called Sign of Times," Albany, N.Y. *Times Union,* April 21, 2006, A11.
7. Amnesty International, "U.S. Congress Gives Green Light to Human Rights Violations in the 'War on Terror,'" September 29, 2006. Available online. URL: http://web.amnesty.org/pages/stoptorture=060930=features=eng.

Appendix A
Documents

1. Maryland Toleration Act, April 21, 1649

Forasmuch as in a well governed and Christian Common Wealth matters concerning Religion and the honor of God ought in the first place to be taken into serious consideration and endeavored to bee settled. Be it therefore . . . enacted . . . That whatsoever person or persons within this Province . . . shall from henceforth blaspheme God, . . . or shall deny our Saviour Jesus Christ to bee the sonne of God, or shall deny the holy Trinity the ffather sonne and holy Ghost, or the Godhead of any of the said three persons of the Trinity or the Unity of the Godhead . . . shall be punished with death and confiscation or forfeiture of all his or her lands. . . .

And whereas the inforceing of the conscience in matters of Religion hath frequently fallen out to be of dangerous Consequence in those commonwealthes where it hath been practised. And for the more quiett and peaceable governement of this Province, and the better to preserve mutuall Love and unity amongst the Inhabitants thereof, Be it Therefore . . . enacted . . . that noe person or persons whatsoever within this Province or the Islands, Ports, Harbors, Creekes, or havens thereunto belonging professing to believe in Jesus Christ, shall from henceforth bee in any waies troubled, Molested or discountenanced for or in respect of his or her religion nor in the free exercise thereof within this Province or the Islands thereunto belonging nor any way compelled to the beleife or exercise of any other religion against his or her consent, soe as they be not unfaithfull to the Lord Proprietary, or molest or conspire against the civill Government established or to bee established in this Province under him or his heires. And that all & every person and persons that shall presume Contrary to this Act and the true intent and meaning thereof directly or indirectly either in person or estate willfully to wronge disturbe trouble or molest any person whatsoever within this Province professing to believe in Jesus Christ for or in respect of his or her religion or the free exercise thereof within this Province other than is provided for in this Act that such person or persons soe offending, shalbe compelled to pay trebble damages to the party soe wronged or molested, and for every such offence shall also forfeit 20 s. sterling in money or the value thereof . . . , Or if the parties soe offending as aforesaid shall refuse or bee unable to recompense the party soe wronged, or to satisfy such ffyne or forfeiture, then such offender shall be severely punished by publick whipping & imprisonment during the pleasure of the Lord proprietary, or his Lieutenant or cheife Governor of this Province. . . .

2. An Act to Establish A Uniform Rule of Naturalization, March 26, 1790

Section 1

Be it enacted by the Senate and House of Representatives of the United States of America in Congress assembled, That any alien, being a free white person, who shall have resided within the limits and under the jurisdiction of the United States for the term of two years, may be admitted to become a citizen thereof, on application to any common law court of record, in any one of the states wherein he shall have resided for the term of one year at least, and making proof to the satisfaction of such court, that he is a person of good character, and taking the oath or affirmation prescribed by law, to support the constitution of the United States, which oath or affirmation such court shall administer; and the clerk of such court shall record such application, and the proceedings thereon; and thereupon such person shall be considered as a citizen of the United States. And the children of such persons so naturalized, dwelling within the United States, being under the age of twenty-one years at the time of such naturalization, shall also be considered as citizens of the United States. And the children of citizens of the United States, that may be born beyond sea, or out of the limits of the United States, shall be considered as natural born citizens: *Provided,* That the right of citizenship shall not descend to persons whose fathers have never been resident in the United States: *Provided also,* That no person heretofore proscribed by any state, shall be admitted a citizen as aforesaid, except by an act of the legislature of the state in which such person was proscribed.

Approved, March 26, 1790.

3. The Alien and Sedition Acts, 1798

1. The Naturalization Act, June 18, 1798

An Act supplementary to and to amend the act, entitled "An act to establish an uniform rule of naturalization, and to repeal the act heretofore passed on that subject."

SECTION 1

Be it enacted by the Senate and House of Representatives of the United States of America in Congress assembled, That no alien shall be admitted to become a citizen of the United States, or of any state, unless in the manner prescribed in the act, entitled "An act to establish an uniform rule of naturalization; and to repeal the act heretofore passed on that subject," he shall have declared his intention to become a citizen of the United States, five years, at least, before his admission, and shall, at the time of his application to be admitted, declare and prove, to the satisfaction of the court having jurisdiction in the case, that he has resided within the United States fourteen years, at least, and within the state or territory where, or for which such court is at the time held, five years, at least, besides conforming to the other declarations and proofs, by the said act required, any thing therein to the contrary hereof notwithstanding: *Provided,* that any alien, who was residing within the limits, and under the jurisdiction of the United States, before the twenty-ninth day of January, one thousand seven hundred and ninety-five, may, within one year after the passing of this act—and any alien who shall have made the declaration of his intention to become a citizen of the United States, in conformity to the provisions of the act, intituled, "An act to establish an uniform rule of naturalization, and to repeal the act heretofore passed on the subject," may, within four years of having made the declaration aforesaid, be admitted to become a citizen, in the manner prescribed by the said act, upon his making proof that he has resided five years, at least, within the limits, and under the jurisdiction of the United States: *And provided also,* that no alien, who shall be a native, citizen, denizen or subject of any nation or state with whom the United States shall be at war, at the time of his application, shall be then admitted to become a citizen of the United States.

SECTION 2

And be it further enacted, That it shall be the duty of the clerk, or other recording officer of the court before whom a declaration has been, or shall be made, by any alien, of his intention to become a citizen of the United States, to certify and transmit to the office of the Secretary of State of the United States, to be there filed and recorded, an abstract of such declaration, in which, when hereafter made, shall be a suitable description of the name, age, nation, residence and occupation, for the time being, of the alien; such certificates to be made in all cases, where the declaration has been or shall be made, before the passing of this act, within three months thereafter. . . .

SECTION 4

And be it further enacted, That all white persons, aliens (accredited foreign ministers, consuls, or agents, their fami-

lies and domestics, excepted) who, after the passing of this act, shall continue to reside, or who shall arrive, or come to reside in any port or place within the territory of the United States, shall be reported, if free, and of the age of twenty-one-years, by themselves, or being under the age of twenty-one years, or holden in service, by their parent, guardian, master or mistress in whose care they shall be, to the clerk of the district court of the district. . . . who shall be authorized by the President of the United States to register aliens: And report . . . shall be made in all cases of residence . . .within forty-eight hours of first arrival or coming into the territory of the United States, and shall ascertain the sex, place of birth, age, nation, place of allegiance or citizenship, condition or occupation, and place of actual or intended residence of the alien. . . .

SECTION 5

And be it further enacted, That every alien who shall . . . .refuse or neglect to make such report, and to receive a certificate thereof, shall forfeit and pay the sum of two dollars; and any justice of the peace, or other civil magistrate, who has authority to require surety of the peace, shall and may, on complaint to him made thereof, cause such alien to be brought before him, there to give surety of the peace and good behaviour during his residence within the United States, or for such term as the justice or other magistrate shall deem reasonable, and until a report and registry of such alien shall be made . . .and in failure of such surety, such alien shall and may be committed to the common gaol, and shall be there held, until the order which the justice or magistrate shall and may reasonably make, in the premises, shall be performed. . . .

2. The Alien Act, June 25, 1798

An Act concerning aliens.

SECTION 1

Be it enacted by the Senate and House of Representatives of the United States of America in Congress assembled, That it shall be lawful for the president of the United States at any time during the continuance of this act, to *order* all such *aliens* as he shall judge dangerous to the peace and safety of the United States, or shall have reasonable grounds to suspect are concerned in any treasonable or secret machinations against the government thereof, to depart out of the territory of the United States . . . .And in case any alien, so ordered to depart, shall be found at large within the United States after the time limited in such order for his departure, . . .every such alien shall, on conviction thereof, be imprisoned for a term not exceeding three years, and shall never after be admitted to become a citizen of the United States.

SECTION 2

And be it further enacted, That it shall be lawful for the President of the United States, whenever he shall deem it necessary for the public safety, to order to be removed out of the territory thereof, any alien who may or shall be in prison in pursuance of this act, and to cause to be arrested and sent out of the United States such of those aliens as shall have been ordered to depart therefrom . . . .in all cases where, in the opinion of the President, the public safety requires a speedy removal. . . .

3. The Alien Enemies Act, July 6, 1798

An Act respecting Alien enemies.

SECTION 1

Be it enacted by the Senate and House of Representatives of the United States of America in Congress assembled, That whenever there shall be declared war between the United States and any foreign nation or government, or any invasion or predatory incursion shall be perpetrated, attempted, or threatened against the territory of the United States, by any foreign nation or government, ...all natives, citizens, denizens or subjects of the hostile nation or government, being males of the age of fourteen years and upwards, who shall be within the United States, and not actually naturalized, shall be liable to be apprehended, restrained, secured and removed, as alien enemies. . . .

4. The Sedition Act, July 14, 1798

An Act in addition to the act, entitled "An act for the punishment of certain crimes against the United States."

SECTION 1

Be it enacted by the Senate and House of Representatives of the United States of America in Congress assembled, That if any person shall unlawfully combine or conspire together, with intent to oppose any measure or measures of the government of the United States, which are or shall be directed by proper authority, or to impede the operation of any law of the United States, or to intimidate or prevent any person holding a place of office in or under the government of the United States, from undertaking, performing or executing his trust or duty; and if any person or persons, with the intent as aforesaid, shall counsel, advise or attempt to procure any insurrection, riot, unlawful assembly, or combination, whether such con-

spiracy, threatening, counsel, advise or attempt shall have the proposed effect or not, he or they shall be deemed guilty of a high misdemeanor, and on conviction, before any court of the United States having jurisdiction thereof, shall be punished by a fine not exceeding five thousand dollars, and by imprisonment during a term not less than six months nor exceeding five years; and further, at the discretion of the court may be holden to find sureties for his good behaviour in such sum, and for such time, as the said court may direct.

SECTION 2

That if any person shall write, print, utter, or publish, or shall cause or procure to be written, printed, uttered or published, or shall knowingly and willingly assist or aid in writing, printing, uttering or publishing any false, scandalous and malicious writing or writings against the government of the United States, or either house of the Congress of the United States, or the President of the United States, with intent to defame the said government, or either house of the said Congress, or the said President, or to bring them, or either of them, into contempt or disrepute, or to excite against them, or either or any of them, the hatred of the good people of the United States, or to stir up sedition within the United States, or to excite any unlawful combination therein, for opposing or resisting any law of the United States, or any act of the President of the United States, done in pursuance of any such law, or of the powers in him vested by the constitution of the United States, or to resist, oppose or defeat any such law or act, or to aid, encourage or abet any hostile designs of any foreign nation against the United States, their people or government, then such persons, being thereof convicted before any court of the United States having jurisdiction thereof, shall be punished by a fine not exceeding two thousand dollars, and by imprisonment not exceeding two years. . . .

4. South Carolina Immigration Bill, 1866

An act for the encouragement and protection of European immigration, and for the appointment of a commissioner and agents, and for other purposes therein expressed.

Be it enacted by the Senate and House of representatives, now met and sitting in General Assembly, and by the authority of the same, that for the purpose of encouraging, promoting, and protecting European immigration to and in this state, the sum of $10,000 be appropriated from the contingent found, to be expended under the direction of the government, for the purposes and in the manner hereinafter provided.

2. That the governor, by and with the advice and consent of the Senate, shall appoint a commissioner of immigration . . . .

3. That it shall be the duty of said commissioner of immigration to advertise in all the gazettes of the state for lands for sale; to cause such lands after having been duly laid off, platted and described, at the expense of the owner or owners of said lands. To be appraised by three disinterested persons. . . . And in case such lands be selected by any immigrants, to superintend the transfer of title and other necessary instruments and proceedings of conveyance.

4. That the said commissioner shall periodically publish, advertise, and cause to be distributed in the Northern and European ports and states, descriptive lists of such lands as have been registered and offered for sale, together with this act, and a statement of such advantages as this state offers in soil, climate, productions, social improvements, etc., to the industrious, orderly, and frugal European immigrant. . . .

6. That the said commissioner shall be specially charged with the protection of the immigrants in the proper selection of their lands; in the procurement of their transportation; in the guarding of them against fraud, chicanery, and peculation; in their temporary location in proper and reasonable places of board and lodging on their arrival; and in making all such regulations and provisions as may be in any manner necessary or conducive to their welfare. And all officials of the state are hereby required to aid and assist him in the objects aforesaid whenever requested.

5. Treaty Between the United States and China, Concerning Immigration, November 17, 1880

By the President of the United States of America

A PROCLAMATION

Whereas a Treaty between the United States of America and China, for the modification of the existing treaties between the two countries, by providing for the future regulation of Chinese immigration into the United States, was concluded and signed at Peking in the English and Chinese languages, on the seventeenth day of November in the year of our Lord one thousand eight hundred and eighty, the original of the English text of which Treaty is word for word as follows:

Whereas in the eighth year of Hsien Feng, Anno Domini 1858, a treaty of peace and friendship was concluded between the United States of America and China, and to which were added, in the seventh year of Tang Chih, Anno Domini 1868, certain supplementary articles to the advantage of both parties, which supplementary articles were to be perpetually observed and obeyed:—and

Whereas the government of the United States, because of the consistently increasing immigration of Chinese laborers to the territory of the United States, and the embarrassments consequent upon such immigration, now desires to negotiate a modification of the existing Treaties which shall not be in direct contravention of their spirit:—. . .

Article I
Whenever in the opinion of the Government of the United States, the coming of Chinese laborers to the United States, or their residence therein, affects or threatens to affect the interests of that country, or to endanger the good order of the said country or of any locality within the territory thereof, the Government of China agrees that the Government of the United States may regulate, limit, or suspend such coming or residence, but may not absolutely prohibit it. The limitation or suspension shall be reasonable and shall apply only to Chinese who may go to the United States as laborers, other classes not being included in the limitations. . . .

Article II
Chinese subjects, whether proceeding to the United States as teachers, students, merchants, or from curiosity, together with their body and household servants, and Chinese laborers who are now in the United States, shall be allowed to go and come of their own free will and accord, and shall be accorded all the rights, privileges, immunities and exemptions which are accorded to the citizens and subjects of the most favored nations.

Article III
If Chinese laborers, or Chinese of any other class, now either permanently or temporarily residing in the territory of the United States, meet with ill treatment at the hands of any persons, the government of the United States will exert all its power to devise measures for their protection and to secure to them the same rights, privileges, immunities and exemptions as may be enjoyed by the citizens or subjects of the most favored nation, . . .

Article IV

The high contracting Powers having agreed upon the foregoing articles, whenever the Government of the United States shall adopt legislative measures in accordance therewith, such measures will be communicated to the Government of China. . . .

Done at Peking, this seventeenth day of November, in the year of our Lord, 1880. Kuanghsu, sixth year, tenth moon, fifteenth day.

JAMES B. ANGELI [seal]
JOHN F. SWIFT [seal]
WM. HENRY TRESCOT [seal]
PAO CHUN [seal]
LI HUNGTSAO [seal]

And whereas the said Treaty has been duly ratified on both parts and the respective ratifications were exchanged at Peking on the 19th day of July 1881:

Now, therefore, be it known that I, Chester A. Arthur, President of the United States of America, have caused the said treaty to be made public to the end that the same and every article and clause thereof may be observed and fulfilled with good faith by the United States and the citizens thereof.

In witness whereof, I have hereunto set my hand and caused the seal of the United States to be affixed.

Done in Washington this fifth day of October in the year of our Lord one thousand eight hundred and eighty-one, and of the Independence of the United States the one hundred and sixth.

By the President   CHESTER A. ARTHUR
JAMES G. BLAINE,
Secretary of State

6. Chinese Exclusion Act, May 6, 1882

An act to execute certain treaty stipulation relating to the Chinese. Whereas, in the opinion of the Government of the United States the coming of Chinese laborers to this country endangers the good order of certain localities within the territory thereof: Therefore,

Be it enacted by the Senate and House of Representatives of the United States of America in Congress assembled, That from and after the expiration of ninety days next after the passage of this act, and until the expiration of ten years next after the passage of this act, the coming of Chinese laborers to the United States be, and the same is hereby, suspended; and during such suspension it shall not be lawful for any Chinese

laborer to come, or, having so come after the expiration of said ninety days, to remain within the United States.

Section 2

That the master of any vessel who shall knowingly bring within the United States on such vessel, and land or permit to be landed, any Chinese laborer, from any foreign port or place, shall be deemed guilty of a misdemeanor, and on conviction thereof shall be punished by a fine of not more than five hundred dollars for each and every such Chinese laborer so brought, and may be also imprisoned for a term not exceeding one year.

. . .

Section 6

That in order to the faithful execution of articles one and two of the treaty of this act before mentioned, every Chinese person other than a laborer who may be entitled by said treaty and this act to come within the United States, and who shall be about to come to the United States, shall be identified as so entitled by the Chinese Government in each case, such identity to be evidenced by a certificate issued under the authority of said government, which certificate shall be in the English language or (if not in the English language) accompanied by a translation into English, stating such right to come, and which certificate shall state the name, title, or official rank, if any, the age, height, and all physical peculiarities, former and present occupation or profession, and place of residence in China of the person to whom the certificate is issued and that such person is entitled conformably to the treaty in this act mentioned to come within the United States. . . .

Section 14

That hereafter no State court or court of the United States shall admit Chinese to citizenship; and all laws in conflict with this act are hereby repealed.

Section 15

That the words "Chinese laborer," whenever used in this act, shall be construed to mean both skilled and unskilled laborers and Chinese employed in mining.

Approved, May 6, 1882.

7. Theodore Roosevelt's Annual Message to Congress, December 3, 1901

. . . Our present immigration laws are unsatisfactory. There should be a comprehensive law enacted with the object of working a three-fold improvement over our present system. First, we should aim to exclude absolutely not only all persons who are known to be believers in anarchistic principles or members of anarchistic societies, but also all persons who are of a low moral tendency or of unsavory reputation. This means that we should require a more thorough system of inspection abroad and a more rigid system of examination at our immigration ports, the former being especially necessary.

The second object of a proper immigration law ought to be to secure by a careful and not merely perfunctory educational test some intelligent capacity to appreciate American institutions and act sanely as American citizens. This would not keep out all anarchists, for many of them belong to the intelligent criminal class. But it would do what is also in point—that is, tend to decrease the sum of ignorance, so potent in producing the envy, suspicion, malignant passion, and hatred of order out of which anarchistic sentiment inevitably springs. Finally, all persons should be excluded who are below a certain standard of economic fitness to enter our industrial field as competitors with American labor. There should be a proper proof of personal capacity to earn an American living and enough money to insure a decent start under American conditions. This would stop the influx of cheap labor, and the resulting competition which gives rise to so much of bitterness in American industrial life, and it would dry up the springs of the pestilential social conditions in our great cities, where anarchistic organizations have their greatest possibility of growth.

Both the educational and economic tests in a wise immigration law should be designed to protect and elevate the general body politic and social. A very close supervision should be exercised over the steamship companies which mainly bring over the immigrants, and they should be held to a strict accountability for any infraction of the law.

8. Reports of the Department of Commerce and Labor, 1908

To section I of the Immigration Act approved February 20, 1907, a proviso was attached reading as follows:

That whenever the President shall be satisfied that passports issued by any foreign government to its citizens to go to any other country than the United States or to any insular possession of the United States or to the Canal Zone are being used for the purpose of enabling the holders to come to the continental territory of the United States to the detriment of labor conditions therein, the President may refuse to permit such citizens of the country issuing such passports to enter the continental territory of the United States from such other country or from such insular possessions or from the Canal Zone.

This legislation was the result of a growing alarm, particularly on the Pacific Coast and in states adjacent to Canada and Mexico, that labor conditions would be seriously affected by a continuation of the then existing rate of increase in admissions to this country of Japanese of the laboring classes. The Japanese government had always maintained a policy opposed to the emigration to continental United States of its subjects belonging to such classes; but it had been found that passports granted by said subjects to such subjects entitling them to proceed to Hawaii or to Canada or Mexico were being used to evade the said policy and gain entry to continental United States.

On the basis of the above-quoted provision, the President, on March 14, 1907, issued a proclamation excluding from continental United States "Japanese or Korean laborers, skilled or unskilled, who have received passports to go to Mexico, Canada, or Hawaii, and come therefrom.". . .

In order that the best results might follow from an enforcement of the regulations, an understanding was reached with Japan that the existing policy of discouraging the emigration of its subjects of the laboring classes to continental United States should be continued and should, by cooperation of the governments, be made as effective as possible. This understanding contemplates that the Japanese government shall issue passports to continental United States only to such of its subjects as are nonlaborers or are laborers who, in coming to the continent, seek to resume a formerly acquired domicile; to join a parent, wife, or children residing there; or to assume active control of an already possessed interest in a farming enterprise in this country; so that the three classes of laborers entitled to receive passports have come to be designated "former residents," "parents, wives, or children of residents," and "settled agriculturalists."

With respect to Hawaii, the Japanese government of its own volition stated that, experimentally at least, the issuance of passports to members of the laboring classes proceeding thence would be limited to "former residents" and "parents, wives, and children of residents." The said government has also been exercising a careful supervision over the subject of the emigration of its laboring class to foreign continuous territory.

It will be seen, therefore, that the report for the past fiscal year covers a novel phase of the immigration question, viz., the exclusion from the continental portion of this country of certain classes of aliens, such exclusion being based in part upon the provision of law mentioned, but principally upon the mutual understanding of the two countries affected, and to be brought about largely by the said two countries uniting upon a policy, agreed by both to be necessary and desirable, one of the countries exercising control over the departure and the other over the admission of the persons whose emigration and immigration it is desired mutually to control.

Source: Washington, D.C.: Government Printing Office, 1909, pp. 221–222.

9. William Howard Taft's Veto of the Literacy Test for Immigrants, February 14, 1913

To the Senate:

I return herewith, without my approval, Senate Bill No. 3175.

I do this with great reluctance. The bill contains many valuable amendments to the present immigration law which will insure greater certainty in excluding undesirable immigrants.

The bill received strong support in both Houses and was recommended by an able commission after an extended investigation and carefully drawn conclusions.

But I can not make up my mind to sign a bill which in its chief provision violates a principle that ought, in my opinion, to be upheld in dealing with our immigration. I refer to the literacy test. For the reasons stated in Secretary [of Commerce Charles] Nagel's letter to me, I can not approve that test. The Secretary's letter accompanies this.

WM. H. TAFT
February 12, 1913

My Dear Mr. President:

. . . .I am of the opinion that this provision [the literacy test] cannot be defended upon its merits. It was originally urged as a selective test. For some time, recommendations in its support upon that ground have been brought to our attention. The matter has been considered from that point of view, and I became completely satisfied that upon that ground the test could not be sustained. The older argument is now abandoned, and in the later

conferences, at least, the ground is taken that the provision is to be defended as a practical measure to exclude a large proportion of undesirable immigrants from certain countries. The measure proposes to reach its results by indirection and is defended purely upon the ground of practical policy, the final purpose being to reduce the quantity of cheap labor in this country.

I cannot accept this argument. No doubt the law would exclude a considerable percentage of immigration from southern Italy, among the Poles, the Mexicans, and the Greeks. This exclusion would embrace probably in large part undesirable but also a great many desirable people, and the embarrassment, expense, and distress to those who seek to enter would be out of all proportion to any good that can possibly be promised for this measure.

My observation leads me to the conclusion that so far as the merits of the individual immigrant are concerned the test is altogether overestimated. The people who come from the countries named are frequently illiterate because opportunities have been denied them. The oppression with which these people have to contend in modern times is not religious, but it consists of a denial of the opportunity to acquire reading and writing. Frequently the attempt to learn to read and write the language of a particular people is discouraged by the government, and these immigrants in coming to our shores are really striving to free themselves from the conditions under which they have been compelled to live.

10. An Act to Limit the Immigration of Aliens into the United States, and for Other Purposes (Johnson-Reed Act), May 26, 1924

Be it enacted by the Senate and House of Representatives of the United States in Congress assembled, That this Act may be cited as the "Immigration Act of 1924."

. . .

Preferences Within Quotas

SECTION 6

(a) In the issuance of immigration visas to quota immigrants preference shall be given—

(1) To a quota immigrant who is the unmarried child under 21 years of age, the father, the mother, the husband, or the wife, of a citizen of the United States who is 21 years of age or over; and

(2) To a quota immigrant who is skilled in agriculture, and his wife, and his dependent children under the age of 16 years, if accompanying or following to join him. The preference provided in this paragraph shall not apply to immigrants of any nationality the annual quota for which is less than 300.

(b) The preference provided in subdivision (a) shall not in the case of quota immigrants of any nationality exceed 50 per centum of the annual quota for such nationality. Nothing in this section shall be construed to grant to the class of immigrants specified in paragraph (1) of subdivision (a) a priority in preference over the class specified in paragraph (2).

Numerical Limitations

Section 11

(a) The annual quota of any nationality shall be 2 per centum of the number of foreign-born individuals of such nationality resident in continental United States as determined by the United States census of 1890, but the minimum quota of any nationality shall be 100.

(b) The annual quota of any nationality for the fiscal year beginning July 1, 1927, and for each fiscal year thereafter, shall be a number which bears the same ratio to 150,000 as the number of inhabitants in continental United States in 1920 having that national origin (ascertained hereinafter provided in this section) bears to the number of inhabitants in continental United States in 1920, but the minimum quota of any nationality shall be 100.

(c) For the purpose of subdivision (b) national origin shall be ascertained by determining as nearly as may be, in respect of each geographical area which under section 12 is to be treated as a separate country . . . .the number of inhabitants in the continental United States in 1920 whose origin by birth or ancestry is attributable to such geographical area. Such determination shall not be made by tracing the ancestors or descendants of particular individuals, but shall be based upon statistics of immigration and emigration, together with rates of increase of population as shown by successive decennial United States censuses, and such other data as may be found to be reliable.

(d) For the purposes of subdivisions (b) and (c) the term "inhabitants of continental United States in 1920" does not include (1) immigrants from geographical areas specified in subdivision (c) of section 4 or their descendants, (2) aliens ineligible to citizenship or their descendants, (3) the descendants of slave immigrants, or (4) the descendants of American aborigines.

(e) The determination provided for in subdivision (c) of this section shall be made by the Secretary of State, the Secretary of Commerce, and the Secretary of Labor, jointly. . . .

Nationality

Section 12

(a) For the purposes of this Act nationality shall be determined by country of birth, treating as separate countries the colonies, dependencies, or self-governing dominions, for which separate enumeration was made in the United States census of 1890; except that (1) the nationality of a child under twenty-one years of age not born in the United States, accompanied by its alien parent nor born in the United States, shall be determined by the country of birth of such parent if such parent is entitled to an immigration visa. . . .

(b) The Secretary of State, the Secretary of Commerce, and the Secretary of Labor, jointly, shall, as soon as feasible after the enactment of this Act, prepare a statement showing the number of individuals of the various nationalities resident in continental United States as determined by the United States census of 1890, which statement shall be the population basis for the purposes of subdivision (a) of section 11. . . .

(e) Such officials shall, jointly, report annually to the President the quota of each nationality under subdivision (a) of section 11, together with the statements, estimates, and revisions provided for in this section. The President shall proclaim and make known the quotas so reported and thereafter such quotas shall continue, with the same effect as if specifically stated herein, for all fiscal years for which quotas are in effect as proclaimed under subdivision (e) of section 11, and shall be final and conclusive for every purpose.

Exclusion from the United States

Section 13

(a) No immigrant shall be admitted to the United States unless he (1) has an unexpired immigration visa or was born subsequent to the issuance of the immigrant visa of the accompanying parent, (2) is of the nationality specified in the visa in the immigration visa, (3) is a non-quota immigrant. . . .

Deportation

SECTION 14

(a) Any alien who at any time after entering the United States is found to have been at the time of entry not entitled under this Act to enter the United States, or to have remained therein for a longer time than permitted under this Act or regulation made thereunder, shall be taken into custody and deported

. . .

Burden of Proof

SECTION 23

Whenever any alien attempts to enter the United States the burden of proof shall be upon such alien to establish that he is not subject to exclusion under any provision of the immigration laws; and in any deportation proceedings against any alien the burden of proof shall be upon such alien to show that he entered the United States lawfully, and the time, place, and manner of such entry into the United States, but in presenting such proof he shall be entitled to the production of his immigration visa, if any, or of any other documents concerning such entry, in the custody of the Department of Labor

. . .

Approved, May 26, 1924

11. Proclamation of Calvin Coolidge Announcing the Immigration Quotas for the Years 1924–1925, June 30, 1924

By the President of the United States A Proclamation

Whereas it is provided by the act of Congress approved May 26, 1924, entitled "An act to limit the immigration of aliens into the United States, and for other purposes" that—

"The annual quota of any nationality shall be two per centum of the number of foreign-born individuals of such nationality resident in continental United States as determined by the United States census of 1890, . . .

"The Secretary of State, the Secretary of Commerce, and the Secretary of Labor, jointly, shall, as soon as feasible after the enactment of this act, prepare a statement show-

ing the number of individuals of the various nationalities resident in continental United States as determined by the United States census of 1890, which statement. . . .

"Such officials shall, jointly, report annually to the President the quota. . . . The President shall proclaim and make known the quotas so reported.". . .

Now, therefor, I, Calvin Coolidge, President of the United States of America acting under and by virtue of the power vested in me by the aforesaid act of Congress, do hereby proclaim and make known that on and after July 1, 1924, and throughout the fiscal year 1924–1925, the quota of each nationality provided in said Act shall be as follows:

Country or area of birth	Quota 1924–1925
Afghanistan	100
Albania	100
Andorra	100
Arabian peninsula	100
Armenia	124
Australia, including Papua, Tasmania, and all islands appertaining to Australia	121
Austria	785
Belgium	512
Bhutan	100
Bulgaria	100
Cameroon (proposed British mandate)	100
China	100
Czechoslovakia	3,073
Danzig, Free State of	228
Denmark	2,789
Egypt	100
Esthonia	124
Ethiopia (Abyssinia)	100
Finland	170
France	3,954
Germany	51,277
Great Britain and Northern Ireland	34,007
Greece	100
Hungary	473
Iceland	100
India	100
Iraq (Mesopotamia)	100
Irish Free State	28,567
Italy, including Rhodes, Dodekanesia, and Castellorizzo	3,845
Japan	100
Latvia	142
Liberia	100

Liechtenstein	100
Lithuania	344
Luxembourg	100
Monaco	100
Morocco (French and Spanish Zones and Tangier)	100
Muscat (Oman)	100
Nauru (proposed British mandate)	100
Nepal	100
Netherlands	1,648
New Zealand (including appertaining islands)	100
Norway	6,453
New Guinea (and other Pacific Islands under proposed Australian mandate)	100
Palestine (with Trans-Jordan, proposed British mandate)	100
Persia	100
Poland	5,982
Portugal	503
Ruanda and Urundi (Belgium mandate)	100
Rumania	603
Russia, European and Asiatic	2,248
Samoa, Western (proposed mandate of New Zealand)	100
San Marino	100
Siam	100
South Africa, Union of	100
South West Africa (proposed mandate of Union of South Africa)	100
Spain	131
Sweden	9,561
Switzerland	2,081
Syria and the Lebanon (French mandate)	100
Tanganyika (proposed British mandate)	100
Togoland (proposed British mandate)	100
Togoland (French mandate)	100
Turkey	100
Yap and other Pacific islands (under Japanese mandate)	100
Yugoslavia	671

GENERAL NOTE.—The immigration quotas assigned to the various countries and quota-areas should not be regarded as having any political significance whatever, or as involving recognition of new governments, or of new boundaries, or of transfers of territories except as the United States Government has already made such recognition in a formal and official manner. . . .

CALVIN COOLIDGE

12. The Immigration and Nationality Act (McCarran-Walter Act), June 27, 1952

An Act

To revise the laws relating to immigration, naturalization, and nationality; and for other purposes.

Be it enacted by the Senate and the House of Representatives of the United States of America in Congress assembled, That this Act, divided into titles, chapters, and sections, according to the following table of contents, may be cited as the "Immigration and Nationality Act.". . .

Title II—Immigration

CHAPTER 1—QUOTA SYSTEM
Numerical Limitations; Annual Quota based upon national origin; minimum quotas

SECTION 201

(a) The annual quota of any quota area shall be one-sixth of 1 per centum of the number of inhabitants in the continental United States in 1920, which number, except for the purpose of computing quotas for quota areas within the Asia-Pacific triangle, shall be the same number heretofore determined under the provision of section 11 of the Immigration Act of 1924, attributable by national origin to such quota are: *Provided,* That the quota existing for Chinese persons prior to the date of enactment of this Act shall be continued, and, ...the minimum quota for any quota area shall be one hundred.

(b) The determination of the annual quota of any quota area shall be made by the Secretary of State, the Secretary of Commerce, and the Attorney General, jointly. Such officials shall, jointly, report to the President the quota of each quota area, and the President shall make known the quotas so reported. . . .

(c) There shall be issued to quota immigrants chargeable to any quota (1) no more immigrant visas in any fiscal year than the quota for such year, and (2) in any calendar month of any fiscal year, no more immigrant visas than 10 per centum of the quota for such year. . . .

SECTION 202

(a) . . . .For the purposes of this Act, the annual quota to which an immigrant is chargeable shall be determined by birth within a quota area. . . .

CHAPTER 2—QUALIFICATIONS FOR ADMISSION OF ALIENS; Travel Control of Citizens and Aliens General Classes of Aliens Ineligible to Receive Visas and Excluded from Admission

SECTION 212

(a) Except as otherwise provided in this Act, the following classes of aliens shall be ineligible to receive visas and shall be excluded from admission into the United States:

(1) Aliens who are feeble-minded;

(2) Aliens who are insane;

(3) Aliens who have had one or more attacks of insanity;

(4) Aliens afflicted with psychopathic personality, epilepsy, or a mental defect;

(5) Aliens who are narcotic drug addicts or chronic alcoholics;

(6) Aliens who are afflicted with tuberculosis in any form, or with leprosy, or any dangerous contagious disease;

(7) Aliens not comprehended within any of the foregoing classes who are certified by the examining surgeon as having a physical defect, disease, or disability, when determined by the consular or immigration officer to be of such a nature that it may affect the ability of the alien to earn a living . . . ;

(8) Aliens who are paupers, professional beggars, or vagrants;

(9) Aliens who have been convicted of a crime involving moral turpitude (other than a purely political offense) or aliens who admit having committed such a crime, or aliens who admit committing acts which constitute the essential elements of such a crime. . . . ;

. . . .(11) Aliens who are polygamists, or who practice polygamy or advocate the practice of polygamy;

(12) Aliens who are prostitutes or who have engaged in prostitution, or aliens coming to the United States solely, principally, or incidentally to engage in prostitution; aliens who directly or indirectly procure or attempt to procure, or who have procured or attempted to procure or to import, prostitutes or persons for the purpose of prostitution or for any other immoral purpose; . . . or aliens coming to the United States to engage in any other unlawful commercialized vice, whether or not related to prostitution;

(13) Aliens coming to the United States to engage in any immoral sexual act;

(14) Aliens coming to the United States for the purpose of performing skilled or unskilled labor, if the Secretary of Labor has determined and certified to the Secretary of State and to the Attorney General that (A) sufficient workers in the United States who are able, willing, and qualified are available at the time . . . .and place . . . .to perform such skilled or unskilled labor . . .;

(15) Aliens who, in the opinion of the consular officer at the time of application for a visa . . ., are likely to become public charges;

. . . .(18) Aliens who are stowaways;

. . . .(25) Aliens . . . .over sixteen years of age, physically capable of reading, who cannot read and understand some language or dialect;

. . . .(27) Aliens who the consular officer or the Attorney General knows or has reason to believe seek to enter the United States solely, principally, or incidentally to engage in activities which would be prejudicial to the public interest, or endanger the welfare, safety, or security of the United States;

(28) Aliens who are, or at any time have been, members of any of the following classes:

(A) Aliens who are anarchists;

(B) Aliens who advocate or teach, or who are members of or affiliated with any organization that advocates or teaches, opposition to all organized government;

(C) Aliens who are members of or affiliated with (i) the Communist Party of the United States, (ii) any other totalitarian party of the United States, (iii) the Communist Political Association, (iv) the Communist or any other totalitarian party of any state of the United States, (v) any section, subsidiary, branch, affiliate, or subdivision of any such association or party . . .,

. . . .(31) Any alien who at any time shall have, knowingly and for gain, encouraged, induced, assisted, abetted, or aided any other alien to enter or to try to enter the United States. . . .

. . . .(e) Whenever the President finds that the entry of any aliens or of any class of aliens into the United States would be detrimental to the interests of the United States, he may . . . .suspend the entry of all aliens or any class of aliens as immigrants or nonimmigrants, or impose on the entry of aliens any restrictions he may deem to be appropriate. . . .

13. Harry S. Truman's Veto of the McCarran-Walter Immigration Act, June 25, 1952 (82nd Congress, 2nd Session, House Document 520)

I return herewith, without my approval, H. R. 5678, the proposed Immigration and Nationality Act.

. . . .H. R. 5678 is an omnibus bill which would revise and codify all of our laws relating to immigration, naturalization, and nationality. A general revision and modernization of these laws unquestionably is needed and long overdue, particularly with respect to immigration. But this bill would not provide us with an immigration policy adequate for the present world situation. Indeed, the bill, taking all of its provisions together, would be a step backward and not a step forward. In view of the crying need for reform in the field of immigration, I deeply regret that I am unable to approve H. R. 5678.

. . . .In one respect, the bill recognizes the great international significance of our immigration and naturalization policy, and takes a step to improve existing laws. All racial bars to naturalization would be removed, and at least some minimum immigration quota would be afforded to each of the free nations of Asia.

I have long urged that racial or national barriers to naturalization be abolished. This was one of the recommendations in my civil rights message to Congress on February 2, 1948. The House of Representatives unanimously passed a bill to carry it out.

But now this most desirable provision comes before me embedded in a mass of legislation which would perpetuate injustices of long standing against many other nations, hamper the efforts we are making to rally the men of the East and West alike to the cause of freedom, and intensify the repressive and inhumane aspects of our immigration procedures. The price is too high, and, in good conscience, I cannot agree to pay it.

. . . .The bill would continue, practically without change, the national origins quota system, which was enacted into law in 1924 and put into effect in 1929. This quota system—always based upon assumptions at variance with our American ideals—long since out of date and more than ever unrealistic in the face of present world conditions.

. . . .As I stated in my message to Congress on March 24, 1952, ..."Our present system is not only inadequate to meet present emergency needs, it is also an obstacle to the development of an enlightened and satisfactory policy for the long-run future." . . .

With the idea of quotas in general there is no quarrel. Some numerical limitations must be set so that immigration will be within our capacity to absorb. But the overall limitation of numbers imposed by the national origins quota system is too small for our needs today, and the country-by-country limitations create a pattern that is insulting to large numbers of our finest citizens, irritating to our allies abroad, and foreign to our purposes and ideals.

. . . .The idea behind this discriminatory policy was, to put it baldly, that Americans with English names were better people and better citizens than Americans with Italian or Greek or Polish names. It was thought that people of west European origins made better citizens than Rumanians or Yugoslavs or Ukrainians or Hungarians or Balts or Austrians. Such a concept is utterly unworthy of our traditions and our ideals. It violates the great political doctrine of the Declaration of Independence that "all men are created equal." It denies the humanitarian creed inscribed beneath the Statue of Liberty proclaiming to all nations, "Give me your tired, your poor, your huddled masses yearning to breathe free." It repudiates our basic religious concepts, our belief in the brotherhood of man, and in the words of St. Paul that "there is neither Jew nor Greek, there is neither bond nor free . . .for ye are all one in Jesus Christ."

The basis of this quota system was false and unworthy in 1924. It is even worse now. At the present time this quota system keeps out the very people we want to bring in. It is incredible to me that in this year of 1952, we should again be enacting into law such a slur on the patriotism, the capacity, and the decency of a large of our citizenry.

. . . .Today, we are "protecting" ourselves, as we were in 1924, against being flooded by immigrants from eastern Europe. This is fantastic. The countries of eastern Europe have fallen under the Communist yoke—they are silenced, fenced off by barbed wire and minefields—no one passes their borders but at the risk of his life. We do not need to be protected from immigrants from these countries—on the contrary, we want to stretch out a helping hand, to save those who are brave enough to escape from barbarism, to welcome and restore them against the day when their countries will, as we hope, be free again. But this we cannot do, as we would like to do, because the quota for Poland is only 6,500, as against the 138,000 exiled Poles, all over Europe, who are asking to come to these shores; because the quota for the now subjugated Baltic countries is little more than 700—against the 23,000 Baltic refugees imploring us to admit them to a new life here; because the quota for Rumania is only 289, and some 30,000 Rumanians, who have managed to escape the labor camps and the mass deportations of their Soviet masters, have asked our help. These are only a few examples of the absurdity, the cruelty of carrying over into this year of 1952 the isolationist limitations of our 1924 law. . . .

In no other realm of our national life are we so hampered and stultified by the dead hand of the past as we are in this field of immigration. We do not limit our cities to their 1920 boundaries—we do not hold our corporations to their 1920 capitalizations—we welcome progress and change to meet changing conditions in every sphere of life, except in the field of immigration.

The time to shake off this dead weight of past mistakes is now. The time to develop a decent policy of immigration—a fitting instrument for our foreign policy and a true reflection of the ideals we stand for, at home and abroad—is now. . . .

. . . .I am asked to approve the reenactment of highly objectionable provisions now contained in the Internal Security Act of 1950—a measure passed over my veto shortly after the invasion of South Korea. Some of these provisions would empower the attorney general to deport any alien who has had a purpose to engage in activities "prejudicial to the public interest" or "subversive to national security." No standards or definitions are provided to guide discretion in the exercise of powers so sweeping. To punish undefined "activities" departs from traditional American insistence on established standards of guilt. To punish an undefined "purpose" is thought control.

These provisions are worse than the infamous Alien Act of 1798, passed in a time of national fear and distrust of foreigners, which gave the President power to deport an alien "dangerous to the peace and safety of the United States." Alien residents were thoroughly frightened and citizens much disturbed by that threat to liberty.

Such powers are inconsistent with our democratic ideals. . . . Once fully informed of such vast discretionary powers vested in the attorney general, Americans now would and should be just as alarmed as Americans were in 1798 over less drastic powers vested in the President.

These conclusions point to an underlying condition which deserves the most careful study. Should we not undertake a reassessment of our immigration policies and practices in the light of the conditions that face in the second half of the twentieth century The great popular interest which this bill has created, and the criticism which it has stirred up, demand an affirmative answer. I hope the Congress will agree to a careful reexamination of this entire matter.

To assist in this complex task, I suggest the creation of a representative commission of outstanding Americans to examine the basic assumptions of our immigration policy, the quota system and all that goes with it, the effect of our present immigration and nationality laws, their administration, and the ways in which they can be brought into line with our national ideals and our foreign policy. . . .

HARRY S. TRUMAN
The White House, *June 25, 1952.*

14. Excerpts from the Report of the President's Commission on Immigration and Naturalization

Introduction

. . .

We Hold These Truths . . .

1. America was founded upon the principle that all men are created equal, that differences of race, color, religion, or national origin should not be used to deny equal treatment or equal opportunity.

2. America historically has been the haven for the oppressed of other lands.

3. American national unity has been achieved without national uniformity.

4. Americans have believed in fair treatment for all.

5. America's philosophy has always been one of faith in our future and belief in progress.

6. American foreign policy seeks peace and freedom, mutual understanding and a high standard of living for ourselves and our world neighbors.

. . .

What We Believe

The Commission believes that immigration has given strength to this country not only in manpower, new industries, inventiveness, and prosperity, but also in new ideas and new culture. Immigrants have provided a continuous flow of creative abilities that have enriched our nation.

The Commission believes that an outstanding characteristic of the United States is its great cultural diversity within an overriding national unity. . . .

The Commission believes that our present immigration laws—

Flout fundamental American traditions and ideals,

Display a lack of faith in America's future,

Damage American prestige and position among other nations,

Ignore the lessons of the American way of life.

. . . .The Commission believes that our present immigration law should be completely rewritten.

. . .

Part VI: Conclusions and Recommendations

Conclusions

The immigrations and nationality law embodies policies and principles that are unwise and injurious to the nation.

It rests upon an attitude of hostility and distrust against all aliens.

It applies discriminations against human beings on account of national origin, race, creed and color.

It ignores the needs of the United States in domestic affairs and foreign policies.

It contains unnecessary and unreasonable restrictions and penalties against individuals.

It is badly drafted, confusing and in some respects unworkable.

It should be reconsidered and revised from beginning to end.

Recommendations

Throughout this report are various recommendations, appearing in the chapters in which particular subjects are discussed, the more important ones are briefly restated here. . . .

The Quota System

1. The national origins quota system should be abolished.

2. There should be a unified quota system, which would allocate visas without regard to national origin, race, creed, or color.

3. The maximum annual quota immigration should be one-sixth of 1 percent of the population of the United States, as determined by the most recent census. Under the 1950 census, quota immigration should be open to 215,162 immigrants annually, instead of the 154,657 now authorized.

4. All immigration and naturalization functions now in the Department of State and the Department of Justice should be consolidated into a new agency. . . .

5. The maximum annual quota of visas should be distributed . . . on the basis of the following five categories

The Right of Asylum
Reunion of Families
Needs in the United States
Special Needs in the Free World

Source: Whom We Shall Welcome, 1953
(pp. xii–xv, 263–64)

15. John F. Kennedy's Address to Congress, July 23, 1963

I am transmitting herewith, for the consideration of the Congress, legislation revising and modernizing our immigration laws. More than a decade has elapsed since the last substantial amendment to these laws. I believe there exists a compelling need for the Congress to re-examine and make certain changes in these laws.

The most urgent and fundamental reform I am recommending relates to the national origins system of selecting immigrants. Since 1924 it has been used to determine the number of quota immigrants permitted to enter the United States each year. Accordingly, although the legislation I am transmitting deals with many problems which require remedial action, it concentrates attention primarily upon revision of our quota system. The enactment of this legislation will not resolve all of our important problems in the field of immigration law. It will, however, provide a solid basis upon which we can build in developing an immigration law that serves the national interest and reflects in every detail the principles of equality and human dignity to which our nation subscribes.

Present legislation establishes a system of annual quotas to govern immigration from each country. Under this system, 156,700 quota immigrants are permitted to enter the United States each year. The system is based upon the national origins of the population of the United States in 1920. The use of the year 1920 is arbitrary. It rests upon the fact that this system was introduced in 1924 and the last prior census was in 1920. The use of a national origins system is without basis in either logic or reason. It neither satisfies a national need nor accomplishes an international purpose. In an age of interdependence of nations, such a system is an anachronism, for it discriminates among applicants for admission into the United States on the basis of accident of birth.

Because of the composition of our population in 1920, the system is heavily weighted in favor of immigration from northern Europe and severely limits immigrations from southern and eastern Europe and other parts of the world. An American citizen with a Greek father or mother must wait at least eighteen months to bring his parents here to join him. A citizen whose married son or daughter, or brother or sister, is Italian cannot obtain a quota number for an even longer time. Meanwhile, many thousands of quota numbers are wasted because they are not wanted or needed by nationals of the countries to which they are assigned.

I recommend that there be substituted for the national origins system a formula governing immigration to the United States which takes into account (1) the skills of the immigrant and their relationship to our need; (2) the family relationship between immigrant and persons already here, so that the reuniting of families is encouraged and (3) the priority of registration. Present law grants a preference to immigrants with special skills, education or training. It also grants a preference to various relatives of

United States citizens and lawfully resident aliens. But it does so only within a national origins quota. It should be modified so that those with the greatest ability to add to the national welfare, no matter where they were born, are granted the highest priority. The next priority should go to those who seek to be reunited with their relatives. As between applicants with equal claims the earliest registrant should be the first admitted.

Many problems of fairness and foreign policy are involved in replacing a system so long entrenched. The national origins system has produced large backlogs of applications in some country, and too rapid a change might, in a system of limited immigration, so drastically curtail immigration in some countries the only effect might be to shift the unfairness from one group to another. A reasonable time to adjust to any new system must be provided if individual hardships upon persons who were relying on the present system are to be avoided. In addition, any new system must have sufficient flexibility to allow adjustments to be made when it appears that immigrants from nations closely allied to the United States will be unduly restricted in their freedom to furnish the new seed population that has so long been a source of strength to our nation.

Accordingly I recommend:

First, that existing quotas be reduced gradually, at the rate of 20 percent a year. The quota numbers released each year should be placed in a quota reserve pool, to be distributed on a new basis.

Second, that natives in no one country receive over 10 percent of the total quota numbers authorized in any one year. This will insure that the pattern of immigration is not distorted by excessive demand from any one country.

Third, that the President be authorized, after receiving recommendations from a seven-man Immigration Board, to reserve up to 50 percent of the unallocated quota numbers to persons disadvantaged by the change in the quota system, and up to 20 percent to refugees whose sudden dislocation requires special treatment. The Immigration Board will be composed of two members appointed by the Speaker of the House of Representatives, two members appointed by the President Pro Tempore of the Senate, and three members appointed by the President. In addition to its responsibility for formulating recommendations regarding the use of the quota reserve pool, the Board will make a continuous study of our immigration policy. . .

. . In order to remove other existing barriers to the reuniting of families, I recommend two additional improvements in the law:

First, parents of American citizens, who now have a preferred quota status, should be accorded nonquota status.

Second, parents of alien residents in the United States, who now have no preference, should be accorded a preference, after skilled specialists and other relatives of citizens and alien residents.

These changes will have little effect on the number of immigrants admitted. They will have a major effect upon the individual hardships many of our citizens and residents now face in being separated from their parents.

In addition, I recommend the following changes in the law in order to correct certain deficiencies and improve its general application.

1. *Changes in the Preference Structure.* At present, the procedure under which specially skilled or trained workers are permitted to enter this country too often prevents talented people from applying for visas to enter the United States. It often deprives us of immigrants who would be helpful to our economy and our culture. This procedure should be liberalized so that highly trained or skilled persons may obtain a preference without requiring that they secure employment here before emigrating. In addition, I recommend that a special preference be accorded workers with lesser skills who can fill specific needs in short supply in this country.

2. *Nonquota status for natives of Jamaica, Trinidad and Tobago should be granted.* Under existing law, no numerical limitation is imposed upon the number of immigrants coming from Canada, Mexico, Cuba, Haiti, the Dominican Republic, the Canal Zone or any independent country in Central or South America. But the language of the statute restricts this privilege to persons born in countries in the Caribbean area which gained their independence prior to the date of the last major amendment to the immigration and nationality statutes, in 1952. This accidental discrimination against the newly independent nations of the Western Hemisphere should be corrected.

2. *Persons afflicted with mental health problems should be admitted provided certain standards are met.* Today, any person afflicted with a mental disease or mental defect, psychotic personality, or epilepsy, and any person who has suffered an attack of mental illness, can enter this country only if a private bill is enacted for his benefit. Families which are able and willing to care for a mentally ill child or parent are often forced to choose between living in the United

States and leaving their loved ones behind and not living in the United States but being able to see and care for their loved ones. Mental illness is not incurable. It should be treated like other illnesses. I recommend that the Attorney General, at his discretion and under proper safeguards, be authorized to waive those provisions of the law which prohibit the admission to the United States of persons with mental problems when they are close relatives of United States citizens and lawfully resident aliens.

3. *The Secretary of State should be authorized, in his discretion, to require reregistration of certain quota immigrant visa applicants and to regulate the time of payment of visa fees.* This authority would bring registration lists up to date, terminate the priority of applicants who have refused to accept a visa, and end the problem of "insurance" registrations by persons who have no present intention to emigrate. . .

As I have already indicated the measures I have outlined will not solve all problems of immigration. Many of them will require additional legislation: some cannot be solved by one country. But the legislation I am submitting will insure that progress will continue to be made toward our ideals and toward the realization of humanitarian objectives. The measures I have recommended will help eliminate discrimination between peoples and nations on a basis that is unrelated to any contribution that immigrants can make and is inconsistent with our traditions of welcome. Our investment in new citizens has always been a valuable source of strength.

Source: John F. Kennedy, *A Nation of Immigrants*, Appendix D, pp. 102–107.

16. California Proposition 187, 1994

SECTION 1. Findings and Declaration.

The People of California find and declare as follows:

That they have suffered and are suffering economic hardship caused by the presence of illegal aliens in this state.

That they have suffered and are suffering personal injury and damage caused by the criminal conduct of illegal aliens in this state.

That they have a right to the protection of their government from any person or persons entering this country unlawfully.

Therefore, the People of California declare their intention to provide for cooperation between their agencies of state and local government with the federal government, and to establish a system of required notification by and between such agencies to prevent illegal aliens in the United States from receiving benefits or public services in the State of California.

SECTION 5. Exclusion of Illegal Aliens from Public Social Services.

Section 10001.5 is added to the Welfare and Institutions Code, to read:

10001.5 (a) in order to carry out the intention of the People of California that only citizens of the United States and aliens lawfully admitted to the United States may receive the benefits of public social services and to ensure that all persons employed in the providing of those services shall diligently protect public funds from misuse, the provisions of this section are adopted.

(b) A person shall not receive any public services to which he or she may be otherwise entitled until the legal status of that person has been verified as one of the following:

(1) A citizen of the United States.
(2) An alien lawfully admitted as a permanent resident.
(3) An alien lawfully admitted for a temporary period of time.

(c) If any public entity in this state to whom a person has applied for public social services determines or reasonably suspects, based upon the information provided to it, that the person is an alien in the United States in violation of federal law, the following procedures shall be followed by the public entity:

(1) The entity shall not provide the person with benefits or services.
(2) The entity shall, in writing, notify the person of his or her apparent illegal immigration status, and that the person must either obtain legal status or leave the United States.
(3) The entity shall also notify the State Director of Social Services, the Attorney General of California, and the United States Immigration and Naturalization Service of the apparent illegal status, and shall provide additional information that may be requested by any other public entity.

SECTION 6. Exclusion of Illegal Aliens from Publicly Funded Health Care.

Chapter 1.3 . . . is added to Part 1 of Division 1 of the Health and Safety Code, to read:

. . . 130. (a) In order to carry out the intention of the People of California that, excepting emergency medical care as required by federal law, only citizens of the United States and aliens lawfully admitted to the United States may receive the benefits of publicly-funded health care, and to ensure that all persons employed in the providing of those services shall diligently protect public funds from misuse, the provisions of this section are adopted.

(b) A person shall not receive any health care services from a publicly-funded health care facility, to which he or she is otherwise entitled until the legal status of that person has been verified as one of the following:

(1) A citizen of the United States.
(2) An alien lawfully admitted as a permanent resident.
(3) An alien lawfully admitted for a temporary period of time.

. . .

SECTION 7. Exclusion of Illegal Aliens from Public Elementary and Secondary Schools.

Section 48215 is added to the Education Code, to read:
. . . 48215. (a) No public elementary or secondary school shall admit, or permit the attendance of, any child who is not a citizen of the United States, an alien lawfully admitted as a permanent resident, or a person who is otherwise authorized under federal law to be present in the United States.

(b) Commencing January 1, 1995, each school district shall verify the legal status of each child enrolling in the school district for the first time in order to ensure the enrollment or attendance only of citizens, aliens lawfully admitted as permanent residents, or persons who are otherwise authorized to be present in the United States.

. . . (e) Each school district shall provide information to the State Superintendent of Public Instruction, the Attorney General of California, and the United States Immigration and Naturalization Service regarding any enrollee or pupil, or parent or guardian, attending a public elementary or secondary school in the school district

determined or reasonably suspected to be in violation of federal immigration laws.

. . .

SECTION 8. Exclusion of Illegal Aliens from Public Postsecondary Educational Institutions.
Section 66010.8 is added to the Education Code, to read:
66010.8 (a) No public institution of postsecondary education shall admit, enroll, or permit the attendance of any person who is not a citizen of the United States, an alien lawfully admitted as a permanent resident in the United States, or a person who is otherwise authorized to be present in the United States.

. . .

SECTION 9. Attorney General Cooperation with the INS.

Section 53069.65 is added to the Government Code, to read:
. . . Whenever the state or a city, or a county, or any other legally authorized local government entity with jurisdictional boundaries reports the presence of a person who is suspected of being present in the United States in violation of federal immigration laws to the Attorney General of California, that report shall be transmitted to the United States Immigration and Naturalization Service. The Attorney General shall be responsible for maintaining on-going and accurate records of such reports, and shall provide any additional information that may be requested by any other government agency.

. . .

17. The Smart Border Declaration and Action Plan, 2001
The Smart Border Declaration

Building a Smart Border for the 21st Century on the Foundation of a North American Zone of Confidence

The terrorist actions of September 11 were an attack on our common commitment to democracy, the rule of law and a free and open economy. They highlighted a threat to our public and economic security. They require our governments to develop new approaches to meet these challenges. This declaration commits our governments to work together to address these threats to our people, our institutions and our prosperity.

Public security and economic security are mutually reinforcing. By working together to develop a zone of confidence against terrorist activity, we create a unique opportunity to build a smart border for the 21st century; a border that securely facilitates the free flow of people and commerce; a border that reflects the largest trading relationship in the world.

Our countries have a long history of cooperative border management. This tradition facilitates both countries' immediate responses to the attacks of September 11. It is the foundation on which we continue to base our cooperation, recognizing that our current and future prosperity and security depend on a border that operates efficiently and effectively under all circumstances.

Action Plan

The attached Action Plan for Creating a Secure and Smart Border includes the measures already identified by our colleagues as well as new initiatives. Four pillars support the action plan:

1. The secure flow of people

We will implement systems to collaborate in identifying security risks while expediting the flow of low risk travelers.

We will identify security threats before they arrive in North America through collaborative approaches to reviewing crew and passenger manifests, managing refugees, and visa policy coordination.

We will establish a secure system to allow low risk frequent travelers between our countries to move efficiently across the border.

2. The Secure Flow of Goods

We will implement a system to collaborate in identifying high risk goods while expediting a flow of low risk goods.

We will identify security threats arriving from abroad by developing common standards for screening cargo before it arrives in North America, while working to clear goods at the first port of entry.

We will adopt compatible security standards at production and distribution facilities to minimize security threats. We will expedite the flow of low risk traffic between our countries by harmonizing commercial processes at the border.

We will expedite the flow of low risk goods between our countries by establishing secure procedures to clear goods from the border, including at rail yards and at marine ports.

3. Secure Infrastructure

We will relieve congestion at key crossing points by investing reciprocally in border infrastructure and identifying technological solutions that will help to speed movement across the border.

We will identify and minimize threats to our critical infrastructure, including the airports, ports, bridges, tunnels, pipelines and powerlines that link our countries.

4. Coordination and Information sharing in the Enforcement of these objectives.

We will put the necessary tools and legislative framework in place to ensure that information and intelligence is shared in a timely and coherent way within our respective countries as well as between them.

Next Steps

We will meet again early in the new year to review the critical paths that we have asked our officials to develop for realizing each of the objectives set out in the action plan. We will consult regularly to ensure continued progress on this plan to achieve the goals outlined as quickly as possible.

This joint action plan is an important step. Our governments are committed to building on this plan to continually identify and implement measures that can be taken to secure a smart border.

These measures are regarded by both governments as matters of the highest priority.

Action Plan for Creating a Secure and Smart Border

THE SECURE FLOW OF PEOPLE

1. Biometric Identifiers

Jointly develop on an urgent basis common biometric identifiers in documentation such as permanent resident cards, NEXUS, and other travel documents to ensure greater security.

2. Permanent Resident Cards

Develop and deploy a secure card for permanent residents which includes a biometric identifier.

3. Single Alternative Inspection System

Resume NEXUS pilot program, with appropriate security measures, for two-way movement of pre-approved travelers at Sarnia-Port Huron, complete pilot project evaluation and expand a single program to other areas along the land border. Discuss expansion to air travel.

4. Refugee/Asylum Processing

Review refugee/asylum practices and procedures to ensure that applicants are thoroughly screened for security risks and take necessary steps to share information on refugee and asylum claimants.

5. Handling of Refugee/Asylum Claims

Negotiate a safe third-country agreement to enhance the handling of refugee claims.

6. Visa Policy Coordination

Initiate joint review of respective visa waiver lists and share look-out lists at visa issuing offices.

7. Air Preclearance

Finalize plans/authority necessary to implement the Preclearance Agreement signed in January 2001. Resume intransit preclearance at Vancouver and expand to other airports per Annex I of the Agreement.

8. Advance Passenger Information / Passenger Name Record

Share Advance Passenger Information and agreed-to Passenger Name Records on flights between Canada and the United States, including in-transit flights. Explore means to identify risks posed by passengers on international flights arriving in each other's territory.

9. Joint Passenger Analysis Units

Establish joint units at key international airports in Canada and the United States.

10. Ferry Terminals

Review customs and immigration presence and practices at international ferry terminals.

11. Compatible Immigration Databases.

Develop jointly an automated database, such as Canada's Support System for Intelligence, as a platform for information exchange, and enhance sharing of intelligence and trend analysis.

12. Immigration Officers Overseas

Increase number of Canadian and U.S. immigration officers at airports overseas and enhance joint training of airline personnel.

13. International Cooperation

Undertake technical assistance to source and transit countries.

THE SECURE FLOW OF GOODS

14. Harmonized Commercial Processing

Establish complementary systems for commercial processing, including audit-based programs and partnerships with industry to increase security. Explore the merits of a common program.

15. Clearance away from the Border

Develop an integrated approach to improve security and facilitate trade through away-from-the-border processing for truck/rail cargo (and crews), including inland preclearance/post-clearance, international zones and pre-processing centers at the border, and maritime port intransit preclearance.

16. Joint Facilities

Establish criteria, under current legislation and regulations, for the creation of small, remote joint border facilities. Examine the legal and operational issues associated with the establishment of international zones and joint facilities, including armed protection or the arming of law enforcement officers in such zones and facilities.

17. Customs Data

Sign the Agreement on Sharing Data Related to Customs Fraud, exchange agreed upon customs data pursuant to NAFTA, and discuss what additional commercial and trade data should be shared for national security purposes.

18. Intransit Container Targeting at Seaports

Jointly target intransit marine containers arriving in Canada/U.S. by exchanging information and analysts. Work in partnership with the industry to develop advance electronic commercial manifest data for marine containers arriving from overseas.

SECURE INFRASTRUCTURE

19. Infrastructure Improvements

Work to secure resources for joint and coordinated physical and

technological improvements to key border points and trade corridors

aimed at overcoming traffic management and growth challenges,

including dedicated lanes and border modeling exercises.

20. Intelligent Transportation Systems

Deploy interoperable technologies in support of other initiatives to facilitate the secure movement of goods and people, such as transponder applications and electronic container seals.

21. Critical Infrastructure Protection

Conduct binational threat assessment on trans-border infrastructure and identify necessary additional protection measures, and initiate assessment for transportation networks and other critical infrastructure.

22. Aviation Security

Finalize Federal Aviation Administration-Transport Canada agreement on comparability/equivalence of security and training standards.

COORDINATION AND INFORMATION SHARING IN THE ENFORCEMENT OF THESE OBJECTIVES

23. Integrated Border and Marine Enforcement Teams

Expand IBET/IMET to other areas of the border and enhance communication and coordination.

24. Joint Enforcement Coordination

Work toward ensuring comprehensive and permanent coordination of law enforcement, anti-terrorism efforts and information sharing, such as by strengthening the Cross-Border Crime Forum and reinvigorating Project Northstar.

25. Integrated Intelligence

Establish joint teams to analyze and disseminate information and intelligence, and produce threat and intelligence assessments. Initiate discussions regarding a Canadian presence in the U.S. Foreign Terrorist Tracking Task Force.

26. Fingerprints

Implement the Memorandum of Understanding to supply equipment and training that will enable the RCMP to access FBI fingerprint data directly via real time electronic link.

27. Removal of Deportees

Address legal and operational challenges to joint removals, and coordinate initiatives to encourage uncooperative countries to accept their nationals.

28. Counter-Terrorism Legislation

Bring into force legislation on terrorism, including measures for the designation of terrorist organizations.

29. Freezing of Terrorist Assets

Exchange advance information on designated individuals and organizations in a timely manner.

30. Joint Training and Exercises

Increase dialogue and commitment for the training and exercise programs needed to implement the joint response to terrorism guidelines. Joint counter-terrorism training and exercises are essential to building and sustaining effective efforts to combat terrorism and to build public confidence.

Ottawa, Canada, December 12, 2001

18. Supreme Court Decision in *Zadvydas v. Davis*, June 28, 2001

SUPREME COURT OF THE UNITED STATES

Nos. 99–7791 and 00–38
Kestutis Zadvydas, Petitioner
v.
Christine G. Davis and Immigration and Naturalization Service

ON WRIT OF CERTIORARI TO THE UNITED STATES COURT OF APPEALS FOR THE FIFTH CIRCUIT

ON WRIT OF CERTIORARI TO THE UNITED STATES COURT OF APPEALS FOR THE NINTH CIRCUIT

Justice Breyer delivered the opinion of the Court.

When an alien has been found to be unlawfully present in the United States and a final order of removal has been entered, the Government ordinarily secures the alien's removal during a subsequent 90-day statutory "removal period," during which time the alien normally is held in custody.

A special statute authorizes further detention if the Government fails to remove the alien during those 90 days. It says:

"An alien ordered removed [1] who is inadmissible . . . [2] [or] removable [as a result of violations of status requirements or entry conditions, violations of criminal law, or reasons of security or foreign policy] or [3] who has been determined by the Attorney General to be a risk to the community or unlikely to comply with the order of removal, may be detained beyond the removal period and, if released, shall be subject to [certain] terms of supervision. . . ."

In these cases, we must decide whether this post-removal-period statute authorizes the Attorney General to detain a removable alien indefinitely beyond the removal period or only for a period reasonably necessary to secure the alien's removal. We deal here with aliens who were admitted to the United States but subsequently ordered removed. Aliens who have not yet gained initial admission to this country would present a very different question. See infra, at 12–14. Based on our conclusion that indefinite detention of aliens in the former category would raise serious constitutional concerns, we construe the statute to contain an implicit "reasonable time" limitation, the application of which is subject to federal court review.

I

A

The post-removal-period detention statute is one of a related set of statutes and regulations that govern detention during and after removal proceedings. While removal proceedings are in progress, most aliens may be released on bond or paroled. 66 Stat. 204, as added and amended, 110 Stat. 3009–585, 8 U.S.C. § 1226(a)(2), (c) (1994 ed., Supp. V). After entry of a final removal order and during the 90-day removal period, however, aliens must be held in custody. §1231(a)(2). Subsequently, as the post-removal-period statute provides, the Government "may" continue to detain an alien who still remains here or release that alien under supervision. §1231(a)(6).

. . .

B

1

We consider two separate instances of detention. The first concerns Kestutis Zadvydas, a resident alien who was born, apparently of Lithuanian parents, in a displaced persons camp in Germany in 1948. When he was eight years old, Zadvydas immigrated to the United States with his parents and other family members, and he has lived here ever since.

Zadvydas has a long criminal record, involving drug crimes, attempted robbery, attempted burglary, and theft. He has a history of flight, from both criminal and deportation proceedings. Most recently, he was convicted of possessing, with intent to distribute, cocaine; sentenced to 16 years' imprisonment; released on parole after two years; taken into INS custody; and, in 1994, ordered deported to Germany. See 8 U.S.C. § 1251(a)(2) (1988 ed., Supp. V) (delineating crimes that make alien deportable).

In 1994, Germany told the INS that it would not accept Zadvydas because he was not a German citizen. Shortly thereafter, Lithuania refused to accept Zadvydas because he was neither a Lithuanian citizen nor a permanent resident. In 1996, the INS asked the Dominican Republic (Zadvydas' wife's country) to accept him, but this effort proved unsuccessful. In 1998, Lithuania rejected, as inadequately documented, Zadvydas' effort to obtain Lithuanian citizenship based on his parents' citizenship; Zadvydas' reapplication is apparently still pending.

The INS kept Zadvydas in custody after expiration of the removal period. In September 1995, Zadvydas filed a petition for a writ of habeas corpus under 28 U.S.C. § 2241 challenging his continued detention. In October 1997, a Federal District Court granted that writ and ordered him released under supervision. *Zadvydas v. Caplinger*, 986 F. Supp. 1011, 1027—1028 (ED La.). In its view, the Government would never succeed in its efforts to remove Zadvydas from the United States, leading to his permanent confinement, contrary to the Constitution.

The Fifth Circuit reversed this decision. *Zadvydas v. Underdown*, 185 F.3d 279 (1999). It concluded that Zadvydas' detention did not violate the Constitution because eventual deportation was not "impossible," good faith efforts to remove him from the United States continued, and his detention was subject to periodic administrative review. *Id.*, at 294, 297. The Fifth Circuit stayed its mandate pending potential review in this Court.

2

The second case is that of Kim Ho Ma. Ma was born in Cambodia in 1977. When he was two, his family fled, taking him to refugee camps in Thailand and the Philippines and eventually to the United States, where he has lived as a resident alien since the age of seven. In 1995, at age 17, Ma was involved in a gang-related shooting, convicted of manslaughter, and sentenced to 38 months' imprisonment. He served two years, after which he was released into INS custody.

In light of his conviction of an "aggravated felony," Ma was ordered removed. See 8 U.S.C. § 1101(a)(43)(F) (defining certain violent crimes as aggravated felonies), 1227(a)(2)(A)(iii) (1994 ed., Supp. IV) (aliens convicted of aggravated felonies are deportable). The 90-day removal period expired in early 1999, but the INS continued to keep Ma in custody, because, in light of his former gang membership, the nature of his crime, and his planned participation in a prison hunger strike, it was "unable to conclude that Mr. Ma would remain nonviolent and not violate the conditions of release."

In 1999 Ma filed a petition for a writ of habeas corpus under 28 U.S.C. § 2241. A panel of five judges in the Federal District Court for the Western District of Washington, considering Ma's and about 100 similar cases together, issued a joint order holding that the Constitution forbids post-removal-period detention unless there is "a realistic chance that [the] alien will be deported" (thereby permitting classification of the detention as "in aid of deportation"). *Binh Phan v. Reno*, 56 F. Supp. 2d 1149, 1156 (1999). The District Court then held an evidentiary hearing, decided that there was no "realistic chance" that Cambodia (which has no repatriation treaty with the United States) would accept Ma, and ordered Ma released.

The Ninth Circuit affirmed Ma's release. *Kim Ho Ma v. Reno*, 208 F.3d 815 (2000). It concluded, based in part on constitutional concerns, that the statute did not authorize detention for more than a "reasonable time" beyond the 90-day period authorized for removal. And, given the lack of a repatriation agreement with Cambodia, that time had expired upon passage of the 90 days. *Id.*, at 830–831.

3

Zadvydas asked us to review the decision of the Fifth Circuit authorizing his continued detention. The Government asked us to review the decision of the Ninth Circuit forbidding Ma's continued detention. We granted writs in both cases, agreeing to consider both statutory and related constitutional questions. See also *Duy Dac Ho v. Greene*, 204 F.3d 1045, 1060 (CA10 2000) (upholding Attorney General's statutory and constitutional authority to detain alien indefinitely). We consolidated the two cases for argument; and we now decide them together.

II

We note at the outset that the primary federal habeas corpus statute, 28 U.S.C. § 2241 confers jurisdiction upon the federal courts to hear these cases. See § 2241(c)(3) (authorizing any person to claim in federal court that he or she is being held "in custody in violation of the Constitution or laws … of the United States"). Before 1952, the federal courts considered challenges to the lawfulness of immigration-related detention, including challenges to the validity of a deportation order, in habeas proceedings. Beginning in 1952, an alternative method for review of deportation orders, namely actions brought in federal district court under the Administrative Procedure Act (APA), became available. And in 1961 Congress replaced district court APA review with initial deportation order review in courts of appeals. . . . The 1961 Act specified that federal habeas courts were also available to hear statutory and constitutional challenges to deportation (and exclusion) orders. These statutory changes left habeas untouched as the basic method for obtaining review of continued custody after a deportation order had become final. See *Cheng Fan Kwok v. INS*, 392 U.S. 206, 212, 215–216 (1968) (holding that §1105a(a) applied only to challenges to determinations made during deportation proceedings and motions to reopen those proceedings).

More recently, Congress has enacted several statutory provisions that limit the circumstances in which judicial review of deportation decisions is available. But none applies here. One provision, 8 U.S.C. § 1231(h) (1994 ed., Supp. V), simply forbids courts to construe that section "to create any … procedural right or benefit that is legally enforceable"; it does not deprive an alien of the right to rely on 28 U.S.C. §2241 to challenge detention that is without statutory authority.

Another provision, 8 U.S.C. § 1252(a)(2)(B)(ii) (1994 ed., Supp. V), says that "no court shall have jurisdiction to review" decisions "specified … to be in the discretion of the Attorney General." The aliens here, however, do not seek review of the Attorney General's exercise of discretion; rather, they challenge the extent of the Attorney General's authority under the post-removal-period detention statute. And the extent of that authority is not a matter of discretion. See also, e.g., § 1226(e) (applicable to certain detention-related decisions *in period preceding entry*

of final removal order); § 1231(a)(4)(D) (applicable to assertion of causes or claims *under § 1231(a)(4)*, which is not at issue here); §§ 1252(a)(1), (a)(2)(C) (applicable to judicial review of "final order[s] of removal"); § 1252(g) (applicable to decisions "to commence proceedings, adjudicate cases, or execute removal orders").

We conclude that § 2241 habeas corpus proceedings remain available as a forum for statutory and constitutional challenges to post-removal-period detention. And we turn to the merits of the aliens' claims.

III

The post-removal-period detention statute applies to certain categories of aliens who have been ordered removed, namely inadmissible aliens, criminal aliens, aliens who have violated their nonimmigrant status conditions, and aliens removable for certain national security or foreign relations reasons, as well as any alien "who has been determined by the Attorney General to be a risk to the community or unlikely to comply with the order of removal." see .. 8 CFR § 241.4(a) (2001). It says that an alien who falls into one of these categories "may be detained beyond the removal period and, if released, shall be subject to [certain] terms of supervision." . . .

The Government argues that the statute means what it literally says. It sets no "limit on the length of time beyond the removal period that an alien who falls within one of the Section 1231(a)(6) categories may be detained." Hence, "whether to continue to detain such an alien and, if so, in what circumstances and for how long" is up to the Attorney General, not up to the courts.

"[I]t is a cardinal principle" of statutory interpretation, however, that when an Act of Congress raises "a serious doubt" as to its constitutionality, "this Court will first ascertain whether a construction of the statute is fairly possible by which the question may be avoided." . . . We have read significant limitations into other immigration statutes in order to avoid their constitutional invalidation. See *United States v. Witkovich*, 353 U.S. 194, 195, 202 (1957) (construing a grant of authority to the Attorney General to ask aliens whatever questions he "deem[s] fit and proper" as limited to questions "reasonably calculated to keep the Attorney General advised regarding the continued availability for departure of aliens whose deportation is overdue"). For similar reasons, we read an implicit limitation into the statute before us. In our view, the statute, read in light of the Constitution's demands, limits an alien's post-removal-period detention to a period reasonably necessary to bring about that alien's removal from the United States. It does not permit indefinite detention.

A

A statute permitting indefinite detention of an alien would raise a serious constitutional problem. The Fifth Amendment's Due Process Clause forbids the Government to "depriv[e]" any "person . . . of . . . liberty . . . without due process of law." Freedom from imprisonment—from government custody, detention, or other forms of physical restraint—lies at the heart of the liberty that Clause protects. See *Foucha v. Louisiana*, 504 U.S. 71, 80 (1992). And this Court has said that government detention violates that Clause unless the detention is ordered in a criminal proceeding with adequate procedural protections, see *United States v. Salerno*, 481 U.S. 739, 746 (1987), or, in certain special and "narrow" non-punitive "circumstances," *Foucha, supra*, at 80, where a special justification, such as harm-threatening mental illness, outweighs the "individual's constitutionally protected interest in avoiding physical restraint." *Kansas v. Hendricks*, 521 U.S. 346, 356 (1997) The proceedings at issue here are civil, not criminal, and we assume that they are nonpunitive in purpose and effect. There is no sufficiently strong special justification here for indefinite civil detention—at least as administered under this statute. The statute, says the Government, has two regulatory goals: "ensuring the appearance of aliens at future immigration proceedings" and "[p]reventing danger to the community." But by definition the first justification—preventing flight—is weak or nonexistent where removal seems a remote possibility at best. As this Court said in *Jackson v. Indiana*, 406 U.S. 715 (1972), where detention's goal is no longer practically attainable, detention no longer "bear[s] [a] reasonable relation to the purpose for which the individual [was] committed." *Id.*, at 738.

The second justification—protecting the community—does not necessarily diminish in force over time. But we have upheld preventive detention based on dangerousness only when limited to specially dangerous individuals and subject to strong procedural protections. Compare *Hendricks, supra*, at 368 (upholding scheme that imposes detention upon "a small segment of particularly dangerous individuals" and provides "strict procedural safeguards") and *Salerno, supra*, at 747, 750–752 (in upholding pretrial detention, stressing "stringent time limitations," the fact that detention is reserved for the "most serious of crimes," the requirement of proof of dangerousness by clear and convincing evidence, and the presence of judicial safeguards), with *Foucha, supra*, at 81–83 (striking down insanity-related detention system that placed burden on detainee to prove nondangerousness). In cases in which preventive detention is of potentially *indefinite* duration, we have also demanded that the dangerousness rationale be accompanied by some other special circumstance,

such as mental illness, that helps to create the danger. See *Hendricks, supra*, at 358, 368.

The civil confinement here at issue is not limited, but potentially permanent. . . . The provision authorizing detention does not apply narrowly to "a small segment of particularly dangerous individuals," *Hendricks, supra*, at 368, say suspected terrorists, but broadly to aliens ordered removed for many and various reasons, including tourist visa violations. . . , cf. *Hendricks*, 521 U.S., at 357–358 (only individuals with "past sexually violent behavior and a present mental condition that creates a likelihood of such conduct in the future" may be detained). And, once the flight risk justification evaporates, the only special circumstance present is the alien's removable status itself, which bears no relation to a detainee's dangerousness. . . .

Moreover, the sole procedural protections available to the alien are found in administrative proceedings, where the alien bears the burden of proving he is not dangerous, without (in the Government's view) significant later judicial review. This Court has suggested, however, that the Constitution may well preclude granting "an administrative body the unreviewable authority to make determinations implicating fundamental rights." . . . The Constitution demands greater procedural protection even for property. See *South Carolina v. Regan*, 465 U.S. 367, 393 (1984) (O'Connor, J., concurring in judgment); *Phillips v. Commissioner*, 283 U.S. 589, 595–597 (1931) (Brandeis, J.). The serious constitutional problem arising out of a statute that, in these circumstances, permits an indefinite, perhaps permanent, deprivation of human liberty without any such protection is obvious.

The Government argues that, from a constitutional perspective, alien status itself can justify indefinite detention, and points to *Shaughnessy v. United States ex rel.* Mezei, 345 U.S. 206 (1953), as support. That case involved a once lawfully admitted alien who left the United States, returned after a trip abroad, was refused admission, and was left on Ellis Island, indefinitely detained there because the Government could not find another country to accept him. The Court held that Mezei's detention did not violate the Constitution. *Id.*, at 215–216.

Although Mezei, like the present cases, involves indefinite detention, it differs from the present cases in a critical respect. As the Court emphasized, the alien's extended departure from the United States required him to seek entry into this country once again. His presence on Ellis Island did not count as entry into the United States. Hence, he was "treated," for constitutional purposes, "as if stopped at the border." *Id.*, at 213, 215. And that made all the difference.

The distinction between an alien who has effected an entry into the United States and one who has never entered runs throughout immigration law. See *Kaplan v. Tod*, 267 U.S. 228, 230 (1925) (despite nine years' presence in the United States, an "excluded" alien "was still in theory of law at the boundary line and had gained no foothold in the United States"); *Leng May Ma v. Barber*, 357 U.S. 185, 188–190 (1958) (alien "paroled" into the United States pending admissibility had not effected an "entry"). It is well established that certain constitutional protections available to persons inside the United States are unavailable to aliens outside of our geographic borders. See *United States v. Verdugo-Urquidez*, 494 U.S. 259, 269 (1990) (Fifth Amendment's protections do not extend to aliens outside the territorial boundaries); *Johnson v. Eisentrager*, 339 U.S. 763, 784 (1950) (same). But once an alien enters the country, the legal circumstance changes, for the Due Process Clause applies to all "persons" within the United States, including aliens, whether their presence here is lawful, unlawful, temporary, or permanent. See *Plyler v. Doe*, 457 U.S. 202, 210 (1982); Mathews v. Diaz, 426 U.S. 67, 77 (1976); *Kwong Hai Chew v. Colding*, 344 U.S. 590, 596–598, and n. 5 (1953); *Yick Wo v. Hopkins*, 118 U.S. 356, 369 (1886); cf. *Mezei, supra*, at 212 ("[A]liens who have once passed through our gates, even illegally, may be expelled only after proceedings conforming to traditional standards of fairness encompassed in due process of law"). Indeed, this Court has held that the Due Process Clause protects an alien subject to a final order of deportation, see *Wong Wing v. United States*, 163 U.S. 228, 238 (1896), though the nature of that protection may vary depending upon status and circumstance. . . .

In *Wong Wing, supra*, the Court held unconstitutional a statute that imposed a year of hard labor upon aliens subject to a final deportation order. That case concerned substantive protections for aliens who had been ordered removed, not procedural protections for aliens whose removability was being determined. Compare *post*, at 2–3 (Scalia, J., dissenting). The Court held that punitive measures could not be imposed upon aliens ordered removed because "all persons within the territory of the United States are entitled to the protection" of the Constitution. 163 U.S., at 238 (citing *Yick Wo*, supra, at 369 (holding that equal protection guarantee applies to Chinese aliens)); see also *Witkovich*, 353 U.S., at 199, 201 (construing statute which applied to aliens ordered deported in order to avoid substantive constitutional problems). And contrary to Justice Scalia's characterization, see *post*, at 2–4, in *Mezei* itself, both this Court's rejection of Mezei's challenge to the procedures by which he was deemed excludable and its rejection of his challenge to continued detention rested upon a basic territorial distinction. See *Mezei, supra*, at 215 (holding that Mezei's presence on Ellis Island was not "considered

a landing" and did "not affec[t]" his legal or constitutional status (internal quotation marks omitted).
. . . .

The Government also looks for support to cases holding that Congress has "plenary power" to create immigration law, and that the judicial branch must defer to executive and legislative branch decisionmaking. . . . In these cases, we focus upon those limitations. In doing so, we nowhere deny the right of Congress to remove aliens, to subject them to supervision with conditions when released from detention, or to incarcerate them where appropriate for violations of those conditions. . . . The question before us is not one of " 'confer[ring] on those admitted the right to remain against the national will' " or " 'sufferance of aliens' " who should be removed. . . . Rather, the issue we address is whether aliens that the Government finds itself unable to remove are to be condemned to an indefinite term of imprisonment within the United States.
. . . .

Finally, the Government argues that, whatever liberty interest the aliens possess, it is "greatly diminished" by their lack of a legal right to "liv[e] at large in this country." Brief for Respondents in No. 99–7791, at 47; see also *post*, at 2–3 (Scalia, J., dissenting) (characterizing right at issue as "right of release into this country"). The choice, however, is not between imprisonment and the alien "living at large." Brief for Respondents in No. 99–7791, at 47. It is between imprisonment and supervision under release conditions that may not be violated. . . . And, for the reasons we have set forth, we believe that an alien's liberty interest is, at the least, strong enough to raise a serious question as to whether, irrespective of the procedures used, cf. *post*, at 18–21 (Kennedy, J., dissenting), the Constitution permits detention that is indefinite and potentially permanent.

B

Despite this constitutional problem, if "Congress has made its intent" in the statute "clear, 'we must give effect to that intent.'" . . . We cannot find here, however, any clear indication of congressional intent to grant the Attorney General the power to hold indefinitely in confinement an alien ordered removed. And that is so whether protecting the community from dangerous aliens is a primary or (as we believe) secondary statutory purpose. Cf. *post*, at 4, 5–6 (Kennedy, J., dissenting). After all, the provision is part of a statute that has as its basic purpose effectuating an alien's removal. Why should we assume that Congress saw the alien's dangerousness as unrelated to this purpose?

The Government points to the statute's word "may." But while "may" suggests discretion, it does not necessarily suggest unlimited discretion. In that respect the word "may" is ambiguous. Indeed, if Congress had meant to authorize long-term detention of unremovable aliens, it certainly could have spoken in clearer terms. Compare 8 U.S.C. § 1537(b)(2)(C) (1994 ed., Supp. V) ("If no country is willing to receive" a terrorist alien ordered removed, "the Attorney General may, notwithstanding any other provision of law, retain the alien in custody" and must review the detention determination every six months).   The Government points to similar related statutes that require detention of criminal aliens during removal proceedings and the removal period, and argues that these show that mandatory detention is the rule while discretionary release is the narrow exception. . . . But the statute before us applies not only to terrorists and criminals, but also to ordinary visa violators, see *supra*, at 11; and, more importantly, post-removal-period detention, unlike detention pending a determination of removability or during the subsequent 90-day removal period, has no obvious termination point.
. . . .

In early 1996, Congress explicitly expanded the group of aliens subject to mandatory detention, eliminating provisions that permitted release of criminal aliens who had at one time been lawfully admitted to the United States . . . . And later that year Congress enacted the present law, which liberalizes pre-existing law by shortening the removal period from six months to 90 days, mandates detention of certain criminal aliens during the removal proceedings and for the subsequent 90-day removal period, and adds the post-removal-period provision here at issue. . . .

We have found nothing in the history of these statutes that clearly demonstrates a congressional intent to authorize indefinite, perhaps permanent, detention. Consequently, interpreting the statute to avoid a serious constitutional threat, we conclude that, once removal is no longer reasonably foreseeable, continued detention is no longer authorized by statute. See 1 E. Coke, Institutes *70b ("*Cessante ratione legis cessat ipse lex*") (the rationale of a legal rule no longer being applicable, that rule itself no longer applies).

IV

The Government seems to argue that, even under our interpretation of the statute, a federal habeas court would have to accept the Government's view about whether the implicit statutory limitation is satisfied in a particular case, conducting little or no independent review of the matter. In our view, that is not so. Whether a set of particular circumstances amounts to detention within, or beyond, a period reasonably necessary to secure removal is determinative of whether the detention is, or is not, pursuant to statutory authority. The basic federal habeas corpus statute grants the federal courts authority to answer that question. . . . In doing so the courts carry out what this Court has described as the "historic purpose of the writ," namely "to relieve detention by executive authorities without judicial trial.". . .

In answering that basic question, the habeas court must ask whether the detention in question exceeds a period reasonably necessary to secure removal. It should measure reasonableness primarily in terms of the statute's basic purpose, namely assuring the alien's presence at the moment of removal. Thus, if removal is not reasonably foreseeable, the court should hold continued detention unreasonable and no longer authorized by statute. In that case, of course, the alien's release may and should be conditioned on any of the various forms of supervised release that are appropriate in the circumstances, and the alien may no doubt be returned to custody upon a violation of those conditions. . . . And if removal is reasonably foreseeable, the habeas court should consider the risk of the alien's committing further crimes as a factor potentially justifying confinement within that reasonable removal period. See *supra*, at 10–11.
. . . .

While an argument can be made for confining any presumption to 90 days, we doubt that when Congress shortened the removal period to 90 days in 1996 it believed that all reasonably foreseeable removals could be accomplished in that time. We do have reason to believe, however, that Congress previously doubted the constitutionality of detention for more than six months. . . . Consequently, for the sake of uniform administration in the federal courts, we recognize that period. After this 6-month period, once the alien provides good reason to believe that there is no significant likelihood of removal in the reasonably foreseeable future, the Government must respond with evidence sufficient to rebut that showing. And for detention to remain reasonable, as the period of prior post-removal confinement grows, what counts as the "reasonably foreseeable future" conversely would have to shrink. This 6-month presumption, of course, does not mean that every alien not removed must be released after six months. To the contrary, an alien may be held in confinement until it has been determined that there is no significant likelihood of removal in the reasonably foreseeable future.

V

The Fifth Circuit held Zadvydas' continued detention lawful as long as "good faith efforts to effectuate . . . deportation continue" and Zadvydas failed to show that deportation will prove "impossible." 185 F.3d, at 294, 297. But this standard would seem to require an alien seeking release to show the absence of any prospect of removal—no matter how unlikely or unforeseeable—which demands more than our reading of the statute can bear. The Ninth Circuit held that the Government was required to release Ma from detention because there was no reasonable likelihood of his removal in the foreseeable future. But its conclusion may have rested solely upon the "absence" of an "extant or pending" repatriation agreement without giving due weight to the likelihood of successful future negotiations. Consequently, we vacate the decisions below and remand both cases for further proceedings consistent with this opinion.

It is so ordered

19. H.R. 5005: Homeland Security Act, January 23, 2002

One Hundred Seventh Congress
of the
United States of America
AT THE SECOND SESSION

Begun and held at the City of Washington on Wednesday, the twenty-third day of January, two thousand and two
An Act
To establish the Department of Homeland Security, and for other purposes

Be it enacted by the Senate and House of Representatives of the United States of America in Congress assembled,

. . . . .

Title I – Department of Homeland Security

SEC. 101. Executive Department; Mission.
(a) ESTABLISHMENT – There is established a Department of Homeland Security, as an executive department of the United States within the meaning of Title 5, United States Code.
(b) MISSION.
(1) IN GENERAL—The primary mission of the Department is to—
(A) prevent terrorist attacks within the United States;
(B) reduce the vulnerability of the United States to terrorism;

(C) minimize the damage, and assist in the recovery, from terrorist attacks that do occur within the United States;
(D) carry out all functions of entities transferred to the Department, including by acting as a focal point regarding natural and manmade crises of emergency planning;
(E) ensure that the functions of the agencies and subdivisions within the Department that are not related directly to securing the homeland are not diminished or neglected except by specific Act of Congress;
(F) ensure that the overall economic security of the United States is not diminished by efforts, activities, and programs aimed at securing the homeland; and
(G) monitor connections between illegal drug trafficking and terrorism, coordinate efforts to sever such connections and otherwise contribute to efforts to interdict illegal drug trafficking.
(2) In carrying out the mission described in Paragraph (1), and as further described in this Act, the Department's primary responsibility shall include—
(A) information analysis and infrastructure protection;
(B) chemical, biological, radiological, nuclear, and related countermeasures;
(C) border and transportation security;
(D) emergency preparedness and response; and
(E) coordination (including the provision of training and equipment with other executive agencies, with state and local government personnel, agencies, and authorities, with the private sector, and with other entities.

20. H.R. 4437: Border Protection, Antiterrorism, and Illegal Immigration Control Act (Sensenbrenner Bill), December 16, 2005

109th CONGRESS
2nd Session

AN ACT

To amend the Immigration and Nationality Act to strengthen enforcement of the immigration laws, to enhance border security, and for other purposes.

Be it enacted by the Senate and the House of Representatives of the United States of America in Congress assembled,

SECTION I. SHORT TITLE; TABLE OF CONTENTS.

(a) SHORT TITLE.—This Act may be cited as the "Border Protection, Antiterrorism, and Illegal Immigration Control Act of 2005."

. . .

TITLE I—SECURING UNITED STATES BORDERS

Sec. 101. ACHIEVING OPERATIONAL CONTROL ON THE BORDER.

(a) In General—No later than 18 months after the date of the enactment of this Act, the Secretary of Homeland Security shall take all actions the Secretary determines necessary and appropriate to achieve and maintain operational control over the entire international land and maritime borders of the United States, to include the following—

(1) systematic surveillance of the international land and maritime borders of the United States through more effective use of personnel and technology, such as unmanned aerial vehicles, ground-based sensors, satellites, radar coverage, and cameras;

(2) physical infrastructure enhancements to prevent unlawful entry by aliens into the United States and facilitate access to the international land and maritime borders by United States Customs and Border Protection such as additional checkpoints, all weather access roads, and vehicle barriers;

(3) hiring and training as expeditiously as possible additional Border Patrol agents authorized under section 5202 of the Intelligence Reform and Terrorism Prevention Act of 2004 (Public Law 1089-458); and

(4) increasing deployment of United States Customs and Border Protection personnel to areas along the international land and maritime borders of the United States where there are high levels of unlawful entry by aliens and other areas likely to be impacted by such increased deployment.

(b) Operations Control Defined—In this section the term 'operational control' means the prevention of all unlawful entries into the United States, including entries by terrorists, other unlawful aliens, instruments of terrorism, narcotics, and other contraband.

(c) Report—Not later than one year after the date of the enactment of this Act and annually thereafter, the Secretary shall submit to Congress a report on the progress made toward achieving and maintaining operational control over

the entire international land and maritime borders of the United States in accordance with this section.

SEC. 102. NATIONAL STRATEGY FOR BORDER SECURITY

(a) Surveillance Plan—Not later than six months after the date of the enactment of this plan, the Secretary of Homeland Security shall submit to the appropriate congressional committees a comprehensive plan for the systematic surveillance of the international land and maritime borders of the United States. The plan shall include the following:

(1) An assessment of existing technologies employed on such borders.

(2) A description of whether and how new surveillance technologies will be compatible with existing surveillance technologies.

(3) A description of how the United States Customs and Border Protection is working, or is expected to work, with the Directorate of Science and Technology of the Department of Homeland Security to identify and test surveillance technology.

(4) A description of the specific surveillance technology to be deployed.

(5) The identification of any obstacles that may impede full implementation of such deployment.

(6) A detailed estimate of all costs associated with the implementation of such deployment and continued maintenance of such technologies.

(7) A description of how the Department of Homeland Security is working with the Federal Aviation Administration on safety and airspace control issues associated with the use of unmanned aerial vehicles in the National Airspace System.

(b) National Strategy for Border Security—Not later than one year after the date of the enactment of this Act, the Secretary of Homeland Security, in consultation with the heads of other appropriate Federal agencies, shall submit to the appropriate congressional committees a National Strategy for Border Security to achieve operational control over all ports of entry into the United States. The Secretary shall update the Strategy as needed and shall submit to the appropriate congressional committee, not later than 30 days after each such update, the updated Strategy. The National Strategy for Border Security shall include the following:

(1) The implementation timeline for the surveillance plan described in subsection (a).

(2) An assessment of the threat posed by terrorists and terrorist groups that may try to infiltrate the United States at points along the international land and maritime borders of the United States.

(3) A risk assessment of all ports of entry to the United States and all portions of the international land and maritime borders of the United States, except for ports of entry and facilities subject to vulnerability assessments under section 70102 or 70103 of title 46, United States Code, with respect to—

(A) preventing the entry of terrorists, other unlawful aliens, instruments of terrorism, narcotics, and other contraband into the United States; and

(B) protecting critical infrastructure at or near such ports of entry or borders.

(4) An assessment of all legal requirements that prevent achieving and maintaining operation control over the entire international land and maritime borders of the United States.

(5) An assessment of the most appropriate, practical, and cost-effective means of defending the international land and maritime borders of the United States against threats to security and illegal transit, including intelligence capacities, technology, equipment, personnel, and training needed to address security vulnerabilities.

(6) An assessment of staffing needs for all border security functions, taking into account threat and vulnerability information pertaining to the borders and the impact of new security programs, policies, and technologies.

. . .

SEC. 103. IMPLEMENTATION OF CROSS-BORDER SECURITY AGREEMENTS.

(a) In General—Not later than six months after the date of the enactment of this Act, the Secretary of Homeland Security shall submit to the appropriate congressional committees (as defined in section 102(g) a report on the implementation of the cross-border security agreements signed by the United States with Mexico and Canada, including recommendations on improving cooperation with such countries to enhance border security.

(b) Updates—The Secretary shall regularly update the Committee on Homeland Security of the House of Representatives concerning such implementation.

. . .

SEC. 106. SECURE COMMUNICATION.

The Secretary of Homeland Security shall, as expeditiously as practicable, develop and implement a plan to ensure clear and secure two-way communication capabilities, including the specific use of satellite communications—

(1) among all Border patrol agents conducting operations between ports of entry;

(2) between Border Patrol agents and their respective Border Patrol stations;

(3) between Border Patrol agents and residents in remote areas along the international border who do not have mobile communications, as the Secretary determines necessary; and

(3) between all appropriate Department of Homeland Security border security agencies and State, local, and tribal law enforcement agencies.

SEC. 107. PORT OF ENTRY INSPECTION PERSONNEL.

In each of fiscal years 2007 through 2010 the Secretary of Homeland Security shall, subject to the availability of appropriations, increase by not less than 250 the number of positions for full-time active duty port of entry inspectors. There are authorized to be appropriated to the Secretary such sums as may be necessary for each such fiscal year to hire, train, equip, and support such additional inspectors under this section.

SEC. 108. CANINE DETECTION TEAMS.

In each of fiscal years 2007 through 2011, the Secretary of Homeland Security shall, subject to the availability of appropriations, increase by not less than 25 percent above the number of such positions for which funds were allotted for the preceding fiscal year the number of trained detection canines for use at United States ports of entry and along the international land and maritime borders of the United States.

. . .

SEC. 114. REPORT ON PROGRESS IN TRACKING TRAVEL OF CENTRAL AMERICAN GANGS ALONG INTERNATIONAL BORDERS.

Not later than one year after the enactment of this Act, the Secretary of Homeland Security shall report to the Committee on Homeland Security of the House of Representatives on the progress of the Department of Homeland Security in tracking the travel of Central American gangs across the international border of the United States.

SEC. 118. SENSE OF CONGRESS REGARDING ENFORCEMENT OF IMMIGRATION LAWS.

(a) Findings—Congress finds the following:

(1) A primary duty of the Federal Government is to secure the homeland and ensure the safety of United States citizens and lawful residents.

(2) As a result of the terrorist attacks on September 11, 2001, perpetrated by al Qaeda terrorists on United States soil, the United States is engaged in a Global War on Terrorism.

(3) According to the National Commission on Terrorist Attacks Upon the United States, up to 15 of the 9/11 hijackers could have been intercepted or deported through more diligent enforcement of immigration laws.

(4) Four years after these attacks, there is still a failure to secure the borders of the United States against illegal entry.

(5) The failure to enforce immigration laws in the interior of the United States means that illegal aliens face little or no risk of apprehension or removal once they are in the country.

(6) If illegal aliens can remain in the United States with impunity, so, too, can terrorists enter and remain while they plan, rehearse, and then carry out their attacks.

(7) The failure to control and to prevent illegal immigration into the United States increases the likelihood that terrorists will succeed in launching catastrophic or harmful attacks on United States soil.

(8) There are numerous immigration laws that are currently not being enforced.

(9) Law enforcement officers are often discouraged from enforcing the laws by superiors.

(b) Sense of Congress—It is the sense of Congress that the President, the Attorney General, Secretary of State, Secretary of Homeland Security, and other Department Secretaries should immediately use every tool available to them to enforce the immigration laws of the United States, as enacted by Congress.

. . .

TITLE XIII—ELIMINATION OF CORRUPTION AND PREVENTION OF IMMIGRATION BENEFITS FROM FRAUD.

. . .

Sec. 3
SENSE OF CONGRESS ON SETTING A MANAGEABLE LEVEL OF IMMIGRATION.

It is the sense of Congress that the immigration and naturalization policy shall be designed to enhance the economic, social, and cultural well-being of the United States of America.

21. Excerpts from President George W. Bush, "A Nation of Laws and Immigrants," a speech delivered on May 15, 2006

I've asked for a few minutes of your time to discuss a matter of national importance—the reform of America's immigration system.

The issue of immigration stirs intense emotions, and in recent weeks Americans have seen those emotions on display. On the streets of major cities, crowds have rallied in support of those in our country illegally. At our southern border, others have organized to stop illegal immigrants from coming in. . . . tonight I will make it clear where I stand and where I want to lead our country on this vital issue.

. . . I support comprehensive immigration reform that will accomplish five clear objectives.

First, the United States must secure its borders. This is a basic responsibility of a sovereign nation. Our objective is straightforward: The border would be open to trade and lawful immigration and shut to illegal immigrants, as well as criminals, drug dealers, and terrorists.

. . . Second, to secure our border, we must create a temporary worker program. The reality is that there are many people on the other side of our border who will do anything to come to America to work and build a better life. . . .

Third, we need to hold employers to account for the workers they hire. It is against the law to hire someone who is in this country illegally. Yet businesses often cannot verify the legal status of their employees because of the widespread problem of document fraud. Therefore, comprehensive immigration reform must include a better system for verifying documents and work eligibility. A key part of that system should be a new identification card for every legal foreign worker. . . .

Fourth, we must face the reality that millions of illegal immigrants are here already. They should not be given an automatic path to citizenship. This is amnesty, and I oppose it. Amnesty would be unfair to those who are here lawfully, and it would invite further waves of illegal immigration. . . .

Fifth, we must honor the great American tradition of the melting pot, which has made us one nation out of many peoples. The success of our country depends upon helping newcomers assimilate into our society and embrace our common identity as Americans. . . .

Americans are bound together by our shared ideals, an appreciation of our history, respect for the flag we fly, and an ability to speak and write the English language. . . .

Appendix B
Biographies of Major Personalities

Abbott, Edith (1876–1957) *social worker, educator*
Edith Abbott received a Ph.D. in political economics at the University of Chicago in 1905 and taught that subject at Wellesley College before joining the Chicago School of Civics and Philanthropy in 1908. In 1920 she helped incorporate that school into the University of Chicago as the School of Social Administration and from 1924 to 1942 served as its dean. Abbott lived for 10 years at Chicago's Hull-House, where she worked with Jane Addams for the protection of the underprivileged and immigrants. She was a member of an advisory committee on emigration of the International Labor Organization and was president of the National Association of Social Workers and the National Conference of Social Work. Abbott founded (1927), edited, and wrote extensively for the magazine *Social Service Review*. Her books *Immigration: Select Documents and Case Records* (1924) and *Historical Aspects of the Immigration Problem* (1926) have become classics in the field.

Adamic Louis (Alojzij Adamic) (1899–1951) *translator, writer*
Born Alojzij Adamic in Slovenia, Austria-Hungary (later Yugoslavia), Adamic came to the United States at the age of 14. After a successful career as a translator of Slavic literature, he became a writer in English of original essays and fiction on the immigrant experience in 1925. His best-selling *The Native Returns: An American Immigrant Visits Yugoslavia and Discovers His Old Country* (1934) was an important account of contemporary Yugoslavia through the eyes of an immigrant, and his *From Many Lands* (1940) was an influential examination of the immigrant in America.

Adams, John (1735–1826) *second president of the United States*
A prime mover in the decision to separate from England, Adams was a founding father of the United States, serving as its second president from 1797 to 1801. He proposed the controversial Alien and Sedition Acts of 1798, empowering the government to deport or punish natives or citizens of hostile nations in the United States and to punish those who expressed anti-American sentiments.

Addams, Jane (1860–1935) *social reformer*
After a wide-ranging education in literature, art, languages, philosophy, and medicine, Jane Addams directed her energies to the aid of the underprivileged. She campaigned vigorously for better public housing, welfare, improved child-labor laws, prison reform, and protection of the rights of immigrants and working women. An exponent of cultural pluralism, she encouraged immigrants in the ethnic neighborhoods of Chicago to preserve their cultural heritages, celebrate their native holidays, and maintain their own customs and languages. In 1898 she founded Hull-House, a pioneer community center offering educational, recreational, and social services. Hull-House was an important center for social reform and a sympathetic haven for immigrant workers. Devoted to feminist and pacifist causes, Addams was active in building organizations of women in many European countries. She served as president of the Women's International League of Peace and Freedom after World War I and shared the Nobel Peace Prize in 1931.

Aldrich, Thomas Bailey (1836–1907) *author, editor*
A popular writer of short stories and novels and a minor poet, Aldrich was editor of the *Atlantic Monthly* from 1881 to 1890. In 1882 he published in that magazine a poem, "The Unguarded Gate," warning against the dangers of aliens entering the United States. Widely read and quoted, it articulated America's growing suspicion and fear of immigration.

Antin, Mary (1881–1949) *Polish immigrant, author*
Mary Antin's father, an unsuccessful businessman, emigrated from Poland to Boston in 1891; the rest of the family followed three years later. A talented writer from an early age, she translated a collection of her letters to Poland and published them in 1899. Her experience as a Jewish immigrant was to remain her principal subject. A series of autobiographical articles first appearing in *The Atlantic Monthly* was published in 1912 as *The Promised Land* with great popular success. This moving memoir and her collection of essays *They Who Knock at Our Gates* (1914) were influential in counteracting a rising tide of opposition to immigration in the United States.

Arthur, Chester Alan (1829–1886) *twenty-first president of the United States*
A dedicated abolitionist, Arthur often undertook the defense of fugitive slaves. During the Civil War, he served as state engineer-in-chief and later as quartermaster-general, with the rank of brigadier general. He campaigned for Ulysses S. Grant and was rewarded with the lucrative appointment of collector of the Port of New York in 1871. When James A. Garfield was elected president in 1880, Arthur was called on to serve as vice president. He became president when Garfield was assassinated the next year and held office from 1881 to 1885. He promoted civil service reform, appealed for federal aid to education, and encouraged American participation in numerous international conferences, but was often without the support of Congress. He vigorously opposed the Chinese Exclusion Act of 1882, but it was passed over his veto. Although popular with the voters, Arthur did not please his party, and he was denied the nomination for election after one term.

Belmont, August (1813–1890) *financier, politician*
Belmont immigrated to the United States from Germany in 1837 and established a private banking firm, in which he became one of the wealthiest men in the country. His contribution to the presidential campaign of Franklin Pierce

brought him the post of minister to the Netherlands (1853–57) and he served as the national leader of the Democratic Party from 1857 to 1872. In 1862 he bought the *New York World*, which became the leading voice of his party.

Benjamin, Judah Philip (1811–1884) *senator from Louisiana, Confederate secretary of war and secretary of state*
Trained as a lawyer, Benjamin was one of the first Jewish members of the U.S. Senate, representing Louisiana from 1853 to 1861. When the Civil War began, he remained loyal to the South and served as attorney general (1861), secretary of war (1861–62), and secretary of state (1862–65) of the Confederate States. At the end of the war he escaped to England and resumed the practice of law.

Beverley, Robert (ca. 1673–1722) *historian, clerk of the general assembly of Virginia*
The son of a middle-class family from Yorkshire, England, who had immigrated to Virginia in 1663, Beverley was educated in England and returned to Virginia as a clerk. As a government official he was a member of the assembly for several sessions from 1699 to 1706. Dissatisfied with an early history of Virginia he read, he produced a brief volume of his own, *History and Present State of Virginia*, in 1705. A lively and candid account, it has remained popular through the centuries since its publication. Beverley's indiscreet comments on contemporary public affairs led to his dismissal from office in 1705, and he retired to his estate, where he cultivated grapes, speculated in real estate, and served as a magistrate.

Birkbeck, Morris (1764–1825) *pioneer, writer*
A prosperous Quaker in England, Birkbeck opposed both the government and the Church of England and immigrated to the United States in 1817. He organized a large colony in Illinois called Albion and wrote extensively about the experience. His *Notes on a Journey in America from the Coast of Virginia to the Territory of Illinois* (1817) and *Letters from Illinois* (1818) were very successful in both England and the United States, and he campaigned succesfully against slavery in Illinois. As both a writer and the president of the first agricultural society in Illinois, Birkbeck was influential in drawing settlers to the American West.

Bradford, William (1590–1657) *colonial leader, governor of the Plymouth Colony*
Born to a prosperous family in Yorkshire, England, Bradford became a Puritan at the age of 16 and three years

later, in 1606, accompanied the congregation of his Separatist church in their immigration to Amsterdam, Holland. After a year there and another 11 in Leyden, Bradford joined the small group that sailed for the New World on the *Mayflower* in 1620. The second governor of the Plymouth Colony, he ruled for all but five years from 1621 until 1657, being elected annually 30 times. His incorruptible honesty and great administrative abilities did much to preserve the colony in its difficult beginnings, and his history of the colony, written about 1651, is one of our best sources of information on the period.

Buchanan, Patrick Joseph (1938–) *writer, television commentator, presidential candidate*

Pat Buchanan received degrees in English and philosophy from Georgetown University in 1961 and a master's in journalism from Columbia University in 1962. In 1966 he began to work as a researcher for Richard Nixon. After Nixon's election, he continued as a White House advisor and a speechwriter for Vice President Spiro Agnew, and from 1985 to 1987 he served President Ronald Reagan as White House communications director. In 1992 and 1996 he unsuccessfully sought the Republican Party nomination for president, and in 2000 he won that of the Reform Party. Identified as a "traditional conservative," Buchanan has opposed abortion and homosexual rights and strongly supported immigration reduction and increased border security in both syndicated newspaper columns and such books as *State of Emergency: How Illegal Immigration Is Destroying America* (2006).

Bull, Ole Bornemann (1810–1880) *Norwegian violinist, founder of a Norwegian colony in Pennsylvania*

The most celebrated virtuoso of his time, Ole Bull founded the national theater in his native Norway. In the course of one of his successful concert tours of North America, he conceived the idea of founding a Norwegian colony in Pennsylvania in 1852 and purchased 120,000 acres in Potter County for that purpose. Many of his fellow Norwegians came to the United States in response to his promotion. The land proved less suitable for farming than he had thought, however, and his colony of Oleana failed. Bull lost more than $70,000 in the project and spent many years touring in both the United States and Europe on behalf of the immigrants he had led to the New World. His ill-fated venture inspired a popular ballad making fun of unrealistic utopian schemes.

Burlingame, Anson (1820–1870) *diplomat*

Burlingame represented New York in the House of Representatives from 1855 to 1861, and from 1861 to 1867 he served as the American minister to China. In 1868 he was appointed by the Chinese government to head a delegation to the United States, where he drew up a treaty that established the rights of Chinese and Americans to visit each other's country on equal terms, thus initiating friendly relations between the two nations. The Burlingame Treaty remained in force until 1880, when anti-Chinese sentiment in the United States called for its amendment and eventual cancellation.

Bushnell, Horace (1802–1876) *clergyman, social activist*

After obtaining a law degree from Yale in 1831, Bushnell entered the divinity school and was ordained a Congregationalist pastor in 1833. An influential theologian, he wrote widely on religious topics and, while in California for his health in 1856, was instrumental in founding what became the University of California in Berkeley. Bushnell wrote numerous articles and pamphlets and from the 1830s campaigned actively against an open immigration policy, which he felt threatened America's racial purity.

Cabot, John (Giovanni Caboto) (ca. 1450–ca. 1499) *Italian mariner, explorer*

Born in Italy, Giovanni Caboto moved to England in 1484 and Anglicized his name to John Cabot. In 1497 he obtained a license from the English king Henry VII to explore the New World in search of a route to Asia. He landed in either present-day Labrador, Newfoundland, or Cape Breton Island in Canada and claimed the region for England. He was probably lost at sea on his second voyage westward in 1498.

Cahan, Abraham (1860–1951) *editor, author*

Born in Lithuania, Cahan immigrated to the United States in 1882 in flight from political persecution for his radical activities. He wrote for newspapers and magazines and became a major voice for social reform and the rights of labor. He became the editor-in-chief of the *Daily Forward*, the leading Yiddish-language newspaper in the United States, and wrote several novels. His theme was almost always the alienation of Jewish immigrants in New York, of whose experience he provided a valuable record.

Calvert, George (first baron Baltimore)
(ca. 1580–1632) *statesman, colonizer*

Calvert was a member of an old Yorkshire family who joined the British court and became a member of Parliament in 1609. Ten years later he was appointed secretary of state and a member of the Privy Council. In 1621 he founded a colony in Newfoundland; soon afterward he was converted to the Roman Catholic faith and received the title of Lord Baltimore in the Irish peerage. In 1625, when Charles I became king, Calvert had to resign his office because of his religious conversion. Finding the climate of Newfoundland unbearable, he abandoned his colony in 1628 and four years later was granted a charter for a large tract of land north of Virginia. Calvert died before the charter was issued, but it was taken by his son Cecilius (1605–75), who established the Maryland colony in 1632 as a haven for English Roman Catholics.

Celler, Emmanuel (1888–1981) *U.S. representative from New York*

A graduate of New York City schools and of Columbia University, from which he received a law degree in 1912, Celler entered politics as a delegate to the Democratic state convention and a representative from Brooklyn. An active proponent of immigration reform, he sponsored several amendments to the 1965 immigration bill.

Champlain, Samuel de (ca. 1567–1635) *explorer, pioneer*

Called "the Father of New France," Champlain was the son of a ship captain and was given his first command of a ship in the French navy in 1599. In 1603 he sailed to Canada under the French flag and explored the St. Lawrence River. He founded Port Royal in Nova Scotia and in 1608 established the city of Quebec on the St. Lawrence. The French king Henry IV appointed him lieutenant-governor of the settlement, where he maintained a fur-trading post. In 1629 the English conquered Quebec and took him to England as a prisoner, but when Canada was restored to France he returned as lieutenant-governor. Champlain served as governor of Canada from 1633 until his death.

Charles II (1630–1685) *king of England*

The son of King Charles I, who was deposed and executed, he attempted to reclaim the throne but was defeated by Oliver Cromwell in 1651. After Cromwell's death in 1658, he returned to England, where he was crowned Charles II in 1660. He attempted unsuccessfully to pro-cure tolerance for English Catholics and Puritans by a declaration in 1662 and granted a royal charter to the Rhode Island Colony as a haven for religious dissidents the next year. Charles II became a Catholic on his deathbed in 1685.

Chastellux, François-Jean de Beauvoir, marquis de
(1734–1788) *French army general, writer*

A major-general in the French Army, Chastellux served with Rochambeau in the American Revolutionary army under George Washington. After traveling for some years in the country he helped liberate, he returned to Paris, where he wrote extensively on philosophy, political science, and history. His popular book *Travels in North-America 1780–82*, published in 1786, describes the natural history of the country and the character of its inhabitants. A highly popular account of frontier life, it was influential in attracting immigrants from Europe to the new nation.

Chavez, Cesar Estrada (1927–1993) *Mexican labor leader and activist*

Mexican American Cesar Chavez left school after the eighth grade and worked as a migrant farm laborer. In 1952 he began working as an organizer for the Community Service Organization, a civil rights group in California dedicated to securing justice for the Latino Community. In 1956 he directed his attention specifically to agricultural labor and cofounded the National Farm Workers Association (NFWA), which later became the United Farm Workers (UFW). Protesting the exploitation of farm labor, the use of pesticides, and the employment of illegal immigrants as temporary replacement workers, his organization led many strikes, demonstrations, and boycotts.

Cleveland, Steven Grover (1837–1908) *twenty-second and twenty-fourth president of the United States*

Cleveland was mayor of Buffalo, New York (1881–82), and governor of New York (1883–85), accomplishing numerous reforms in both offices. He served as both the 22nd (1885–89) and 24th president (1893–97). His presidency was marked by a strong international stand. Cleveland vetoed a restrictive immigration bill in 1897 in part because of the literacy requirement it included.

Cobbett, William (1763–1835) *journalist*

After taking up residence in the United States in 1792 as a political refugee from England, Cobbett became one of the most influential and controversial pamphleteers in the new nation. Deliberately confrontational, he took an openly pro-British stand and was often threatened with violence. His savage sarcasm and prickly personality earned him the nickname Peter Porcupine, which he took as a pseudonym, launching *Porcupine's Gazette and Daily Advertiser* in 1797. Sued for libel and attacked on all sides, he returned to England in 1800 but returned to America in 1817. For the next two years he farmed and wrote extensively, opposing English immigration to the United States and disputing Morris Birkbeck's promotion of settlement in the prairie lands in the West.

Corsi, Edward (1896–1965) *political activist, public official*

A native of Italy, Corsi was brought to the United States in 1907 and grew up in great poverty in New York City. After graduating from Fordham University Law School he became director of a settlement house in an Italian section of New York, providing a variety of services to Italian immigrants, and wrote extensively on social problems of his countrypeople for the public press. In 1931 President Herbert Hoover appointed Corsi U.S. commissioner of immigration at Ellis Island; Franklin Roosevelt reappointed him to that post in 1933. During his three years as commissioner he succeeded in generating federal funds for the renovation of the facility. He was named special assistant on refugee and immigration problems by Secretary of State John Foster Dulles in 1954, but after being accused of communist sympathies by Francis E. Walter, chairman of the House Sub-committee on Immigration and cosponsor of the 1952 McCarran-Walter Immigration Act, he was dismissed. New York governor W. Averill Harriman appointed Corsi to the state's Committee on Refugees (1954–55) and the State Unemployment Insurance Board (1958–65). Corsi worked actively and effectively to promote a liberal immigration policy and was influential in awakening public awareness of the contributions of immigrants.

Crèvecoeur, Michel-Guillaume-Jean de (1735–1813) *writer*

After immigrating to the United States from France in 1759, Crèvecoeur farmed in Orange County, New York, where he wrote *Letters from an American Farmer*, an account of daily life in America and a perceptive early analysis of the emerging American personality. Immensely popular in its French translation, the book presented so idyllic a picture of farm life in his adopted country that more than 500 families left France to settle on the Ohio River as a result of it. Crèvecoeur later was made French consul in New York and became a close friend of Washington, Franklin, and Jefferson.

Dillingham, William Paul (1843–1923) *senator from Vermont*

Son of a distinguished attorney and governor of Vermont, he filled many offices in that state, serving four terms in the legislature from 1876 to 1886, as tax commissioner from 1882 to 1888, and as governor from 1888 to 1890. He was elected to the U.S. Senate on the Republican ticket in 1900 and held that seat until his death. Dillingham was made chairman of a special commission on immigration in 1907. The commission produced a 41-volume report, the largest study of immigration in history, examining the subject from every aspect. In 1913 he introduced a bill based on his study and designed to limit immigration annually to 10 percent of the number of people of each nationality already in the country. The bill was defeated because the entry of the United States in World War I almost completely suspended immigration, but in 1920 he renewed the proposal. The second Dillingham bill was vetoed by President Wilson, but in 1921 his restrictionist ideas were accepted, with the quotas reduced to 3 percent. Although it was a temporary measure, the Dillingham Bill of 1921 established a quota policy that was incorporated into subsequent legislation and remained the basis of immigration law for the next 44 years.

Donnelly, Ignatius (1831–1901) *congressman, political reformer*

Born in Philadelphia, Donnelly studied law but devoted his talents to the Republican Party and became lieutenant-governor of Pennsylvania in 1859. As a congressman from 1863 to 1869, he supported his party's policies but left it to speak and write for economic and political reform. Along with eccentric writings intended to prove the historical truth of Atlantis and Francis Bacon's authorship of the plays attributed to William Shakespeare, Donnelly wrote widely warning of a Jewish conspiracy to take control of the world. His futuristic novel *Caesar's Column: A Story of the Twentieth Century* (1891) was influential in stimulating anti-immigration sentiment.

Duden, Gottfried (1785–1855) *pioneer, writer*

A German lawyer who observed that his native country was overcrowded, Duden traveled to America in 1824 to explore the possibility of a German settlement. He settled in Missouri and traveled around the region until 1827, when he returned to Germany and wrote a glowing account of America. *Report on a Journey to the Western States of North America and a Stay of Several Years along the Missouri,* published in 1828, presented so appealing a picture of life in America that it drew nearly 40,000 German immigrants to the Missouri River valley.

du Pont de Nemours, Eleuthère Irénée (1771–1834) *industrialist*

E. I. du Pont was the son of a prominent French economist, Pierre du Pont de Nemours, whose defense of his country's king during the French Revolution led to his imprisonment and immigration to the United States in 1799. E. I. du Pont worked in his father's printing plant in Paris until it was closed by the new French government in 1797 and immigrated to the United States in 1800. He established a gunpowder plant near Wilmington, Delaware, where the business generated one of the largest family fortunes in the country.

Fillmore, Millard (1800–1874) *thirteenth president of the United States*

Vice president under Zachary Taylor, Fillmore inherited the presidency on Taylor's death in office, serving from 1850 to 1853. He promoted expansion in the West, establishing a naval expedition to negotiate a commercial treaty with Japan. An opponent of liberal immigration policy, Fillmore ran for president in 1856 on the American (Know-Nothing) Party ticket, losing by one of the largest majorities in American history.

Ford, Henry (1863–1947) *industrialist, pioneer automobile manufacturer*

A machinist by trade, Ford worked as chief engineer for the Edison Illuminating Company in Detroit until 1899, when he founded an automobile company. He founded the Ford Motor Company, the world's largest automobile producer, and was a pioneer in mass production with his innovative assembly-line method. In 1918 Ford purchased the *Dearborn* (Michigan) *Independent,* in which he published anti-Semitic editorials regularly from 1920 until 1922. Political and economic pressure forced him to drop the subject in that year, but he resumed the campaign in 1924. His articles were collected into a four-volume work called *The International Jew,* which continued to be influential for many years. His accusations of a Jewish conspiracy against America had a great following in Nazi Germa-

ny, and in 1938 Ford accepted the Grand Cross of the German Eagle from the German government. Ford later recanted his policy and publicly apologized for his apparent support of Hitler, but his anti-Semitic campaign had helped to support the restrictive immigrant legislation that prevented many Jews from escaping Nazi Germany.

Franklin, Benjamin (1706–1790) *political leader, diplomat, inventor*

Boston-born Franklin worked as an apprentice printer until, in 1729, he purchased and began to publish the Pennsylvania *Gazette.* Already known for his wise and witty writing, he became the clerk of the Pennsylvania Assembly in 1736 and served as a member of it from 1751 to 1764. He also held the office of deputy postmaster general for the colonies and represented Pennsylvania, Georgia, New Jersey, and Massachusetts as colonial agent in England during the 1760s. During his long and varied career, Franklin invented an efficient stove; performed important experiments with electricity; helped organize what became the American Philosophical Society and the University of Pennsylvania; and sponsored a city police force, a fire department, a circulating public library, and a city hospital in Philadelphia. As a delegate to the Second Continental Congress in 1775, he helped draft the Declaration of Independence; after the Revolutionary War he helped negotiate a peace treaty with England, signed in 1783. Although he encouraged emigration to the new country, Franklin was fearful of ethnic diversity and worked to maintain cultural and linguistic unity in the United States.

Frick, Henry Clay (1849–1919) *industrialist*

Frick, who had little formal education, recognized the importance of industrial expansion following the U.S. Civil War and organized a company to supply coke to steel mills in Pittsburgh, Pennsylvania in 1871. A millionaire by the age of 30, he became chairman of Carnegie Steel Company in 1889 and director of J. P. Morgan's United States Steel in 1901. Frick was known as a ruthless employer, using violent means to counter strikes by immigrant coke workers.

Gilbert, Sir Humphrey (ca. 1539–1583) *navigator, explorer*

Sir Humphrey Gilbert shared with his half brother, Sir Walter Raleigh, a belief in a northwest passage to China and India and the courage to venture out to find it. He wrote a book on the subject, *Discourse* (1576) that so impressed Queen Elizabeth I that she gave him a charter to explore and colonize any land he found in the New World. Gilbert made two expeditions (1579 and 1583) to look for a marine route to the East, exploring the north coast of Newfoundland, in present-day Canada, on the second. More daring than skilled, he had trouble with his crews on both trips, and his ship sank in a storm on his second voyage home.

Goldman, Emma (1869–1940) *anarchist writer, political activist*
An immigrant from Lithuania at the age of 17, Goldman worked for workers' and women's rights, among other liberal causes. She was arrested and briefly jailed for agitation in New York City in 1893. In 1906 she founded the magazine *Mother Earth*, which she edited until 1917. In that year she was again jailed for her public protests against military conscription, instituted as United States involvement in World War I approached. She remained in prison until 1919, when she was deported to the newly formed Soviet Union. Equally critical of Russia's social order, she left in 1921. She traveled widely, seeking and protesting political and social injustice wherever she found it, until her death in Canada.

Gompers, Samuel (1850–1924) *labor leader*
Born in London to a working-class family that had emigrated from Holland, Gompers was brought to the United States in 1863. Apprenticed to his father, a cigar maker, he joined the cigar maker union in 1864 and became active in organized labor. He was instrumental in the founding of the American Federation of Labor (AFL) in 1886 and was its leader every year for the rest of his life except 1924. Gompers supported the open-door policy in American immigration until the end of World War I, but he then came to favor immigration restriction on the grounds of both the economic threat of foreign labor to American employment opportunities and its danger to American cultural and racial unity. He actively opposed Chinese and Filipino immigration and prohibited Chinese membership in the AFL.

Grant, Madison (1865–1930) *naturalist, activist for immigration restriction*
A wealthy aristocrat whose family was socially prominent in New York City from colonial times, Grant attended Yale University and received a law degree from Columbia. With no need to earn a living, he devoted his energies to his two main interests, naturalism and the study of ethnic groups. He promoted wildlife protection and wilderness preser-

vation; helped found the New York Zoological Society, the American Bison Society, and the Save-the-Redwoods League; and served for many years as the president of the Bronx Zoo. Convinced that racial mixture would result in the reversion to a primitive type, he strongly opposed the admission of foreign workers whom he saw as a threat to the racial purity of the American people. His popular book *The Passing of the Great Race* (1916) warned of "race suicide" and called for immigration restriction to protect the "Nordic races" in America from "mongrelization." From 1922 until he died, he was vice president of the Immigration Restriction League. Grant's writings contributed to the establishment of a restrictive immigration policy in the United States, and his racist views were reflected in the Johnson-Reed Act of 1924, which established national quotas for admission to the United States.

Hammond, John (ca. 1613–1663) *writer, lawyer*
Hammond emigrated from England to Virginia as a voluntary indentured servant around 1636, and after completing his seven years of service he became a farmer and lawyer. In 1654 he became an innkeeper and the proprietor of a ferry in Maryland. In 1656 he wrote a pamphlet, *Leah and Rachel, or the Two Fruitful Sisters Virginia and Maryland*, considered one of the best 17th-century tracts promoting immigration to America. In it he praises the country as a land of opportunity but cautions the newcomer on its risks.

Harrison, Benjamin (1833–1901) *twenty-third president of the United States*
The grandson of President William Henry Harrison, Benjamin Harrison served in the Union army in the Civil War, attaining the rank of brigadier general. He was a senator from Ohio from 1881 to 1887. As president (1889–93), Harrison supported the revision of the naturalization laws restricting Asian immigration.

Hayes, Rutherford Birchard (1822–1893) *nineteenth president of the United States*
The Ohio-born lawyer served in the Union army during the Civil War, attaining the rank of brigadier general; in the House of Representatives from 1865 to 1867; and as governor of Ohio from 1868 to 1872 and from 1876 to 1877, when he was elected president on the Republican ticket. During his single term (1877–1881) he helped reconcile the post–Civil War differences between North and South and vetoed a bill limiting Chinese immigration on the grounds that it violated the Burlingame Treaty.

Hirsch, Baron de (Maurice de Hirsch) (1831–1896) *German businessman, philanthropist*

Born Freiherr Moritz von Hirsch auf Gereuth, Baron de Hirsch devoted his considerable fortune to aiding his fellow Jews, especially those of the Middle East and Russia. He founded the Jewish Colonization Association to help Asian and European Jews relocate anywhere they could find sanctuary from oppression, and in 1891 he established a fund specifically to support and educate Jewish immigrants in the United States.

Hoover, John Edgar (1895–1972) *director of the FBI*

The son of a government employee, J. Edgar Hoover received a law degree from George Washington University in 1917 and upon graduation became a clerk in the Department of Justice and was placed in charge of the Alien Registration Section of the Bureau of Investigation (renamed the Federal Bureau of Investigation in 1935). He became assistant director of the bureau in 1912 and director in 1924. His work led to the deportation of many aliens he defined as radicals and anarchists. A profound believer in the subversive intentions of international communism, he contributed significantly to the anti-immigrant hysteria during the "Red Scare" and the cold war.

Hutchinson, Anne (ca. 1591–1643) *religious leader*

The daughter of a dissident Church of England minister, Anne Hutchinson was persecuted as a Puritan and immigrated to America in 1634. She became an influential member of the Massachusetts Bay Colony, where she held private prayer meetings at home defending the principle of personal good work, rather than divine grace, as a means to salvation. Denounced for teaching men and for failing to honor church officials, she was banished from the colony in 1637 and joined Roger Williams in Rhode Island. After her husband died in 1642, she moved to the Dutch colony on Long Island, where she and 13 of her 14 children were killed in an Indian massacre the next year. Charged with behavior "unseemly for one of her sex" and with encouraging women to rebel, she provided women with a model of independence and resourcefulness and is regarded as the earliest feminist in the New World.

Jogues, Isaac (1607–1646) *missionary, martyr*

Jogues was born to a noble family in France and became a Jesuit in 1636. He became a missionary to the Huron Indians in Canada that same year. He made a dangerous journey through the wilderness and was captured and mutilated by the Iroquois. After a year as a slave in an Indian village, he was rescued by the Dutch and taken to New Amsterdam (now New York City), of which he wrote an important early description. He went back to France in 1644 but returned to his missionary duties in Canada, where he was killed by the Mohawk the next year. Jogues was beatified by Pope Pius XI as a martyr in 1925.

Johnson, Albert (1869–1957) *newspaper editor, politician, anti-immigration activist*

Johnson became a reporter in Missouri at the age of 19 and went on to work for newspapers in St. Louis and Washington, D.C., as a news editor and managing editor. In 1898 he became the editor of the ultra-conservative *Tacoma* (Washington) *News* and began to campaign against the admission of Japanese immigrants. In 1912 he led a movement to smash a labor union strike and won a seat in Congress as a Republican from Washington. Although he continued editing and publishing newspapers, he served for the next 20 years in the House of Representatives. In 1919 he was appointed chairman of the House Committee on Immigration and Naturalization and worked energetically to restrict the admission of foreigners. He introduced a bill to limit European immigrants to 3 percent of the number of each nationality already in the country according to the census of 1910, and after a veto by President Wilson the bill was passed in 1921. Following Senator David Reed's "national origins" plan of establishing quotas discriminating against southern Europeans and excluding all Asians, he cosponsored the conservative Reed-Johnson Act, which passed into law in 1924. Johnson was defeated for office in 1932.

Kalb, Johann (Baron de Kalb) (1721–1780) *soldier*

A German soldier who entered the French army and rose to the rank of brigadier general, Kalb was inspired by the American struggle for independence and came with the marquis de Lafayette to the New World to fight in the Revolutionary War. Claiming the title of baron in order to justify a commission in the Continental army, he received the rank of major general under George Washington and fought heroically as Baron de Kalb in New Jersey, Maryland, and South Carolina, where he died in battle.

Kalm, Peter (1716–1779) *Swedish botanist, writer*

A distinguished botanist who studied with Carolus Linnaeus, the father of modern botanical classification, Kalm was sponsored by the Swedish Academy of Science to tour North America in search of plants that could be grown profitably in Sweden. A friend of Benjamin Franklin and other distinguished American naturalists, Kalm traveled extensively in the Northeast and Canada. His three-volume *Travels into North America* (1753–61, published in English in 1770–71) was the first detailed scientific report of the New World. Its perceptive and objective account of the social conditions, politics, and history of Pennsylvania, New Jersey, New York, and southern Canada provided Europe with one of its first accurate pictures of conditions in America, and its translations into German, Dutch, and French influenced many in their decision to immigrate to the New World.

Kearney, Denis (1847–1907) *anti-immigrant labor agitator*

Irish-born Kearney immigrated to the United States in 1868 and became a citizen eight years later. He developed a prosperous business in carting merchandise in San Francisco and joined organized labor representing the Draymen and Teamsters' Union. He spoke powerfully in open-air meetings against railroad companies, banks, and local politicians, earning a reputation as an agitator. His most passionate oratory was directed against the Chinese, whom he saw as threatening American labor. He was often arrested for "incendiary" statements but was always acquitted. Kearney was instrumental in organizing the Workingmen's Party of California in 1877 and spoke repeatedly on the necessity of ending Chinese labor competition, ending most of his speeches with a cry of "The Chinese must go!" The party had considerable influence during the 1870s, and Kearney is credited with (or blamed for) spearheading the campaign that led to the Chinese Exclusion Act of 1882. His and his party's influence faded during the following years, and Kearney retired in 1888.

Kennedy, John Fitzgerald (1917–1963) *thirty-fifth president of the United States*

The great-grandson of Irish immigrants, Kennedy served as a member of the House of Representatives (1947–53) and senator (1953–60) from Massachusetts before being elected the first Catholic president of the United States (1960–63). He confronted the Soviet presence in Cuba, signed a nuclear test-ban treaty, and launched the Peace Corps. Kennedy worked for a more liberal immigration policy for many years and made a formal proposal for new legislation in his last year. Although he was assassinated in 1963, his proposal was largely responsible for the major revision in immigration law of 1965.

Kocherthal, Josua von (Josua Harrsch) (1669–1719) *Lutheran clergyman, leader of German immigrants to America*

Born Josua Harrsch in the Kocher Valley in Swabia, from which he took his pseudonym, Kocherthal visited the British colony of Carolina in 1706 and published an enthusiastic account of his trip to encourage German immigration to the New World. In 1708 he recruited 53 followers in Frankfurt, of whom he succeeded in leading 41 to form a German colony in America. He settled 15 families in Newburgh, New York. So effective was his promotion of the American venture that he was able to return to New York State with 2,344 "Palatines" (natives of the Palatinate, a province of Germany) in 1710, initiating the largest non-English-speaking migration to British North America of the 18th century.

Korematsu, Fred (1919–2005) *World War II internment camp resister*

Fred Korematsu, a 23-year-old welder born in Oakland, California, of Japanese immigrants, was jailed in 1942 when he refused to join his family in the internment camp established for all people of Japanese ancestry shortly after the United States entered World War II. Soon after his arrest, an official of the American Civil Liberties Union (ACLU) asked him to participate in a legal action against the government attacking the constitutionality of the exclusion directive on the grounds of racial discrimination. *Korematsu v. the United States of America* became one of the landmark cases in U.S. immigration history, finally reaching the Supreme Court in 1944. It ruled against him by a vote of 6–3, but the conviction was overturned in 1983, and five years later the federal government provided reparations and apologies to survivors among the 120,000 Japanese Americans relocated during World War II. A symbol of civil rights, Korematsu was awarded the Medal of Freedom, the nation's highest civilian award, by President Clinton in 1998.

Kosciusko, Thaddeus (1746–1817) *Polish patriot, hero of the American Revolution*

While a captain in the Polish army, Kosciusko was drawn to the American cause and in 1776 came to the country to serve in the Revolutionary army. He was appointed chief engineer in charge of the construction of the fort at West Point from 1778 to 1780 and became adjutant to General Washington. In 1784 he returned to Poland, where he became a general in the Polish army and commander in chief of the rebel forces in 1794. In 1797 he returned to

America, where Congress honored his war service with a land grant in Ohio. Kosciusko went to France in 1798, where he continued his fight for the freedom of Poland.

Lafayette, marquis de (Marie-Joseph-Paul-Yves-Roch-Gilbert du Motier) (1757–1834) *French officer, statesman active in American Revolution*

A wealthy French aristocrat, Lafayette came to America at the age of 19 to serve in the war for independence and was made a major general without pay or command. He joined General Washington's staff and served with distinction in several important military campaigns, including the battle that led to the defeat of General Cornwallis in 1781. He returned to France the following year and played a prominent part in the French Revolution, in which he was made the commander of the French National Guard. He returned to America in 1784, and in 1803 he was rewarded for his service with a large land grant in Louisiana and later a township in Florida. His grave in Paris was covered with earth from Bunker Hill as a token of American gratitude for his contribution to the Revolutionary War.

La Guardia, Fiorello Henry (1882–1947) *politician, mayor of New York*

Born in New York City to Italian immigrants, La Guardia traveled with his family to Europe in his teens and at the age of 19 took a job with the U.S. consulate in Budapest. Fluent in Yiddish, Italian, German, French, and various Slavic languages, he worked as an interpreter at the consulate in Trieste and at 20 became the American consul in Fiume. He attended law school in New York while working as an interpreter at Ellis Island and in 1916 was elected to Congress. La Guardia was a highly decorated war hero, holding the rank of major in World War I, and he served for 15 years in the U.S. House of Representatives. Elected mayor of New York in 1933, he was the first to serve three consecutive terms (1934–45) and also the first American of Italian ancestry to hold that office. La Guardia fought corruption and supported slum clearance and low-cost housing.

La Salle, René-Robert Cavelier (sieur de La Salle) (1643–1687) *explorer, pioneer settler*

A French nobleman, La Salle was one of the first to explore and settle the region near present-day Montreal, Canada, where he established a lucrative fur-trading post around 1666. Louis XIV gave him large land grants and trading privileges in the western area of North America

in 1673 and 1678. In 1682 La Salle explored the Mississippi River, sailing to the Gulf of Mexico, and claimed the entire Mississippi Valley for the French king, naming it Louisiana. After King Louis appointed him viceroy of North America, he organized an expedition to colonize the continent in 1684 but was murdered by his own men.

Lazarus, Emma (1849–1887) *poet*

Emma Lazarus was born into a cultivated Spanish–Jewish family in New York and studied languages and classical literature from an early age. Her first book, published in 1867, included poems and translations from German and was favorably noted by Ralph Waldo Emerson, and her novel *Alide* (1874) won the praise of Russian novelist Ivan Turgenev. Lazarus's poetry and fiction showed her great pride in her Jewish heritage and her concern for the persecuted Jews of Europe. From 1881 she dedicated herself to helping new immigrants to the United States in both social work and writing. Her sonnet "The New Colossus" (1883) was widely quoted as a statement of America's generous immigration policy; it was engraved on a plaque fixed to the base of the Statue of Liberty in 1886.

Lodge, Henry Cabot (1850–1924) *political leader, historian*

The son of a wealthy and aristocratic Boston family, Lodge received both a law degree and a Ph.D. in history from Harvard, where he taught for several years. A political independent, he was elected to the Massachusetts House of Representatives as a Republican in 1878 and served in the U.S. Congress from 1887 to 1893, when he was elected to the U.S. Senate. Lodge was a moderate conservative, campaigning powerfully for American entry into World War I and, as chairman of the Senate Foreign Relations Committee, opposing President Wilson's efforts on behalf of the League of Nations. He supported the protective tariff and a strong military force and became one of the nation's leading spokesmen for national expansion. Lodge vigorously supported restriction of immigration and sponsored a literacy bill, providing for the exclusion of any immigrant who could not read, that was passed by Congress in 1896 but vetoed by President Cleveland.

Logan, James (1674–1751) *colonial statesman, scholar*

The son of a Scottish clergyman of the Established Church, Logan converted to Quakerism, then became the secretary of William Penn in 1699 and accompanied the Quaker leader to Pennsylvania. He was a member of the Provincial Council from 1703 to 1747 and became its president, serving as the chief executive of the province from 1736 to 1738. He was a judge from 1726 and chief justice of the Pennsylvania Supreme Court from 1731 to 1739. A distinguished scientist, he made significant contributions to the study of botany and astronomy. Logan was highly successful in land investment and in trade with the Indians, and he left a library of more than 3,000 books to the city of Philadelphia.

Lyon, Matthew (1749–1822) *newspaperman, congressman, entrepreneur*
Born in Ireland, Lyon entered the United States in 1764 as a redemptioner (a type of indentured servant). He signed the Declaration of Independence, served in the Revolutionary War, and was elected to the House of Representatives from Vermont in 1796. While serving in the House, he founded a newspaper, and after publishing a letter criticizing President John Adams, he became the first citizen indicted under the Sedition Act of 1798 for "maligning the government." He was fined $1,000 and sentenced to four months in prison but was reelected from jail as a martyr for civil liberties. The fine was later refunded to his heirs by Congress, which declared the Sedition Act unconstitutional.

Madison, James (1751–1836) *fourth president of the United States*
A major figure in the creation and adoption of the U.S. Constitution, Madison represented his native Virginia in the House of Representatives (1789–97), served as secretary of state (1801–09), and was U.S. president (1809–17). Madison strongly opposed Adams's Alien and Sedition Laws.

Mazzei, Filippo (1730–1816) *Italian physician, political agent for American colonies*
Mazzei lived and worked as a wine merchant in London from 1755 to 1773, when he immigrated to Virginia to introduce a wine industry in the New World. A political philosopher whose ideas influenced his friend Thomas Jefferson, he was employed to represent the United States in Europe from 1779 to 1783 and sent important information to Jefferson during those years.

McCarran, Patrick Anthony (1876–1954) *senator from Nevada*

The son of two Irish immigrants, McCarran was elected a member of the Nevada legislature while still in law school in 1903 and began practicing law two years later. He served as a district attorney and justice of the Nevada State Supreme Court, of which he was chief justice from 1917 to 1919. He was elected to the U.S. Senate on the Democratic ticket in 1932. His career in Congress included the sponsorship of numerous bills, including legislation establishing the Civil Aeronautics Authority in 1938. In 1950 he authored the Internal Security Act, targeting communists and communist sympathizers in response to cold war hysteria. McCarran is best remembered for the 1952 Immigration and Naturalization Act, which he cosponsored with Congressman Francis E. Walter. Codifying the many amendments to the Johnson-Reed Act of 1924, the McCarran-Walter Act reinforced the quota laws based on national origins and dictated a restrictionist immigration policy that remained in force until 1965.

McCarthy, Joseph Raymond (1908–1957) *senator from Wisconsin*
McCarthy practiced law from 1935 to 1939, when he was elected a circuit court judge in Wisconsin. In 1946 he became a senator from that state and in February 1950 became a national figure when he delivered a speech charging that the State Department was "infested" with communists. With only the most shadowy evidence, he continued to accuse government officials of being involved in a conspiracy to betray the country until 1954, when the Senate officially censured him. McCarthy's effective campaign against what he perceived as communist influence was influential in renewing the Red Scare in America.

Meissner, Doris Marie (1942–   ) *commissioner of the U.S. Immigration and Naturalization Service*
Doris Meissner is a graduate of the University of Wisconsin who served as a special assistant to the attorney general in 1973–74, as assistant director of the Office of Policy and Planning in 1975, as executive director of the Cabinet Committee on Illegal Aliens in 1976, and as deputy attorney general from 1977 to 1980. In 1981 she was appointed acting commissioner of the INS and then held the post of executive associate commissioner until 1986. On October 18, 1993, she was sworn in as the commissioner of the INS, where she served for the next seven years. After retiring on November 18, 2000, she rejoined the Carnegie Endowment for International Peace, for which she had earlier served as director of the Immigration Policy Project.

Morse, Samuel Finley Breese (1791–1872) *artist, inventor, political activist*

A prominent portrait painter, Morse was the founder and first president of the National Academy of Design, but he became better known for his invention of the magnetic telegraph about 1832. An ardent anti-Catholic, he wrote a violent attack on America's liberal immigration policy entitled *Imminent Danger to the Free Institutions of the United States Through Immigration* in 1835 and the next year ran for the office of mayor of New York City on the native American "Know-Nothing" ticket.

Mühlenberg, John Peter Gabriel (1746–1807) *Lutheran clergyman, Revolutionary War general*

The American-born son of a German immigrant Lutheran minister, Mühlenberg was ordained in 1772 but left the pulpit to serve in the Continental army in 1776. He organized a German regiment and was made a brigadier general in 1777. He served under Baron Friedrich von Steuben in 1780 and saw action in several major campaigns. Mühlenberg was later a member of the United States House of Representatives (1789–91, 1793–95, 1799–1801) and the U.S. Senate (1801).

Muir, John (1838–1914) *naturalist*

The Scottish-born Muir was fascinated by stories of the forests and wildlife of North America before he immigrated to the United States at the age of 10. He toured widely throughout the country, recording his observations in several important books, and his reverence for nature was a major influence in shaping the conservation and environmental movement in the United States. From the 1880s he campaigned eloquently for the establishment of Yosemite National Park, approved by Congress in 1890. His experiences as a young immigrant are recorded movingly in his memoir *The Story of My Boyhood and Youth* (1913).

Oglethorpe, James Edward (1696–1785) *English soldier, philanthropist, colonist of Georgia*

As a member of the British Parliament from 1722 to 1754, Oglethorpe was active in prison reform and organized a project for a colony in America of men released from debtor's prison. In 1732 he received a royal charter for a colony in southern Carolina, to which he gave the name Georgia, and he led a group of immigrants there the following year. He administered the colony and as general of its troops successfully defended it against the Spanish in 1742.

Paine, Thomas (1737–1809) *pamphleteer*

One of the most influential supporters of the revolutionary cause in the colonies, Paine emigrated from England in 1774 and worked as a journalist in Philadelphia. In 1776 he published *Common Sense*, in which he argued eloquently for American independence. He fought in the Revolutionary War and from 1776 to 1783 issued six numbers of *Crisis*, a periodical urging patriotism for the emerging nation. From 1777 to 1779 he was secretary to Congress's committee on foreign affairs and then became clerk of the Philadelphia Assembly. He returned to England in 1787 and in 1792 published *The Rights of Man*, supporting the French Revolution and calling on England to abolish the monarchy. He was convicted of treason in England in 1792 and banished to France, where he fell afoul of the government again and was imprisoned. American minister James Monroe secured his release as an American citizen, and he returned to the United States in 1802.

Palmer, Alexander Mitchell (1872–1936) *member of the House of Representatives and attorney general*

Palmer supported progressive legislation in Congress (1909–15), sponsoring women's suffrage and a bill prohibiting child labor. As attorney general (1919–21), he took a strong stand against radicals and was responsible for many raids against suspected aliens in 1919 and 1920. The Palmer Raids, often based on insufficient evidence, reflected and heightened the Red Scare hysteria of the period.

Pastorius, Franz Daniel (1651–1720) *lawyer, colonizer, writer*

Born to a prosperous family in Franconia, Germany, Pastorius practiced law successfully in Frankfurt for several years but became drawn to religion due to his increasing dissatisfaction with the state of European society. He was appointed to represent a group of Frankfurt Quakers and Mennonites who wanted to immigrate to William Penn's new colony in America in 1683. As their agent he acquired 15,000 acres in Pennsylvania, where he founded Germantown. Pastorius became the settlement's first mayor and served the community in various capacities until his death. Fluent in seven languages, he wrote extensively on spiritual, political, and scientific matters.

Penn, William (1644–1718) *religious reformer, founder of Pennsylvania*

Penn studied law for two years at Oxford University but was expelled for his religious nonconformist views. He joined the Society of Friends (Quakers) and became active as a religious and political pamphleteer. When he inherited a large financial claim against Charles II from his father, Admiral Sir William Penn, he received a tract of land in the New World as payment and established the province of Pennsylvania as a "Holy Experiment" dedicated to religious toleration and democratic government. He promoted immigration to North America, describing in glowing terms the rich opportunities of the New World and offering liberal terms for purchase and rental of land. Penn was always fair and honorable in his dealings with the Native American population, with whom his colony enjoyed peaceful relations, and he attempted to reduce the evils of slavery in Pennsylvania. He was the author of some 42 books and pamphlets championing religious freedom and political equality.

Priestley, Joseph (1733–1804) *English clergyman, chemist*

Priestley made several important contributions to the understanding of electricity and chemistry while serving as a minister in Leeds and Birmingham, England. After his house and personal effects were burned by an angry mob because of his sympathy for the French Revolution, Priestley immigrated to the United States in 1794. His enthusiastic letters back to England describing the good life available to immigrants in America influenced many to follow his example.

Pulaski, Casimir (1747–1779) *Polish soldier in the American Revolution*

After a daring career as a revolutionary in his native Poland, Count Pulaski fled to Turkey and later to France before immigrating to the United States with a letter of introduction from Benjamin Franklin to George Washington in 1777. He volunteered for the Continental army and was made a general. He organized an independent cavalry troop, fought valiantly, and was killed in the Battle of Savannah, Georgia.

Raleigh, Sir Walter (ca. 1554–1618) *English courtier, navigator*

A favorite of Queen Elizabeth I, Raleigh fought along with his half brother Sir Humphrey Gilbert against the Span-

iards in 1578. After Gilbert's death, he received the same patent allowing him to explore and take in the queen's name any land in America. He sent an expedition to explore the coast from Florida to North Carolina in 1584 and named the coast Virginia in honor of the queen. In 1585 he sent settlers to colonize the coast, but the project was abandoned the next year. Another attempt also failed, and Raleigh gave up his rights to the new land. After Elizabeth's death, political enemies convinced her successor, James I, that Raleigh opposed the new king, and he was imprisoned in 1603. Released in 1616, he made an expedition to South America and attacked a Spanish settlement against royal orders. When he returned in 1618, he was charged with treason and beheaded.

Reed, David Aiken (1880–1953) *senator*

The son of a Pennsylvania lawyer and business associate of Andrew Carnegie, Reed became a protégé of financier Andrew Mellon, a powerful figure in the Republican Party, and with his help was appointed to fill a vacant seat in the Senate for Pennsylvania in 1922. Reed took an isolationist position, opposing American membership in the League of Nations, recognition of the Soviet Union, and President Roosevelt's New Deal policies. Particularly hostile to liberal immigration policies, he developed a national-origins principle that sought to preserve the racial status quo by favoring northern Europeans. This method of allotting fixed quotas for immigration along national lines was enshrined in the Reed-Johnson Immigration Act of 1924. Reed's identification with big-money interests and his attacks on organized labor cost him his seat in the Senate in 1934.

Ridge, Thomas Joseph (Tom Ridge) (1945–   ) *congressman, governor, secretary of Homeland Security*

Tom Ridge graduated from the Dickinson School of Law in Pennsylvania in 1972. He was in private practice and served as assistant district attorney in Pennsylvania until 1982, when he entered politics as a member of the Republican Party. He was elected to Congress in 1983 and served six consecutive terms. In 1995 he was elected governor of Pennsylvania, resigning from that position in 2001 to become the first director of the Office of Homeland Security when the office was created after the terrorist attack of September 11. He signed the Canada–U.S. Smart Border Declaration in 2001. With the passage of the Homeland Security Act of 2002, which created a cabinet-level Department of Homeland Security, he became its first secretary. Ridge resigned in 2004 and joined the board of directors of Home Depot, Inc.

Root, Elihu (1845–1937) *politician, diplomat, senator from New York*

Root served as secretary of war (1899–1904) and secretary of state (1905–09) before joining the Senate, where he served from 1910 to 1915. He worked to strengthen friendly relations with South America and helped establish a civil government in Puerto Rico. A strong supporter of the League of Nations, he helped frame the statute for the World Court in 1920. Root opposed a liberal immigration policy for the United States and supported literacy test for applicants.

Rynning, Ole (1809–1838) *Norwegian immigrant leader, writer*

Rynning was a schoolmaster who studied the economic problems of the laborers and farmers of his country and concluded that emigration provided a solution. In 1837 he organized a group of 84 emigrants and set sail for the United States. Fifty-three of the band made their way to the Beaver Creek region in Iroquois country about 70 miles south of Chicago, but a combination of bad climate and malaria, to which Rynning fell victim, caused the colony to disband. Rynning's description of the country written during the year of his colony's existence, *A True Account of America for the Information and Help of Peasant and Commoner*, known as the "America Book," was published in Norway in 1839. Regarded as one of the most dependable and informative of all immigrant guidebooks, it created a sensation and inspired many Norwegians to immigrate to the United States.

Sacco, Nicola (1891–1927) and Bartolomeo Vanzetti (1888–1927) *anarchists*

Both Nicola Sacco and Bartolomeo Vanzetti immigrated to the United States from Italy in 1908; Sacco worked as an edge-trimmer in a shoe factory and Vanzetti was a fish peddler. Dedicated to the principles of anarchism, they were arrested in 1920 for a murder committed during a payroll robbery of the shoe factory where Sacco worked, and although the evidence was insufficient they were convicted in 1920 because of the anti-immigrant hysteria of the time. The Sacco-Vanzetti case became a subject of international controversy.

Schurz, Carl (1829–1906) *politician, reformer*

Born near Cologne, Germany, Schurz participated in the unsuccessful revolutionary movement of 1848–49 in Germany and, like other "Forty-Eighters," fled to the United States in 1852. After studying law, he began to practice in Milwaukee, Wisconsin, in 1859 and campaigned for Abraham Lincoln in his first presidential campaign. After Lincoln's election in 1860, Schurz was appointed U.S. minister to Spain, where he served until 1862. He fought with distinction at Second Bull Run, Chancellorsville, and Gettysburg in the Civil War and was made major general in 1863. He worked as a journalist from 1865 to 1868 and served as senator from Missouri from 1869 to 1875 and as U.S. secretary of the interior from 1877 to 1881. The first German American to hold the rank of senator and serve in the national cabinet, Schurz was influential in formulating the principles of the Republican Party in the United States.

Seligman, Joseph (1819–1880) *merchant, civil leader, philanthropist*

A model of the self-made man rising from his low origins as an immigrant, Seligman began as a clothes peddler immediately after his immigration from Germany in 1837. Seligman established a dry-goods store in Alabama and with his brothers founded an international banking firm in New York City in 1862. A friend of Ulysses S. Grant, Seligman helped the Union during the Civil War and negotiated numerous contracts with the Treasury Department. In New York City he fought corruption in politics. Seligman was made head of the New York City Rapid Transit Commission and was active in Jewish organizations, providing extensive support for immigrants. The refusal of the Grand Union Hotel in Saratoga, New York, to admit him in 1877 was a widely publicized example of anti-Semitism.

Sensenbrenner, Frank James (F. James Sensenbrenner) (1943–) *U.S. representative from Wisconsin*

F. James Sensenbrenner received a law degree from the University of Wisconsin in 1968 and from that year until 1975 served in the Wisconsin state assembly. He was elected to the state senate in 1975 and as a Republican to the national House of Representatives in 1978, where he played an important role in the impeachment of President Clinton in 1998 and introduced the USA PATRIOT Act to the House in 2001. A strong advocate of stiffening the penalties for employing or aiding illegal immigrants, Sensenbrenner sponsored the controversial House of

Representatives bill 4437, the Border Protection, Anti-terrorism, and Illegal Immigration Control Act of 2005, which passed in the House on December 16 by a vote of 329 to 182 and became known as the Sensenbrenner Bill.

Serra, Junípero (1713–1784) *missionary priest, religious leader*

The Franciscan priest was a professor of philosophy in his native Spain before immigrating to Mexico City in 1750. After working as a missionary to the Indians there, he became president of the missions of Lower California in 1768, and from 1769 to 1782 he founded missions in San Diego, Monterey, San Antonio, San Luis Obispo, San Francisco, and elsewhere. He introduced cattle, sheep, and European farming methods and converted many Native Americans of the area to Christianity. A controversial figure, Serra fought for Indian rights, but also harshly punished those who did not follow Christian rules. Some California Indian tribes believe his work contributed to Indian enslavement in early California. Fray Serra was one of the most influential figures in the introduction of Christianity and European civilization to the American West. He was elevated to sainthood by the Catholic Church in 1988.

Simpson, Alan Kooi (1931–) *senator from Wyoming*

Alan Simpson graduated from the University of Wyoming Law School and began practice in 1958. He served in the Wyoming House of Representatives from 1964 to 1977 and in 1978 was elected as a Republican to the United States Senate, where he has held several posts, including that of Republican whip from 1985 to 1995. In 1986 he cosponsored the controversial Immigration Reform and Control Act (IRCA, also known as the Simpson-Mazzoli Act), which tightened security at the borders and restrictions against illegal aliens but also provided amnesty for certain undocumented workers.

Smith, John (1580–1631) *military adventurer, colonist, historian*

After an adventurous youth as a soldier in Europe and Turkey, Smith joined in the Virginia Company's enterprise in the New World as one of the governing council of the colony. A courageous and realistic leader, he was instrumental in helping the often-impractical colonists adapt to their new environment, organizing the 600 immigrants who joined the survivors of the first settlement

and introducing the cultivation of Indian corn. According to his own account, he was captured by Indians and saved from death by the intercession of the chief's daughter Pocahontas. That and other stories in his popular *Generall Historie of Virginia, New-England, and the Summer Isles* (1624) have been criticized as exaggerated, but his several volumes of history and description were influential in promoting immigration to the New World.

Specter, Arlen (1930–) *senator from Pennsylvania*

After graduating from the Yale Law School in 1956, Arlen Specter practiced in Philadelphia before entering politics. As a member of the Democratic Party, he served as Chief Counsel on the Warren Commission investigating the assassination of President John F. Kennedy. He later became a Republican and ran unsuccessfully for mayor of Philadelphia in 1973, senator in 1976, and governor in 1978. He was elected senator in 1980, 1986, 1992, 1998, and 2004 and sought the Republican presidential nomination in 1996 but was defeated by Bob Dole. A moderate conservative, Specter has established a record as prochoice and anti–gun control and is opposed to wiretapping without a legal warrant. A staunch supporter of the Immigration Reform amd Control Act (IRCA), he has voted against limiting welfare for immigrants and spoken in favor of a guest-worker program with a path to citizenship, extending Social Security rights to illegal aliens, and providing visas to skilled workers.

Standish, Miles (1584–1656) *soldier, American colonist*

After a career as a mercenary soldier in the Netherlands, British-born Miles Standish accompanied the Pilgrims on the *Mayflower* to the New World in 1620. He was appointed captain and put in charge of the defense of the colony, where he negotiated with Indians for land and supplies and later became treasurer and member of the governor's council.

Steuben, Friedrich Wilhelm Ludolph Gerhard Augustin von (Baron Steuben) (1730–1794) *German soldier*

A captain in the Prussian army, von Steuben came to America in 1777 with a recommendation from Benjamin Franklin to General Washington. Appointed inspector general of the army at Valley Forge, he trained the Continental army, was made a major general, and fought successfully at Monmouth and Yorktown. He became a naturalized citizen of the United States in 1783 and made his home in New York City.

Stoddard, Thomas Lothrop (1883–1950)
anti-immigration propagandist
With a family extending back to colonial Massachusetts, a law degree from Boston University, and a Ph.D. from Harvard, Stoddard was a respected lecturer and writer on world affairs and race. His most famous book, *The Rising Tide of Color Against White-World Supremacy* (1920), warned strongly against the danger to white civilization of the Asian and African races, and the next year his *The New World of Islam* outlined the same threat from the Near East. Stoddard was a disciple of Madison Grant, whose belief in the superiority of the "Nordic race" and fear of its pollution by the "lesser" Alpine and Mediterranean peoples he shared. Stoddard's *Racial Realities of Europe* (1924), *Reforging America* (1927), *Clashing Tides of Color* (1927) and other books all urged white solidarity and were influential in promoting restrictionist immigration policies.

Strong, Josiah (1847–1916) *clergyman, social reformer*
A Congregationalist pastor deeply concerned with the problems of the worker, Strong predicted class warfare, which he saw as threatened by increased immigration. His influential books *Our Country* (1885) and *The New Era* (1893) warned against foreigners as corrupters of government, causes of crime and immorality, and recruits for socialism. Strong founded the League for Social Service, calling for a Christian solution to social and economic problems, in 1898.

Stuyvesant, Peter (ca. 1610–1672) *Dutch political administrator in America*
An employee of the Dutch West India Company, Stuyvesant served in Brazil and became governor of Curaçao, the largest island of the Netherlands Antilles, in 1643. While leading a military force against a French fort on the island of St. Maarten the next year, he lost his right leg. In 1647 Stuyvesant was appointed director-general of New Netherland. During his 17 years of vigorous rule, he conciliated the Indians of the region, strengthened the trading post's defenses, expelled the Danish from Delaware (1655) and annexed the territory, and established the boundary between the Dutch and English colonies of Connecticut. A member of the Dutch Reformed Church, he enforced religious laws strictly and tried to suppress the Lutheran Church and the entry of Jews. This intol-

erance and his dictatorial manner made him personally unpopular, and when the English occupied the colony in 1664, his subjects refused to support him and the colony was surrendered without a fight.

Taft, William Howard (1857–1930) *twenty-seventh president of the United States*
Taft served as a judge of the Ohio Superior Court, U.S. solicitor general (1890–1902), U.S. Circuit Court judge (1892–1900), governor of the Philippine Islands (1901–04), secretary of war (1904–08), and chief justice of the U.S. Supreme Court (1921–30). As president (1909–13), Taft vetoed a restrictionist immigration bill presented to Congress in 1913.

Tocqueville, Alexis-Charles-Henri Maurice Clérel de (Alexis de Tocqueville) (1805–1859)
French writer, political analyst
Alexis de Tocqueville was born to a family of landed aristocracy in France. He studied law in Paris and was appointed a magistrate at Versailles. In 1831 he was commissioned by the government to go to America to report on the penal system; he published his report in 1833. Two years later he published his most important work, *Democracy in America*, which was awarded a prize by the French Academy the next year. The first systematic analysis of American democracy, the book provided an insightful account of the culture of the young country and the impact of its immigrant population. It was very popular internationally and was translated into many languages.

Truman, Harry S. (1884–1972) *thirty-third president of the United States*
After sitting as a senator of his native Missouri (1935–45), Truman was vice president under President Franklin Delano Roosevelt (1945) and inherited the presidency (1945–53) in that year. Truman worked for a liberal postwar policy. He vetoed the repressive Internal Security Act in 1950 and the restrictive immigration act proposed by Senator McCarran and Representative Walter in 1952, but both were passed over his veto.

Unonius, Gustaf (1810–1902) *Swedish pioneer in North America*
An educated Swede working as a government official in the university town of Uppsala, Sweden, Unonius was drawn to the New World in 1840 by its social equality and the economic opportunities it afforded. He founded a small Swedish colony, which he called

New Uppsala, in Wisconsin, and his enthusiastic letters home describing his venture, published in English in two volumes as *A Pioneer in Northwest America, 1841–58*, attracted many of his countrymen to the New World. The colony foundered, and he left it for New York in a few years to become a Lutheran minister. He later returned to Stockholm, but his example was influential in the westward spread of Swedish immigrants in the United States.

Walter, Francis Eugene (1894–1963) *U.S. representative from Pennsylvania*

After practicing law for 13 years, Walter was elected to the U.S. House of Representatives on the Democratic ticket in 1932 and retained his seat there until his death. He strongly opposed a bill for the establishment of a permanent Committee on Un-American Activities in the 79th Congress in 1945 but during the next Congress, in 1948, he supported a subversive activities control bill. In 1948 he introduced into the House a bill doubling the number of displaced persons allowed to enter the United States. In 1949 he reluctantly became the second-ranking Democrat on the House Un-American Activities Committee, and in March of that year he introduced a bill to deprive American communists of citizenship. In 1950, as chairman of the House Judiciary Subcommittee on Immigration Affairs, he introduced a bill to enable Americans who had lost their citizenship by voting in the Italian election to regain it, and another to increase the number of war refugees admitted to the United States. He also proposed a bill to remove racial barriers to naturalization. Walter was active throughout his career in investigating communist activities and sponsoring immigration-reform legislation. His most influential contribution was his successful introduction, with Senator Pat McCarran, of the 1952 Immigration and Naturalization Act, establishing precise immigration quotas for admission to the United States from each country.

West, Thomas (Lord Delaware, Baron De La Warre) (1577–1618) *colonist*

The 12th baron De La Warre, West was an English soldier who became a member of the council of the Virginia Company in 1609 and successfully recruited 400 new immigrants to the colony in 1610. He became its governor the same year and saved it from dissolving. The colony of Delaware was named for him.

Williams, Roger (1603–1684) *clergyman, political reformer, colonizer*

An ordained minister of the Church of England, Williams was opposed to the idea of a state church and was persecuted in England for his democratic political beliefs. He immigrated to Massachusetts in 1631 but refused a pulpit in the Boston church because it was dependent on the English church. His insistence that only the Indians owned the land and that the government had no power to impose a religion on the people resulted in his banishment from Massachusetts in 1635, and he went to live among the Indians. The next year Williams and a few faithful followers received from the Indians a tract of land on which they founded the city of Providence. Dedicated to democratic principles, the separation of church and state, and religious toleration, the community became the first city of Rhode Island. Williams secured a charter for the Providence plantation in 1644 and served as its president from 1654 to 1657.

Wilson, Thomas Woodrow (1856–1924) *twenty-eighth president of the United States*

A professor of jurisprudence and political economy, Wilson was president of Princeton University from 1902 to 1910 and governor of New Jersey from 1911 to 1913. He accomplished many reforms as governor. As U.S. president (1913–21) he was unable to maintain American neutrality in World War I or to bring the United States into the League of Nations after it. Like his predecessor, William Howard Taft, he vetoed an immigration bill calling for a literacy test in 1915, but a similar bill was passed over his veto in 1917.

Winthrop, John (1588–1649) *colonial leader*

Dissatisfied with both the church and the government of England, Winthrop left his law practice in London to become governor of the Massachusetts Bay Company in 1630. A devout Puritan, he did much to define the religious and political principles of his colony, and during his nearly 20 years as governor and deputy governor of Massachusetts he worked to limit immigration to those accepting Puritan theology. When the New England Confederacy, incorporating the several colonies of the region, was formed in 1643 to protect the colonists from the Native Americans, Winthrop became its first president.

Zangwill, Israel (1864–1926) *English playwright and novelist*

A popular writer of light fiction and editor of a humorous magazine, Zangwill won great success with his 1898 novel *The Children of the Ghetto*, depicting the life of Jewish immigrants in London. His most famous work was the play *The Melting Pot* (1908), dealing with intermarriage and the fusion of races in America. Much admired by President Theodore Roosevelt, it provided a slogan for the American dream of racial harmony, and its title was to enter the national vocabulary. Zangwill was active in international Zionism and founded the Jewish Territorial Organization for the Settlement of the Jews Within the British Empire, of which he was president from 1905 to 1925.

Ziglar, James W. (1945–) *commissioner of the Immigration and Naturalization Service*

Mississippi-born James W. Ziglar is a graduate of George Washington University law school and had a long career as an investment banker before entering public service. Leaving his position as a managing director of PaineWebber Inc. in 1998, he was elected sergeant at arms of the U.S. Senate, where he was chief protocol and law enforcement officer. In 2001 he was appointed commissioner of the Immigration and Naturalization Service. Criticized in the conservative press for leniency, he retired on November 30, 2002, as the last commissioner of the INS.

Appendix C
Maps

413

Distributions by Regions of the Six Most Numerous Foreign-Born White Groups, 1930

More than 500,000 people to the region

100,000 to 500,000 people to the region

25,000 to 100,000 people to the region

Fewer than 25,000 people to the region

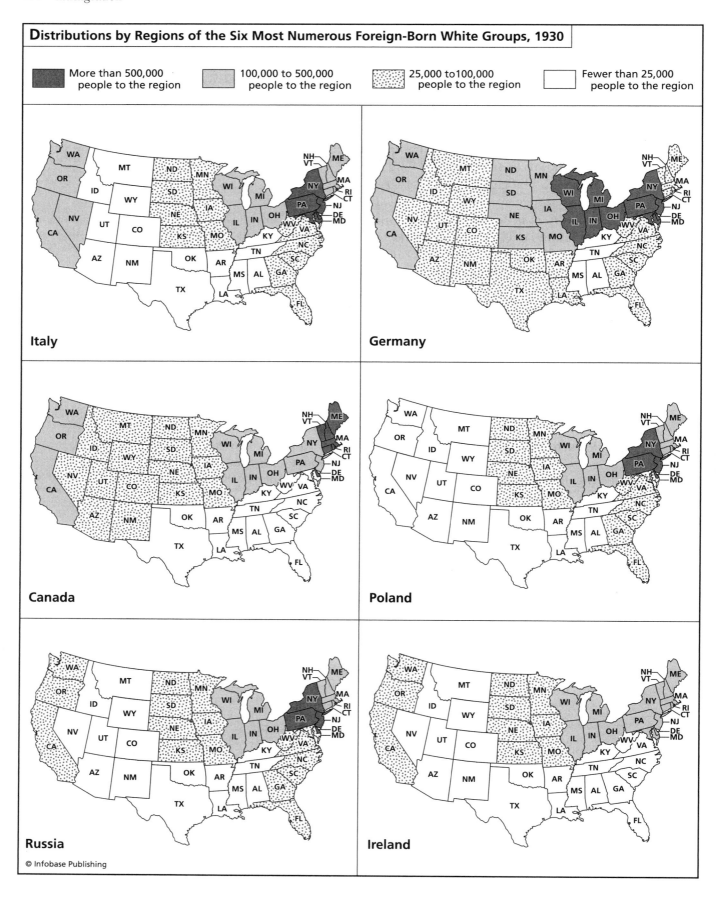

Italy

Germany

Canada

Poland

Russia

Ireland

© Infobase Publishing

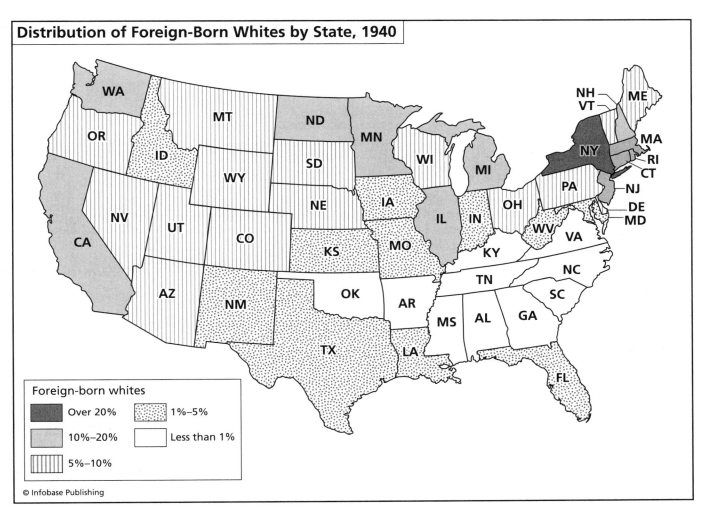

Distribution of Foreign-Born Whites by State, 1940

Foreign-born whites

- Over 20%
- 10%–20%
- 5%–10%
- 1%–5%
- Less than 1%

© Infobase Publishing

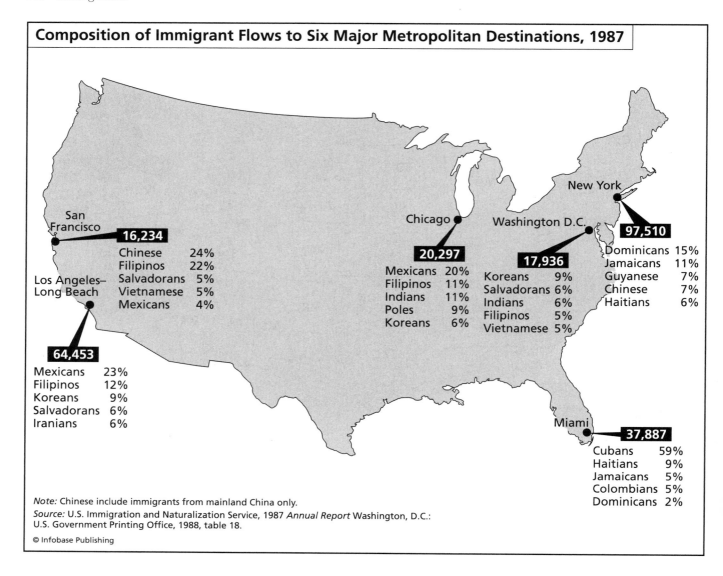

Composition of Immigrant Flows to Six Major Metropolitan Destinations, 1987

San Francisco — 16,234

Chinese	24%
Filipinos	22%
Salvadorans	5%
Vietnamese	5%
Mexicans	4%

Los Angeles–Long Beach — 64,453

Mexicans	23%
Filipinos	12%
Koreans	9%
Salvadorans	6%
Iranians	6%

Chicago — 20,297

Mexicans	20%
Filipinos	11%
Indians	11%
Poles	9%
Koreans	6%

Washington D.C. — 17,936

Koreans	9%
Salvadorans	6%
Indians	6%
Filipinos	5%
Vietnamese	5%

New York — 97,510

Dominicans	15%
Jamaicans	11%
Guyanese	7%
Chinese	7%
Haitians	6%

Miami — 37,887

Cubans	59%
Haitians	9%
Jamaicans	5%
Colombians	5%
Dominicans	2%

Note: Chinese include immigrants from mainland China only.

Source: U.S. Immigration and Naturalization Service, 1987 *Annual Report* Washington, D.C.: U.S. Government Printing Office, 1988, table 18.

© Infobase Publishing

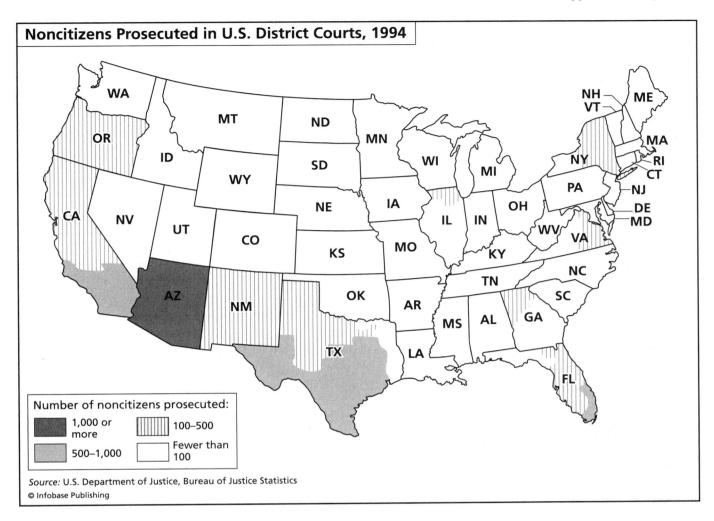

Noncitizens Prosecuted in U.S. District Courts, 1994

Number of noncitizens prosecuted:

- 1,000 or more
- 500–1,000
- 100–500
- Fewer than 100

Source: U.S. Department of Justice, Bureau of Justice Statistics
© Infobase Publishing

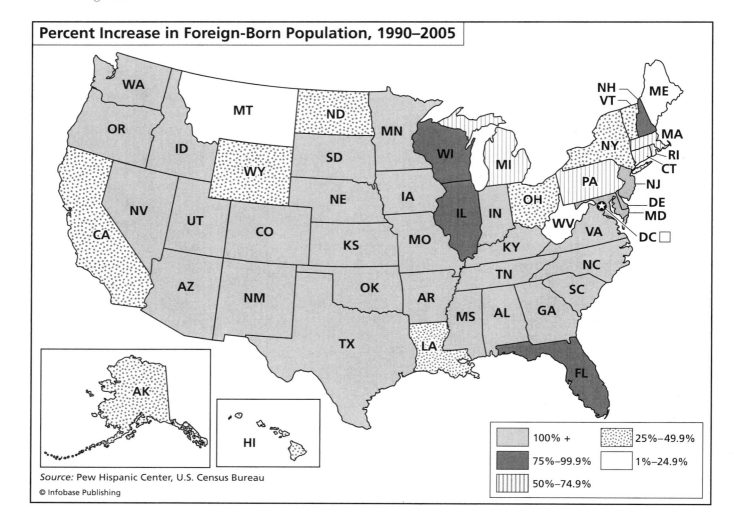

Percent Increase in Foreign-Born Population, 1990–2005

Legend:
- 100% +
- 75%–99.9%
- 50%–74.9%
- 25%–49.9%
- 1%–24.9%

Source: Pew Hispanic Center, U.S. Census Bureau

© Infobase Publishing

Appendix D
Graphs and Tables

1. Persons Obtaining Legal Permanent Resident Status in the United States, Fiscal Years 1820–2005
2. Persons Obtaining Legal Permanent Resident Status in the United States by Region and Country of Last Residence, Fiscal Years 1820–2005
3. Immigration to the United States from Northern and Western Europe and Southern and Eastern Europe, 1820–1923
4. Immigrants Admitted to the United States by Region of Birth, 1820–1979
5. Immigrants and Their Children in the United States, 1870–2040
6. Reasons for Emigrating, 1933–1945
7. Refugee Arrivals, in the United States, Fiscal Years 1980–2005
8. U.S. Immigration Admissions, 1990–1999
9. Apprehensions of Undocumented Immigrants, 1991–1999
10. Origins of 9.1 Million Legal Immigrants Arriving in the United States, 1991–2000
11. Origins of 7 Million Undocumented Immigrants in the United States, 2000

419

Persons Obtaining Legal Permanent Resident Status in the United States, Fiscal Years 1820–2005

Year	Number	Year	Number	Year	Number	Year	Number	Year	Number
1820	8,385	1859	121,282	1898	229,299	1937	50,244	197 6[1]	499,093
1821	9,127	1860	153,640	1899	311,715	1938	67,895	197 7	458,755
1822	6,911	1861	91,918	1900	448,572	1939	82,998	1978	589,810
1823	6,354	1862	91,985	1901	487,918	1940	70,756	1979	394,244
1824	7,912	1863	176,282	1902	648,743	1941	51,776	198 0	524,295
1825	10,199	1864	193,418	1903	857,046	1942	28,781	198 1	595,014
1826	10,837	1865	248,120	1904	812,870	1943	23,725	198 2	533,624
1827	18,875	1866	318,568	1905	1,026,499	1944	28,551	198 3	550,052
1828	27,382	1867	315,722	1906	1,100,735	1945	38,119	198 4	541,811
1829	22,520	1868	138,840	1907	1,285,349	1946	108,721	1985	568,149
1830	23,322	1869	352,768	1908	782,870	1947	147,292	1986	600,027
1831	22,633	1870	387,203	1909	751,786	1948	170,570	1987	599,889
1832	60,482	1871	321,350	1910	1,041,570	1949	188,317	1988	641,346
1833	58,640	1872	404,806	1911	878,587	1950	249,187	1989	1,090,172
1834	65,365	1873	459,803	1912	838,112	1951	205,717	1990	1,535,872
1835	45,374	1874	313,339	1913	1,197,892	1952	265,520	1991	1,826,595
1836	76,242	1875	227,498	1914	1,218,480	1953	170,434	1992	973,445
1837	79,340	1876	169,986	1915	326,700	1954	208,177	1993	903,916
1838	38,914	1877	141,857	1916	298,826	1955	237,790	1994	803,993
1839	68,069	1878	138,469	1917	295,403	1956	321,625	1995	720,177
1840	84,066	1879	177,826	1918	110,618	1957	326,867	1996	915,560
1841	80,289	1880	457,257	1919	141,132	1958	253,265	1997	797,847
1842	104,565	1881	669,431	1920	430,001	1959	260,686	1998	653,206
1843	52,496	1882	788,992	1921	805,228	1960	265,398	1999	644,787
1844	78,615	1883	603,322	1922	309,556	1961	271,344	2000	841,002
1845	114,371	1884	518,592	1923	522,919	1962	283,763	2001	1,058,902
1846	154,416	1885	395,346	1924	706,896	1963	306,260	2002	1,059,356
1847	234,968	1986	334,203	1925	294,314	1964	292,248	2003	703,542
1848	226,527	1887	490,109	1926	304,488	1965	296,697	2004	957,883
1849	297,024	1888	546,889	1927	335,175	1966	323,040	2005	1,122,313
1850	369,980	1889	444,427	1928	307,255	1967	361,972		
1851	379,466	1890	455,302	1929	279,678	1968	454,448		
1852	371,603	1891	560,319	1930	241,700	1969	358,579		
1853	368,645	1892	579,663	1931	97,139	1970	373,326		
1854	427,833	1893	439,730	1932	35,576	1971	370,478		
1855	200,877	1894	285,631	1933	23,068	1972	384,685		
1856	200,436	1895	258,536	1934	29,470	1973	398,515		
1857	251,306	1896	343,267	1935	34,956	1974	393,919		
1858	123,126	1897	230,832	1936	36,329	1975	385,378		

[1] Includes the 15 months from July 1, 1975, to September 30, 1976, because the end date of fiscal years was changed from June 30 to September 30.

Source: U.S. Department of Homeland Security.

Persons Obtaining Legal Permanent Resident Status in the United States, by Region and Selected Country of Last Residence, Fiscal Years 1820–2005

Region and Country of Last Residence[1]	1820 to 1829	1830 to 1839	1840 to 1849	1850 to 1859	1860 to 1869	1870 to 1879	1880 to 1889	1890 to 1899	1900 to 1909
Total	128,502	538,381	1,427,337	2,814,554	2,081,26 1	2,742,137	5,248,568	3,694,294	8,202,388
Europe	99,272	422,771	1,369,259	2,619,680	1,877,726	2,2 51,878	4,638,677	3,576,411	7,572,569
Austria-Hungary[2,3,4]	–	–	–	–	3,375	60,127	314,787	534,059	2,001,376
Austria[2,4]	–	–	–	–	2,700	54,529	204,805	268,218	532,416
Hungary[2]	–	–	–	–	483	5,598	109,982	203,350	685,567
Belgium	28	20	3,996	5,765	5,785	6,991	18,738	19,642	37,429
Bulgaria[5]	–	–	–	–	–	–	–	52	34,651
Czechoslovakia[6]	–	–	–	–	–	–	–	–	–
Denmark	173	927	671	3,227	13,553	29,278	85,342	56,671	61,227
Finland	–	–	–	–	–	–	–	–	–
France[7]	7,694	39,330	75,300	81,778	35,938	71,901	48, 193	35,616	67,735
Germany[3,4]	5,753	124,726	385,434	976,072	723,734	751,769	1,445,181	579,072	328,722
Greece	17	49	17	32	51	209	1,807	12,732	145,402
Ireland[8]	51,617	170,672	656,145	1,029,48 6	427,419	422,264	674,061	405,710	344,940
Italy	430	2,225	1,476	8,643	9,853	46,296	267,660	603,76 1	1,930,475
Netherlands	1,105	1,377	7,624	11,122	8,387	14,267	52,715	29,349	42,463
Norway-Sweden[9]	91	1,149	12,389	22,202	82, 937	178,823	586,441	334,058	426,981
Norway[9]	–	–	–	–	16,068	88,644	185,111	96,810	182,542
Sweden[9]	–	–	–	–	24,224	90,179	401,330	237,248	244,439
Poland[3]	19	366	105	1,087	1,886	11,016	42, 910	107,793	–
Portugal[10]	177	820	196	1,299	2,083	13, 971	15,186	25,874	65,154
Romania	–	–	–	–	–	–	5,842	6,808	57,322
Russia[3,11]	86	280	520	423	1,670	35,177	182,698	450,101	1,501,301
Spain[12]	2,595	2,010	1,916	8,795	6,966	5,540	3,9 95	9,189	24,818
Switzerland	3,148	4,430	4,819	24,423	21,124	25,212	81,151	37,020	32,541
United Kingdom[8,13]	26,336	74,350	218,572	445,322	532,956	578,447	810,900	328,759	469,518
Yugoslavia[14]	–	–	–	–	–	–	–	–	–
Other Europe	3	40	79	4	9	590	1,070	145	514
Asia	34	55	121	36,080	54,408	134,128	71,151	61,285	299,836
China	3	8	32	35,933	54,028	133,139	65,797	15,268	19,884
Hong Kong	–	–	–	–	–	–	–	–	–
India	9	38	33	42	50	166	247	102	3,026
Iran	–	–	–	–	–	–	–	–	–
Israel	–	–	–	–	–	–	–	–	–
Japan	–	–	–	–	138	19 3	1,583	13,998	139,712
Jordan	–	–	–	–	–	–	–	–	–
Korea	–	–	–	–	–	–	–	–	–
Philippines	–	–	–	–	–	–	–	–	–
Syria	–	–	–	–	–	–	–	–	–
Taiwan	–	–	–	–	–	–	–	–	–
Turkey	19	8	45	94	129	382	2,478	27,510	127,999
Vietnam	–	–	–	–	–	–	–	–	–
Other Asia	3	1	11	11	63	248	1,046	4,407	9,215
America	9,655	31,905	50,516	84,145	130,292	345,010	524,82 6	37,350	277,809
Canada and Newfoundland[15,16]	2,297	11,875	34,285	64,171	117,978	324,310	492,865	3,098	123,067
Mexico[16,17]	3,835	7,187	3,069	3,446	1,957	5,133	2,405	734	31,188
Caribbean	3,061	11,792	11,803	12,447	8,751	14,285	27,323	31,480	100,960
Cuba	–	–	–	–	–	–	–	–	–
Dominican Republic	–	–	–	–	–	–	–	–	–
Haiti	–	–	–	–	–	–	–	–	–
Jamaica[18]	3,061	11,792	11,803	12,447	8,751	14,285	27,323	31,480	100,960
Other Caribbean[18]	57	94	297	512	70	173	279	649	7,341
Central America	–	–	–	–	–	–	–	–	77
Belize	–	–	–	–	–	–	–	–	–
Costa Rica	–	–	–	–	–	–	–	–	–
El Salvador	–	–	–	–	–	–	–	–	–
Guatemala	–	–	–	–	–	–	–	–	–
Honduras	–	–	–	–	–	–	–	–	–
Nicaragua	–	–	–	–	–	–	–	–	–
Panama[19]									

See footnotes at end of table.

Persons Obtaining Legal Permanent Resident Status in the United States, by Region and Selected Country of Last Residence, Fiscal Years 1820–2005
– Continued

Region and Country of Last Residence[1]	1910 to 1919	1920 to 1929	1930 to 1939	1940 to 1949	1950 to 1959	1960 to 1969	1970 to 1979	1980 to 1989	1990 to 1999
Total	6,347,380	4,295,510	699,375	856,608	2,499,26 8	3,213,749	4,248,203	6,244,379	9,775,398
Europe	4,985,411	2,560,340	444,399	472,524	1,404,97 3	1,133,443	825,590	668,866	1,348,612
Austria-Hungary[2,3,4]	1,154,727	60,891	12,531	13,574	113,015	27,590	20,387	20,437	27,529
Austria[2,4]	589,174	31,392	5,307	8,393	81,354	17,571	14,239	15,374	18,234
Hungary[2]	565,553	29,499	7,224	5,181	31, 661	10,019	6,148	5,063	9,295
Belgium	32,574	21,511	4,013	12,473	18,885	9,647	5,413	7,028	7,077
Bulgaria[5]	27,180	2,824	1,062	449	97	59 8	1,011	1,124	16,948
Czechoslovakia[6]	–	101,182	17, 757	8,475	1,624	2,758	5,654	5,678	8,970
Denmark	45,830	34,406	3,470	4,549	10,918	9,797	4,405	4,847	6,189
Finland	–	16,922	2,438	2,230	4,923	4,310	2,829	2,569	3,970
France[7]	60,335	54,842	13,761	36,954	50,113	46,975	26, 281	32,066	35,945
Germany[3,4]	174,227	386,634	119,107	119,506	576,905	209,616	77,142	85,752	92,207
Greece	198,108	60,774	10,599	8,605	45,153	74,173	102,370	37, 729	25,403
Ireland[8]	166,445	202,854	28,195	15,701	47, 189	37,788	11,461	22,210	65,384
Italy	1,229,916	528,133	85,053	50,509	184,576	200,11 1	150,031	55,562	75,992
Netherlands	46,065	29,397	7,791	13,877	46,703	37,918	10,373	11,234	13,345
Norway-Sweden[9]	192,445	170,329	13, 452	17,326	44,224	36,150	10,298	13,941	17,825
Norway[9]	79,488	70,327	6,901	8,326	22,806	17, 371	3,927	3,835	5,211
Sweden[9]	112,957	100,002	6,551	9,0 00	21,418	18,779	6,371	10,106	12,614
Poland[3]	–	223,316	25,555	7,577	6,4 65	55,742	33,696	63,483	172,249
Portugal[10]	82,489	44,829	3,518	6,765	13,928	70, 568	104,754	42,685	25,497
Romania	13,566	67,810	5,264	1,254	914	2,339	10,774	24,753	48,136
Russia[3,11]	1,106,998	61,604	2,463	605	453	2,329	28,132	33,311	433,427
Spain[12]	53,262	47,109	3,669	2,774	6,880	40,793	41,718	22,783	18,443
Switzerland	22,839	31,772	5,990	9,904	17,577	19,193	8,536	8,316	11,768
United Kingdom[8,13]	371,878	341,552	61,813	131,794	195,709	220,213	133,218	153,644	156,182
Yugoslavia[14]	–	49,215	6,920	2,039	6,9 66	17,990	31,862	16,267	57,039
Other Europe	6,527	22,434	9,978	5,584	11,756	6,845	5,245	3,447	29,087
Asia	269,736	126,740	19,231	34,532	135,844	358,60 5	1,406,544	2,391,356	2,859,899
China	20,916	30,648	5,874	16,072	8,836	14,060	17,627	170,897	342,058
Hong Kong	–	–	–	–	13,781	67,047	117,350	112,132	116,894
India	3,478	2,076	554	1,692	1,850	18,638	147,997	231,64 9	352,528
Iran	–	208	198	1,144	3,195	9,059	33,763	98,141	76,899
Israel	–	–	–	98	21,376	30,911	36, 306	43,669	41,340
Japan	77,125	42,057	2,683	1,557	40,651	40,956	49,392	44,150	66,582
Jordan	–	–	–	–	4,899	9,2 30	25,541	28,928	42,755
Korea	–	–	–	83	4,845	27,048	241 ,192	322,708	179,770
Philippines	–	–	391	4,099	17,245	70,660	337 ,726	502,056	534,338
Syria	–	5,307	2,188	1,179	1,091	2,432	8,086	14,534	22,906
Taiwan	–	–	–	–	721	15, 657	83,155	119,051	132,647
Turkey	160,717	40,450	1,327	754	2,980	9,464	12,209	19,208	38,687
Vietnam	–	–	–	–	290	2,9 49	121,716	200,632	275,379
Other Asia	7,500	5,994	6,016	7,854	14,084	40,494	174,484	483,601	637,116
America	1,070,539	1,591,278	230,319	328,435	921,61 0	1,674,172	1,904,355	2,695,329	5,137,743
Canada and Newfoundland[15,16]	708,715	949,286	162,703	160,911	353,169	433,128	179,267	156 ,313	194,788
Mexico[16,17]	185,334	498,945	32,709	56,158	273,847	441,824	621,218	1,009,586	2,757,418
Caribbean	120,860	83,482	18,052	46,194	115,661	427,23 5	708,850	790,109	1,004,687
Cuba	–	12,769	10,641	25,976	73,221	202,030	256,49 7	132,552	159,037
Dominican Republic	–	–	1,026	4,802	10,219	83,552	139,249	221,552	359,818
			156	823	3,787	28,992	55,166	121 ,406	177,446
Haiti	–	–	–	–	7,397	62,218	130,226	193,874	177,143
Jamaica[18]	120,860	70,713	6,229	14,593	21,037	50,443	127,712	120,725	131,243
Other Caribbean[18]	15,692	16,511	6,840	20,135	40,201	98,560	120,374	339,376	610,189
Central America	40	285	193	433	1,133	4,185	6,747	14,964	12,600
Belize	–	–	431	1,965	4,044	17,975	12,405	25,017	17,054
Costa Rica	–	–	597	4,885	5,094	14,405	29,428	137,418	273,017
El Salvador	–	–	423	1,303	4,197	14,357	23, 837	58,847	126,043
Guatemala	–	–	679	1,874	5,320	15,078	15, 651	39,071	72,880
Honduras	–	–	405	4,393	7,812	10,383	10, 911	31,102	80,446
Nicaragua	–	–	1,452	5,2 82	12,601	22,177	21,395	32,957	28,149
Panama[19]									

See footnotes at end of table.

Persons Obtaining Legal Permanent Resident Status in the United States, by Region and Selected Country of Last Residence, Fiscal Years 1820–2005

– Continued

Region and Country of Last Residence[1]	2000	2001	2002	2003	2004	2005
Total	841,002	1,058,902	1,059,356	703,542	957,88 3	1,122,373
Europe	131,920	176,892	177,059	102,546	135,66 3	180,449
Austria-Hungary[2, 3, 4]	2,009	2,303	4,004	2,176	3,689	4,569
Austria[2, 4]	986	996	2,650	1,160	2,442	3,002
Hungary[2]	1,023	1,307	1,354	1,016	1,247	1,567
Belgium	817	997	834	515	746	1,031
Bulgaria[5]	4,779	4,273	3,476	3,706	4,042	5,451
Czechoslovakia[6]	1,407	1,911	1,854	1,472	1,8 71	2,182
Denmark	549	732	651	435	568	714
Finland	377	497	365	230	346	549
France[7]	4,063	5,379	4,567	2,926	4,209	5,035
Germany[3, 4]	12,230	21,992	20,977	8,061	10,270	12,864
Greece	5,113	1,941	1,486	900	1,213	1,473
Ireland[8]	1,264	1,531	1,400	1,002	1,518	2,083
Italy	2,652	3,332	2,812	1,890	2,495	3,179
Netherlands	1,455	1,888	2,296	1,321	1,713	2,150
Norway-Sweden[9]	1,967	2,544	2,082	1,516	2,0 11	2,264
Norway[9]	508	582	460	385	457	472
Sweden[9]	1,459	1,962	1,622	1,131	1,554	1,792
Poland[3]	9,750	12,308	13,274	11,004	14,048	14,837
Portugal[10]	1,373	1,611	1,301	808	1,062	1,084
Romania	6,506	6,206	4,515	3,305	4,078	6,431
Russia[3, 11]	43,156	54,838	55,370	33,513	41,959	60,395
Spain[12]	1,390	1,875	1,588	1,102	1,453	2,002
Switzerland	1,339	1,786	1,493	862	1,193	1,465
United Kingdom[8, 13]	14,427	20,118	17,940	11,155	16,680	21,956
Yugoslavia[14]	11,960	21,854	28,051	8,270	13,213	19,249
Other Europe	3,337	6,976	6,723	6,377	7,286	9,486
Asia	254,932	336,112	325,749	235,339	319,025	382,744
China	41,804	50,677	55,901	37,342	50,280	64,921
Hong Kong	7,181	10,282	7,938	5,015	5,421	5,004
India	38,938	65,673	66,644	47,032	65,507	79,140
Iran	6,481	8,003	7,684	4,696	5,898	7,306
Israel	3,871	4,892	4,907	3,686	5,206	6,963
Japan	7,688	10,424	9,106	6,702	8,655	9,929
Jordan	4,476	5,106	4,774	4,008	5,186	5,430
Korea	15,107	19,728	19,917	12,076	19,441	26,002
Philippines	40,465	50,644	48,493	43,133	54,651	57,656
Syria	2,255	3,542	3,350	2,046	2,549	3,350
Taiwan	9,457	12,457	9,932	7,168	9,314	9,389
Turkey	2,702	3,463	3,914	3,318	4,491	6,449
Vietnam	25,159	34,537	32,372	21,227	30,074	30,832
Other Asia	49,348	56,684	50,817	37,890	52,352	70,373
America	392,461	470,794	477,363	305,936	408,972	432,748
Canada and Newfoundland[15, 16]	21,289	29,991	27,142	16,447	22,439	29,930
Mexico[16, 17]	171,445	204,032	216,924	114,758	173,711	157,992
Caribbean	84,250	96,384	93,914	67,498	82,116	91,378
Cuba	17,897	25,832	27,435	8,685	15,385	20,651
Dominican	17,373	21,139	22,386	26,112	30,063	27,366
Republic	21,977	22,470	19,151	11,924	13,695	13,496
Haiti	15,603	15,031	14,507	13,045	13,581	17,775
Jamaica[18]	11,400	11,912	10,435	7,732	9,392	12,090
Other Caribbean[18]	60,331	72,504	66,298	53,283	61,253	52,636
Central America	774	982	983	616	888	901
Belize	1,390	1,863	1,686	1,322	1,811	2,479
Costa Rica	22,301	30,876	30,472	27,854	29,297	20,891
El Salvador	9,861	13,399	15,870	14,195	18,655	16,475
Guatemala	5,851	6,546	6,355	4,582	5,339	6,825
Honduras	18,258	16,908	9,171	3,503	3,842	3,196
Nicaragua	1,896	1,930	1,761	1,211	1,421	1,869
Panama[19]						

See footnotes at end of table.

Persons Obtaining Legal Permanent Resident Status in the United States, by Region and Selected Country of Last Residence, Fiscal Years 1820–2005

— Continued

Region and Country of Last Residence[1]	1910 to 1919	1920 to 1929	1930 to 1939	1940 to 1949	1950 to 1959	1960 to 1969	1970 to 1979	1980 to 1989	1990 to 1999
Other Central America	15,652	16,226	2,660	–	–	–	–	–	–
South America	39,938	43,025	9,990	19,662	78,418	250,754	273,608	399,862	570,624
Argentina	–	–	1,067	3,108	16,346	49,384	30,303	23,442	30,065
Bolivia	–	–	50	893	2,759	6,205	5,635	9,798	18,111
Brazil	–	4,627	1,468	3,653	11,547	29,238	18,600	22,944	50,744
Chile	–	–	347	1,320	4,669	12,384	15,032	19,749	18,200
Colombia	–	–	1,027	3,454	15,567	68,371	71,265	105,494	137,985
Ecuador	–	–	244	2,207	8,574	34,107	47,464	48,015	81,358
Guyana	–	–	131	596	1,131	4,546	38,278	85,886	74,407
Paraguay	–	–	33	85	576	1,249	1,486	3,518	6,082
Peru	–	–	321	1,273	5,980	19,783	25,311	49,958	110,117
Suriname	–	–	25	130	299	612	714	1,357	2,285
Uruguay	–	–	112	754	1,026	4,089	8,416	7,235	6,062
Venezuela	–	–	1,155	2,182	9,927	20,758	11,007	22,405	35,180
Other South America	39,938	38,398	4,010	7	17	28	97	61	28
Other America[20]	–	29	25	25,375	60,314	22,671	1,038	83	37
Africa	8,867	6,362	2,120	6,720	13,016	23,780	71,408	141,990	346,416
Egypt	–	1,063	781	1,613	1,996	5,581	23,543	26,744	44,604
Ethiopia	–	–	10	28	302	804	2,588	12,927	40,097
Liberia	–	–	35	37	289	841	2,391	6,420	13,587
Morocco	–	–	73	879	2,703	2,880	1,967	3,471	15,768
South Africa	–	–	312	1,022	2,278	4,360	10,002	15,505	21,964
Other Africa	8,867	5,299	909	3,141	5,448	9,314	30,917	76,923	210,396
Oceania	12,339	9,860	3,306	14,262	11,353	23,630	39,980	41,432	56,800
Australia	11,280	8,404	2,260	11,201	8,275	14,986	18,708	16,901	24,288
New Zealand	–	935	790	2,351	1,799	3,775	5,018	6,129	8,600
Other Oceania	1,059	521	256	710	1,279	4,869	16,254	18,402	23,912
Not Specified[20, 21]	488	930	–	135	12,472	119	326	305,406	25,928

See footnotes at end of table.

Persons Obtaining Legal Permanent Resident Status in the United States, by Region and Selected Country of Last Residence, Fiscal Years 1820–2005
— Continued

Region and Country of Last Residence[1]	2000	2001	2002	2003	2004	2005
Other Central America	–	–	–	–	–	–
South America	55,143	67,880	73,082	53,946	69,452	100,811
Argentina	2,472	3,426	3,791	3,193	4,672	6,945
Bolivia	1,744	1,804	1,660	1,365	1,719	2,164
Brazil	6,767	9,391	9,034	6,108	10,247	16,331
Chile	1,660	1,881	1,766	1,255	1,719	2,354
Colombia	14,125	16,234	18,409	14,400	18,055	24,710
Ecuador	7,624	9,654	10,524	7,022	8,366	11,528
Guyana	5,255	7,835	9,492	6,373	5,721	8,772
Paraguay	394	464	413	222	324	523
Peru	9,361	10,838	11,737	9,169	11,369	15,205
Suriname	281	254	223	175	170	287
Uruguay	396	516	499	470	750	1,110
Venezuela	5,052	5,576	5,529	4,190	6,335	10,870
Other South America	12	7	5	4	5	12
Other America[20]	3	3	3	4	1	1
Africa	40,790	50,009	56,002	45,559	62,623	79,701
Egypt	4,323	5,333	6,215	3,928	6,590	10,296
Ethiopia	3,645	4,620	6,308	5,969	7,180	8,380
Liberia	1,225	1,477	1,467	1,081	1,540	1,846
Morocco	3,423	4,752	3,188	2,969	3,910	4,165
South Africa	2,814	4,046	3,685	2,088	3,335	4,425
Other Africa	25,360	29,781	35,139	29,524	40,068	50,589
Oceania	5,928	7,201	6,495	5,076	6,954	7,432
Australia	2,694	3,714	3,420	2,488	3,397	4,090
New Zealand	1,080	1,347	1,364	1,030	1,420	1,457
Other Oceania	2,154	2,140	1,711	1,558	2,137	1,885
Not Specified[20, 21]	14,971	17,894	16,688	9,086	24,646	39,299

– Represents zero or not available.

[1] Data for years prior to 1906 refer to country of origin; data from 1906 to 2005 refer to country of last residence.

[2] Data for Austria and Hungary not reported separately for all years during 1860 to 1869, 1890 to 1899, 1900 to 1909.

[3] From 1899 to 1919, data for Poland included in Austria-Hungary, Germany, and the Soviet Union.

[4] From 1938 to 1945, data for Austria included in Germany.

[5] From 1899 to 1910, included Serbia and Montenegro.

[6] Currently includes the Czech Republic and Slovak Republic.

[7] From 1820 to 1910, included Corsica.

[8] Prior to 1926, data for Northern Ireland included in Ireland.

[9] Data for Norway and Sweden not reported separately until 1869.

[10] From 1820 to 1910, included Cape Verde and Azores Islands.

[11] From 1820 to 1920, data refer to the Russian Empire. Between 1920 and 1990 data refer to the Soviet Union. From 1991 to present, the data refer to the Russian federation, Armenia, Azerbaijan, Belarus, Georgia, Kazakhstan, Kyrgyzstan, Moldova, Russia, Tajikistan, Ukraine, and Uzbekistan.

[12] From 1820 to 1910, included the Canary Islands and Balearic Islands.

[13] Since 1925, data for United Kingdom refer to England, Scotland, Wales, and Northern Ireland.

[14] Currently includes Bosnia-Herzegovina, Croatia, Macedonia, Slovenia, Serbia, and Montenegro.

[15] Prior to 1911, data refer to British North America. From 1911, data include Newfoundland.

[16] Land arrivals not completely enumerated until 1908.

[17] No data available for Mexico from 1886 to 1893.

[18] Data for Jamaica not reported separately until 1953. Prior to 1953, Jamaica was included in British West Indies.

[19] From 1932 to 1972, data for the Panama Canal Zone included in Panama.

[20] Included in 'Not Specified' until 1925.

[21] Includes 32,897 persons returning in 1906 to their homes in the United States.

Note: From 1820 to 1867 figures represent alien passenger arrivals at seaports; from 1868 to 1891 and 1895 to 1897 immigrant alien arrivals; from 1892 to 1894 and 1898 to 2005 immigrant aliens admitted for permanent residence; from 1892 to 1903 aliens entering by cabin class were not counted as immigrants. Land arrivals were not completely enumerated until 1908. For this table, fiscal year 1843 covers nine months ending September 1843, fiscal years 1832 and 1850 cover 15 months ending December 31 of the respective years, and fiscal year 1868 covers six months ending June 30, 1868.

Source: U.S. Department of Homeland Security

Immigration to the United States from Northern and Western Europe and Southern and Eastern Europe, 1820–1923

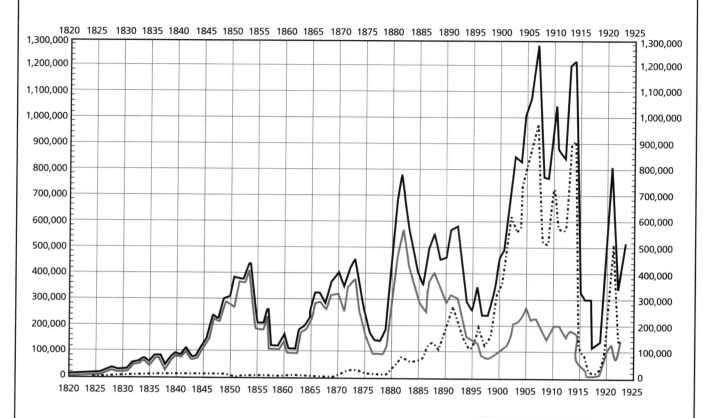

Northern and western Europe

Southern and eastern Europe

All countries

Immigrants Admitted to the United States by Region of Birth, 1820–1979

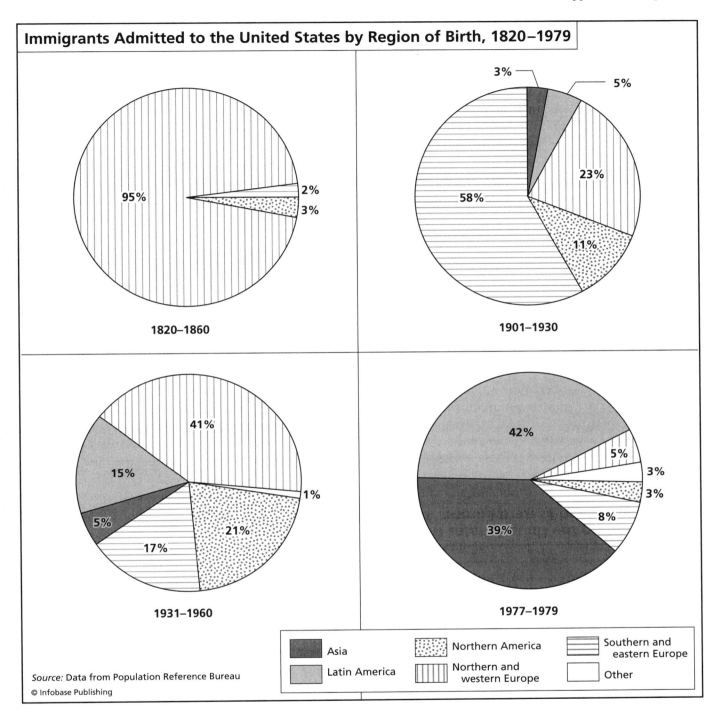

1820–1860

1901–1930

1931–1960

1977–1979

Legend:
- Asia
- Latin America
- Northern America
- Northern and western Europe
- Southern and eastern Europe
- Other

Source: Data from Population Reference Bureau
© Infobase Publishing

Immigrants and Their Children in the United States, 1870–2040

Percentage of Population

	1870	1910	1970	2040 (est.)
Children of immigrants	14%	20%	12%	13%
Immigrants	14%	15%	5%	14%

■ Immigrants   ▤ Children of immigrants

Source: Data from Peter Brimelow, *Alien Nation*, New York: Random House, 1995.

© Infobase Publishing

Reasons for Emigrating, 1933–1945

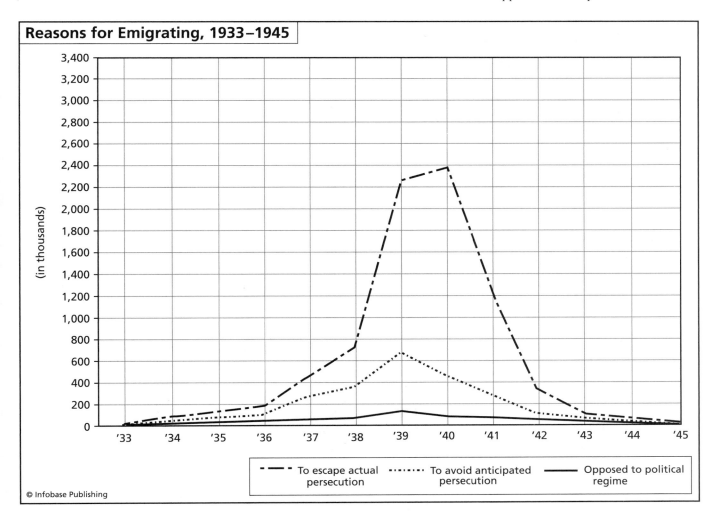

Refugee Arrivals in the United States, Fiscal Years 1980–2005

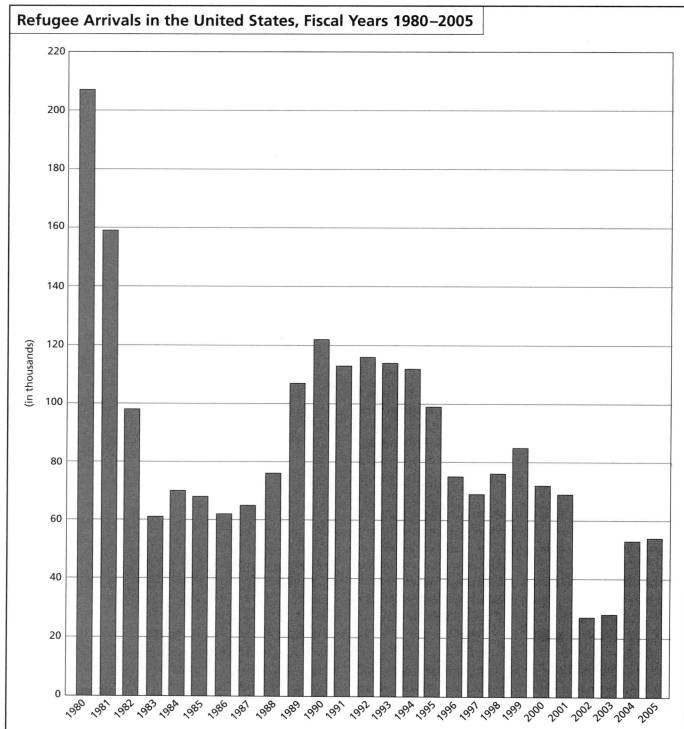

Note: Data series began following the Refugee Act of 1980. Excludes Amerasian immigrants except in fiscal years 1989 to 1991.

Source: U.S. Department of State, Bureau of Population, Refugees and Migration (PRM), Office of Admissions, Refugee Processing Center (RPC).

© Infobase Publishing

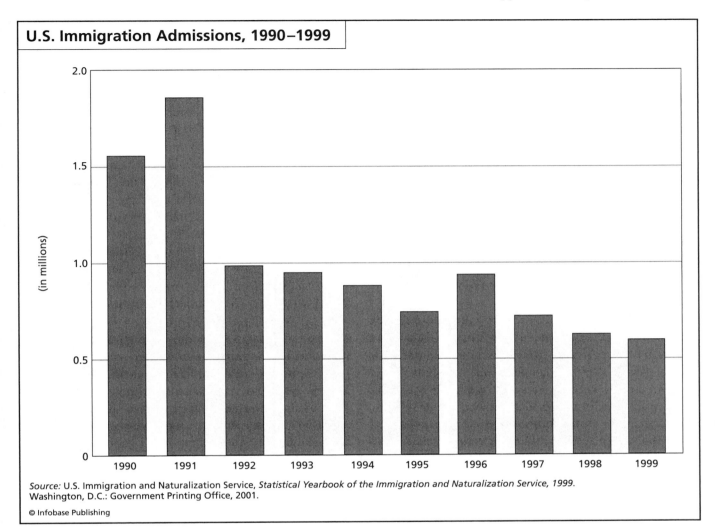

U.S. Immigration Admissions, 1990–1999

Source: U.S. Immigration and Naturalization Service, *Statistical Yearbook of the Immigration and Naturalization Service, 1999.* Washington, D.C.: Government Printing Office, 2001.

© Infobase Publishing

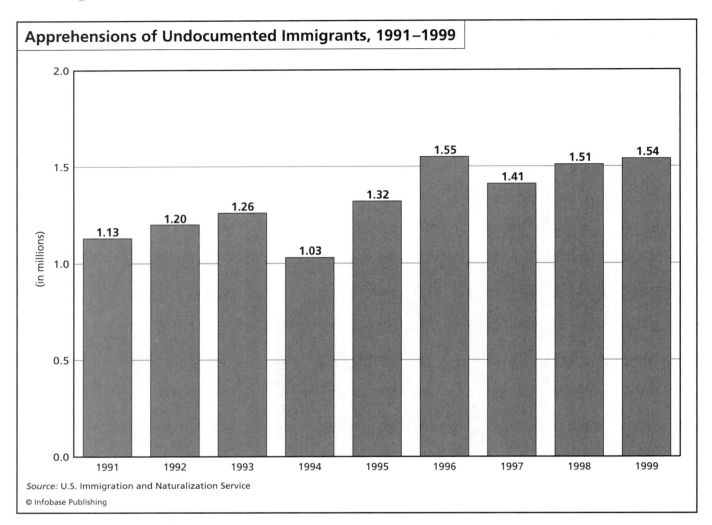

Apprehensions of Undocumented Immigrants, 1991–1999

(in millions)

1991 — 1.13
1992 — 1.20
1993 — 1.26
1994 — 1.03
1995 — 1.32
1996 — 1.55
1997 — 1.41
1998 — 1.51
1999 — 1.54

Source: U.S. Immigration and Naturalization Service

© Infobase Publishing

Origins of 9.1 Million Legal Immigrants Arriving in the United States, 1991–2000

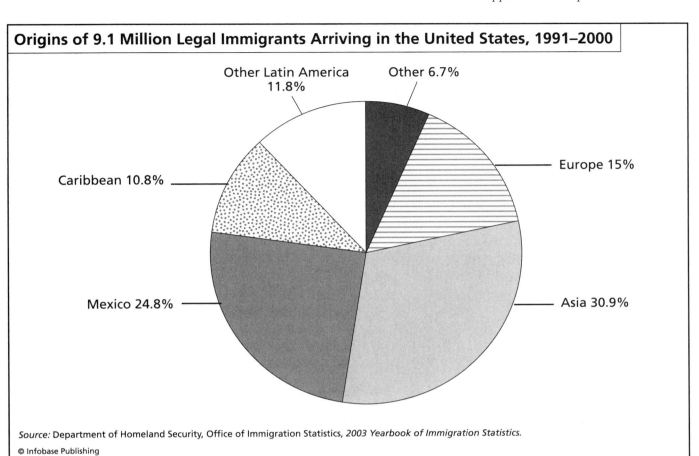

Other Latin America
11.8%

Other 6.7%

Caribbean 10.8%

Europe 15%

Mexico 24.8%

Asia 30.9%

Source: Department of Homeland Security, Office of Immigration Statistics, *2003 Yearbook of Immigration Statistics.*

© Infobase Publishing

Origins of 7 Million Undocumented Immigrants in the United States, 2000

Canada, 0.7%

Asia, 4.6%

Unknown, 11.4%

South America, 5.5%

Caribbean, 2.4%

Central America, 6.7%

Mexico, 68.7%

Source: Office of Policy and Planning, U.S. Immigration and Naturalization Service,
Estimates of the Unauthorized Immigrant Population Residing in the United States: 1990–2000, January 31, 2003.

© Infobase Publishing

Glossary

AILF   See American Immigrant Law Foundation.

alien   A person not a citizen or a national of the country.

America fever   The intense interest in and yearning for immigration to America experienced in Scandinavia in the 1830s, sparked by Norwegian immigrant Ole Rynning's travel book *A True Account of America* (1838).

American Immigrant Law Foundation (AILF   A Chicago-based advocacy group promoting a more liberal immigration policy.

anchor babies   Children born in the United States to illegal immigrants, so-called because, as U.S. citizens, they "anchor" their parents in the country.

asylum   Temporary refuge provided to aliens unable or unwilling to return to their countries because of persecution based on race, religion, or political opinion. According to the United States Citizenship and Immigration Services (USCIS), asylees in the United States "are eligible to adjust to lawful permanent status after one year of continuous residence." See also **refugee**.

BCBP   See **Bureau of Customs and Border Protection.**

bracero   Mexican contract laborer admitted to the United States under a 1942 treaty. The bracero program, which officially ended in 1964, accounted for nearly 5 million Mexican farm and railroad workers in 21 states across the United States South and Southwest. The word is from the Spanish *brazo*, "arm," used for manual laborers.

Bureau of Customs and Border Protection (BCBP)   The agency under the Department of Homeland Security (DHS) charged with enforcing United States borders.

CIRA   See **Comprehensive Immigration Reform Act of 2006.**

citizenship   The status, acquired by birth or naturalization, conferring all the rights and protections provided by the government.

Comprehensive Immigration Reform Act of 2006 (CIRA)   Senate Bill 2611, calling for increased security along America's southern border. It includes provisions for an increase in guest workers and permits illegal immigrants to apply for citizenship.

Department of Homeland Security (DHS)   A federal department whose functions include those formerly carried out by the Immigration and Naturalization Service (INS).

deportation   The formal expulsion of an alien found guilty of violating the immigration laws; see also *removal*.

DHS   See **Department of Homeland Security.**

displaced person   A person removed from his or her homeland because of war. In 1948 U.S. President Harry Truman signed the Displaced Persons Act, which remained in force until 1952, allowing a total of nearly 400,000 otherwise ineligible immigrants from Europe into the United States.

diversity visa   A visa given in an annual visa lottery. See **visa lottery.**

emigrant   A person who leaves a country to establish a permanent residence in another.

eugenics   The science of improving the quality of the human race by selective breeding. The principles of eugenics were used as a justification for excluding certain ethnic groups from American immigration in the 1920s.

forty-eighter   One of a group of 4,000 to 10,000 Germans who emigrated to America as refugees from a failed political revolution and social reform movement beginning in 1848. They had a significant influence on the cultural and political life of the German-American community and inspired many in their homeland to follow their example and relocate in the United States.

Golden Land   Term for America among Eastern European Jews from about the 1880s to the 1920s because of America's economic and social opportunities.

435

green card Popular name for the encoded document issued by the United States Citizenship and Immigration Services (USCIS) showing lawful permanent residence; officially *Permanent Resident Card* or *L-155*. Originally green but now pink, it authorizes its holder to live and work permanently in the United States.

headright A grant of land offered by a colonial administration to a settler for each immigrant whose indenture was purchased. The Virginia Company's headright was 50 acres, offered to any landowner who brought one indentured worker to the colony or to any family who came on its own.

ICE See **Immigration and Customs Enforcement.**

Illegal Immigration Reform and Immigrant Responsibility Act of 1996 (IIRAIRA) An act that established rigid requirements for admission to the United States.

IIRAIRA See **Illegal Immigration Reform and Immigrant Responsibility Act.**

IMMACT 90 See **Immigration Act of 1990.**

immigrant A person who enters a foreign country to establish a permanent residence there.

Immigration Act of 1990 (IMMACT 90) An act that increased the number of immigrants allowed to enter the United States, revised the grounds for exclusion and deportation, revised naturalization requirements, and made other fundamental changes in federal immigration law.

Immigration and Naturalization Service (INS) The original name of the United States immigration processing and enforcement bureau before its functions were transferred from the Justice Department to the Department of Homeland Security on March 1, 2003. The present-day bureau is called the **United States Citizenship and Immigration Services (USCIS).**

immigration depot A receiving station for immigrants at a port of entry. The largest immigration depots in the United States have been Ellis Island in New York and Angel Island in San Francisco; others have operated in Boston, Philadelphia, and Baltimore.

Immigration and Customs Enforcement (ICE) The investigative arm of the United States Department of Homeland Security (DHS) responsible for the security of the national borders.

INS See **Immigration and Naturalization Service.**

Immigration Reform and Control Act of 1986 (IRCA) An act that tightened the laws regarding entry to and residence in the United States and established penalties for employers of illegal aliens.

indenture A contract by which someone sells his or her service for a period of time or is sentenced for a crime for a term of service by a court. Many early 18th-century immigrants from England came to America as indentured workers.

IRCA See **Immigration Reform and Control Act of 1986.**

melting pot A metaphor for the United States as a country in which immigrants of different races mingle and are fused into a single community. The term was given popularity by Israel Zangwill's 1908 play *The Melting Pot* dealing with intermarriage and the American dream of racial harmony.

nativism Anti-immigrant sentiment based on the fear that the culture and economy of the native country is threatened by the presence of foreigners. This political philosophy was especially prevalent in the United States during the 1830s, was originally directed at the Catholic Church, and favored native-born Americans over immigrants in employment, public office, and voting privilege.

naturalization The process of becoming a citizen, usually requiring permanent residence for five years in the United States.

Operation Gatekeeper A program implemented by the U.S. Border Patrol in 1994 to improve the security of the 2,000-mile U.S.–Mexican border. The crackdown has increased the number of arrests of undocumented immigrants

"Other than Mexican" (OTM) Term used for undocumented non-Mexicans crossing the U.S.-Mexican border.

padrone [Italian: master, employment agent] A man who controls and finds employment for Italian laborers in the United States, usually for a high percentage of the worker's pay.

passenger act A law enacted by the United States regulating the number of passengers and the conditions of passage for immigrants from England to the United States. Several passenger acts were passed in the early 19th century after the first passed by England in 1803 to limit the emigration of skilled labor.

patroon Owner of an estate in New Netherlands (present-day New York and New Jersey), which was granted by the Dutch government in return for an agreement to settle 50 Dutch families on it.

penal transportation Deportation to a colony by the British courts of convicted felons who would serve their sentences as indentured laborers. The practice, which accounted for some 50,000 forced migrations to America, was discontinued after the Revolutionary War.

quota laws A series of statutes limiting immigration into the United States by imposing national quotas based on previous immigration statistics. The first of the laws establishing how many members of each race or nationality could enter the country, called the Johnson Bill, was passed in 1921.

race suicide The destruction of the race by the admission into a country of other races deemed inferior, as conceived by anti-immigration forces in the United States in the early 20th century. A term given prominence by Madison Grant in his inflammatory nativist book *The Passing of the Great Race* (1916), it suggested that the ethnic stock of Northern Europe then predominant in the United States was in danger of pollution if inferior African, Asian, and Southern and Eastern European immigrants were allowed into the country.

redemptioner Immigrant from Germany who, like English indentured laborers, sold his or her services to American landowners for a period of time in return for passage. Approximately half of the German immigrants who came to colonial America were redemptioners.

refugee According to Section 101(a)(42) of the Immigration and Nationality Act, "any person who is outside any country of such person's nationality . . . and who is unable or unwilling to return to, and who is unable or unwilling to provide himself or herself of the protection of that country because of persecution or a well-founded fear of persecution on account of race, religion, nationality, membership in a particular social group, or political opinion. . . ." See also **asylum.** A refugee differs from an asylee or asylum-seeker in receiving that status before coming to the country that grants refuge, whereas asylum may be granted only after arrival.

Scotch-Irish The descendants of Scottish immigrants to North Ireland, mostly from the Irish province of Ulster,

who constituted a large percentage of the wave of immigration to the American colonies from around 1718.

steerage The lowest deck of a transport vessel, near the steering mechanism, to which passengers traveling at the cheapest rate are assigned. The majority of immigrants arriving in the United States during the late 19th and early 20th century were compelled to travel in this least comfortable part of the ship.

STOPIT See **Stop the Out-of-Control Problems of Immigration Today.**

Stop the Out-of-Control Problems of Immigration Today (STOPIT) An organization that seeks to limit immigration to the United States.

undocumented Illegally present in the United States, used of aliens working without legal permission.

United States Citizenship and Immigration Services (USCIS) The immigration and processing bureau formerly known as the Immigration and Naturalization Service, now a part of the Department of Homeland Security.

United States Visitor and Immigration Status Technology (US-VISIT) A Department of Homeland Security (DHS) program responsible for border management and control. The US-VISIT Act, enacted January 5, 2004, calls for the fingerprinting and digital photographing of everyone entering and leaving the United States.

USCIS See **United States Citizenship and Immigration Service.**

US-VISIT See **United States Visitor and Immigration Status Indicator Technology.**

visa An endorsement placed on a passport allowing the bearer to apply for entry to the country granting it. The United States issues visas in various categories indicating the purpose of the intended entry. Some examples are visitor (B), temporary worker (H), student (F or J), athlete or entertainer (P), and religious worker (R).

visa lottery An annual mail-in lottery, established in 1990, in which 40,000 "diversity" visas—raised to 55,000 in 1994—were distributed at random to countries that were considered underrepresented in United States immigration. Forty percent of the allotment were specifically designated for natives of Ireland. The visa lottery created the first opportunities in modern times for foreign nationals to immigrate without immediate relatives to sponsor them or jobs for which there was a labor shortage in America. The visa lottery was abolished by the Border Protection, Antiterrorism, and Illegal Immigration Control Act of 2005, H.R. 4437.

war bride   A woman admitted to the United States outside the quota limitations because she is the wife of a member of the U.S. armed forces. The War Brides Act of 1946 provided for entry to the country of wives, husbands, and children of American service personnel.

wetback   Pejorative term for an illegal alien from Mexico, from Spanish slang *mojado* (wet), based on the idea of the Mexican gaining entry illegally by swimming across the Rio Grande, the river that separates the United States and Mexico.

Bibliography

Abbott, Edith. *Historical Aspects of the Immigration Problem.* Chicago: University of Chicago Press, 1926.

———. *Immigration: Select Documents and Case Records.* Chicago: University of Chicago Press, 1924.

Abbott, Grace. *The Immigrant and the Community.* New York: The Century Company, 1917.

Adamic, Louis. *From Many Lands.* New York: Harper & Brothers, 1940.

———. *Laughing in the Jungle: The Autobiography of an Immigrant in America.* New York: Harper & Brothers, 1932.

———. *My America, 1928–1938.* New York: Da Capo Press, 1976; first published 1938.

———. *A Nation of Nations.* New York: Harper & Brothers, 1944.

———. *The Native Returns: An American Immigrant Visits Yugoslavia and Discovers His Old Country.* New York: Harper & Brothers, 1934.

———. *Two-Way Passage.* New York: Harper & Brothers, 1941.

———. *What's Your Name?* New York: Harper & Brothers, 1942.

Adams, John. *The Works of John Adams, Second President of the United States, with a Life of the Author, Notes, and Illustrations, by his Grandson Charles Francis Adams,* 10 vols. Freeport, N.Y.: Books for Libraries Press, 1969; first published 1850–56.

Adler, Lenore. *Migration, Immigration and Emigration: International Perspective.* New York: Praeger, 2003.

Adler, Mortimer J., et al., eds. *The Annals of America,* 19 vols. Chicago: Encyclopedia Britannica, Inc., 1968.

Agueros, Jack. *The Immigrant Experience.* New York: The Dial Press, 1971.

Alba, Richard D. *Italian Americans: Into the Twilight of Ethnicity.* New York: Prentice Hall, 1985.

Albers, Richard. *Remaking the American Mainstream: Assimilation and Contemporary Immigration.* Cambridge, Mass.: Harvard University Press, 2002.

Alexseev, Mikhail A. *Immigration Phobia and the Security Dilemma: Russia, Europe, and the United States.* New York: Cambridge University Press, 2005.

Amfitheatrof, Erik. *The Children of Columbus: An Informal History of the Italians in the New World.* Boston: Little, Brown and Company, 1973.

Anbinder, Tyler. *Nativism and Slavery: The Northern Know-Nothings and the Politics of the 1880s.* New York: Oxford University Press, 1992.

Anderson, Robert Charles. *The Great Migration Begins: Immigrants to New England, 1620–1633,* 3 vols. Boston: New England Historic Genealogy Society, 1995.

Andersons, Edgars, ed. *Cross Road Country—Latvia.* Waverly, Iowa: Gramata, 1953.

Andrews, Edward Deming. *The People Called Shakers: A Search for the Perfect Society.* New York: Dover Publications, 1963; first published 1953.

Antin, Mary. *From Plotzk to Boston.* New York: M. Wiener, 1986; first published 1899.

———. *The Promised Land.* Boston: Houghton, Mifflin & Company, 1969; first published 1912.

———. *They Who Knock at Our Gates: A Complete Gospel of Immigration.* Boston: Houghton, Mifflin & Company, 1914.

Appel, John J. *The New Immigration.* New York: G. P. Putnam, 1971.

Archdeacon, Thomas J. *Becoming American: An Ethnic History.* New York: The Free Press, 1983.

Argus, M. K. *Moscow-on-the-Hudson.* New York: Harper & Brothers, 1951.

Ashabrenner, Brent. *The New Americans: Changing Patterns in United States Immigration.* New York: Dodd Mead and Co., 1983.

———. *Our Beckoning Borders: Illegal Immigration to America.* New York: Cobblehill Books/Dutton, 1996.

Auster, Lawrence. *The Path to National Suicide: An Essay on Immigration and Multiculturalism.* Monterey, Va.: American Immigration Control Foundation, 1990.

Axtell, James, William J. Baker, and Orm Överland. *America Perceived.* West Haven, Conn.: Pendulum Press, 1974.

Bailey, Thomas A. *Voices of America.* New York: The Free Press, 1976.

Bailyn, Bernard. *The Peopling of North America: An Introduction.* New York: Alfred A. Knopf, 1986.

———. *Voyagers to the West: A Passage in the Peopling of America on the Eve of the Revolution.* New York: Alfred A. Knopf, 1986.

Baird, Charles Washington. *History of the Huguenot Emigration to America.* Baltimore, Md.: Genealogical Publishing Company, 1973; first published 1885.

Balch, Emily Greene. *Our Slavic Fellow Citizens.* New York: Arno Press, 1969; first published 1910.

Ballagh, James Curtis. *White Servitude in the Colony of Virginia.* New York: Burt Franklin, 1969; first published 1895.

Bandon, Alexandra. *Mexican Americans.* New York: New Discovery Books, 1993.

———. *West Indian Americans.* New York: New Discovery Books, 1994.

Barkai, Avraham. *Branching Out: German-Jewish Immigration to the United States, 1820–1914.* New York: Holmes & Meier, 1944.

Barzini, Luigi. *O America: When You and I Were Young.* New York: Harper & Row, 1977.

———. *The Italians.* New York: Atheneum, 1964.

Baxter, W. T. *The House of Hancock.* Cambridge, Mass.: Harvard University Press, 1945.

Bean, Frank D., and Gillian Stevens. *America's Newcomers and the Dynamics of Diversity.* New York: Russell Sage, 2003.

Beard, Annie E. S. *Our Foreign-Born Citizens.* New York: Thomas Y. Crowell Company, 1955.

Beard, Charles A., and Mary R. Beard. *The Rise of American Civilization.* New York: The Macmillan Company, 1940; first published 1927.

Beck, Louis J. *New York's Chinatown.* New York: Bohemia Publishing Company, 1898.

Beck, Roy. *The Case against Immigration: The Moral, Economic, Social, and Environmental Reasons for Reducing U.S. Immigration Back to Traditional Levels.* New York: W. W. Norton & Company, 1996.

Benét, Steven Vincent. *Western Star.* New York: Farrar & Rinehart, 1943.

Bercovici, Konrad. *It's the Gypsy in Me.* Englewood Cliffs, N.J.: Prentice Hall, Inc., 1941.

Berger, Josef, and Dorothy Berger, eds. *Diary of America.* New York: Simon & Schuster, 1957.

Bernard, William S., et al. *American Immigration Policy: A Reappraisal.* New York: Harper & Brothers, 1950.

Berthoff, Rowland Tappan. *British Immigrants in Industrial America, 1790–1850.* Cambridge, Mass.: Harvard University Press, 1953.

Beverley, Robert. *The History and Present State of Virginia.* Chapel Hill: University of North Carolina Press, 1947; first published 1705.

Billington, Roy Allen. *The Protestant Crusade, 1800–1860: A Study of the Origins of American Nativism.* Chicago: Quadrangle Books, 1938.

Birkbeck, Morris. *An Address to the Farmers of Great Britain; With an Essay on the Prairie of the Western Country.* London, England: J. Ridgway, 1818.

———. *Letters from Illinois.* New York: Da Capo Press, 1970; first published 1818.

———. *Notes on a Journey in America from the Coast of Virginia to the Territory of Illinois.* New York: Augustus M. Kelley, 1971; first published 1818.

Blau, Joseph L., and Salo W. Baron. *The Jews of the United States, 1790–1840: A Documentary History.* New York: Columbia University Press, 1963.

Blegen, Theodore Christian. *Land of Their Choice: The Immigrants Write Home.* Minneapolis: University of Minnesota Press, 1955.

———. *Norwegian Migration to America, 1825–1860.* New York: Arno Press, 1969; first published 1931.

Blegen, Theodore Christian, and Martin B. Ruud. *Emigrant Songs and Ballads.* Minneapolis: University of Minnesota Press, 1936; first published 1911.

Blumenthal, Shirley, and Jerome S. Ozer. *Coming to America: Immigrants from the British Isles.* New York: Delacorte Press, 1980.

Bodnar, John E. *Immigrant Industrialization: Ethnicity in an American Mill Town, 1870–1940.* Pittsburgh, Pa.: University of Pittsburgh Press, 1977.

———. *The Transplanted: A History of Immigrants in Urban America.* Bloomington: Indiana University Press, 1985.

Bodnar, John E., Roger Simon, and Michael P. Weber. *Lives of Their Own: Blacks, Italians, and Poles in Pittsburgh, 1900–1960.* Urbana: University of Illinois Press, 1981.

Bogardus, Emory Stephen. *Immigration and Race Attitudes.* Englewood, N.J.: Jerome S. Ozer, 1971; first published 1928.

———. *The Mexican in the United States.* Los Angeles, Calif.: University of Southern California Press, 1934.

Bogen, Elizabeth. *Immigration in New York.* New York: Praeger, 1987.

Bojer, Johan. *The Emigrants.* New York: The Century Company, 1925.

Bok, Edward. *The Americanization of Edward Bok: The Autobiography of a Dutch Boy Fifty Years After.* New York: Charles Scribner's Sons, 1922.

Bonner, Arthur. *Alas! What Brought Thee Hither? The Chinese in New York, 1800–1950.* Madison, N.J.: Fairleigh Dickinson University Press, 1997.

Boorstin, Daniel J. *The Americans: The Colonial Experience.* New York: Random House, 1958.

———. *The Americans: The Democratic Experience.* New York: Random House, 1973.

———. *The Americans: The National Experience.* New York: Random House, 1965.

Borjas, George J. *Heaven's Door: Immigration Policy and the American Economy.* Princeton, N.J.: Princeton University Press, 2001.

Bouvier, Leon F., and Robert W. Gardner. *Immigration to the United States: The Unfinished Story.* Washington, D.C.: Population Reference Bureau, 1986.

Bouvier, Leon F., and Lindsey Grant. *How Many Americans? Population, Immigration and the Environment.* San Francisco: Sierra Books, 1994.

Brace, Charles Loring. *The Norse Folk; or A Visit to the Homes of Norway and Sweden.* New York: Charles Scribner's Sons, 1857.

Bradford, William. *Of Plymouth Plantation.* New York: Capricorn Books, 1962; written 1651, first published 1856.

Brandenburg, Broughton. *Imported Americans: The Story of the Experiences of a Disguised American and his Wife Studying the Immigration Question.* New York: F. A. Stokes, 1904.

Breckenridge, Sophonisba P. *New Homes for Old.* New York: Harper & Brothers, 1921.

Bremer, Frederika. *The Homes of the New World; Impressions of America.* New York: Harper & Brothers, 1853.

Briggs, John W. *An Italian Passage: Immigrants to Three American Cities, 1890–1930.* New Haven, Conn.: Yale University Press, 1978.

Brimelaw, Peter. *Alien Nation: Common Sense About America's Immigration Disaster.* New York: Random House, 1995.

Bromwell, William J. *History of Immigration to the United States.* New York: Arno Press, 1969; first published 1856.

Brown, Francis R., and Joseph S. Roucek. *One America: The History, Contributions, and Present Problems of Our Racial and National Minorities.* New York: Prentice Hall, 1952; first published 1937.

Brown, Lawrence Guy. *Immigration: Cultural Conflicts and Social Adjustments.* New York: Longmans, Green and Co., 1933.

Brownstone, David M., Irene M. Franck, and Douglass L. Brownstone. *Island of Hope, Island of Tears.* New York: Rawson, Wade Publishers, 1979.

Bruce, J. Campbell. *The Golden Door: The Irony of Our Immigration Policy.* New York: Random House, 1954.

Bruns, Jette. *Hold Dear, as Always: Jette, a German Immigrant Life in Letters.* Columbia: University of Missouri Press, 1988.

Buchanan, Patrick J. *The Death of the West: How Dying Populations and Immigrant Invasions Imperil Our Country and Civilization.* New York: Thomas Dunne Books, 2002.

———. *State of Emergency: How Illegal Immigration Is Destroying America.* New York: Thomas Dunne Books, 2006.

Buell, Raymond Leslie. *Japanese Immigration.* Boston: World Peace Foundation, 1924.

Bulosan, Carlos. *America Is in the Heart: A Personal History.* New York: Harcourt, Brace & Co., 1946.

Burlend, Rebecca. *A True Picture of Immigration: or, Fourteen Years in the Interior of America.* Chicago: Lakeside Press, 1936; first published 1848.

Burn, James Dawson. *Three Years among the Working Classes in the United States during the War.* London, England: Smith, Elder & Co., 1865.

Bye, Erik. *Blow, Silver Wind: A Story of Norwegian Immigration to America.* Minneapolis, Minn.: Norwegian Cultural Institute, 1980.

Byrne, Stephen. *Irish Immigration to the United States.* New York: Appleton, 1969; first published 1873.

Cahan, Abraham. *The Rise of David Levinsky.* New York: Harper & Brothers, 1917.

Capaldi, Nicolas, ed. *Immigration: Debating the Issues.* Amherst, Mass.: Prometheus Books, 1997.

Capek, Thomas. *The Czechs (Bohemians) in America.* Boston: Houghton, Mifflin & Company, 1920.

Carnegie, Andrew. *Autobiography of Andrew Carnegie.* Garden City, N.Y.: Doubleday Doran, 1933; first published 1920.

Cavanah, Frances, ed. *We Came to America: An Anthology.* Philadelphia: Macrae Smith Company, 1954.

Cavanaugh, Francis P. *Immigration Restrictions at Work Today: A Study of the Administration of Immigration Restrictions by the United States.* Washington, D.C.: Catholic University Press, 1928.

CBS News. *60 Minutes Verbatim: Who Said What to Whom.* New York: Arno Press, 1980.

Chan, Sucheng. *Asian Americans: An Interpretative History.* Boston: Twayne Publishers, 1991.

Chastellux, marquis de, François Jean de Beauvoir. *Travels in North America, 1780, 1781, & 1782.* Chapel Hill: University of North Carolina Press, 1963; first published 1786.

Chavez, Leo R. *Covering Immigration: Popular Images and the Politics of the Nation.* Berkeley, Calif.: University of California Press, 2001.

Chen, Jack. *The Chinese of America: From the Beginning to the Present.* San Francisco, Calif.: Harper & Row, 1980.

Chickering, Jesse. *Immigration into the United States.* Boston: Charles C. Little, 1848.

Chin, Tung Pok, and Winifred C. Chin. *Paper Son: One Man's Story.* Philadelphia, Pa.: Temple University Press, 2000.

Christowe, Stoyen. *This Is My Country.* New York: Carrick and Evans, 1938.

———. *My American Pilgrimage.* Boston: Little, Brown and Company, 1947.

Clark, Amy Elizabeth. *Peter Porcupine in America: The Career of William Cobbett, 1752–1800.* Philadelphia: Gettysburg, 1939.

Coan, Peter Morton. *Ellis Island Interviews: In Their Own Words.* New York: Facts On File, 1997.

Cobbett, William. *Peter Porcupine in America: Pamphlets on Republicanism and Revolution.* Ithaca, N.Y.: Cornell University Press, 1994; first published 1796.

Codrescu, Andrei. *Road Scholar: Coast to Coast Late in the Century.* New York: Hyperion Press, 1993.

Cohen, Felix S. *Immigration and National Welfare.* New York: League for Industrial Democracy, 1940.

Cohen, Rose. *Out of the Shadow.* New York: George H. Doran Co., 1918.

Colbert, David, ed. *Eyewitness to America: 500 Years of America in the Words of Those Who Saw It Happen.* New York: Pantheon Books, 1997.

Cole, Stewart, and Mildred Wiese Cole. *Minorities and the American Promise.* New York: Harper & Brothers, 1954.

Coleman, Elizabeth. *Chinatown, U.S.A.* New York: The John Day Company, 1946.

Coleman, Terry. *Going to America: A History of Emigrants from Great Britain and Ireland to America in the Mid-Nineteenth Century.* New York: Pantheon Books, 1972.

Colton, Calvin. *Manual for Emigrants to America.* London, England: Westley & Davis, 1832.

Commager, Henry Steele. *Immigration and American History.* Minneapolis: University of Minneapolis Press, 1961.

———, ed. *America in Perspective.* New York: Random House, 1947.

———, ed. *Living Ideas in America.* New York: Harper & Brothers, 1951.

Commager, Henry Steele, and Allan Nevins. *The Heritage of America.* Boston: Little, Brown and Company, 1951; first published 1939.

Commons, John Rogers. *Races and Immigrants in America.* New York: A. M. Kelley, 1967; first published 1907.

Conley, Ellen Alexander. *The Chosen Shore: Stories of Immigrants.* Berkeley: University of California Press, 2004.

Conway, Alan. *The Welsh in America: Letters from Immigrants.* Minneapolis: University of Minnesota Press, 1961.

Conway, Russell H. *Why the Chinese Emigrate and the Means They Adopt for the Purpose of Reaching America.* New York: Lee & Shepard, 1871.

Coolidge, Mary Roberts. *Chinese Immigration.* New York: Arno Press, 1969; first published 1909.

Coppa, Frank J., and Thomas J. Curran. *The Immigrant Experience in America.* Boston: Twayne Publishers, 1976.

Corbach, Otto. *The Open Door.* London, England: Jonathon Cape, 1933.

Cornelius, James M. *The English Americans.* New York: Chelsea House, 1990.

Corsi, Edward. *In the Shadow of Liberty.* New York: The Macmillan Company, 1935.

———. *Paths to the New World.* New York: Anti-Defamation League of B'nai B'rith, 1956; first published 1953.

Cose, Ellis. *A Nation of Strangers: Prejudice, Politics, and the Populating of America.* New York: Morrow, 1992.

Countryman, Edward. *Americans: A Collision of Histories.* New York: Hill and Wang, 1996.

Cournos, John. *Autobiography.* New York: G. P. Putnam, 1935.

Covelle, Leonard. *The Heart Is the Teacher.* New York: McGraw Hill, 1958.

Cozic, Charles, ed. *Illegal Immigration.* San Diego, Calif.: Greenhaven Press, 1997.

Crèvecoeur, Michel-Guillaume-Jean de. *Letters from an American Farmer.* Franklin Center, Pa.: Franklin Library, 1982; first published 1782.

Cunz, Dieter. *The Maryland Germans.* Princeton, N.J.: Princeton University Press, 1948.

———. *They Came from Germany: The Stories of Famous German-Americans.* New York: Dodd, Mead, 1966.

Curran, Henry C. *Pillar to Post.* New York: Charles Scribner's Sons, 1941.

Daché, Lilly, and Dorothy Roe Lewis. *Talking through My Hats.* New York: Coward-McCann, Inc., 1946.

Dalton, Humphrey, ed. *Will America Drown? Immigration and the Third World Population Explosion.* Washington, D.C.: Scott-Townsend, 1993.

D'Angelo, Pascal. *Son of Italy.* New York: Arno Press, 1975; first published 1924.

———. *Coming to America: A History of Immigration and Ethnicity in American Life.* New York: HarperCollins Publishers, 1990.

Daniels, Roger. *Asian Americans: Chinese and Japanese in the United States since 1850.* Seattle: University of Washington Press, 1988.

Daniels, Roger. *Guarding the Golden Door: American Immigration Policy and Immigrants since 1882.* New York: Farrar, Straus and Giroux, 2004.

David, Henry. *The History of the Haymarket Affair.* New York: Farrar & Rinehart, 1936.

Davie, Maurice Rea. *World Immigration with Special Reference to the United States.* New York: The Macmillan Company, 1949; first published 1936.

Davie, Maurice Rea, et al. *Refugees in America.* New York: Harper & Brothers, 1947.

Davis, David Brion, and Steven Mintz. *The Boisterous Sea of Liberty: A Documentary History of America from Discovery through the Civil War.* New York: Oxford University Press, 1998.

Davis, Jerome. *The Russian Immigrant.* New York: Arno Press, 1969; first published 1922.

Davis, Marilyn P. *Mexican Voices, American Dreams: An Oral History of Mexican Immigration to the United States.* New York: Henry Holt, 1990.

Davis, Mike, and Justin Akers Chacón. *No One Is Illegal: Fighting Racism and State Violence on the U.S.–Mexico Border.* Chicago: Haymarket Books, 2006.

Day, Clarence. *After All.* New York: Alfred A. Knopf, 1936.

De Jong, David Cornel. *With a Dutch Accent.* New York: Harper & Brothers, 1944.

Dennis, Lawrence. *The Coming American Fascism.* New York: Harper & Brothers, 1936.

Desmond, Humphrey Joseph. *The Know-Nothing Party. A Sketch.* Washington, D.C.: The New Century Press, 1904.

Dickens, Charles. *American Notes.* New York: International Publishing Corp., 1985; first published 1842.

Dickson, R. *Ulster Immigration to Colonial America, 1718–1775.* London, England: Routledge & Kegan Paul, 1966.

Diffendorffer, Frank Ried. *The German Immigration into Pennsylvania through the Port of Philadelphia from 1710 to 1775.* Baltimore, Md.: Genealogical Publishing Co., 1979; first published 1900.

di Franco, J. Philip, *The Italian Americans.* New York: Chelsea House, 1988.

Dimont, Max I. *The Jews in America: The Roots, History and Destiny of American Jews.* New York: Simon & Schuster, 1978.

Dina, Hasia. *Hungering for America: Italian, Irish, and Jewish Foodways in the Age of Migration.* Cambridge, Mass.: Harvard University Press, 2003.

Dinnerstein, Leonard, and David M. Reimers. *Ethnic Americans: A History of Immigration.* New York: HarperCollins Publishers, 1988; first published 1981.

Divine, Robert A. *American Immigration Policy, 1924–1952.* New Haven, Conn.: Yale University Press, 1957.

Dollar, Charles M., and Gary W. Reichard. *American Issues: A Documentary Reader.* New York: Glencoe/McGraw-Hill, 1994; first published 1988.

Dougherty, John E. *Illegals: The Imminent Threat Posed by Our Unsecured U.S.–Mexican Border.* Nashville, Tenn.: Nelson Current, 2004.

Dow, Mark. *American Gulag: Inside U.S. Immigration Prisons.* Berkeley: University of California Press, 2004.

Drake, Samuel Gardner. *Biography and History of the Indians of North America, from Its First Discovery.* Boston: B. B. Munsey, 1851; first published 1834.

Duden, Gottfried. *Report on a Journey to the Western States of North America and a Stay of Several Years along the Missouri.* Columbia: State Historical Society of Missouri, 1880; first published 1829.

Duncan, Hannibal Gerald. *Immigration and Assimilation.* Boston: D. C. Heath, 1933.

Duus, Olaus Fredrik. *Frontier Parsonage: The Letters of Olaus Fredrik Duus, Norwegian Pastor in Wisconsin, 1855–1858.* Northfield, Minn.: Norwegian-American Historical Association, 1947.

Easum, Chester Verne. *The Americanization of Carl Schurz.* Chicago: The University of Chicago Press, 1929.

Eaton, Allen H. *Immigrant Gifts to American Life.* New York: Russell Sage Foundation, 1932.

Eddis, William. *Letters from America, Historical and Descriptive: Comprising Occurrences from 1769 to 1777, Inclusive.* London, England: Printed for the Author, 1792.

Ellis, David Maldwyn. *New York State and City.* Ithaca, N.Y.: Cornell University Press, 1979.

Elovitz, Paul H., and Charlotte Kahn, eds. *Immigrant Experiences: Personal Narratives and Psychological Analysis.* Madison, N.J.: Fairleigh Dickinson University Press, 1997.

Emsden, Katharine, ed. *Coming to America: A New Life in a New Land.* Carlisle, Mass.: Discovery Enterprises, Ltd., 1993.

Erickson, Charlotte. *American Industry and the European Immigrant, 1860–1885.* Cambridge, Mass.: Harvard University Press, 1957.

———. *Invisible Immigrants: The Adaptation of English and Scottish Immigrants in Nineteenth-Century America.* Coral Gables, Fla.: University of Miami Press, 1973.

Ernest, Robert. *Immigrant Life in New York City 1825–1863.* Port Washington, N.Y.: King's Crown Press, 1965; first published 1949.

Esteves, Sandra Maria. *Tropical Rains: A Bilingual Downpour.* Bronx, N.Y.: African Caribbean Theater, 1984.

Ets, Marie Hall. *Rosa: The Life of an Italian Immigrant.* Minneapolis, Minn.: University of Minnesota Press, 1970.

Evans, J. Martin. *America: The View from Europe.* San Francisco, Calif.: The San Francisco Book Company, 1976.

Ewen, Elizabeth. *Immigrant Women in the Land of Dollars: Life and Culture on the Lower East Side, 1890–1925.* New York: Monthly Review, 1985.

Fairchild, Henry Pratt. *Greek Immigration to the United States.* New Haven, Conn.: Yale University Press, 1911.

———. *Immigration: A World Movement and Its American Significance.* New York: The Macmillan Company, 1928; first published 1925.

———. *The Melting-Pot Mistake.* Boston: Little, Brown and Company, 1926.

———, ed. *Immigrant Backgrounds.* New York: J. Wiley & Sons, 1927.

Faust, Albert Bernhardt. *The German Element in the United States, with Special Reference to Its Political, Moral, Social, and Educational Influence.* New York: The Steuben Society of America, 1927.

Faux, William. *Memorable Days in America: Being a Journal of a Tour to the United States, Principally Undertaken to Ascertain . . . the Condition and Probable Prospects of British Emigrants.* London, England: W. Simpkin and R. Marshall, 1823.

Feldber, Michael. *The Philadelphia Riots of 1844: A Study in Ethnic Conflict.* Westport, Conn.: Greenwood Press, 1975.

———. *Race and Nationality in American Life.* Boston: Little, Brown and Company, 1957.

Fenton, Heike, and Melvin Hecker. *The Greeks in America, 1528–1977.* Dobbs Ferry, N.Y.: Oceana Publications, 1978.

Fermi, Laura. *Illustrious Immigrants: The Intellectual Migration from Europe, 1930–1941.* Chicago: University of Chicago Press, 1971; first published 1968.

Fields, Harold. *The Refugee in the United States.* New York: Oxford University Press, 1938.

Firth, C. H. *The American Garland; Being a Collection of Ballads Relating to America, 1563–1759.* Oxford, England: Oxford University Press, 1915.

Fischer, David Hackett. *Albion's Seed: Four British Folkways in America.* New York: Oxford University Press, 1989.

Fisk, John. *The Dutch and Quaker Colonies in America.* Boston: Houghton, Mifflin & Company, 1927; first published 1899.

Fleming, Donald, and Bernard Bailyn, eds. *The Intellectual Migration: Europe and America, 1930–1960.* Cambridge, Mass.: Harvard University Press, 1969.

Fleming, Thomas J. *The Golden Door: The Story of American Immigration.* New York: W. W. Norton & Company, 1970.

Flom, George Tobias. *A History of Norwegian Immigration to the United States from the Earliest Beginning Down to the Year 1848.* Bowie, Md.: Heritage Books, 1992; first published 1909.

Flynn, Elizabeth Gurley. *I Speak My Own Piece: Autobiography of "The Rebel Girl".* New York: Masses & Mainstream, 1955.

Foerster, Robert Franz. *Italian Immigration of Our Times.* Cambridge, Mass.: Harvard University Press, 1919.

Foner, Nancy, ed. *New Immigrants in New York City.* New York: Columbia University Press, 1987.

Foner, Nancy. *In a New Land: A Comparative View of Immigration.* New York: New York University Press, 2005.

Forbes, Robert Bennet. *The Voyage of the Jamestown on Her Errand of Mercy.* Boston: Eastburn Press, 1847.

Force, Peter, ed. *Tracts and Other Papers, Relating Principally to the Origin, Settlement, and Progress of the Colonies in North America, from the Discovery of the Country to the Year 1776,* 4 vols. Washington, D.C.: P. Force, 1836–46.

Ford, Henry J. *The Scotch-Irish in America.* Princeton, N.J.: Princeton University Press, 1915.

Forster, Walter O. *Zion on the Mississippi: The Settlement of the Saxon Lutherans in Missouri, 1839–1841.* St. Louis, Mo.: Concordia Publishing House, 1953.

Fountas, Angela Jane, ed. *Coming of Age Biculturally: First Generation Women Reflect on Identity.* San Francisco and New York: Avalon Publishing Group, 2005.

Fox, Paul. *The Poles in America.* New York: Arno Press, 1970; first published 1922.

Franklin, Benjamin. *The Works of Benjamin Franklin,* 10 vols. Edited by Jared Sparks. Boston: Whittemore, Niles & Hall, 1856.

Furer, Howard B. *The British in America, 1578–1970.* Dobbs Ferry, N.Y.: Oceana Publications, 1972.

Galarzo, Ernesto. *Barrio Boy.* Notre Dame, Ind.: University of Notre Dame Press, 1971.

Gales, Joseph, ed. *The Debates and Proceedings in the Congress of the United States, with an Appendix Containing Important State Papers and Public Documents, and All the Laws of a Pub-*

lic Nature, 42 vols. Washington, D.C.: Gales & Seaton, 1834–56.

Galicich, Anne. *The German Americans.* New York: Chelsea House, 1989.

Gallico, Paul. *Mrs. 'Arris Goes to New York* (1960). In *Gallico Magic.* Garden City, N.Y.: Nelson Doubleday, Inc., 1967.

Gambino, Richard. *Blood of my Blood.* Garden City, N.Y.: Doubleday & Co., 1974.

Gamio, Manuel. *The Mexican Immigrant.* Chicago: University of Chicago Press, 1931.

———. *Mexican Immigration to the United States: A Study of Human Migration and Adjustment.* Chicago: University of Chicago Press, 1930.

Garis, Roy L. *Immigration Restriction: A Study of the Opposition to and the Regulation of Immigration into the United States.* New York: The Macmillan Company, 1927.

Gavit, John Palmer. *Americans by Choice.* New York: Harper & Brothers, 1922.

Gay, Ruth. *Unfinished People: Eastern European Jews Encounter America.* New York: W. W. Norton & Company, 1996.

Geiser, Karl Frederick. *Redemptioners and Indentured Servants in the Colony and Commonwealth of Pennsylvania.* New Haven, Conn.: Tuttle, Morehouse & Taylor Co., 1901.

Gerber, David A., and Alan M. Kraut, eds. *American Immigration and Ethnicity: A Reader.* New York: Palgrave Macmillan, 2005.

Gernand, Renée. *The Cuban Americans.* New York: Chelsea House, 1995.

Gerstle, Mary. *American Crucible: Race and Nation in the Twentieth Century.* Princeton, N.J.: Princeton University Press, 2002.

Gibson, Otis. *The Chinese in America.* Cincinnati, Ohio: Hitchcock & Walden, 1877.

Gish, Theodore, and Richard Spuler. *Eagle in the New World: German Immigration to Texas and America.* College Station: Texas A&M University Press, 1986.

Glazer, Nathan. *Clamor at the Gates: The New American Immigration.* San Francisco, Calif.: Institute for Contemporary Studies, 1985.

———. *The New Immigration: A Challenge to American Society.* San Diego, Calif.: San Diego State University Press, 1988.

Glazer, Nathan, and Daniel Patrick Moynihan. *Beyond the Melting Pot.* Cambridge, Mass.: MIT Press, 1970; first published 1963.

Glenn, Evelyn Nakano. *Unequal Freedom: How Race and Gender Shaped American Citizenship and Labor.* Cambridge, Mass.: Harvard University Press, 2004.

Glenn, Susan Anita. *Daughters of the Shtetl: Life and Labor in the Immigrant Generation.* Ithaca, N.Y.: Cornell University Press, 1990.

Glitz, Albrecht, and Christian Dustmann. *Immigration, Jobs and Wages: Theory, Evidence and Opinion.* Cambridge, Mass.: Harvard University Press, 2004.

Goodnight, Lynn, et al. *Changing the Immigration Policy of the United States.* Lincolnwood, Ill.: National Textbook Company, 1994.

Graham, Otis J. *Unguarded Gates: A History of America's Immigration Crisis.* Lanham, Md.: Rowman & Littlefield, 2004.

Graham, Stephen. *With Poor Immigrants to America.* New York: The Macmillan Company, 1914.

Grant, Lindsey, ed. *Elephants in the Volkswagen: Facing Tough Questions about Our Overcrowded Country.* New York: Freeman, 1992.

Grant, Madison. *The Passing of the Great Race, or, The Racial Bias of European History.* 2d ed., rev. New York: Charles Scribner's Sons, 1918.

Grant, Madison, and Charles Stewart Davison, eds. *The Alien in our Midst, or "Selling Our Birthright for a Mess of Pottage."* New York: The Galton Publishing Company, 1930.

Greenleaf, Barbara Kaye. *American Fever: The Story of American Immigration.* New York: Four Winds Press, 1970.

Griffin, William D. *The Irish in America.* Dobbs Ferry, N.Y.: Oceana Publications, 1973.

Guillet, Edwin C. *The Great Migration: The Atlantic Crossing by Sailing Ship since 1770.* Toronto, Canada: University of Toronto Press, 1963; first published 1937.

Hakluyt, Richard. *The Principal Navigations, Voyages, Traffiques, and Discoveries of the English Nation.* Cambridge, England: Cambridge University Press, 1965; first published 1589.

Hall, Bruce Edward. *Tea That Burns: A Family Memoir of Chinatown.* New York: The Free Press, 1998.

Hall, Prescott Farnsworth. *Immigration and Its Effects on the United States.* New York: Henry Holt, 1907.

Halych, Wasil. *Ukrainians in the United States.* Chicago: University of Chicago Press, 1937.

Hamilton, Alexander. *The Works of Alexander Hamilton,* 12 vols. Edited by Henry Cabot Lodge. New York: G. P. Putnam's Sons, 1904.

Hamilton, Alexander, James Madison, and John Jay. *The Federalist Papers.* New York: Penguin Books, 1961; first published 1787–88.

Hammond, John. *Leah and Rachel, or Two Fruitfull Sisters, Virginia and Maryland,* in Force, Peter, ed., *Tracts and Other Papers. Volume 3, #14;* first published 1656.

Handlin, Oscar. *The Americans: A New History of the People of the United States.* Boston: Little, Brown and Company, 1963.

———. *Boston's Immigrants, 1790–1880: A Study of Acculturation.* Cambridge, Mass.: Harvard University Press, 1991; first published 1941.

———, ed. *Children of the Uprooted.* New York: G. Braziller, 1966.

———, ed. *Immigration as a Factor in American History.* New York: Spectrum Books, 1959.

———. *Race and Nationality in American Life.* Boston: Little, Brown and Company, 1957.

———, ed. *This Was America.* Cambridge, Mass.: Harvard University Press, 1949.

———. *The Uprooted.* Boston: Little, Brown/Atlantic Monthly Press, 1973; first published 1951.

Hanna, Charles A. *The Scotch-Irish; or, The Scot in North Britain, North Ireland, and North America.* New York: G. P. Putnam's Sons, 1902.

Hansen, Marcus Lee. *The Atlantic Migration, 1607–1868.* Cambridge, Mass.: Harvard University Press, 1940.

Hansen, Marcus Lee, *The Immigrant in American History.* Cambridge, Mass.: Harvard University Press, 1940.

———, and John B. Brebner. *The Mingling of the Canadian and American Peoples.* New Haven, Conn.: Yale University Press, 1940.

Hardin, Garrett. *The Immigration Dilemma: Avoiding the Tragedy of the Commons.* Washington, D.C.: FAIR, 1995.

Harkness, George Elma. *The Church and the Immigrant.* New York: George H. Doran, 1921.

Harrower, John. *Journal of John Harrower, an Indentured Servant in the Colony of Virginia, 1774–1776.* New York: Holt, Rinehart and Winston, 1963.

Hartmann, Edward George. *Americans from Wales.* Boston: Christopher Publishing House, 1967.

Hasanovitz, Elizabeth. *One of Them: Chapters from a Passionate Autobiography.* Boston: Houghton Mifflin, 1918.

Haugen, Einar Ingvald, and Camilla Cai. *Ole Bull.* Madison: University of Wisconsin Press, 1993.

Hawgood, John A. *The Tragedy of German America: The Germans in the United States of America during the Nineteenth Century—and After.* New York: G. P. Putnam's Sons, 1940.

Hawks, Francis Lister. *History of North Carolina,* 2 vols. Spartanburg, N.C.: Reprint Company, 1961; first published 1857–58.

Hayes, Helene. *U.S. Immigration Policy and the Undocumented: Ambivalent Laws, Furtive Lives.* Westport, Conn.: Greenwood Publishing Group, 2001.

Hayworth, J. D., with Joe Eule. *Whatever It Takes: Illegal Immigration, Border Security and the War on Terror.* Washington, D.C.: Regnery Publishing, 2001.

Heaton, Eliza O. *The Steerage: A Sham Immigrant Voyage to New York in 1888.* Brooklyn, N.Y.: Eagle Press, 1919.

Heer, David. *Immigration in America's Future.* Boulder, Colo.: Westview Press, 1996.

Henry, Patrick. *Patrick Henry: Life, Correspondence and Speeches,* 3 Vols. Edited by William Wirt Henry. New York: Burt Franklin, 1969; first published 1891.

Herrick, Cheesman A. *White Servitude in Pennsylvania: Indentured and Redemption Labor in the Colony and Commonwealth.* Freeport, N.Y.: Books for Libraries Press, 1970; first published 1926.

Higham, John. *Send These to Me: Jews and Other Immigrants in Urban America.* New York: Atheneum, 1975.

———. *Strangers in the Land: Patterns of American Nativism, 1860–1925.* New York: Atheneum, 1970; first published 1955.

Hill, S. S. *Emigrant's Introduction to an Acquaintance with the British American Colonies, and the Present Condition and Prospects of Colonists.* London, England: Parbury and Company, 1837.

———. *To Be an American: Cultural Pluralism and the Rhetoric of Assimilation.* New York: New York University Press, 1997.

Hing, Bill Ong. *Defining America through Immigration Policy.* Philadelphia, Pa.: Temple University Press, 2004.

———. *Deporting Our Souls: Values, Morality, and Immigration Policy.* New York: Cambridge University Press, 2006.

Hoexter, Corinne K. *From Canton to California: The Epic of Chinese Immigration.* New York: Four Winds, 1976.

Hoff, Rhoda. *America's Immigrants: Adventures in Eyewitness History.* New York: Henry Z. Walck, 1967.

Holt, Hamilton, ed. *The Life Stories of Undistinguished Americans, as Told by Themselves.* New York: Routledge, 1990; first published 1906.

Hondagneu-Sotelo, Pierrette. *Gender and U.S. Immigration: Contemporary Trends.* Berkeley: University of California Press, 2003.

Honour, Hugh. *The New Golden Land: European Images of America from the Discoveries to the Present Time.* New York: Pantheon Books, 1976.

Hourwich, Isaac Aaronvich. *Immigration and Labor: The Economic Aspects of European Immigration to the United States.* New York: B. W. Huebsch, 1922; first published 1912.

Howe, Frederick C. *The Confessions of a Reformer.* New York: Charles Scribner's Sons, 1925.

Howe, Irving, and Kenneth Libo. *How We Lived.* New York: R. Marek Publishers, 1979.

Howitt, Emanuel. *Selections from Letters Written during a Tour through the United States, in the Summer and Autumn of 1819.* Nottingham, England: J. Dunn, 1820.

Humphrey, Hubert H. *The Stranger at Our Gates: America's Immigration Policy.* New York: Public Affairs Committee, 1954.

Hutchinson, Edward Prince. *Immigrants and Their Children, 1850–1950.* New York: J. Wiley & Sons, 1956.

Imlay, Gilbert. *The Immigrants.* Gainesville, Fla.: Scholars' Facsimiles and Reprints, 1964; first published 1794.

Iorizzo, Luciano John. *Italian Immigration and the Padrone System.* New York: Arno Press, 1980; first published 1966.

Isaacs, Julius. *Economics of Migration.* London, England: Kegan, Paul, Trench, Trubner & Co., 1947.

Isbister, John. *The Immigration Debate: Remaking America.* West Hartford, Conn.: Kumarian Press, 1996.

Isely, Elise Dubach, as told to her son Bliss Isely. *Sunbonnet Days.* Caldwell, Idaho: Caxton Printers, 1935.

Itchihashi, Yamoto. *Japanese in the United States: A Critical Study of Japanese Immigrants and Their Children.* New York: Arno Press, 1969; first published 1932.

Jackson, Kenneth T. *The Ku Klux Klan in the City, 1915–1930.* New York: Oxford University Press, 1967.

Jacoby, Tamar. *Reinventing the Melting Pot: The New Immigrants and What It Means to Be American.* New York: Basic Books, 2004.

Jager, A. *The Emigrant; The Life, Experiences, and Humorous Adventures of A. Jager, Emigrant to South America in 1882, to Australia in 1885, and to California in 1908.* Los Angeles: Southern California Printing Co., 1908.

Janson, Florence Edith. *The Background of Swedish Immigration, 1840–1930.* Chicago: University of Chicago Press, 1931.

Jaworski, Irene D. *Becoming American: The Problems of Immigrants and Their Children.* New York: Harper & Brothers, 1960; first published 1950.

Jay, John. *The Correspondence and Public Papers of John Jay,* 4 vols. Edited by Henry P. Johnston. New York: G. P. Putnam's Sons, 1890–93.

Jefferson, Thomas. *The Works of Thomas Jefferson: Published by Order of Congress from the Original Manuscripts Deposited in the Department of State,* 9 vols. New York: Townsend MacCoun, 1884.

———. *The Writings of Thomas Jefferson,* 10 vols. New York: G. P. Putnam's Sons, 1892–99.

Jenks, Jeremiah W., and Lauck W. Jett. *The Immigration Problem: A Study of American Immigration Conditions and Needs.* London, England: Funk and Wagnalls, 1922; first published 1917.

Jensen, Carl Christian. *An American Saga.* Boston: Little, Brown and Company, 1927.

Jensen, Merrill, ed. *English Historical Documents,* Volume 9: *American Colonial Documents to 1776.* New York: Oxford University Press, 1955.

Jick, Leon A. *The Americanization of the Synagogue, 1820–1870.* Hanover, N.H.: University Press of New England, 1976.

Johnson, Kevin R. *The "Huddled Masses" Myth: Immigration and Civil Rights.* Philadelphia, Pa.: Temple University Press, 2004.

Johnson, Stanley Currie. *The History of Emigration from the United Kingdom to North America, 1763–1912.* New York: E. P. Dutton & Co., 1913.

Jones, Maldwyn Allen. *American Immigration.* Chicago: University of Chicago Press, 1960.

———. *Destination America.* New York: Holt, Rinehart and Winston, 1976.

Jones, Mary Harris. *Autobiography of Mother Jones.* Chicago: C. H. Ker, 1925.

Jordan, Terry G. *German Seed in Texas Soil: Immigrant Farmers in Nineteenth-Century Texas.* Austin: University of Texas Press, 1966.

Joseph, Samuel. *Jewish Immigration to the United States from 1881 to 1910.* New York: Arno Press, 1969; first published 1914.

Kahler, Max V. *Immigration and Aliens in the United States.* New York: Bloch, 1936.

Kalm, Peter. *Travels into North America.* Barre, Mass.: Imprint Society, 1972; first published in Swedish 1753–61 and in English 1770.

Kapp, Friedrich. *Immigration and the Commissioners of Emigration of the State of New York.* New York: The Nation Press, 1870.

Karp, Abraham J. *Golden Door to America: The Jewish Immigrant Experience.* New York: The Viking Press, 1976.

Katzman, David M., and William M. Tuttle, Jr., eds. *Plain Folk: The Life Stories of Undistinguished Americans.* Urbana: University of Illinois Press, 1982.

Kawakami, Kiyoshi Karl. *Asia at the Door: A Study of the Japanese Question in Continental United States, Hawaii and Canada.* New York: Fleming H. Revell, 1914.

Kennedy, John F. *A Nation of Immigrants.* New York: Harper & Row, 1986; first published 1964.

Kent, Donald P. *Refugee Intellectual: The Americanization of the Immigrants of 1933–1941.* New York: Columbia University Press, 1953.

Kessner, Thomas, and Betty Boyd Caroli. *The Golden Door: Italian and Jewish Immigrant Mobility in New York City, 1880–1915.* New York: Oxford University Press, 1977.

———. *Today's Immigrants, Their Stories.* New York: Oxford University Press, 1973.

Kettner, James H. *The Development of American Citizenship, 1608–1870.* Chapel Hill: University of North Carolina Press, 1978.

Kherdian, David. *Finding Home.* New York: Greenwillow Press, 1981.

Kingsbury, Susan Myra, ed. *The Records of the Virginia Company of London.* Washington, D.C.: Government Printing Office, 1906–1985.

Kinkead, Gwen. *Chinatown: A Portrait of a Closed Society.* New York: HarperCollins Publishers, 1992.

Kirkpatrick, Clifford. *Intelligence and Immigration.* Baltimore, Md.: Williams and Wilkins, 1926.

Knaplund, Paul. *Moorings Old and New: Entries in an Immigrant's Log.* Madison: The State Historical Society of Wisconsin, 1963.

Knight, J. *Important Extracts from Original and Recent Letters Written by Englishmen, in the United States of America, to Their Friends in England,* 2nd Series. Manchester, England: M. Wilson, 1818.

Konvitz, Milton Ridvas. *Civil Rights in Immigration.* Ithaca, N.Y.: Cornell University Press, 1953.

Kraus, Michael. *The Atlantic Civilization: 18th Century Origins.* Ithaca, N.Y.: Cornell University Press, 1949.

———. *Immigration: The American Mosaic.* New York: Van Nostrand, 1955.

Krueger, Mas Amadeus Paulus. *Second Fatherland: The Life and Fortunes of a German Immigrant.* College Station: Texas A & M University Press, 1976.

Kunz, W. S. *Chinese in American Life: Some Aspects of Their History, Status, Problems, and Contributions.* Seattle: University of Washington Press, 1962.

Kurelek, William. *They Sought a New World: The Story of European Immigration to North America.* Montreal, Canada: Tundra Books, 1985.

Kuropas, Myron B. *To Preserve a Heritage: The Story of the Ukranian Immigration in the United States.* New York: The Ukranian Museum, 1984.

La Guardia, Fiorello H. *The Making of an Insurgent: An Autobiography, 1882–1919.* Philadelphia: J. B. Lippincott and Co., 1948.

Lai, Him Mark, et al. *Island: Poetry and History of Chinese Immigrants on Angel Island, 1910–1940.* San Francisco: Hoc Doi, 1980.

Lamphere, Louise, Alex Stepick, and Guillermo Grenier. *Newcomers in the Workplace.* Philadelphia: Temple University Press, 1994.

Larson, Laurence M. *The Log Book of a Young Immigrant.* Northfield, Minn.: Norwegian-American Historical Association, 1939.

Lasker, Bruno. *Filipino Immigration to the Continental United States and Hawaii.* Chicago: University of Chicago Press, 1931.

Laufer, Peter. *Wetback Nation: A Case for Opening the Mexican-American Border.* Lanham, Md.: Ivan R. Dee, Publisher, 2006.

Lazarus, Emma. *The Poems of Emma Lazarus,* 2 vols. Boston: Houghton, Mifflin & Company, 1889.

Learned, Marion Dexter. *The Life of Francis Daniel Pastorius, the Founder of Germantown.* Philadelphia: Campbell, 1908.

Lehner, Ernst and Johanna. *How They Saw the New World.* New York: Tudor, 1966.

Lengyel, Emil. *Americans from Hungary.* Philadelphia: J. B. Lippincott and Co., 1948.

Leonard, Ira M., and Robert D. Parmet. *American Nativism, 1830–1860.* New York: Van Nostrand Reinhold, 1971.

Lestechinsky, Jacob. *Jewish Migration for the Past 100 Years.* New York: Yiddish Scientific Institute, 1944.

Levin, Shmarya. *Childhood in Exile.* New York: Harcourt Brace, 1929.

Levitt, Peggy. *The Transnational Villagers.* Berkeley: University of California Press, 2001.

Levy, Peter B., ed. *100 Key Documents in American Democracy.* Westport, Conn.: Greenwood Press, 1994.

Lewis, Edward R. *America: Nation or Confusion: A Study of Our Immigration Problems.* New York: Harper & Brothers, 1928.

Leyburn, James Graham. *The Scotch-Irish: A Social History.* Chapel Hill: University of North Carolina Press, 1962.

———. *Jewish Pioneers in America, 1492–1848.* New York: Brentano's, 1931.

Lieberson, Stanley. *A Piece of the Pie: Blacks and White Immigrants since 1880.* Berkeley: University of California Press, 1980.

Lin, Ann Chih, ed.; Nicole W. Green, author. *Immigration.* Washington, D.C.: C.Q. Press, 2002.

Lin Yutang. *Chinatown Family.* New York: John Day Co., 1948.

———. *The Vigil of a Nation.* New York: John Day Co., 1945.

Lips, Eva. *Rebirth in Liberty*. New York: Flamingo Publishing Co., 1942.

Litwack, F. Leon. *North of Slavery: The Negro in the Free States, 1790–1860*. Chicago: University of Chicago Press, 1965.

Long, John. *John Long's Voyages and Travels of an Indian Trader in the Years 1768–1788*. Chicago, Ill.: R. R. Donnelly & Sons Company, 1922; first published 1791.

Look Before You Leap; or A Few Hints to Such Artizans, Mechanics, Labourers, Farmers, and Husbandmen, as Are Desirous of Emigrating to America, Being a Genuine Collection of Letters, from Persons Who Have Emigrated. . . . London, England: W. Row, 1796.

Lopreato, Joseph. *Italian Americans*. New York: Random House, 1970.

Lucas, Henry Stephen, ed. *Dutch Immigrant Memoirs and Related Writings*. Grand Rapids, Mich.: Eerdmans Publishing Co., 1997.

———. *Netherlanders in America: Dutch Immigration to the United States and Canada, 1789–1950*. Ann Arbor, Mich.: University of Michigan Press, 1955.

Lyman, Stanford, Jr. *Chinese Americans*. New York: Random House, 1974.

Maclean, Annie Marion. *Modern Immigration: A View of the Situation in Immigrant Receiving Countries*. Philadelphia: J. B. Lippincott and Co., 1925.

Maguire, John Francis. *The Irish in America*. New York: Arno Press, 1960; first published 1868.

Maisel, Albert Q. *They All Chose America*. New York: Nelson, 1957.

Malkin, Michelle. *Invasion: How America Still Welcomes Terrorists, Criminals, and Other Foreign Menaces to Our Shores*. Washington, D.C.: Regnery Publishing, 2004.

Mangano, Antonio. *Sons of Italy: A Social and Religious Study of the Italians in America*. New York: Missionary Education Movement of the United States and Canada, 1917.

Manners, Ande. *Poor Cousins*. New York: Coward, McCann & Geoghegan, 1973.

Marden, Charles F. *Minorities in American Society*. New York: American Book Co., 1952.

Massey, Douglas S. *Worlds in Motion: Understanding World Migration at the End of the Millennium*. New York: Oxford University Press, 2005.

Mattson, Hans. *Reminiscences: The Story of an Emigrant*. St. Paul, Minn.: D. D. Merrill, 1891.

Mayo-Smith, Richmond. *Emigration and Immigration: A Study in Social Science*. New York: Charles Scribner's Sons, 1908.

McBain, Ed. *Another Part of the City*. New York: Warner Books, 1986.

McCabe, James D., Jr. *Lights and Shadows of New York Life*. New York: Farrar, Straus & Giroux, 1970; first published 1872.

McNeil, William H., and Rush S. Adams. *Human Migration: Patterns and Policies*. Bloomington: Indiana University Press, 1978.

Melcher, Ernest O. *Life Transplanted*. New York: The William-Frederick Press, 1956.

Meltzer, Milton. *The Hispanic Americans*. New York: Thomas Y. Crowell, 1982.

Melville, Herman. *Redburn, His First Voyage*. New York: The Library of America, 1983; first published 1849.

Mesick, Jane. *The English Traveler in America, 1785–1835*. New York: Columbia University Press, 1922.

Meyerhoff, Barbara. *Remember Our Days*. New York: Simon & Schuster, 1978.

Miller, Kenneth Dexter. *The Czecho-Slovaks in America*. New York: G. H. Doran, 1922.

———. *We Who Are American*. New York: Friendship Press, 1943.

Miller, Kerby A. *Emigrants and Exiles: Ireland and the Irish Exodus to North America*. New York: Oxford University Press, 1985.

Miller, Kerby A., and Paul Wagner. *Out of Ireland: The Story of Irish Emigration to America*. Washington, D.C.: Elliott & Clark Publishers, 1994.

Miller, Olga Katzin. *Migration, Emigration, Immigration*. Logan, Utah: The Everton Publishers, Inc., 1974.

Miller, Randall, ed. *Germans in America: Retrospect and Prospect*. Philadelphia: The German Society of Philadelphia, 1984.

Millman, Joel. *The Other Americans: How Immigrants Renew Our Country, Our Economy, and Our Values*. New York: The Viking Press, 1997.

Mills, Nicholas. *Arguing Immigration: Are the New Immigrants a Wealth of Diversity . . . or a Crushing Burden?* New York: Touchstone, 1994.

Mims, Edwin, Jr. *American History and Immigration*. Bronxville, N.Y.: Sarah Lawrence College Press, n.d.

Mitau, Martin, ed. *Cathay in Eldorado: The Chinese in California*. San Francisco: Book Club of California, 1972.

Mittelberger, Gottlieb. *Journey to Pennsylvania in the Year 1750 and Return to Germany in the Year 1754*. Cambridge, Mass.: Harvard University Press, 1960; first published 1756.

Moltman, Günter, ed. *Germans to America: 300 Years of Immigration 1683–1983*. Stuttgart, Germany: Institute for Foreign Cultural Relations, 1982.

Moquin, Wayne, and Charles Van Doren, eds. *A Documentary History of the Italian Americans*. New York: Praeger Publishers, 1975.

Morison, Samuel Eliot. *The Oxford History of the American People*. New York: Oxford University Press, 1965.

———. *The European Discovery of America*. New York: Oxford University Press, 1971.

Morse, Dean W. *Pride against Prejudice: Work in the Lives of Older Blacks and Young Puerto Ricans*. Montclair, N.J.: Allanheld, Osmun & Co., 1980.

Morse, Samuel Finley Breese. *Imminent Danger to the Free Institutions of the United States through Foreign Immigration, and the Present State of the Naturalization Laws*. New York: Arno Press, 1969; first published 1835.

Muir, John. *The Story of My Boyhood and Youth*. Boston: Houghton, Mifflin & Company, 1913.

Mulder, William. *Homeward to Zion: The Mormon Migration from Scandinavia*. Minneapolis, Minn.: University of Minnesota Press, 1957.

Munsterberg, Hugo. *The Americans*. Garden City, N.Y.: Doubleday, Page, 1914.

Murray, Robert K. *Red Scare: A Study in National Hysteria*. Minneapolis: University of Minnesota Press, 1955.

Myers, Albert Cook. *Immigration of the Irish Quakers into Pennsylvania, 1682–1750*. Swarthmore, Penn.: published by the author, 1902.

Myers, Gustavus. *History of Bigotry in the United States*. New York: Capricorn Books, 1960; first published 1943.

Namias, June. *First Generation: In the Words of Twentieth-Century American Immigrants*. Boston: Beacon Press, 1978.

Natella, Arthur A., ed. *The Italians in America, 1513–1974*. Dobbs Ferry, N.Y.: Oceana Publications, 1975.

Neidle, Cecyle S. *The New Americans*. New York: Twayne Publishers, 1967.

Nelson, Brent. *America Balkanized: Immigration's Challenge to Government*. Monterey, Va.: American Immigration Control Foundation (AICF), 1994.

Ness, Immanuel. *Immigrants, Unions, and the New U.S. Labor Market*. Philadelphia, Pa.: Temple University Press, 2005

Nettle, George. *A Practical Guide for Emigrants to North America . . . With Full Information Respecting . . . Matters Requisite for the Emigrant to Become Acquainted with Before Embarking*. London, England: Simpkin, Marshall & Company, 1850.

Nevins, Allen, ed. *America through British Eyes*. New York: Oxford University Press, 1948.

Nguyen, Tram. *We Are All Suspects Now: Untold Stories from Immigrant America after 9/11*. Boston: Beacon Press, 2005.

Nichols, Thomas Low. *Lecture on Immigration and Right of Naturalization*. New York: Burgess, Stringer and Company, 1845.

Novotny, Ann. *Strangers at the Gate: Ellis Island, Castle Garden, and the Great Migration to America*. Riverside, Conn.: The Chatham Press, 1971.

O'Connor, Richard. *The German-Americans*. New York: Little, Brown and Company, 1968.

O'Connor, Thomas H. *The Boston Irish: A Political History*. Boston: Back Bay Books, 1995.

Odorizzi, Irene M. Planinsek. *Footsteps through Time*. Reston, Va.: Washington Landmark Tours, 1978.

O'Grady, Joseph P. *How the Irish Became Americans*. New York: Twayne Publishers, 1973.

Olmsted, Frederick Law. *A Journey through Texas: or A Saddle-Trip on the Southwestern Frontier*. Austin: University of Texas Press, 1978: first published 1857.

Olsen, Laurie. *Crossing the Schoolhouse Border: Immigrant Students and the California Public Schools*. San Francisco: California Tomorrow, 1988.

O'Neill, Teresa, ed. *Immigration: Opposing Viewpoints*. San Diego, Calif.: Greenhaven Press, 1992.

Oni-Eseleh, Ohiro D. *In Pursuit of Dreams: The Truth About Immigration*. Baltimore: Erica House, 1999.

Ono, Kent A., and John M. Sloop. *Shifting Borders: Rhetoric, Immigration, and California's Proposition 187*. Philadelphia, Pa.: Temple University Press, 2002.

Orebaugh, David D. *Crime, Degeneracy and Immigration: Their Interrelations and Interreactions*. Boston: R. G. Badger, 1929.

Orth, Samuel P. *Our Foreigners: A Chronicle of Americans in the Making*. New Haven, Conn.: Yale University Press, 1920.

Padover, Saul K., ed. *Thomas Jefferson on Democracy*. New York: New American Library, 1967.

Paine, Thomas. *Common Sense*. Indianapolis, Ind.: The Bobbs-Merrill Company, 1953; first published 1770.

Panunzio, Constantine M. *Immigration Crossroads*. New York: The Macmillan Company, 1927.

———. *The Soul of an Immigrant*. New York: The Macmillan Company, 1921.

Papashvili, George, and Helen Papashvili. *Anything Can Happen*. New York: Harper & Brothers, 1945.

Peck, Ira, Steven Jantzen, and Daniel Rosen, *American Adventures*. Austin, Tex.: Steck-Vaughn Company, 1983; first published 1970.

Peckham, Howard Henry, ed. *Narratives of Colonial America, 1704–1765.* Chicago: R. R. Donnelley & Sons, 1971.

Pellegrini, Angelo Maria. *Immigrant's Return.* New York: The Macmillan Company, 1952.

Percival, John. *The Great Famine: Ireland's Potato Famine, 1845–1851.* London, England: BBC Books, 1995.

Perea, Juan F. *Immigrants Out: The New Nativism and the Anti-Immigrant Impulse in the United States.* New York: New York University Press, 1997.

Peters, Clarence A. *The Immigration Problem.* New York: H. W. Wilson, 1948.

Pinkwater, D. Manus. *The Hoboken Chicken Emergency.* Englewood Cliffs, N.J.: Prentice Hall, 1977.

Polenberg, Richard. *One Nation Divisible: Class, Race, and Ethnicity in the United States since 1938.* New York: The Viking Press, 1980.

Portes, Alejandro, and Rubén G. Rumbaut. *Immigrant America: A Portrait.* 1990. Reprint, Berkeley: University of California Press, 1996.

———. *Legacies: The Story of the Immigrant Second Generation.* Berkeley and New York: University of California Press and Russell Sage, 2001.

Potter, George. *To the Golden Door.* Boston: Little, Brown and Company, 1960.

Powderly, Terence. *The Path I Trod: Autobiography of Terence Powderly.* New York: Columbia University Press, 1940.

Pozzetta, George E., ed. *Assimilation, Acculturation, and Social Mobility.* New York: Garland Publishers, 1991.

———. *Contemporary Immigration and American Society.* New York: Garland Publishers, 1991.

———. *Emigration and Immigration: The Old World Confronting the New.* New York: Garland Publishers, 1991.

———. *Immigrant Family Patterns: Demography, Fertility, Housing, Kinship, and Urban Life.* New York: Garland Publishers, 1991.

———. *Immigrants on the Land: Agriculture, Rural Life, and Small Towns.* New York: Garland Publishers, 1991.

———. *Themes in Immigration History.* New York: Garland Publishers, 1991.

———. *Unions and Immigrants: Organization and Struggle.* New York: Garland Publishers, 1991.

Pula, James S. *Polish Americans: An Ethnic Community.* New York: Twayne Publishers, 1995.

Puskas, Julianna. *From Hungary to the United States.* Budapest, Hungary: Akademiai Kiado, 1982.

Qualey, Carlton Chester. *Norwegian Settlement in the United States.* Northfield, Minn.: The Norwegian-American Historical Association, 1938.

Quigley, Hugh. *The Irish Race in California and on the Pacific Coast.* San Francisco: A. Roman & Co., 1878.

Raaen, Aagot. *Grass of the Earth: Immigrant Life in the Dakota Country.* St. Paul, Minn.: Minnesota Historical Society Press, 1994; first published 1950.

Rademaker, John Adrian. *These Are Americans: The Japanese-Americans in Hawaii in World War II.* Palo Alto, Calif.: Pacific Books, 1951.

Raeder, Ole Munch. *America in the Forties: The Letters of Ole Munch Raeder.* Minneapolis, Minn.: University of Minnesota Press, 1929.

Ravage, Marcus Eli. *An American in the Making: The Life Story of an Immigrant.* New York: Dover Publications, 1971; first published 1917.

Reeves, Pamela. *Ellis Island: Gateway to the American Dream.* New York: Crescent Books, 1993.

Reeves, Richard. *President Kennedy: Profile of Power.* New York: Simon & Schuster, Inc., 1993.

Reimers, David. *Unwelcome Strangers: American Identity and the Turn against Immigration.* New York: Columbia University Press, 1998.

———. *Still the Golden Door: The Third World Comes to America.* New York: Columbia University Press, 1992.

Renkiewicz, Frank, ed. *The Poles in America, 1608–1972.* Dobbs Ferry, N.Y.: Oceana Publications, 1973.

———. *The Polish Presence in Canada and America.* Toronto, Canada: Multicultural History Society of Ontario, 1982.

Rhodes, James Ford. *History of the United States, 1850–1877.* New York: The Macmillan Company, 1899.

Riis, Jacob A. *The Battle with the Slums.* New York: Patterson Smith, 1969; first published 1902.

———. *How the Other Half Lives.* New York: Dover Books, 1971; first published 1890.

———. *The Making of an American.* New York: The Macmillan Company, 1920; first published 1901.

———. *Neighbors: Modern Stories of the Other Half.* New York: The Macmillan Company, 1914.

Rippley, La Vern. *The German-Americans.* Boston: Twayne Publishers, 1976.

Rips, Gladys Nadler. *Coming to America: Immigrants from Southern Europe.* New York: Delacorte Press, 1981.

Rischin, Moses. *The Promised City: New York's Jews 1870–1914.* New York: Harper & Row, 1962.

———, ed. *The Jews of North America.* Detroit, Mich.: Wayne State University Press, 1987.

Robbins, Albert. *Coming to America: Immigrants from Northern Europe.* New York: Delacorte Press, 1981.

Roberts, Kenneth Lewis. *Why Europe Leaves Home.* Indianapolis, Ind.: The Bobbs-Merrill Co., 1922.

Roberts, Peter. *The New Immigration: A Study of the Industrial and Social Life of Southeastern Europeans in America.* New York: The Macmillan Company., 1912.

Rodrigues, Richard. *Hunger of Memory.* Boston: R. R. Godine, 1982.

Roediger, David R. *Working Toward Whiteness: How America's Immigrants Became White.* New York: Basic Books, 2005.

Roleff, Tamara K., ed. *Immigration.* San Diego, Calif.: Greenhaven Press, 1998.

Rolle, Andrew F. *The American Italians: Their History and Culture.* Belmont, Calif.: Wadsworth Publishing Co., 1972.

Rose, Peter I. *Tempest Tost: Race, Immigration, and the Dilemma of Diversity.* New York: Oxford University Press, 1997.

Rose, Philip M. *The Italians in America.* New York: G. H. Doran, 1922.

Rosenfeld, Max. *Pushcarts and Dreamers: Stories of Jewish Life in America.* New Brunswick, N.J.: Thomas Yoseloff, 1967.

Ross, Edward Alsworth. *The Old World in the New: The Significance of Past and Present Immigration to the American People.* Englewood, N.J.: Jerome S. Ozer, 1971; first published 1914.

Rubio-Marin, Ruth. *Immigration as a Democratic Challenge.* New York: Cambridge University Press, 2000.

Rumbaut, Rubén G., and Alejandro Portes. *Ethnicities: Children of Immigrants in America.* Berkeley and New York: University of California Press and Russell Sage, 2001.

Rushmore, Elsie. *Immigrant Backgrounds.* New York: Russell Sage Foundation Library, 1920.

Rynning, Ole. *True Account of America for the Information and Help of Peasant and Commoner.* Edited by Theodore C. Blegen. Freeport, N.Y.: Books for Libraries Press, 1971; first published 1838.

Safford, Victor. *Immigration Problems: Personal Experiences of an Official.* New York: Dodd Mead, 1925.

Salins, Peter D. *Assimilation American Style: An Impassioned Defense of Immigration and Assimilation as the Foundation of American Greatness and the American Dream.* New York: Basic Books, 1997.

Saloutos, Theodore. *The Greeks in the United States.* Cambridge, Mass.: Harvard University Press, 1964.

———. *They Remember America: The Story of the Repatriated Greek-Americans.* Berkeley: University of California Press, 1956.

Salyer, Ivey E. *Laws Harsh as Tigers: Chinese Immigrants and the Shaping of Modern Immigration Law.* Chapel Hill: University of North Carolina Press, 1995.

Sandberg, Neil C. *Ethnic Identity and Assimilation: The Polish American Community.* New York: Praeger, 1974.

Sandemeyer, Elmer Clarence. *The Anti-Chinese Movement in California.* Urbana: University of Illinois Press, 1939.

Sanders, Ronald. *Shores of Refuge: A Hundred Years of Jewish Immigration.* New York: Schocken Books, 1988.

Sanderson, John Philip. *Republican Landmarks: The Views and Opinions of American Statesmen on Foreign Immigration.* Philadelphia: J. B. Lippincott and Co., 1856.

Sandler, Martin, *Immigrants.* New York: HarperCollins Publishers, 1995.

Sandler, Martin, Edwin C. Rozwenc, and Edward C. Martin. *The People Make a Nation.* Boston: Allyn & Bacon, Inc., 1971.

Santoli, Al. *New Americans: An Oral History: Immigrants and Refugees in the U.S. Today.* New York: Viking, 1988.

Sawada, Mitziko. *Tokyo Life, New York Dreams: Urban Japanese Visions of America, 1890–1924.* Berkeley: University of California Press, 1996.

Schappes, Morris Urman. *A Documentary History of the Jews of the United States, 1654–1875.* New York: The Citadel Press, 1952; first published 1950.

Schermerhorn, R. A. *These Our People: Minorities in American Culture.* New York: Nelson, 1957.

Schiro, George J. *Americans by Choice: History of the Italians in Utica.* Utica, N.Y.: Thomas J. Griffiths Sons, 1940.

Schlesinger, Arthur M., Jr. *The Disuniting of America: Reflections on a Multicultural Society.* New York: W. W. Norton & Company, 1992, 1949.

Schoener, Allon, ed. *Portal to America: The Lower East Side, 1870–1925.* New York: Holt, Rinehart and Winston, 1967.

Schrader, Frederick Franklin. *The Germans in the Making of America.* Boston: Stratford Company, 1942.

Schrier, Arnold. *Ireland and the American Emigration, 1850–1900.* Minneapolis: University of Minnesota Press, 1958.

Schurz, Carl. *Reminiscences of Carl Schurz.* New York: The McClure Co., 1907–08.

Scott, Franklin D. *Emigration and Immigration.* New York: The Macmillan Company, 1963.

Scourby, Alice. *The Greek Americans.* Boston: Twayne Publishers, 1984.

Scrope, G. Poulett. *Extracts of Letters from Poor People Who Emigrated Last Year to Canada and the United States.* London, England: James Ridgway, 1832.

Seller, Maxine Schwartz. *To Seek America.* Englewood, N.J.: Jerome S. Ozer, 1977.

———, ed. *Immigrant Women.* Albany: State University of New York Press, 1994; first published 1981.

Senior, Clarence. *Strangers Then Neighbors: From Pilgrims to Puerto Ricans.* New York: Anti-Defamation League of the B'nai B'rith, 1961.

Seward, George F. *Chinese Immigration in Its Social and Economical Aspects.* New York: Charles Scribner's Sons, 1881.

Sexton, Patricia Cayo. *Spanish Harlem.* New York: Harper & Row, 1965.

Shannon, William Vincent. *The American Irish: A Political and Social Portrait.* New York: The Macmillan Company, 1963.

Shapiro, Mary J. *Gateway to Liberty: The Story of the Statue of Liberty and Ellis Island.* New York: Vintage Books, 1986.

Shepperson, Wilbur Stanley. *British Emigration to North America: Projects and Opinions in the Early Victorian World.* Oxford, England: Blackwell, 1957.

Shippen, Katherine B. *Passage to America: The Story of the Great Migration.* New York: Harper & Brothers, 1950.

Sih, Paul K. T., and Leonard B. Allen, eds. *The Chinese in America.* New York: St. John's University Press, 1976.

Silving, Helen. *Immigration Laws of the United States.* New York: Oceana Publications, 1948.

Simon, Emily Parker. *Strong as the People.* New York: Friendship Press, 1943.

Simon, Julian. *The Economic Consequences of Immigration.* Cambridge, Mass.: Basil Blackwell/CATO Institute, 1989.

Simon, Rita J., and Susan H. Alexander. *The Ambivalent Welcome: Print Media, Public Opinion and Immigration.* Westport, Conn.: Praeger, 1993.

Smith, Abbot Emerson. *Colonists in Bondage: White Servitude and Convict Labor in America 1607–1776.* New York: W. W. Norton & Company, 1971; first published 1947.

Smith, James Morton. *Freedom's Fetters: The Alien and Sedition Laws and American Civil Liberties.* Ithaca, N.Y.: Cornell University Press, 1966; first published 1950.

Smith, John. *Travels and Works of John Smith, President of Virginia, and Admiral of New England, 1580–1631,* 2 vols. New York: Burt Franklin, 1910; first published 1624.

Smith, Page. *A New Age Begins: A People's History of the American Revolution,* 2 vols. New York: McGraw-Hill Book Company, 1976.

Smith, Sid. *The Settlers' New Home: or, Whether to Go, and Whither?* London, England: J. Kendrick, 1850.

Smith, William. *An Emigrant's Narrative, or a Voice from the Steerage.* New York: W. Smith, 1850.

Smith, William Carlson. *Americans in the Making: The Natural History of the Assimilation of Immigrants.* New York: Appleton-Century, 1939.

———. *Americans in Process: A Study of Our Citizens of Oriental Ancestry.* Ann Arbor, Mich.: Edwards Brothers, 1937.

Solomon, Barbara Miller. *Ancestors and Immigrants: A Changing New England Tradition.* Cambridge, Mass.: Harvard University Press, 1956.

Sorin, Gerald. *A Time for Building: The Third Migration, 1880–1920.* Baltimore, Md.: Johns Hopkins University Press, 1992.

Stacy, Palmer, and Wayne Lutton. *The Immigration Time Bomb.* Monterey, Va.: The American Immigration Control Foundation, 1985.

Starr, Dennis. *The Italians of New Jersey: A Historical Introduction and Bibliography.* Newark, N.J.: New Jersey Historical Society, 1985.

Stegner, Wallace E. *One Nation.* Boston: Houghton, Mifflin & Company, 1945.

Steinbeck, John. *Travels with Charlie.* New York: The Viking Press, 1962.

Steiner, Edward Alfred. *From Alien to Citizen: The Story of My Life in America.* New York: Fleming H. Revell, 1914.

———. *The Immigrant Tide: Its Ebb and Flow.* New York: Fleming H. Revell, 1909.

———. *On the Trail of the Immigrant.* New York: Arno Press, 1969; first published 1906.

Steiner, Jesse Frederick. *The Japanese Invasion: A Study in the Psychology of Interracial Contacts.* Chicago: A. C. McClurg, 1917.

Stephenson, George M. *A History of American Immigration, 1820–1924.* Boston: Ginn and Company, 1926.

Stevenson, Robert Louis. *The Amateur Immigrant: From the Clyde to Sandy Hook.* Chicago: Stone and Kimball, 1895.

———. *Across the Plains: With Other Memories and Essays.* New York: Nelson, 1892.

Stoddard, Theodore Lothrop. *Re-forging America.* New York: Charles Scribner's Sons, 1927.

———. *The Rising Tide of Color against White World-Supremacy.* Westport, Conn.: Negro Universities Press, 1970; first published 1920.

Strong, Josiah. *Our Country: Its Possible Future and Its Present Crisis.* New York: Baker and Taylor, 1885.

Suarez-Orozco, Carola, and Marcelo Suarez-Orozco. *Children of Immigrants.* Cambridge, Mass.: Harvard University Press, 2001.

———, and Desiree Qin-Hilliard. *The New Immigration: An Interdisciplinary Reader.* New York: Routledge, 2004.

Sutton, Constance R., and Elsa M. Cheney, eds. *Caribbean Life in New York City: Sociocultural Dimensions.* New York: Center for Migration Studies of New York, 1987.

Swierenga, Robert P., ed. *The Dutch in America: Immigration, Settlement, and Cultural Change.* New Brunswick, N.J.: Rutgers University Press, 1985.

Taft, Donald Reed, and Richard Robbins. *International Migrations: The Immigrant in the Modern World.* New York: Ronald Press, 1955.

Takaki, Ronald. *A Larger Memory: A History of Our Diversity, with Voices.* Boston: Little, Brown and Company, 1998.

———. *Strangers from a Different Shore: A History of Asian Americans.* Boston: Little, Brown and Company, 1998; first published 1989.

Taylor, Bayard. *Northern Travel. Summer and Winter Pictures. Sweden, Denmark, and Lapland.* New York: G. P. Putnam, 1883.

Taylor, Phillip. *The Distant Magnet: European Emigration to the U.S.A.* New York: Harper Torch Books, 1972.

TenBroek, Jacobus, Edward N. Barnhart, and Floyd W. Matson. *Prejudice, War, and the Constitution.* Berkeley: University of California Press, 1968; first published 1954.

Thomas, William I., and Florian Znaniecki. *The Polish Peasant in Europe and America.* Urbana: University of Illinois Press, 1996; first published 1918.

Thompson, Francis V. *Schooling of the Immigrant.* New York: Harper & Brothers, 1920.

Thomson, E. H. *The Emigrant's Guide to the State of Michigan.* New York: Office of the Michigan Agency for Emigration, 1849.

Thorek, Max. *A Surgeon's World: An Autobiography.* Philadelphia: J. B. Lippincott and Co., 1943.

Thorpe, Francis Newton. *The Federal and State Constitutions, Colonial Charters, and Other Organic Laws of the States, Territories, and Colonies Now or Heretofore Forming the United States of America,* 7 vols. Buffalo, N.Y.: W. S. Hein, 1933; first published 1909.

Tichenor, Daniel J. *Dividing Lines: The Politics of Immigration Control in America.* Princeton, N.J.: Princeton University Press, 2002.

Tocqueville, Alexis de. *Democracy in America.* London, England: Oxford University Press, 1952; first published 1835–39.

Tomasi, Lydio, ed. *Italian Americans: New Perspectives in Italian Immigration and Ethnicity.* New York: Center for Migration Studies of New York, Inc., 1985.

Traverso, Edmund. *Immigration: A Study in American Values.* Boston: D. C. Heath, 1964.

Trefousse, Hans L. *Carl Schurz: A Biography.* Knoxville: University of Tennessee Press, 1982.

Tse, Lucy. *Why Don't You Learn English? Separating Fact from Fallacy in the U.S. Language Debate.* New York: Teachers College Press, 2001.

Tyler, Poyntz, ed. *Immigration and the United States.* New York: The H. W. Wilson Co., 1956.

Ueland, Andreas. *Recollections of an Immigrant.* New York: Minton, Balch and Co., 1929.

Ungar, Sanford J. *Fresh Blood: The New American Immigrants.* New York: Simon & Schuster, 1995.

United States Commission on Human Rights. *The Tarnished Golden Door: Civil Rights Issues in Immigration, a Report.* Washington, D.C.: Commission on Human Rights, 1980.

United States Commission on Immigration. *Immigration and Crime.* Washington, D.C.: Government Printing Office, 1911.

United States Congress. *Statements and Recommendations Submitted by Societies and Organizations Interested in the Subject of Immigration.* Washington, D.C.: Government Printing Office, 1911.

United States Department of Commerce and Labor. *Reports of the Department of Commerce and Labor,* 9 vols. Washington, D.C.: Government Printing Office, 1905–13.

United States Immigration Commission, *Reports of the Immigration Commission* (the Dillingham Report), 41 vols. Washington, D.C.: Government Printing Office, 1911.

United States President's Commission on Immigration and Naturalization, *Whom We Shall Welcome: A Report of the President's Commission on Immigration and Naturalization.* Washington, D.C.: Government Printing Office, 1953.

Unonius, Gustaf. *A Pioneer in Northwest America, 1841–1858: The Memoirs of Gustaf Unonius.* 2 vols. Minneapolis: University of Minnesota Press, 1950–60.

Vinson, John. *Immigration Out of Control: The Interests against America.* Monterey, Va.: American Immigration Control Foundation (AICF), 1992.

Visser, Margaret. *The Way We Are.* Winchester, Mass.: Faber and Faber, 1996; first published 1994.

Wakin, Edward. *Enter the Irish-Americans.* New York: Thomas Y. Crowell Co., 1976.

Walch, Timothy. *Immigrant America: European Ethnicity in the United States.* New York: Garland Publishers, 1994.

Waldinger, Roger D. *Through the Eye of the Needle: Immigrants and Enterprise in New York's Garment Trades.* New York: New York University Press, 1986.

Waldinger, Roger. *How the Other Half Works: Immigration and the Social Organization of Labor.* Berkeley: University of California Press, 2004.

Wareing, John. *Emigrants to America: Indentured Servants Recruited in London, 1718–1733.* Baltimore, Md.: Genealogical Publishing Co., 1985.

Warne, Frank Julian. *The Immigrant Invasion.* New York: Dodd Mead, 1913.

———. *The Slav Invasion and the Mine Workers: A Study in Immigration.* Philadelphia: J. B. Lippincott and Co., 1904.

———. *The Tide of Immigration.* New York: D. Appleton & Co., 1916.

Washington, George. *The Writings of George Washington,* 14 vols. New York: G. P. Putnam's Sons, 1889–93.

Watts, Julie R. *Immigration Policy and the Challenge of Globalization: Unions and Employers in an Unlikely Alliance.* Ithaca, N.Y.: Cornell University Press, 2002.

Weatherford, Doris. *Foreign and Female: Immigrant Women in America, 1840–1930.* New York: Facts On File, 1995.

Weiss, Feri Felix. *The Sieve, or, Revelations of the Man Mill, Being the Truth about American Immigration.* Boston: Page, 1921.

Welfling, Mary E. *The Ole Bull Colony in Potter County.* Coudersport, Penn.: Potter County Historical Society, 1952.

Wheeler, Carl F. *The Immigrant Experience: The Anguish of Becoming American.* New York: Dial Press, 1971.

Whelpley, James Davenport. *The Problem of the Immigrant.* London, England: Chapman & Hall, 1905.

Wierzbicki, Susan. *Beyond the Immigrant Enclave: Network Change and Assimilation.* New York: LFB Scholarly Publishing, 2004.

Williamson, Chilton, Jr. *The Immigration Mystique: America's False Conscience.* New York: HarperCollins/Basic Books, 1996.

Winthrop, John. *The Winthrop Papers,* 5 vols. Boston: Massachusetts Historical Society, 1929–47.

Winthrop, R. C. *Life and Letters of John Winthrop,* 2 vols. Boston: Ticknor & Fick's, 1864.

Wittke, Carl Frederick. *The Irish in America.* Baton Rouge, La.: Louisiana State University Press, 1956.

———. *Refugees of Revolution: The German Forty-Eighters in America.* Philadelphia: University of Pennsylvania Press, 1952.

———. *We Who Built America: The Saga of the Immigrant.* New York: Dial Press, 1939.

Wolfe, Alan. *One Nation, After All.* New York: The Viking Press, 1998.

Woodham-Smith, Cecil. *The Great Hunger: Ireland 1845–1849.* London, England: Penguin Books, 1991; first published 1962.

Woods, Robert Archey. *Americans in Process.* Boston: Houghton, Mifflin & Company, 1902.

Woofter, T. J. *Races and Ethnic Groups in American Life.* New York: McGraw-Hill, 1933.

Worth, Richard. *Africans in America.* New York: Facts on File, 2004.

Wright, Louis Booker, ed. *The Elizabethans' America: A Collection of Early Reports by Englishmen on the New World.* Cambridge, Mass.: Harvard University Press, 1965.

Wrobel, Paul. *Our Way: Family, Parish, and Neighborhood in a Polish-American Community.* Notre Dame, Ind.: University of Notre Dame Press, 1979.

Wu, Charles L. *Attitudes toward Negroes, Jews and Orientals in the United States.* Columbus, Ohio: H. L. Hedrick, 1930.

Wust, Klaus. *The Virginia Germans.* Charlottesville, Va.: University of Virginia Press, 1969.

Wust, Klaus, and Heinz Moos, eds. *Three-Hundred Years of German Immigration in North America, 1683–1983.* Baltimore, Md.: Moos Publishing, 1983.

Xenides, J. P. *The Greeks in America.* San Francisco: R. & E. Research Associates, 1972; first published 1922.

Yans-McLaughlin, Virginia, and Marjorie Lightman. *Ellis Island and the Peopling of America.* New York: The New Press, 1997.

Yearley, Clifton K., Jr. *Britons in American Labor.* Westport, Conn.: Greenwood Press, 1974.

Yezierska, Anzia. *All I Could Never Be.* New York: Brewer, Warren, & Putnam, 1932.

———. *Children of Loneliness: The Story of Immigrant Life in America.* New York: Funk & Wagnalls, 1923.

———. *Hungry Hearts.* Boston: Houghton, Mifflin & Company, 1948; first published 1920.

———. *Salome of the Tenements.* Chicago: University of Chicago Press, 1982; first published 1923.

Yoshido, Chisato. *Illegal Immigration and Economic Welfare.* New York: Springer-Verlag, 2002.

Young, Alexander, ed. *Chronicles of the First Planters of the Colony of Massachusetts Bay, from 1623 to 1636.* Boston: C. C. Little and J. Brown, 1846.

Zabrowska, Magdalena J. *How We Found America: Reading Gender through East European Immigrant Narratives.* Chapel Hill: University of North Carolina Press, 1995.

Zakrzewska, Maria Elizabeth. *A Woman's Quest.* New York: Appleton & Co., 1924.

Zangwill, Israel. *The Melting Pot: Drama in Four Acts.* New York: Arno Press, 1975; first published 1909.

Zempel, Solvieg. *In Their Own Words: Letters from Norwegian Immigrants.* Minneapolis: University of Minnesota and the Norwegian-American Historical Association, 1991.

Ziegler, Benjamin Munn, ed. *Immigration, an American Dilemma.* New York: D. C. Heath, 1953.

Zielonka, David M., and Robert J. Wechman. *The Eager Immigrants: A Survey of the Life and Americanization of Jewish Immigrants to the United States.* Champaign, Ill.: Stipes Publishing Company, 1972.

Zolbert, Aristide R. *A Nation by Design: Immigration Policy in the Fashioning of America.* Cambridge, Mass.: Harvard University Press, 2006.

Index

Locators in *italic* indicate illustrations. Locators in **boldface** indicate main entries/topics and biographies. Locators followed by *m* indicate maps. Locators followed by *t* indicate graphs and tables. Locators followed by *g* indicate glossary entries. Locators followed by *c* indicate chronology entries.

A

G